Trade, Labour and Sustainable Development

ELGAR STUDIES IN LABOUR LAW

Series Editor: Adelle Blackett, *Professor of Law, Canada Research Chair in Transnational Labour Law and Development, and Director of the Labour Law and Development Research Laboratory, McGill University, Canada*

This series studies labour law in context and embraces accounts that rethink founding narratives of labour law, including employment and social security; centres themes that engage with labour law's peripheries such as reproductive labour, labour informality and precarious work; and invites close, grounded reflection on labour law's future. It seeks to foster critical engagement with boundary-crossing in fields like migration law, trade and investment law, human rights law, environmental law, and law and development. It welcomes interdisciplinary approaches to labour law that hone insights from and contribute to critical legal theories, legal geography, pluralist approaches to law, economic sociology of law, and third world approaches to international law, to name a few. It is interested in labour law's methods and encourages the study of international and comparative labour law, the operation of labour law across multiple governance levels, and the emergence of transnational labour law. Both monographs and edited collections are welcomed.

For a full list of Edward Elgar published titles, including the titles in this series, visit our website at www.e-elgar.com.

Trade, Labour and Sustainable Development

Leaving No One in the World of Work Behind

Tonia Novitz

Professor of Labour Law, University of Bristol Law School, UK

ELGAR STUDIES IN LABOUR LAW

Edward Elgar PUBLISHING

Cheltenham, UK • Northampton, MA, USA

Published by
Edward Elgar Publishing Limited
The Lypiatts
15 Lansdown Road
Cheltenham
Glos GL50 2JA
UK

Edward Elgar Publishing, Inc.
William Pratt House
9 Dewey Court
Northampton
Massachusetts 01060
USA

A catalogue record for this book
is available from the British Library

Library of Congress Control Number: 2024930592

This book is available electronically in the **Elgar**online
Law subject collection
http://dx.doi.org/10.4337/9781786430533

Printed on elemental chlorine free (ECF)
recycled paper containing 30% Post-Consumer Waste

ISBN 978 1 78643 052 6 (cased)
ISBN 978 1 78643 053 3 (eBook)

Printed and bound in the USA

Contents

Series preface

Professor Tonia Novitz is at the forefront of scholarship offering close, rigorous engagements with sustainable development in labour law and global trade. By scrutinizing the relevant United Nations sustainable development goals alongside international labour standards, and analysing regional and international trade and financial initiatives with technical precision and care, she reaches beyond familiar accounts to demonstrate the interdependence of all three pillars of sustainable development law.

Professor Novitz's contribution to Elgar Studies in Labour Law is mature, comprehensive and timely. We thank her in particular for significantly furthering the series' disciplinary boundary-crossing ambition. Her work takes development seriously, and in the process helps to imagine sustainable futures for us all.

Adelle Blackett
Montreal, 6 March 2024

Acknowledgements

The research for this book was assisted by funding from the World Universities Network (WUN) and the Institute of Advanced Studies (IAS) at the University of Bristol, which enabled a visiting fellowship at the University of Auckland in 2017 where I was very fortunate to work with international lawyers, Caroline Foster and Jane Kelsey who generously shared their exceptional expertise on international trade law.

This book has also benefitted from opportunities to contribute to two exciting projects: one on 'Sustainable markets for responsible trade' (SMART) led by Beate Sjåfjell at the University of Oslo funded by the European Union's Horizon 2020 research and innovation programme under grant agreement No 693642 (2015–2020); and the other funded by the Swedish Research Council on 'An inclusive and sustainable Swedish labour law – the ways ahead' (2017–2021) led by Petra Herzfeld Olsson at the University of Stockholm. I learnt a great deal from Beate and Petra, but also from the many and various contributors to both projects and my thanks go to them all. That said, the views given here are my own and should not be taken to reflect the views of the European Commission, the Swedish Research Council, or other participants in these two projects.

It should also be acknowledged that this book is the culmination of a long process of academic engagement in this field of study. Its beginnings lie with the LLM unit on 'International Law of Trade and Aid' that Rachel Murray and I designed together and co-taught from 2004 onwards. The book's content reflects the critical investigations that followed as we developed and changed the content, teaching delivery, co-tutors and even the name of that course. This book further draws on countless lively conversations in seminars not only with fellow teachers, but with University of Bristol students taking this and other courses, whose probing questions and enthusiasm have led me to explore various issues I might otherwise have missed. It has been one of the joys of academic life to see these students go on to both practical and academic work in which their policy reach and legal craft exceed mine.

Much (although not all) of my research in this field since 2004 has appeared in various publications, some sole authored and others written in collaboration with colleagues (past and present) at the University of Bristol, such as Rutvica Andrijasevic, Katie Bales, Alan Bogg, Manoj Dias-Abey, Michael Ford, Clair Gammage, Lydia Hayes, Lydia Medland, Margherita Pieraccini, Phil Syrpis, and Charlotte Villiers. I owe them an enormous debt and see this book as the outcome of all they have taught me over the years. This monograph is, after all, predominantly an attempt to bring these threads of mutual learning and our energetic debates together. Where appropriate, many of these co-authored and co-edited publications are credited in the footnotes in the chapters that follow, but any errors (and any questionable assertions) remain my own. Also, my experience of collective representation and action in the University and College Union (UCU), particularly at Bristol, has been memorable and instructive; I am grateful to these UCU colleagues for their solidarity and inspiration, on which this book builds.

In addition, I am very grateful for encouragement and advice from the other international and European labour lawyers I have been fortunate to work with, especially the editor of this series, Adelle Blackett, and also Janice Bellace, Chelo Chacartegui, Nicola Countouris, Valerio De Stefano, Ruth Dukes, Franz Christian Ebert, Stein Evju, Keith Ewing, Colin Fenwick, Judy Fudge, John Hendy KC, John Howe, Claire La Hovary, Julia López López, Klaus Lörcher, David Mangan, Shae McCrystal, Guy Mundlak, Marco Rocca, Supriya Routh, Beryl ter Haar, Lisa Tortell, and Jeffrey Vogt.

In the end, this book would not have been possible without the love and support of friends and family through good and bad times. They include the fabulous Brown, Kendall, Mahanty, Pylas, Marshall/Simpson and Syrpis families; and of course Shreya Atrey, Nina Boeger, Kaye Burling, Jane Chamberlin, Jasmine Chua, Sarah Coe, Jackie Greenwood, Susan Lamb, Louise McMullan, Jule Mulder, Devyani Prabhat, Beatriz Rodriguez, Albert Sanchez-Graells, Kirsty Real, Dimitra Simeonidou, Teresa Swift and Melanie Thomas. I also owe many thanks to my ever-generous neighbours on Clift Road (too numerous to name here) for the fun and revelry, but also incredible kindness in times of need. Finally, boundless credit has to go to my mother, Rosemary Du Plessis who makes everything possible; to my father David Novitz who remains my touchstone; to my wise brother Julian Novitz and the wonderful Sabita Naheswaran; and to my sons, Alex Syrpis and Kris Syrpis, whose childhood I have treasured and whose future is now unfolding.

'As we embark on this collective journey, we pledge that no one will be left behind.'
– Preamble, United Nations (UN), Transforming our World: The 2030 Agenda for Sustainable Development, General Assembly, 70th Session, A/Res/70/1, New York, 2015.

This book draws on sources available on 1 September 2023 and all web references provided were last accessed on 1 October 2023.

Abbreviations

ACT/EMP	ILO Bureau for Employers' Activities
ACTRAV	ILO Bureau for Workers' Activities
AfCFTA	African Continental Free Trade Agreement
AFL-CIO	American Federation of Labor and Congress of Industrial Organizations
BEE	Business Enabling Environment (World Bank)
BRICS	Brazil, Russia, India, China and South Africa
CAO	Compliance Advisor/Ombudsman (World Bank)
CBDR	Common but Differentiated Responsibility
CCAS	ILO Conference Committee on the Application of Standards
CDP	UN Committee for Development Policy
CEACR	ILO Committee of Experts on the Application of Conventions and Recommendations
CETA	Comprehensive Economic Trade Agreement concluded between Canada and the EU
CFA	ILO Governing Body Committee on Freedom of Association
CRTA	WTO Committee on Regional Trade Arrangements
CSF	Civil Society Forum
CSO	Civil Society Organisation
CSPF	Civil Society Policy Forum
CSR	Corporate Social Responsibility
DAG	Domestic Advisory Group
DB	Doing Business
DSU	WTO Dispute Settlement Understanding
EBA	EU 'Everything But Arms' Arrangement
EC	European Communities

ECHR	European Convention on Human Rights
ECOSOC	UN Economic and Social Council
EFTA	European Free Trade Area
EPZ	Export Processing Zone
ESF	Environmental and Social Framework
ETUC	European Trade Union Confederation
ETUI	European Trade Union Institute
EU	European Union
EWI	Employing Workers Index
FTA	Free Trade Agreement
GATS	General Agreement on Trade in Services
GATT	General Agreement on Tariffs and Trade
GCCs	Global Commodity Chains
GFA	Global Framework Agreement
GPNs	Global Production Networks
GSP	Generalized System of Preferences
GSP+	EU Special Incentive Arrangement for Sustainable Development and Good Governance
GUF	Global Union Federation
GVCs	Global Value Chains
HLPF	UN High Level Political Forum
HR	Human Resources
IBRD	International Bank for Reconstruction and Development
ICCPR	International Covenant on Civil and Political Rights 1966
ICESCR	International Covenant on Economic, Social and Cultural Rights 1966
ICFTU	International Confederation of Free Trade Unions
ICJ	International Court of Justice
ICSID	International Centre for Settlement of Investment Disputes
IDA	International Development Agency
IEI	International Economic Institution
IEO	Independent Evaluation Office

IFA	International Framework Agreement
IFC	International Finance Corporation
IFI	International Financial Institution
ILAW	International Lawyers Assisting Workers
ILC	International Labour Conference
ILO	International Labour Organization
IPEC	International Programme on the Elimination of Child Labour
IPEC+	International Programme on the Elimination of Child Labour and Forced Labour
ISDS	Investor-State Dispute Settlement
ISO	International Organization for Standardisation
IMF	International Monetary Fund
IOE	International Organization of Employers
ITC	International Trade Centre (WTO)
ITO	International Trade Organization
ITUC	International Trade Union Confederation
LDC	Least Developed Country
MDG	Millennium Development Goal
MFN	'Most Favoured Nation' principle
MGOs	Major Groups and other Stakeholders
MIGA	Multilateral Investment Guarantee Agency
MNE	Multinational Enterprise
NGO	Non-governmental Organisation
OECD	Organization for Economic Co-operation and Development
PR	Public Relations
PRSP	Poverty Reduction Strategy Paper (IMF)
PS	Performance Standard
RMG	Ready Made Garment
ROO	Rules of Origin
SAP	Structural Adjustment Programme
SDG	Sustainable Development Goal
SDR	Special Drawing Right

SDT	Special and Differential Treatment
SPS Agreement	Agreement on Santitary and Phytosanitary Measures
SSCM	Sustainability Supply Chain Management
SSDS	State–State Dispute Settlement
TBT Agreement	Agreement on Technical Barriers to Trade
TCA	EU–UK Trade and Cooperation Agreement
TEU	Treaty on the European Union
TFAF	Trade Facilitation Agreement Facility
TFEU	Treaty on the Functioning of the European Union
TPRM	Trade Policy Review Mechanism
TRIPs	Agreement on Trade-Related Aspects of Intellectual Property Rights
TSD	Trade and Sustainable Development (chapter in an EU FTA)
UDHR	Universal Declaration of Human Rights 1948
UK	United Kingdom of Great Britain and Northern Ireland
ULG	Universal Labour Guarantee
UN	United Nations
UNCITRAL	United Nations Commission on International Trade Law
UNCTAD	UN Conference on Trade and Development
UNDRIP	United Nations Declaration on the Rights of Indigenous Peoples 2007
UNGA	UN General Assembly
UNGPs	UN Guiding Principles on Business and Human Rights
US	United States of America
USMCA	Agreement between the United States of America, the United Mexican States and Canada
USTR	Office of the US Trade Representative
VNR	Voluntary National Report
WBCSD	World Business Council for Sustainable Development
WCED	World Commission on Environment and Development
WCL	World Confederation of Labour
WHO	World Health Organization
WTO	World Trade Organization

1. An introduction to trade, labour and sustainable development

1. INTRODUCTION

The impact of global trade on labour is alarming. There are growing disparities in income between those with capital who trade, those who manage that process and those who work.[1] Those who work are more often exposed to enduring material and social inequalities, and the COVID-19 pandemic exposed the scale of increasing poverty.[2] COVID-19 and the war in Ukraine also revealed the potential fragility of global supply chains, reliant on subcontracting work to the places in the world where labour is cheaper.[3] The costs of insecurity have been disproportionately borne by working people, who as consumers struggle to be able to purchase basic goods and services essential to their survival and for whom inflationary pressures have affected the buying power of their wages, any social security provision available and (as they grow older) the value of their pensions. Access to work and job security has meanwhile been undermined, reinforcing pre-existing vulnerabilities of female,

[1] Thomas Piketty, *Capital in the Twenty-First Century* (Harvard University Press 2014); Ann Harrison, John McLaren and Margaret McMillan, 'Recent Perspectives on Trade and Inequality' (2011) 3(1) *Annual Review of Economics* 261; Thomas M. Flaherty and Ronald Rogowski, 'Rising Inequality as a Threat to the Liberal International Order' (2021) 75(2) *International Organization* 495.

[2] Konstantinos Angelopoulos, Spyridon Lazarakis, Rebecca Mancy and Max Schroeder, *Pandemic-Induced Wealth and Health Inequality and Risk Exposure* (2021) CESifo Working Paper No. 9474 available at: http://dx.doi.org/10.2139/ssrn.3985772; from a gender equality perspective, see Meraiah Foley and Rae Cooper, 'Workplace Gender Equality in the Post-pandemic Era: Where To Next?' (2021) 63(4) *Journal of Industrial Relations* 463.

[3] For the impact of COVID-19, see International Labour Organization (ILO) Monitor, *COVID-19 and the World of Work*, 2nd ed. (ILO 2020). For the effects of the Russian invasion of Ukraine, see for example Ebru Orhan, 'The Effects of the Russia–Ukraine War on Global Trade' (2022) 8(1) *Journal of International Trade, Logistics and Law* 141.

younger and older workers.[4] Yet, at the same time, immense profits for those with capital can still be achieved. The richest have seen their wealth increase dramatically during the pandemic.[5]

These contemporary concerns also must be considered alongside other issues. For example, there is greater awareness that, without changing modes of production and delivery of services – namely, how work is carried out – environmental harms will follow, such as those connected to climate change and loss of biodiversity.[6] There is also alarm that the way in which migration for work is regulated can generate shocking forms of labour exploitation, generating escalating campaigns for change.[7]

Simultaneously, workers' national-level experience of the effects of global trade has sparked rebellion against established regulatory modes and international institutions, with forms of nationalism emerging such as 'Brexit' (British exit of the European Union).[8] Bilateral and multilateral trade arrangements have been placed under stress for other geo-political reasons, a key example being the reluctance to implement the trade agreement concluded tentatively

---

[4] See, for example, Humayun Kabir, Myfanwy Maple and Kim Usher, 'The Impact of COVID-19 on Bangladeshi Readymade Garment (RMG) Workers' (2021) 43(1) *Journal of Public Health* 47; and Abi Adams-Prassl, Teodora Boneva, Marta Golin and Christopher Rauh, 'Inequality in the Impact of the Coronavirus Shock: Evidence from Real Time Surveys' IZA DP No. 13183 (2020) available at: https://covid-19.iza.org/wp-content/uploads/2020/04/dp13183.pdf.

[5] As documented in Uwe Gneiting, Nicholas Lusiani and Irit Tamir, 'Power, Profits and the Pandemic: From Corporate Extraction for the Few to an Economy that Works for All' (2021) available at: http://dx.doi.org/10.2139/ssrn.3956244.

[6] Paolo Tomassetti, 'From Treadmill of Production to Just Transition and Beyond' (2020) 26(4) *European Journal of Industrial Relations* 439.

[7] For example, the International Trade Union Confederation (ITUC) campaign discussed in *Qatar: Profit and Loss* (ITUC 2016); and Business and Human Rights Resource Centre, 'Qatar: Fears that poor living conditions for migrant workers linked to sharp rise in coronavirus cases' available at: www.business-humanrights.org/en/qatar-fears-that-poor-living-conditions-for-migrant-workers-linked-to-sharp-rise-in-coronavirus-cases.

[8] Italo Colantone and Piero Stanig, *Global Competition and Brexit* (2016) BAFFI CAREFIN Centre for Applied Research on International Markets, Banking, Finance and Regulation available at: https://papers.ssrn.com/sol3/papers.cfm?abstract_id=2870313; discussed in Tonia Novitz, 'Freedom of Association: Its Emergence and the Case for Prevention of Its Decline' in Janice Bellace and Beryl ter Haar (eds), *Research Handbook on Labour, Business and Human Rights Law* (Edward Elgar Publishing 2019). See, in a US context, Thomas J. Schoenbaum and Daniel C.K. Chow, 'The Peril of Economic Nationalism and a Proposed Pathway to Trade Harmony' (2019) 30 *Stanford Law and Policy Journal* 115.

between China and the US in January 2020.[9] In this context, the conduct of the International Monetary Fund (IMF), the World Bank Group and the World Trade Organization (WTO) is attracting growing scrutiny.[10] The International Labour Organization (ILO) and the World Health Organization (WHO) have also drawn critical attention.[11] It is evident that the relationship between trade and labour is highly contested and the subject of active debate.

This book seeks to look behind the veil of the ostensibly separate disciplinary remits of international 'trade law' and 'labour law', breaking down barriers between what might seem to be discrete systems, highlighting their connections and shared problems. This is done by primarily examining regulatory actions taken in public international law institutions, whether through standard-setting and supervision of such standards, or through the promulgation of soft law recommendatory instruments and programmatic activities. In so doing, the ways in which ostensibly separate systems 'communicate' are considered, not only at the level of global governance and international law, but also in terms of normative input into regional and national legal and regulatory systems.[12] This book also recognises the emergence of 'transnational law',

---

[9] Available at: https://ustr.gov/about-us/policy-offices/press-office/press-releases/2020/january/economic-and-trade-agreement-between-government-united-states-and-government-peoples-republic-china; for critical analysis just prior to the coronavirus pandemic, see Caroline Freund, Maryla Maliszewska, Aaditya Mattoo and Michele Ruta, *When Elephants Make Peace: The Impact of the China–US Trade Agreement on Developing Countries* (World Bank 2020) available at: https://elibrary.worldbank.org/doi/abs/10.1596/1813-9450-9173. For subsequent tensions in US–Chinese trade relations, see the 'Symposium on Gregory Shaffer: Governing the Interface of US–China Trade Relations' (2022) *AJIL Unbound* available at: www.cambridge.org/core/journals/american-journal-of-international-law/ajil-unbound-by-symposium/gregory-shaffer-governing-the-interface-of-u-s-china-trade-relations.

[10] See, for example, Alexander Kentikelenis, Daniela Gabor, Isabel Ortiz, Thomas Stubbs, Martin McKee and David Stuckler. 'Softening the Blow of the Pandemic: Will the International Monetary Fund and World Bank Make Things Worse?' (2020) *The Lancet Global Health* available at: https://doi.org/10.1016/S2214-109X(20)30135-2; and Stephen Woolcock, *Reforming the WTO, Part 1: Why World Trade Rules Are Looking Shaky. LSE Brexit* (20 Apr 2020) available at: http://eprints.lse.ac.uk/104285/.

[11] For example Jonathan Z. Ludwig, 'Chernobyl, Coronavirus, and the Art of the Authoritarian Cover-Up: Who Is to Blame, and What Is to be Done?' *SAGE* 1 (2020); and the 'Symposium on Transnational Futures of International Labor Law' special issue (2019) 113 *AJIL Unbound* available at: www.cambridge.org/core/journals/american-journal-of-international-law/ajil-unbound-by-symposium/transnational-futures-of-international-labor-law.

[12] Cf. Niklas Luhmann, 'Operational Closure and Structural Coupling: The Differentiation of the Legal System' (1992) 13 *Cardozo Law Review* 1419; Gunther Teubner, *Law as an Autopoietic System* (Blackwell 1993), at 35; and Simon Deakin,

which bridges and anticipates complex interplays between public and private law settings, as well as norms applied at multiple levels.[13]

The apparent problems of 'fragmentation' of international law,[14] for example between ILO and WTO norms,[15] could be addressed in any number of ways.[16] For example, it has been suggested that recourse to the more technical and 'mechanistic' legal provisions of the Vienna Convention on the Law of Treaties[17] could assist in the interpretation of different instruments, so as to determine their relative priority.[18] However, in this book these tensions are examined in relation to a broader aspiration for 'sustainable development', an objective which has been presented on the global stage as offering an overarching unifying holistic solution to the reconciliation of trade and labour norms.[19]

'Legal Evolution: Integrating Economic and Systemic Approaches' (2011) 7(3) *Review of Law and Economics* 659.

[13] See Kevin Kolben, 'Transnational Labor Regulation and the Limits of Governance' (2011) 12(2) *Theoretical Inquiries in Law* 403; Adelle Blackett and Anne Trebilcock, 'Conceptualising Transnational Labour Law' in Adelle Blackett and Anne Trebilcock (eds), *Research Handbook on Transnational Labour Law* (Edward Elgar Publishing 2015); Anne Trebilcock, 'Why the Shift from International to Transnational Law is Important for Labour Standards' in Henner Gott (ed.), *Labour Standards in International Economic Law* (Springer 2018), at 57–65; Adelle Blackett, 'On Social Regionalism in Transnational Labour Law' (2020) 159(4) *International Labour Review* 591, 607–9. Note that the focus of this book relates to trade *between* states, rather than *within* states, although the latter will be relevant to the former.

[14] Martti Koskenniemi and Päivi Leino, 'Fragmentation of International Law? Postmodern Anxieties' (2002) 15(3) *Leiden Journal of International Law* 553; and International Law Commission (Study Group), *Fragmentation of International Law: Difficulties arising from the Diversification and Expansion of International Law: Report of the Study Group of the International Law Commission/finalized by Martti Koskenniemi* (UN 2006) Doc. A/CN.4/L.682, at 361–2, para. 474 available at: https://digitallibrary.un.org/record/574810.

[15] Natalia Delgado, 'Towards Work Liberalization: The WTO Discourse on Labour Standards and Policy' (2019) 35(4) *International Journal of Comparative Labour Law and Industrial Relations* 455.

[16] A range of options are for example explored by Anne Trebilcock, 'The ILO as an Actor in International Economic Law: Looking Back, Gazing Ahead' in Marc Bungenberg, Markus Krajewski, Christian J. Tams, Jörg Philipp Terhechte and Andreas R. Ziegler (eds), *European Yearbook of International Economic Law 2019* (Springer 2019), at 21 et seq.

[17] Vienna Convention on the Law of Treaties concluded 23 May 1969; for further discussion see Chapter 3 of this book, text accompanying nn.103 and 172, and Chapter 5 of this book, text accompanying n.119.

[18] Chantal Thomas, 'Convergences and Divergences in International Legal Norms on Migrant Labor' (2011) 32 *Comparative Labour Law and Policy Journal* 404, 429 and 433.

[19] For the germination of such an argument made in relation to the Millennium Development Goals, see Ellen Hey, 'The MDGs Archaeology, Institutional

In this context, the terms 'sustainability' and 'sustainable development' are used interchangeably, despite the view taken by certain scholars that the former represents a goal while the latter is the process.[20] Rather, both are taken to be terms concerned with a particular vision of substance and process, which have the potential to have a profound effect on world policy-making. In particular, the apparent global consensus on the 17 'Sustainable Development Goals' (SDGs) adopted by the United Nations (UN) General Assembly in the 2030 Agenda offers a significant point of reference.[21] In this way, we might understand 'sustainability' (or 'sustainable development') as the attempt to pull together and reconcile normative communications from different 'systems' under a single umbrella.[22]

There is much that is appealing in the way that the narrative of sustainable development seeks to combine economic, environmental and social objectives, and does so with attention to equality within and between states, including a determination that no one is to be left behind. The idea of a common cause prevailing across all international institutions, public and commercial, would also alleviate the perceived need for clearer normative hierarchies and could aid in the resolution of interactional tensions between the activities of international organisations.[23] However, it has yet to be determined whether this is an actual realisable vision or merely a comforting mirage.

In this book, the emergence of 'sustainable development' as a normative discourse on the world stage is mapped with reference to the relationship between trade and labour, beginning with the historical account presented in this chapter, which is then followed by interrogation of sustainable development's constitutive economic, environmental and social aims in Chapter 2. The emerging application of a sustainable development narrative at the ILO is

Fragmentation and International Law: Human Rights', International Environmental and Sustainable (Development) Law (March 21, 2009). Available at: https://ssrn.com/abstract=1366345. For consideration of the unifying capacity of the sustainable development goals, see for example Christina Voigt (ed.), *Sustainable Development as a Principle of International Law: Resolving Conflicts between Climate Measures and WTO Law* (Brill 2009).

[20] See discussion in Margherita Pieraccini and Tonia Novitz, 'Sustainability and Law: A Historical and Theoretical Overview' in Margherita Pieraccini and Tonia Novitz (eds), *Legal Perspectives on Sustainability* (Bristol University Press 2020), 10–11.

[21] United Nations (UN), Transforming Our World: The 2030 Agenda for Sustainable Development, General Assembly, 70th Session, A/Res/70/1, New York, 2015 ('UN 2030 Agenda').

[22] Ralf Rogowski, *Reflexive Labour Law in the World Society* (Edward Elgar Publishing 2013), chs 1–3.

[23] Henner Gött, *The Law of Interactions Between International Organizations* (Springer 2020).

considered in Chapter 3, while Chapter 4 critically analyses the extent to which sustainable development is promoted in international economic institutions, such as the IMF, World Bank Group and WTO. Chapter 5 examines the translation of sustainable development into the chapters of free trade agreements. Chapter 6 then examines how public and private regulation of multinational corporate governance in global supply chains is being reshaped in response to sustainable development objectives. Each chapter explores both the potential of this normative framing around sustainable development and its limitations when applied to the relationship between trade and labour.

Recent studies of global supply chains highlight complex interactions between law, policy and practice,[24] and 'multilayered' intersections between global, regional and national-level spheres of regulation.[25] They also reveal dramatic changes in what the ILO has come to describe as the 'world of work',[26] which can no longer be understood as limited to industrial relations associated with manufacturing and goods to be traded, or even the conversion of labour into 'services' to be supplied within and across borders, but encompasses more complex forms of subcontracting and delegation of tasks. Examples include the platform and gig economy, but also other forms of self-employment that create multitudes of so-called business 'entrepreneurs' who nevertheless remain dependent on the supply of their labour to survive and can experience 'unacceptable forms of work'.[27]

Accordingly, a broader interdisciplinary literature informs the analysis of power, which this chapter introduces and to which this book repeatedly returns, including the question as to which key actors (emanating from different states,

---

[24] Discussed in Stefano Ponte, Gary Gereffi and Gale Raj-Reichert (eds), *Handbook on Global Value Chains* (Edward Elgar Publishing, 2019); 'Special Issue: Global Value Chains and their Employment Relations Consequences' (2021) 59(1) *British Journal of Industrial Relations (BJIR)* 3; and Donatella Alessandrini, 'Global Value Chains, Development and the *Long Duree* of Trade and Investment Law' (2022) 35 *Leiden Journal of International Law* 619.

[25] Jonathan Morris, Jean Jenkins and Jimmy Donaghey, 'Uneven Development, Uneven Response: The Relentless Search for Meaningful Regulation of GVCs' (2021) 59(1) *BJIR* 3, 11–12.

[26] See preamble to the International Labour Organization (ILO) Declaration on Social Justice for a Fair Globalization 2008 available at: www.ilo.org/wcmsp5/groups/public/---ed_norm/---declaration/documents/genericdocument/wcms_371208.pdf. See also International Labour Organisation (ILO) Convention No. 190 on Violence and Harassment 2019, Article 2.

[27] For a European perspective, see Jeff Kenner, Isabella Florczak and Marta Otto (eds), *Precarious Work: The Challenge for Labour Law in Europe* (Edward Elgar Publishing 2019); for global analysis, see Deirdre McCann and Judy Fudge, 'Unacceptable Forms of Work: A Multidimensional Model' (2017) 156(2) *International Labour Review* 147.

business and labour) can and should have voice and exercise forms of control in the current complex international legal regime (or regimes) related to trade. The circumstances of all those at work are, it is argued here, generated by contemporary forms of trade. For this reason, we might expect their voices to play a role in reshaping the parameters of what is deemed acceptable at international, regional and national levels.[28] The power of different actors and the resources that they can access (both communicative and material)[29] will be determinative of what a sustainable development discourse can deliver. It may be important to recognise that labour is not homogeneous, such that we need to appreciate the different forms work can take and in which countries and circumstances this may be the case.

This book calls for public international law and institutions to include those engaged in this wider 'world of work' (across the globe in diverse circumstances) within the necessary discussions regarding sustainable development and 'just transition'.[30] To do so could be the start of the 'deep structural transformation'[31] that would be needed to address current forms of fragmentation which have been manifested in the tensions between the legal trade and labour regimes – even though it is conceded that the inclusion of diverse forms of collective voice at work can only be a necessary rather than a sufficient condition for such an achievement. Accordingly, each of the chapters in this book, whose content was briefly outlined above, considers not only the extent to which sustainable development features in that setting, but also the scope for hearing and responding to collective voices of those at work in myriad different ways across the globe.

This chapter seeks to introduce some of the context and concepts which will enable a reader to both engage with the legal dimensions of this study and their

---

[28] For recent exploration of the scope of solidarity in this respect, see Julia López López (ed.), *Inscribing Solidarity: Debates in Labor Law and Beyond* (Cambridge University Press 2022).

[29] See Stefan Schmalz, Carmen Ludwig and Edward Webster, 'The Power Resources Approach: Developments and Challenges' (2018) 9 *Global Labour Journal* 113; and Tonia Novitz, 'Multi-level Disputes relating to Freedom of Association and the Right to Strike: Transnational Systems, Actors and Resources' (2020) 36(4) *International Journal of Comparative Labour Law and Industrial Relations* 471, 478–9.

[30] David Doorey, 'Just Transitions Law: Putting Labour Law to Work on Climate Change' (2017) 30(2) *Journal of Environmental Law and Practice* 201; Dimitris Stevis, Edouard Morena and Dunja Krause, 'Introduction: The Genealogy and Contemporary Politics of Just Transitions' in Edouard Morena, Dunja Krause and Dimitris Stevis (eds), *Just Transitions: Social Justice in the Shift towards a Low-carbon World* (Pluto Press 2020).

[31] Delgado n.15 above, at 482.

significance. It starts with a brief explanation of historical treatment of labour in the sphere of trade law. The chapter then goes on to clarify one of the key terms used throughout the book, that of 'development'. In particular, this part explains the relevance of identification of so-called 'developing' (as opposed to 'developed') countries, which has technical implications for the application of international trade instruments; this part also interrogates usage of the terms 'Global North' and 'Global South', which may be geographically inexact but are commonly used in contemporary academic literature. The chapter then addresses the issues of 'power' between capital and labour but also across the divide between such countries. The chapter goes on to chart how a variety of international instruments pertaining to sustainable development have, to date, addressed issues of trade and labour in the context of power-based inequalities. The chapter closes by considering the promise, perils and preconditions for sustainability in this context, highlighting the key arguments presented in this book.

2. HISTORICAL TREATMENT OF LABOUR IN THE CONTEXT OF TRADE

In the period immediately after the Second World War, in the bargain that was 'embedded liberalism',[32] it was understood that trade was centred on goods. The predominant policy concern reflected in trade law lay with fair competition among manufacturers within and between States. This premise enabled adoption of national, regional and eventually global labour standards that regulated terms for hire of workers, so that their maltreatment could not be used as a basis for competitive advantage. Workers and their employers were expected to prosper in ways that enabled the formation of a consumer base for the manufactured products supplied. Workers' collective voice was to be managed internally to each domestic economy, through traditional mechanisms involving trade unions, collective bargaining and industrial action. The participation of workers in political parties and their influence within an electoral system enabled not just friendly society protections and regulation of terms and conditions of employment under trade union auspices, but in the post-war system normalised adoption of social welfare provision, at least in so-called developed countries in the Global North.[33] This ideal may now

---

[32] See for the origins of this term, John Ruggie, 'International Regimes, Transactions and Change: Embedded Liberalism in the Post-war Economic Order' (1982) 36(2) *International Organization* 385.

[33] T.H. Marshall, *Citizenship and Social Class* (Cambridge University Press 1950), 10 et seq; see also K.D. Ewing, 'The Function of Trade Unions' (2005) 34(1) *Industrial Law Journal* 1.

be regarded as merely one of the potential 'varieties of capitalism',[34] and in the past 70 or more years, a more liberal (or neoliberal) global market order has arguably been made manifest and encouraged.[35] This book considers the difficulties that arise now when labour standards have to be transposed into a particular variety of capitalism in which the commercial benefits of trade and its financialisation are strongly prioritised. The book also examines the manifold forms that trade and its regulation now take.

The initial potential for integration of protection of trade and labour standards protection acknowledged by the Havana Charter, the draft constitution of the putative International Trade Organization (ITO), was not replicated in the Marrakesh Agreement Establishing the WTO of 1994.[36] This notional separation of trade and labour has since been made even more stark in the Singapore Declaration, which set out the demarcated parameters of WTO and ILO competence.[37] Moreover, in addition to the long extant General Agreement on Tariffs and Trade 1948 (the GATT), which was provisionally agreed when the constitution of an ITO could not be, and which later came under WTO auspices, more significant now is the regulation of trade in services. This is reflected in the adoption of the General Agreement on Trade in Services (GATS) under the 1994 WTO Agreement. Trade in services, facilitated also by free trade agreements (FTAs) outside a WTO framework, allows forms of off-shore provision enabled often by new modes of technological development, supply-chain contracting and temporary migrant delivery of work not envisaged in 1948.[38] Additionally, trade can now have multiple transnational dimensions through global supply chains, such that corporate entities or franchises operate in complex cross-border assembly of manufactured items and provision of services that no longer map onto neatly state-bordered

---

[34] Cf. Peter A. Hall and David Soskice (eds), *Varieties of Capitalism: The Institutional Foundations of Comparative Advantage* (Oxford University Press 2001).

[35] Matthew Sparke, 'Comparing and Connecting Territories of Illiberal Politics and Neoliberal Governance' (2020) 8(1) *Territory, Politics, Governance* 95. On this transition, see also Ruth Dukes and Wolfgang Streeck, *Democracy at Work: Contract, Status and Post-industrial Justice* (Polity 2022), especially chs 3 and 4.

[36] See the Havana Charter for an International Trade Organisation, available at: www.jus.uio.no/english/services/library/treaties/15/15-02/ito.xml; and Marrakesh Agreement Establishing the World Trade Organisation, available at: www.wto.org/english/docs_e/legal_e/04-wto.pdf.

[37] See the Singapore Declaration of the WTO Ministerial Conference 1996 recognising the competence of the ILO to 'set and deal' with core labour standards, available at: www.wto.org/english/thewto_e/minist_e/min96_e/wtodec_e.htm.

[38] Philip L. Martin, *GATS, Migration and Labour Standards* DP/165/2006 (ILO 2006); Joanna Howe and Rosemary Owens (eds), *Temporary Labour Migration in the Global Era: The Regulatory Challenges* (Hart 2016).

commercial frames.[39] This makes limited national-level provision for exercise of collective worker voice problematic, if it is to have any influence on the conduct of trans-border trade. Finally, contemporary diverse forms of trade in goods and services raise the spectre of a panoply of different modes of work which have not previously come within the sphere of conventional forms of trade union representation.[40]

Collective labour rights created at the national level are now under threat. There have been increasing challenges to existing mechanisms for protection of labour standards at national level, and even to those proffered by the ILO, as well as other UN agencies and human rights institutions.[41] Much of this also has to do with expectations of financial management of national economies,[42] which are promoted by international financial institutions engaged in lending, perhaps most notably the IMF and the World Bank Group.[43] It is suggested that this evolving historical regulatory matrix, when combined with private corporate conduct utilising the opportunities it provides, is shaping the changing modes through which labour is hired. Additionally, following the global financial crisis, a global health (and associated debt) crisis and a war-time food and fuel supply crisis, there is a resultant preoccupation with constrained public spending and private economic growth. National governments and supranational institutions are increasingly deferential to the legal entitlements of commercial entities trading in goods, services and finance, seeking investment opportunities, bidding for public procurement contracts and seeking regularisation of competition. In this context, there is a danger that labour standards will be seen merely as barely tolerable limitations on freedoms to trade.[44]

---

[39] David Weil, *The Fissured Workplace: Why Work Has Become So Bad for So Many and What Can Be Done to Improve It* (Harvard University Press 2014); Jeremias Prassl, *The Concept of the Employer* (Oxford University Press 2015).

[40] For an exploration of trade union adaptation to new forms of work, see Virginia Doellgast, Nathan Lillie and Valeria Pulignano (eds), *Reconstructing Solidarity: Labour Unions, Precarious Work, and the Politics of Institutional Change in Europe* (Oxford University Press 2018).

[41] For discussion in relation to the right to strike, for example, see Jeffrey Vogt, Janice Bellace, Lance Compa, K.D. Ewing, Lord Hendy QC, Klaus Lörcher and Tonia Novitz, *The Right to Strike in International Law* (Hart 2020).

[42] Wolfgang Streeck, *How Will Capitalism End?* (Verso 2016).

[43] Franz Christian Ebert, 'A Public Law Perspective on Labour Governance by International Financial Institutions: The Case of the IMF's Article IV Consultations' (2020) 17(1) *International Organizations Law Review* 105.

[44] See Case C-438/05 *ITF and FSU v Viking Line* (2007) ECR I-10779 (2007); and Case C-341/05 *Laval un Partneri v Svenska Byggnadsarbetareförbundet* (2007) ECR I-11767. Cf. Mark Freedland and Jeremias Prassl (eds) *Viking, Laval and Beyond* (Hart 2014); and Stein Evju (ed.) *Cross-border Services, Posting of Workers, and Multilevel*

3. DEFINITIONAL PROBLEMS WITH 'DEVELOPMENT' AND OTHER TERMINOLOGY

On the issue of 'development' in 'sustainable development' and what is a 'developing country', the following clarification may be helpful. There is no universal stable or clear definition of so-called developed and developing countries,[45] although there is widespread acknowledgement of the power imbalances between such states. The World Bank classifies countries as high, middle or low income depending on gross national income (GNI), while the IMF has used the terms 'advanced countries, developing countries and countries in transition'.[46]

There is no simple formula that can be applied to defend the classification of economic development, which may explain why '[t]here is no established convention for the designation of developed and developing countries or areas in the United Nations system'.[47] The lack of a common practice may also be attributed to the decision taken at the UN Conference on Trade and Development (UNCTAD) to support the practice of 'self-declaration' of so-called developing countries, which were often newly de-colonised states seeking political influence and concessions on the international stage. It was at UNCTAD that the 'Group of 77', initially consisting of 77 self-declared developing countries, started to act as a united lobby in the international community. From the 'Declaration of the 77'[48] onwards their sheer numbers meant that their individual lack of wealth was not necessarily an impediment to exercising influence on the international stage. Accordingly, these states who identified as 'developing' countries

> attached cardinal importance to democratic procedures which afford no position of privilege in the economic and financial, no less than in the political spheres. Furthermore, the developing countries would stress the need for continued evolution

---

Governance (University of Oslo 2013); also Alain Supiot, 'A Legal Perspective on the Economic Crisis of 2008' (2010) 149(2) *International Labour Review* 151.

[45] Aoife O'Donoghue and Ntina Tzouvala, 'TTIP: The Rise of the "Mega-market" Trade Agreements and Its Potential Implications for the Global South' (2016) 8(2) *Trade Law and Development* 30, 33–6.

[46] Elimma C. Ezeani, *The WTO and its Development Obligation* (Anthem Press 2012), 23.

[47] UNCTAD, *Handbook of Statistics 2021* available at: https:// hbs .unctad .org/ classifications/. See, for an identical statement, the UN Statistics Division Code, cited in Ezeani n.46 above, 19.

[48] Joint Declaration of the Seventy-Seven Developing Countries made at the Conclusion of the UN Conference on Trade and Development, Geneva, 15 June 1964 available at: www.g77.org/doc/Joint%20Declaration.html.

in the institutional field, leading not merely to the progressive strengthening of the machinery that is now contemplated, but also to the ultimate emergence of a comprehensive international trade organization.[49]

Today, states may face difficult choices regarding whether they wish to be identified as 'developing countries'. The adjective 'developing' can be viewed as patronising. It is suggestive of the aspiration to become like wealthier 'developed' countries, and emulate uncritically their social, political and economic systems, when these may be flawed in various ways. It also has pejorative connotations, which could be detrimental for example in attracting investment. However, states may need to be recognised as 'developing' to benefit from certain trade concessions, for example under the World Trade Organization (WTO) 'special and differential treatment' (SDT) provisions.[50] This makes the uncertainty of the systems via which categorisation is made more problematic and subject to power capture.[51] The result is that many claims that countries can make for dispensations in trade tend to be linked to specific economic thresholds. The aim seems to be to promote clarity regarding eligibility, for example regarding certain concessions under the GATT or under a Generalised System of Preferences (GSP), which may set out conditions for 'graduation' for stronger or emerging economies.[52]

In particular, the categorisation of a country as a 'least developed country' (LDC) has tangible benefits in international economic law. This is a more technical term than that of 'developing country', which has been defined by the UN since 1971.[53] The Committee for Development Policy (CDP), a sub-

---

[49] Ibid., Article 6.

[50] See Part IV of the General Agreement on Tariffs and Trade (GATT) adopted in 1965 and also appended to the GATT, the Enabling Clause: 'Differential and More Favourable Treatment Reciprocity and Fuller Participation of Developing Countries' – Decision of 28 November 1979 L/4903. For further discussion see this chapter at text accompanying n.88 and n.125; also Chapter 4 at text accompanying n.269 et seq.

[51] Clara Weinhardt and Till Schöfer, 'Differential Treatment for Developing Countries in the WTO: The Unmaking of the North–South Distinction in a Multipolar World' (2022) 43(1) *Third World Quarterly* 74.

[52] See disregard of India's claims to entitlement to quantitative restrictions under Article XVIII declined by the Appellate Body due to an IMF finding that the achievement of India's 'development plan' and management of structural conditions was possible without this. See Decision of the Appellate Body, India – Quantitative Restrictions on Imports of Agricultural Textile and Industrial Products, WT/DS90/AB/R, adopted 6 August 1999. Cf. the application of safeguarding measures under Article XIX of the GATT which cannot be applied to developing countries whose import share is 3 per cent or less from the application of safeguard measures, unless the total share of imports from all such countries exceeds 9 per cent.

[53] See https://unctad.org/topic/least-developed-countries/recognition.

sidiary body of the UN Economic and Social Council (ECOSOC) maintains a list of LDCs, which it reviews every three years.[54] The three criteria applied by the CDP are: (1) per capita income; (2) what are termed 'human assets' (namely indicators of nutrition, health, school enrolment and literacy); and (3) 'economic vulnerability' (indicators of natural and trade-related shocks, physical and economic exposure to shocks, and smallness and remoteness).[55] Countries can graduate from LDC status,[56] and when they do so are supported by UNCTAD as concessions made for them are removed.[57] Notably, there is no room 'for states to "regress" into the category', the assumption being that all states will progress in 'development' terms.[58] Just as 'development' is a sliding scale apparently oriented in an upwards trajectory, it is also vital to acknowledge the continuum of least developed, developing and emerging economies.[59] In recent years, the most powerful of the latter, the BRICS (Brazil, Russia, India, China and South Africa) and the MINT economies (Mexico, Indonesia, Nigeria and Turkey), have become significant trade actors which have formed alliances, although their capacity to transform the multilateral trading and investment system does seem to remain constrained.[60]

An alternative to use of the terms 'developed' and 'developing' stems from the so-called Brandt line, which partitions the wealthier 'Global North' from the 'Global South'.[61] This binary is also problematic, since the continuum of industrialisation and wealth in the global economy does not neatly fit with

---

[54] The list as at 24 November 2021 consisted of 46 countries comprising 880 million people, available at: www.un.org/development/desa/dpad/wp-content/uploads/sites/45/publication/ldc_list.pdf.

[55] See www .un .org/ development/ desa/ dpad/ least -developed -country -category .html.

[56] Six countries have done so to date: Botswana (1994), Cape Verde (2007), Maldives (2011), Samoa (2014), Equatorial Guinea (2017) and Vanuatu (2020).

[57] For issues arising when there is an absence of support, see Isaiah Frank, 'The Graduation Issue for LDCs' (1979) 13 *Journal of World Trade Law* 289; and Mustafizur Rahman and Debapriya Bhattacharya, *Graduating LDCs in an Evolving WTO: Options and Strategies* (Friedrich-Ebert-Stiftung & Centre for Policy Dialogue 2019).

[58] O'Donoghue and Tzouvala n.45, 38. They observe however that the European Union recognises more LDC states than are acknowledged at the UN.

[59] Gordon H. Hanson, 'The Rise of Middle Kingdoms: Emerging Economies in Global Trade' (2012) 26(2) *Journal of Economic Perspectives* 41.

[60] For helpful analysis of their influence and status, see Li Li, 'BRICS: A Limited Role in Transforming the World' (2019) 43(6) *Strategic Analysis* 499; and Adeolu Durotoye, 'The MINT Countries as Emerging Economic Power Bloc: Prospects and Challenges' (2014) 4(5) *Developing Country Studies* 1.

[61] See Willy Brandt, *North-South: A Programme for Survival: Report of the Independent Commission on International Development Issues* (MIT Press 1980) and Willy Brandt, *Common Crisis North-South: Cooperation for world recovery* (Food and

this simple geographical distinction. Nevertheless, on the basis that the terms 'North' and 'South' are widely used and are usually regarded as less offensive than the connotations around 'development', these terms are used here unless dictated by reference to primary legal materials and secondary sources which refer to 'developing countries'.[62]

This book has its inevitable limitations, having been written from the perspective of an academic lawyer who has been resident in the UK for the past 30 years. Given that the UK has been a member of the European Union (EU) for most of that time, and that EU regulation has been the subject of my research over decades, my aim has been to make its workings accessible to scholars based in other countries. I also realise that scholarship originating in the Global North will be over-represented in this book, but my aim has been to search out other sources, available in English, from the Global South and so-called emerging economies and include these perspectives. There is no doubt room for further analysis of the preliminary findings presented here in a broader context in more specific settings, reflecting the relationship between trade and labour relations in spaces that this book has not accessed and does not represent. Indeed, that research agenda is one which this author would welcome in the attempt to craft regulatory solutions to the obvious problems flagged here, and to evaluate the utility of sustainable development objectives in doing so.

4. ISSUES OF POWER

The issue of 'power' is one to which this book returns repeatedly. It is an issue raised in every chapter and therefore also demands attention and definition, although that task is not straightforward. In this context, Steven Lukes' classic typology of 'power' may be helpful.[63]

First and foremost, power can be understood as the situation where 'A exercises power over B when A affects B in a manner contrary to B's interests'.[64] Where an employer possesses the material resources relative to a worker (or group of workers) to dictate terms and conditions of service, their preferences will take precedence, and they can be understood to hold superior bargaining power. Indeed, famously, Otto Kahn-Freund observed that 'the relation between an employer and an isolated employee or worker is typically a relation

---

Agriculture Organization of the United Nations 1983) available at http://agris.fao.org/agris-search/search.do?recordID=XF2015040077.

[62] Also explained in Novitz n.8 above, at 232.

[63] Steven Lukes, *Power: A Radical View*, 1st ed. (Macmillan 1974).

[64] Ibid, 27; described originally by Robert A. Dahl, 'The Concept of Power' (1957) 2(3) *Behavioral Science* 201, 202–3 as 'A has power over B to the extent that he can get B to do something that B would not otherwise do'.

between a bearer of power and one who is not a bearer of power. In its inception it is an act of submission, in its operation it is a condition of subordination.'[65] In this context, collective representation of workers' interests through collective bargaining and industrial action (including a right to strike) becomes crucial as a means by which to compensate for this dyadic subordination.[66]

It may be worth noting that some workers are more vulnerable than others, reflecting the paradox of precarity,[67] so that those who do not have the bargaining power to be hired on terms compatible with a standard employment relationship then struggle to claim the protection of domestic labour laws (including access to collective labour rights), which they need more than others.[68] The exclusion of certain types of work in various ways from formal legal recognition, which can be linked to forms of racial prejudice, sexual discrimination and responses to disability (for example), can lead to a scenario where there is less opportunity to organise effectively in response.[69] Given the higher incidence of informality in the Global South,[70] a geographical distributional problem to which this book also returns in later chapters, the scale of bargaining power of some multinational enterprises as employers is further enhanced.

Less blatant and more insidious versions of power are also identified by Lukes. A second dimension of power relates to the ability to set the agenda (to include or exclude matters) for the policy debates to the detriment of

---

[65] Otto Kahn-Freund, *Labour and the Law* (Stevens 1972), 8. See also Lord Wedderburn, 'Labour Law and the Individual in Post-Industrial Societies' in Lord Wedderburn, Max Rood, Gerard Lyon-Caen, Wolfgang Däubler and Paul van der Heijden (eds), *Labour Law in the Post-Industrial Era* (Aldershot 1994), 44, who likewise identified as an enduring feature of the employment relationship the relative subordination of the worker.

[66] See Vogt et al n.41; also Tonia Novitz, *International and European Protection of the Right to Strike* (Oxford University Press 2003).

[67] Mark Freedland, *The Contract of Employment and the Paradoxes of Precarity* (2016) University of Oxford Legal Research Paper Series Paper No 37/2016.

[68] Regarding these current challenges for platform workers, see Anthony Forsyth, *The Future of Unions and Worker Representation: The Digital Picket Line* (Bloomsbury Publishing 2022); see also Chapter 2 of this book, text accompanying nn. 70–8.

[69] Cf. Adelle Blackett and Colleen Sheppard, 'Collective Bargaining and Equality: Making Connections' (2003) 142 *International Labour Review* 419; and Etienne Pataut and Sophie Robin-Olivier, *The Future of Labour Law*, White Paper 23 (International Law Association 2023), 13–17.

[70] For discussion see contributions to Supriya Routh and Vando Borghi (eds), *Workers and the Global Informal Economy: Interdisciplinary Perspectives* (Routledge 2016).

another.[71] Lukes is best known for his third radical critique of a further ideological dimension of power, which enables the shaping of preferences where 'A may exercise power over B [...] by influencing, shaping or determining his very wants'.[72] The interesting point may however be that there is no single identifiable actor which achieves the deception and indoctrination of the other. Rather, as Peter Digeser has suggested, preference shaping can be achieved through social practices, normalising certain preferences.[73] Understood in this way, the exercise of power may be structural, as agents are disciplined into understanding and internalising certain roles and actions, which are not only economically, but also socially and politically, constituted. In this way, there may be a shift from seeing power as binary or 'dyadic' (between 'A' and 'B') to instead seeing it as based on collective alliances, in which vested interests may be served in more diffuse ways.[74]

In this context, various labour lawyers have investigated the potential for neo-Republican theory and the idea of 'non-domination' (advocated by Philip Pettit, Frank Lovett and others)[75] to resist exercise of arbitrary power in the employment relationship. Views range from advocacy of caution in the application of what remains a contested field of democratic theory,[76] to a partial application of the principles advocated by republican theorists,[77] and even an

---

[71] Lukes n.63, 16; citing Peter Bachrach and Morton S. Baratz, 'Two Faces of Power' (1962) 56 *The American Political Science Review* 947.

[72] Lukes n.63, 23.

[73] Peter Digeser, 'The Fourth Face of Power' (1992) 54(4) *The Journal of Politics* 977.

[74] Mark P. Dallas, Stefano Ponte, and Timothy J. Sturgeon, 'Power in Global Value Chains' (2019) 26(4) *Review of International Political Economy* 666, 672 cite Foucault's analysis as a basis for understanding 'constitutive' and 'diffuse' power, which cannot be attributed to a single agent.

[75] See Philip Pettit, *Republicanism: A Theory of Freedom and Government* (OUP 1999); Frank Lovett and Philip Pettit, 'Neorepublicanism: A Normative and Institutional Research Program' (2009) 12 *Annual Review of Political Science* 11; and Frank Lovett, *A General Theory of Domination and Justice* (OUP 2010). For an outline of the potential relevance of their respective theories to labour law, see the detailed examination offered by David Cabrelli and Rebecca Zahn, 'Civic Republican Political Theory and Labour Law' in Hugh Collins, Gillian Lester and Virginia Mantouvalou, *Philosophical Foundations of Labour Law* (OUP 2018).

[76] Alan Bogg, 'Republican Non-Domination and Labour Law: New Normativity or Trojan Horse?' (2017) 33(3) *International Journal of Comparative Labour Law and Industrial Relations* 391.

[77] David Cabrelli and Rebecca Zahn, 'Theories of Domination and Labour Law: An Alternative Conception for Intervention?' (2017) 33(3) *International Journal of Comparative Labour Law and Industrial Relations* 339.

emphatic embrace of the possibilities.[78] Certainly, this is an evolving field of analysis.

However, despite the potential promise of this theoretical approach, my focus goes beyond a concern with what might be understood as 'arbitrary'. Instead, this book engages more broadly with the arguably more wide-ranging three dimensions of power identified above, which can assist our understanding not only of the dynamics of bargaining power between capital and labour, but also of the interactions between states and other powerful actors in international relations. Such a view of power may explain how certain states, sometimes in alliance with particular employer representatives, can utilise opportunities for their preferences to prevail within institutions, including the content of instruments adopted and scrutiny of their implementation.[79] Those alliances can seek to make those at work act in ways that do not serve their interests (under the first dimension of power). They can achieve that aim by setting the agenda of international organisations. In doing so, they may garner support to establish and maintain rules of trade which, respectively, further the balance of payments position (for a state or group of states) and boost profit margins (for certain modes of business). This is a manifestation of the second dimension of power. Externally to that institution, they may simultaneously use their own economic resources and related forms of media and other influence in ways that normalise the exclusion of the preferences of other actors, reflecting exercise of a third dimension of power. Hybrid transnational practices, such as the combined private and public operation of global value chains, may be better explained through this conceptually rich apparatus which provides a multi-dimensional account of power.[80]

There remains scope also, as contemporary power resource theorists have observed, for trade unions and other representatives of those at work, such as non-governmental organisations, to utilise institutional resources, involving media communications, academic research, coordinated litigation strategies and other forms of 'societal power', to gain greater agency in transnational

---

[78] Dáire MacCormack-George, 'Philip Pettit's Republicanism and Labour Law; A Defence' (2021) 37(4) *International Journal of Comparative Labour Law and Industrial Relations* 417; and Ricardo M. Buendia Esteban, 'Examining Recent Initiatives to Ensure Labour Rights for Platform Workers in the European Union to Tackle the Problem of Domination' (2022) 28(4) *Transfer: European Review of Labour and Research* 475.

[79] Cf. Tonia Novitz and Phil Syrpis, 'Assessing Legitimate Structures for the Making of Transnational Labour Law: The Durability of Corporatism' (2006) 35(4) *Industrial Law Journal* 367 and 380–1.

[80] Dallas, Ponte and Sturgeon n.74; and see also Stefano Ponte, *Business, Power and Sustainability in a World of Global Value Chains* (Zed Books 2019).

labour regulation,[81] including in the sphere of trade.[82] Nevertheless, we may also understand the conventional legal frameworks operating regarding international labour standards and global trade as having their own ideological impacts; the question is whether the narrative of 'sustainable development' has potential to disrupt prior normative conventions and enable change.

5. THE PROMISE OF 'SUSTAINABLE DEVELOPMENT' IN INTERNATIONAL INSTRUMENTS AND POLICY

The final section of this introductory chapter offers a review of relevant international institutional engagement with sustainable development over the past 50 years (from 1972 to the present day). This is an opportunity to extrapolate some key foundational principles that may underlie the so-called hybrid and contested concept[83] of sustainable development. While acknowledging the reasons for opposition to a sustainable development approach, it is argued that its potential application and significance remain worthy of interrogation in relation to trade and labour. The chapter concludes by considering how (despite potential obstacles) the promise of sustainability could be realised in relation to crafting regulation of the trade–labour linkage and the preconditions for doing so, which are considered in the remainder of the book.

---

[81] Schmalz et al n.29; see also Christian Lévesque and Gregor Murray, 'Understanding Union Power: Resources and Capabilities for Renewing Union Capacity' (2010) 16(3) *Transfer: European Review of Labour and Research* 333.

[82] Pedro Mendonca and Dragoş Adăscăliţei, 'Trade Union Power Resources within the Supply Chain: Marketisation, Marginalisation, Mobilisation' (2020) 34(6) *Work, Employment and Society* 1062; Huw Thomas and Mark Anner, 'Dissensus and Deadlock in the Evolution of Labour Governance: Global Supply Chains and the International Labour Organization (ILO)' (2022) *Journal of Business Ethics* forthcoming, available at: https://link.springer.com/article/10.1007/s10551-022-05177-z#citeas.

[83] See Frances Flanagan and Caleb Goods, 'Climate Change and Industrial Relations: Reflections on an Emerging Field' (2022) 64(4) *Journal of Industrial Relations* 479, 482 on 'sustainable development' as a 'hybrid labour–environment concept'; also Steve Connelly, 'Mapping Sustainable Development as a Contested Concept' (2007) 12(3) *Local Environment* 259; and Fred P. Gale, *The Political Economy of Sustainability* (Edward Elgar Publishing 2018). Cf. Justice Mensah, 'Sustainable Development: Meaning, History, Principles, Pillars, and Implications for Human Action' (2019) 5(1) *Cogent Social Science* 1653531.

5.1 An Overview of International Initiatives Addressing Sustainable Development

The obvious starting point for any historical review is the 1972 Declaration agreed at the UN Stockholm Conference on Environment and Development, which did not expressly refer to sustainable development, but sought 'the preservation and enhancement of the human environment'.[84] Nor did the Declaration discuss 'trade' explicitly, but the issue of work was acknowledged,[85] with the statement in Principle 8 that 'Economic and social development is essential for ensuring a favorable living and working environment for man and for creating conditions on earth that are necessary for the improvement of the quality of life'. In a contemporary context where employment extends beyond the conventional workplace and into the wider community,[86] this statement continues to have considerable resonance.

The issue of equality within and between states (at different levels of 'development') was also raised by the 1972 Declaration, which observed:

> In the developing countries most of the environmental problems are caused by under-development. Therefore, the developing countries must direct their efforts to development, bearing in mind their priorities and the need to safeguard and improve the environment. For the same purpose, the industrialized countries should make efforts to reduce the gap between themselves and the developing countries.[87]

This seems to have been a nod to emerging policy initiatives relating to 'special and differential treatment' (SDT) in favour of so-called developing countries in the context of world trade, designed to address power imbalances between the Global North and South.[88]

In 1983, the UN General Assembly welcomed the creation of the World Commission on Environment and Development,[89] which produced in 1987 what came to be known as the 'Brundtland Report' (named after the chair of the Commission). This is the source of the world-renowned statement that sustainable development is concerned with meeting 'the needs of the present without compromising the ability of future generations to meet their own

---

[84] Declaration of the UN Conference on the Human Environment (1972) UN Doc. A/Conf.48/14.

[85] Ibid, paras 3, 5 and 6.

[86] Paolo Tomassetti, 'Labor Law and Environmental Sustainability' (2018) 40 *Comparative Labour Law and Policy Journal* 61, 63.

[87] Declaration of the UN Conference on the Human Environment (1972) UN Doc. A/Conf.48/14, preamble, para. 4.

[88] See this chapter, text accompanying n.50 above.

[89] UNGA RES 38/161 of 19 December 1983.

needs', which entails consideration 'of the long term as well as the short-term advantages and disadvantages of alternative actions'.[90] In other words, *inter*-generational justice (between present and future generations) as well as *intra*-generational justice (addressing for example relative poverty within a single generation) are both regarded as vital for sustainable development. In this way, the Brundtland Report prompted attention to both geographical and temporal distributive justice.[91]

The Brundtland Report recognised problems related to trade, both insofar as items could be traded which were dangerous to health and safety at work, as well as the wider environment,[92] and in the sense that systemic material inequalities in trade undermined sustainable development.[93] The servicing of debt to IFIs was seen as impeding attention by government to environmental and social issues in 'many countries, especially in Africa and Latin America'.[94] Recognising the common dependence of so-called developing counties on export of agricultural and other primary produce such as timber, the report called for international institutions to take greater account of the impact of trade rules on the environment.[95] Further, the Brundtland Commission observed the increased establishment of chemical and pollutive industries in developing countries, posing risks of hazardous industrial accidents, prompting trade unions to press for action by management and authorities that was not always forthcoming.[96] Otherwise, the Commission's focus was more on 'work opportunities' than on the regulation of the terms and conditions of work, even in the context of trade.[97]

---

90 World Commission on Environment and Development (WCED), *Our Common Future* (Oxford University Press 1987), 51.

91 For discussion, see William M. Lafferty and Oluf Langhelle, 'Sustainable Development as Concept and Norm' in William M. Lafferty and Oluf Langhelle (eds) *Towards Sustainable Development* (Palgrave Macmillan 1999). For an attempt to concretise these objectives, see Erling Holden, Kristin Linnerud and David Banister, 'Sustainable Development: Our Common Future Revisited' (2014) 26 *Global Environmental Change* 130.

92 WCED n.90 above, Introduction, para. 16.

93 Ibid, para. 19: 'Trade barriers in the wealthy nations – and in many developing nations – make it hard for African nations to sell their goods for reasonable returns, putting yet more pressure on ecological systems. Aid from donor nations has not only been inadequate in scale, but too often has reflected the priorities of the nations giving the aid, rather than the needs of the recipients.'

94 Ibid, para. 78.

95 Ibid, paras 37 and 38.

96 Ibid, chapter 8.

97 Ibid, chapter 2.

The Brundtland Report can be distinguished from the UN Declaration on the Right to Development 1986,[98] which focused on 'economic, social, cultural and political development, in which all human rights and fundamental freedoms can be fully realized', but made no specific mention of trade or labour, or even issues relating to environmental or inter-generational justice. Article 2(1) did however stress that 'The human person is the central subject of development and should be the active participant and beneficiary of the right to development'. All persons were to have the responsibility for and the ability to actively, freely and meaningfully participate in policy-making connected to development. Moreover, under Article 8(2), 'states should encourage popular participation in all spheres as an important factor in development' and in the full realisation of all human rights. In this way, development was linked to individual and collective human agency, in a way which may be linked to later acknowledgement of the importance of participatory engagement to the ambition of *sustainable* development.

The Rio Declaration (known as 'Agenda 21') on Environment and Development 1992[99] reverted to many of the concerns raised by the Brundtland Report, with Principle 3 stating: 'The right to development must be fulfilled so as to equitably meet developmental and environmental needs of present and future generations.' Intra-generational justice was also recognised in Principle 5 seeking to eradicate poverty 'in order to decrease the disparities in standards of living and better meet the needs of the majority of the people of the world', while Principle 6 attended to 'The special situation and needs of developing countries'. Principle 12 recognised the importance of the 'international economic system' and 'trade policy' in achieving the Rio Declaration's other objectives, while Principle 15 adopted the 'precautionary principle' whereby 'Where there are threats of serious or irreversible damage, lack of full scientific certainty shall not be used as a reason for postponing cost-effective measures to prevent environmental degradation'. Perhaps most significant was the appreciation in Principle 10 of the desirability of participation in environmental decision-making (arguably also drawing on the entitlement established in the UN Declaration on the Right to Development): 'environmental issues are best handled with the participation of all concerned citizens.' This principle was given force in Europe through what has come to be known as the Aarhus Convention of 1998,[100] which set out three aspects of participatory

---

[98] UN Declaration on the Right to Development 1986 UNGA RES/41/128 of 4 December 1986.

[99] Rio Declaration on Environment and Development 1992 A/CONF.151/26 of 14 June 1992. Available at: www.un-documents.net/rio-dec.htm.

[100] United Nations Economic Commission for Europe (UNECE) Convention on Access to Information, Public Participation in Decision-Making and Access to Justice

environmental justice: access to environmental information, participation in environmental decision making and access to justice in environmental matters. This initiative was followed by the Escazú Agreement in 2018, in which Latin American and Caribbean states have also made commitments to 'Information, Public Participation and Justice in Environmental Matters'.[101]

In comparison, the eight Millennium Development Goals (MDGs) adopted by the UN General Assembly (UNGA) in 2000 were criticised for the top-down imposition of social, economic and environmental standards without scope for extensive participatory engagement or reflection, which led to capture of the process by vested interests.[102] That lack of concern with encouragement of civil society participation was also arguably evident in the Johannesburg World Summit on Sustainable Development, where the dialogue session was shortened and had no official input into the outcome document.[103] The Johannesburg Plan of Action (2002)[104] ultimately sought to integrate the three 'independent and mutually reinforcing pillars', namely the economic, social and environmental dimensions of sustainable development, while (in a now familiar way) focussing on poverty eradication prominent in MDG 1.[105] By 2010, the International Court of Justice had also formally recognised the principle of 'sustainable development' as a means by which to mediate between economic and environmental interests, although the social pillar was arguably neglected in the *Pulp Mills* case.[106]

Rio+20 in 2012 sought to promote the 'green economy', a tool designed to promote environmental issues but notably also economic growth. Rio+20

---

in Environmental Matters, 25 June 1998, which entered into force on 20 October 2001, available at: https://unece.org/DAM/env/pp/documents/cep43e.pdf.

[101] Regional Agreement on Access to Information, Public Participation and Justice in Environmental Matters in Latin America and the Caribbean, Escazú, 4 March 2018, which entered into force on 22 April 2021 available at: https://treaties.un.org/Pages/ViewDetails.aspx?src=IND&mtdsg_no=XXVII-18&chapter=27&clang=_en.

[102] Jan Vandemoortele, 'The MDG Conundrum: Meeting the Targets Without Missing the Point' (2009) 27(4) *Development Policy Review* 355.

[103] Tom Waas, Jean Hugé, Aviel Verbruggen and Tarah Wright, 'Sustainable Development: A Bird's Eye View' (2011) 3(10) *Sustainability* 1637. See for more detailed analysis Pieraccini and Novitz n.20, 19–20.

[104] Available at: www.un-documents.net/jburgdec.htm.

[105] Article 1.2 Johannesburg Plan of Action 2002.

[106] *Case Concerning Pulp Mills on the River Uruguay*, ICJ Judgment (20 April 2010), discussed in Virginie Barral, 'Sustainable Development in International Law: Nature and Operation of an Evolutive Legal Norm' (2012) 23(2) *European Journal of International Law* 377; see also Clair Gammage and Tonia Novitz, 'The Concept of Sustainability and its Application' in Clair Gammage and Tonia Novitz (eds), *Sustainable Trade, Investment and Finance: Toward Responsible and Coherent Regulatory Frameworks* (Edward Elgar Publishing 2019), 3–6.

is however as notable for the decision to pursue development of the SDGs adopted in 2015 and for introducing the High Level Political Forum (HLPF), which operates now as a mechanism for scrutiny of their implementation.[107]

The SDGs are the successor to these incremental international policy developments. The 2030 Agenda adopted the methodology of the MDGs, namely the use of goals, targets and indicators, and deployed the HLPF in attempts to coordinate or (as it has been termed) 'orchestrate' implementation of the SDGs.[108] Despite concerns that the deliberative process preceding adoption of the SDGs gave precedence to certain business interests,[109] this was a richer and more extensive process than had hitherto been seen in Johannesburg or Rio. The result was a very full agenda and set of objectives concerning 'people, planet, prosperity, peace and partnership', including not only specific environmental goals but also detailed social and economic aspirations (while making it clear that the latter are subject to the concerns raised by other SDGs).

Among the noteworthy goals established by the UNGA Resolution relevant to labour are: SDG 1, which addresses poverty; SDG 4, promoting education; SDG 5, concerning gender equality; SDG 8, advocating sustainable growth, employment and decent work; and SDG 10, seeking equality within and between states. SDG 16 raises the issue of good governance, highlighting the importance of access to justice but also of 'strong institutions'. Indeed, this 'institutional dimension' of sustainable development has been described as a fourth pillar entailing 'the capacity to ensure conditions of stability, democracy, participation, information, training and justice'.[110] Under SDG target 16.7, the aim is to '[e]nsure responsive, inclusive, participatory and representative decision-making at all levels', which one might assume would include workers' representatives, especially trade unions. In this way, many of the principles espoused in the Aarhus Convention at European level were given global application.[111] The UN Special Rapporteur has argued that target 16.10

---

107 Documentation relating to the decision-making at Rio+20 can be accessed at: https://sustainabledevelopment.un.org/rio20.

108 Kenneth W. Abbott and Steven Bernstein, 'The High-level Political Forum on Sustainable Development: Orchestration by Default and Design' (2015) 6(3) *Global Policy* 222. Cf. Tonia Novitz and Margherita Pieraccini, 'Agenda 2030 and the Sustainable Development Goals: "Responsive, Inclusive and Participatory Decision-making"?' in Pieraccini and Novitz n.19, 53–60.

109 See Lou Pingeot, *Corporate Influence in the Post-2015 Process* Working Paper (Misereor, Brot für die Welt and Global Policy Forum, 2014); and Regina Scheyvens, Glenn Banks and Emma Hughes, 'The Private Sector and the SDGs: The Need to Move beyond "Business as Usual"' (2016) 24(6) *Sustainable Development* 371.

110 Valentina Cagnin, *Labour Law and Sustainable Development* (Wolters Kluwer 2020), 23.

111 See Aarhus Convention n.100.

which sets out the need to respect 'fundamental rights' should be understood to include freedom of association, and thereby collective bargaining and a right to strike.[112]

Notably, any promotion of sustainable development through trade is not to be pursued by unilateral measures but rather through the global partnership more broadly envisaged in SDG 17. This contemplates a variety of actions, including provision of finance to assist countries in the Global South (targets 17.2–17.5), transfer of technologies (targets 17.6–17.8), capacity building (target 17.9) and 'a universal, rules-based, open, non-discriminatory and equitable multilateral trading system' (target 17.10). The latter is to also entail greater export capacity and access to markets for the least developed countries (targets 17.11 and 17.12). Trade is to be fair across the globe. This is consistent with the statement in the preamble to the 2030 Agenda that the use of 'unilateral economic, financial or trade measures not in accordance with international law and the Charter of the United Nations' is to be prevented where this will 'impede the full achievement of economic and social development, particularly in developing countries'.[113]

'Policy coherence' is viewed as a crucial path to both 'global macroeconomic stability' (target 17.13) and sustainable development (target 17.14). Moreover, while each country is to have the autonomy to craft their own 'policies for poverty eradication and sustainable development' (target 17.15), there is also a collective responsibility imposed on a global multi-stakeholder partnership (targets 17.16 and 17.17). These are not only obligations imposed on state actors, but also international and regional organisations of which they are members, as well as business and civil society.[114] The partnerships can consist of 'public, public–private and civil society' actors. Their actions will be grounded in attention to statistical data (under targets 17.18 and 17.19).

All the SDGs intersect and operate together, but perhaps SDG 8 is most significant for our purposes, insofar as it offers an attempt to reconcile what have long between regarded as potentially conflicting objectives concerned with 'economic growth' and 'decent work', while avoiding 'environmental

---

112 Report of the Special Rapporteur on the Rights to Freedom of Peaceful Assembly and Association, 7 August 2018, A/73/279, paras. 6 and 58, also paras. 87–89.

113 See the 2030 Agenda n.21 above, para. 30.

114 Elena Sondermann and Cornelia Ulbert, 'Transformation through "Meaningful" Partnership? SDG 17 as Metagovernance Norm and Its Global Health Implementation' (2021) 9(1) *Politics and Governance* 152; Patrick Holden, 'Finding Common Ground? European Union and European Civil Society Framing of the Role of Trade in the Sustainable Development Goals' (2019) 57(5) *Journal of Common Market Studies* 956. See also the UN 2030 Agenda n.21, para 29 and at para 67 mentioning the UN Guiding Principles on Business and Human Rights (discussed further in Chapter 6 of this book).

degradation'. We will examine more closely the content and nuances of SDG 8 in the next chapter when considering the economic case for regulation of labour in the context of trade and the desirability of 'growth'.[115] SDG 8 targets address the eradication of forced labour, the elimination of child labour and the elimination of discrimination. 'Freedom of association and collective bargaining' appear in an indicator (8.8.2) adopted subsequently and, as noted above, are understood to be incorporated into SDG target 16.10.[116] SDG 8 also goes further to include, for example, trafficking and modern slavery in SDG target 8.7 and recognition of the need for protection of the working conditions and environment for migrant workers in target 8.8. The more specific issue of transaction costs of migrant worker remittances is dealt with in SDG target 10.10. In SDG target 10.7 comes the injunction to 'facilitate orderly, safe, regular and responsible migration and mobility of people, including through the implementation of planned and well-managed migration policies'.

Moreover, SDG 8 has to be seen as connected to and supplemented by attention to gender equality in SDG 5 and inequality more broadly in SDG 10. SDG 5 aims to 'Achieve gender equality and empower all women and girls'. Of particular relevance to an interpretation and application of SDG 8 may be the broad SDG target 5.1 to 'end all forms of discrimination' and target 5.4 relating to women's 'unpaid care and domestic work'. This raises issues as to the ambit of 'work' which should be subjected to regulation. Indeed, Sandra Fredman has pointed to the potentially transformational aspects of SDG 5 in that it operationalises female representation in decision-making alongside the concrete norms that feed into enabling their effective representation.[117] If we see SDG 8 as connected to collective worker voice – of girls and women as well as boys and men – then SDG 5 has considerable significance for what might be termed broadly 'the world of work'.

SDG 10 addresses 'reduction of inequality within and among countries', and refers to social and economic inclusion and outcomes, including wages in target 10.4 and labour share of GDP in the attached indicator. In a context

---

[115] See Chapter 2 of this book, text accompanying nn. 32–9. See also Halliki Kreinin and Ernest Aigner, 'From "Decent Work and Economic Growth" to "Sustainable Work and Economic Degrowth": A New Framework for SDG 8' (2022) 49(2) *Empirica* 281; and Johannes Euler, 'The Commons: A Social Form that Allows for Degrowth and Sustainability' (2019) 30(2) *Capitalism Nature Socialism* 158.

[116] See Tonia Novitz, 'Sustainable Development Goal 8: Promote Sustained, Inclusive, and Sustainable Economic Growth, Full and Productive Employment, and Decent Work for All' in Jonas Ebbesson and Ellen Hey (eds), *Cambridge Handbook on the United Nations Sustainable Development Goals and International Law* (Cambridge University Press 2022), 213–15.

[117] Sandra Fredman, *Working Together: Human Rights, the Sustainable Development Goals and Gender Equality* (The British Academy 2018).

where inequalities of income are growing starkly between management and labour,[118] this SDG is of considerable significance in relation to the interpretation of the objectives set out in SDG 8. In particular, the cross-section of SDG 8 and 10 raises questions regarding the ways in which paid work and collective bargaining which enhances remuneration of workers can redistribute income.[119] SDG targets 10.2. and 10.3 suggest attention to an anti-discriminatory framework can assist in the interpretation and application of SDG targets 8.5 and 8.8. concerning 'decent work' and 'labour rights', if these are to be for 'all'.[120]

There are also some important references to trade issues in the 2030 Agenda, which should also be flagged at this point. An example is SDG 2, which is concerned with 'sustainable agriculture', and sets out a target 2.b that seeks to 'correct and prevent trade restrictions and distortions in world agricultural markets'. These restrictions are likely to have particular effects on countries in the Global South, given their frequent specialisation in exports of primary produce.[121] Further, target 8.A seeks to 'Increase Aid for Trade support for developing countries, in particular least developed countries, including through the Enhanced Integrated Framework for Trade-Related Technical Assistance to Least Developed Countries'. As observed above, SDG 17 and its associated targets also make repeated reference to the needs of 'developing' and 'least developed countries' in the context of trade. Nevertheless, it is interesting that despite this explicit reference to 'developing countries' in SDG targets, sensitivity to the stigma of the term would seem to have led the UN Statistics Division to decide that it will not use 'developing country' as a statistical category when collating data regarding the Sustainable Development Goal indicators.[122]

In more substantive terms, partnering aid with trade enables the building of capacity at national level in the Global South, with the potential to enhance human functionings and capabilities without which decent work becomes unlikely.[123] That objective is consistent with reference to promotion of 'capa-

---

[118] Thomas Piketty, *Capital in the Twenty-First Century* (Harvard University Press 2014); Lydia Hayes and Tonia Novitz, 'Trade Unions and Economic Inequality' (2021) 4(1) *Institute of Employment Rights Journal* 118.

[119] Florence Jaumotte and Carolina Buitron, *Inequality and Labor Market Institutions* (IMF Discussion Note 15/14 2015).

[120] Novitz n.116, 214.

[121] Cf. Discussion in the WCED Brundtland Report, text accompanying n 95 above.

[122] See Onno Hoffmeister, *Development Status as a Measure of Development* UNCTAD Research Paper no. 46 (UN 2020), 3.

[123] Cf. Martha Nussbaum, *Creating Capabilities: The Human Development Approach* (Harvard University Press 2011); and Amartya Sen, *Development as Freedom* (Oxford University Press 1999).

bilities' in the preamble to the 2030 Agenda and SDG 17 targets.[124] This attention by the 2030 Agenda to issues of substantive equality in the trade sphere fortifies the principle of SDT mentioned above,[125] which receives specific attention in SDG target 10.8.

Moreover, if we recognise trade as commerce as having palpable effects on the environment that will need to be remedied, then we may need to think about SDG 8's objective of 'decent work' as connected to facets of 'just transitions' associated with environmental needs.[126] Changing the terms of trade in goods and services to ensure environmental standards set by SDGs are met can affect jobs in manufacturing, but also the terms of work supplied through, for example, agencies and migration. In this context, concerns of labour and the environment connect, with a need for attention to protection of SDG 4 targets regarding re-training and meaningful access to forms of learning to ensure employment promotion. Additionally SDGs 1 and 10 stress that social protection that will enable such transitions without the workers affected falling into poverty. Further, if climate change disrupts industry and agriculture then what the current ILO Director-General, Gilbert F. Houngbo, has termed 'decent work' aspects of social justice instantiated in SDGs 1, 4 and 10 become relevant again, including the protections contemplated in SDG 8.8 for 'climate refugees' or migrants whose movement across borders has been encouraged by such changes.[127] We might further expect the design of policies for employment promotion and social protection, which as we will see are notable features of the ILO's longstanding commitment to 'decent work',[128] to also encompass 'social dialogue' and human rights protections in line with SDG 16 and promoted under the broad umbrella of global partnership fostered by SDG 17.[129]

The UN has developed a reflexive soft law process for regular review of state compliance with particular SDGs through the HLPF understood as 'orchestration', involving voluntary national reports (VNRs) by states for

---

[124] See the 2030 Agenda n.21 above, paras 35 and 28.

[125] See text accompanying nn.50 and 88 above.

[126] For an impressive overview of contemporary concerns regarding 'just transitions', see Edouard Morena, Dunja Krause and Dimitris Stevis (eds), *Just Transitions: Social Justice in the Shift towards a Low-carbon World* (Pluto Press 2020).

[127] *Report of the Director-General: Advancing Social Justice* (ILO 2023), 25–6.

[128] On the substance of 'decent work' established by the ILO (employment promotion, social protection, social dialogue and fundamental principle and rights at work), see Chapter 3 of this book, text accompanying nn.107–51.

[129] See International Labour Office, *Time to Act for SDG 8: Integrating Decent Work, Sustained Growth and Environmental Integrity* (ILO 2019), and further discussion of these issues regarding environmental rationales for trade regulation in Chapter 2 in text accompanying nn.113 et seq.

review.[130] The UN seeks significant assistance from international institutions such as the ILO, in both assessing the satisfaction of the various indicators attached to each goal and target,[131] and more generally the measures required to achieve the goals.[132] Civil society, including trade unions and non-governmental organisations (NGOs) recognised by ECOSOC, come within the ambit of 'major groups and other stakeholders' (MGOs) invited to attend the HLPF annual review process and participate in 'side-events'.[133] The problem is that the VNRs, as their title indicates, are indeed 'voluntary' and state-centred, while the eight days which has been allocated for their review and scrutiny seems inadequate.[134] It is to be hoped that the SDG Summit held on 18–19 September 2023, which marks the midway point for achievement of the SDGs, will regenerate interest in their achievement.[135] Where the SDGs have arguably been effective is in their incorporation into other instruments and supervisory mechanisms relating to trade and labour, as discussed in Chapters 3 to 6 of this book. They also have continued to have resonance on the international stage, for example, the UN Conference on Trade and Development (UNCTAD) in the Bridgetown Covenant of 2021 drew on the 2030 Agenda, the SDGs and principles of sustainable development to make commitments to address the exploitation of those in 'informal and unpaid work' (who are predominantly women)[136] and address the impact of digital technologies on labour markets.[137]

5.2 Principles of Sustainable Development related to Trade and Labour

From this review, we can extrapolate the following principles as foundational to a sustainability approach. It is evident from these international initiatives

---

[130] See Abbott and Bernstein n.108. For argument for a more 'robust' supervisory system, see Qerim Qerimi, 'The Ambitious Modesty of the High-Level Political Forum on Sustainable Development' (2022) 13(2) *Global Policy* 281.

[131] See the contribution made by ILO statistics available at: https://ilostat.ilo.org/topics/sdg/; and *Decent Work and the Sustainable Development Goals: A Guidebook on SDG Labour Market Indicators* (ILO 2018), the ILO being responsible for gathering data on 17 SDG indicators.

[132] International Labour Office, *Time to Act for SDG 8: Integrating Decent Work, Sustained Growth and Environmental Integrity* (ILO 2019).

[133] Novitz and Pieraccini n.108.

[134] Qerimi n.130, 284–5.

[135] See www.un.org/en/conferences/SDGSummit2023.

[136] United Nations Conference on Trade and Development (UNCTAD), The Bridgetown Covenant: From inequality and vulnerability to prosperity for all TD/L.435, 6 October 2021, 10, para. 57.

[137] Ibid, para. 58.

that what is 'sustainable' is also 'durable' in the longer term, durability being a synonym for sustainability. That assessment of durability is brought to bear on the economic, social and environmental 'pillars' of development.[138]

Labour might seem to fit simply in the sphere of the social pillar (or 'social sustainability'), being a vital part of access to community, the necessities of life and overall social well-being and agency.[139] However, it is argued in this book that labour also has dimensions relevant to the other two pillars of sustainable development. The statement in the preamble to the 2030 Agenda that the SDGs are 'integrated and indivisible' is pertinent here.[140] Work in a capitalist society involves the production of income for both the person working and those who profit from that work (from a Marxist material explanation of exploitation).[141] Moreover, labour is connected intrinsically to the environment in which work takes place, whether this is the factory or the office, or, as was evident during the COVID-19 pandemic, at home or in the streets.[142]

Analysis of the durability of social and legal policy in the trade sphere in relation to the three pillars of sustainable development will further require reflection on *intra-generational* fair distribution of resources within and between countries, as well as what has been termed *inter-generational* justice that looks to the well-being of not only present but future generations. A notable feature of a shared sustainable development agenda therefore is concern with issues of equality and capabilities, entailing resistance to 'entrenched social injustice', which is arguably evident in SDG 10 as well as SDG 8.[143] As the Preamble to the 2030 Agenda says at the outset: 'No one will be left behind.'[144] This is significant, insofar as the current climate crisis and other environmental harms can be linked to what have been described as 'patterned hierarchies' and distributional injustice,[145] as well as forms of social discrimination and domi-

[138] Ben Purvis, Yong Mao and Darren Robinson, 'Three Pillars of Sustainability: In Search of Conceptual Origins' (2019) 44(3) *Sustainability Science* 681.

[139] Cf. Erich Grießler and Beate Littig, 'Social Sustainability: A Catchword between Political Pragmatism and Social Theory' (2005) 8(1–2) *International Journal of Sustainable Development* 65.

[140] 2030 Agenda n.21, Preamble and Declaration, paras 5 and 18.

[141] Karl Marx, *Capital* (Wordsworth 2013); Anne-Laure Fayard, 'Notes on the Meaning of Work: Labor, Work, and Action in the 21st Century' (2021) 30(2) *Journal of Management Inquiry* 207, 209.

[142] See Tomassetti n.86 who regards the idea of a discrete workplace as now anachronistic.

[143] As described by Nussbaum n.123 above, at 18–19. See citation of her earlier work in Grießler and Littig n.139, 75.

[144] 2030 Agenda n.21, preamble and Declaration, para. 4; versions of this phrase are repeated throughout.

[145] Anna Grear, 'Towards "Climate Justice"? A Critical Reflection on Legal Subjectivity and Climate Injustice: Warning Signals, Patterned Hierarchies, Directions

nance.[146] The focus on decarbonisation in policy reform has been criticised by environmental scholars who wish to avoid 'carbon fundamentalism'[147] and see a need to address 'issues of equality and exclusion'.[148]

In this way also, under a sustainability model, the three pillars of economic, social and environmental goals can come into play together – although it is less clear how any conflicts between objectives should be prioritised. As Flanagan and Goods have observed: 'Questions of how each sustainability goal should be achieved relative to, or in combination with, the others are rarely mandated.'[149] The interactions between SDGs and their relative priorities seem likely to be the subject of continued debate and deliberation.

It emerges from mapping the succession of international instruments outlined above and contestation between application of the three 'pillars' in the sphere of trade and labour that sustainable development is not a simple static end-goal, but an active dynamic process of reflection and readjustment.[150] Over time, the significance of participatory engagement by stakeholders has become increasingly prominent. While it is obvious that future generations are not here to be represented today and younger persons also lack many opportunities for democratic engagement, there is an intention to widen access to political voice for various under-represented constituencies affected by economic, environmental and social change. If 'no one will be left behind', then everyone must be recognised and their interests reflected in decision-making processes.

This participatory approach builds on a legacy of environmental policy adjustments as 'just transitions', dating from the engagement of Canadian and United States unions in the 1970s in changes to working practices and alleviating the burden of such changes on workers.[151] Engagement with worker representatives and engagement in social dialogue and collective bargaining is also

---

for Future Law and Policy' (2014) 5 *Journal of Human Rights and the Environment* 103, 111 and 127. See also Julia Dehm, 'Reflections on Paris: Thoughts Towards a Critical Approach to Climate Law' (2018) *Quebec Journal of International Law* 61.

[146] Tomassetti n.6 above, at 441 and 452.

[147] Gopal Dayaneni, 'Carbon Fundamentalism vs. Climate Justice' (2009) 16(2) *Race, Poverty & the Environment* 7.

[148] Ed Atkins, *A Just Energy Transition: Getting Decarbonisation Right in a Time of Crisis* (Bristol University Press 2023), 7.

[149] Flanagan and Goods n.83, 482.

[150] So much is clear from the progression of international instruments and reports discussed above, and, in a contemporary setting, reference to the 2030 Agenda in the ILO World Employment and Social Outlook Report, *The Role of Digital Labour Platforms in Transforming the World of Work* (Geneva: ILO, 2021), 113, 174 and 222 available at: www.ilo.org/global/research/global-reports/weso/2021/WCMS_771749/lang--en/index.htm.

[151] Stevis et al n.30 above, 9.

recommended by the ILO 2015 'Tripartite Guidelines for a Just Transition'.[152] The 'imperatives of a just transition of the workforce and the creation of decent work' were acknowledged in the preamble to the Paris Agreement concluded that year, even if no mechanisms were created through that medium to realise such participatory engagement.[153] We return to the significance of the 'just transition' principle in Chapter 2.[154]

5.3 The Potential Dangers of a Sustainability Approach

While it is possible to identify certain foundational normative principles which underlie a sustainability discourse, that is not to say that its current influence in policy-making is uncontroversial. Sustainable development is not a straightforward candidate for achievement of normative cohesion in the treatment of trade and labour. A number of objections have been raised, which come from a variety of viewpoints.

One concern raised was that there was an insufficient link made between the SDGs and extant human rights standards established under UN institutions.[155] However, the preamble to the 2030 Agenda at least states the intention to preserve the obligation of all states to 'respect, protect and promote human rights' under international law,[156] including explicit reference to 'the right to development'.[157] A fairer comment may be that the content of the SDGs themselves (and their targets and indicators) has been selective and variable in the treatment of human rights norms. It has been argued that a trade-conditionality approach should be based not on the nebulous and flexible policies associated with sustainable development but on more tangible human rights protections reflecting 'fundamental principles and rights at work'.[158] The strength of that

---

[152] *Guidelines for a Just Transition Towards Environmentally Sustainable Economies and Societies For All* (ILO 2015) available at: www.ilo.org/wcmsp5/groups/public/---ed_emp/---emp_ent/documents/publication/wcms_432859.pdf.

[153] Available at: https://unfccc.int/sites/default/files/english_paris_agreement.pdf. See for comment on this issue, Pataut and Robin-Olivier n.69, 62.

[154] See Chapter 2 of this book, text accompanying nn.168–84.

[155] See Thomas Pogge and Mitu Sengupta, 'The Sustainable Development Goals (SDGs) as Drafted: Nice Idea, Poor Execution' (2015) 24(3) *Washington International Law Journal* 571 at 573; and V.P. Nanda, 'The Journey from the Millennium Development Goals to the Sustainable Development Goals' (2016) 44 *Denver Journal of International Law and Policy* 389, 404.

[156] UN 2030 Agenda n.21 above, for example paras 8, 10 and 19.

[157] Ibid, paras 10 and 35.

[158] Connelly n.83. For criticism of this shift towards a sustainability approach in an EU trade context due to its uncertainty, see Lore Van den Putte and Jan Orbie, 'EU Bilateral Trade Agreements and the Surprising Rise of Labour Provisions' (2015) 31(3) *International Journal of Comparative Labour Law and Industrial Relations*

objection will be considered further in Chapter 2, in relation to human rights arguments which have been understood to be part of the social rationale for protection of labour standards in trade.

Linking sustainable development objectives to labour standards in the context of trade has also been opposed by 'deep ecologists', but for different reasons. Their concern is not with the enforcement of human rights but rather with giving priority in policy-making to the Ecocene, or, in other words, environmental concerns.[159] If environmental issues are indeed to be prioritised over the Anthropocene, then we might expect labour standards to be only a limited and supplementary aspect of sustainable development. Moreover, even the term sustainable development becomes suspect, to the extent that (for example under the 2030 Agenda) it is acknowledged to be 'people-centred'.[160]

An approach to trade policy in which ecology is the central focus would make work-related issues more peripheral. Issues concerning labour might only seem relevant in the context of achievement of necessary transitions to ensure environmental protections.[161] The arguments associated with this standpoint are a helpful reminder of the tensions which sustainability attempts, as a discourse, to bridge. These issues are again addressed further in Chapter 2.[162]

The application of a sustainability approach to trade can also be criticised on the basis that this flexible (and contested) discourse can be used by business to obstruct the imperatives of established UN human rights norms and dilute the strict legal obligations arising from, for example, ILO standards.[163] This concern was voiced at the time of adoption of the SDGs.[164] The willingness

---

263 at 281–2; in terms of the limited enforceability of such clauses, see Lorand Bartels, 'Human Rights and Sustainable Development Obligations in EU Free Trade Agreements' (University of Cambridge Legal Studies Research paper Series Paper No. 24/2012 2012).

[159] Merle Jacobs, 'Sustainable Development and Deep Ecology: An Analysis of Competing Traditions' (1994) 18(4) *Environmental Management* 477. For a history of these tensions, see Pieraccini and Novitz n.20, 25–8. Note the omission of discussion of labour and work-related issues in the UNGA discussions which resulted in the Request for an advisory opinion of the International Court of Justice on the obligation of States in respect of climate change. See UNGA A/77/L.58 and UNGA resolution 77/276 of 29 March 2023.

[160] The 2030 Agenda n.21, para. 74(e).

[161] For the role of global trade unions in this species of engagement with 'just transitions', see Dimitris Stevis and Romain Felli, 'Global Labour Unions and Just Transition to a Green Economy' (2015) 15(1) *International Environmental Agreements* 29.

[162] Chapter 2 of this book, text accompanying nn.133–84.

[163] For acknowledgement of business interests advocating a sustainability approach, see Diane F. Frey, 'Economic Growth, Full Employment and Decent Work: The means and ends in SDG 8' (2017) 21(8) *The International Journal of Human Rights* 1164.

[164] See Pingeot n.109; Scheyvens et al n.109.

of big business to adopt and utilise a sustainable development agenda has been evident in 'Vision 2050' proposed by the World Business Council for Sustainable Development (WBCSD), which sets out a sustainable development agenda from a business perspective. Issued originally in 2010, the WBCSD vision did not initially contemplate much more than freer trade.[165] To the extent that labour standards were considered, and this was minimal, the aims seemed to be concerned with greater flexibility for employers; for example: 'Broader and more flexible concepts of work as well as virtual mobility give people and companies different options and conditions for employment.'[166]

However, the 2050 Agenda was updated in 2021 as 'Time to Transform'. It now contains explicit recognition of the role that labour unions can play in protecting more vulnerable workers and easing fuel transitions.[167] The identification of problems with systemic inequalities exposed by the COVID-19 pandemic, with reference to the principle that no one should be left behind,[168] suggests an ideological shift on the part of business that is not perhaps easily dismissed, even though concrete concessions may be more difficult to achieve. Moreover, there would be dangers in ceding the field of sustainability-based policy, especially where it concerns trade and labour markets, to employers at global, regional, national or local levels. Instead, it is argued in this book that it is necessary for the concerns of those at work to be represented in policy and legal debates concerning sustainable development and trade.

5.4 Preconditions for Realisation of a Sustainable Trade–Labour Linkage

Much controversy over the 'trade–labour linkage' has been concerned with whether access to trade should be conditional on compliance with certain labour standards and the legal or other regulatory measures that would entail.[169] However, this terminology, and consequent debates, can obscure the fact that,

---

[165] WBCSD, *Vision 2050* (2010) available at: www.wbcsd.org/Overview/About-us/Vision_2050/Resources/Vision-2050-The-new-agenda-for-business, especially at 10 and 20.

[166] Ibid, 16.

[167] WBCSD, *Vision 2050 Time to Transform* (2021) available at: www.wbcsd.org/contentwbc/download/11765/177145/1, especially at 12 and 30.

[168] Ibid., 21.

[169] Christian Barry and Sanjay G. Reddy, 'International Trade and Labor Standards: A Proposal for Linkage' (2006) 39 *Cornell International Law Journal* 545; Sandra Polaski, 'The Strategy and Politics of Linking Trade and Labor Standards: An Overview of Issues and Approaches' in Kimberly A. Elliott (ed.), *Handbook on Globalisation and Labour Standards* (Edward Elgar Publishing 2022).

in reality, trade and labour have always been and remain interdependent.[170] So much is already evident from the introductory material covered in this chapter, and more evidence follows in this book.

The terms of trade profoundly affect the ways in which labour is hired, impacting on the daily lives of those at work across the globe and in different occupations and sectors, whether hired formally as workers or otherwise. Moreover, access to labour is built into trade law, an example being 'trade in services', discussed further in Chapters 4 and 5 of this book, which enables temporary movement of natural persons to enable cross-border service provision by employees. Accordingly, exploration of the implications of a sustainable development approach in this book will not so much forge a new connection between two unrelated aspects of international law (for that fragmented vision of separate spheres for trade and labour was always a fallacy),[171] but rather assist in explicating how these ties arise and what that might mean for better regulation.

The aim of this book is not to assert that a sustainable development perspective is uncontroversial or even that it will always necessarily be beneficial, but to acknowledge that this is an emergent approach which has gained considerable ideological traction and is therefore deserving of attention. For this reason, Chapters 3 to 6 identify how the emerging sustainable development discourse has been adopted and (to varying degrees) implemented by the ILO, by IFIs, by the WTO, in preferential (or 'free') trade agreements and in the context of corporate social responsibility. This is an opportunity to examine the extent to which the paradigm of 'sustainable development' is now impacting on regulation of the relationship between trade and labour. The observations made will explain why this shift in discourse has had relatively little effect today, although it still has the potential to do so.

However, this book is not only concerned with a 'mapping exercise' but is also normatively grounded. Chapter 2 will continue by examining closely the economic, social and environmental pillars of sustainable development and how they offer reasons for protecting labour standards in trade. In this way, this book offers a critique of the various concrete ways in which a sustainable development approach to the intersection of trade and labour can be understood, with reference to the connections between substantive normative 'pillars' that are regarded as crucial to sustainability.

---

[170] Adelle Blackett, 'On Social Regionalism in Transnational Labour Law' (2020) 159(4) *International Labour Review* 591, 610. See also Chapter 7, text accompanying n.5.

[171] Cf. n.14 above.

Sustainable development objectives (or, in the words of the 2030 Agenda, 'goals' and 'targets') often converge to operate in complementary ways, but may also diverge. It is an appreciation of these complexities that this book seeks to prompt. The argument being made is that more attention needs to be paid to the synergies and tensions identified. For example, it does not seem viable in the longer term to merely pursue labour and environmental aims as twin tracks to sustainable development operating in parallel. It would be preferable to interrogate how the different pillars may inter-relate and the ways in which these relationships can be addressed. In this way, the case may be made to widen the scope of labour standards to be protected on the global stage, even beyond the 'core' that are currently acknowledged. Where there are obvious conflicts, decisions will have to be made as to what values to prioritise and when.

Such normative questions require attention to the ways in which decisions regarding sustainable policy-making around trade and labour are made. The route to a less fragmented approach therefore lies not only in the substantive content of the 2030 Agenda, but in the procedural expectations inherent in SDGs 16 and 17, namely the notion of participatory good governance by multiple actors and at multiple levels. This would entail inclusive engagement in decision-making by all those affected by the policies, laws and regulatory mechanisms to be adopted.

This argument for inclusive participatory engagement as a facet of sustainable development has two dimensions in this book. The first is that it is vital that working people be represented in these decisions. That can be achieved, at least in part, by including trade unions at local, national, regional and international levels. But it is further argued here that challenge is to ensure inclusion of all those engaged in work, whether formal or informal, home state or migrant, recognising the limitations of current national, regional and international laws which define the term 'worker' too narrowly and thereby exclude too many of those at work from access to collective voice and influence. This observation renders relevant other civil society organisations, ideally where members are represented,[172] but also NGOs which cannot claim to be representative of an interested membership but that do have the capacity to highlight injustice to those in the world of work.[173]

---

[172] Beate Kohler-Koch and Christine Quittkat, 'What Is Civil Society and Who Represents Civil Society in the EU? Results of an Online Survey among Civil Society Experts' (2009) 28(1) *Policy and Society* 11; Nicole Bolleyer and Patricia Correa, 'Member Influence and Involvement in Civil Society Organizations: A Resource Dependency Perspective on Groups and Parties' (2022) 70(2) *Political Studies* 519.

[173] See Adelle Blackett, *Everyday Transgressions: Domestic Workers' Transnational Challenge to International Labor Law* (Cornell University Press/ILR Press 2019); and

The second is that there must be inclusive representation of those at work, not only in all sectors of the labour market (where work is bought and sold in a multiplicity of ways) but in all parts of the 'world'. In that sense the expression of 'world of work' (used at the ILO) is understood in this book not only to be a means to broaden the coverage of who counts as a 'worker', but also to expand the geographical remit of that inquiry to encompass all parts of the globe. For that reason, as labour can be represented also by states where democratic mechanisms enable this, this book examines how those in the Global South gain voice in the international institutions that are the subject of this study.

If no one is to be left behind when trade and labour rules are forged, such that viable compromises and sustainable solutions are to be adopted at national, regional and international levels, more inclusive access for those at work is key. The contribution of this book is to identify these preconditions for realising the promise of sustainable development for the relationship between trade and labour, and to consider the extent to which they are recognised or lacking in current international and transnational policy formation.

Andreas Bieler and Jörg Nowak (eds), *Labour Conflicts in the Global South* (Routledge 2022).

2. Reconciling three rationales for protection of labour standards in sustainable trade

1. INTRODUCTION TO THE RELEVANCE OF THE THREE PILLARS

This chapter sets out the case that can be made for protection of labour standards in trade from a 'sustainable development' perspective. Building on the historical survey of sustainable development instruments in Chapter 1, this case can be made in various ways, in 'economic', 'social' and 'environmental' terms reflecting the three pillars of sustainability, each of which would have implications for the identification of labour standards to be protected and the manner of their protection. The aim is to identify substantive norms which would be desirable as a basis for trade regulation, but also to recognise how participatory, transparent and inclusive decision-making can achieve synergies between these types of arguments and even resolve conflicts.

Sustainable development as a rationale for regulation of trade already holds sway.[1] The 2030 Agenda adopted by the United Nations (UN) General Assembly makes reference to both the need to protect 'decent work' and the terms of trade.[2] This connection had already been forged by the European Union (EU), which places protections of labour standards under the heads of 'sustainable development' and 'human rights and good governance' in instruments relating to generalised trade preferences[3] and free trade agreements

[1] For background and discussion prior to 2015, see Olivier De Schutter, *Trade in the Service of Sustainable Development: Linking Trade to Labour Rights and Environmental Standards* (Bloomsbury/Hart 2015).

[2] United Nations (UN), Transforming Our World: The 2030 Agenda for Sustainable Development, General Assembly, 70th Session, A/Res/70/1, New York, 2015 ('The 2030 Agenda').

[3] Regulation (EU) No 978/2012 of the European Parliament and of the Council of 25 October 2012 applying a scheme of generalised tariff preferences and repealing Council Regulation (EC) No 732/2008 OJ L 303/1 31.10.2012. At the time of writing, the European Commission is proposing continuation of this scheme, regarding which see European Commission, *Proposal for a Regulation of the European Parliament*

(FTAs). For example, the European Commission has observed that trade and sustainable development (TSD) chapters inserted in EU FTAs require 'the effective implementation of the International Labour Organization (ILO) conventions [...] that each party has ratified' and respect for 'core ILO principles as set out in the 1998 ILO Declaration on Fundamental Principles and Rights at Work'.[4] These chapters also include obligations to comply with the Multilateral Environmental Agreements (MEAs) ratified by the parties.

Further, apart from *de facto* connections made in international instruments between sustainable development, trade and labour, the suggestion made here is that a sustainability approach may have certain advantages in normative terms which deserve consideration. 'Economic', 'social' and 'environmental' justifications for protection of labour standards in trade have traditionally been treated as discrete and independent. A holistic perspective on these 'three pillars' of sustainable development presumes that they are interconnected and demands analysis of their interactions.[5]

The 17 Sustainable Development Goals (SDGs) are stated in the preamble to the 2030 Agenda to be 'integrated and indivisible' and to 'balance the three dimensions of sustainable development: the economic, social and environmental'.[6] This may be of assistance when addressing interactions between trade and labour, if we regard working life as 'relational'. The recognition of indivisibility makes sense, given that work is not only an activity performed for an employer; rather, those who do that work are connected to their 'family, community, and environment' in ways that are deeply intertwined.[7] Moreover, this intersection between labour and the environment is not only personal but structural; for example, the dynamics of labour relations have to be understood in the context of usage of work in agriculture and fossil fuels as a basis for

---

and of the Council on applying a generalised scheme of tariff preferences and repealing Regulation (EU) No 978/2012 of the European Parliament and of the Council COM(2021) 579 22.9.2021 available at: https://eur-lex.europa.eu/legal-content/EN/TXT/PDF/?uri=CELEX:52021PC0579&from=EN.

4 European Commission, *Communication on the Power of Trade Partnerships: Together for green and just economic growth* COM(2022) 409 final, 22 June 2022, at 2.

5 Ben Purvis, Yong Mao and Darren Robinson, 'Three Pillars of Sustainability: In Search of Conceptual Origins' (2019) 44(3) *Sustainability Science* 681.

6 See the 2030 Agenda n.2 above, preamble, para. 1; and see Sara Seck, 'Transnational Labour Law and the Environment: Beyond the Bounded Autonomous Worker' (2018) 33(2) *Canadian Journal of Law and Society* 137, 155.

7 Sara Seck, 'Relational Law and the Reimagining of Tools for Environmental and Climate Justice' (2019) 31(1) *Canadian Journal of Women and Law* 151, 158; Ania Zbyszewska, 'Regulating Work with People and "Nature" in Mind: Feminist Reflections' (2018) 40(1) *Comparative Labor Law and Policy Journal* 9 at 22–4.

manufacturing.[8] A sustainability approach may thereby assist in challenging the past dominance of economic rationales for trade promotion and regulation, opening space for greater consideration of the working environment in both social and ecological terms. Additionally, the scope of labour standards deserving of protection in the context of trade, which have often been limited to what are deemed 'human rights',[9] or what the ILO terms 'core' or 'fundamental' labour standards,[10] could be extended by adopting a wider sustainable development perspective responding to environmental issues and their connection to work.[11]

Recognising the synergies and tensions between economic, social and environmental reasons for regulation does however pose questions as to how they should be concretised in legal frameworks addressing trade and labour. The final part of this chapter considers how challenging questions could be addressed, arguing that this requires participatory engagement by all those affected across the globe and in all kinds of work. Suggestions are made as to how this could be achieved through collective bargaining, protest and various forms of social dialogue, with attention to entrenched power imbalances. In so doing, this chapter lays the foundations for the more technical legal analysis of trade and labour institutions and practices which follows in the book.

2. ECONOMIC UNDERSTANDINGS OF THE RELATIONSHIP BETWEEN TRADE AND LABOUR

There are numerous economic rationales for recognising the ways in which labour markets shape trade and vice versa. Various facets of this often instrumental and utilitarian vision of arguments for trade and labour market regu-

---

[8] Frances Flanagan and Caleb Goods, 'Climate Change and Industrial Relations: Reflections on an Emerging Field' (2022) 64(4) *Journal of Industrial Relations* 479; and Paolo Tomassetti, 'Energy Transition: A Labour Law Retrospective' (2022) 52(1) *Industrial Law Journal* 34.

[9] See Thomas Cottier, Joost Pauwelyn, and Elisabeth Bürgi Bonanomi (eds), *Human Rights and International Trade* (Oxford University Press 2005); Lorand Bartels, *Human Rights Conditionality in the EU's International Agreements* (Oxford University Press 2005).

[10] For information regarding the ILO Declaration on Fundamental Principles on Rights at Work 1998 and its amendment in 2022, as well as current 'fundamental ILO Conventions', see https://libguides.ilo.org/c.php?g=657806&p=4649148. This is discussed further in Chapter 3 of this book at text accompanying nn.75–104.

[11] An argument introduced in Tonia Novitz, 'Labour Standards and Trade: Need We Choose between "Human Rights" and "Sustainable Development"?' in Henner Gött (ed), *Labour Standards in International Economic Law* (Springer 2018).

lation are examined here. Issues regarding the uncritical pursuit of economic growth are identified, alongside the need to consider social norms as a basis for crafting terms of fair competition in trade.

2.1 The Instrumental Economic Case for Labour Regulation

The construction and regulation of labour markets can be understood as shaping the potential economic benefits of trade (whether within or beyond the nation state). Notable here are the assertions made by Adam Smith in 1776 regarding the ways in which 'division of labour' enhances profitability of trade and the lowering of prices for consumers.[12] David Ricardo in 1817 identified the utility of comparative advantage, with reference to a country's specialisation in supplying certain kinds of products, utilising certain forms of labour and thereby trade.[13] Workers then gain advantages as consumers when goods become cheaper.

Ricardo's identification of comparative advantage as an issue has fostered other economic theorisation regarding regulation of labour markets. An example is the conversion of his assumptions into the Heckscher–Ohlin theory, which addresses labour as a factor of production.[14] This theory posits that production will move to the site most specialised and suitable for its purposes. So, labour-intensive production will gravitate towards labour-abundant countries, while capital-intensive production will tend to be based in capital-abundant countries. Tariffs in trade may then be seen as a way of protecting wages in labour-intensive industries.[15]

This theorisation led to expectations that trade and migration will operate as 'substitutes between countries that have different factor endowments', such that we should not expect migration from labour-abundant countries where work is readily available due to this kind of specialisation (in response to comparative advantage). However, as Chantal Thomas has observed, this is

---

[12] Adam Smith, *An Inquiry into the Nature and Causes of the Wealth of Nations* Rev. ed. (Penguin 1979), Book 1, chapter 1 'Of the Division of Labour' and chapter III 'That the Division of Labour Is Limited by the Extent of the Market'; also chapter VIII 'Of the Wages of Labour', which suggests that division of labour leads not only to wages commensurate to productivity but also to cheaper goods.

[13] David Ricardo, *On the Principles of Political Economy and Taxation* (Penguin 1971). For later conversion into the Heckscher–Ohlin theory, see for example Mark Blaug, *The Methodology of Economics: Or How Economists Explain* (Cambridge University Press 2009) ch 11, who also addresses the Stolper–Samuelson model, which posited the potential role of tariffs in protecting wages in labour-intensive industries.

[14] Gunnar Heckscher, Eli Filip Heckscher, and Bertil Ohlin, *Heckscher-Ohlin Trade Theory* (MIT Press 1991).

[15] As discussed in Blaug n.13 above.

palpably false.[16] That assumption also neglects the complex push–pull factors which generate migration,[17] and the economic benefits that both high- and low-skilled migrants can bring in terms of productivity.[18]

Moreover, economic justifications for regulation of the labour market are inherently limited. They are primarily utilitarian in their formulation, being concerned with what is regarded as the effective facilitation of profitable trade rather than their concrete effects on those people whose labour provides the basis for those profits.

Another difficulty with reliance on early attempts to theorise the connections between trade and labour is the assumptions on which they are based. For example, as Bob Hepple observed, Ricardo assumed that capital was unlikely to be mobile but will remain linked to one country, thereby connecting the fortunes of a state to its domestic manufacturers. By the time Hepple was writing in 2005, he could confidently confirm that this was patently no longer the case in the global economy, as multinational enterprises (MNEs) relocated or utilised subsidiaries according to the most advantageous tax and regulatory environments.[19] This provides a useful reminder that the economic fortunes of states and employers may not always be straightforwardly aligned in the ways that Ricardo posited. That shift poses difficulties for state-oriented regulation of trade and labour on the world stage.

In particular, the model offered by Ricardo and others does not easily map onto the realities of global supply chain arrangements. His was a model that places states at its centre, rather than the forms of subcontracting from a 'lead firm' downwards that characterise global supply chains. The literature on global supply chains is rich and varied and it is not possible to do full justice to its dimensions in this brief discussion, which is continued in Chapter 6 of this book.[20] The ILO has defined 'supply chains' as 'the cross-border organization of the activities required to produce goods or services and bring them

---

[16] Chantal Thomas, 'Migration and International Economic Asymmetry' in Alvaro Santos, Chantal Thomas and David Trubek (eds), *World Trade and Investment Law Reimagined: A Progressive Agenda for an Inclusive Globalization* (Anthem Press 2019), 241–56.

[17] Cf. Saskia Sassen, *The Mobility of Labour and Capital: A Study in International Investment and Labor Flow* (University of Cambridge Press 1998).

[18] Florence Jaumotte, Ksenia Koloskova and Sweta C. Saxena, 'This Is the Impact of Migration on Productivity' (2017) *World Economic Forum*, available at: www.weforum.org/agenda/2017/01/this-is-the-impact-of-migration-on-productivity/.

[19] Bob Hepple, *Labour Laws and Global Trade* (Hart 2005), 23.

[20] Terence K. Hopkins and Immanuel Wallerstein, 'Commodity Chains in the World Economy prior to 1800' (1986) 10(1) *Review* 157 at 159 cited in Gary Gereffi and Miguel Korzeniewicz (eds), *Commodity Chains and Global Capitalism* (Prager 1994) at 2. See also Chapter 6 of this book, text accompanying n.17 et seq.

to consumers through inputs and various phases of development, production and delivery'.[21] MNEs will thereby ensure production of component parts of goods and may even provide delivery of services across multiple sites, rather than being tied to one state.[22]

The supply chain process tends to involve subcontracting from an MNE based in one country to a business entity in another and may also entail the establishment of subsidiaries to carry out the lead firm's business, or other forms of investment.[23] For these reasons, whether goods or services originate from a particular state can be difficult to detect, resulting in the controversy over 'rules of origin'.[24] If production of goods or supply of services cannot be mapped onto the state, trade rules based on Ricardo's notion of comparative advantage may be unhelpful.

Moreover, Ricardo and Smith seem to have been more concerned with the productive outcomes of regulation of labour markets, rather than labour conditionality in trade. That preoccupation can be detected in the contemporary arguments for and against labour market regulation. On the one side is concern that labour standards can add costs for producers of goods or supply of services, which can lead to a competitive disadvantage in trade.[25] In this context, not only laws but the lawful operations of trade unions have been viewed as unduly restricting the free market order.[26] This concern has generated a call for 'deregulation' of labour markets, which, as we will see in Chapter 4, was

---

21 ILO, *Report IV: Decent Work in Global Supply Chains*, ILC, 105th Session (ILO 2016), 2.

22 Daria Taglioni and Deborah Winkler, 'Making Global Value Chains Work for Development' (2014) *The World Bank – Economic Premise*, Number 143, 1–2 and 8.

23 David A. Wuttke, Constantin Blome, and Michael Henke, 'Focusing the Financial Flow of Supply Chains: An Empirical Investigation of Financial Supply Chain Management' (2013) 145(2) *International Journal of Production Economics* 773; Philipp Wetzel and Erik Hofmann, 'Supply Chain Finance, Financial Constraints and Corporate Performance: An Explorative Network Analysis and Future Research Agenda' (2019) 216 *International Journal of Production Economics* 364.

24 Rules of origin have not been set by the WTO but are often established in FTAs. See WTO *Technical Information on Rules of Origin* available at: www.wto.org/english/tratop_e/roi_e/roi_info_e.htm. See Gabriel Felbermayr, Feodora Teti and Erdal Yalcin, 'Rules of Origin and the Profitability of Trade Deflection' (2019) 121 *Journal of International Economics* 103248.

25 For critical but helpful explanation of this view, see Eddy Lee, 'Globalization and Labour Standards: A Review of Issues' (1997) 136(2) *International Labour Review* 173.

26 See Friedrich A. Hayek, *1980s Unemployment and the Unions: Essays on the Impotent Price Structure of Britain and Monopoly in the Labour Market*, 2nd ed. (Institute of Economic Affairs 1984); and Richard A. Posner, 'Some Economics of Labor Law Author' (1984) 51(4) *The University of Chicago Law Review* 988.

evident in the 'Doing Business Report' of the World Bank from 2003 to 2022.[27] It should be noted that such a 'deregulatory strategy' is actually, ironically, usually more closely associated with placing greater (and more complex) constraints on trade union activity than enabling the 'free' operation of a market order.[28]

From the 1990s onwards there has been compelling evidence to demonstrate that protection of labour standards assists in the efficient and effective production of goods and delivery of services.[29] For example, the Organisation for Economic Co-operation and Development (OECD) has found that 'proper implementation of some core labour standards can support economic development, permitting an expansion in trade' and that 'concerns expressed by certain developing countries that core standards would negatively affect their economic performance or their international competitive position are unfounded; indeed, it is theoretically possible that the observance of core standards would strengthen the long-term economic performance of all countries'.[30] Obviously, ensuring an adequate wage for workers and allowing time in which such wages can be spent ensures the consumer base which enables trade and thereby profit. International Monetary Fund (IMF) economists have advocated collective bargaining rights, which enhance redistribution of income from capital to labour, enabling greater spending power and capitalist economies to 'grow'.[31]

---

27 See Chapter 4 of this book, text accompanying n.104 et seq.

28 For the UK experience, see Sandra Fredman, 'The New Rights: Labour Law and Ideology in the Thatcher Years' (1992) 12(1) *Oxford Journal of Legal Studies* 24; more recently comparable observations have been made in India and Thailand. See Atul Sood, Paaritosh Nath and Sangeeta Ghosh, 'Deregulating Capital, Regulating Labour: The Dynamics in the Manufacturing Sector in India' (2014) 49 (26/27) *Economic and Political Weekly* 58; and John Lawler and Chokechai Suttawet, 'Labour Unions, Globalization and Deregulation in Thailand' (2000) 6(3) *Asia Pacific Business Review* 214 at 226 et seq.

29 Simon Deakin and Frank Wilkinson, 'Rights versus Efficiency? The Economic Case for Transnational Labour Standards' (1994) 23 *Industrial Law Journal* 289.

30 OECD, *Trade, Employment and Labour Standards: A Study of Core Workers' Rights and International Trade* (OECD 1996), at 11 and 3, respectively. This view was recently cited and endorsed in the Report of the Panel of Experts (2020) Proceeding constituted under Article 13.15 of the EU-Korea Free Trade Agreement, 25 January 2021, at para. 88, available at: https://trade.ec.europa.eu/doclib/docs/2021/january/tradoc_159358.pdf, referring also to ILO, *Handbook on Assessment of Labour Provisions in Trade and Investment Arrangements* (ILO 2017), 18.

31 See Florence Jaumotte and Carolina Buitron, *Inequality and Labor Market Institutions* (IMF Staff Discussion Note 15/14, 1 July 2015). Also, see World Bank, *World Development Report 2019: The Changing Nature of Work* (World Bank Group 2019); and OECD *Policy Responses to New Forms of Work* (OECD 2019), both of which seek to promote productive work which also provides the worker with disposable income as a consumer.

Nevertheless, these are economic instrumental arguments for national-level labour laws, not proposals for reshaping of international laws relating to trade to ensure that such labour standards prevail.

2.2 The Pursuit of Economic Growth

Commitment to 'economic growth' pervades the 2030 Agenda, in particular SDG 8, in which the link is made with 'decent work'. This connection is also deserving of attention.[32] SDG target 8.2 contemplates achieving 'economic growth' through 'higher levels of economic productivity' involving 'diversification, technological upgrading and innovation, including through a focus on high-value added and labour-intensive sectors'. In other words, the objective is to achieve growth through investment in change and potentially, accompanying that change, investment in labour, presumably skills and training. The accompanying indicator 8.2.1 requires measurement of the '[a]nnual growth rate of real GDP per employed person', which is difficult to reconcile with the notion that 'labour is not a commodity'.[33]

It does seem, however, that, in the aftermath of the pandemic and the onset of the Ukraine war, the 7 per cent growth rate envisaged for least developed countries is unlikely to be realised.[34] Even before these events, there were questions as to whether this should be a priority.[35] These targets associated with growth and those connected to employment (such as targets 8.3, 8.5, 8.6 and 8.b) do however have to be read in tandem with the rest of the 2030 Agenda and other SDGs, targets and indicators. It may be telling that the aim of target 8.4 is to 'decouple' economic growth from environmental degrada-

[32] See discussion of synergies in International Labour Office, *Time to Act for SDG 8: Integrating Decent Work, Sustained Growth and Environmental Integrity* (ILO 2019), x and 2. See also Tonia Novitz, 'Sustainable Development Goal 8: Promote Sustained, Inclusive, and Sustainable Economic Growth, Full and Productive Employment, and Decent Work for All' in Jonas Ebbesson and Ellen Hey (eds), *Cambridge Handbook on the United Nations Sustainable Development Goals and International Law* (Cambridge University Press 2022).

[33] The first ILO Constitution to be found in Part XIII of the Treaty of Versailles 1919 stated in Section II (Article 427) that 'labour should not be regarded merely as a commodity or article of commerce', repeated in Article I(a) of the ILO Declaration on Philadelphia 1944.

[34] See the IMF, *World Economic Outlook: Gloomy and More Uncertain* (IMF 2022), released 26 July 2022 and available at: www.imf.org/en/Publications/WEO/Issues/2022/07/26/world-economic-outlook-update-july-2022.

[35] UN Department of Economic and Social Affairs, *Sustainable Development Outlook 2019: Gathering Storms and Silver Linings* (UN 2019), 2, 11 and 16.

tion, while in target 8.9 promotion of jobs in tourism is to be limited to what is 'sustainable'.

Similarly, as noted above, trade is clearly conceived of in the 2030 Agenda as a route to economic success, but only on 'inclusive' terms that ensure non-discriminatory and fair processes and outcomes which 'leave no one behind'. The kinds of inequalities now being witnessed in global supply chains, made manifest by the pandemic which were outlined in Chapter 1, are not acceptable by-products of trade from a sustainability perspective, which takes account of not only economic but social and environmental concerns. In response to such concerns, there has been active advocacy by academic commentators and civil society of 'managed degrowth',[36] and concern that a 'productivist' approach to the economy cannot enable the forms of structural changes needed to prevent climate crisis and other ecological harms.[37] The implications for labour of degrowth in terms of availability of jobs and terms and conditions of hire are unclear and currently being debated,[38] but it has been suggested that forms of shared non-profit ownership should flourish which could provide greater benefits for communities as a whole, including those who work within them.[39] If growth is to be achieved through trade, SDG 17.10 suggests that this can be achieved through an 'equitable multilateral trading system', presumably based on rules set regarding fair terms of competition.

---

[36] The leading text is Giorgos Kallis, 'In Defence of Degrowth' (2011) 70(5) *Ecological Economics* 873; for application in contemporary circumstances, see Peter Wells, Wessam Abouarghoub, Stephen Pettit and Anthony Beresford, 'A Socio-technical Transitions Perspective for Assessing Future Sustainability following the COVID-19 Pandemic' (2020) 16(1) *Sustainability: Science, Practice and Policy* 29, 33–4. See also Chapter 1 of this book, at text accompanying n115.

[37] Pasi Heikkurinen, Toni Ruuska, Anna Kuokkanen and Sally Russell, 'Leaving Productivism Behind: Towards a Holistic and Processual Philosophy of Ecological Management' (2021) 20(1) *Philosophy of Management* 21; and Tony Fitzpatrick, 'Paradigm Lost? Blocking the Path to Ecosocial Welfare and Post-productivism' in Christopher Deeming (ed.), *The Struggle for Social Sustainability: Moral Conflicts in Global Social Policy* (Policy Press 2021).

[38] From an eco-feminist perspective, see Anna Saave and Barbara Muraca, 'Rethinking Labour/Work in a Degrowth Society' in Nora Räthzel, Dimitris Stevis and David Uzzell (eds), *The Palgrave Handbook of Environmental Labour Studies* (Palgrave Macmillan 2021); for the claim that this would enable the Global South to insist on fair prices for labour, see Jason Hickel, 'What Does Degrowth Mean? A Few Points of Clarification' (2021) 18(7) *Globalizations* 1105, 1109–10.

[39] See Tomassetti n.8, on a commons approach to cooperative ownership of energy sources and the implications for labour relations, 64–7.

2.3 Establishing Terms of Fair Competition

Linked to an economic rationale is the notion that labour standards can be used not merely to regulate domestic labour markets to enhance profits or growth, but to be included in setting fair terms of competition in trade. Indeed, this is a recurrent theme in a recent monograph by Aneta Tyc, who, in her history of the development of workers' rights in the context of global trade rules, discusses how fair competition is vital to an understanding of the place of labour rights in international law.[40] Such terms of competition clearly have to be transparent to be fair, but further difficulties arise in relation to how they are set and applied. While we can imagine the fair rules of trade being determined by strategic means reflecting perceived self-interest, such as game theory, even then it is difficult to achieve this without some reference to a normative foundation reflecting the longer-term interests of the parties and those who will be affected by their conduct.[41]

It is not difficult to envisage circumstances in which states seek to enable the businesses based there to compete in international trade markets by lowering the price of goods (or services) for export and to do so by lowering labour standards.[42] Another possibility is that a state seeks to attract investment, and thereby boost capacity for trade, by reducing labour law protections.[43] Employers may then seek to take advantage of such a legal framework to reduce labour costs and increase profits.

'Dumping' under standard world trade rules, established under Article VI of the General Agreement on Tariffs and Trade (GATT), establishes the entitlement of a state to take compensatory measures when 'products of one country are introduced into the commerce of another country at less than the *normal*

---

[40] Aneta Tyc, *Global Trade, Labour Rights and International Law* (Routledge 2021), ch 1.

[41] For a brilliant exploration of possibilities, see Maayan Menashe, 'The Race to the Bottom Revisited: International Labour Law, Global Trade and Evolutionary Game Theory' (2020) 40(1) *Oxford Journal of Legal Studies* 53.

[42] For a helpful history of these concerns and their manifestation in domestic and international law, see Steve Charnovitz, 'The Influence of International Labour Standards on the World Trading Regime – A Historical Overview' (1987) 126 *International Labour Review* 565; more recently see Etienne Pataut and Sophie Robin-Olivier, *The Future of Labour Law*, White Paper 23 (International Law Association 2022), 8–9 and 38.

[43] Also see regarding attempts to attract investment by diminishing protective practices, rather than labour laws *per se*, Fangjin Ye, 'The Impact of Bilateral Investment Treaties (BITs) on Collective Labor Rights in Developing Countries' (2020) 15(4) *The Review of International Organizations* 899.

value'.[44] The term 'social dumping' has been linked to 'the gaining of unfair competitive advantage [...] through unacceptably low social standards'.[45] The question then is what labour standards are unacceptably low so as to render the price 'abnormal', which goes beyond mere acquisition of a legitimate comparative advantage.[46] When we talk about 'social' dumping, the argument being made is that the economic gain is illegitimate because it violates established norms or evades accepted forms of regulation.[47]

The essence of 'social dumping' would seem to be a short-term advantage conferred on those employers and the states which derive benefits from such commercial activities, despite having longer-term flaws, such as a failure to invest in infrastructure and talent or the long-term welfare of workers and citizens.[48] Arguably, as we have seen in the second part of this chapter, orientation towards policy that is sustainable or 'durable' offers a basis to challenge such short-term gains and the costs that accompany them.

The other facet of so-called social dumping is its presumptive spiralling effects.[49] If one trade competitor can violate labour rights, then the risk is that

---

[44] As discussed by Francis Maupain, *The Future of the International Labour Organization in the Global Economy* (Hart 2013), 136.

[45] See Phil Syrpis, *EU Intervention in Domestic Labour Law* (OUP 2007), 41; also Tonia Novitz, 'Collective Bargaining and Social Dumping in Posting and Procurement – What Might Come from Recent Court of Justice Case Law and the Proposed Reform of the Posting of Workers Directive?' in Albert Sanchez-Graells (ed), *Smart Public Procurement and Labour Standards: Pushing the Discussion after RegioPost* (Hart 2018), 215; and Tonia Novitz, 'Addressing "Social Dumping" and "Unfair Competition": An Analysis of EU Pillar Initiatives from a Sustainability Perspective' in Ann-Christine Hartzén, Andrea Iossa and Elena Karageorgiou (eds), *Law, Solidarity and the Limits of Social Europe: Constitutional Tensions for EU Integration* (Edward Elgar Publishing 2022).

[46] Magdalena Bernaciek, *Social Dumping: Political Catchphrase or Threat to Labour Standards?* (ETUI 2012).

[47] Daniel Vaughan-Whitehead, *EU Enlargement versus Social Europe? The Uncertain Future of the European Social Model* (Edward Elgar Publishing 2003), 325. See also Erik Bengtsson, 'Social Dumping Cases in the Swedish Labour Court in the Wake of *Laval*, 2004–2010' (2016) 37(1) *Economic and Industrial Democracy* 23 at 24; citing Bernaciek n.46, 26.

[48] See for example, Simon Deakin and Frank Wilkinson, 'The Law and Economics of the Minimum Wage' (1992) *The Journal of Law and Society* 379, 385–6: '[L]ow pay represents a subsidy enabling otherwise uncompetitive firms and sectors to survive. Under these circumstances, regulation is necessary to create an environment in which firms compete not on the basis of low pay but through high labour quality and technological and organizational innovation.'

[49] As discussed by Brian Bercusson and Cynthia Estlund, 'Regulating Labour in the Wake of Globalisation: New Challenges, New Institutions' in Brian Bercusson and Cynthia Estlund (eds), *Regulating Labour in the Wake of Globalisation: New Challenges, New Institutions* (Hart 2008), 4, who refer to a 'downward spiral'.

others will be tempted to follow suit to achieve short-term gains regardless of long-term consequences. This fear of a 'race to the bottom' helps to explain why in 1919 the ILO Constitution included a statement acknowledging that 'the failure of any nation to adopt humane conditions of labour is an obstacle in the way of other nations which desire to improve the conditions in their own countries'.[50]

It has been suggested by prominent labour lawyers, such as Bob Hepple, that the so-called race to the bottom is largely a fiction, since productivity gains lie in increasing wages as well as working conditions alongside a stable social policy infrastructure.[51] That view accords with the instrumental case for labour standards offered by IMF and OECD findings, highlighted above.[52] However, in the context of the global financial crisis of 2007–10, there was greater emphasis on short-term gains by employers and the states in which they are based.[53] Perhaps Hepple's observations hold true for the period of time in which he was writing, during a period of relative stability, but given current pressures once again for short-term economic recovery driven by the pandemic and the Ukraine war, negative competition seems likely to come to the fore once again. In this scenario, the case for taking further steps in times of crisis to safeguard fair terms of competition in trade (both environmental and social) can be, and is being, made.[54] Yet, competition is not all that is at stake. From a broader sustainability perspective, the aim is not only to prevent destructive patterns of competition but also to infuse the normative foundation of trade with social and environmental aspirations, both of which can be linked to the conditions in which people work.

Moreover, there are dangers in failing to recognise that the formal terms of fair competition in trade, set for example by the GATT or in other contexts by the World Trade Organization (WTO), can perpetuate substantive injustice. A wealth of contemporary evidence suggests that current trade rules do not necessarily enhance the lives of workers generally, and certainly not of all workers in all states.[55] Deeply entrenched divisions in wealth and prospects

---

[50] Treaty of Versailles 1919, Part XIII, Section 1. See Tyc n.40 above.

[51] Hepple n.19 above, 13–16.

[52] See this chapter, text accompanying nn.30 and 31 above.

[53] Alain Lipietz, 'Fears and Hopes: The Crisis of the Liberal-productivist model and Its Green Alternative' (2013) 37(1) *Capital & Class* 127; see also Daniel Vaughan-Whitehead (ed.), *The European Social Model in Crisis: Is Europe Losing Its Soul?* (Edward Elgar Publishing/ILO 2015).

[54] Clive L. Spash, 'The Economy as if People Mattered: Revisiting Critiques of Economic Growth in a Time of Crisis' (2021) 18(7) *Globalizations* 1087.

[55] See Thomas Piketty, *Capital in the Twenty-First Century* (Harvard University Press 2014).

within states, but also between the 'Global North' and the 'Global South',[56] have not been shifted by current rules of trade, despite the initial assertion that the latter would be able to trade their way out of poverty.[57] It is therefore apparent that not only will the terms of trade matter, in terms of construction of rules of fair competition, but so will their effects on those who work for a living. In that sense, social concerns can feed into the construction of what are 'fair' rules in the sense of 'process-oriented' regulation, but also what are regarded as acceptable outcomes.

3. SOCIAL RATIONALES

An analysis focused on economic benefits exposes how labour relations and global trade are in many ways co-constitutive but does not engage so fully with other ethical reasons for the protection of labour standards. This brings us to a series of 'social' rationales for labour rights in international trade. This part of the chapter considers the impact of current trade patterns on the world of work and the case for human rights to be embedded in trade, alongside arguments for even more generous and wide-ranging labour protections. The relevance of these reasons for protection of labour standards in trade are also considered from the perspective of sustainable development.

3.1 The Transformation of Work in Response to Trade

It seems sensible to begin here with the effects of contemporary trade on the world of work, which do not seem sustainable. There is a social case to be made which recognises the limitations of neo-liberal capitalism based on short-term profit,[58] and responds to the resultant precarity experienced in labour markets.[59] The demand for ever-growing profits leads to attempts

---

[56] Branko Milanovic, *Global Inequality: A New Approach for the Age of Globalization* (Harvard University Press 2016); Miriam Ronzoni, 'Global Labour Injustice: A Critical Overview' in Yossi Dahan, Hanna Lerner and Faina Milman-Sivan (eds), *Global Justice and International Labour Rights* (Cambridge University Press 2016).

[57] See T. Ademola Oyejide, 'Development Dimensions in Multilateral Trade Negotiations' in Mike Moore (ed.), *Doha and Beyond: The Future of the Multicultural Trading System* (Cambridge University Press 2004).

[58] Peter A. Hall and David Soskice, *Varieties of Capitalism: The Institutional Foundations of Comparative Advantage* (Oxford University Press, 2001); cf. Kim M. Willey, *Stock Market Short-Termism: Law, Regulation, and Reform* (Palgrave Macmillan 2019).

[59] Tonia Novitz, 'Social Sustainability, Labour and Trade: Forging Connections' in Margherita Pieraccini and Tonia Novitz (eds), *Legal Perspectives on Sustainability*

to cut the costs of labour through transnational multiple sites of production, service delivery and distribution demanded by business and in which states are complicit.[60] Current methods of manufacture and supply of services, building on recent technological developments, have generated extensive cross-border sites for transnational production and delivery driven by the interests of corporate and commercial actors. Subcontracting across territorial state boundaries enables multinational enterprises and even their smaller subcontractors to exploit differences between legal frameworks and access the benefits of diminished regulatory costs in particular countries. The commercial enterprise can be attracted to the site of any given country by its government, offering inducements for investment, enabling the many and varied contractual arrangements which allow movement of capital and productive distribution. Those engaged in work then become ever more distant from the shareholders (and other forms of investors) who profit from their labour.[61]

Rapid growth and diversification in trade through the operation of global supply chains has led to shifts in work relations, namely who does the work, how the work is performed, and for whom.[62] While these are sometimes described as 'global value chains', in examining the evidence academic commentators have argued that these are better described as 'global poverty chains', as subcontracting leads to production and service delivery where wage rates are cheapest, or even below subsistence level for the state concerned.[63] In this process, the way in which labour is converted to trade in services can lead to commodification of the most vulnerable workers, for example in the setting of 'global care chains'.[64] The use of domestic work in informal but

(Bristol University Press 2020), 159–85. See more generally, Jeff Kenner, Izabela Florczak and Marta Otto (eds), *Precarious Work: The Challenge for Labour Law in Europe* (Edward Elgar Publishing 2019).

60 Wolfgang Streeck, *How Will Capitalism End?* (Verso 2016) at 1 and 205; see also Ruth Dukes and Wolfgang Streeck, *Democracy at Work: Contract, Status and Post-Industrial Justice* (Polity 2022), 57–82.

61 For a fuller analysis, see Tonia Novitz, 'Supply Chains and Temporary Migrant Labour: The Relevance of Trade and Sustainability Frameworks' in Diamond Ashiagbor (ed.), *Re-imagining Labour Law for Development* (Hart 2019).

62 Leah Vosko, *Managing the Margins: Gender, Citizenship and the International Regulation of Precarious Employment* (Oxford University Press 2010); and Guy Standing, *The Precariat: The New Dangerous Class* (Bloomsbury 2014).

63 Charlotte Villiers, 'Collective Responsibility and the Limits of Disclosure in Regulating Global Supply Chains' (2018) 23 *Deakin Law Review* 143; Benjamin Selwyn, 'Poverty Chains and Global Capitalism' (2019) 23(1) *Competition & Change* 71.

64 See Arlie Hochschild, 'Global Care Chains and Emotional Surplus Value in Will Hutton and Anthony Giddens (eds), *On the Edge: Living with Global Capitalism* (Jonathan Cape 2000), 131; Nicola Yeates, 'Global Care Chains: A State-of-the-art

also increasingly commercialised settings via transnational supply through agencies has expanded, despite attempts at regulation in international, regional and domestic fora.[65]

Another feature of these global supply chains is the emergence of 'export processing zones' (EPZs), in which countries seek to attract foreign investment by lowering regulatory standards regarding tax, environmental standards and labour laws.[66] These began with identification of particular geographical locations within a country devoted to labour-intensive production and became associated with a decline in labour standards protections within those circumscribed areas. EPZs (or, as they are now often termed, 'special economic zones') have since evolved to apply sector-wide to services as well as goods and can involve a wider range of regulatory freedoms.[67] There can even be subcontracting of migrant labour transported from another country into these zones to reduce labour costs to as little as possible. As Jennifer Gordon observes, this cuts local workers out of the picture, while migrants in these zones can be exposed to shocking forms of exploitation where they 'work long hours for low wages under conditions that restrict their autonomy, with little to no bargaining power, access to legal mechanisms, or political recourse to challenge the problems they face'.[68]

Additionally, in the Global South, the size of the informal economy outside the sphere of regulated 'employment' has raised issues for those seeking to regulate the terms of trade.[69] In the Global North, there has been an increase in the hiring of agency workers, migrant workers, casual workers on zero- or minimum-hour contracts and platform workers no longer engaged through a standard employment relationship.[70] Migrant workers may be additionally

---

Review and Future Directions in Care Transnationalization Research' (2012) 12(2) *Global Networks* 135; and Ann Stewart, *Gender, Law and Justice in Global Markets* (Cambridge University Press 2011).

65 See Adelle Blackett, *Everyday Transgressions: Domestic Workers' Transnational Challenge to International Labor Law* (Cornell University/ILR Press 2019); Jennifer Gordon, 'Regulating the Human Supply Chain' (2017) 102 *Iowa Law Review* 445.

66 See Jennifer Gordon, 'In the Zone: Work at the Intersection of Trade and Migration' (2022) 23(2) *Theoretical Inquiries in Law* 147, 151–7.

67 See Douglas Zeng, 'The Past, Present and Future of Special Economic Zones and Their Impact' (2021) 24 *Journal of International Economic Law* 259.

68 Gordon n.66, 182.

69 Discussed in Supriya Routh and Vando Borghi (eds), *Workers and the Global Informal Economy: Interdisciplinary Perspectives* (Routledge 2016), although it would be a mistake to view the informal economy as wholly unregulated, see Supriya Routh, 'Examining the Legal Legitimacy of Informal Economic Activities' (2022) 31(2) *Social and Legal Studies* 282.

70 See for early identification of this issue as a global phenomenon, see Leah Vosko, *Temporary Work: The Gendered Rise of a Precarious Employment Relationship*

disadvantaged when working in their destination (the 'host state' country) by virtue of linguistic differences; a failure of knowledge and ability to access domestic legal remedies; difficulty in accessing trade union representation; and isolation, which may be due to the geographical situation of their housing or just the lack of immediate support from family, friends and their community in their country of origin. The resultant potential for their vulnerability and exploitation is well documented.[71] Established trade unions have sought to engage with precarious workers and those at work not usually deemed 'workers', with varying degrees of success.[72] What has also been documented is the rise of what have been termed 'syndicalist' unions,[73] 'independent' (or 'indie') unions'[74] and, in the US, 'worker centers',[75] which seek to represent the needs of an increasing number of marginalised members of the labour market and mobilise their collective bargaining strength.

Shifts in employment status (and their consequences) have been linked to cross-border subcontracting prompted by competitive trade pressures.[76] There

---

(University of Toronto Press 2000); and Guy Davidov, 'Who Is a Worker?' (2005) 34 *Industrial Law Journal* 57. More recently, see Mark Graham and Mohammed Anwar, 'The Global Gig Economy: Towards a Planetary Labour Market?' (2019) 24(4) *First Monday* 21.

[71] For a recent empirical study and review of past literature, see Anna Boucher, 'What Is Exploitation and Workplace Abuse? A Classification Schema to Understand Exploitative Workplace Behaviour towards Migrant Workers' (2022) 27(4) *New Political Economy* 629.

[72] Heather Connolly, Stefania Marino and Miguel Martinez Lucio, *The Politics of Social Inclusion and Labor Representation: Immigrants and Trade Unions in the European Context* (Cornell University Press 2019); and Miguel Martinez Lucio and Stephen Mustchin, 'The Politics and Diversity of Worker Representation: The Increasing Fluidity and Challenge of Representation' in Gregor Gall (ed.), *Handbook of the Politics of Labour, Work and Employment* (Edward Elgar Publishing 2019).

[73] Niklas Selberg, 'The Laws of Illegal Work and Dilemmas in Interest Representation on Segmented Labor Markets: A Propos Irregular Migrants in Sweden' (2014) 35 *Comparative Labor Law and Policy Journal* 247; Edmund Heery, 'Unions and the Organising Turn: Reflections after 20 Years of Organising Works' (2014) 26(4) *The Economic and Labour Relations Review* 545.

[74] Manoj Dias-Abey, 'Mobilizing for Recognition: Indie Unions, Migrant Workers, and Strategic Equality Act Litigation' (2022) 38(2) *International Journal of Comparative Labour Law and Industrial Relations* 137; and Vera Weghmann, 'Theorising Practice: Independent Trade Unions in the UK' (2022) 2(1) *Work in the Global Economy* 132.

[75] Janice Fine and Jennifer Gordon, 'Strengthening Labor Standards Enforcement through Partnerships with Workers' Organizations' (2010) 38(4) *Politics & Society* 552; and Nik Theodore, 'Regulating Informality: Worker Centers and Collective Action in Day-labor Markets' (2020) 15(1) *Growth and Change* 144.

[76] ILO, *Report IV: Decent Work in Global Supply Chains*, ILC, 105th Session, Geneva (ILO, 2016).

are crises in the treatment of those at work, but also understandings of what is 'work'. Flexible work, contemplated explicitly by *Vision 2050* back in 2010,[77] resulted in exclusion from access to standard legal protections, such as minimum terms and conditions of hire, as well as those relating to trade union representation, encompassing access to information and consultation rights, collective bargaining and lawful industrial action.[78] The erosion of terms on which labour is hired, now being led by patterns of trade involving fragmented supply of goods and services, cannot be durable in the longer term. Moreover, this trend is blatantly inconsistent with the notion that 'no one will be left behind', since inequalities between those who are workers and others in the 'world of work' will be entrenched.

3.2 A Human Rights Approach Spanning Civil, Political, Social, Economic and Cultural Rights

A human rights approach which incorporates labour rights is not instrumental. It is not designed to further the profitability of world trade, but rather to temper its application and set the boundaries of fair competition.[79] Human rights as 'trumps'[80] have come to be recognised in the legal regulation of trade as imperatives, being the entitlements of human beings which their dignity demands. Examples of recognition of the importance of human rights protections to trade, which will be examined more closely in this book, include Article XX of the GATT and Article XIV of the General Agreement on Trade in Services (GATS),[81] and terms set out in FTAs.[82]

In the period after the Second World War, international emphasis was placed on the protection of labour standards as human rights which were linked to fair terms of trade.[83] For example, the ILO Declaration of Philadelphia 1944 proclaimed that certain labour rights (such as freedom of association) could

---

77 See WBCSD, Vision 2050 (2010) available at: www .wbcsd .org/ Overview/ About-us/Vision_2050/Resources/Vision-2050-The-new-agenda-for-business, especially at 10 and 20; also Chapter 1, text accompanying nn.165–6.

78 As outlined in Tonia Novitz, 'Changes in Employment Status under Austerity and Beyond – Implications for Freedom of Association' (2016) 39(1) *Dublin University Law Journal* 27.

79 See Philip Alston (ed.), *Labour Rights as Human Rights* (Oxford University Press 2005); and Virginia Mantouvalou, 'Are Labour Rights Human Rights?' (2012) 3 European Labour Law Journal 151.

80 Ronald Dworkin, *Taking Rights Seriously* (Duckworth 1977).

81 See Chapter 4 of this book.

82 See Chapter 5 of this book.

83 Virginia Leary, 'The Paradox of Workers' Rights as Human Rights' in Lance Compa and Stephen Diamond (eds), *Human Rights, Labour Rights and International*

be considered human rights and, notably, that protection of social justice was not to be compromised by economic and financial policies.[84] Other significant initiatives were the UN Charter 1945, the preamble to which sought 'to reaffirm faith in fundamental human rights, in the dignity and worth of the human person, in the equal rights of men and women and of nations large and small', such that the UN institutions envisaged were 'to establish conditions under which justice and respect for the obligations arising from treaties and other sources of international law can be maintained', while also promoting 'social progress and better standards of life in larger freedom'.

The ostensibly soft law and declaratory Universal Declaration of Human Rights 1948 (UDHR) went further, notably asserting the human rights of all 'without distinction' based on territorial borders (Articles 1 and 2); prohibiting slavery, servitude and the slave trade (Article 4); protecting freedom of association (Article 20), the right to work and the right to fair terms and conditions, including equal remuneration and the entitlement to form and join trade unions (Article 23), as well as the right to 'reasonable limitation of working hours and periodic holidays with pay' (Article 24) and to a standard of living adequate for 'health and well-being' (Article 25).[85]

In the wake of the Cold War, the international community distinguished between civil and political rights of individuals and collective socio-economic rights, with the latter being more controversial.[86] This distinction explains the parallel adoption of the International Covenant on Civil and Political Rights (ICCPR) and the International Covenant on Economic, Social and Cultural Rights 1966 (ICESCR) adopted in 1966 (which together with the UDHR are commonly termed 'the International Bill of Human Rights'). Moreover, as decolonisation progressed after the Second World War, a third generation of human rights came to be identified. These encompass rights that often have a civil, political and social aspect but which are best understood as the rights of 'peoples', such as for example the rights to self-determination and to development.[87]

It has been claimed that labour rights termed 'socio-economic' are less amenable to enforcement than 'civil and political' rights, being characterised

---

Trade (Philadelphia: University of Pennsylvania Press, 1996). See also discussion of the Havana Charter in Chapter 4 of this book at text accompanying nn.181 et seq.

[84] ILO, Declaration of Philadelphia 1944, Article II(C).

[85] See Nicolas Valticos, 'International Labour Standards and Human Rights: Approaching the Year 2000' (1998) 138 *International Labour Review* 135.

[86] Ibid, 138.

[87] James Crawford, *The Rights of Peoples* (Oxford University Press 1988); Peter Jones, 'Human Rights, Group Rights, and Peoples' Rights' (1999) 21 *Human Rights Quarterly* 80.

as progressive rather than immediate, group-oriented as opposed to individual, and resource-dependent. In short, many labour rights could be regarded as not so much justiciable as policy-oriented.[88] Yet, collective labour rights have traversed both categories, with freedom of association and the right to form and join trade unions treated as a species of a civil and political right under Article 22 of the ICCPR, while the rights to engage in collective bargaining and to take strike action have been recognised as socio-economic entitlements under Article 8 of the ICESCR. In practice, as has been argued by many commentators, the two species of collective labour rights inevitably overlap, as the findings of supervisory bodies have since observed.[89]

There has been a growing trend towards regarding these entitlements as 'indivisible', traversing traditional boundaries in a variety of ways,[90] possessing both individual and collective dimensions[91] and offering a range of options for enforcement.[92] We see echoes of this assertion of indivisibility in the discourse of sustainable development and the 2030 Agenda.[93] The creation of an individual complaints procedure with respect to the ICESCR and by virtue of the now operative San Salvador Protocol to the American Convention on Human Rights[94] may indicate that these prejudices are gradually being overcome in the international community. The claim to indivisibility in the 2030 Agenda arguably gains resonance from these earlier assertions that civil, polit-

---

[88] For an example, see Ivan Hare, 'Social Rights as Fundamental Human Rights' in Bob Hepple (ed), *Social and Labour Rights in a Global Context: International and Comparative Perspectives* (Cambridge University Press 2002).

[89] In the ECHR context, see *Demir and Baykara v Turkey* Application No 34503/97, 12 November 2008, discussed in Keith Ewing and John Hendy, 'The Dramatic Implications of Demir and Baykara' (2010) 39 *Industrial Law Journal* 2. See more recently, 'Freedom of Association, Including the Right to Form and Join Trade Unions', Joint statement by the Committee on Economic, Social and Cultural Rights and the Human Rights Committee, 23 October 2019, E/C.12/2019/3-CCPR/C/2019/1, which states that the right to strike is 'corollary to the effective exercise of the right to form and join trade unions'.

[90] Ariel Zylberman, 'The Indivisibility of Human Rights' (2017) 36(4) *Law and Philosophy* 389.

[91] Tonia Novitz, 'Are Social Rights Necessarily Collective Rights? A Critical Analysis of the Collective Complaints Protocol to the European Social Charter' (2002) *European Human Rights Law Review* 50.

[92] See Mantouvalou n.79.

[93] See 2030 Agenda n.2, Preamble and Declaration, paras 5 and 18.

[94] Optional Protocol (GA resolution A/RES/63/117) to the International Covenant on Economic, Social and Cultural Rights which provides the Committee competence to receive and consider communications; and Additional Protocol to the American Convention on Human Rights in the area of Economic, Social and Cultural Rights 'Protocol of San Salvador' available at: www.oas.org/es/sedi/ddse/documentos/Protocolo%20San%20Salvador/English/1.%20Protocol.pdf.

ical, social, economic and cultural rights are interconnected.[95] Civil, political and socio-economic human rights of migrant workers have also been acknowledged, not only at the ILO,[96] but in the UN context in instruments such as the International Convention on the Protection of Rights of all Migrant Workers and Members of their Families 1990,[97] and the Protocol to Suppress and Punish Trafficking in Persons, Especially Women and Children 2004.[98]

Recognition under international human rights law of the rights of peoples and their claims to economic, political and cultural self-determination has been more complex. This matters for our purposes, since there is (for example) potential for indigenous peoples to combine cultural claims relating to protection of the environment and those who work on the land, as observed by Sara Seck, who has potently illustrated the problems with perpetuation of siloed thinking in these fields.[99] The ILO has played a role in promoting the rights of indigenous peoples in the context of labour as far as its mandate would permit, in particular through ILO Conventions Nos 107 and 169,[100] the latter providing for rights to participation, consultation and self-management for indigenous peoples.[101] ILO engagement with these issues arguably provided the foundations for the 2007 UN Declaration on the Rights of Indigenous Peoples (UNDRIP),[102] which sets out rights of indigenous peoples 'to free, prior and informed consent' (if not veto), alongside the entitlement to develop priorities and strategies for the exercise of the right to development (Article 23) and rights to property and to financial and technical assistance from states (Article 39). UNDRIP is only a declaratory instrument and arguably still places development as an objective of self-determination in an economic rather than an

---

95 See on 'indivisibility', the 2030 Agenda, n.2, Declaration, paras 5, 15 and 85.

96 See ILO Migration for Employment Convention (Revised), 1949 (No. 97); also Migrant Workers (Supplementary Provisions) Convention, 1975 (No. 143); and chapter 3 of this book, text accompanying n.85.

97 Available at: www.ohchr.org/EN/ProfessionalInterest/Pages/CMW.aspx.

98 Available at: www .unodc .org/ unodc/ treaties/ CTOC/ . See also the Global Compact for Migration adopted in 2018 available at: https://refugeesmigrants.un.org/sites/default/files/180713_agreed_outcome_global_compact_for_migration.pdf; and Antoine Pécoud, 'Philosophies of Migration Governance in a Globalizing World' (2020) 18(1) *Globalizations* 103.

99 See Seck n.6, 138–41.

100 ILO Indigenous and Tribal Populations Convention, 1957 (No. 107); and ILO Indigenous and Tribal Peoples Convention, 1989 (No. 169).

101 See the 'Convention No. 169 Toolbox' available at: www.ilo.org/global/topics/indigenous-tribal/toolbox/lang--en/index.htm.

102 See text and resources available at: www .un .org/ development/ desa/ indigenouspeoples/declaration-on-the-rights-of-indigenous-peoples.html.

environmental and social frame.[103] However, there have been attempts at the UN, by John Knox among others, to challenge these ostensible limitations.[104]

This issue of self-determination in the context of human rights of peoples matters, in at least three ways. One is the broad treatment of 'work' or 'labour' in this setting: 'the consideration of land-based livelihoods reminds us that industrial labour is not the only "work" that merits attention.'[105] This is arguably aided by thinking in terms of human rights rather than employment status.[106] A second notable aspect of peoples' rights under international law is the promotion of the right to collective voice in the form of participation and consultation (at the ILO) and consent (later at the UN); the extent to which this is a right for those at work (broadly understood) will be relevant to the trade–labour linkage and its regulation. Finally, appreciation of peoples' rights and the ways in which the environment and labour are intrinsically connected for many indigenous communities offers a basis for a growing realisation that this is true not only in terms of specific cultural histories but also in more extensive ways, potentially for all contemporary workers, drawing on Seck's understanding of 'a relational worker constituted by porous boundaries' between themselves and their families, communities and physical environment.[107]

3.3 Which Labour Standards Should Be Recognised as So 'Fundamental' as to Be Terms of Trade?

What has been even less clear is *which* labour standards will be treated as so fundamental that they are to be regarded as terms of trade, as opposed to broader facets of social policy that might be desirable but are not imperative. This is an issue which has been explored at the ILO, where certain ILO

---

[103] Sarah A. Radcliffe, 'Geography and Indigeneity III: Co-articulation of Colonialism and Capitalism in Indigeneity's Economies' (2020) 44(2) *Progress in Human Geography* 374, 383–4.

[104] As initially UN Independent Expert and later Special Rapporteur on the Issue of Human Rights Obligations Relating to the Enjoyment of a Safe, Clean, Healthy and Sustainable Environment; see for example reports UN Doc A/HRC/25/53 (2014) and UN Doc A/HRC/37/59, (2018); discussed by Seck n.6 at 146–8.

[105] Seck n.6, at 141.

[106] Valerio De Stefano, 'Non-Standard Work and Limits on Freedom of Association: A Human Rights-Based Approach' (2017) 46(2) *Industrial Law Journal* 185.

[107] See Seck n.6, 151–3; see also Zbyszewska n.7, 21: 'if we take seriously the suggestion that as we transform (nonhuman) nature it simultaneously transforms us (that we coevolve), why should not labor law have something to say about the worker's capacity to relate to the nonhuman others or materials with which they are coengaging, coworking, cotransforming, and about the quality of that relation or its impact on the worker?'

Conventions have been identified as 'fundamental' and certain labour rights as 'core' under the 1998 ILO Declaration on Fundamental Principles and Rights at Work, with the result that they map broadly onto civil and political rights and have been treated by certain actors, such as the EU, as enforceable when included in trade instruments as a species of human rights protection aligned with 'sustainable development and good governance'.[108] The content and limitations of this approach to selection of labour rights as human rights at the ILO is discussed further in Chapter 3, which explores the relevance of the concept of 'decent work' entailing employment promotion, social protection and social dialogue as well as the promotion of 'fundamental principles and rights at work'.[109] It is worth observing at this stage that the notion of decent work in SDG 8 is not merely limited to a human rights approach but encompasses a broader range of socio-economic aspects of well-being, in relation to, for example, the 'working environment' broadly understood of migrant workers and those in precarious employment (under SDG 8.8).[110]

Famously, Roberto Unger identified a right as 'a loaded gun that the right-holder may shoot at will in his corner of town. Outside that corner the other licensed gunmen may shoot him down.'[111] While Unger's observations were aimed at the domestic legal system and its governance, some of these nevertheless hold true for the idea of rights in the international law realm, insofar as these fail to appreciate 'those areas of social existence where people stand in a relationship of heightened mutual vulnerability and responsibility toward each other'.[112] Vidya Kumar has elaborated on this objection, by identifying the ways in which international legal treatment of labour rights as human rights can serve to depoliticise the fundamental subordination inherent in labour relations while enabling claims for employers. Further, she observes that 'the narrative of convergence' around core labour standards as human rights 'depoliticises the conflicts between workers in developing nations and developed nations'.[113] This concern would also seem to lie at the root of Philip Alston's objection that identification of ILO core labour standards as 'human rights'

---

[108] In practice, see 2012 Regulation n.3, Article 9. Cf. Christopher McCrudden and A.C.L. Davies, 'A Perspective on Trade and Labour Rights' (2000) *Journal of International Economic Law* 43.

[109] See Chapter 3 of this book, text accompanying nn.107 et seq.

[110] See Chapter 1 of this book, text accompanying nn.116 et seq.

[111] Roberto M. Unger, 'The Critical Legal Studies Movement' (1983) 96 *Harvard Law Review* 563, 597.

[112] Ibid.

[113] Vidya Kumar, 'Rethinking the Convergence of Human Rights and Labour Rights in International Law: Depoliticisation and Excess' in Ruth Buchanan and Peer Zumbansen, *Law in Transition: Human Rights, Development and Transitional Justice* (Bloomsbury 2014), 136.

would reflect 'those labour practices in relation to which developed countries are thought to perform well and on which at least some of the major exporting developing countries are thought to perform poorly'.[114]

Imbalances of power between the Global North and the Global South, not to mention between capital and labour, are difficult to recognise within an economic or even a human rights discourse when approached in a formalistic way.[115] While it might seem advantageous to apply global standards (based on universally accepted human rights) for fair competition rather than a unilateral set of rules and there is evidence that compliance with core labour standards can promote productivity, there is a danger that the rules of the game will still be set with reference to the preferences of western industrialised countries. These may impair export opportunities of those countries that need to boost their economies, diverting breaches of core labour standards to non-export industries, while any sanctions imposed could impede rather than boost development, harming rather than helping those at work in the Global South.[116]

It has been suggested that labour standards protections are better determined through collective bargaining rather than application of human rights norms, as the former is a more reflexive form of regulation engaging with the concrete needs and desires of those at work, enabling them more agency and the achievement of benefits above a bare minimum.[117] That caution has been stated primarily in the domestic realm but is also worth considering in terms of transnational trade regulation. While there is some degree of consensus in the Global North that human rights constraints should be placed on trade, how they apply to labour and/or the Global South remains contentious, especially at the WTO.[118]

---

114 Philip Alston, '"Core Labour Standards" and the Transformation of the International Labour Rights Regime' (2004) 15 *European Journal of International Law* 457, 466 and 487.

115 Although note the assertion by scholars that a more substantive approach is realisable. E.g. Sandra Fredman, *Human Rights Transformed: Positive Rights and Positive Duties* (Oxford University Press 2008).

116 Kofi Addo, 'The Correlation Between Labour Standards and International Trade' (2002) 36(2) *Journal of World Trade* 285; cf. Hans-Michael Wolffgang and Wolfram Feuerhake, 'Core Labour Standards in World Trade Law: The Necessity for Incorporation of Core Labour Standards in the World Trade Organization' (2002) 36(5) *Journal of World Trade* 883.

117 Kevin Kolben, 'Labour Rights as Human Rights?' (2010) 50 *Virginia Journal of International Law* 449.

118 Tonia Novitz and Colin Fenwick, 'The Application of a Human Rights Discourse to Labour Relations: Translation of Theory into Practice' in Colin Fenwick and Tonia Novitz (eds) *Human Rights at Work* (Onati/Hart 2010).

In this context, it is worth briefly noting the attempts made by Amartya Sen and Martha Nussbaum to offer a more substantive approach to realisation of human rights, by placing these apparently abstract entitlements in a more concrete context which evaluates the extent to which persons have the 'capabilities' to exercise their notional freedoms.[119]

Sen has offered a vision of 'development as freedom'[120] not merely oriented to negative protections from interference by the state, but also going beyond broader social policy planning.[121] He has sought recognition of 'both *processes* that allow freedom of actions and decisions, and the actual *opportunities* that people have',[122] taking account of human 'functionings', namely 'the various things a person may value doing or being'.[123] While acknowledging how workers' capabilities can be significant,[124] he has not been prescriptive as to the ways in which they should be realised, recognising 'the heterogeneity of distinct components of freedom as well as the need to take note of different persons' diverse freedoms' such that they cannot simply be placed in a universal hierarchical order.[125]

While Martha Nussbaum also appreciated that 'capabilities have a very close relationship to human rights',[126] unlike Sen she has listed 'Central Human Capabilities' based on her understanding of human dignity.[127] Placed among these is 'affiliation', namely the ability 'to engage in various forms of social interaction', which entails protection of 'freedom of assembly and political speech' as well as the institutions which assist in doing so.[128] Nussbaum recognises the 'architectonic' quality of this capability which can be vital to

---

[119] For discussion of the relevance of this analysis to labour law, see Judy Fudge, 'The New Discourse of Labour Rights: From Social to Fundamental Rights?' (2007) 29 *Comparative Labor Law and Policy Journal* 29; and most recently contributors to Brian Langille (ed), *The Capability Approach to Labour Law* (Oxford University Press 2019).

[120] Amartya Sen, *Commodities and Capabilities* (North-Holland 1985); Amartya Sen, *Development as Freedom* (Oxford University Press 1999).

[121] Cf. Isaiah Berlin, 'Two Concepts of Liberty' in *Four Essays on Liberty* (Oxford University Press 1969), 121–6.

[122] Sen (1999) n.120 above, 17.

[123] Ibid, at 75.

[124] Ibid, 27–30 and 112–16.

[125] Ibid, 33.

[126] Martha Nussbaum, 'Capabilities as Fundamental Entitlements: Sen and Social Justice' (2003) 9 *Feminist Economics* 33 at 36. See also Martha Nussbaum, 'Capabilities and Human Rights' (1997) 66 *Fordham Law Review* 273.

[127] Martha Nussbaum, *Women and Human Development: The capabilities approach* (Cambridge University Press 2000), ch 1.

[128] Nussbaum (2003) n.126 above, 41–2.

the achievement of others;[129] further, she acknowledges its links to the collective voice of those at work seeking to address systemic inequality (arguably of the kinds identified in SDG 5 and SDG 10 as being problematic).[130] In other words, collective bargaining (and collective action) can be understood as 'enabling rights' in the world of work.

As this section of the chapter has established, there have been attempts to address the stark social injustices arising from current forms of global trade by insisting at a minimum on certain human rights protections. These have had their limitations as a mechanism for fostering fairer trade. In part this may be due to the dominance of individualistic civil and political rights, which may not reflect the collective concerns of labour. The extension of protection of meaningful economic, social and cultural rights, including the rights of indigenous peoples, has been helpful. However, a capabilities discourse, as constructed by Sen and Nussbaum, prompts attention not only to human rights per se, but to how they are to be accessed and actualised. It is this attention to human agency which makes the notion of capabilities so compelling. Powerful arguments have also been made that framing environmental protections in terms of capabilities can assist in enabling people to resist climate change and protect biodiversity.[131] Moreover, we will see that social and ecological objectives can also connect in the context of strategic human rights litigation. There are important synergies as well as potential conflicts to be explored in this context.

4. ENVIRONMENTAL RATIONALES

The protection of labour standards in trade has been stated explicitly by the EU to be linked to sustainability, as noted earlier in this chapter.[132] In this way, matters such as adherence to international labour standards, at least those relating to freedom of association, child labour, forced labour and discrimina-

---

[129] Martha Nussbaum, *Creating Capabilities: The human development approach* (Harvard UP 2011), 33–9.

[130] Martha Nussbaum, 'Labour Law and the Capabilities Approach' in Langille n.119, 80.

[131] See also Peter Andersson, Niklas Bruun, Petra Herzfeld Olsson, Tonia Novitz and Erik Sjödin, 'Assessing the Swedish Labour Law Model through a Social Sustainability Lens' (2022) 2 *Retfærd* 75, 90–2; Breena Holland, 'Justice and the Environment in Nussbaum's "Capabilities Approach": Why Sustainable Ecological Capacity Is a Meta-capability' (2008) 61(2) *Political Research Quarterly* 319; Rosie Day, 'A Capabilities Approach to Environmental Justice' in Ryan Holifield, Jayajit Chakraborty and Gordon Walker (eds), *The Routledge Handbook of Environmental Justice* (Routledge 2017).

[132] See this chapter, nn.3 and 4.

tion, have been enforceable as a species of trade conditionality, regardless of their connection (or not) to other environmental concerns. The first issue that therefore needs to be considered under this head is whether, from an environmental perspective, this treatment of labour standards as a facet of sustainable development should be viewed as permissible even when there is no obvious ecological link. I shall argue here that this is a defensible approach, from the perspective of both intra- and inter-generational justice; however, any design of social policy (involving implementation of labour rights as human rights, and other labour standards) must take account of environmental concerns.

This section then goes on to consider what should happen where environmental objectives clash with social and economic concerns, including those concerning labour standards, endorsing a 'planetary boundaries' approach. Moreover, it is argued that environmental arguments can and should be applied to make sense of the importance of protection of whistleblowers at work, which offers a case for extending the remit of protection of labour standards in trade from the current remit of ILO fundamental principles to, for example, protections from dismissal and detriment.

This section also examines the ways in which environmental objectives can be pursued through human rights claims and other labour standards, alongside the significance of a 'just transition' approach which can be seen as a manifestation of freedom of association. It is argued that also, in terms of effectiveness and durability of policy-making, the shaping and implementation of green transitions should incorporate collective bargaining and representation of a wide range of those in the broader world of work.

4.1 Should the Focus of Sustainability Be Ecological?

Environmental concerns dominate the 2030 Agenda and are most evident in SDG 2 (agriculture), SDG 6 (water), SDG 7 (energy), SDG 9 (industry, innovation and infrastructure), SDG 11 (sustainable cities and communities), SDG 12 (responsible consumption and production), SDG 13 (climate change), SDG 14 (oceans and seas), as well as SDG 15 (ecosystems and biodiversity on land). There has been debate regarding the sufficiency of these environmental standards, which reflect, but do not always replicate as a minimum, other extant international instruments.[133] However, it is easy to see the normative case for their protection even if merely in the minimal form expounded in the

[133] See Duncan French and Louis J. Kotzé, *Sustainable Development Goals: Law, Theory and Implementation* (Edward Elgar Publishing 2018), 3; Tonia Novitz and Margherita Pieraccini, 'Agenda 2030 and the Sustainable Development Goals: Responsive, Inclusive, Participatory and Representative Decision-Making?' in Pieraccini and Novitz n.59 above, 51–2.

2030 Agenda, so that there is an expectation that states within the international community will regulate trade and investment in ways consistent with the achievement of these goals.

There is some uncertainty as to how these environmental norms, intrinsic to sustainability, relate to economic and social goals set out in the 2030 Agenda. It has after all been asserted that sustainable development is a principle primarily concerned with environmental objectives to which matters such as labour standards must, ultimately, be viewed as subsidiary. The notion that sustainability is predominantly an ecological principle has been the dominant view taken by legal academic commentators such as Klaus Bosselmann[134] and Virginie Barral.[135]

Arguably, the insertion into the 2030 Agenda of other SDGs setting out discrete norms, for example, poverty (SDG 1), health (SDG 3), education (SDG 4), gender (SDG 5), work (SDG 8) and equality (SDG 10), suggests that the international community does not accept a solely environmental orientation for sustainable development, but more a view that economic, social and environmental factors all contribute to inter- and intra-generational justice, both of which are crucial. The inclusion of protection from child labour in both SDG 8.7 and SDG 16.2 has much to do with intra-generational justice (distributive justice between present generations in terms of access to education and thereby wealth) and makes us acknowledge children as part of future generations whose interests deserve protection even if they currently lack the means or capacity for democratic representation. While child labour can and has been used in pollutant industries, such as mining, this is not the only basis for objection to the treatment of children whose individual functionings and collective capabilities are harmed. Indeed, there is the irony that their labour can be used to facilitate transitions to sustainable vehicles, and we should place a red line around instrumental use of children in that way.[136]

In her conception of 'Doughnut Economics', Kate Raworth has offered a helpful conception of how economic, social and environmental objectives (such as those set out in the 2030 Agenda) could co-exist and be respected. Her

---

134 Klaus Bosselmann, *The Principle of Sustainability: Transforming Law and Governance*, 2nd ed. (Routledge 2016).

135 Virginie Barral, 'Sustainable Development in International Law: Nature and Operation of an Evolutive Legal Norm' (2012) 23(2) *European Journal of International Law* 377, 380.

136 Benjamin K. Sovacool, 'When Subterranean Slavery Supports Sustainability Transitions? Power, Patriarchy, and Child Labor in Artisanal Congolese Cobalt Mining' (2021) 8(1) *The Extractive Industries and Society* 271; Cristiana Panella and Thierry De Putter, 'The Invisible Lives of Cobalt Miners and Green Traceability Discourses' (2022) 38(5) *Anthropology Today* 13.

argument is that social and economic goals will have to be constrained by the need to live within 'planetary boundaries'. The environment will set a limit, but it remains possible to respect each person's entitlement to the resources they need for a 'social foundation' of rights below which no one should fall.[137] Indeed, meeting those needs and preventing inequalities will have positive ecological benefits. This means that it is appropriate under SDG 16.2 to 'end abuse, exploitation, trafficking and all forms of violence against and torture of children' (which may have nothing directly to do with environmental concerns but much to do with intra-generational and inter-generational justice), but the policies put in place to do so must fall within the boundaries of what the planet can provide.[138] There are likely to be synergies and connections between the maintenance of environmental standards and protection of labour standards and workers' rights. Child labour cannot therefore be addressed without reference to the resources available and the ecological effects of programmatic and other measures. To use a hypothetical example, a child labour programme which compensated for the costs of children's education by employing adults in the community in a polluting industry (for example a local mine which created effluent endangering the adults' health and that of their families) would be highly problematic and would have to be rethought and implemented in another way. Other options and measures to address child labour would have to be taken instead.

For comparable reasons, it would be a mistake to see jobs merely as instrumental for an environmental agenda. Employment promotion is certainly an important facet of 'decent work' as envisaged both in SDG 8 and at the ILO.[139] However, it is arguably not enough that 'green jobs' are created; rather, the jobs created must meet the basic standards established universally by human rights norms and reflect the other aspirations of 'decent work'. Evidence to date is that the wages paid in the renewables sector do not match those available in oil and gas and that serious health and safety concerns have been raised

---

[137] Kate Raworth, *Doughnut Economics: Seven Ways to Think Like a 21st Century Economist* (Cornerstone Books 2017), briefly illustrated at 11. For her analysis of the problematic treatment of labour, see 188–91.

[138] For earlier presentation of this argument, see Tonia Novitz, 'Engagement with Sustainability at the International Labour Organization and Wider Implications for Collective Worker Voice' (2020) 159(4) *International Labour Review* 463, 465 and 469; and Tonia Novitz, 'Tripartism as Sustainable Governance' in George P. Politakis, Tomi Kohiyama and Thomas Lieby (eds), *ILO 100: Law for Social Justice* (ILO 2019), 341.

[139] See Chapter 1 of this book, text accompanying n.128; and Chapter 3, text accompanying n.141.

by working practices.[140] For the intersection of environmental and labour concerns to be fully interrogated, the normative standing of labour rights requires attention jointly and severally with environmental objectives. In this context, we may also wish to argue for forms of educational and social assistance which facilitate changes to ensure environmental well-being. To do so would also be consistent with the recognition that patterned inequalities have a well-documented role in generating environmental and other crises.[141]

4.2 Whistleblowing and Environmental Protections

One example of an important potential connection between environmental protections and labour standards is the case for assisting and shielding whistleblowers from the wrath of employers and managers, when they expose ecological harms that they have detected at work. After all, 'workers are the most immediate knowers of possible non-compliance by the company with its environmental obligations'.[142] Matters suitable for whistleblowing should at a minimum include identification of issues regarding 'safe and healthy working conditions' under Article 7 of the ICESCR, or 'a safe and healthy working environment' under amended Article 2 of the 1998 Declaration on Fundamental Principles and Rights at Work.[143] There may also in practice be some overlap between the conditions in which work is carried out and welfare of the wider community. For example, use of certain chemicals harmful to those in a workplace may lead to the leak of pollutants harmful to others in the locality; or, indeed, the place where work is carried out may be at home or on the streets, such that again an employer's actions or execution of an employer's instructions may have effects beyond those immediately hired to do the work.[144] Indeed, given the relationship of all workers to their wider

---

[140] Ed Atkins, *A Just Energy Transition: Getting Decarbonisation Right in Times of Crisis* (Bristol University Press 2023), 117–18.

[141] For recent acknowledgement of these connections, see Report of the Director-General, *Advancing Social Justice*, International Labour Conference, 111th Session, 2023, especially chs 2 and 3.

[142] Juan Escribano Gutierrez, 'Labour and Environmental Sustainability: Summary of Literature Reviews' (2020), 1–2 available at: http://agreenment.adapt.it/wp-content/uploads/2020/11/comparative_report_agreenment_final.pdf.

[143] Resolution on the inclusion of a safe and healthy working environment in the ILO's framework of fundamental principles and rights at work, ILC.110/Resolution1, 10 June 2022 available at: www.ilo.org/wcmsp5/groups/public/---ed_norm/---relconf/documents/meetingdocument/wcms_848632.pdf. See also Chapter 3 of this book, text accompanying n.90 et seq.

[144] Cf. Paolo Tomassetti, 'From Treadmill of Production to Just Transition and Beyond' (2020) 26(4) *European Journal of Industrial Relations* 439.

community and environment, one might expect that whistleblowing should be permitted also with respect to wider communal harms, including those which are environmental.[145]

This is interesting (and problematic) because there is no specific instrument concerned with environmental whistleblowing at work so far adopted by the ILO.[146] Arguably, protection from violence and harassment for voicing environmental concerns can be regarded as covered by international human rights instruments and the 2019 ILO Convention No. 190 on Violence and Harassment at Work.[147] Reprisal by way of dismissal might seem a lesser sanction, but given the impact on those dependent on working for a living, there is a strong case for making protection from termination available for environmental whistleblowing. At present, the ILO Termination of Employment Convention No. 158 of 1982 only protects whistleblowers where there has been the actual 'filing of a complaint or the participation in proceedings against an employer involving alleged violation of laws or regulations or recourse to competent administrative authorities' (under Article 5(c)).[148] This will not cover the scenario where there has been no legal action but another form of public disclosure; a limitation which has not kept pace with legal initiatives elsewhere.[149] In this sense, the ability of those in the world of work or their representatives to speak out about environmental and social harms seems unduly limited.

It is notable that neither protection from dismissal nor whistleblowing are currently treated as a fundamental labour right protected under current mainstream trade conditionality provisions. There is also the issue that an ever-increasing number of those who labour in both the Global North and the Global South are not formally regarded as workers eligible for protection from dismissal or termination of contractual relations.[150] In this way, it is possible that a more holistic sustainable development perspective, which recognises connections between environmental and labour concerns, could be

---

[145] See text accompanying n.7 above.

[146] For an excellent review of measures taken to date regarding whistleblowing in international, regional and domestic laws, see Iheb Chalouat, Carlos Carrión-Crespo and Margherita Licata, *Law and Practice on Protecting Whistle-Blowers in the Public and Financial Services Sectors* (ILO 2019).

[147] Such as the ICCPR and ICESCR, discussed in text accompanying nn.87–9 above.

[148] Chalouat et al n.146, at 5.

[149] Cf. Directive (EU) 2019/1937 of the European Parliament and of the Council of 23 October 2019 on the protection of persons who report breaches of Union law OJ L 305/17, 26.11.2019, Article 15.

[150] Claire La Hovary and Jordi Agustí Panareda, 'What Is Work? A Malleable Notion in the ILO's Legal Pursuit of Social Justice' in Politakis et al, n.138.

the basis for revisiting the foundations of employment status (and definition of a 'worker') and labour norms to take account of precarious sub-contracted work. This issue may also prompt action beyond a conventional 'fundamental labour rights' matrix to recognise the significance of a wider range of labour standards not currently mentioned, for example, in SDG 8.[151]

4.3 Environmental Claims as Human Rights

Another way in which environmental and so-called social rationales intersect is the increasing framing of ecological concerns within a human rights paradigm. The most recent example is the unanimous adoption by the UNGA on 28 July 2022 of a Resolution declaring that access to a clean, healthy environment is a universal human right.[152] It is not entirely clear what are the implications of linking environmental concerns to a human rights legal framework. Presumably, it offers the opportunity for environmental imperatives to trump other objectives at least sometimes, and to demand attention. This is, after all, a strategy deployed by the labour movement and one which has had some successes.[153] While sometimes a blunt instrument and one whose ambit is contested,[154] what seems appealing is the 'universal' dimension to human rights claims: all people's lives matter wherever they are, across national borders. This chimes with what we know about environmental impacts that also have no respect for 'man-made' borders.[155]

A more concrete revelation of how a human rights approach may be deployed can be found in the case brought by Claudia Duarte Agostinho and five others against Portugal and 32 other states which are members of the Council of Europe. This case was filed on 30 November 2020 by six Portuguese young persons who lack access to the standard democratic processes which would enable them to hold their own state and the EU to account on climate change. Instead, they brought their claim under the European Convention on Human Rights (ECHR) against all EU member states and also countries with whom

---

151 Cf. Chapter 1 of this book, text accompanying nn.116 et seq.

152 Resolution A/76/L75 reported at https://news.un.org/en/story/2022/07/1123482. The eight abstentions however included China and Russia.

153 As discussed in contributions to Colin Fenwick and Tonia Novitz (eds), *Human Rights at Work* (Onati/Hart 2010); and more recently in Janice Bellace and Beryl ter Haar (eds), *Research Handbook on Labour, Business and Human Rights Law* (Edward Elgar Publishing, 2019).

154 See this chapter above, text accompanying nn.88 et seq.

155 Tonia Novitz, 'Sustainability as Solidarity Unbound: Labour Rights and Collective Voice in the United Nations Sustainable Development Goals and the European Union' in Julia Lopez-Lopez (ed.), *Inscribing Solidarity: Debates in Labor Law and Beyond* (Cambridge University Press 2022), 27.

the EU has significant trade relations, namely Norway, Russia, Switzerland, Turkey, Ukraine and the UK. The claims made are based on Article 2 (the right to life) and Article 8, the text of which provides for the right of 'everyone' to 'respect for his private and family life, his home and his correspondence'. The statement of alleged violations says that the latter must be understood to apply more generally to 'a healthy, protected environment'. The claimants also argue age discrimination in relation to the lack of action taken on climate change, as the interferences with their rights under Articles 2 and 8 are more acute than for older generations – this is a claim for intergenerational equity. They allege shared responsibility of all the state parties for 'multiple internationally wrongful acts'. No mention of work or labour is made in the claim filed, but there is mention of the significance of case law requiring the European Court of Human Rights to take account of elements of international law, which also enables the Convention to be viewed as a living instrument.[156]

The case has been fast-tracked by the European Court of Human Rights and (at the time of writing) judgment is expected from the Grand Chamber.[157] There have been a number of third party interventions to date, most of which have been made public, although the State responses have not been released publicly. One such intervention was made by the Council of Europe Commissioner for Human Rights, which stressed 'that environment and human rights are interdependent'; human rights are not only the casualty of ecological damage but 'are also the key to rolling it back'.[158] The Commissioner rejected the past approach which insulated environmental considerations from international human rights law. She linked her assertions to more general acceptance by Council of Europe states and their support for recognition of a right to a healthy environment at the UN level.[159] She considered that there arise certain obligations for states to take preventative actions accordingly in response to the threat of climate change and the rights of the child.[160] Moreover, she highlighted the significance of 'enabling rights and guarantees' such as the participatory

---

156 See Klaus Lörcher, 'The New Social Dimension in the Jurisprudence of the European Court of Human Rights (ECtHR): The Demir and Baykara Judgment, its Methodology and Follow-up' in Filip Dorssemont, Klaus Lörcher, and Isabelle Schömann (eds), *The European Convention on Human Rights and the Employment Relation* (Hart 2013).

157 Referral to the Grand Chamber was made on 30 June 2022, according to: https://climate-laws.org/geographies/international/litigation_cases/duarte-agostinho-and-others-v-portugal-and-32-other-states and the case is currently due to be heard in September 2023.

158 Third Party Intervention by the Council of Europe Commissioner for Human Rights, CommDH(2021)16, 5 May 2021. Stated twice at paras 7 and 37.

159 Ibid, paras 8 and 15.

160 Ibid, paras 20–8.

entitlements recognised in the Aarhus Convention.[161] Her conclusion was that these rights to participation in decision-making should include access before the European Court of Human Rights and she recommended accordingly a generous approach to standing requirements to enable children to pursue their human rights claims regarding climate change.[162]

An interesting question is what might be the further implications of such a case in the world of work, if the ECHR's ambit is extended in this way, as a 'living instrument'. There has been a rapid growth in strategic human rights litigation relating to climate change, as has been acknowledged by Grainne De Búrca in her book on *Reframing Human Rights in a Turbulent Era*.[163] She celebrates 'human rights experimentalism' and the mobilisation of the discourse of human rights 'used by many progressive social, environmental, indigenous, labour and other movements'.[164] De Búrca's suggestion is that human rights claims can be helpful where the project is a dynamic one, which is 'activated, shaped, and given its meaning and impact through the ongoing mobilization of affected populations, groups and individuals, and through their iterative engagement with an array of domestic and international institutions and processes over time'.[165] While she and others make minimal reference to the rights of those at work, it is possible that environmental and labour claims could be united in these forms of strategic litigation.

It is evident that environmental harms generated in the workplace may provide workers with grounds to claim for compensation under Article 4 of the ECHR (in terms of a right to life), as well as for harms to their private life and bodily integrity under Article 8. In the *Vilnes* case, it was established that workers have a right to information regarding risks to their health and safety.[166] I have argued elsewhere that it is also possible to envisage a case being made for workers to claim collective rights to information and consultation and even to organise under Article 11 of the ECHR to challenge health and life-damaging workplace practices, including pollution which affects health at work.[167] Moreover, we might expect the European Court of Human Rights

---

161 Ibid, para. 29.

162 Ibid, para. 35 et seq.

163 Grainne de Búrca, *Reframing Human Rights in a Turbulent Era* (Oxford University Press 2021).

164 Ibid, 2.

165 Ibid, 3–4.

166 Appns nos 52806/09 and 22703/10 *Vilnes and Others v. Norway*, 5 December 2013; see also Appn no. 31612/09 *Pavlov v Russia*, 11 October 2022 and the Concurring Opinion of Judge Serghides, paras 4–5 citing labour standards established under the European Social Charter in this respect.

167 As discussed in Tonia Novitz, 'Human Rights as a Regulatory Tool for "Just Transition" in Europe and Beyond' (2023) 39(3/4) *International Journal of Comparative Labour Law and Industrial Relations* 439.

should be alert by virtue of Article 14 to discriminatory aspects of the ways in which disproportionate burdens are borne by certain groups of workers in relation to pollutants, greenhouse gases and even damage to biodiversity. This brings us to our final piece of the environmental matrix, namely the issue of just transition and how this could be facilitated (or otherwise) by trade unions.

4.4 Just Transitions

It is widely acknowledged that there is potential for the short-term interests of trade union members, for example in the retention of jobs in a particular industry, to clash with longer-term ecological concerns.[168] This tension is well documented where workers have opposed closure of worksites despite the pollutants which affect local communities. In such a context we may find a 'trade-off' between different human rights exercised by different portions of civil society,[169] although there is also the possibility that, when those engaged in such work live in or adjacent to the local community, their interests may well coincide. Indeed, as residents, workers may also have an incentive to promote employer attention to environmental issues that would otherwise have profound consequences for inter- and intra-generational justice.

For such reasons, trade unions have sought 'just transitions' to subsidised and gradually improved environmentally sustainable production and delivery of services, redeploying and reskilling workers so as to avoid unemployment. The very term 'just transition' was first coined by US and Canadian union leaders as far back as the 1970s, most notable being the leading roles played by Tony Mazzochi of the US Oil, Chemical and Atomic Workers International Union (OCAW) who proposed a 'Superfund for Workers' and Brian Kohler of the Canadian Energy and Chemical Workers Union (ECWU).[170] They acknowledged that the work performed by their members could be environ-

---

[168] See Béla Galgóczi, 'The Changing Role of Trade Unions in the Sustainable Development Agenda' (2014) 24 *International Review of Sociology* 59, 63.

[169] For example between the human right to health and other human rights in a context where freedom is systematically constrained. See Areli Valencia, 'Human Rights Trade-offs in a Context of "Systemic Lack of Freedom": The Case of the Smelter Town of La Oroya, Peru' (2014) 13(4) *Journal of Human Rights* 456; and Areli Valencia, *Human Rights Trade-Offs in Times of Economic Growth: The Long-term Capability Impacts of Extractive-led Development* (Palgrave Macmillan 2016).

[170] See Dimitris Stevis and Romain Felli, 'Global Labour Unions and Just Transition to a Green Economy' (2015) 15(1) *International Environmental Agreements* 29, 32; Béla Galgóczi, 'Just Transition on the Ground: Challenges and Opportunities for Social Dialogue' (2020) 26(4) *European Journal of Industrial Relations* 367; also Dimitris Stevis, Edouard Morena and Dunja Krause, 'Introduction: The Genealogy and Contemporary Politics of Just Transitions' in Edouard Morena, Dunja Krause and

mentally harmful, but wanted to prompt reconsideration of the ways in which changes would be effected to ensure the protection of those at work in this process. In so doing, they challenged 'the perception of environmental protection as a "jobs killer"'.[171] The determination to achieve 'just transitions' has been a notable feature of policies seeking to phase out coal mining in countries as diverse as Germany[172] and South Africa.[173] The point is also that transitions to 'green jobs' will entail transitions to 'precarious jobs' unless there is introduction of forms of portable training alongside state support for the emergent industries.[174] In this way, there is arguably a connection to be made here between 'just transitions' and the stress placed on education in employment promotion and in state provision of social protection inherent in the ILO notion of 'decent work'.[175]

Currently, in the EU, the European Commission is seeking to shift to a 'circular economy' as part of the new European Green Deal, to avoid wastage and instead enable repair of products and more effective recycling.[176] In response, the European Trade Union Confederation (ETUC) is pushing for greater social dialogue regarding the impact of these transitions, regarding such matters as health and safety and gender equality, as well as private and public funding to 'promote quality employment, innovation, reskilling and upskilling'.[177] There are indications that the European Commission and the social partners now do accept the need for these kinds of 'just transitions',[178] but progress is argu-

---

Dimitris Stevis (eds), *Just Transitions: Social Justice in the Shift towards a Low-carbon World* (Pluto Press 2020), 9 et seq.

[171] Atkins n.140, 23.

[172] Judson Abraham, 'Just Transitions for the Miners: Labor Environmentalism in the Ruhr and Appalachian Coalfields' (2017) 39(2) *New Political Science* 218; Atkins n.140, 25.

[173] See the Joint Statement on the Just Energy Transition Partnership (JET-P) for South Africa established in 2021 with support from the EU, UK and US reported at: www.gov.uk/government/news/joint-statement-international-just-energy-transition-partnership; discussed in Atkins n.140, 148.

[174] Atkins n.140, 127.

[175] See Chapter 3 of this book, text accompanying nn.107 et seq.

[176] Communication from the Commission to the European Parliament, the Council, the European Economic and Social Committee and the Committee of the Regions: A new Circular Economy Action Plan for a cleaner and more competitive Europe COM/2020/98 final, 11.3.2020.

[177] See *European Social Partners' Project on Circular Economy and the World of Work* (2021) and summary available at: www.etuc.org/en/publication/european-social-partners-project-circular-economy-and-world-work-0.

[178] European Commission, *Communication on a Strong Social Europe for Just Transitions* COM(2020) 14 final 14.1.20; Porto Social Summit, Porto Social Commitment, 7 May 2021 available at: www.2021portugal.eu/en/porto-social-summit/porto-social-commitment/.

ably slow. The ETUC's endeavours build upon the foundations of the ILO Guidelines on Just Transitions 2015,[179] agreed by an ILO Tripartite Meeting of Experts on Sustainable Development, Decent Work and Green Jobs. The Guidelines stress the potential for trade unions to exercise influence as social partners, referring to 'collective bargaining' and 'collective agreements'.[180]

While just transition is not mentioned in the 2030 Agenda, the preamble to the 2015 Paris Agreement takes 'into account the imperatives of a just transition of the workforce and the creation of decent work and quality jobs'.[181] A case has also been made by David Doorey for adoption of broader and more far-reaching 'Just Transitions Law' to enable progressive accommodation of worker and broader societal needs in facilitating a shift to a low carbon and greener economy, guided by a 'theory of justice', which envisages a wider programme for assistance.[182] There is a strong case for environmental and social transitions to draw on structural support from government and public institutions and yet, at the same time, it is evident that the dynamism and connection offered by collective bargaining as a route to reform should not be forgotten or neglected.[183] The latter is a vital way in which to build socio-political acceptance of change as well as acceptance from market actors; which is more likely to be achieved where certain conditions are met, such as fairness in procedure and design, inclusiveness, transparency (shared information) and shared authority contributing to decision-making.[184] Indeed, it is argued in the final section of this chapter that engagement with collective labour rights and representatives from a wider world of work offers potential to reconcile the economic, environmental and social rationales for regulatory reform of trade and its effects on labour.

---

[179] ILO Guidelines for a just transition towards environmentally sustainable economies and societies for all (hereafter ILO Just Transitions Guidelines 2015) available at: www.ilo.org/wcmsp5/groups/public/---ed_emp/---emp_ent/documents/publication/wcms_432859.pdf discussed in Chapter 3 of this book, text accompanying nn.203 et seq. See, for analysis, Sebastian Sabato and Boris Fronteddu, *A Socially Just Transition through the European Green Deal?* (European Trade Union Institute 2020).

[180] ILO Guidelines n.179, paras 16–18. Whether by intention or design, there is no mention of a right to strike.

[181] See Navraj Singh Ghaleigh, *Just Transitions for Workers: When Climate Change Met Labour Justice*. Edinburgh School of Law Research Paper No. 2019/30 (University of Edinburgh 2019).

[182] David J. Doorey, 'Just Transitions Law: Putting Labour Law to Work on Climate Change' (2017) 30(2) *Journal of Environmental Law and Practice* 201.

[183] Stevis et al n.170, observe at 19 that despite 'the global diffusion of just transition', the concept remains 'firmly rooted in the union movement', having (at 22) 'multiple functions for workers and organised labour'.

[184] Atkins n.140, 57–8.

5. RECONCILING DIFFERENT RATIONALES: THE IMPORTANCE OF ENGAGEMENT WITH THE WORLD OF WORK

This chapter has examined the different justifications which can be offered for approaching the connections between trade and labour from a sustainable development perspective. Twenty years ago Lafferty and Langhelle were adamant that there was no need to identify any hierarchy between the economic, social and environmental pillars of sustainable development; rather, it was necessary to challenge policy which does not take any or all of these into consideration.[185] This holistic view is consistent with the contemporary 2030 Agenda, which would have us believe that economic, social and environmental objectives are inter-related, indivisible and ultimately reconcilable. But can this be the case?

From the perspective of autopoietic theory and reflexive law, there is cause to be wary of treating different 'systems' as if they had the same internal normative rationales.[186] When economic, social and environmental systems collide, they can cause disruption or 'perturbations'.[187] Of course, systems may be normatively closed yet potentially open to communication, but the outcomes of such communication may not be straightforward adaptation. They are likely to depend on the modes of contestation by relevant interested agents,[188] reflecting their relative capabilities, functionings and resources, which prompts attention to 'social choice, deliberative mechanisms, and [...] power'.[189]

While regulatory creativity is to be encouraged,[190] it is not only communication which shapes legal systems, but the effects of relative wealth and privilege which can be weaponised through institutions such as the ILO and

---

[185] William M. Lafferty and Oluf Langhelle, 'Sustainable Development as Concept and Norm' in William M. Lafferty and Oluf Langhelle (eds) *Towards Sustainable Development* (Palgrave Macmillan 1999), 13.

[186] See, for example, Niklas Luhmann, *Social Systems* (first printed 1984 (in German), Stanford University Press 1995); and Gunther Teubner, *Law as an Autopoietic System* (Blackwell 1993).

[187] See Ralf Rogowski, *Reflexive Labour Law in the World Society* (Edward Elgar Publishing 2013), chs 1–3.

[188] Simon Deakin, 'Legal Evolution: Integrating Economic and Systemic Approaches' (2011) 7(3) *Review of Law and Economics* 659 at 677.

[189] See Fudge n.119, 65.

[190] Deirdre McCann, Sangheon Lee, Patrick Belser, Colin Fenwick, John Howe and Malte Luebker (eds), *Creative Labour Regulation: Indeterminacy and Protection in an Uncertain World* (ILO/Palgrave Macmillan 2014).

WTO as they seek to regulate trade from social and economic perspectives.[191] Moreover, the agency of relevant actors may be constrained by the systems (for example of trade law) within which they operate. Here there is perhaps a useful analogy to be drawn with Lukes' third concept of power, namely that an internal view of the system may influence, shape or determine our desires and choices.[192] For this reason, it seems preferable not merely to cite the indivisibility of the pillars of sustainable development, but to recognise and confront their potential tensions and trade-offs.

That is not to suggest there is a simple formula which will enable hierarchical priorities to be determined; rather, we might understand this as a complex process which requires participatory, democratic and reflexive engagement comparable to Sen's insistence on democratic processes aimed at identifying and realising capabilities.[193] Also, we may have to acknowledge that different decisions could be taken at different times depending on the best evidence available, but that these should be transparent. In other words, to avoid the crises which tensions between the economic and social (and environmental) can create, we need institutions which can address these and debate them openly and responsibly. In so doing, it may be possible to inculcate the intra-generational justice that sustainable development demands while acknowledging responsibility for future generations, not able to be represented in that process.[194]

It has been asserted by Dani Rodrik that what is needed is taming of the process of 'hyper-globalisation' and a return to governance by the 'nation state' as 'the only game in town when it comes to providing the regulatory and legitimizing arrangements on which markets rely'.[195] That is not the solution that is advocated in this book, for several reasons. One is that international institutions have the capacity for prompting reflection by national governments, which might otherwise fall prey to pandering to populism, designing regulation designed to secure short-term electoral gains that please a majority of voters rather than longer-term benefits. As Alvaro Santos has observed, the 'democratic deficit, lack of legitimacy, and loss of voice and accountability' that Rodrik detects at the global level in relation to trade regulation can also be

---

[191] Eric Tucker, 'Labor's Many Constitutions (and Capital's Too)' (2011–12) 33 *Comparative Labor Law and Policy Journal* 355.

[192] Steven Lukes, *Power: A Radical View*, 1st ed. (Macmillan 1974), 23; see discussion in Chapter 1 of this book, text accompanying n. 63 et seq.

[193] See Sen (1999) n.120.

[194] Erling Holden, Kristin Linnerud, and David Banister, 'Sustainable Development: Our Common Future Revisited' (2014) 26 *Global Environmental Change* 130, 132.

[195] Dani Rodrik, *Straight Talk on Trade: Ideas for a Sane World Economy* (Princeton University Press 2018), 13–14.

true of the nation state,[196] even though these failings are manifested in different forms.

Another objection to Rodrik's proposition is that states are not distinct entities in the way that the Westphalian system has pretended. Ecological evidence indicates that what one government does inside its state borders affects another.[197] Also, the experience of the ILO over the last century is that the failure of one state to regulate its labour markets will have effects on others.[198] A legacy of colonialism,[199] alongside the effects of cross-border pollution, means that a government in one country may have compelling ethical obligations to assist a government in another.[200] Moreover, the contemporary operation of global supply chains creates forms of interdependence fostering exploitation,[201] which require transnational regulation on the world stage, as well as regional, national and local solutions. The luxury of deliberation merely at the level of the nation state is no longer feasible in practical terms and can hardly be seen as legitimate. Rather, we might pay attention to how meaningful participation and voice from those affected by trade policy can be fed into international institutions and other forms of transnational regulation.

In this context, social dialogue and collective bargaining may operate as mechanisms that can prevent destabilising countermovement and thereby enable durability of policy-making in the realm of trade and labour at local, national, regional and global levels. Incorporation of the needs of present and future generations could be achieved through deliberative mechanisms, although this would require greater sensitivity to the power differentials

---

196 Ibid, 29; Alvaro Santos, 'Reflecting on *Straight Talk on Trade*' in Santos et al n.16, 56.

197 Cf. Will Hickey, *The Sovereignty Game: Neo-Colonialism and the Westphalian System* (Palgrave Macmillan 2020); Saskia Sassen, *Losing Control? Sovereignty in the Age of Globalization* (Columbia University Press 1996).

198 See the enduring preamble to the ILO Constitution, stating: 'the failure of any nation to adopt humane conditions of labour is an obstacle in the way of other nations which desire to improve the conditions in their own countries'. Available at: www.ilo.org/hanoi/Whatwedo/Publications/WCMS_818973/lang--en/index.htm.

199 Adelle Blackett, 'Theorizing Emancipatory Transnational Futures of International Labor Law' (2019) 113 *American Journal of International Law* 390, 392.

200 See for example the appeals from Bangladesh following flooding attributed to the global climate crisis in 2021, as reported in Nan Powart, 'Call for Compensation for Effects of Climate Crisis in Bangladesh' *The National*, 7 November 2021. Also note the decision finally taken at the COP 27 to establish and operationalise 'a fund to compensate vulnerable nations for "loss and damage" from climate-induced disasters' which is arguably a new and significant manifestation of the principle of 'common but differentiated responsibility' (CBDR) ; for further information see www.un.org/en/climatechange/cop27.

201 See Chapter 6 of this book; also Atkins n.140, ch 8.

between potential policy actors than has traditionally been the case. A sustainable development rationale could prompt greater inclusiveness in the voices that shape trade rules and, thereby, their effect on labour markets and social, economic and environmental conditions globally. This will depend on enabling the capabilities and ensuring the influence of those at work who are currently systematically disadvantaged and dispossessed, such that there can be meaningful redistribution of power and thereby economic wealth (as well as other social and environmental goods) within and between states.

5.1 Expectation of Countermovement from Those in the World of Work

In 1944 Karl Polanyi offered an account of the inherent tensions between the economic and the social, between markets and their regulation, which cannot be wholly resolved, but where an imbalance results in forms of 'countermovement'.[202] This account has proven to have enduring influence as a basis for understanding numerous issues relating to the relationship between trade and labour, including how they may intersect and conflict.

Polanyi resisted claims that markets (such as those relating to transnational trade) should be self-regulating and that economic rationales should always prevail.[203] 'To allow the market mechanism to be sole director of the fate of human beings and their natural environment, indeed, even of the amount and use of purchasing power, would result in the demolition of society.'[204] In particular, he identified land, labour and money as 'fictitious commodities', not 'produced for sale', and which had particular features which demonstrated that they should not be traded like other items. Land, for example, is not made; rather, nature exists independently of human commerce or attempts to tame its use. Labour is a human activity not neatly detachable from other facets of workers' lives and cannot be 'stored'. Money is a representation of the power to purchase created by banking or state finance and, as such, caution must be exercised in exposing its value to the vagaries of the market representing supply and demand.[205] Polanyi considered that economic orders can and should be 'embedded' in the social orders that they serve; when they cease to do

---

[202] See Karl Polanyi, *The Great Transformation: The Political and Economic Origins of Our Time* (Beacon Press 2001) 2nd paperback ed.

[203] Cf. Friedrich A. Hayek, 'Economics and Knowledge' (1937) 4(13) *Economica* 33; and Friedrich A. Hayek, *The Road to Serfdom* (Dymock's 1944), discussed in Damien Cahill, 'Polanyi, Hayek and Embedded Neoliberalism' (2018) 15(7) *Globalizations* 977, 985–91. See also n.26 above.

[204] Polanyi n.202, 76.

[205] Ibid, 75.

so and operate according to a separate economic motive, some correction is required. This trichotomy may be helpful in terms of also understanding tensions arising, not only between the economic and the social, but also between the environment and these two spheres.

Polanyi recognised the limited capacity of markets to self-correct, appreciating the need for their political regulation to achieve their re-embedding in our 'complex society'. A period of market building or 'economic reconstruction' could be expected to prompt induce a 'countermovement': 'human society would have been annihilated but for protective counter-moves which blunted the action of this self-destructive mechanism'.[206] This can be understood as a kind of 'double movement so that 'the extension of market organization in respect to genuine commodities was accompanied by its restriction in respect of fictitious ones'.[207] Pressure for market expansion would be counteracted by societal resistance requiring some market contraction. Countermovement was described by Polanyi as 'a network of measures and policies [...] integrated into powerful institutions designed to check the action of the market relative to land, labor and money'.[208] One difficulty with that description is that it might seem to discount the ways in which state action can be co-opted for market-led purposes and the ways in which the state can 'embed' market values in law and practice (as Polanyi himself acknowledged).[209] Rather, protective countermovement instantiated in law and regulation may be better seen as linked to action prompted by civil society,[210] and, as we have seen in recent times, that action can be environmentally motivated as well as reflecting social concerns.[211]

There is a fundamental question here: who are the representatives of society whose voice offers such effective countermovement?[212] Nancy Fraser has expressed concern that Polanyi idealised society in an almost communitarian fashion, failing to recognise how established social norms may also be a source of injustice, for example in relation to the treatment of women and the most

---

206 Ibid, 79. See also discussion in Fudge n.119, 32–3.

207 Polanyi n.202, 79.

208 Ibid.

209 Bernard Barber, 'All Economies Are "Embedded": The Career of a Concept and Beyond' (1995) 62(2) *Social Research* 387; and Cahill n.203, 980 who stresses this point is made in Polanyi n.202, 250.

210 Fred Block, 'Introduction' to Polanyi n.202, xviii.

211 See Benjamin J. Richardson (ed.), *From Student Strikes to the Extinction Rebellion: New Protest Movements Shaping Our Future* (Edward Elgar Publishing 2020).

212 Diamond Ashiagbor, Prabha Kotiswaran and Amanda Perry-Kessaris, 'Introduction: Moving towards an Economic Sociology of Law' (2013) 40 *Journal of Law and Society* 1.

marginalised outliers in a particular social structure.[213] It is also evident that racial prejudice can be socially embedded in market systems.[214] Perhaps, in our current era of complex global commodity and supply chains, where 'multiple public and private actors' interact in a variety of ways,[215] we might better understand countermovement not as a reflection of a single homogeneous society, but as complex and conflicted, offering opportunities to 'integrate social protection with emancipation'.[216] Contemporary civil society might demand labour standards as a facet of corporate social responsibility from multinational employers in the context of trade,[217] or reflect the concerns of green movements, seeking regulatory changes simultaneously to the management of land and labour, for the benefit of the ecocene.[218] In these ways, perceptions of the scope of legitimate social and environmental objectives would seem to have shifted since Polanyi's analysis in 1944, alongside our understanding of the relationships between his fictitious commodities of land, labour and money, which could now broadly tally with sustainability objectives encompassing environmental, social and economic concerns.[219]

In the absence of the corrective process of 'double movement', Polanyi predicted negative consequences, including irrational regulatory choices based on sentiment rather than practicality. He gave as an example an increase in tariff barriers in response to national protectionist interests, which raised costs of

---

[213] Nancy Fraser, 'Can Society Be Commodities All the Way Down? Post-Polanyian Reflections on Capitalist Crisis' (2014) 43(4) *Economy and Society* 541, 544.

[214] See also the powerful analysis offered by Diamond Ashiagbor, 'Race and Colonialism in the Construction of Labour Markets and Precarity' (2021) 50(4) *Industrial Law Journal* 506; and Adelle Blackett, 'Racial Capitalism and the Contemporary International Law on Slavery: (Re)membering *Hacienda Brasil Verde*' (2022) 25 *Journal of International Economic Law* 334.

[215] See Ernst Langthaler and Elke Schüßler, 'Commodity Studies with Polanyi: Disembedding and Re-Embedding Labour and Land in Contemporary Capitalism' (2009) 44(2) *Österreichische Zeitschrift für Soziologie* 209, 213.

[216] Fraser n.213, 554.

[217] Lilian Moncrieff, 'Karl Polanyi and the Problem of Corporate Social Responsibility' (2015) 42(3) *Journal of Law and Society* 434, 446–50; cf. Ronaldo Munck, *Globalization and Contestation: The New Great Counter-Movement* (Routledge 2006).

[218] See Diana Stuart, Ryan Gunderson and Brian Petersen, 'Climate Change and the Polanyian Counter-movement: Carbon Markets or Degrowth?' (2019) 24(1) *New Political Economy* 89; also Margherita Pieraccini and Tonia Novitz, 'Sustainability and Law: A Historical and Theoretical Overview on Pluralising Sustainability' in Pieraccini and Novitz n.59 above, 28–30.

[219] Tonia Novitz, 'Past and Future Work at the International Labour Organization: Labour as a Fictitious Commodity, Countermovement and Sustainability' (2020) 17(1) *International Organizations Law Review* 10, 12 and 28.

goods.[220] He was also aware 'of reactionary forces striving for a re-embedding of markets, fascism framed as "national socialism" being a prime example of the latter'.[221] An equivalent today may be found in contemporary populism and authoritarian government.[222]

It follows that, while spontaneous countermovement from angry representatives of civil society could correct markets, the potential extremity of responses to market expansion would be better tempered by more consistent democratic, participatory and egalitarian forms of ongoing institutional governance of markets.[223] In a complex society, we could accept regulatory constraints imposed by the state in order to achieve 'more abundant freedom for all' that cannot be achieved by markets governed solely by a profit motive.[224] Integration of markets in society could prevent the separation of politics and economics (with its attendant dangers),[225] and this could be plausibly achieved not only through state regulation, but by states acting within international organisations.[226] In other words, the 'embeddedness' that Polanyi sought could be mapped onto the identification of distinct varieties of capitalism operating in legal and political institutions at national, regional and international levels.[227] Indeed, he welcomed the emergence of international institutions such as the ILO designed to mediate tensions between economic and social forces, hoping that a new international economic (and legal) order would emerge.[228]

Applying Polanyi's analysis to the sphere of international trade, what can it tell us? First, this analytical frame suggests that economic systems established to foster trade and investment markets are likely to require correctives,

---

[220] Fred Block, 'Karl Polanyi and the Writing of *The Great Transformation*' (2003) 32 *Theory and Society* 275, 296–8.

[221] Langthaler and Schüßler n.215 above, 214.

[222] Tonia Novitz, 'Freedom of Association: Its Emergence and the Case for Prevention of Its Decline' in Bellace and ter Haar n.153 above; and Alan Bogg and Mark Freedland, 'Labour Law in the Age of Populism: Towards Sustainable Democratic Engagement' in Julia López López (ed.), *Collective Bargaining and Collective Action: Labour Agency and Governance in the 21st Century?* (Hart 2018).

[223] Block n.210, 300–1.

[224] Polanyi n.202, 268.

[225] Ibid., 263.

[226] Gareth Dale, 'In Search of Karl Polanyi's International Relations Theory' (2016) 42 *Review of International Studies* 401, 419.

[227] Diamond Ashiagbor, 'Unravelling the Embedded Liberal Bargain: Labour and Social Welfare Law in the Context of EU Market Integration' (2013) 19(3) *European Law Journal* 303, 306 citing Hall and Soskice n.54. See also Fikret Adaman, Pat Devine, and Begum Ozkaynak, 'Reinstituting the Economic Process: (Re)embedding the Economy in Society and Nature' (2003) 13(2) *International Review of Sociology/ Revue Internationale de Sociologie* 357, 360.

[228] See Polanyi n.202, chs 16, 17 and 18; and Dale n.226 above, 404–20.

especially to the extent that they engage with trade of land, labour or money. Our concern is predominantly with the impacts of trade on labour, although, as we have seen, the environment (including air, land and water) is not easily severed from its regulation. The essential social aspect of labour means that, when economic objectives prevail at the expense of the needs of workers, their families and their communities, we can expect countermovement. This could take unpleasant nationalistic forms, such as 'British jobs for British workers' or 'America first', seeking to prevent domestic workers from what is perceived to be unfair market competition from foreign sources.[229]

The process of 'double movement' might also take gentle and perhaps more rational forms of re-balancing of legal institutions, such as the relative influence of the ILO and WTO,[230] or the availability of structural funding and projects which ameliorate the harsher impacts of trade competition on workers.[231] What Polanyi's analysis offers us is a springboard for further questions, regarding who controls the government of any given state and, indeed, the international institutions with which he was becoming enamoured. The source of the voices of effective social movements and civil society groups that he considers may prompt 'counter-movement' also deserve our attention. Are these heterogeneous or homogeneous, and how do they access power? Where, for example, do domestic trade unions or their international federations, fit within this conceptual framework? Moreover, how do we factor in concerns not only with clashes between economic and social objectives, but between potentially the economic, social and environmental facets of sustainable development, which are now to be a source of reference in the context of trade?

5.2 Deliberative Democracy Tempered by Attention to Power Dynamics

We could in this context consider deliberative democratic justifications aimed at increasing transparency, inclusion of debate by interested parties and, thereby, the quality of decision-making when determining trade-offs between economic, social and environmental rationales for regulatory intervention in trade and labour. Advocates of deliberative theories of governance, among

---

[229] Novitz n.222 above, 249–52.

[230] Tucker n.191 above.

[231] In an EU context, see the European Social Fund Plus, outlined on the European Commission website at: https://ec.europa.eu/european-social-fund-plus/en. For comparable ILO projects and programmes, see Chapter 3 of this book at text accompanying n. 285 et seq.

which Jürgen Habermas has played a leading role,[232] consider such discursive processes to be the best model for democratic participation in international institutions.[233] From the 1990s onwards, international institutions have sought to respond to calls for good governance, which extends beyond forms of state control to engagement with civil society.[234] For example, the WTO and the World Bank Group have been criticised for their lack of deliberative participatory mechanisms enabling the exercise of influence by civil society organisations. Their absence has generated challenges to the legitimacy of their policies.[235]

The endorsement of 'deliberative democracy' can be regarded as a response to a broader 'legitimacy crisis'; a crisis which for example arises where trade regulation enables profits but also social or environmental harms, generating rebellious 'countermovement' from workers and other members of civil society.[236] In this context, law operates as a potential medium through which a link can be made between market systems, bureaucratic institutions and the 'lifeworld', offering scope for greater legitimacy.[237]

The claim made by deliberative theorists is that, in a pluralist global society, legal norms cannot merely appeal to shared substantive values. Instead, in a complex society, law needs to connect to free and open communication from self-organising communities of free and equal citizens.[238] Informal communicative action in the public sphere can then be fed into more formal politi-

---

232 Jürgen Habermas, *Between Facts and Norms: Contributions to a Discourse Theory of Law and Society* transl. William Rehg (MIT 1996); and Amy Gutmann and Dennis F. Thompson, *Why Deliberative Democracy?* (Princeton University Press 2004).

233 This approach has also been cautiously endorsed by Philip Pettit as an advocate of republican theory to the extent that 'contestatory institutions' are available for people 'to make their voice heard'. See Philip Pettit, 'Depoliticizing Democracy' (2004) 17(1) *Ratio Juris* 52, 62. Cf. Chapter 1 of this book, text accompanying n.75 et seq.

234 See, for discussion of this literature, James N. Rosenau, 'Governance, Order and Change in World Politics' in James N. Rosenau and Ernst-Otto Czempiel (eds), *Governance Without Government: Order and Change in World Politics* (Cambridge University Press 1992), 4; and Markus Jachtenfuchs, 'The Governance Approach to European Integration' (2001) 39 *Journal of Common Market Studies* 245.

235 Ilan Kapoor, 'Deliberative Democracy and the WTO' (2004) 11(3) *Review of International Political Economy* 522; Richard Higgott and Eva Erman, 'Deliberative Global Governance and the Question of Legitimacy: What Can We Learn from the WTO?' (2010) 36(2) *Review of International Studies* 449; Ruth Houghton, 'Looking at the World Bank's Safeguard Reform through the Lens of Deliberative Democracy' (2019) 32(3) *Leiden Journal of International Law* 465.

236 Cf. Polanyi's view of 'countermovement' discussed in text accompanying nn.202 et seq.

237 Habermas n.232, 56.

238 Ibid, xli.

cal processes.[239] The pragmatics of communication, which involve making a genuine effort to understand and relate to the words of another, is said to be what makes this process possible.[240] While an 'ideal speech situation' may not always realisable,[241] its creation entails, as a minimum, the establishment of a framework of basic rights upon which civil society can rely, although it is not clear from Habermas' writing whether he would include effective provision of socio-economic rights alongside civil and political rights.[242] In this sense a deliberative theory of international justice is dependent on the protection of human rights discussed earlier in this chapter, relying on their promotion by international institutions through processes of deliberation. The two are co-original.[243]

International legal norms then adopted by any international institution, for example in the context of trade and labour, can then be regarded as legitimate where all affected individuals could agree to them in a rational discourse centred on practical reason.[244] The best check to ensure that this has been achieved is the 'third generation' operationalisation of deliberative democratic theory,[245] such that availability of transparent information and deliberative debate by interested parties is facilitated by the institution concerned. Moreover, decisions taken must be able to be explained and justified to those affected.[246] In this way, through a dynamic process, durable and arguably sustainable policy-making could (at least in theory) be achievable.

---

[239] Ibid, 304–8.

[240] Jürgen Habermas, *Communication and the Evolution of Society* (Beacon Press 1979), 1–68.

[241] Robert Alexy, *A Theory of Legal Argumentation: The Theory of Rational Discourse as Theory of Legal Justification* transl. Ruth Adler and Neil MacCormick (Clarendon Press 1989), 119–24.

[242] See Habermas n.232, 77; and Constantin Stamatis, 'The Idea of Deliberative Democracy: A Critical Appraisal' (2001) 14 *Ratio Juris* 390.

[243] Habermas n.232, 104.

[244] Ibid, at 107–8.

[245] Stephen Elstub, 'The Third Generation of Deliberative Democracy' (2010) 8 *Political Studies Review* 291. Or the shift from a 'theoretical statement' to a working theory, for which see Simone Chambers, 'Deliberative Democratic Theory' (2003) 6 *Annual Review of Political Science* 307.

[246] Amy Gutmann and Dennis F. Thompson, *Democracy and Disagreement* (The Belknap Press 1996); as discussed in John Boswell and Jack Corbett, 'Deliberative Bureaucracy: Reconciling Democracy's Trade-off Between Inclusion and Economy' (2018) 66(3) *Political Studies* 618. Cf. Laura Scherera, Paul Behrensa, Arjan de Koninga, Reinout Heijungsa, Benjamin Sprechera, Arnold Tukkera, 'Trade-offs between Social and Environmental Sustainable Development Goals' (2018) 90 *Environmental Science and Policy* 65.

Habermas has argued that communicative action can be fostered by international and European institutions to create social solidarity in a pluralistic society.[247] He saw the traditional Westphalian system as under threat, 'as a consequence of the growing interdependence of global society and transnational economy'. In this context, '[t]he traditional line between foreign and domestic economic policies, in particular, has become blurred, while both the autonomy and sovereignty of formerly independent nation States have become increasingly undermined'.[248] Given the weakness of the nation state as a political entity,[249] he considered that the UN can, and should, impose the fundamental principles of the international legal order, for example in relation to 'peace-keeping, human rights politics and protection against global ecological, technological and criminal risks'. Habermas has been more a proponent of multi-level governance than of a new world state, arguing for regulation by not only a reformed international organisation, but also nation states and a horizontal network of transnational regimes. He has appreciated that such change is viable only to the extent that there is an expansion of communicative action and civil solidarity beyond national borders, which transnational social movements (such as labour and environmental lobbyists) and international institutions themselves may promote.[250]

The difficulty is that a deliberative democratic approach, as advocated by Habermas, does seem to assume altruism or neutrality of international institutions as law-makers.[251] He considers that the countries of the Global North which dominate these institutions will learn from further discussions 'about their distorted understanding and selective practice of human rights in the past and, maybe, at present'. Nevertheless, he considers that the normative

---

[247] Jürgen Habermas, 'The European Nation-State and the Pressures of Globalization' (1999) *New Left Review* 46 and Jürgen Habermas, 'Why Europe Needs a Constitution' (2001) *New Left Review* 11.

[248] See further the exploration of this issue in Adelle Blackett, 'Global Governance, Legal Pluralism and the Decentered State: A Labor Law Critique of Codes of Corporate Conduct' (2001) *Indiana Journal of Global Legal Studies* 401; and more recently, Streeck n.60 above.

[249] Cf. Rodrik n.195.

[250] Jürgen Habermas, 'Kant's Idea of Perpetual Peace, with the Benefit of Two Hundred Years' Hindsight' in James Bohman and Matias Lutz-Bachmann (eds), *Perpetual Peace: Essays on Kant's Cosmopolitan Ideal* (MIT 1997), 113 and 131–3. See also Jürgen Habermas, 'A Short Reply' (1999) 12 *Ratio Juris* 445 at 450–1.

[251] William Rasch, 'A Just War? Or Just a War? Schmitt, Habermas and the Cosmopolitan Orthodoxy' (2000) 21 *Cardozo Law Review* 1665; and Danilo Zolo, 'A Cosmopolitan Philosophy of International Law? A Realist Approach' (1999) 12 *Ratio Juris* 428, especially at 438–9.

substance of human rights will withstand the accusation that they are merely a reflection of western traditions.[252]

There remain however controversies as to how such rights should be applied and instantiated and even how civil society actors should participate in international law-making and supervisory processes.[253] For example, de Búrca has acknowledged that civil society can be bureaucratic[254] and 'illiberal, exclusionary, repressive',[255] and concedes that that the Global North can be over-represented in NGO activities.[256] There has even been considerable controversy over the extent to which 'comitology', discursive debate in committee structures, is conducive to deliberative democracy.[257] Moreover, if law-making should be informed by the 'lifeworld', one would assume that decisions should be taken as close to those whom they affect as is feasible, so at local, national or regional levels rather than internationally. For example, where labour standards are at issue, those at work should be involved. Also, if international law is to serve a communicative as opposed to a coercive purpose, there may be some legitimate debate as to the circumstances in which 'hard law' should be imposed by international institutions (for example, through economic sanctions), versus 'soft law' mechanisms which serve as a tool by which to inform those participating in the policy formation across the world.

Arguably, we can detect the influence of this theoretical basis in, for example, attempts by John Ruggie to promote corporate accountability.[258] Indeed, the promotion by the UN of Guiding Principles on Human Rights, which has the potential to influence the terms of fair competition in global

[252] Habermas (1999) n.247, 452; and Angela Ward, 'International Order, Political Community, and the Search for a European Public Philosophy' (1999) 22 *Fordham International Law Journal* 930.

[253] For a range of views, see Joshua Cohen and Charles Sabel, 'Directly Deliberative Polyarchy' (1997) 3 *European Law Journal* 313; James Bohman, 'International Regimes and Democratic Governance: Political Equality and Influence in Global Institutions' (1999) 75 *International Affairs* 499; and John S. Dryzek, 'Transnational Democracy' (1999) 7 *Journal of Political Philosophy* 30.

[254] de Búrca n.163 above, 30.

[255] Ibid, 32.

[256] Ibid, 218.

[257] Christian Joerges, 'Deliberative Supranationalism – Two Defences' (2002) 8(1) *European Law Journal* 133; cf. deliberative argument for strengthening the European Parliament, outlined in Erik O. Eriksen, 'Getting to Agreement: Mechanisms of Deliberative Decision-making' (2018) 10(3) *International Theory* 374.

[258] See 'Guiding Principles on Business and Human Rights: Implementing the United Nations "Protect, Respect and Remedy" Framework' available at: www.ohchr.org/Documents/Publications/GuidingPrinciplesBusinessHR_EN.pdf.

trade, has been termed a species of 're-embedded liberalism', and has been linked to deliberative democratic values.[259]

A deliberative democratic approach may have benefits in terms of its inclusive participatory assumptions, and the options it presents regarding regulatory strategy. It also chimes with a systems theory approach based on communicative and reflexive procedural interaction between economic, social and legal systems. Moreover, it prompts attention to regulating not so much in accordance with universal dictates but rather with what those most affected by regulation may want. Further, it has been argued that deliberation has 'transformative' potential, enabling radical rethinking of policy positions which have been taken for granted, enabling for example meaningful transitions towards sustainability.[260] In these ways it can be argued that deliberative democratic approaches to policy-making have the capacity to enable access to important decision-making processes for trade unions and civil society organisations representing those engaged in all forms of work.

However, deliberative democratic theory has tended to skirt over problems of power in communicative action.[261] There have been calls for protection of protest and other forms of activism, as meaningful debate cannot neatly be contained within institutional structures given their systemic biases.[262] It is in this context that claims have been made for protection of a right to strike, which Alan Bogg has argued is not inconsistent with deliberative democracy, if that theoretical framework is complemented by attention to power dynamics in the context of labour relations.[263] Acceptance of such an entitlement would seem to be crucial if collective bargaining is to be enabled, which will not merely amount to 'collective begging'.[264] Voice without any access to influence is unlikely to be meaningful.

---

259 Steen Vallentin and David Murillo, 'Ideologies of Corporate Responsibility: From Neoliberalism to "Varieties of Liberalism"' (2021) *Business Ethics Quarterly* 1.

260 Marit Hammond, 'Sustainability as a Cultural Transformation: The Role of Deliberative Democracy' (2020) 29(1) *Environmental Politics* 173.

261 Although this issue is now receiving greater attention, regarding which see Nicole Curato, Marit Hammond and John B. Min, *Power in Deliberative Democracy: Norms, Forums, Systems* (Palgrave Macmillan 2019).

262 See regarding this John S. Dryzek, *Deliberative Democracy and Beyond: Liberals, Critics, Contestations* (Oxford University Press 2002); Iris Marion Young, 'Activist Challenges to Deliberative Democracy' (2001) 29(5) *Political Theory* 670; and Anna Drake, *Activism, Inclusion and the Challenges of Deliberative Democracy* (UBC Press 2021).

263 Alan Bogg, *The Democratic Aspects of Trade Union Recognition* (Hart 2011), 270–1.

264 Eric Tucker has traced the history of this expression back to 1921, for which see his contribution, 'Can Worker Voice Strike Back? Law and the Decline and Uncertain

Arguably, deliberative democracy has now achieved a paradigm shift in international institutions, such that 'affected persons and groups by now participate in many areas of global rule- and law-making', which addresses problems of legitimacy and improves the quality of decision-making, but there remain concerns as to who should be included in such participatory processes.[265] This is perhaps not altogether surprising, considering the ongoing debates on how those at work should be represented through trade unions and national legal structures.[266] Nevertheless, it remains problematic that, in the context of international and regional labour law, there are blatant difficulties securing engagement with collective representatives of those engaged in atypical, precarious and migrant work; even when such representatives exist, their limited resources may affect their capacity to offer meaningful representation. In this sense, 'capability for voice' is relevant.[267] The relative lack of power of even traditional trade unions can be juxtaposed with the resistance of employers to respect for established international labour standards at the ILO and the soft law processes set up by the Guiding Principles on Business and Human Rights.[268] These attempts made by influential corporate actors to undermine human and labour rights protections in UN institutions and agencies indicate that the instantiation of deliberative democracy can be difficult to achieve.

It has been argued that more may need to be done to engage with the 'political economy of sustainability', which requires 'multi-stakeholder governance', ensuring that the stakeholders assembled for decision-making purposes 'have a strong claim to speak on behalf of the constituency they claim to

---

Future of Strikes' in Alan Bogg and Tonia Novitz (eds), *Voices at Work: Continuity and Change in the Common Law World* (Oxford University Press 2014), 458.

[265] Jan Sändig, Jochen von Bernstorff and Andreas Hasenclever, 'Affectedness in International Institutions: Promises and Pitfalls of Involving the Most Affected' (2018) 3(5–6) *Third World Thematics: A TWQ Journal* 587.

[266] Guy Mundlak, *Organizing Matters: Two Logics of Trade Union Representation* (Edward Elgar 2020); Michael Ford and Tonia Novitz, 'There Is Power in a Union? Revisiting Trade Union Functions in 2019' in Alan Bogg, Jake Rowbottom, and Alison Young (eds), *The Constitution of Social Democracy: Essays in Honour of Keith Ewing* (Hart 2020), 261–86.

[267] Jean-Michel Bonvin and Francesco Laruffa, 'Deliberative Democracy in the Real World: The Contribution of the Capability Approach' (2018) 28(2) *International Review of Sociology* 216. See also Richard Hyman and Rebecca Gumbrell-McCormick, '(How) Can International Trade Union Organisations Be Democratic?' (2020) 26(3) *Transfer* 253.

[268] See Janice R. Bellace, 'Pushback on the Right to Strike: Resisting the thickening of soft law' in Adelle Blackett and Anne Trebilcock (eds), *Research Handbook on Transnational Labour Law* (Edward Elgar Publishing 2015), 191–2; also further discussion of the employers' group resistance at the ILO in Chapter 3 of this book and limited corporate social responsibility in Chapter 6 of this book.

represent' and that decision-making will not be limited to majority voting or 'disempower minorities and hinder the deliberation required to generate more inclusive, creative compromises'.[269] There is potential to link here the notion of 'just transition' to the elements of procedural justice stressed in the 1998 Aarhus Convention,[270] namely that environmental (and related social) costs should not be disproportionately experienced or borne by those who are both most vulnerable and least responsible for ecological harms, such as indigenous peoples, vulnerable communities and the poor.[271] Indeed, the arguments for 'democratising work' from combined environmental and social perspectives have been persuasively presented by activists and academics alike.[272] While there is perhaps a gradual shift in opinion taking place towards recognition of the need for a 'worker-centred' trade policy, there is little scope at present for inclusive representation of the world's most vulnerable workers so that no one is left behind.[273] This is most obviously the case in developing countries of the Global South where informality prevails, but is also increasingly becoming a feature of the Global North. In this way, the very structure of the global labour market and growing reliance on supply chains and fissured work obstructs forms of democratic engagement and even, given the limited coverage of labour law in relation to those not deemed 'workers', their ability to engage in collective bargaining and to strike.[274] Despite this, perhaps as

---

[269] Fred P. Gale, *The Political Economy of Sustainability* (Edward Elgar Publishing 2018), especially at 145–6.

[270] United Nations Economic Commission for Europe (UNECE) Convention on Access to Information, Public Participation in Decision-Making and Access to Justice in Environmental Matters, 25 June 1998, which entered into force on 20 October 2001, available at: https://unece.org/DAM/env/pp/documents/cep43e.pdf. See also, regarding the Escazú Agreement, Chapter 1 of this book, text accompanying n.101.

[271] See Flanagan and Goods n.8, 484; citing Darryn Snell, 'Trade Unions and Environmental Justice' in Nora Räthzel, Dimitris Stevis and David Uzzell (eds), *The Palgrave Handbook of Environmental Labour Studies* (Springer 2021). See also on the relationship between inequalities and climate change and the necessity of partnership with NGOs and trade unions in that context, J. Mijin Cha, 'A Just Transition: Why Transitioning Workers into a New Clean Energy Economy Should Be at the Center of Climate Change Policies' (2017) 29(2) *Fordham Environmental Law Review* 196.

[272] See Isabelle Ferreras, Julie Battilana and Dominique Méda (eds) *Democratize Work: The Case for Reorganizing the Economy* (Chicago University Press 2022); and Atkins n.140, 128–31.

[273] Desirée LeClercq, 'Invisible Workers' (2022) 116 *AJIL Unbound* 107.

[274] See, for example, Tonia Novitz, 'Collective Labour Rights for Working People: The Legal Framework Established by the International Labour Organization' and Alan Bogg, 'Economic Coordination as Freedom of Association' in Sanjukta Paul, Shae McCrystal and Ewan McGaughey (eds), *The Cambridge Handbook of Labor in Competition Law* (Cambridge University Press 2022).

a form of 'counter-movement', it has been observed by the authors of a recent International Law Association report on the 'Future of Work' that

> a very new relationship is being forged between NGOs and Trade Unions on the one hand, and between NGOs and Trade Unions in the North and the South, on the other. These alliances based on complementarities of expertise and modes of action augurs for a reconfiguration of actors at the global level.[275]

The application of representative democratic processes, the terms of debates, the institutions in which they take place and the permissible outcomes are all issues which will guide the analysis in this book of the connections between trade law and labour law. A case is made for ongoing preservation under trade rules of labour's access to dissent, protest and activism. It is suggested that this should be understood as multi-faceted, including engagement in standard-setting as well as scrutiny of the implementation of such standards, within international institutions, or at regional or national level.

In Chapters 3 and 4, which set out the functions of the ILO, IMF, World Bank Group and WTO, I examine the ways in which all these international institutions seek to establish their legitimacy and by what means. The ILO is an unusual UN agency, in that its legitimacy is derived not only from the consent of states to its operations but from its tripartite structure, engaging national and global representation of 'workers' and 'employers' in the adoption of standards, as well as scrutiny of their implementation. Here, the language of human rights (civil, political, socio-economic and cultural) has permeated and social justice is, at least in theory, to take precedence over economic objectives. By way of contrast, the IMF and World Bank operate as financial institutions, sensitive to the needs of their investors, but also have obligations to pursue global stability. While not overly deferential to the ILO, they seek to bolster their administrative operations by forms of consultation with civil society stakeholders, including trade unions and NGOs representing atypical workers. In the WTO formal parity of treatment is pursued as a way of determining fair terms of trade, with some recognition however of the structural power imbalance experienced by the Global South and the need for exceptions regarding public policy, including prohibition of prison labour and potentially other forms of unfair trade and social dumping. There is minimal opportunity for trade union engagement, other than at an annual Public Forum in which civil society is more broadly represented and within a now fiercely contested dispute settlement process. In all four institutions, there is growing emergence of 'sustainable development' as an institutional objective and as a source of legitimacy, although there is significant variance in its treatment.

---

275 Pataut and Robin-Olivier n.42, 27.

Chapter 5 interrogates the ways in which FTAs concluded by nation states build on internationally established structures, focussing on EU practices which entail the inclusion of trade and sustainable development (TSD) chapters. Trade–labour policy cannot be regarded simply as bilaterally (or even multilaterally) determined by state actors, but is determined within the legal and legitimacy frameworks established by the ILO and WTO, in particular with reference to the potential for aid, conditional lending and other forms of mediation from the IMF and World Bank institutions. The scope for influence over FTA content and implementation from civil society, including trade unions, emerges as extremely limited, even in the EU where considerable steps have been taken to recognise their entitlement to engagement in trade regulatory processes. Chapter 6 analyses the scope for private governance and public–private initiatives in the context of the global supply chains operating in trade, observing once again the permeation of norms accepted in UN institutions and agencies, such as the ILO. The scope for those at work to shape corporate governance policies, for example through global framework agreements, is considered here. Accordingly, in all these scenarios, we return to the issue of voices of those in the world of work and their potential influence.

3. A sustainable role for the International Labour Organization in regulating trade?

1. INTRODUCTION

The International Labour Organization (ILO) is the specialist United Nations (UN) agency responsible for setting and promoting implementation of labour standards across the world. Over the past century, the ILO has sought to address the parameters of fair competition in trade, such that employers (and the states in which they are based) cannot compete on the basis of exploitative labour standards. Its competence to do so is well established, affirmed for example in the 1996 World Trade Organization (WTO) Singapore Ministerial Declaration.[1] Engagement with concerns relating to sustainable development has been more recent, but again is arguably reflected in the UN 2030 Agenda,[2] with the specific insertion of the ILO term 'decent work' in Sustainable Development Goal (SDG) 8.[3] This chapter maps the history of ILO treatment of trade and sustainability in relation to labour standards. Addressing underlying controversies over competence and process, the aim is to explain why ILO influence over the terms of trade has to date been cautious, subtle and largely indirect.

This analysis begins with discussion of the origins of the ILO as a facet of the peace settlement of 1919 accompanying creation of the League of Nations, alongside the emergence of the ILO in its role as a UN agency after the Second World War. The second part of the chapter examines the implications of the

---

1 Singapore WTO Ministerial Declaration WT/MIN(96)/DEC, 18 December 1996 Article 4.

2 United Nations General Assembly (UNGA) Resolution on the 2030 Agenda 25 September 2015 A/RES/70/1.

3 ILO Resolution on Advancing Social Justice through Decent Work 2016, International Labour Conference (ILC) 105th Session. See also Background Note by the International Labour Organization for the UN High-Level Political Forum 11–20 July 2016, New York, available at: www.ilo.org/global/topics/sdg-2030/WCMS_510121/lang--en/index.htm.

strategic decision to focus on 'core' or 'fundamental' labour standards by identifying certain Conventions and 'principles and rights at work', which became a reference point for trade conditionality. The third part of the chapter considers the ways in which the ILO has engaged with a sustainable development agenda. It emerges that the International Labour Office has become more assertive in arguing that freedom of association and collective bargaining are 'enabling rights' vital to sustainability. Finally, the chapter outlines the scope and ambitions of current and potential future ILO activities relevant to the interaction between trade and labour, drawing on a sustainable development rationale, in relation to international economic institutions, corporate governance, trade conditionality and global supply chains.

On the one hand, the ILO seems well placed to push for a multi-level sustainable development agenda to the extent that the Organization satisfies the preconditions identified in the first chapter of this book. If the efficacy of a sustainable trade–labour linkage requires protection of freedom of association and promotion of collective bargaining, the ILO's constitutional tripartite structure offers a promising normative base. Similarly, the ILO has sought respect for human rights and capabilities, which emerge not only in various landmark ILO declaratory instruments but also in the selection of 'core' labour standards (taken to represent accepted 'fundamental principles and rights at work') which we find commonly incorporated into free trade agreements across the globe. It was argued in Chapter 2 that a sustainable trade–labour linkage may need to go beyond this core, and in this respect other ILO Conventions and Recommendations not yet given such status may still be significant. Further, this chapter will detail the emergence of a broader 'decent work' objective that could be vital to management of just transition (entailing employment promotion, lifelong learning and social protection, as well as social dialogue and the fundamental principles identified above). It is evident from ILO actions from 2015 onwards that sustainable development has become a crucial part of its mandate, and that means greater engagement also with trade-related concerns.

However, there are potential obstructions to representative participatory engagement with a trade–labour linkage at the ILO, which are identified in this chapter. One such obstacle is the complex demarcation of competencies between different UN agencies, which the ILO would have to overcome to address a combination of trade and labour issues, even when grounded in a global desire to achieve sustainable development. Another barrier has been the ILO's past institutional hesitance to enable representation of all those in the wider 'world of work', such as informal labour markets, particularly from the Global South, not traditionally represented within the ILO's tripartite structure.[4] Arguably, it is possible to see a shift from the dominance of a Global North agenda to greater inclusion of a wider variety of actors from other places, but that change remains tentative and experimental. A further stumbling block has been a tendency to address supply chain regulation primarily in terms of corporate social responsibility rather than with reference to trade and investment.[5]

This chapter identifies these hurdles but also appreciates that they may not be insurmountable. Promising recent initiatives include the 2023 Strategy on Supply Chains, which would enable research into trade and investment concerns;[6] a new strategy on just transition endorsed at the International Labour Conference;[7] and the advocacy by the incoming ILO Director-General, Gilbert F. Houngbo, of a 'Global Coalition for Social Justice' linked to sustainable development objectives.[8] Their scope and viability are also examined here.

2. THE CONSTITUTIONAL FOUNDATIONS OF THE ILO AND THEIR CONNECTIONS TO 'FAIR COMPETITION' IN TRADE

The ILO Constitution is most concerned with identification of the preconditions for enduring 'social justice', which the preamble to Part XIII of the 1919 Treaty of Versailles stated was vital to the achievement of 'universal peace'.[9] Aspirations for a sustainable and peaceful international community are examined here alongside recognition of the role that international labour standards could play in setting terms of fair competition in trade.

Examination of these constitutional norms would be incomplete without appreciation of the tripartite structure of the ILO, which offered in 1919

---

4 See Chapter 1 of this book, text accompanying n.70.

5 Cf. Tonia Novitz, 'Supply Chains and Temporary Migrant Labour: The Relevance of Trade and Sustainability Frameworks' in Diamond Ashiagbor (ed.), *Re-imagining Labour Law for Development* (Hart 2019).

6 A five-year *ILO Strategy on Decent Work in Supply Chains* GB.347/INS/8, 27 February 2023, 10 at paras 22–3.

7 ILO Resolution concerning a just transition towards environmentally sustainable economies and societies for all 2023, ILC.111/Resolution V, ILC, 111th Session.

8 *Update on the Global Coalition for Social Justice* GB.347/INS/4, 20 February 2023; *Report of the Director-General*: *Advancing Social Justice* (ILO 2023).

9 Treaty of Versailles 1919, Part XIII, preamble, [1919] UKTS 4 (Cmd. 153). See the reiteration of this objective by the current ILO Director-General, Gilbert F. Houngbo, stressed in an interview on 3 October 2022 at: www.ilo.org/global/about-the-ilo/newsroom/news/WCMS_857344/lang--en/index.htm. For his initial call for a 'Global Coalition for Social Justice' on 2 November 2022, see www.ilo.org/global/about-the-ilo/newsroom/news/WCMS_859985/lang--en/index.htm.

a unique model for international governance. After a century in operation, this quest for ever-improving participatory engagement in determining the contours and implementation of 'decent work' can offer a useful reference point for further initiatives in the international community, especially regarding the potential role of collective worker voice in achieving sustainable development objectives in the context of trade.

The first section examines the terms of the first ILO Constitution in 1919, which endeavoured to promote not only protection of labour standards, but also fair trade and participatory engagement of worker and employer representatives in the governance of the Organization. The second section considers the emphasis placed on human rights in the ILO Declaration of Philadelphia in the aftermath of the Second World War II, which sought to enable social justice to take priority over utilitarian economic objectives.

2.1 The 1919 ILO Constitution and the Conditions for Social Justice

The formal establishment of the ILO, in 1919, was part of the process aimed at ending the tensions arising from the First World War. The intention was to ensure a basic level of protection for workers in member states, which would reward returning servicemen for their war efforts, offering an incentive to resist Bolshevist revolution.[10]

The founders of the ILO considered that a lasting (or sustainable) 'universal peace' after the First World War could be established only 'through the promotion and development of social justice'.[11] What was to be regarded as 'just' would ultimately be determined by a limited number of industrialised states, as was reflected in the membership of the Commission on International Labour Legislation.[12] Within that carefully circumscribed group of countries, there was to be a significant trade union steer as to the objectives of the Commission. Samuel Gompers, president of the American Federation of Labour, was elected President by the Commission's members. He steered the drafting in a bold direction, supporting proposals from UK delegates, Edward Phelan and Harold

---

[10] George N. Barnes, *History of the International Labour Office* (London: Williams and Norgate, 1926), 80; Mark F. Imber, *The USA, ILO, UNESCO and IAEA: Politicization and Withdrawal in the Specialised Agencies* (Macmillan 1989), 43.

[11] Victor-Yves Ghebali, *The International Labour Organization: A Case-study on the Evolution of UN Specialised Agencies* (Martinus Nijhoff 1989), 62–5.

[12] For the terms of reference, see ILO, *Report and Minutes of the Commission on International Labour Legislation, Peace Conference, Paris 1919* (Tipografia 1921), v. See also Barnes n.10, 38.

Butler, which shaped the radical institutional form that the ILO was to take.[13] Their combined vision, alongside the political compromises which had to be made, were reflected in the text of Part XIII of the 1919 Treaty, the preamble to which stated that 'conditions of labour exist involving such injustice, hardship, and privation to large numbers of people as to produce unrest so great that the peace and harmony of the world are imperilled; and an improvement of those conditions is urgently required'. Under Gompers' leadership the Commission offered a dynamic and participatory model for tripartite deliberation which has arguably been shown to be durable, as the ILO celebrated its centenary in 2019.[14]

The ILO proposed in 1919 was constructed on the platform of earlier political experiments: the International Working Men's Association (the 'First International'), which sought to promote international collective organisation of workers; the 'Second International', aimed at promotion of international labour standards;[15] and the inter-governmental International Association for Labour Legislation.[16] The latter, which operated an 'International Labour Office' in Basel until 1919, had succeeded in gaining state agreement to two Berne Conventions in 1906: the first preventing nightwork for women and the second concerning prohibition of the use of white (yellow) phosphorus in the manufacture of matches.[17] The Berne Convention on the making of matches addressed issues of health and safety at work and beyond, since white phosphorous was notorious for the disabling and life-threatening condition of 'phossy jaw' for those who produced and sold these matches.[18] In this way

---

13 *Report and Minutes of the Commission* n.12, 47–8. See also proceedings of the Commission, related by Edward Phelan (later to become a Director of the ILO) in James Thompson Shotwell, *The Origins of the International Labour Organization* (Columbia University Press 1934), Vol. I, 127–98; and Antony E. Alcock, *History of the International Labour Organisation* (Macmillan 1971), 18–31.

14 Janice Bellace, 'The ILO and Tripartism: The Challenge of Balancing the Three-Legged Stool' in George P. Politakis, Tomi Kohiyama and Thomas Lieby (eds), *ILO 100: Law for Social Justice* (ILO 2019), especially at 291–301.

15 See G. M. Stekloff, *History of the First International* (Martin Lawrence Limited 1928). Cf. Alvin W. Gouldner, 'Marx's Last Battle: Bakunin and the First International' 11(6) *Theory and Society* 853; and Gerry Rodgers, Eddy Lee, Lee Swepston and Jasmien Van Daele, *The ILO and the Quest for Social Justice 1919–2009* (International Labour Office 2009), 4.

16 See Alcock n.13, 3–11; and Aneta Tyc, *Global Trade, Labour Rights and International Law* (Routledge 2021), ch 1.

17 Carter Goodrich, 'Labor Legislation and the International Frontier' (1941) 15(4) *Social Service Review* 661, 663.

18 Regarding the latter, see the fuller discussion at Lowell J. Satre, 'After the Match Girls' Strike: Bryant and May in the 1890s' (1982) 26(1) *Victorian Studies* 7; and Tonia Novitz, 'Changing Collective Representation and Action to Meet the

a precedent had already been set for addressing harmful working conditions, which could otherwise reduce the costs of labour attached to goods, creating a potential competitive advantage for unscrupulous employers. So, the objective of such initiatives was not only workers' welfare but the terms of fair competition in trade.

The preamble to Part XIII of the Versailles Treaty proclaimed that 'the failure of any nation to adopt humane conditions of labour is an obstacle in the way of other nations which desire to improve the conditions of their own countries'.[19] George Barnes, the UK Government Representative at Versailles, reflected subsequently:

> Labour regulation had become a necessity in order to safeguard the relatively high standards of life in the advanced countries [...] That [...] is an insular sort of argument to use in favour of an organization with humanitarian outlook, but at least it is a practical one [...] the need had arisen for levelling out industrial competition between nations by raising the conditions of labour in the lower paid countries.[20]

Karl Polanyi likewise described the ILO as having been created 'in order to equalize conditions of competition between states'.[21] It does seems that those States victorious after the First World War sought to use the ILO to regulate trade relations such that the labour standards adopted by Western European States would not lead to any competitive disadvantage vis-à-vis other nations.[22] However, the statement in Article 427 to the effect that 'differences of climate, habits and customs of economic opportunity and industrial tradition, make

---

Challenges: Historical Lessons and Contemporary Learning' in Alysia Blackham, Miriam Kullmann and Ania Zbyszewska (eds), *Theorising Labour Law in a Changing World: Towards Inclusive Labour Law* (Hart 2019).

[19] For the significance of this statement, see Anne Trebilcock, 'The ILO as an Actor in International Economic Law: Looking Back, Gazing Ahead' in Marc Bungenberg, Markus Krajewski, Christian J. Tams, Jörg Philipp Terhechte and Andreas R. Ziegler (eds) *European Yearbook of International Economic Law 2019* (Springer 2020), 5.

[20] Barnes n.10, 35–7 and 45–7. See for a similar view, Archibald Chisholm, *Labour's Magna Charta: A Critical Study of the Labour Clauses of the Peace Treaty and of the Draft Conventions and Recommendations of the Washington International Labour Conference* (Longmans 1925), 10–11. Cf. Ghebali n.11, 14.

[21] Karl Polanyi, *The Great Transformation: The Political and Economic Origins of our Time* (Beacon Press, 2001, 2nd paperback ed), 27–8; see also Adelle Blackett, 'On Social Regionalism in Transnational Labour Law' (2020) 159(4) *International Labour Review* 591, 593.

[22] Barnes n.10, 79: 'If [the ILO] is not supported by the great industrial countries of Europe, it must assuredly lose in moral prestige, because for good or ill those countries lead the world in labour and industrial activities generally. Above all else, the International Labour Organisation must justify itself to the European organised industrialised democracies.'

strict uniformity in the conditions of labour difficult of immediate attainment' has also been cited as an early example of the principle of 'common but differentiated responsibility' (CBDR) at international law, which has had further application in the context of global environmental law subsequently.[23]

There was certainly awareness of China and Japan as potential trade competitors in this context.[24] That competitive agenda has been described as permeating 'the constitution and subsequent history of the ILO'.[25] Further, there was the statement that 'labour should not be regarded merely as a commodity or article of commerce' set out (twice) in Article 427 of the 1919 Treaty. This can be regarded as an injunction against slavery or even just commodification of labour. In a trade context, it can also be read as resistance to trade in labour, admitting only of trade in goods in respect of which the input of workers into the value of those goods should be protected, at least through basic workers' rights.[26]

There were two parts to the first ILO Constitution set out in Part XIII of the Treaty of Versailles in 1919. The preamble to Section I set out the Organization of Labour's objectives, while the ways in which the ILO was to operate were detailed in Articles 387–426. Section II consisted of Article 427 detailing the 'General Principles' consisting of 'nine guiding points' of 'special and urgent importance'.[27] Article 389 set out the role of the 'General Conference of Representatives of the Members' (now known as the International Labour Conference), which was to make the ultimate decisions, while a 'Governing Body' would exercise executive powers. The Governing Body was initially dominated by Western European powers and has since been reformed, although ten nations of 'chief industrial importance' retain unelected seats.[28]

---

[23] Rowena Maguire, 'The Role of Common But Differentiated Responsibility in the 2020 Climate Regime (2013) 4 *Carbon and Climate Law Review* 260, 261.

[24] Alcock n.13, 3–16.

[25] Harold Butler, *The International Labour Organization* (OUP 1939), 7–8.

[26] Tonia Novitz, 'Freedom of Association: Its Emergence and the Case for Prevention of Its Decline' in Janice Bellace and Beryl Ter Haar (eds), *Business, Labour and Human Rights* (Edward Elgar Publishing 2019), 242.

[27] See Albert Thomas, 'Preface' in *The International Labour Organization: The First Decade* (Allen & Unwin 1931), 31.

[28] For background to this controversy, see Stephen Hughes and Nigel Haworth, *The ILO Involvement in Economic and Social Policies in the 1930s* (ILO 2019), 18. As of 2023, the Governing Body consists of 56 titular members (28 governments, 14 employers and 14 workers), with 66 deputy members (28 governments, 19 employers and 19 workers). The majority of government members are elected but ten titular seats are permanently reserved for 'states of chief industrial importance': Brazil, China, France, Germany, India, Italy, Japan, the Russian Federation, the United Kingdom and the United States. Employer and worker members are elected separately in their individual capacity. See for an explanation, www.ilo.org/gb/about-governing-body/lang-

Both the International Labour Conference and the Governing Body would receive administrative assistance from the 'International Labour Office' led by a 'Director'.[29]

An innovative and unique feature of the ILO was the unprecedented tripartite nature of the International Labour Conference and Governing Body,[30] which was daring and adventurous.[31] Tripartism was described by Albert Thomas, the first ILO Director, as 'the smoke and dust of practical politics, which may get things smudged, but gets them done'.[32] This system of governance was designed to ensure the ILO's enduring relevance and responsiveness to the needs of its constituencies;[33] for, while 'all codification is abstract', 'institutions are living things'.[34] As Alain Supiot has put it: 'Social Justice is a principle of action.'[35] The constitutional guarantee of 'freedom of association' was the basis for this tripartite constitution, and so it was not surprising that the second principle listed of 'special and urgent importance' (after the statement that labour was not a commodity) was: 'The right of association for all lawful purposes by the employed as well as by the employers'.

The drafting and adoption of labour standards at the ILO came to be understood to be the joint responsibility of representatives of employers, workers and governments. So, too, did supervision of implementation of those standards by bodies such as the ILO Conference Committee on the Application of Standards (the CCAS) from 1926[36] and the Governing Body Committee on Freedom of Association (the CFA) from 1951.[37] While governments tend to be more influential (being half of the state delegates at any International Labour Conference), employer and worker representatives have at least received formal parity of treatment. Governments have the most influence

---

-en/index.htm and for membership from 2021 to 2024, www.ilo.org/wcmsp5/groups/public/@ed_norm/@relconf/@reloff/documents/meetingdocument/wcms_083528.pdf.

29 Later to become the 'Director-General'.

30 Claire La Hovary, 'A Challenging Ménage à Trois? Tripartism in the International Labour Organization' (2015) 12(1) *International Organizations Law Review* 204, 205–6.

31 Albert Thomas, 'The International Labour Organisation – Its Origins, Development and Future' (1921) 1 *International Labour Review* 5, 11.

32 Ibid, 9.

33 Ibid, 16.

34 Ibid, 7. See also Bellace n.14.

35 Alain Supiot, *The Spirit of Philadelphia: Social Justice vs the Total Market* (Verso 2012), 97.

36 International Labour Office, *The Committee on the Application of Standards of the International Labour Conference: A Dynamic and Impact Built on Decades of Dialogue and Persuasion* (ILO 2011), 11.

37 International Labour Office, *Freedom of Association: Compilation of Decisions of the Committee on Freedom of Association* (ILO 2018), 1.

at the ILO, but cannot act without consulting and responding to the concerns of these social actors, especially since the adoption of any ILO Convention or Recommendation requires a two-thirds majority of all the delegates at the International Labour Conference.[38] Initially, only the English and French texts of Conventions were to be authoritative; it is only for Conventions adopted from 2023 onwards that the Spanish texts also acquired that status.[39]

In Polanyian terms, the first ILO Constitution can be read as reflecting a determination to respond to and regulate conflicting social and market demands.[40] Tripartite governance could be regarded as a form of 'counter-movement' in response to the exploitative treatment of labour prior to the First World War, recognising the need to extinguish the practices of sweated labour through agreement reached between states, while giving interested social actors scope to deliberate on priorities, standards and actions. What was missing from this analysis of the plight of 'labour' was any real discussion of 'land' and/or 'money', that is, the other two fictitious commodities which Polanyi was later to identify. The only monetary and environmental issues were raised, not under Article 427, but in the preamble to Section 1 of Part XIII recognising that 'improvement was urgently required' regarding, *inter alia*, 'the provision of an adequate living wage, the protection of the worker against sickness, disease and injury arising out of his employment'.

The limitations of ILO competence relating to trade and money were to be exposed during the depression of the 1930s and the 'beggar thy neighbour' trading practices associated with ever higher tariffs. Standard-setting in the ILO slowed, although dialogue with affected governments, employers and workers increased. ILO economists proposed new research-based policies challenging 'existing orthodoxies on monetary policy, price stability and employment' arguing for 'internationally coordinated public work programmes' and mechanisms to enable a stable exchange rate of monetary exchange, but failed to achieve influence at the World Economic Conferences led by the League of Nations.[41]

38 See ILO Constitution, Article 19.

39 See ILO Resolution concerning the final provisions of international labour Conventions 2023 ILC.111/Resolution II, ILC 111th Session, establishing a new standard final clause, 'Article H': 'The French and English, French and Spanish versions of the texts of this Convention shall both be authentic are equally authoritative.'

40 See Polanyi n.21; discussed in Chapter 2 of this book at nn.202 et seq.

41 See Anthony M. Endres and Grant Fleming, 'International Economic Policy in the Interwar Years: The Special Contribution of ILO Economists' (1996) 135 *International Labour Review* 207; Hughes and Haworth n.28, 20; Rodgers et al n.15, 172–6; and Trebilcock n.19, 7.

2.2 Human Rights in the Declaration of Philadelphia and the Aftermath of the Second World War

The functions of the ILO were revisited after the Second World War, when the Declaration of Philadelphia 1944 repeated in Article I(a) that 'Labour is not a commodity' and reiterated the ILO's commitment to freedom of association,[42] which was later to become the subject of ILO Conventions Nos 87 and 98 and be made subject to specific supervisory mechanisms, the Fact-Finding and Conciliation Commission on Freedom of Association and the CFA.[43]

Moreover, 'freedom of expression and of association' were said to be 'essential to sustained progress'.[44] This was not perhaps tantamount to an expression of the need for sustainability or sustainable development, pre-dating the evolution of that concept as charted in Chapter 1 of this book.[45] Nevertheless, there is an appreciation here of concerns with intra-generational justice, such that Article I(c) states that 'poverty anywhere constitutes a danger to prosperity everywhere', sentiments arguably echoed decades later in the 2030 Agenda and SDG 1.

The Declaration of Philadelphia also recognised the potential for labour standards to be recognised as human rights,[46] arguably drawing on the political accord which was later to underlie the adoption of the UN Universal Declaration of Human Rights of 1948.[47] In Article II(a) it is declared that 'all human beings, irrespective of race, creed or sex, have the right to pursue both their material well-being and their spiritual development in conditions of freedom and dignity, of economic security and equal opportunity'; while paragraph (b) of the same Article states that 'the attainment of the conditions in which this shall be possible must constitute the central aim of national and

---

42 Declaration of Philadelphia 1944, Art. I(b), Art. I(d), and Art. III(e).

43 ILO Freedom of Association and Protection of the Right to Organise Convention, 1948 (No. 87) and Right to Organise and Collective Bargaining Convention, 1949 (No. 98). See Henner Gött, 'Interactions Between International Organizations: Approaching a Neglected Governance Dimension' (2020) 17(1) *International Organizations Law Review* 75, 82–5; and Tonia Novitz, *International and European Protection of the Right to Strike* (Oxford University Press 2003), 114–20 and 188–91.

44 Declaration of Philadelphia 1944, Art. I(b) and Art. III(e).

45 See Chapter 1 of this book, text accompanying nn.83 et seq.

46 See Virginia A. Leary, 'Lessons from the Experience of the ILO' in Philip Alston (ed.), *The United Nations and Human Rights: A Critical Reappraisal* (Oxford University Press 1992), 591.

47 See UNGA Resolution 217 A (III) of 10 December 1948. ILO, *Report of the Committee of Experts on the Application of Conventions and Recommendations: General Report and Observations concerning Particular Countries*, Report III (Part IA) (ILO 1998) ILC, 86th Session, 16–17.

international policy'. Alain Supiot has described this as 'the link established between spiritual freedoms and material security'.[48]

There was also appreciation in Article III of the significance of freedom of association in the form of 'the effective recognition of the right of collective bargaining, the co-operation of management and labour in the continuous improvement of productive efficiency, and the collaboration of workers and employers in the preparation and application of social and economic measures'.[49] Worker and employer representatives, 'enjoying equal status with those of governments', were to join with states in 'free discussion and democratic decision with a view to promotion of the common welfare'.[50] One can detect both economic motives and social claims being recognised simultaneously here, and an expectation that these objectives would underlie the operation of the ILO, while also being pursued in member states.

The express recognition of various socio-economic rights included the commitment to achieve 'adequate protection for the life and health of workers in all occupations' in Article III(g); the working environment was considered vital. A proclamation in Article IV served as a helpful prelude to subsequent UN debates regarding connections between trade and development, advocating for example effective international and national action, listing 'measures to expand production and consumption, to avoid severe economic fluctuations, to promote the economic and social advancement of the less developed regions of the world, to assure greater stability in world prices of primary products, and to promote a high and steady volume of international trade'. The Philadelphia Conference pledged full ILO cooperation with international bodies entrusted with such responsibilities. As Sandrine Kott has explained, in this way the ILO came to play a role as 'a social agent of economic globalisation', which came into tension with its constitutional mission of 'social justice'.[51] On the one hand, the ILO's predominant constitutional concern remained with promoting the well-being of those at work, but at the same time, as a UN agency, its role was to collaborate with other such agencies rather than challenge the economic vision that they pursued. Initially this was not problematic, to the extent that a Keynesian economic approach offered a form of 'embedded lib-

[48] Supiot n.35, 13.

[49] Lee Swepston, 'Human Rights and Freedom of Association: Development through ILO Supervision' (1998) 137 *International Labour Review* 169, 170.

[50] Declaration of Philadelphia 1944, Art. I(d).

[51] Sandrine Kott, 'ILO: Social Justice in a Global World? A History in Tension' in Christophe Gironde and Gilles Carbonnier (eds), *The ILO@100: Addressing the Past and Future of Work and Social Protection* (Brill Nijhoff 2019), 34.

eralism' attractive to many western ILO members,[52] so that scrutiny of fiscal orthodoxy and trade relations established on the global stage was not often deemed necessary. Indeed, the oversight that the Bretton Woods institutions provided following the 'beggar they neighbour' policies of the 1930s was widely welcomed.[53]

Of particular interest in relation to trade was the assertion in Article II(c) of the Declaration that economic and financial policies, whether national or international, should be accepted 'only insofar as they may be held to promote and not to hinder' the achievement of the Organization's 'fundamental objective', namely 'social justice'. Moreover Article II(d) recognised the 'responsibility of the International Labour Organization to examine and consider all international economic and financial policies and measures in the light of this fundamental objective'. The purpose of the ILO was not merely to be competitive regulation; rather, priority was to be given to social justice rather than utilitarian economic efficiencies.[54] The ability of the ILO to scrutinise (rather than only respond to the perceived dictates of) economic policy was an important addition to its competence,[55] if one which has been difficult subsequently to reconcile with the specialist competence of other UN agencies. In particular, as we shall see, the subsequent adoption of a 'Washington Consensus' by the Bretton Woods institutions-promoted deregulation of labour standards created considerable tension.[56]

Section II of Part XIII (Article 427) of the Treaty of Versailles was removed, as the 1944 Declaration was annexed to the ILO Constitution and the ILO became an official UN agency[57] alongside others, such as the Bretton Woods institutions: an International Bank for Reconstruction and Development

---

52 John Ruggie, 'International Regimes, Transactions and Change: Embedded Liberalism in the Post-war Economic Order' (1982) 36(2) *International Organization* 385.

53 Cf. this chapter, text accompanying n.41.

54 See Ghebali n.11, at 62–3, 78–80 and 81–6.

55 *Future Policy, Programme and Status of the International Labour Organisation* (ILO 1944), 7–10.

56 See John Williamson, 'A Short History of the Washington Consensus' (2009) 15 *Law and Business Review of the Americas* 7; Peter Bakvis, 'The World Bank's Doing Business Report: A last fling for the Washington Consensus?' (2009) 15(3–4) *Transfer: European Review of Labour and Research* 419. See further discussion in Chapter 4 of this book, text accompanying nn.63 et seq.

57 The text of the agreement can be found in XXIX No. 4 *Official Bulletin* 15.11.46, 293. See for the substance of these negotiations, Alcock n.13, 188–204; and L.B. Sohn, 'The Contribution of the International Labour Organization to the Development of the Concept of Economic, Social and Cultural Rights' in R-J Dupuy (ed.), *Mélanges en l'honneur de Nicolas Valticos* (Éditions A. Pedone 1999).

(IBRD) and an International Monetary Fund (IMF). An International Trade Organisation (ITO) was planned for, but never materialised.[58]

Under the original Havana Charter intended to create the ITO, it was recognised that 'all countries have a common interest in the achievement and maintenance of fair labour standards related to productivity, and thus in the improvement of wages and working conditions as productivity may permit', but also that 'unfair labour conditions, particularly in production for export, create difficulties in international trade, and, accordingly, each Member shall take whatever action may be appropriate and feasible to eliminate such conditions within its territory'.[59] Notably, this did not permit obvious trade conditionality, but rather self-regulation by the putative members of the ITO. However, ITO members who were also ILO members were to 'cooperate' with the ILO 'in giving effect to this undertaking', as was the ITO itself.[60] In the end, the failure of the US Congress to ratify the Havana Charter led to the General Agreement on Tariffs and Trade (the GATT) being adopted provisionally in the absence of an ITO, and the ILO's status as a reference point for regulation of trade was never cemented.[61]

Nevertheless, standard-setting at the ILO in the post-Second World War period flourished. Numerous Conventions and Recommendations were adopted by the International Labour Conference, apparently galvanised by the constitutional principles that had been established in 1919 but supplemented in 1944. These came to be known, at least colloquially, as an International Labour Code.[62] In 1969 the ILO was awarded the Nobel Peace Prize for its services

---

[58] Alcock n.13, 188–202; C. Wilfred Jenks, 'Co-ordination in International Organization: An Introductory Survey' (1951) 28 *British Yearbook of International Law* 29 at 43–8; see also Guy Fiti Sinclair, 'C. Wilfred Jenks and the Futures of International Organizations Law' (2020) 31(2) *European Journal of International Law* 525.

[59] See the Havana Charter for an ITO, available at: www .jus .uio .no/ english/ services/library/treaties/15/15-02/ito.xml, Article 7.

[60] Ibid; for discussion, see Clair Wilcox, 'The London Draft of a Charter for an International Trade Organization' (1947) 37(2) *The American Economic Review* 529; and, more briefly, Trebilcock n.19, 8–9.

[61] John Jackson, *Sovereignty, the WTO and Changing Fundamentals of International Law* (Cambridge University Press 2006), 93; Andreas F. Lowenfeld, *International Economic Law* (Oxford University Press 2008), 28–30.

[62] See the original *International Labour Code: A Systematic Arrangement of the Conventions and Recommendations adopted by the International Labour Conference, 1919–1939* (ILO 1941); and Neville N. Rubin, *Code of International Labour Law: Law, Practice and Jurisprudence* (Cambridge University Press 2005).

to world peace through the promotion of social justice, although there were challenges ahead.[63]

In a period of decolonisation, the ILO came under pressure to meet what Wilfred C. Jenks described as the 'challenge of universality'.[64] With a wider membership at the ILO, the dominance of Western European states could no longer be assumed. Tensions arose during the Cold War[65] and as previous colonial territories became independent.[66] Extreme differentials in wealth, and thereby the balance of power between states in the so-called Global North and the de-colonised 'developing states' of the Global South,[67] gradually and increasingly became the subject of debate.[68] Arguments against the formal parity of treatment of states in international trade began, with reference to the idea of 'special and differential treatment' (SDT), although this was not a notion that gained obvious traction at the ILO. Instead, a fairly wide margin of appreciation was permitted to states regarding the manner of implementation of ILO constitutional and Convention obligations, which would allow for differences in wealth and capacity.[69]

Towards the end of the Cold War period, calls were made for a reduction in ILO standard-setting,[70] in part to boost economic growth of post-Socialist

---

[63] Steve Hughes, 'The International Labour Organisation' (2005) 10(3) *New Political Economy* 413; Laurence Helfer, 'The ILO at 100: Institutional Innovation in an Era of Populism' (2019) 113 *American Journal of International Law* 396.

[64] C. Wilfred Jenks, 'The Challenge of Universality' (1959) 53 *American Society of International Law Proceedings* 85.

[65] See Alcock n.13, 284–305 and 318–37; Imber n.10, 51–2 and 65–6.

[66] On the role of the Group of 77 within the ILO, see Ghebali n.11, 41–2; and regarding US temporary withdrawal in response to assertion of their concerns which had profound effects on the US budget, see Stephen I. Schlossberg, 'United States Participation in the ILO' (1989) 11 *Comparative Labor Law Journal* 48, 68–71.

[67] See for discussion of these terms, Chapter 1 of this book at text accompanying nn.45–62.

[68] Branko Milanovic, *Global Inequality: A New Approach for the Age of Globalization* (Harvard University Press 2016); Miriam Ronzoni, 'Global Labour Injustice: A Critical Overview' in Yossi Dahan, Hanna Lerner and Faina Milman-Sivan (eds), *Global Justice and International Labour Rights* (Cambridge University Press 2016).

[69] Note, in particular, the controversial 'flexibility' clause, which has been introduced into particular Conventions in order to ensure that 'universal' ILO standards cater for the special domestic circumstances of its members. Discussed in G. Chike Okogwu, 'Labour Standards across Different Levels of Development' in Werner Sengenberger and Duncan Campbell (eds), *International Labour Standards and Economic Interdependence* (ILO International Institute for Labour Studies 1994), 154–7.

[70] Efren Cordova, 'Some Reflections on the Overproduction of International Labour Standards' (1993) 14 *Comparative Labor Law Journal* 138.

states and to address unemployment in the Global North. As the role of the ILO shifted and became less concerned with acting as a debating chapter for East–West concerns, and international standards ceased to be regarded as a way to avert socialism, the employers' group began to challenge the pertinence of ILO standards, even those which had previously been regarded as well-established, such as the scope of freedom of association.[71] As the relevance of the ILO was questioned, the ILO budget also came under threat.[72]

The Director-General of the ILO responded by initiating studies of the continuing relevance and efficacy of ILO standards[73] – an initiative which provided the foundation for identification of the 'core' or 'fundamental' labour standards promulgated by the ILO today, which have become regarded as a legitimate basis for trade conditionality.

3. IDENTIFICATION OF 'FUNDAMENTAL' ILO STANDARDS, DECENT WORK AND THE CONSEQUENCES FOR TERMS OF TRADE

In 1994, the ILO tripartite Governing Body took the decision to establish a 'Working Party' on the social dimension of the liberalisation of international trade. The aim was to discover whether consensus could be reached on the viability of a 'social clause' in trade agreements. Such consensus was not achievable, due to stark divisions of opinion between countries and between social actors, but the remit of the Working Party was widened to consider the social impact of globalisation through the investigation of country-based case studies. The Working Party concluded that there should be protection of 'social pillars' through domestic policies, in response to market-led globalisation.[74] However, this proposal made little headway. Instead, other develop-

---

71 ILC, 81st session, 1994, ILC, Report of the Committee on the Application of Standards: Submission, Discussion and Adoption at 28/90, Alfred Wisskirchen (Employers' adviser, Germany; Employer Vice-Chairman of the Committee on the Application of Standards). See Alfred Wisskirchen, 'The Standard-setting and Monitoring Activity of the ILO: Legal Questions and Practical Experience' (2005) 144 *International Labour Review* 253.

72 Janice Bellace, 'The ILO Declaration of Fundamental Principles and Rights at Work' (2001) 17 *International Journal of Comparative Labour Law and Industrial Relations* 269, 271.

73 See *Report of the Director-General: Defending Values, Promoting Change* (ILO 1994); See *Report of the Director-General: Promoting Employment* (ILO 1995).

74 These social pillars were identified as: education and training; social safety nets; labour law and industrial relations; and respect for core labour standards. See Governing Body Working Party on the Social Dimension of Globalization, *Country Studies on the Social Impact of Globalization* GB.276/WP/SDL/1 (ILO 1999).

ments at the ILO, namely recognition of core labour standards, adoption of a 'Decent Work Agenda' and challenges to tripartism, have done more to shape ILO influence over the terms of global trade.

In this section of the chapter we examine these developments. We first consider the initiative taken to promote fundamental ILO standards by identifying 'core Conventions' and constitutional obligations through the 1998 Declaration on Fundamental Principles and Rights at Work. The implications of this prioritisation of labour standards in the context of trade are considered alongside the ILO's subsequent attempt to address the effects on labour of globalisation through the creation of a 'Decent Work Agenda', which has subsequently received explicit recognition in the 2030 Agenda and SDG 8. The section concludes by discussing the employers' walkout in 2012, which presented a challenge to tripartite mechanisms in the ILO and collective labour rights in ILO member states. Again, the implications for ILO influence on the terms of cross-border trade will be discussed.

3.1 'Fundamental' ILO Standards

Allegations of 'over-production' of ILO standards led to a decision to review and rationalise ILO Conventions which were binding on member states.[75] This involved prioritisation of the ratification of certain Conventions over others. In particular, Michel Hansenne (ILO Director-General from 1989–99) identified certain so-called core or fundamental ILO Conventions relating to: freedom of association, the right to organise and collective bargaining (ILO Conventions Nos 87 and 98); prohibition of forced labour (Conventions Nos 29 and 105); prevention of child labour (initially Convention No.138 to which Convention No.182 was later added); and discrimination (Conventions Nos 100 and 111).[76] This strategy has given prominence to these Conventions, so that they are now widely seen as a helpful reference point for trade conditionality, particularly in the EU, as will be discussed further in Chapter 5. The attention to these 'core' standards led not only to the further elaboration on child labour and adoption of Convention No. 182, which was designated as 'core', but also to a further Protocol of 2014 to Convention No. 29.[77] The 2014 Forced Labour Protocol,

---

[75] See Cordova n.70.

[76] Also note four other 'priority' (or 'governance') ILO Conventions identified in the Follow-up to the Declaration on Social Justice for a Fair Globalization 2008, available at: www.ilo.org/global/standards/introduction-to-international-labour-standards/conventions-and-recommendations/lang--en/index.htm.

[77] See the Protocol of 2014 to the Forced Labour Convention, 1930 (No. 29) and the Forced Labour (Supplementary Measures) Recommendation 2014 (No. 203) availa-

drawing on the initiative taken in the Palermo Protocol on Trafficking,[78] recognises that certain groups of workers are at 'a higher risk of becoming victims of forced or compulsory labour, especially migrants' and proposes measures accordingly.

Hansenne's endeavour culminated in the identification of four 'core' labour standards in Article 2 of the ILO Declaration of Fundamental Principles and Rights at Work 1998,[79] referred to in the WTO Singapore Ministerial Declaration of 1996.[80] They were:

(a) freedom of association and the effective recognition of the right to collective bargaining;
(b) the elimination of all forms of forced or compulsory labour;
(c) the effective abolition of child labour; and
(d) the elimination of discrimination in respect of employment and occupation.

These were labour standards regarding which all members had prior obligations under the then ILO Constitution (as supplemented by the Declaration of Philadelphia, which had been appended to the original text of the Treaty of Versailles), regardless of whether those states had ratified related ILO Conventions. These labour standards had been recognised already within the UN framework as civil and political rights, and were therefore more likely to attract consent from a post-Cold War constituency led by an emergent Western liberal democratic consensus.[81] This human rights approach asserted the universal character of these labour standards, prioritising them over other economic objectives.[82] However, there was also a danger, soon flagged, that this approach could unduly limit other legitimate ILO objectives,[83] arguably dimin-

---

ble at: www.ilo.org/dyn/normlex/en/f?p=NORMLEXPUB:12100:0::NO::P12100_ILO_CODE:P029.

[78] UN Convention Against Transnational Organized Crime 2000; also Protocol against the Smuggling of Migrants by Land, Sea and Air 2004 and Protocol to Suppress and Punish Trafficking in Persons, Especially Women and Children 2004 (the Palermo Protocol') available at: www.unodc.org/unodc/treaties/CTOC/.

[79] See www.ilo.org/declaration/lang--en/index.htm.

[80] See n.1 above.

[81] Cf. Francis Fukyama, *The End of History and the Last Man* (Free Press 1992), which celebrated the 'triumph' of Western liberal ideology.

[82] See comment from Christopher McCrudden and A.C.L. Davies, 'A Perspective on Trade and Labour Rights' (2000) *Journal of International Economic Law* 43.

[83] Jill Murray, 'Taking Social Rights Seriously: Is there a Case for Institutional Reform of the ILO?' in Colin Fenwick and Tonia Novitz (eds), *Human Rights at Work: Perspectives on Law and Regulation* (Hart 2010).

ishing the influence of a larger International Labour Code.[84] For example, they could be said to detract attention from ILO Conventions concerning migrant work, that provide for the entitlements of such workers to equality of treatment and protection of their human rights, which is likely to be of considerable significance in the context of contemporary global supply chains and movement for work.[85]

Some academic commentators were accepting of this strategic selective approach. For example, Brian Langille endorsed this protection of process rights, as opposed to substantive outcomes, which he viewed as being more achievable for developing countries conducive to capacity (and capability) building in the Global South.[86] Notably, this selection of standards had also been endorsed by OECD studies as compatible with the trade aspirations of developing countries.[87] Others, however, were alarmed by this prioritisation of ILO norms, which marked a problematic retreat from insistence on the socio-economic entitlements of workers and compliance with a wider range of ILO Conventions.[88]

---

[84] See Rubin n.62.

[85] See ILO Migration for Employment Convention (Revised), 1949 (No. 97); also Migrant Workers (Supplementary Provisions) Convention, 1975 (No. 143). For comment on their enduring relevance and scope of implementation, see Judy Fudge, 'Precarious Migrant Status and Precarious Employment: The Paradox of International Rights for Migrant Workers' (2012–13) 34 *Comparative Labor Law and Policy Journal* 95; Joo-Cheong Tham, 'Equality and Community for Migrant Workers' in Alan Bogg, Jacob Rowbottom and Alison Young (eds), *The Constitution of Social Democracy: Essays in Honour of Keith Ewing* (Bloomsbury Publishing 2020); and Petra Herzfeld Olsson, 'The Role of Effective Enforcement in International Law on Labour Migration' (2020) 17(1) *International Organizations Law Review* 206.

[86] Brian Langille, 'Core Labour Standards – The True Story (Reply to Alston)' (2005) 16 *European Journal of International Law* 409, 431. This view is consistent with later publications such as Brian Langille, 'Imagining Post Geneva Consensus Labor Law for Post Washington Consensus Development' (2009) 31 *Comparative Labor Law and Policy Journal* 523; and Brian Langille, '"Hard Law Makes Bad Cases": The International Labour Organization (Nervously) Confronts New Governance Institutions' (2016) 32(4) *International Journal of Comparative Labour Law and Industrial Relations* 407.

[87] Discussed by Steve Charnovitz, 'Trade, Employment and Labour Standards: The OECD Study and Recent Developments: The OECD Study and Developments in the Trade and Labour Standards Debate' (1997) 11 *Temple International and Comparative Law Journal* 131.

[88] Philip Alston, '"Core Labour Standards" and the Transformation of the International Labour Rights Regime' (2004) 15 *European Journal of International Law* 457; Philip Alston, 'Facing Up to the Complexities of the ILO's Core Labour Standards Agenda' (2005) 16 *European Journal of International Law* 457; Philip Alston and James Heenan, 'Shrinking the International Labour Code' (2004) 36(2/3) *International*

One concern relating to the selective content of Article 2 of the 1998 Declaration has now been addressed. As early as 1997, Bob Hepple observed that health and safety was a problematic omission from the 'core'.[89] In June 2022, the International Labour Conference remedied this omission by placing in Article 2 an entitlement to 'a safe and healthy working environment', while giving 'fundamental' status also to Conventions Nos 155 and 187.[90] This Resolution made clear that the amendment stemmed from appreciation of the need for ILO activity in response to the COVID-19 pandemic,[91] in which the Organization had sought to work in collaboration with the World Health Organisation (WHO).[92]

The text of the 1998 Declaration reveals some awareness of the ways in which the newly identified core labour standards could be applied in a trade scenario.[93] Article 1 of the 1998 Declaration states that 'the specific circumstances' of States must be considered when assessing compliance. Article 5 stresses that 'labour standards should not be used for protectionist trade purposes' and that 'the comparative advantage of any country should in no way be called into question', arguably echoing the terms of the WTO Singapore

Law and Politics 221; Guy Standing, 'The ILO: An Agency for Globalization' (2008) 39(3) *Development and Change* 355, 367–8.

89 Bob Hepple, 'New Approaches to International Labour Regulation' (1997) 26 *Industrial Law Journal* 353, 359.

90 See ILO Resolution on the inclusion of a safe and healthy working environment in the ILO's framework of fundamental principles and rights at work 2022, ILC.110/Resolution1, ILC 110th Session. For background, see Zahra Yusifli and Colin Fenwick, 'Workers' Rights and Human Rights: Toward a New Fundamental Principle?' in Kimberley Elliott (ed.), *Handbook on Globalisation and Labour Standards* (Edward Elgar Publishing 2022). For changes to reporting requirements for Conventions Nos 155 and 187 to shift from a six-year to a three-year reporting cycle, see ILO Governing Body, *Minutes of the Legal Issues and International Labour Standards Section* GB.347/LILS/PV (ILO 2023), 22–4; and for consequential amendments of other ILO Conventions and Recommendations in 2003, see Safe and Healthy Working Environment (Consequential Amendments) Convention, 2023 (No. 191); and the Safe and Healthy Working Environment (Consequential Amendments) Recommendation, 2023 (No. 207).

91 ILO Resolution on the inclusion of a safe and healthy working environment 2022 n.90, Preamble: 'Mindful of the vital importance of occupational safety and health, as compellingly demonstrated by the COVID-19 pandemic and its profound and transformative impact on the world of work.'

92 See ILO resources at: www.ilo.org/global/topics/coronavirus/lang--en/index.htm; and WHO Press Release at: www.who.int/news/item/23-02-2022-ilo-who-step-up-collaboration-to-address-health-emergencies-and-promote-healthier-and-safer-working-populations.

93 See Hepple n.89, 360–2.

Ministerial Declaration two years earlier.[94] The aim seems to have been to evade ILO endorsement of the introduction of a social clause, which would have been highly controversial.[95] As one commentator observed contemporaneously: 'The Declaration reduces pressures on other international bodies, particularly the WTO, to adopt coercive trade sanctions as the appropriate means of enhancing workers' rights and improving working conditions.'[96] Instead, the Declaration set out a 'follow-up' procedure, consisting of 'annual review' of conduct of member states that had not ratified 'core' ILO Conventions and a thematic 'global report' on the scale of compliance with each of the core labour standards to be carried out every four years.[97]

That said, the reality was that Article 2 of the 1998 Declaration became a touchstone for the legitimacy of labour conditionality included in free trade agreements (FTAs), despite protestations that the instrument would be 'non-binding'.[98] By 2019, an International Labour Report could observe that FTAs concluded by the US tend to make reference to the 'rights stated in the ILO 1998 Declaration and its follow-up', while the EU tends to require compliance with 'internationally recognized core labour standards as contained in the ILO fundamental Conventions'.[99] It is also notable that the 2022 International Labour Conference Resolution amending the 1998 Declaration contained a 'saving clause' in Article 5, which declared 'that nothing in this resolution shall be construed as affecting in any unintended manner the rights and obligations of a Member arising from existing trade and investment agree-

---

[94] See n.1 above; also Hilary Kellerson, 'The ILO Declaration of 1998 on Fundamental Principles and Rights: A Challenge for the Future' (1998) 137 *International Labour Review* 223, 225.

[95] The insertion of paragraph 5 was demanded by 113 government representatives and five observers (including China) as recorded in Bob Hepple, *Labour Laws and Global Trade* (Hart 2005), 61.

[96] Christopher R. Coxson, 'The 1998 ILO Declaration on Fundamental Principles and Rights at Work: Promoting Labor Law Reforms Through the ILO as an Alternative to Imposing Coercive Trade Sanctions' (1998) 17 *Dickinson Journal of International Law* 469, 504.

[97] For the most recent reports, see www.ilo.org/declaration/lang--en/index.htm; see also ILO Governing Body, Review of annual reports under the follow-up to the ILO Declaration on Fundamental Principles and Rights at Work (1998), as amended in 2022 GB.347/INS/3, 24 February 2023 (ILO 2023).

[98] Cf. Desirée LeClercq, 'Integrating Non-binding Labour Standards in Binding Trade Agreements: The ILO's Feedback Loop' (2023) 26(3) *Journal of International Economic Law* 542–58.

[99] See, for analysis, *Labour Provisions in G7 Trade Agreements: A Comparative Perspective* (ILO 2019), 24.

ments between States'.[100] In other words, reference to the 1998 Declaration in an FTA will not denote any obligation to comply with a 'healthy and safe working environment' until expressly incorporated in the instrument in question.[101] While this would almost certainly be the position in any case under international law, the political sensitivity of the issue meant that it required clarification in advance. This is an acknowledgement by ILO delegates today of the use to which Article 2 of the 1998 Declaration has in fact been put.

Notably, prior to the 2022 Resolution, certain FTAs had already made express reference to obligations regarding a safe and healthy working environment;[102] but it will depend on the particular wording and context of an FTA, which merely makes reference to the 1998 Declaration, whether such rights and obligations can be regarded by the parties as intended.[103] It is less clear what will be the implication of adding a fifth fundamental principle with respect to other international instruments which draw on the 1998 Declaration. These currently include the UN Global Compact (1999), the UN Guiding Principles on Business and Human Rights (2011) and the OECD Guidelines for Multinational Enterprises (1976, as revised).[104]

The relationship of the broader principles set out in the 1998 Declaration with the precise text of the fundamental ILO Conventions remains unclear when applied in a trade context.[105] The approach of the expert panel in the EU–Korea FTA dispute was to find that ILO Conventions Nos 87 and 98 should be regarded as relevant to whether Korea had complied with the principle of freedom of association as established under the 1998 Declaration, even though Korea had not ratified those Conventions at the time of the hearing, on the basis that this would be consistent with the supervisory findings of the ILO

---

[100] ILO Resolution on the inclusion of a safe and healthy working environment 2022 n.90.

[101] See *Report VII: Inclusion of safe and healthy working conditions in the ILO's framework of fundamental principles and rights at work* ILC, 110th Session, 2022, para 14 and paras 31–3.

[102] See UK–Australia Free Trade Agreement (FTA), Article 21.1 and 21.4, signed 16 December 2021 and available at: www.gov.uk/government/collections/free-trade-agreement-between-the-united-kingdom-of-great-britain-and-northern-ireland-and-australia; and UK–NZ FTA, Article 23.5, signed on 22 February 2022 and available at: www.gov.uk/government/collections/free-trade-agreement-between-the-united-kingdom-of-great-britain-and-northern-ireland-and-new-zealand.

[103] In all probability, such interpretation would take place with reference to the Vienna Convention on the Law of Treaties 1969, which came into force on 27 January 1980, and is at the time of writing ratified by 116 states. See https://treaties.un.org/Pages/showDetails.aspx?objid=080000028003902f.

[104] Discussed in Chapter 6 of this book. See Trebilcock n.19, 15.

[105] Cf. Laurence R. Helfer, 'Monitoring Compliance with Unratified Treaties: The ILO Experience' (2008) 71 *Law and Contemporary Problems* 193.

CFA, which has long held that these instruments merely reflect the obligations of all ILO members under the ILO Constitution.[106] However, that interpretation would seem to turn on the precise wording of the terms the parties use in the FTA in question and the apparent intention of the parties.

3.2 The Effect of a 'Decent Work Agenda'

To counter concerns regarding the narrow scope of the fundamental labour rights identified by the ILO under Hansenne, the next incoming ILO Director-General (from 1999–2012), Juan Somavia, sought to pursue a broader 'Decent Work Agenda' and, in so doing, open the way for 'a more substantive policy debate on development issues and rights at work within the ILO'.[107] He attributed his response to the practical concerns of those in the labour market in his country of origin, Chile, and to the fact that he was the first ILO Director-General to hail from the Global South.[108]

This was a four-pronged notion of 'decent work', which would encompass fundamental principles and rights at work, but also promotion of job opportunities, social protection and social dialogue.[109] The danger was that this was an over-correction in terms of breadth, so that 'decent work' could be viewed as 'a kind of normative potluck',[110] or a 'slogan' and a 'costly diversion' of little substance.[111]

In 2002, the ILO responded to controversies over trade and labour standard linkages by launching a World Commission on the Social Dimension of Globalization 'of eminent personalities'. The aim was to investigate the dynamics and effects of globalisation, 'to better understand people's aspirations and concerns' and 'identify innovative ways of making economic, social and environmental objectives sustainable and mutually reinforcing'.[112] There

---

[106] Report of the Panel of Experts (2020) Proceeding constituted under Article 13.15 of the EU–Korea Free Trade Agreement, 25 January 2021, Panel: Dr J. Murray (Chairperson), Professor L. Boisson de Chazournes and Professor J. Lee, para. 113; available at: https://trade.ec.europa.eu/doclib/docs/2021/january/tradoc_159358.pdf. See regarding the evolution of CFA findings on this issue and their constitutional foundations, Novitz n.41, 192–9.

[107] *Report of the Director-General: Decent Work* (ILO 1999), 8.

[108] Marieke Louis, 'Who Decides? Representation and Decision-making at the International Labour Organization' in Gironde and Carbonnier (eds) n.51, 45.

[109] ILO Declaration on Social Justice for a Fair Globalisation 2008.

[110] Francis Maupain, *The Future of the International Labour Organization in the Global Economy* (Hart 2013), 54.

[111] Guy Standing, 'The International Labour Organization' (2010) 15(2) *New Political Economy* 307, 314.

[112] www.ilo.org/public/english/wcsdg/commission/objectives.htm.

were therefore echoes of a sustainable development discourse in its mission statement. Moreover, this model of bringing together people 'able to bring to bear expertise, judgment and experience from different perspectives'[113] can be regarded as a precedent for the later Global Commission on the Future of Work which reported in 2019.[114] Both are notable for ILO determination to attempt to access a wide range of views beyond the traditional industrial settings, which had been familiar sites of trade union representation, and across the globe. A series of regional dialogues was held by the World Commission, which emphasised constructive deliberative dialogue rather than the conflictual approach adopted by some participants.[115] However, some interesting findings did emerge. For example, in the context of debate between representatives of the Global North and the Global South within the WTO, the World Commission conceded that 'a conversation between a cat and a mouse is not a conversation'.[116]

Concrete proposals for reform included achievement of good governance at national level, such as respect for human rights under the law and delivery of essential public goods such as health care and education.[117] National governments were to promote the ILO concept of 'decent work',[118] and to take forward the 'dialogues' begun by the World Commission.[119] Regional integration was recommended as a 'stepping stone' for management of global forces, building capabilities to take advantage of global opportunities, offering a useful redistributive mechanism and improving conditions under which people connect to the global economy, enabling a 'voice' in global governance for poorer countries (and their workers).[120] Moreover, reform of global governance was recommended to promote transparency and democratic accountability.[121] It was recommended that the ILO be a key actor in international cooperation or 'policy coherence' with the World Bank, the IMF and the WTO, in 'policy

---

113 ILO Governing Body Working Party on the Social Dimension of Globalization, *Enhancing the Action of the Working Party on the Social Dimension of Globalization: Next Steps* GB.282/WP/SDG/1, 282nd Session of the ILO Governing Body (ILO 2001), paras 4 and 6.

114 See text accompanying nn.226 et seq. below.

115 See for example *Regional Dialogue: Africa* (Arusha, February 2003), 2. See www.ilo.org/public/english/wcsdg/consulta/africa/index.htm.

116 ILO World Commission on the Social Dimension of Globalization, *A Fair Globalization: Creating Opportunities for All* (ILO 2004), 22.

117 Ibid, 55–64.

118 Ibid, 64.

119 Ibid, 132.

120 Ibid, 71–4.

121 Ibid, 76–91.

development dialogues' and a 'Globalization Policy Forum'.[122] In this respect, it was claimed that the tripartite structure of the ILO offered a unique advantage for the representation of government, management and labour. It was also recommended that these other international economic institutions should develop mechanisms for dialogue and decision more aligned with participatory inclusion of civil society.[123] As we shall see in Chapter 4 of this book, governance of international economic institutions has moved slightly in this direction, but has yet to even remotely replicate the kind of participatory engagement offered at the ILO.[124]

Following the 2004 Report of the World Commission on the Social Dimension on Globalization,[125] the ILO International Labour Conference adopted the Declaration on Social Justice for a Fair Globalization 2008.[126] The idea of 'decent work' was curiously absent from the title of the 2008 Declaration, which instead placed emphasis on 'social justice' in a way that was reminiscent of the original 1919 ILO Constitution.[127] In terms of substance, the 'Decent Work Agenda' was given immediate attention in Article I(A) and described as consisting of 'four equally important strategic objectives':

(i) promoting employment …
(ii) developing and enhancing measures of social protection – social security and labour protection – which are sustainable and adapted to national circumstances …
(iii) promoting social dialogue and tripartism …
(iv) respecting, promoting and realizing the fundamental principles and rights at work, which are of particular significance, as both rights and enabling conditions that are necessary for the full realization of all the strategic objectives …

In respect of (iv), it was clear that the rights to freedom of association and collective bargaining were a vital aspect of 'fundamental principles and rights at work' but also 'enabling rights' for achievement of other facets of decent work, being linked also to social dialogue and tripartism. Once again, it was observed under Article I(A)(iv) that 'the violation of fundamental principles and rights at work cannot be invoked or otherwise used as a legitimate compar-

---

122 Ibid, 124.
123 Ibid, 135–6.
124 See Chapter 4 of this book below.
125 ILO World Commission n.116.
126 ILO Declaration on Social Justice for a Fair Globalization adopted by the International Labour Conference at its Ninety-seventh Session, Geneva, 10 June 2008 available at: http://staging2.ilo.org/wcmsp4/groups/public/---dgreports/---cabinet/documents/publication/wcms_099766.pdf.
127 Maupain n.110, 58.

ative advantage and that labour standards should not be used for protectionist trade purposes'.

The preamble begins by identifying that globalisation, 'characterized by the diffusion of new technologies, the flow of ideas, the exchange of goods and services, the increase in capital and financial flows, the internationalization of business and business processes and dialogue as well as the movement of persons, especially working women and men, is reshaping the world of work'. This idea of a broader conception of work than that often regulated under national employment, labour and social security laws has since raised significant debate at the ILO. There had been a lack of tripartite will to pursue standard-setting via a Convention to ensure an inclusive approach to the question of 'employment' or 'worker status', with the adoption instead of an Employment Relationship Recommendation No. 198 in 2006 seeking to encourage member states to 'formulate and apply a national policy [...] in order to guarantee effective protection for workers who perform work in the context of an employment relationship'.[128] However, the 2008 Declaration's wording of 'the world of work' potentially offered more promise, as was later reflected in the proposal for a 'Universal Labour Guarantee' and the coverage of ILO Convention No. 190 at the ILO's centenary.[129]

The Declaration says little otherwise about global 'trade' *per se*. Instead, trade is mentioned again only at Article II(C), where the impact of trade and financial markets are considered in relation to their impact on 'employment'. There it is stressed that 'the ILO's role' is 'to evaluate those employment effects to achieve its aim of placing employment at the heart of economic policies'. This seems like a tentative explanation of the ILO's reason to expand its global normative competence, reassuring state parties and other international institutions that ILO policy interventions will be limited just to 'employment', rather than asserting wholesale the legitimacy of ILO concern with trade as intrinsically connected to work and labour conditions. An interesting question

---

[128] *The Employment Relationship: An Annotated Guide to ILO Recommendation No. 198* (ILO 2007) available at: www.ilo.org/wcmsp5/groups/public/---ed_dialogue/---dialogue/documents/publication/wcms_172417.pdf. For analysis, see Mark Freedland. 'Application of Labour and Employment Law Beyond the Contract of Employment' (2007) 146(1) *International Labour Review* 3; Breen Creighton and Shae McCrystal, 'Who Is a Worker in International Law' (2016) 37(3) *Comparative Labor Law and Policy Journal* 691; Valerio De Stefano, 'Not as Simple as It Seems: The ILO and the Personal Scope of International Labour Standards' (2021) 160(3) *International Labour Review* 387; and Tonia Novitz, 'Collective Labour Rights for Working People: The Legal Framework Established by the International Labour Organization' in Sanjukta Paul, Shae McCrystal and Ewan McGaughey (eds), *The Cambridge Handbook of Labor in Competition Law* (Cambridge University Press 2022).

[129] See this chapter below, text accompanying nn.239 and 251.

is the extent to which the 2008 Declaration actually influenced policy initiatives of the international economic institutions, which is discussed further in Chapter 4 of this book.

The focus of enforcement of the 2008 Declaration set out in an Annex 'Follow-up to the Declaration' was, curiously, not placed on the constituent member states, or the employers which, as commercial entities in the context of globalisation, were gaining profit and causing havoc. Instead, the ILO's gaze was to be diverted inwards. Article II contemplated that it would be for the ILO to 'review' and adapt its institutional practices to further the 'Decent Work Agenda'.[130] The aim seems to have been to redesign ILO activities to make them more facilitative and less critical of states and employers.[131] Added emphasis was placed on ILO provision of 'technical assistance' (in Article II(C)). The intention was to strengthen 'research, information collection and sharing' (in Article II(D)), which would provide the basis for decent work issues to be raised through the International Labour Conference agenda (Article III).

The ILO's internal review processes came at an opportune time for the employers' group, whose bargaining power had been strengthened at the end of the Cold War. The employers' lobby were presented with new opportunities to question long-established standards and supervisory mechanisms under the the 'Standards Review Mechanism' (addressing gaps, overlaps and relevance of existing ILO instruments)[132] and the 'standards initiative' (reviewing ILO supervisory mechanisms),[133] both of which were put in place by virtue of the 2008 Declaration.[134] As Paul van der Heijden has observed, the result is that 'the ILO's monitoring system [...] is being questioned from within the organi-

---

[130] See concerns raised in Tonia Novitz, 'Connecting Freedom of Association and the Right to Strike: European Dialogue with the ILO and Its Potential Impact' (2010) 15(3) *Canadian Labour and Employment Law Journal* 465, 480–1.

[131] Cf. reforms proposed by Bob Hepple, 'Does Law Matter? The Future of Binding Norms' in George P. Politakis (ed.), *Protecting Labour Rights as Human Rights: Present and Future of International Supervision* (ILO 2007) 221; and Hepple n.89, 271–5.

[132] See ILO Standards Review Mechanism Tripartite Working Group, information available at: www.ilo.org/global/standards/WCMS_449687/lang--en/index.htm.

[133] See www.ilo.org/global/about-the-ilo/history/centenary/WCMS_472742/lang--en/index.htm. For the other 'Centenary Initiatives', see www.ilo.org/global/about-the-ilo/history/centenary/lang--en/index.htm.

[134] Claire La Hovary, 'The ILO's Employers' Group and the Right to Strike' (2016) 22(3) *Transfer: European Review of Labour and Research* 401, 404; Francis Maupain, 'A Second Century for What? The ILO at a Regulatory Crossroad' (2020) 17(1) *International Organizations Law Review* 291, 319.

zation and as a result it is in danger to be weakened'.[135] This has been a matter of particular concern given the strong recommendations made by ILO supervisory bodies in response to austerity policies pursued by governments during the global financial crisis which impacted on established labour standards.[136] In that instance, ILO mechanisms presented a bulwark against rapid deterioration of decent work norms, reasserting the centrality of freedom of association and social dialogue, in a manner consistent with the 2008 Declaration.

In response to the wider 'Decent Work Agenda', the International Labour Office also took seriously its role in promoting employment, responding to the global financial crisis by creating in 2009 a 'Global Jobs Pact' aimed at preserving employment in the short term and enhancing labour standards and social protection in the longer term.[137] The ambition seems to have been to accelerate a 'job-rich recovery',[138] mapping onto Articles I(A) and II(C) of the 2008 Declaration. The UN Economic and Social Council (ECOSOC) then encouraged UN member states to 'make full use of the Global Jobs Pact in shaping their policy package'.[139] While there has been criticism that this initiative was limited in scope and impact,[140] it is perhaps notable from an environmental perspective that operationalisation of the Pact has involved the active promotion of 'green jobs',[141] discussed further in the next section of this

---

[135] Paul van der Heijden, 'The ILO Stumbling towards Its Centenary Anniversary' (2018) 15(1) *International Organizations Law Review* 203, 219.

[136] Claire Kilpatrick, 'Taking the Measure of Changing Labour Mobilization at the International Labour Organisation in the Wake of the EU Sovereign Debt Crisis' (2019) 68(3) *International and Comparative Law Quarterly* 665. Discussed in Chapter 4 of this book, text accompanying nn.78 et seq.

[137] See *Recovering from the Crisis: A Global Jobs Pact* (adopted by the International Labour Conference in 2009 and amended in 2022) available at: www.ilo.org/jobspact/about/lang--en/index.htm; and www.ilo.org/wcmsp5/groups/public/---ed_norm/---relconf/documents/meetingdocument/wcms_115076.pdf. See also regarding the Pact's influence in 2009: http://ilo.org/wcmsp5/groups/public/---dgreports/---exrel/documents/genericdocument/wcms_173424.pdf.

[138] See for example, ILO, *Accelerating a Job-rich Recovery in G20 Countries: Building on Experience. An ILO report, with substantive contributions from OECD, to the Meeting of G20 Labour and Employment Ministers* (ILO 2010) which also demonstrates International Office attempts at policy dialogue with other global economic actors, such as the OECD. Available at www.ilo.org/public/libdoc/jobcrisis/download/g20_report_accelerating.pdf.

[139] *Recovering from the Crisis: A Global Jobs Pact* n.137, Introduction by ILO Director-General, Juan Somavia, at 3.

[140] Stephen McBride and Scott Smith, 'In the Shadow of Crisis: Economic Orthodoxy and the Response of Global Labour' (2013) 4(3) *Global Labour Journal* 206, 217.

[141] *Recovering from the Crisis: A Global Jobs Pact* n.137 at para. 11. For academic comment on this positive engagement, see Conseulo Chacartegui, 'Workers'

chapter. The Global Jobs Pact was mentioned expressly in the 2030 Agenda, SDG target 8.b, which is aligned with the commitment in paragraph 67 of the UN General Assembly Resolution to protect 'the labour standards of the International Labour Organization'.[142] More recently, ILO commitment to the Global Jobs Pact was renewed with the amendment of the original instrument in 2022[143] – a step which presaged contemplation of a new strategy to be led by the ILO on just transition, approved by the International Labour Conference in 2023.[144]

The 2022 International Labour Conference 'Resolution concerning the third recurrent discussion on employment' took the 2008 Declaration as its starting point but went even further than the amended Global Jobs Pact.[145] This Resolution recognised the crises which labour faces globally: 'evidenced by high informality, labour rights violations in global supply chains, low productivity, skills mismatches, persistent and rising working poverty, uneven and mostly weak wage growth, labour market inequalities and various forms of discrimination, as well as insecure forms of work.'[146] If anything, the situation is worse than when the 2004 World Commission Report was issued. However, an explicit aim in 2022 was 'making progress on the Sustainable Development Goals (SDGs), especially SDG 8'.[147]

The 2022 Resolution made a firm commitment to the four ingredients of decent work, but also to '[f]acilitating the just transition towards environmentally sustainable and inclusive economies and societies in accordance with the Guidelines for a just transition towards environmentally sustainable economies and societies for all of the International Labour Organization (ILO)'.[148] Notably, the Resolution also attended to problems of 'insecure forms of work', for example in platform work, and issues relating to employment

---

Participation and Green Governance' (2018) 40(1) *Comparative Labor Law and Policy Journal* 89, 99. Regarding the earlier 2007 Green Jobs Initiative operating as a partnership between the United Nations Environment Programme (UNEP), the International Trade Union Confederation (ITUC) and the International Organisation of Employers (IOE), see Kees van der Ree, 'Promoting Green Jobs: Decent Work in the Transition to Low-carbon, Green Economies' in Gironde and Carbonnier n.51, 263.

142 See the 2030 Agenda, n. 2.

143 See www.ilo.org/wcmsp5/groups/public/---ed_norm/---relconf/documents/meetingdocument/wcms_115076.pdf.

144 ILO Resolution concerning a just transition towards environmentally sustainable economies and societies for all 2023 n.6. See further detailed discussion in this chapter, text accompanying n.337.

145 ILO Resolution on the inclusion of a safe and healthy working environment 2022 n.90.

146 Ibid, para. 3.

147 Ibid, para. 6.

148 Ibid, para. 10.

status as well as the necessity to develop '[p]olicies to improve decent work outcomes of trade and supply chains' contemplating 'greater coherence with labour migration policies'.[149] We shall see later in this chapter how these commitments connect to further plans to address global supply chains and just transition and to forge a 'Global Coalition' to do so, which follow from the objectives stated in the ILO 2019 Centenary Declaration linked to sustainable development but also the deeper core value of 'social justice'.[150] Notably, the realisation of these ambitious objectives is to come via 'social dialogue', stated to include 'collective bargaining and tripartite cooperation', which is regarded as 'essential in promoting peace, enabling recovery and building resilience'.[151] It is here, arguably, that difficulties have arisen within the ILO that are likely to have effects in its member states.

3.3 The Benefits of (and Trouble with) Tripartism

The ILO's constitutional foundations are deeply rooted in freedom of association, which underlies its tripartite structures. Accordingly, freedom of association and the effective right to collective bargaining are regarded as crucial enabling rights, for example in Article I(A) of the 2008 Declaration.[152] The tripartite structure of the ILO is evident in the structure of the CFA, created in 1951 to hear complaints alleging breach of the constitutional principle of freedom of association, which is unusual in that instead of the standard 2:1:1 model used in the Conference and Governing Body, equal numbers of government, employer and worker delegates deliberate, assisted by an independent chair.[153] Tripartite deliberation is also manifest in the CCAS, where representatives of the workers' and employers' groups within the ILO sit alongside government delegates to discuss and debate findings of the ILO Committee of Experts on the Application of Conventions and Recommendations (CEACR), so as to determine whether the Conference should discipline a state for its practices by mention in 'a special paragraph'.[154] This remains the norm

---

[149] Ibid, para. 11.

[150] See section 5 of this chapter.

[151] ILO Resolution on the inclusion of a safe and healthy working environment 2022 n.90, paras 13–16.

[152] For a recent reassertion of this claim, see ILO *Social Dialogue Report 2022: Collective bargaining for an inclusive, sustainable and resilient recovery* (ILO 2022), 30.

[153] See Bellace n.14.

[154] See Lee Swepston, 'Supervision of ILO Standards' (1997) 13 *International Journal of Comparative Labour Law and Industrial Relations* 327; and Jean-Michel Servais, *International Labour Law*, 6th ed (Kluwer 2020), Part III.

regarding 'naming and shaming',[155] although further measures can be taken with tripartite approval, such as those adopted by the International Labour Conference in respect of Myanmar in 1999 and Belarus in 2023.[156] While it is the International Court of Justice (ICJ) which has the authority to interpret the ILO Constitution,[157] the ICJ has only done so rarely (on six occasions between 1922 and 1932),[158] and it is only in 2023 that an advisory opinion has been sought concerning freedom of association, namely the scope of Convention No. 87.[159]

Engagement in the ILO's tripartite mechanisms has been facilitated by particular provision made for the employers' and workers' groups through

---

155 On the 'social pressure' placed on states, see Faradj Koliev and James H. Lebovic, 'Shaming into Compliance? Country Reporting of Convention Adherence to the International Labour Organization' (2022) 48(2) *International Interactions* 258; also Faradj Koliev and James H. Lebovic, 'Selecting for Shame: The Monitoring of Workers' Rights by the International Labour Organization, 1989 to 2011' (2018) 62(2) *International Studies Quarterly* 437.

156 See ILO Resolution on the Widespread Use of Forced Labour in Myanmar 1999, ILC 87th Session. See for a precursor, the Declaration concerning the Policy of Apartheid in South Africa discussed by Trebilcock n.19, 9; and also application of this model of temporary suspension of technical assistance and invitations to attend ILO meetings in the ILO Governing Body Resolution concerning the Russian Federation's aggression against Ukraine from the perspective of the mandate of the International Labour Organization (Adopted on March 2022) GB.44/Resolution (ILO 2022) available at: www .ilo .org/ wcmsp5/ groups/ public/ - - -ed _norm/ - - -relconf/ documents/ meetingdocument/ wcms _839998 .pdf; see also *Minutes of the 348th Session of the Governing Body of the International Labour Office* GB.348/PV, 17 June 2023 (ILO 2023), 14–21. The latter was not, however, deliberated upon as part of the International Labour Conference (ILC) supervisory processes – unlike the 2023 action taken at the ILC in relation to Belarus, for which see ILO Resolution concerning the measures recommended by the Governing Body under article 33 of the ILO Constitution on the subject of Belarus 2023 ILC.111/Resolution I (ILO 2023).

157 ILO Constitution, Art. 37(1).

158 As the Permanent Court of International Justice (PCIJ) as it then was, regarding which see Philip Burton, 'Ordering Institutions: The Judicial Function of the Permanent Court of International Justice in Relation to Interwar Organizations' (2021) *International Organizations Law Review* 540, 560–3 and 569–72, in which the Permanent Court of International Justice gradually limited the scope of its own interventions finding that the ILO should be able to interpret its own constituent instrument, 'in the first place at least'; see also Jeffrey Vogt, Janice Bellace, Lance Compa, K.D. Ewing, Lord Hendy QC, Klaus Lörcher and Tonia Novitz, *The Right to Strike in International Law* (Hart 2020), 56 and 179–81.

159 Ebere Osieke, 'The Exercise of the Judicial Function with respect to the International Labour Organization' (1974–5) LXVII *British Yearbook of International Law* 315, 316–19. See https://www.ilo.org/global/topics/freedom-of-association-and-the-right-to-collective-bargaining/advisory-opinion-C87-icj/lang--en/index.htm.

the ILO Bureau for Employers' Activities (ACTEMP)[160] and the Bureau for Workers' Activities (ACTRAV) respectively.[161] Further, on the international stage, the International Organization of Employers (IOE) acts as the secretariat for the employers' group at the ILO, although it operates in a way that is institutionally separate from ACTEMP. The International Trade Union Confederation (ITUC) again is distinct from but collaborates with ACTRAV. Notably, the ILO Director-General from 2012 to 2022, Guy Ryder, was previously Secretary-General of the International Confederation of Free Trade Unions (ICFTU) from 2002 to 2006; this organisation merged with the World Confederation of Labour (WCL) to form the ITUC,[162] of which Ryder was the founding Secretary-General, his term running from 2006 to 2010.[163] In these ways, collective representation of worker and employer interests has been embedded in ILO decision-making. More recently, coalitions of NGOs have been recognised at the ILO in securing adoption of ILO Conventions relating to domestic work and violence and harassment.[164] In this way, their involvement and allyship has been essential to some of the ILO's most significant standard-setting in recent years. However, they remain outside the formal structure of tripartism, which still rests on an attempt to balance the formal powers of employers, workers and governments.[165]

---

160 ILO Bureau for Employers' Activities (ACTEMP) available at: www.ilo.org/actemp/lang--en/index.htm.

161 ILO Bureau for Workers' Activities (ACTRAV) available at: www.ilo.org/actrav/lang--en/index.htm.

162 See Rebecca Gumbrell-McCormick, 'The International Trade Union Confederation: From Two (or More?) Identities to One' (2013) 51(2) *British Journal of Industrial Relations* 240; and Marieke Louis, 'The ILO, Social Partners and the G20: New Prospects for Social Dialogue at the Global Level?' (2016) 16(3) *Global Social Policy* 235, 240–4; discussed further in Tonia Novitz, 'Multi-level Disputes relating to Freedom of Association and the Right to Strike: Transnational Systems, Actors and Resources'(2020) 36(4) *International Journal of Comparative Labour Law* 471.

163 'Biography of Guy Ryder, 10th ILO Director-General' (April 29, 2020), www.ilo.org/global/about-the-ilo/how-the-ilo-works/ilo-director-general/WCMS_205241/lang--en/index.htm.

164 ILO Domestic Workers Convention, 2011 (No. 189); and Violence and Harassment Convention, 2019 (No. 190). See for comment on NGO and civil society roles in their adoption, Adelle Blackett, *Everyday Transgressions: Domestic Workers' Transnational Challenge to International Labor Law* (Cornell University/ILR Press 2019), especially chs 2 and 5; also Eileen Boris, 'From Sexual Harassment to Gender Violence at Work: The ILO's Road to Convention #190' (2022) 19(1) *Labor* 109.

165 Tonia Novitz and Phil Syrpis, 'Assessing Legitimate Structures for the Making of Transnational Labour Law: The Durability of Corporatism' (2006) 35(4) *Industrial Law Journal* 367; Faina Milman-Sivan, 'Representativity, Civil Society, and the EU Social Dialogue: Lessons from the International Labor Organization' (2009) 16 *Indiana*

Notable also are coalitions of government representatives, which exercise influence at the ILO. These include groupings of states from the Global North such as Industrialized Market Economy Countries (IMEC) and the EU. From the Global South, notable groups include the Africa group[166] and the Group of Latin America and Caribbean Countries (GRULAC).[167] They may be regional or cross-cutting geographically depending on alignment of interests, such as the BRICS countries (Brazil, the Russian Federation, India, China and South Africa).[168] The inclusiveness of ILO tripartite governance in terms of geographical reach and full participation of states outside the Global North, as well as non-state actors, remains an active subject of debate in the Office and before the Governing Body.[169]

Tripartism, in the sense of genuine engagement with non-state actors, has also arguably prompted the ILO to take seriously the relative power of employers who are also larger multinational enterprises. The result was the ILO Tripartite Declaration of principles concerning multinational enterprises and social policy (MNE Declaration), adopted in 1977 and most recently revised in 2017,[170] to which we return in Chapter 6 of this book.

However, more recently there has been a significant challenge presented by the employers' group to the ways in which social dialogue and tripartism has operated in the ILO, and simultaneously the scope of ILO norms applicable to national collective labour rights. In 2012 the 'employers' group' at the ILO staged a rebellion within the CCAS, refusing to shortlist cases for consideration by the Committee where they concerned the right to strike, and walking out of the relevant meeting.[171] The group refused to abide by a long-standing

Journal of Global Legal Studies 311; and Guy Mundlak, 'Tri-Plus: Reflections on Opening the ILO's Tripartite Structure' in Politakis et al, n.14.

[166] Louis n.162, 50.

[167] See on GRULAC membership: www.ipu.org/about-ipu/members/geopolitical-groups/grulac-group-latin-america-and-caribbean.

[168] Sixth meeting of the tripartite working group on the full, equal and democratic participation in the ILO's tripartite governance, *Background Note: The Role and Functioning of the Tripartite Screening Group, and the Officers of the Governing Body* (ILO 2023), paras 9–11 available at: www.ilo.org/wcmsp5/groups/public/---dgreports/---jur/documents/genericdocument/wcms_850346.pdf.

[169] ILO Final Report of the tripartite working group on the full, equal and democratic participation in the ILO's tripartite governance GB.347/INS/6, 31 January 2023.

[170] See the current text available at: www.ilo.org/wcmsp5/groups/public/---ed_emp/---emp_ent/---multi/documents/publication/wcms_094386.pdf.

[171] See discussion in Claire La Hovary, 'Employers' Group 2012 Challenge to the Right to Strike' (2013) 42(4) *Industrial Law Journal* 338; Janice Bellace, 'The ILO and the Right to Strike' (2014) 153(1) *International Labour Review* 29; Lee Swepston, 'Crisis in the ILO Supervisory System: Dispute over the Right to Strike' (2013) 29(2) *International Journal of Comparative Labour Law and Industrial Relations* 199.

finding of the CEACR that the right to strike could be considered implicit in the protection of workers' activities under Article 3 of ILO Convention No. 87, even though this had also long been established in another ILO supervisory body, the CFA, and was consistent with principles of treaty interpretation established by the Vienna Convention on the Law of Treaties.[172] Further, the employers' group challenged the authority of the Committee of Experts on the Application of Conventions and Recommendations (CEACR) to make that finding, as only the ICJ had the power to interpret ILO instruments; it said that the appropriateness of state practice should be left to the tripartite decision-making process manifested in the CCAS.[173]

This matters in part because it is hard to conceive how collective bargaining can be effective without recourse by collective labour to the threat of a right to strike.[174] This apparent challenge to international recognition of an entitlement to take industrial action also impinged on the legitimacy of the use of strikes as a means of protest, for example against economic and social policies, which had been established by ILO supervisory bodies.[175] Further, the ILO CFA and CEACR had consistently found, and reiterated in 2012, that ILO constitutional freedom of association rights, including the right to effective collective bargaining and the right to strike, are rights of everyone and not to be demarcated by employment status.[176] That finding could enable more precarious workers, such as those employed by platforms or prevalent in the gig economy, to lawfully engage in collective bargaining and take industrial action to support their claims.[177] The diminution of the influence and authority of the principles

---

[172] See ILO CFA *Compilation* n.37, paras 753–4; and ILO CEACR, *General Survey on Freedom of Association* (ILO 1994), 66; and ILO, *Report of the CEACR on Application of International Labour Standards* (ILO 2014), 73. See Vogt et al n.158, chs 2–7.

[173] ILO Report of the Conference Committee on the Application of Standards, ILC 101st Session, Record of Proceedings (2012), Part I/19-22.

[174] For a summary of these arguments, see Novitz n.43, ch 3; also Chapter 2 of this book at text accompanying nn.263–4.

[175] For the legitimacy of protest action as accepted by ILO supervisory bodies, see ILO, *CFA Compilation* n.37, paras 224 and 763: 'While purely political strikes do not fall within the scope of the principles of freedom of association, trade unions should be able to have recourse to protest strikes, in particular where aimed at criticizing a government's economic and social policies', discussed in Tonia Novitz, 'The Restricted Right to Strike: "Far-Reaching" ILO Jurisprudence on the Public Sector and Essential Services' (2017) 38(3) *Comparative Labor Law and Policy Journal* 353, at 358 and 369–74.

[176] See *Case 2888 (Poland)* Report No 363, March 2012 available at: www.ilo.org/dyn/normlex/en/f?p=1000:50002:0::NO:50002:P50002_COMPLAINT_TEXT_ID:3057194; and CEACR Observation on Poland (2015).

[177] See De Stefano n.128; and Novitz n.128, especially at 18–20.

established by these supervisory bodies affects the relative power of collective labour in ILO member states and thereby (albeit less directly) the influence of the workers' group also at the ILO.[178] This came at a problematic juncture, given that it is arguable that the labour standards set by the ILO regarding collective worker representation and activity need to be expanded and strengthened rather than weakened in the light of workers' legitimate concern with environmental issues and just transitions.[179]

In 2015 the dispute between the employers' and workers' groups was formally settled.[180] However, the IOE continues to contest the operation and influence of ILO supervisory bodies, now focusing on the Committee on Freedom of Freedom of Association.[181] This was a live issue at the International Labour Conference in June 2021.[182] The question whether the right to strike is protected under Convention No. 87 has now been referred to the ICJ, with the hearing due to take place in 2024.[183]

Greater support for a right to strike has been forthcoming instead from the UN human rights system, following the 2018 report of the UN Special Rapporteur on Freedom of Assembly and Freedom of Association[184] and the Joint Statement of the UN Human Rights Committee and Committee on Economic, Social and Cultural Rights, which concluded that the right to strike is 'corollary to the effective exercise of the right to form and join trade

---

178 On analysis and sources of trade union power, see for example Claus Offe and Helmut Wiesenthal, 'Two Logics of Collective Action: Theoretical notes on social class and organizational form' (1980) 1(1) *Political Power and Social Theory* 67; Walter Korpi, 'Power Resources Approach vs. Action and Conflict: On Causal and Intentional Explanations in the Study of Power' (1985) 3(2) *Sociological Theory* 31; and Stefan Schmalz, Carmen Ludwig and Edward Webster, 'The Power Resources Approach: Developments and Challenges' (2018) 9 *Global Labour Journal* 113.

179 See section 5 of Chapter 2 of this book.

180 See ILO Tripartite Meeting on the Freedom of Association and Protection of the Right to Organise Convention, Outcome of the Meeting, 23–25 February 2015, Annex I: Joint Statement and Annex II: Government Group Statement available at: www.ilo.org/wcmsp5/groups/public/---ed_norm/---relconf/documents/meetingdocument/wcms_346764.pdf.

181 Discussed in Vogt n.158, ch 13.

182 Committee on Application of Standards, Geneva, ILC 109th session; the EU statement supporting existing ILO supervisory mechanisms is available at: https:// eeas .europa .eu/ delegations/ un -geneva _en/ 99523/ International %20Labour %20Conference %20109th %20session: %20EU %20Statement %20 - %20Committee %20on%20Application%20of%20Standards.

183 See https://www.ilo.org/global/topics/freedom-of-association-and-the-right-to-collective-bargaining/advisory-opinion-C87-icj/lang--en/index.htm.

184 United Nations (UN) Report of the Special Rapporteur on the Rights to Freedom of Peaceful Assembly and Association, 7 August 2018, A/73/279, paras 6 and 58.

unions'.[185] However, it is peculiar that, due to its tripartite form, the ILO as an institution has greater difficulty making such a statement, such that in the recent reiteration by the International Labour Office of the rights to freedom of association, social dialogue and collective bargaining, mention of the right to strike is minimal; the message is limited to how effective social dialogue can minimise industrial action and how the effects of strikes can be reduced for employers.[186] This reticence by the International Labour Office regarding the right to strike becomes apparent when considering ILO treatment of sustainable development, particularly in the period after adoption of the UN Agenda 2030. A form of tripartite paralysis has operated as a block on securing ILO Conventions on issues such as employment status (for example in the platform economy)[187] and regulation of global supply chains.[188] This has been problematic, given their importance to the world of work globally, and it is significant that in 2023 new measures were being contemplated regarding both. The current scope of the measures now contemplated and their potential connection to a sustainable development (and broad social justice) agenda are examined in the next section of this chapter.

4. SUSTAINABLE DEVELOPMENT AND SOCIAL JUSTICE OBJECTIVES AT THE ILO

In 2013, well in advance of the UN General Assembly adoption of the SDGs,[189] the International Labour Conference adopted a Resolution addressing 'sustainable development, decent work and green jobs', offering a series of 'Conclusions'.[190] Conclusion 1 stated: 'The four pillars of the Decent Work Agenda – social dialogue, social protection, rights at work and employment – are indispensable building blocks of sustainable development and must be

[185] UN 'Freedom of Association, Including the Right to Form and Join Trade Unions', Joint statement by the Committee on Economic, Social and Cultural Rights and the Human Rights Committee, 23 October 2019, E/C.12/2019/3-CCPR/C/2019/1.

[186] See ILO Social Dialogue Report 2022, n.152, at, e.g., 32, 44 and 117. The message relating to strikes taken during the COVID-19 pandemic relating to personal protective equipment (PPE) seems to be that this could have been evaded by 'valuing workers on the front line', as discussed at 150.

[187] Discussed in Claire La Hovary and Jordi Agustí-Panareda, 'What Is Work? A Malleable Notion in the ILO's Legal Pursuit of Social Justice' in Politakis et al, n.14.

[188] Huw Thomas and Mark Anner, 'Dissensus and Deadlock in the Evolution of Labour Governance: Global Supply Chains and the International Labour Organization (ILO)' (2023) 184 *Journal of Business Ethics* 33.

[189] The 2030 Agenda n.2.

[190] ILO Resolution concerning sustainable development, decent work and green jobs 2013, ILC 102nd Session.

at the centre of policies for strong, sustainable and inclusive growth and development'. In this way, the constituents of the International Labour Conference seem to have accepted the role of the ILO in promoting economic growth, which is viewed as consistent with 'development'. In Conclusion 2 'sustainable development' was defined in a familiar manner, as discussed in Chapters 1 and 2 of this book, as meaning 'that the needs of the present generation should be met without compromising the ability of future generations to meet their own needs. Sustainable development has three dimensions – economic, social and environmental – which are interrelated, of equal importance and must be addressed together.' In Conclusion 4, reference was made to a 'just transition for all', which would need to be 'well managed and contribute to the goals of decent work for all, social inclusion and the eradication of poverty'.

That Resolution was arguably the building block on which current ILO (and UN) policy for sustainable development was constructed. Protection of the need for 'decent work' was recognised in SDG 8 of the 2030 Agenda. Further, 'a just transition' involving 'decent work', drawing on ILO Guidelines,[191] was incorporated into the Paris Agreement on Climate Change,[192] and a subsequent Declaration was adopted at COP26.[193] It might seem to follow that decent work is now 'considered the prerequisite for equitable globalization, to reduce poverty and to achieve inclusive and *sustainable* development', representing 'a *paradigm of reference*'.[194] This section of the chapter examines the extent of that influence, before going on to consider the potential significance of ILO initiatives surrounding 'the future of work' from 2019 onwards.

4.1 The Influence of ILO 'Decent Work' on the 2030 Agenda and SDGs

The reference in the 2030 Agenda and SDG 8 to 'decent work' can be regarded as a significant accomplishment for the ILO. It indicates recognition by the international community of the ILO 'Decent Work Agenda' and, thereby, deference to labour standards identified by the ILO as vital to a development

---

[191] ILO Guidelines for a just transition towards environmentally sustainable economies and societies (ILO 2015) available at: www.ilo.org/wcmsp5/groups/public/---ed_emp/---emp_ent/documents/publication/wcms_432859.pdf.

[192] The Paris Agreement under the United Nations Framework Convention on Climate Change 12 December 2015.

[193] Declaration on 'Supporting the Conditions for a Just Transition Internationally: Green Growth, Decent Work, and Economic Prosperity in the Transition to Net Zero' (2021) available at: https://ukcop26.org/supporting-the-conditions-for-a-just-transition-internationally/.

[194] Valentina Cagnin, *Labour Law and Sustainable Development* (Wolters Kluwer 2020), 47.

and redistributive agenda, which have been agreed by employer, worker and government representatives at the tripartite International Labour Conference.[195] Previously, the ILO had successfully sought the addition of a 'decent work' target to Millennium Development Goal 1 on poverty, to 'achieve full and productive employment for all, including women and young people'.[196] The 2030 Agenda arguably gave greater recognition to other facets of the 2008 Declaration on Social Justice for a Fair Globalization, but is by no means a straightforward translation of that instrument.

For example, while Article I(A)(iv) of the 2008 Declaration originally required recognition of all *four* 'fundamental principles and rights at work', this was not obviously reflected in the wording of SDG 8. *Three* out of the four are set out in the SDG 8 targets, namely elimination of discrimination (in target 8.5 and arguably 8.8) and eradication of forced labour and elimination of child labour (in target 8.7); 'freedom of association and collective bargaining' appears only in an 'indicator' 8.8.2, which was adopted later in 2017.[197]

Arguably, 'freedom of association and the effective recognition of the right to collective bargaining' could always be regarded as implicit in the guarantee of 'fundamental rights' under target 16.10, and this was the position taken by a UN special rapporteur who also saw a right to strike as arising from that protection.[198] Francis Maupain has further argued that SDG 16 could usefully be imbued with normative content derived from ILO standards and experience, including its broader constitutional mission of social justice.[199] However, an interesting question is *why* express mention of collective labour rights was omitted, when under Article I(A)(iv) of the 2008 Declaration they are regarded as vital to enable other facets of 'decent work' to be realised (not only in terms of freedom of association and collective bargaining, but also of social dialogue). One might suspect that this was due to the concern articulated by employers regarding the scope of freedom of association from 2012 onwards

---

[195] See the ILO Declaration on Social Justice for a Fair Globalization 2008; also *Report of the Director-General: Decent Work* (ILO 1999); *Report of the Director-General: Reducing the Decent Work Deficit* (ILO 2001).

[196] Diane F. Frey and Gillian MacNaughton, 'A Human Rights Lens on Full Employment and Decent Work in the 2030 Sustainable Development Agenda' (2016) 6(2) *Journal of Workplace Rights* 1, 6.

[197] IISD, *Policy Brief: Getting to 2030: Tracking SDG Indicators for Evidence of Implementation Progress* (2021) available at: http:// sdg .iisd .org/ commentary/ policy-briefs/getting-to-2030-tracking-sdg-indicators-for-evidence-of-implementation -progress/.

[198] Report of the Special Rapporteur on the rights to freedom of peaceful assembly and association, 7 August 2018, A/73/279, paras 6 and 58, also paras 87–9.

[199] Maupain n.110, 326–8.

and the dispute in the ILO relating to the right to strike,[200] bearing in mind the influence business is acknowledged to have had in the drafting of the 2030 Agenda.[201]

Regarding other facets of decent work, such as those stressed in Article I(A)(i) of the 2008 Declaration, SDG target 8.3 is dedicated to promotion of employment. Concerns regarding access of 'women and young people' to full and productive employment raised by the then Director-General, Juan Somavia, in the 'Preface' to the published Declaration are addressed by target 8.5 addressing equality issues and target 8.6 responding to youth unemployment. However, promotion of employment can be regarded as having been grafted problematically onto an economic growth model, for which full employment is not necessarily a priority.[202]

'Social protection' under Article I(A)(ii) of the 2008 Declaration includes both social security and labour protection relating to 'healthy and safe working conditions', as well as 'wages and earnings, hours and other conditions of work'. These were recognised separately in the 2030 Agenda, with SDG target 1.3 concerning protection from poverty and 'nationally appropriate social protection systems and measures for all, including floors'. It is SDG 8.8 which seeks to 'protect labour rights and promote safe and secure working environments for all workers' and goes further than the 2008 Declaration by 'including migrant workers, in particular women migrants, and those in precarious employment'.

Given the apparent ambivalence of the drafters of the 2030 Agenda regarding 'freedom of association' observed above, it is perhaps unsurprising that less was done to address promotion of 'social dialogue and tripartism' contemplated in Article I(A)(iii). Nevertheless, it is arguable that other aspects of SDG 16 reflect, even if indirectly, these participatory concerns. Target 16.6 aims to '[d]evelop effective, accountable and transparent institutions at all levels', presumably nationally and internationally, while target 16.7 is a prompt for 'responsive, inclusive, participatory and representative decision-making at all levels', presumably at all levels of governance, including the workplace. Similarly, SDG 17, in seeking to 'strengthen the means of implementation

---

[200] See text accompanying nn.171–83 above.

[201] Discussed by Lou Pingeot, *Corporate Influence in the Post-2015 Process* Working Paper (Misereor, Brot für die Welt and Global Policy Forum, 2014); and Regina Scheyvens, Glenn Banks and Emma Hughes, 'The Private Sector and the SDGs: The Need to Move beyond "Business as Usual"' (2016) 24(6) *Sustainable Development* 371; and see also Chapter 1 of this book, text accompanying nn.163–6.

[202] Diane F. Frey, 'Economic Growth, Full Employment and Decent Work: The Means and Ends in SDG 8' (2017) 21(8) *The International Journal of Human Rights* 1164.

and revitalize the global partnership for sustainable development' in matters such as trade and finance, contemplates a significant role for 'civil society'. In particular, targets 17.16 and 17.17 acknowledge the role to be played by a wide variety of 'stakeholders' who could be represented in and thereby participate in this regulatory process. However, once again, there are questions to be asked as to why the inclusion of worker representation was not made explicit in SDGs 16 and 17, when this would be expected given established ILO norms. This raises questions regarding the ability of the 2030 Agenda to promote the process for just transition which was contemplated under the 2013 Resolution and later in Guidelines adopted by an ILO tripartite expert meeting in 2015.

4.2 The Impact of the ILO Just Transition Guidelines

In 2015, an ILO Tripartite Meeting of Experts on Sustainable Development, Decent Work and Green Jobs agreed certain non-binding 'Guidelines for a just transition towards environmentally sustainable economies and societies'.[203] Notably, the ILO Guidelines began with repetition of key elements of the 2013 Resolution.[204] As Béla Galgóczi has explained, the ILO understanding of 'just transition' has two features: one concerned with 'outcomes', namely the achievement of meaningful ecological change while ensuring that 'the precepts of decent work' are recognised; the other concerned with 'process', which he describes as 'how we get there from present socio-economic realities'.[205] The ILO Guidelines presented the potential 'outcomes' of just transition in an extremely positive way, contemplating 'net gains in employment' through the improvement of job 'quality' as well as greater social inclusion, while highlighting risks of 'displacement', 'loss of assets and livelihoods', 'forced migration' and 'adverse effects' on 'poor households'.[206] 'Guiding principles' were provided in the ILO Guidelines to govern the scope of the policies adopted for just transition, while identifying 'Key policy areas' and the need for 'Policy coherence'.[207] Notably, an express connection was made with the 2030 Agenda, even though the UNGA Resolution did not mention 'just transition', with the ILO Guidelines stating that governments should 'integrate provisions for a just transition into national plans and policies for the achieve-

---

203 ILO, *Guidelines for a Just Transition* n.191.

204 Ibid, see Part II 'Our vision'.

205 Béla Galgóczi, 'Just Transition on the Ground: Challenges and Opportunities for Social Dialogue' (2020) 26(4) *European Journal of Industrial Relations* 367, 369.

206 ILO, *Guidelines for a Just Transition* n.191, Part III 'Opportunities and challenges'.

207 Ibid, Parts IV–V.

ment of the Sustainable Development Goals and national environmental and climate change action plans'.[208]

The importance of 'process' became clear later in the Guidelines, where it was contemplated that governments and social partners should together 'consider concluding agreements for the implementation of economic, social and environmental policies, including with a view to achieving the Sustainable Development Goals'.[209] Social dialogue and collective agreements 'at all levels' were also acknowledged as a way to achieve such objectives.[210] There was no mention of a right to strike in the document, which is perhaps not surprising given the controversy of that issue at the ILO at the time that the Guidelines were adopted.[211] Curiously, only 'consultation' of the social partners was recognised as helpful for the design of 'macroeconomic and growth policies', which include 'investing public funds into greening the economy' but also the development of 'trade and investment policies'.[212] The scope of the latter is not clear, but is said to involve 'use of trade and investment policies to reach social, economic and environmental sustainability, to facilitate access to environmentally friendly technology, to nurture domestic green industries in their infancy, and to encourage and facilitate green innovation and jobs'.[213] It seems that tripartite agreement could not be reached between the experts drafting the Guidelines, which would enable codetermination on such matters.[214]

The importance of 'just transition' (as connected to 'decent work') was acknowledged subsequently in the Paris Agreement 2015, which recognised in the preamble 'the imperatives of a just transition of the workforce and the creation of decent work and quality jobs in accordance with nationally defined development priorities'. The notion of 'just transition' and the ILO Guidelines subsequently fed into the Paris work programme and the 2018 Solidarity and Just Transition Silesia Declaration.[215] The ILO Guidelines have also provided the foundation for a 'Climate for Jobs Initiative' founded by 46 states after the 2019 United Nations Climate Action Summit. This initiative operates with ILO support, but has its own specific 'donor group', working through an 'international advisory group' advised by an 'international technical group'

---

208 Ibid, para. 15(c).

209 Ibid, para. 16(a).

210 Ibid, paras 17–18.

211 See text accompanying nn.171–83 above.

212 ILO, *Guidelines for a Just Transition* n.191, para. 19.

213 Ibid, para. 19(e)(i).

214 Cf. Article II(c) of the ILO Declaration of Philadelphia 1944, discussed above in this chapter.

215 Navraj Singh Ghaleigh, *Just Transitions for Workers: When Climate Change Met Labour Justice*. Edinburgh School of Law Research Paper No. 2019/30 (University of Edinburgh 2019), 16–19.

and assisted by its own Secretariat. National steering committees work on domestic implementation of agreed policies.[216]

A further Just Transition Declaration was adopted by a selection of countries at the UN Climate Change Conference COP 26, held in Scotland in 2021.[217] This is an interesting development, given that the signatories consist of the European Union (EU), with 12 EU Member States also signing individually and therefore all the more emphatically (Austria, Belgium, Denmark, France, Germany, Greece, Ireland, Italy, the Netherlands, Poland, Spain and Sweden). The other signatories are Canada, New Zealand, Norway, the UK and the United States. This is very much an initiative of states in the Global North and therefore a stark contrast to the 'Climate for Jobs Initiative', which has a broader membership and more Global South membership and engagement.[218] The content of the Declaration also merits attention. It is oriented towards economic growth, but also inclusivity and arguably intra-generational justice, seeking to address poverty and to ensure that 'no one is left behind in the transition to a net zero and climate resilient future'.[219] There is acknowledgement that '[s]ocial dialogue as well as rights at work are indispensable building blocks of sustainable development and must be at the centre of policies for strong, sustainable, and inclusive growth and development'.[220] The Declaration further states that the aim of the signatories is 'to work with relevant international organisations, including the ILO and others'. However, in the elaboration of what is meant by 'support' for and promotion of 'social dialogue' in Article 2, there is no mention of collective bargaining – and it is evident that the social dialogue anticipated will include 'key stakeholders' beyond the social partners representing management and labour 'to ensure no one is left behind'. A boon is the reference to 'capacity building of the participants', which is reminiscent of concerns with capabilities established as a crucial issue in the 2030 Agenda,[221] but this is not obviously a statement which is particularly sensitive to the legitimacy or concerns of collective labour representation.

The other facet of the Declaration, which is arguably interesting for our purposes, is its determination to encourage 'the transition from the informal to

---

[216] Further information is available at: www.climateaction4jobs.org/initiative/.

[217] See information available at: www.ilo.org/global/about-the-ilo/newsroom/news/WCMS_826717/lang--en/index.htm.

[218] See the news item on Mauritania joining the Climate for Jobs Initiative at: www.climateaction4jobs.org/mauritania-joins-the-climate-action-for-jobs-initiative/.

[219] For the text of the Just Transition Resolution at the COP: 'Supporting the Conditions for a Just Transition Internationally – Green Growth, Decent Work, and Economic Prosperity in the Transition to Net Zero', see https://ukcop26.org/supporting-the-conditions-for-a-just-transition-internationally/.

[220] Ibid.

[221] See Chapter 2 of this book, text accompanying n.130.

the formal economy', with 'formalised' work being stated as an ambition in Article 4. This is in line with a traditional ILO approach, but arguably does not go as far as one might hope to address the broader 'world of work' to which labour standards could be applied. Moreover, it may yet be problematic that this Declaration, when acknowledging the importance of protections of human rights by business in supply chains in Article 5, mentions expressly only 'the prohibition of slavery, child labour and forced labour' and at no time refers to 'freedom of association and the effective recognition of collective bargaining'. At least 'occupational health and safety in accordance with the [2008] ILO Declaration' is recognised as included as a vital facet of 'decent work' in both Articles 4 and 5. The signatories have declared that they will 'include information on Just Transitions efforts, where relevant' in their Biennial Transparency Reports, so there should be more information on what these countries have done in due course, and whether this reflects or undermines the ILO vision of 'just transition'.

4.3 A 'Sustainable' Future of Work at the ILO

In 2015, the then ILO Director-General, Guy Ryder, launched a 'Future of Work Initiative' to address the 'current world of work dynamics'.[222] From the various consultations and dialogues set in motion came three significant policy statements all issued at the time of the ILO centenary in 2019, which demonstrated the ILO's newfound embrace of a sustainable development discourse. These are (in order of their publication): the Global Commission on the Future of Work Report;[223] the 2019 Centenary Declaration;[224] and the International Labour Office Report, *Time to Act for SDG 8*.[225] The policies advocated in each could have implications for the role of labour standards in trade, although, as we shall see, that issue is muted and largely glossed over.

---

[222] See ILO, *Report of the Director General: ILO Future of Work Centenary Initiative*, ILC 104th Session (ILO 2015), at 11, para. 47. Available at: www.ilo.org/wcmsp5/groups/public/---ed_norm/---relconf/documents/meetingdocument/wcms_369026.pdf.

[223] ILO Global Commission on the Future of Work, *Work for a Brighter Future* (ILO 2019), Report issued 22 January 2019 available at: www.ilo.org/global/publications/books/WCMS_662410/lang--en/index.htm.

[224] ILO Centenary Declaration for the Future of Work 2019, 21 June 2019 available at: www.ilo.org/wcmsp5/groups/public/@ed_norm/@relconf/documents/meetingdocument/wcms_711674.pdf.

[225] ILO International Labour Office, *Time to Act for SDG 8: Integrating Decent Work, Sustained Growth and Environmental Integrity* (ILO 2019), Report issued 10 July 2019 available at: www.ilo.org/global/publications/books/WCMS_712685/lang--en/index.htm.

4.3.1 The Global Commission on the Future of Work Report

The membership of the Global Commission on the Future of Work was as far-ranging as the World Commission on the Social Dimension of Globalization had been,[226] including not only tripartite representation of governments, employers and workers but also of academics, representatives of NGOs (including an organisation of self-employed women) and the UN Secretary-General's Envoy on Youth.[227] Alert to diverse contemporary concerns, the Global Commission, in its Report titled *Work for a Brighter Future*, made explicit reference to the 2030 Agenda and SDGs.[228] In so doing, the Global Commission identified the conditions for what it termed 'sustainable work'.[229]

Issues relating to the loss of and creation of new jobs were, unsurprisingly, raised at the outset,[230] but there was also a proposal to 'prioritize long-term, sustainable investments that favour human development and protect the planet'.[231] I have argued elsewhere that many of the Global Commission's recommendations can be linked to the 2030 Agenda.[232] For example, the aim to reduce working poverty[233] and provide 'universal social protection from birth to old age'[234] can be regarded as a response to SDGs 1, 8 and 10, while advocacy of 'lifelong learning' from childhood onwards connects with SDG 4.[235] The Commission's promotion of 'a transformative agenda for gender equality' can also plausibly be linked to SDG 5.[236]

The overall policy prescription offered was a new social contract and a 'human-centred agenda', which would entail access to collective voice as a facet of 'social justice'.[237] This proposal was said to be directed at 'renewing the democratic underpinnings of our labour markets, and strengthening social dialogue, giving everybody a voice in shaping the changes underway and the

---

[226] See World Commission Report n.116 and discussion of membership in this chapter at text accompanying n.113 et seq.

[227] Global Commission Report n.223, 71.

[228] Ibid, for example at 10 and 23.

[229] Ibid, 10–13 and 45 et seq.

[230] Ibid, 10.

[231] Ibid, 46 et seq.

[232] Tonia Novitz, 'Sustainable Development Goal 8: Promote Sustained, Inclusive, and Sustainable Economic Growth, Full and Productive Employment, and Decent Work for All' in Jonas Ebbesson and Ellen Hey (eds), *Cambridge Handbook on the United Nations Sustainable Development Goals and International Law* (Cambridge University Press 2022).

[233] Global Commission Report n.223, 11, 18, 24.

[234] Ibid, 35–6, 44.

[235] Ibid, 30–2.

[236] Ibid, 34–5.

[237] Ibid, 11 discusses the link to social dialogue. See also 10–14, 21–3, 38, 54–6.

quality of their working lives'.[238] However, there was little detailed consideration of how collective representation in the wider world of work could be achieved, and the question of the right to strike was not addressed.

The most radical proposal presented by the Global Commission was a new 'Universal Labour Guarantee' (ULG) to apply to everyone engaged in work (regardless of whether they were in a standard employment relationship). The ULG was to have two aspects, the first being those fundamental workers' rights set out in Article 2 of the 1998 Declaration[239] and the second being entitlement to 'a set of basic working conditions: (i) adequate living wage, (ii) limits on hours of work and (iii) safe and healthy workplaces'.[240] This was a proposal subsequently embraced by the workers' group but fiercely resisted by employers.[241] This push towards expansion of what had previously been regarded as 'core' labour standards has nevertheless since reaped rewards in terms of the inclusion of safety and health as a fundamental principle and right at work under the 1998 Declaration.[242] Moreover, recent free trade agreements concluded by the UK make reference to these labour standards.[243] So, in this respect, this policy initiative seems to be having an impact on trade relations, even if the ULG has yet to be fully embraced in the ILO itself and the amendment to Article 2 of the 1998 does not directly import the right to a safe and healthy workplace into FTAs.[244]

---

[238] Ibid, 28.

[239] At that time 'freedom of association and the effective recognition of the right to collective bargaining and freedom from forced labour, child labour and discrimination', as discussed by the Global Commission Report n.223, 39.

[240] Ibid, 39.

[241] Vicente Silva, 'The ILO and the Future of Work: The Politics of Global Labour Policy' (2022) 22(2) *Global Social Policy* 341, 350–1.

[242] See ILO Resolution on the inclusion of a safe and healthy working environment 2022, n.90.

[243] See UK–Australia Free Trade Agreement (FTA), Article 21.4, signed 16 December 2021 and available at: www.gov.uk/government/collections/free-trade-agreement-between-the-united-kingdom-of-great-britain-and-northern-ireland-and-australia; and UK–NZ FTA, Article 23.5, signed on 22 February 2022 and available at: www.gov.uk/government/collections/free-trade-agreement-between-the-united-kingdom-of-great-britain-and-northern-ireland-and-new-zealand.

[244] Cf. Desirée LeClercq, 'Occupational Safety and Health as a New Fundamental Labour Right: Opportunities and Challenges' (12 July 2022). Available at SSRN: https://papers.ssrn.com/sol3/papers.cfm?abstract_id=4161060.

The Global Commission also proposed that the ILO work more closely with the WTO,[245] recognising that

> There are strong, complex and crucial links between trade, financial, economic and social policies. The success of the human-centred growth and development agenda we propose depends heavily on coherence across these policy areas. Trade and financial policies are important means to the material welfare and spiritual development of the person through decent work.[246]

This assertion of the importance of trade to labour is unsurprising, but the difficulty for the ILO will be in securing that formal institutional cooperation and securing its own influence when doing so.[247]

4.3.2 The ILO Centenary Declaration 2019

The 2019 'Centenary Declaration: A New Declaration for the Future of Work' was consciously based on the legacy of the 1998 and 2008 Declarations.[248] This instrument made repeated reference to 'social justice', while reiterating the importance of 'social dialogue' in a wider 'world of work' and those 'people' affected (as opposed only to 'workers').[249] This chimes with use of that term in Convention No. 190 on Violence and Harassment also adopted in 2019, Article 2(1) of which protects not only 'workers' but also 'other persons in the world of work', including 'persons working irrespective of their contractual status' and extends by virtue of Article 2(2) to 'both the formal and informal economy'.[250]

Article III(B) of the Centenary Declaration reaffirmed 'the continued relevance of the employment relationship' but also the rights of 'all workers' to (i) 'their fundamental rights'; (ii) 'an adequate minimum wage, statutory or negotiated'; (iii) 'maximum limits on working time'; and (iv) 'safety and health at work'. This would seem to have been a compromise on the issue of employment status and expansion of fundamental rights, resisting full application of the proposed ULG, but rather deferring to the employers' group opposition allied to that of the US Trump administration.[251] Nevertheless, the

---

245 Global Commission Report n.223, 14.

246 Ibid., 56.

247 See Tonia Novitz, 'Social Sustainability, Labour and Trade: Forging Connections' in Margherita Pieraccini and Tonia Novitz (eds), *Legal Perspectives on Sustainability* (Bristol University Press 2020, 171 et seq; see further Trebilcock n.19, 20.

248 Centenary Declaration n.224, preamble.

249 Ibid; Articles I(A) and III(A).

250 For discussion see Anne Trebilcock, 'What the New Convention on Violence and Harassment Tells Us about Human Rights and the ILO' in Politakis et al n.14.

251 See Silva n.241, 352.

Conference did adopt a supplementary Resolution requesting the Governing Body 'to consider, as soon as possible, proposals for including safe and healthy working conditions in the ILO's framework of fundamental principles and rights at work',[252] an initiative which was we now know was successfully concluded in the summer of 2022.[253] This request resonates with both SDG 3 (concerning 'healthy lives' and 'well-being') and, of course, SDG target 8.8 (discussed above).

The Centenary Declaration also stressed 'freedom of association and the effective recognition of the right to collective bargaining as enabling rights' in Article II(A)(vi) (in a manner reminiscent of Article I(A)(iv) of the 2008 Declaration), and placed expected emphasis on 'social dialogue, including collective bargaining and tripartite cooperation' in Article II(B). Article IV(C) envisaged that the ILO would 'strengthen the capacity of its tripartite constituents to [...] encourage the development of strong and representative social partner organizations' and provide 'strong, influential and inclusive mechanisms of social dialogue'. No mention, however, was made of the right to strike.

The ILO's commitment to sustainable development was placed centre stage in the Centenary Declaration, with Article I appreciating the significance of 'a fair, inclusive and secure future of work' for 'sustainable development'. The Declaration's 'human-centred approach to the future of work' was to put 'workers' rights and the needs, aspirations and rights of all people at the heart of economic, social and environmental policies'.

In terms of trade, the Centenary Declaration does not say much, which may be due to the difficulty of gaining consensus from constituent ILO members. Under Article III(C), there is a call to promote 'sustained, inclusive and sustainable economic growth, full and productive employment and decent work for all' through, inter alia, '(ii) trade, industrial and sectoral policies'. There is no detailed indication of what this might involve. The Declaration does however end with discussion of the importance of 'policy coherence' in Article IV(F), arguably reminiscent of the commitment to 'global partnership' in SDG 17, which states:

> On the basis of its constitutional mandate, the ILO must take an important role in the multilateral system, by reinforcing its cooperation and developing institutional arrangements with other organizations to promote policy coherence in pursuit of its

---

[252] ILO Resolution on the ILO Centenary Declaration for the Future of Work 2019, ILC 108th Session.

[253] See ILO Resolution on the inclusion of a safe and healthy working environment 2022 n.90.

> human-centred approach to the future of work, recognizing the strong, complex and crucial links between social, trade, financial, economic and environmental policies.

This statement is suggestive of further ILO activity in the trade and labour field, especially given the link between economic, environmental and social pillars of sustainable development, although no precise commitments are made regarding the form that this should take. This provision does however provide the basis for subsequent ILO strategies adopted in 2023 regarding global supply chains, proposals for a Global Coalition for Social Justice, and determination to design a strategy regarding just transitions.[254]

4.3.3 The International Labour Office and Time to Act for SDG 8

The International Labour Office's report on *Time to Act for SDG 8* was submitted to the High-Level Political Forum (HLPF) in 2019 as part of the process for scrutiny of implementation of this SDG. Moreover, in so doing, Director-General Guy Ryder explicitly linked the 2019 Centenary Declaration to engagement of the ILO with a sustainable development agenda.[255] This is interesting because the 129-page report that was presented to the HLPF did not require the same consensus as an instrument like the 2019 Declaration, and was able to be bolder in terms of its content.

It is interesting that the Office report engaged with the economic and social tensions at play in SDG, citing Karl Polanyi's 1944 text when observing: 'Economies are embedded in societies. This means that transformative changes in the economy and in the world of work are influenced and shaped by the institutions, structures and organizations that make up society.'[256] The report identified various synergies or 'dynamic interlinkages' between SDG 8 targets and SDGs engaging with economic and social issues.[257] These include, arguably, SDGs 1, 2, 3, 4, 5, 7, 9, 10 and 16.[258] The Office seemed less confident when considering how environmental objectives set out in other SDGs might affect labour, but did appreciate that these should place limits

---

254 See section 4.2 of this chapter.

255 See press release available at: www.ilo.org/global/about-the-ilo/newsroom/news/WCMS_712636/lang--en/index.htm#:~:text=ILO%20Director-General%20Guy%20Ryder%20attended%20the%20HLPF%20from,and%20the%20United%20Nations%20Economic%20and%20Social%20Council. See also for connections between the ILO's broader standards agenda and sustainable development, ILO, *The Rules of the Game: An Introduction to the Standards-related Work of the International Labour Organization*, 4th ed. (ILO 2019), especially at 12–13.

256 International Labour Office Report n.225, 2.

257 Ibid, Executive Summary, x.

258 Ibid, 29 and 32.

on economic growth which should be linked to 'sustainable consumption'.[259] There was also admission of the need for redistribution of economic gains and resources between wealthy and poorer states in the international community.[260] The very different ecological, economic and social performances of different regions were indicative of this imperative.[261]

On the debate regarding 'how environmental, social and economic targets can be balanced',[262] the Report advocated attention to the precepts of 'social justice' as they have been established at the ILO.[263] Indeed, in its conclusion the Report reiterates the significance of Article II(c) of the Declaration of Philadelphia in 1944 to the effect that 'Where there are trade-offs and conflicting interests among SDG targets, social justice, in accordance with the ILO mandate, should be applied as the guiding principle in developing new technologies, institutions and policies that can help strike a balance between the various targets'.[264]

This could be a bold mission, given that ILO expertise seems limited to issues concerning work. That said, as discussed in Chapter 2, child labour can be seen in terms of the well-being of future generations, while working lives are profoundly connected to environmental concerns, so labour is by no means divorced from inter-generational aspirations.[265] The ILO's foray into promotion of green jobs also points to overlaps in competence.[266] Moreover, the ILO can offer procedural mechanisms for determination of the viability of any trade-offs with reference to social justice concerns. Such consensus could be reached 'through social dialogue between the main stakeholders – especially employers, workers and governments, but also civil society organizations'.[267] This observation chimes with the principle of participatory decision-making elaborated in Principle 10 of the Rio Declaration and elaborated further in SDG 16 targets.[268] While this inclusive approach still cannot enable full participation by children and future generations whose voices cannot readily be fully represented at the table where decisions are made, a deliberative approach[269] making a genuine attempt to appreciate and attend to their interests, as well

---

259 Ibid, 35–7.
260 Ibid, 39.
261 Ibid, 40–51.
262 Ibid, 38.
263 Ibid, 39.
264 Ibid, 79.
265 See Chapter 2 of this book, text accompanying n.136.
266 International Labour Office Report n.225, 35. See also this chapter, text accompanying n.190 et seq.
267 International Labour Office Report n.225, 39.
268 See Chapter 1 of this book, text accompanying n.99.
269 See Chapter 2 of this book, text accompanying n.232 et seq.

as those of other forms of life on the planet (plants and animals), could offer a constructive basis for the reconciliation of potential conflicts between SDGs in practice.

The Office advocated a virtuous policy 'spiral' towards realisation of the SDG 8 objectives, which entails various aspects of the Decent Work Agenda but also protection of human rights at work, considering how these can be applied sectorally, nationally and regionally, through state mechanisms such as labour inspection but also through social dialogue.[270] In this context, the Office also envisaged bolstering freedom of association and collective bargaining, especially given the transformation of the world of work that is taking place in the current trade climate. The report advocated 'building the capacity of trade unions to represent workers in non-standard employment arrangements',[271] reflecting expansion in casual, fixed term, part-time, on-call, agency and other forms of subcontracting, as well as disguised self-employment.[272] Concern with the particular vulnerability of female and migrant workers was also expressed with reference to SDG 8.8.[273]

Moreover, a strong case was made for social dialogue in sustainability terms, as the Report recognised that '[t]he full involvement of free, independent, strong and representative employers' and workers' organizations in policy-making and implementation is a powerful governance instrument for sustainable development, since it reinforces democratic ownership, inclusiveness and accountability'.[274] In this way, connections between sustainability, freedom of association, collective bargaining and social dialogue were recognised, if not considered in detail – a trend already familiar from the Global Commission Report and the Centenary Declaration. The right to take collective action (or to strike) was again not addressed at all. However, we need not view that as determinative of whether such a term is ultimately included in trade conditionality, given that the US–Mexico–Canada (USMCA) Labor chapter does (in footnote 6) explicitly recognise a right to strike 'linked to the freedom of association which cannot be realized without protecting the right to strike'.[275]

On the subject of global trade, the Office seemed reluctant to offer extensive recommendations. Of course, as 'Aid for Trade' is an SDG target in 8.a,

---

[270] International Labour Office Report n.225, 53 et seq.
[271] Ibid, 70. See also 33–4 and 70–5.
[272] Ibid, 69.
[273] Ibid, 11, 25, 70 and 71.
[274] Ibid, 74.
[275] Signed in its revised version on 10 December 2019. Available at: https://ustr.gov/sites/default/files/files/agreements/FTA/USMCA/Text/23-Labor.pdf; cf. Vogt et al n.158, 132.

the document could not remain entirely silent on the subject.[276] However, not a great deal was said and what was observed is uncontroversial. SDG target 8.a refers to a WTO initiative launched in 2005, which has sought to ensure that so-called developing and least developed countries have the access to resources that could enable participation in international trade and international trade disputes. The report noted academic research supporting the initiative and its outcomes, but observed that trade support in terms of 'a share of the donor countries' GDP' remained at the exceptionally low rate of 0.1 per cent.[277] Moreover, even those who were enthusiastic about the 'Aid for Trade' initiative from the outset did not see it as a panacea without pursuit of other development policies and reforms.[278] Recent analysis also suggests that the utility of the initiative depends on the quality of governance in the recipient country,[279] and concern has been expressed that the efficacy of the scheme is being assessed only with reference to trade volume rather than its social effects.[280] It was acknowledged in the report that 'structural change' to realise the SDGs would only be possible if an 'integrated policy perspective' was adopted, including 'trade'.[281] An illustration could be the ILO contribution to a 'Skills for Trade and Economic Diversification (STED) programme'.[282] However, a more far-reaching vision was absent from this document. Arguably, the Office could have made a plea to be involved in a global policy partnership concerning trade, which would have been in line with SDG 17,[283] but no such plea was made. This is now a claim being pursued by the current ILO Director-General.[284]

---

[276] International Labour Office Report n.225, 8.

[277] Ibid, 13–14. See endorsement however at 30: '8.a ("Aid for Trade") is essential to create favourable conditions for enterprise development, and also to promote diversification and sustained growth, particularly in developing countries.'

[278] Joseph E. Stiglitz and Andrew Charlton. 'Aid for Trade' (2006) 5(2) *International Journal of Development Issues* 1.

[279] Sena Kimm Gnangnon, 'Effect of Aid for Trade Policy and Regulations on Tariff Policy Volatility: Does Institutional and Governance Quality Matter?' (2019) 7(1) *Economies* 6.

[280] Yakoub Benziane, Siong Hook Law, Anitha Rosland, Muhammad Daaniyall Abd Rahman, 'Aid for Trade Initiative 16 Years On: Lessons Learnt from the Empirical Literature and Recommendations for Future Directions' (2022) 21(1) *Journal of International Trade Law and Policy* 79.

[281] International Labour Office Report n.225, 58.

[282] Ibid., 63.

[283] Cf. Novitz n.247, 172.

[284] See this chapter, n.8.

5. GOING FORWARD: THE ILO AS A FACILITATOR OF INFORMATION, PROGRAMMES, PARTNERSHIPS AND MORE?

In 2019, the ILO seemed to skilfully evade controversies regarding its competence and potential role in trade regulation regarding labour standards. The institution adopted a Centenary Declaration strong on rhetoric but weaker on action.[285] The reason for this disjuncture between 'lofty aspirations and practical achievements' would seem to be the problems with tripartism and representation[286] which were highlighted earlier in this chapter. But could the ILO do more?

In responding to the crises of global capitalism highlighted by the global financial crisis and the COVID-19 pandemic,[287] the ILO has had little to say about addressing either the impact on labour of flawed trade regulation or the underlying structural issues that impede engagement with these problems. Instead, the Organization has carefully carved out a facilitative function, whereby the Office gathers statistics, provides technical assistance, operates various programmes (to which member states can opt in and out) and seeks to develop partnerships with other international institutions. Yet, ILO institutional actors, with reference to a mandate to pursue sustainable development, are now beginning to push for more.

In 2023 the Governing Body endorsed a new strategy regarding global supply chains,[288] while a Resolution was adopted at the International Labour Conference to develop a comparable strategy on 'just transition'. [289] This 'strategy'-focused regulatory approach offers a cautious but creative response to contemporary demands in the global world of work. The recently appointed ILO Director-General, Gilbert F. Houngbo, is also offering a proposal that could be supportive of both strategies: a Global Coalition for Social Justice.[290] These measures may well build effectively on ILO knowledge, expertise and reputational assets established through its role in data-gathering and *ad hoc* programmes and partnerships. In this way, the ILO's apparently hesitant, non-confrontational role may become a more proactive one.

---

285 See this chapter, text accompanying nn.248 et seq.

286 See Helfner n.63, 399–401.

287 See Chapter 1 of this book, text accompanying nn.1–11.

288 ILO *Strategy on Decent Work in Supply Chains* GB.347/INS/8, 27 February 2023.

289 ILO Resolution concerning a just transition 2023 n.7.

290 *Update on the Global Coalition for Social Justice* GB.347/INS/4, 20 February 2023; *Report of the Director-General*: *Advancing Social Justice* (ILO 2023).

5.1 Information: Statistical Advice and Technical Assistance

From 1923 onwards, the ILO has hosted the International Conference of Labour Statisticians, which gathers data and makes policy recommendations on a range of matters, including informal employment, but also the 'Decent Work Indicators' utilised in the ILO's Decent Work programmes.[291] This ILO role has been described as 'Governance by Data'.[292] Most recently, in 2018, the Conference adopted resolutions regarding the assemblage of information relating to SDG indicators for which the ILO has responsibility and also child labour statistics.[293] On the one hand, this information has ostensibly little to do with the regulation of labour standards in the context of trade. Yet, given what we know about how, for example, child labour has been used as a basis for trade conditionality in FTAs, these statistical exercises may also have wider repercussions. Arguably, this role of the ILO as a site of knowledge through statistical data collection seems set to expand. For example, revision of statistical standards on informality (in the hire of labour services) is now planned for discussion at the 2024 International Conference of Labour Statisticians.[294]

The ILO has resisted direct engagement in trade regulation, instead arriving at a position where International Labour Office officials will assist states which choose to include ILO standards in their trade agreements. In this sense the ILO is oriented to being facilitative rather than instructive.[295] Recently, the ILO has established a new 'Labour Provisions in Trade Agreements Hub', essentially an online resource which provides a record of different labour standards provisions inserted into FTAs.[296] This is a source of reference rather than instruction. The problem obviously remains that, in the application of clauses under FTAs, there is a risk of inconsistency of interpretation of ILO instruments which are mentioned therein.[297] In the EU, the European

---

[291] Further information is available at: https://ilostat.ilo.org/about/standards/icls/. See also Trebilcock n.19, 23. Cf. Richard Anker, Igor Chernyshev, Philippe Egger and Farhad Mehran, 'Measuring Decent Work with Statistical Indicators' (2003) 142 *International Labour Review* 147.

[292] Velibor Jakovleski, Scott Jerbi and Thomas Biersteke, 'The ILO's Role in Global Governance: Limits and Potential' in Gironde and Carbonnier n.51, 97–8.

[293] A list of these Resolutions is accessible at: https://ilostat.ilo.org/about/standards/icls/icls-documents/#icls20.

[294] *Minutes of the 348th Session of the Governing Body of the International Labour Office* GB.348/PV, 17 June 2023 (ILO 2023), 12–13.

[295] ILO *Assessment of Labour Provisions in Trade and Investment Arrangements* (ILO 2016); Jakovleski et al n.292, 89–91.

[296] See www.ilo.org/LPhub/.

[297] Discussed in Jordi Agusti-Panareda, Franz Christian Ebert and Desirée LeClercq, *Labour Provisions in Free Trade Agreements: Fostering their Consistency with the*

Commission, when describing its interactions with the ILO, has stated: 'Over the last year the Commission services have intensified exchanges with ILO in order to ensure a coherent approach in the implementation of the ILO conventions. The ILO is ready to provide technical assistance on the ratification and implementation of international labour standards.'[298]

However, the ILO has been reluctant to be involved in direct determination of compliance with trade agreements, corporate codes of conduct or global framework agreements. While enforcement procedures established by states may entail deference to the views of ILO supervisory bodies, this is not insisted upon by the ILO. Proposals have been made for a more active ILO role,[299] and, as we shall see in Chapter 6 of this book, the ILO has demonstrated its capacity to expand its role, given the convening function the Organization adopted with respect to the creation and functioning of the Bangladesh Accord.[300]

However, at least for the time being, it seems to be up to the parties to FTAs, corporate codes or even global framework agreements to select the ILO standards that they wish to include in the text, the attention to be given to the findings of the ILO supervisory bodies, the procedures by which this is assessed and how they are implemented.[301] This means that unequal bargaining power between states and social partners can affect these terms; there is no multilateral global regulation that applies, at least for the time being.

Arguably, the adoption by the ILO Governing Body of the 2023 five-year strategy on decent work in supply chains[302] indicates that the status quo is not effective in terms of dissemination of ILO standards. It is now envisaged that

---

ILO Standard System (ILO 2014); and Jordi Agusti-Panareda, Franz Christian Ebert and Desirée LeClercq, 'ILO Standards and Trade Agreements: A Case for Consistency' (2015) 36 *Comparative Labor Law and Policy Journal* 347.

[298] European Commission Services non-paper, 'Feedback and Way Forward on Improving the Implementation and Enforcement of Trade and Sustainable Development chapters in EU Free Trade Agreements' 26 February 2018, 4; available at: https://trade.ec.europa.eu/doclib/docs/2018/february/tradoc_156618.pdf.

[299] Cf. Antonio Garcia-Muñoz Alhambra, Beryl Ter Haar and Attila Kun, 'Harnessing Public Institutions for Labour Law Enforcement' (2020) 17(1) *International Organizations Law Review* 233.

[300] For the International Accord for Health and Safety in the Textile and Garment Industry and the 2013 and 2018 Accords on Fire and Building Safety in Bangladesh see https://bangladeshaccord.org/resources; also Anne Trebilcock, 'The Rana Plaza Disaster Seven Years On: Transnational Experiments and Perhaps a New Treaty?' (2020) 159(4) *International Labour Review* 545, 555–6.

[301] See regarding this approach in FTAs, Tonia Novitz, 'Sustainable Labour Conditionality in EU Free Trade Agreements? Implications of the EU–Korea Expert Panel Report' (2022) 1 *European Law Review* 3, 5–9 and 15–18.

[302] *ILO Strategy on Decent Work in Supply Chains* GB.347/INS/8, 27 February 2023.

the ILO will 'take a leading role in ensuring decent work in supply chains' and 'use all available ILO means of action' to do so.[303] This will not only involve the setting of substantive standards and supervisory engagement with their breach, for example regarding child or forced labour, but also with the active pursuit of social dialogue, alongside promotion, realisation and respect for freedom of association and the effective recognition of the right to collective bargaining.[304] In the 2023 International Labour Office Report on the strategy, the term 'sustainable' is used in terms of its general meaning, namely what is durable and viable, and there is reference to the Office's work and expertise on SDG 8.8.2.[305]

Predominantly, this is a strategy focused on corporate social responsibility, as is evident from the centrality of the ILO Tripartite Declaration of Principles concerning Multinational Enterprises and Social Policy to International Labour Office-planned activities[306] and to 'promot[ing] international labour standards as the basis of human rights due diligence processes'.[307] However, there is scope here to reach beyond ILO customary reliance on private commercial actors to achieve reform. 'Output 11', a new 'coordinated research agenda', will 'focus on global, regional and bilateral trade and its impact on decent work in supply chains'.[308] The bringing together of examination of 'opportunities and challenges for enterprises' with more concrete facets of international law on trade and investment could be helpful here. This seems to be contemplated under the head of 'policy coherence', where the determination to promote 'policies for fair and rules-based international trade that respects labour standards' is evident, with plans stated to strengthen cooperation with 'other international organizations'.[309]

That said, the focus of the strategy still seems to be on servicing the demands of ILO member states for advice and strengthening their capacity 'to develop and implement trade and investment policies that generate decent work and inclusive growth'.[310] This is not going to be a top-down exercise but rather a cautious and careful evidence-based attempt to effect change. It is also interesting that this strategy is directly linked to the current Director-General's

---

303 Ibid, 5, 'Goals' stated at para. 3.
304 Ibid.
305 Ibid, 6–7.
306 Ibid, 8–10.
307 Ibid, 8, 10 and 12.
308 Ibid, 10 at paras 22–3; although this remains only a research agenda for the time being rather than a call to action.
309 Ibid, 12, paras 32–3.
310 Ibid, 9 and 12, especially see para. 34.

proposal for a Global Coalition for Social Justice.[311] The plan is for the strategy to entail 'cross-Office collaboration' utilizing existing resources but it also contemplates coordination regarding 'the Office's engagement with donors'.[312] A donor-led approach could prove problematic insofar as this could give wealthier Global North states greater strategic influence, which one would hope will be guarded against in the Office.

5.2 Programmes and Partnerships

The ILO is renowned for its contemporary programmes for the promotion of labour standards. These gained prominence from 1992 onwards with the International Programme for the Elimination of Child Labour (IPEC).[313] Others, which have been mentioned already in this chapter, include the Decent Work Country Programmes[314] and the Skills for Trade and Economic Diversification Programme.[315] The ILO strategy on decent work in supply chains will, notably, be coordinated in its implementation within the existing 'priority action programme on decent work in supply chains'.[316] The objective in these programmes has been to offer incentives for implementation of labour standards without incurring the harsh stick of sanctions, such as trade sanctions. This is an approach which has been welcomed by some who recognise the barriers to compliance in certain developing countries in the Global

---

311 Ibid, 12, paras 33–4.

312 Ibid, 14, para. 41.

313 For the current IPEC+ Flagship Programme, see documents available at: www.ilo.org/global/about-the-ilo/how-the-ilo-works/flagships/ipec-plus/lang--en/index.htm.

314 Information regarding the current operation of the Decent Work Country Programmes and their past evaluation from 2006 is available at: www.ilo.org/global/about-the-ilo/how-the-ilo-works/departments-and-offices/program/dwcp/lang--en/index.htm#:~:text=Decent%20Work%20Country%20Programmes%20%28DWCPs%29%20have%20been%20established,as%20a%20key%20component%20of%20national%20development%20strategies. See, for discussion of DWP implementation in Southern Africa, Evance Kalula, Ada Okoye Ordor, and Colin Fenwick, *Labour Law Reforms that Support Decent Work: The Case of Southern Africa* (ILO 2008).

315 See www.ilo.org/skills/areas/skills-training-for-poverty-reduction/WCMS_534303/lang--en/index.htm#:~:text=Skills%20for%20Trade%20and%20Economic%20Diversification%20%28STED%29%20is,Balanced%20Growth%20developed%20by%20the%20ILO%20in%202010.

316 *ILO Strategy on Decent Work in Supply Chains* GB.347/INS/8, 27 February 2023, 3.

South, even though they would acknowledge that there might be longer-term economic benefits if those countries were able to implement such standards.[317]

More recently, a 'Better Work' Programme has been created in partnership between the ILO and the International Finance Corporation (IFC), an arm of the World Bank Group.[318] This initiative is solely focused on the garment industry, but currently covers nine countries and more than 2.4 million workers. The latter is indicative of the ILO's desire to form partnerships more broadly with other international institutions. More importantly, this is conceived as a 'public–private' partnership for decent work, for example between the ILO and the brand H&M.[319] In conjunction with the WTO, the ILO has launched joint research initiatives on trade and employment,[320] as well as skills,[321] but these have been short–term while prolonged cooperation and collaboration do not seem to have been realised.

Since the World Commission Report in 2004, it has been an ongoing aspiration of the ILO to forge partnerships with other international economic institutions. Indeed, the ILO's ambition for policy coherence through cooperation is arguably reflected in SDG 17. As Anne Trebilcock has observed, a past clash of approach between the ILO and other international economic institutions at a time when the 'Washington Consensus' was dominant led to 'informal agreement in the mid-1990s between the ILO, the IMF and the World Bank to exchange drafts of their flagship reports for comment prior to publication', which continues to this day.[322] When the IFC adopted Policy and Performance Standards on Social and Environmental Sustainability, that tension eased a little, but there remain conflicts, which will be discussed further in Chapter 4. A difficulty has been the potential for conflict between international organisations, even UN agencies, on trade and labour matters. This has a long history.[323]

In 2023 the current incumbent ILO Director-General, Gilbert F. Houngbo, declared his intention to launch a Global Coalition for Social Justice, securing

---

317 Cf. Brian A. Langille, 'Eight Ways to Think about International Labour Standards' (1997) 31 *Journal of World Trade* 27; and Langille (2009) n.86.

318 Documentation is available at: https://betterwork.org/about-us/the-programme/.

319 See www.ilo.org/pardev/public-private-partnerships/lang--en/index.htm.

320 See www.ilo.org/global/about-the-ilo/newsroom/news/WCMS_082146/lang--en/index.htm#:~:text=ILO%20and%20WTO%20issue%20new%20joint%20study%20on,both%20organizations%3A%20the%20relationship%20between%20trade%20and%20employment.

321 See www.ilo.org/global/publications/books/WCMS_560500/lang--en/index.htm.

322 Trebilcock n.19, 12.

323 Henner Gött, *The Law of Interactions Between International Organizations* (Springer 2020); Guy Fiti Sinclair, *To Reform the World: International Organizations and the Making of Modern States* (Oxford University Press 2018).

closer partnerships with international agencies, including international financial and trade institutions on matters relating to trade and investment.[324] This is because '[t]he quest for social justice goes beyond the world of work' and so 'cannot be an endeavour for the ILO alone',[325] with each partner expected to 'provide leadership and support in line with its respective mandate and expertise'.[326] Assessing the dynamics of past partnerships in 2019, commentators observed that the ILO was 'playing a secondary, supportive role, even when the issues in question are part of its constitutional mandate'.[327] By way of contrast, in the Coalition envisaged by Houngbo, the ILO will act as a convenor and thereby a leader: 'This is a crucial area where the ILO needs to reinforce its leadership within the multilateral system, leveraging its strong convening power.'[328]

The proposal for this Global Coalition is not only linked to social justice but is presented with reference to sustainable development norms.[329] For example, growing inequalities are said to be 'threatening the achievement of the 2030 Agenda for Sustainable Development'.[330] It is also a proposal intended by Houngbo to chime with the vision presented by the UN Secretary-General in 2021 of a 'Common Agenda' and a renewed social contract.[331]

Houngbo's aim, familiar from the supply chain strategy, is to 'foster fair, rules-based international trade, ensure market access for all and, at the request of Member States, provide coherent advice in relation to labour provisions within trade agreements to support their effective implementation'.[332] There is also a procedural element to the extent that the aim is to build the capacity of tripartite constituents and promote effective social dialogue on matters con-

---

[324] *Update on the Global Coalition for Social Justice* GB.347/INS/4, 20 February 2023, 6–7; and *Report of the Director-General: Advancing Social Justice* (ILO 2023), 29–30.

[325] *Update on the Global Coalition for Social Justice* GB.347/INS/4, 20 February 2023, 4, para. 7.

[326] Ibid, 9, para. 28.

[327] Jakovleski et al n.292, 94.

[328] *Report of the Director-General: Advancing Social Justice* (ILO 2023), 24, para. 70.

[329] *Update on the Global Coalition for Social Justice* GB.347/INS/4, 20 February 2023, 4–7, paras 7, 12–13; on 'just transitions', see also para. 17. On sustainable development, see *Report of the Director-General: Advancing Social Justice* (ILO 2023), for example at 25 et seq.

[330] *Update on the Global Coalition for Social Justice* GB.347/INS/4, 20 February 2023, 4, para. 8.

[331] Ibid, 5, para. 10; *Report of the Director-General: Advancing Social Justice* (ILO 2023), 30, para. 107.

[332] *Update on the Global Coalition for Social Justice* GB.347/INS/4, 20 February 2023, 7, para. 17.

cerning trade and investment.[333] Moreover, the Coalition will not only consist of worker, employer and government representatives and other international organisations but also of 'other stakeholders (from, for example, enterprises, academia and non-governmental organizations) that are committed to increasing their efforts to address social justice deficits'.[334] In this way, trade and decent work can be integrated and just transitions facilitated.[335]

An interesting question is whether engagement with issues concerning sustainable development will be sufficient to create the common cause that Houngbo asserts exists. In tandem with this comes the endorsement by the International Labour Conference of a new strategy for just transition, which again posits the ILO as a leader among UN institutions.[336] The 2023 Resolution calls on the Director-General to devise and budget for a strategy and action plan leading to a programme (or programmes) focused on 'just transition towards environmentally sustainable economies and societies for all' in consultation with the Governing Body. The Director-General will also 'communicate the conclusions to relevant international and regional organizations'.[337] The strategy clearly builds on the 2015 Guidelines, stressing the importance of freedom of association, collective bargaining and social dialogue, which must also be 'inclusive'.[338] In this context, governments ('in consultation with the most representative employer and worker organisations') are to take a variety of actions, including to 'foster inclusive and sustainable trade and investment frameworks, value chains and supply chains that contribute to a just transition and decent work; and effectively implement the Tripartite Declaration of Principles concerning Multinational Enterprises and Social Policy and the United Nations Guiding Principles on Business and Human Rights'.[339] The ILO is to assist its tripartite constituents in doing so, not only through research and technical assistance, but also through showing leadership at the international level, which has a variety of different aspects.[340]

The ILO in this Resolution undertakes to 'reinforce its leadership role, as the only tripartite specialized UN agency representing governments, employers and workers, in advancing a just transition in the multilateral system',[341]

---

333 Ibid.

334 Ibid, 8, para. 25.

335 *Report of the Director-General: Advancing Social Justice* (ILO 2023), 30, para. 106.

336 ILO Resolution concerning a just transition 2023 n.7.

337 Ibid, Preamble.

338 Ibid, 2–3 especially see para 6 and 9–20.

339 Ibid, 4, para. 21(i).

340 Ibid, 6–7, para. 23.

341 Ibid, para. 23(a).

thereby stressing its own unique representative capacity for participatory decision-making while also recognising the importance of drawing in other voices not readily represented, such as indigenous and tribal peoples.[342] The Resolution recognises the need for the ILO to lead on issues that will arise relating to 'labour mobility' (presumably including all forms of migration for work),[343] 'global financial initiatives' and 'collaboration with the international financial institutions' and other key 'relevant international organisations'.[344] Links are made to other ILO initiatives and programmes, and a connection is made with the proposed Global Coalition for Social Justice.[345]

This may be an indication that the ILO's customary hesitance to engage with and comment on issues of trade and investment, even when affecting labour standards, is diminishing. The ILO may emerge not merely as a 'helpmate' and site of statistical and expert knowledge when called upon by corporations, states and regional actors to assist, but could lead on policy changes.[346] Also significant may be the ILO Governing Body commitment to place 'platform work' on the International Labour Conference agenda in 2025.[347] This may be an important first step towards ensuring greater representativity for a key and growing sector in the wider 'world of work' too often deemed as self-employed and excluded from regulation.

6. CONCLUSION

This chapter has mapped the ILO's evolving treatment of the relevance of trade to labour and the Organization's gradual, increasing engagement with sustainable development. The chapter has built on the theoretical and historical observations presented in Chapters 1 and 2 by explaining in more concrete terms how the ILO has encountered and responded to the ways in which labour and trade intersect in practice, reflected in the ILO's constitutional development, international standards adopted, supervisory process, technical assistance and other activities. In this context the chapter has also examined the significance of the ILO's experience with tripartism as a foundation for developing the kinds of participatory governance that sustainable development

---

342 Ibid, para. 23(d).

343 Ibid, para. 23(h) and (o).

344 Ibid, para. 23(k) and (l).

345 Ibid, para. 23(m).

346 *ILO Strategy on Decent Work in Supply Chains* GB.347/INS/8, 27 February 2023 (ILO 2023), Output 10: support provided to ILO constituents.

347 ILO Governing Body, *Minutes of the Policy Development Section* GB.347/POL/PV, 347th Session, Geneva, 13–23 March 2023 (ILO 2023), 3–16.

requires in the international community when regulating the connections between trade and labour.

First, it is evident that the ILO's regulatory authority stems from its protections of freedom of association for workers and employers and the ways in which this constitutional norm enables participatory engagement in standard-setting supervisory mechanisms and policy formation more broadly. Tripartism has offered at least a formal parity of power for employers and workers, which enhances decision-making and ensures decisions are relevant; as such, it is not surprising that the International Labour Office and ILO Director-General offer this as a prescription for designing just transitions across the globe where trade, investment and labour intersect. However, what this chapter also demonstrates is the growing awareness of the ILO that the dynamics of power are complex. Tripartism can operate as a block on the establishment of much-needed new regulation in the world of work, and even on protection of existing standards, through established supervisory mechanisms.

Moreover, there is potential for the exclusion of those most vulnerable, who are arguably in need of the greatest representation. Those in informal work, but also migrants and children at work, struggle to be included in the trade union structures represented at the ILO, and, as such, there is growing recognition of the need for a wider range of stakeholders to be given effective voice. Appreciation of these issues has generated a process of experimentation at the ILO, which Guy Mundlak has described as 'an ongoing learning process that accommodates the differences in logic and methods of operations that characterize the traditional social partners on the one hand and organizations in civil society on the other hand'.[348] We see that those in the world of work have allied to effect changes, for example when NGOs worked together with employer, trade union and government representatives, as well as Office staff, to secure the adoption of Conventions Nos 189 and 190.[349] The importance of inclusive decision-making is also arguably evident in the membership of the ILO World and Global Commissions whose reports provided the basis for the 2008 and Centenary Declarations.[350] There is – as new measures contemplated regarding platform work indicate – a growing realisation that too much everyday work is kept outside the sphere of national, regional and even international labour law. Too many people are currently being 'left behind', despite the injunctions of the 2030 Agenda.[351] The wider 'world of work' needs to be addressed but also

[348] Mundlak n.165, 311, 313 and 334.

[349] ILO Domestic Workers Convention, 2011 (No. 189); and Violence and Harassment Convention, 2019 (No. 190).

[350] See this chapter, text accompanying n.226.

[351] See the 2030 Agenda n.2, Preamble and Declaration, para. 4.

to have a say in the modes of regulation adopted by the global community to secure sustainable development in trade.

Third and finally, that world of work has to be recognised in geographically inclusive terms. Although it has been difficult for countries outside the Global North to exercise influence at the ILO, arguably the appointment of Directors-General from outside Europe and the US – Juan Somavia, originating from Latin America, and Gilbert F. Houngbo, from Africa – has enabled a change in orientation. In 2023, the change in in ILO Conventions' official languages to include Spanish and the wording of the 2023 Resolution on Just Transitions indicated appreciation of that need. This would still appear to be an evolving project at the ILO, but it is one of which the international community could take note.

An interesting question is whether the ambition of 'sustainable development' really can deliver the common cause needed to further cement the cooperation and collaboration sorely needed between the ILO and other financial and trade institutions. It will become apparent that much depends not so much on a stated unity of purpose as on the mechanisms and processes put in place to achieve an accord. Moreover, an overly state-centric approach which does not acknowledge the need to engage with the wider global populace situated in work seems bound to fail. In that sense, the dynamics of ILO engagement with worker and employer representatives and the challenges they encounter are lessons to be taken forward when we think about designing solutions to trade regulation which will impact on a wider 'world of work'.

Chapter 4 evaluates the extent to which lessons learnt at the ILO are reflected in the governance and thereby the policies of the IMF, World Bank or WTO in relation to trade and labour.

4. International economic institutions, their treatment of labour and aspirations for sustainable development

1. INTRODUCTION

This chapter examines the ways in which international economic institutions (IEIs) operate at a global level to regulate labour markets and thereby affect the terms and conditions under which people work. It may be unsurprising from a systems-based analysis[1] that organisations such as the International Monetary Fund (IMF), the World Bank Group and the World Trade Organization (WTO) operate with respect to their own distinctive functional economic objectives, which, as we shall see, are set out in their constitutional foundational documents. These IEIs do not, like the International Labour Organization (ILO), prioritise 'social justice',[2] although there are expectations that, while regulating and thereby stabilising the terms of trade and investment, these institutions will bring social advantages, including for those who labour for a living.

However, these institutions stand accused of deploying neoliberal policies globally to deliver certain benefits to economic interests originating in the Global North, which have resisted more redistributive measures that might enhance welfare and dignity in the world of work.[3] They are characterised

[1] See Chapter 2 of this book above, text accompanying nn.186–92. Cf. Chios Carmody, 'Theory and Theoretical Approaches to WTO Law' (2016) 13(2) *Manchester Journal of International Economic Law* 152, 161, 178 and 181.

[2] See Chapter 3 of this book above.

[3] See for example Quinn Slobodian, *Globalists: The End of Empire and the Birth of Neoliberalism* (Harvard University Press 2018), who charted the influence of the 'Geneva School' and the operations of the IMF, World Bank and WTO from the 1920s to the 1980s. Elli Louka, *The Global Economic Order: The International Law and Politics of the Financial and Monetary System* (Edward Elgar Publishing 2020) sees those institutions as complicit in preservation of a 'minimum' world order, which entailed evasion of a 'maximum world order' that could provide 'a dignified human existence for all'.

as institutions maintaining global governance in which capitalist norms can be 'embedded',[4] while resisting significant redistributive intra-generational justice.[5] This chapter examines how the institutional structures and activities of three IEIs have contributed to current economic, social and environmental crises discussed in Chapters 1 and 2, given the limits on ILO competence and activities identified in Chapter 3. While issues regarding so-called labour conditionality and social clauses are discussed here, and it is conceded that their introduction or strengthening could be conducive to improved labour standards globally, my main concern lies with the ways in which IEIs have erected a legal framework which created structural inequalities and impediments to workers' well-being and flourishing, neither of which is consistent with a sustainable development agenda as identified in Chapters 1 and 2 of this book.

That is not to say that a global economic system should simply be dismantled, returning to forms of more state-centred controls on the terms of trade.[6] Past experiments with that manifestation of capitalism in the early twentieth century do not bode well.[7] As production of goods and delivery of services traverse national borders in various ways (including movement of workers),[8] so too do the environmental and social effects of commerce.[9] Multilateral regulation at the global level seems appropriate in such circumstances.

---

[4] Slobodian n.3 at 16 describes this as 'encasement of the market in a spirit of militant globalism'; see also at 5–7; cf. Chapter 2 of this book, text accompanying nn.209 et seq, relating to 'embedding' liberalism and neoliberalism.

[5] As discussed by Thomas Pogge, 'Recognized and Violated by International Law: The Human Rights of the Global Poor' (2005) 18(4) *Leiden Journal of International Law* 717, 726–727.

[6] Cf. Dani Rodrik, *Straight Talk on Trade: Ideas for a Sane World Economy* (Princeton University Press 2018), 12–14 and his 'normative case for the nation-state' at 54; see also Dani Rodrik, 'A Response to the Comments by Thomas, Gallagher, Shaffer and Santos' in Alvaro Santos, Chantal Thomas and David Trubek (eds), *World Trade and Investment Law Reimagined: A Progressive Agenda for an Inclusive Globalization* (Anthem Press 2019), 60–2.

[7] Cf. Karl Polanyi, *The Great Transformation: The Political and Economic Origins of our Time* (Beacon Press 2001, 2nd paperback ed), chs 16–18; see also the attempts of the ILO to secure international cooperation discussed in Chapter 3 of this book above.

[8] See Chantal Thomas, 'Migration and International Economic Asymmetry' in Santos, Thomas and Trubek n.6, which explains why even if borders are 'closed' people still move for work, with FTAs having sometimes unintended consequences for irregular migration.

[9] See Tonia Novitz, 'Sustainability as Solidarity Unbound: Labour Rights and Collective Voice in the United Nations Sustainable Development Goals and the European Union' in Julia López López (ed.), *Inscribing Solidarity: Debates in Labor Law and Beyond* (Cambridge University Press 2022), 28–9.

While IEIs do now refer to sustainable development in key instruments and policy documents, the 2030 Agenda has yet to be operationalised in a significant way in any of the institutions examined here. What is presented here is an exploration of the case for reform of the constitution and conduct of IEIs, if a sustainable development agenda is to be taken seriously. It is argued that a key facet of such reform would be the inclusion of collective voice from the wider 'world of work' into these institutions, which would act as a multi-faceted touchstone for their normative development and the practical application of such norms.

The next section of the chapter considers the emergence of the Bretton Woods institutions at the time that the ILO became a UN agency. It examines their constitutional origins, such as the Articles of Agreement for the International Monetary Fund (IMF) and the International Bank for Reconstruction and Development (IBRD), and the subsequent evolution of their role in international economic law, alongside their governance and activities. It is argued that the activities of the IMF and World Bank Group (which now encompasses the IBRD alongside other organisations) have shaped the design and application of labour standards in trade. The extent to which ILO standards have influenced these two institutions will also be discussed, together with the extent of recent concessions apparently made to sustainable development in policy-making.

The third section of the chapter examines the regulation of trade, with particular reference to design of the General Agreement on Tariffs in Trade (the GATT), a multilateral instrument which was applied provisionally until being given a firmer legal basis when appended to the Marrakesh Agreement Establishing the World Trade Organization in 1994.[10] The attempt to introduce more effective dispute settlement in 1994 is highlighted, alongside commitments in the Marrakesh Agreement to development and sustainability, which have not been regarded as encompassing protection of labour standards. There is a brief introduction here to the terms of trade envisaged in the GATT and a fuller analysis of the General Agreement on Trade in Services (GATS), the latter having particular implications for temporary movement of workers across borders. The ability of WTO members to take unilateral action to protect labour and environmental standards is considered with reference both to Article XX of the GATT and Article XIV of GATS; the significance of the capacity to establish 'Generalised Systems' (or 'Schemes') for tariff preferences (known as GSP) is also outlined here, together with limitations placed on the discretion of states to do so.

10 Available at: www.wto.org/english/docs_e/legal_e/04-wto.pdf.

2. THE OPERATIONS OF THE IMF AND THE WORLD BANK GROUP: THEIR IMPACTS ON LABOUR STANDARDS AND TERMS OF TRADE

This section of the chapter begins by charting the origins of the Bretton Woods institutions and their constitutional objectives. Issues with their governance and limitations of trade union and other civil society participation in their decision-making processes are identified, alongside the consequences that this has had in terms of policy-making. The origins and unexpected longevity of the Washington Consensus are also examined here, alongside implications for lending conditionality, prescriptions for economic management and impact on labour standards across the globe. This part closes by examining increasing ILO influence on the World Bank, leading to at least partial cessation on prescriptions for 'Doing Business' and the introduction of 'Performance Standards' in project lending for the promotion of environmental and social sustainability, including labour standards.

2.1 The Ambitions of Bretton Woods and Associated Articles of Agreement

In July 1944, delegates from 44 states met at Bretton Woods, New Hampshire.[11] Their aim, as stated by United States (US) President Franklin D. Roosevelt at the time, was 'to talk over proposals for an enduring program of future economic cooperation and peaceful progress'.[12] Reference to a sustainable lasting 'peace' may be compared to the original ILO constitution in the Treaty of Versailles 1919. Detailed rules and mechanisms were to be put in place to prevent the kinds of 'beggar thy neighbour' competition in trade and finance which exacerbated the effects of the Great Depression in the 1930s:

> Commerce is the life blood of a free society. We must see to it that the arteries which carry that blood stream are not clogged again, as they have been in the past, by artificial barriers created through senseless economic rivalries. Economic diseases are highly communicable. It follows, therefore, that the economic health of every

---

[11] 'The Bretton Woods Agreement – I' (1945) 1(2) *The World Today* 71, citing *United Nations Monetary and Financial Conference: Bretton Woods, Final Act and Related Documents, New Hampshire, July 1 to July 22, 1944* (United States Government Printing Office 1944). The text of the Final act and documents is available at: www.cvce.eu/obj/final_act_of_the_bretton_woods_conference_22_july_1944-en-2520351c-0e91-4399-af63-69e4b33ef17a.html.

[12] Statement by Franklin D. Roosevelt, 29 June 1944; available at: www.cvce.eu/en/obj/statement_by_franklin_d_roosevelt_29_june_1944-en-051f8720-94b9-4aee-991b-901dd926a578.html.

> country is a proper matter of concern to all its neighbours, near and distant. Only through a dynamic and a soundly expanding world economy can the living standards of individual nations be advanced to levels which will permit a full realization of our hopes for the future.[13]

On 22 July 1944, the delegates formally agreed upon Articles of Agreement for an International Monetary Fund (the IMF) to stabilise exchange rates and balance of payments transfers in ways that would facilitate trade. The creation of the IMF would be accompanied by the launch of an International Bank for Reconstruction and Development (the IBRD).[14] Article I(ii) of the IMF Articles of Agreement stated that the Fund's objective was '[t]o facilitate the expansion and balanced growth of international trade, and to contribute thereby to the promotion and maintenance of high levels of employment and real income and to the development of the productive resources of all members as primary objectives of economic policy'.[15] Similarly, one of the key 'purposes' of the IBRD, as stated in Article I(iii) of its Articles of Agreement, was '[t]o promote the long range balanced growth of international trade and the maintenance of equilibrium in balances of payments by encouraging international investment for the development of the productive resources of members, thereby assisting in raising productivity, the standard of living and conditions of labour in their territories'. It is therefore apparent that both these soon-to-be UN agencies were intended not only to promote trade, but in so doing to enhance employment and labour conditions, although there was no mention of the ILO in either instrument.

By 1945, 29 states had joined as members of the IMF, which began to operate in 1947.[16] The IMF currently provides surveillance of 'monetary and financial developments' both in member states and the world economy at large,[17] while also offering lending programmes to assist states facing 'balance of payments' difficulties.[18] Likewise, in 1947, the IBRD issued its first loan

---

13 Ibid.

14 See the statements of the Commission to this effect, dated 20 July 1944 available at: www.cvce.eu/en/education/unit-content/-/unit/02bb76df-d066-4c08-a58a-d4686a3e68ff/889e7148-b008-4945-b101-2488fdbf6dad/Resources.

15 IMF Articles of Agreement, 22 July 1944.

16 For this history and early operations, see Andreas Lowenfeld, *International Economic Law,* 2nd ed. (Oxford University Press 2008), ch 18.

17 For detailed analysis of IMF 'surveillance' and its implications for ILO standards, see Franz Christian Ebert, 'A Public Law Perspective on Labour Governance by International Financial Institutions: The Case of the IMF's Article IV Consultations' (2020) 17(1) *International Organizations Law Review* 105.

18 Regarding both activities, see Louka n.3, 2449.

to France for post-war reconstruction.[19] The IBRD currently describes its function as being to provide 'loans, guarantees, risk management products, and advisory services to middle-income and creditworthy low-income countries, as well as by coordinating responses to regional and global challenges'.[20]

This book does not have the scope to examine in detail the original features of the Bretton Woods system, such as the management of exchange rates by the IMF and the collapse of the US dollar tie to the price of gold (the adjusted 'gold-exchange' standard).[21] Nor is there space to examine all aspects of the current operations of the World Bank Group, which includes the IBRD alongside the International Finance Corporation (IFC) (created in 1956, which enables private sector lending for projects without government guarantees to private enterprises), the International Development Agency (IDA) (created in 1960, which provides concessional lending to the world's poorest countries), the International Centre for Settlement of Investment Disputes (ICSID) (established in 1965 by the Convention on the Settlement of Investment Disputes between States and Nationals of Other States, supplemented in 1978 by the Additional Facility) and the Multilateral Investment Guarantee Agency (MIGA) (created in 1988, which provides guarantees for investors against non-commercial risks). Since the creation of the World Bank a large number of influential regional development banks have also been established, presenting challenges to coordinated global policy-making.[22] While their specific policies relating to sustainable development and labour standards can have considerable impact,[23] detailed investigation of the many and diverse activities of these 28 institutions also goes beyond the scope of this book.

At the World Bank, ICSID and MIGA certainly are of importance, given the ways in which incentives for investment and management of disputes over

---

19 See www.worldbank.org/en/archive/history/exhibits/Digitized-Records-World-Bank-First-Loan#:~:text=France%20had%20originally%20applied%20for,signed%20on%20May%209%2C%201947.

20 'International Bank for Reconstruction and Development' (World Bank 2022), available at: www.worldbank.org/en/who-we-are.

21 Louka n.3, chs 8 and 9.

22 For examination of power relations with each other and dynamics vis-à-vis the World Bank Group, see the classic analysis from Roy Culpeper, 'Regional Development Banks: Exploiting Their Specificity (1994) 15(3) *Third World Quarterly* 459; for a more recent interrogation of the implications of their proliferation, see Tyler Pratt, 'Angling for Influence: Institutional Proliferation in Development Banking' (2021) 65(1) *International Studies Quarterly* 95.

23 For example, on the notable role of the European Bank for Reconstruction and Development in promotion of labour standards as human rights, see Mpoki Mwakagali, *International Financial Institutions and Labour Standards: A Legal Study of the Role of These Institutions in the Promotion of Freedom of Association and Collective Bargaining* (Stockholm University 2018), 311–12.

acceptable state conduct in that context have implications for subsequent trade of goods and services. Enforcement of investor protections in bilateral and multilateral trade agreements can be used to seek compensation from a government which seeks to raise environmental or labour standards when these may have financial consequences for an investor, for example on the basis that there has been violation of 'fair and equitable treatment' or 'indirect expropriation'.[24] There is growing consensus that indirect expropriation cannot and should not be successfully claimed when regulatory action is non-discriminatory and 'designed and applied to protect legitimate public welfare objectives' by operation of what has come to be known as the 'police powers' doctrine.[25] Those public welfare objectives would seem to include protection of labour standards, as is evident from Article 11 of the Convention establishing the MIGA and accompanying commentary.[26] Nevertheless, it is also apparent that investors can challenge state regulatory action and succeed, despite the legitimacy of a government's aims, where delays and inconsistencies in procedures are damaging to an investor's commercial interests.[27] The overall potential chilling effects this may have on domestic policies (or 'policy space') for achievement of sustainable development objectives are well-documented.[28] Notably, ICSID

---

[24] *Compania del Desarrollode Santa Elena, S.A. v Republic of Costa Rica*, ICSID Case No. ARB/96/1, Final Award of 17 February 2002, paras 71–2 15 ICSID Rev. 167 (2000): 'where property is expropriated, even for environmental purposes, whether domestic or international, the State's obligation to pay compensation remains.' See also *Técnicas Medioambientales Tecmed, S.A. v United Mexican States*, ICSID Case No. ARB (AF)/00/2, Award of 29 May 2003, at 20, para. 63.

[25] Christian Riffel, 'Indirect Expropriation and the Protection of Public Interests' (2022) 71 *International and Comparative Law Quarterly (ICLQ)* 945, 953; see also Joshua Paine, 'Autonomy to Set the Level of Regulatory Protection in International Investment Law' (2021) 70 *ICLQ* 697, who has argued for protection of proportionate regulatory powers for environmental and labour purposes, subject to a 'least-restrictive means test'.

[26] Riffel n.25, 954.

[27] *Eco Oro Minerals Corp v Republic of Colombia*, ICSID Case No ARB/16/41, Decision on Jurisdiction, Liability and Directions on Quantum, 9 September 2021; discussed in Robert Garden, 'Eco Oro v Colombia: The Brave New World of Environmental Exceptions' (2023) 38(1) *ICSID Review* 17 who concluded at 24 that even 'the deliberate inclusion by treaty drafters of express treaty language to balance States' environmental obligations with the rights of foreign investors does not appear to have brought the desired clarity or outcomes'. The same seems to hold true for labour standards and other social protections.

[28] Kyla Tienhaara, Rachel Thrasher, B. Alexander Simmons and Kevin P. Gallagher, 'Investor-State Dispute Settlement: Obstructing a Just Energy Transition' (2022) *Climate Policy* DOI: 10.1080/14693062.2022.2153102. See specifically on labour as well as environmental standards, Clair Gammage and Tonia Novitz, 'Trade, Investment and Corporate Sustainability' in Beate Sjåfjell and Christopher M.

assists in managing conciliation and arbitration over such issues, but does not do so exclusively.[29]

It may well be significant how ICSID carries out its functions – for example, the amendment of ICSID rules to enable interested non-disputing parties such as NGOs to intervene in investor-state dispute settlement (ISDS), as the *Foresti* arbitration demonstrated.[30] The context that MIGA provides in terms of its constitution and operations will also be important, for example in terms of the conditions placed on guarantees for investors, which may be limited according to compliance with environmental and labour standards; its policies in that regard are discussed below.[31]

Nevertheless, the focus of this chapter will be on those facets of IMF and World Bank Group activities that demonstrate their institutional impact on labour markets and their regulation, as well as the response of these two UN agencies to ILO standards. We will return to issues relating to investment in Chapter 5 when examining the significance of free trade agreements, which can include investment chapters.

2.2 Governance and Civil Society Participation

From a sustainable development perspective which stresses 'global partnership', the first issue of relevance is the dominance of wealthier states in the governance of the IMF and World Bank Group. The voting rights of members of the IMF and World Bank institutions such as the IBRD are determined by the capital that they have provided. This has obvious implications, namely that the wealthiest states set the terms of international economic management

---

Bruner (eds), *Cambridge Handbook of Corporate Law, Corporate Governance and Sustainability* (Cambridge University Press 2019), 25–7; and also Clair Gammage and Tonia Novitz (eds), *Sustainable Trade, Investment and Finance Toward Responsible and Coherent Regulatory Frameworks* (Edward Elgar Publishing 2019).

29 See for example the United Nations Commission on International Trade Law (UNCITRAL) has adopted its own Arbitration Rules (dating from 1976 and revised in 2010 and 2013), which have included UNCITRAL Rules on Transparency in Treaty-based Investor-State Arbitration (the 'Rules on Transparency') since 2013, texts available at: www.uncitral.org/uncitral/en/uncitral_texts/arbitration/2010Arbitration_rules.html; and Judith Levine, 'Navigating the Parallel Universe of Investor-State disputes under the UNCITRAL Rules' (2017) 14(1) *Transnational Dispute Management* (TDM) available at: www.transnational-dispute-management.com/article.asp?key=2434.

30 *Piero Foresti, Laura de Carli & Others v The Republic of South Africa*, ICSID Case No. ARB(AF)/07/01, Award of 4 August 2010.

31 See *MIGA Performance Standards on Environmental and Social Sustainability 1 October 2013* available at: www.miga.org/sites/default/files/archive/Documents/MIGA_Performance_Standards_October_2013.pdf discussed at n.155 below.

when compared to those countries who are dependent on borrowing from these institutions. In other words, money is rewarded with power. Moreover, while a space has been found for consultation of civil society, there is not the same access to decision-making that one finds in the tripartite ILO, which incorporates into its governance structures representatives of employers and workers.[32]

Article XII of the IMF Articles of Agreement established a three-tier governance structure. At the base is a Board of Governors, which usually meets annually and consists of one governor (commonly a minister of finance or representative of the national central bank) and one 'alternate' (a deputy) from each of the 190 member states. The voting influence of those representatives reflects the size of their allocated 'quota'. That quota reflects (roughly) the economic size of the State and how they are expected to pay into the general fund. Of each country's quota, 25 per cent is paid in Special Drawing Rights (SDRs)[33] or other reserve currencies approved by the IMF, with the remainder paid in a country's currency.[34] In response to powerful allegations regarding the injustice of previous allocations, 'voice and participation' reforms were agreed at the IMF in 2010, which have meant a change in quotas and thereby voting power for those members who consented to their quota increases following the Board Reform Amendment in 2016.[35] Notably, the reform of these quotas has also affected access to IMF finance and shares in general allocation of SDRs.[36] As Gabriel Garcia has observed, these changes 'represent a step in the right direction to strengthening the participation of developing countries in IMF governance; however, they do not significantly change the way in which the IMF makes its decisions'.[37] Almost 47 per cent of IMF voting power remains controlled by nine developed countries, and the US vote (of 17 per

---

[32] See the recommendation of the ILO World Commission on the Social Dimension of Globalization that further action be taken by the IMF and World Bank in this respect, discussed in Chapter 3, text accompanying nn.122–3.

[33] A reserve asset issued by the IMF, regarding which see www.imf.org/en/About/Factsheets/Sheets/2023/special-drawing-rights-sdr.

[34] For details, see Louka n.3, 239–44. The current allocation of quotas and thereby voting rights, as reformed in 2016, is available at: www.imf.org/en/About/Factsheets/Sheets/2022/IMF-Quotas.

[35] For one of the key and controversial prompts for reform, see Ngaire Woods, *The Globalizers: The IMF, the World Bank and Their Borrowers* (Cambridge University Press 2006), especially chs 1 and 7. See discussion of the actual reforms in Gabriel Garcia, 'The Rise of the Global South, the IMF and the Future of Law and Development' (2016) 37(2) *Third World Quarterly* 191, 196–7.

[36] See www.imf.org/en/About/Factsheets/Sheets/2022/IMF-Quotas.

[37] Garcia n.35, 197.

cent) is still needed for important decisions to be agreed (which require a qualified vote of 85 per cent).[38] In this way, the veto power of the US is preserved.

On the IMF Executive Board, eight states have sufficient voting power to elect one director each to represent their interests: China, France, Germany, Japan, Russia, Saudi Arabia, the UK and the US.[39] The other 16 Executive Directors are elected for two-year terms by groups of countries known as 'constituencies'.[40] The Managing Director acts as Chair of the Board; notably, the current incumbent – Kristalina Georgieva, appointed in 2019 – was previously CEO of the World Bank from 2017 to 2019 and during that time acted as President of the Bank for three months.[41] This also reveals the ways in which the policies and governance of the two Bretton Woods institutions remain in many ways aligned, both formally and informally. The Managing Director of the Fund has to date always been European (and Georgieva hails from the EU member state of Bulgaria), while the First Deputy Managing Director of the IMF has been a US citizen. The current Deputy, Gita Gopinath, does however hold both Indian and US citizenship, having also been the first female Chief Economist of the Fund (on leave from Harvard University) before taking up this role.[42]

Governance of the World Bank Group takes a broadly comparable form to that of the IMF. There are currently 189 World Bank Group member states, which had to first join the IMF before joining the IBRD.[43] Once a member of the IBRD, states are eligible for membership in the IDA, IFC and MIGA.[44] Membership of ICSID is determined separately, and consists (at the time of writing) of 165 signatory and contracting states.[45] Once again, the IBRD, IFC and MIGA are governed by Boards of Governors and Boards of Executive Directors, while decision-making at ICSID is steered by an annual meeting of an Administrative Council at which each member is represented, chaired

---

38 Ibid.

39 Note that there is overlap but there is not replication of the states of 'Chief Industrial Importance' who keep government seats on the ILO Governing Body, which does not include Saudi Arabia. Cf. Chapter 3 of this book, text accompanying n.28.

40 The current constitution of the Executive Board is available at: www.imf.org/en/About/executive-board/eds-voting-power.

41 Information available at: www.imf.org/en/About/senior-officials/Bios/kristalina-georgieva.

42 See www.imf.org/en/About/Senior-Officials/Bios/gita-gopinath.

43 See www.worldbank.org/en/about/leadership/members; also IBRD Articles of Agreement, Article II, Section 1.

44 See World Bank 'Member Countries' available at: www.worldbank.org/en/about/leadership/members.

45 See 'Database of ICSID Member States' available at: https://icsid.worldbank.org/about/member-states/database-of-member-states.

by the President of the World Bank Group. The controversial convention, as noted, has been for a US representative to be appointed to the role of President of the Group while a European representative acts as Managing Director of the IMF.[46] The current President, Ajay Banga, who took office in June 2023, does not depart in formal terms from this tradition, but is notable as an Indian-born US citizen who has previously acted as chairman of both the US–India Business Council (USIBC) and the International Chamber of Commerce. He has connections to a Global South country but also strong ties with business interests.[47]

As regards voting power, this turns on the level of each country's 'capital subscriptions'. For example, originally each member of the IBRD was allotted 250 basic votes and one vote for each share of capital subscription. Since then, there have been some modest reforms, such that the number of IBRD shares owned by developing and emerging economies rose from 43 per cent in 2010 to 47 per cent at the time of writing, but the US retains its power and borrowing states have little.[48] The overall result seems to continue to be World Bank policy which replicates US preferences,[49] and reform proposals persist both as regards World Bank and IMF governance.[50]

The World Bank Group and IMF together host a Civil Society Policy Forum (CSPF) prior to their 'spring' and annual meetings, which enables session-based discussion of key issues. For example, at the ten-day meeting in April 2022, the CSPF included a session in which the ITUC was involved together with other civil society organisations (CSOs) debating an IMF proposal for a new 'Resilience and Sustainability Trust' to channel SDRs (IMF reserve assets) to vulnerable countries. The IMF proposal was compared and

---

46 Michael Cremens and Michael Kremer, 'The New Role for the World Bank' (2016) 30(1) *Journal of International Economic Perspectives* 53, 62. Cf. Mwangi S. Kimenyi, 'Time to Rethink the Future World Bank President Appointment Process' (2012) *Brookings* available at: www.brookings.edu/opinions/time-to-rethink-the-future-world-bank-president-appointment-process/.

47 See: https://president.worldbankgroup.org/en/president; and www.businesstoday.in/management/leadership/story/ajay-banga-mastercard-ceo-head-us-india-business-council-31519-2012-04-16.

48 Jonathan R. Strand and Kenneth J. Retzl, 'Did Recent Voice Reforms Improve Good Governance within the World Bank?' (2016) 47(3) *Development and Change* 410, 419–21; and Cremens and Kramer n.46, 71.

49 See Richard Clark and Lindsay R. Dolan, 'Pleasing the Principal: US Influence in World Bank Policymaking' (2021) 65(1) *American Journal of Political Science* 36, which charts how lending conditionality can be mapped onto US interests.

50 Daniel Bradlow, 'Global Economic Governance and IMF Governance Reform: A Proposal', African Sovereign Debt Justice Paper Series, Paper III, Afronomicslaw (2021) available at: www.afronomicslaw.org/sites/default/files/pdf/Danny%20Bradlow%20IMF%20Governance%20Reform-Bradlow%20(times%20new%20roman).pdf.

contrasted with a letter sent to the G20 in September 2021 articulating shared 'principles for fair SDR re-channelling'.[51] Proposals can be made by CSOs for session panels, which in practice will include a panellist from either the IMF or the World Bank (or occasionally both institutions). This inclusion of IMF and World Bank representatives is helpful insofar as it promotes dialogue between CSOs and these institutions. The criteria for accepting proposals is not particularly transparent, at least from the website, but it does seem that joint proposals from multiple CSOs are favoured, so organised labour usually needs to find alliances to be heard at the CSPF.[52] Nevertheless, in April 2023, the four-day CSPF did include one session which was solely sponsored by the ITUC titled 'Roadmap to a new social contract? The World Bank and labor in 2023'. This involved not only panellists from the ITUC, but also those representing the American Federation of Labor and Congress of Industrial Organizations (AFL-CIO) and the Barbados Workers' Union, as well as the manager for 'Social Protection and Jobs Global Practice' at the World Bank.[53] This initiative however made up a very small proportion of the overall CSO, IMF and World Bank dialogue taking place at the forum.

There is no provision for integration of CSOs, or worker representatives, in the mainstream decision-making at the IMF or in the World Bank Group. For example, in February 2023, the IMF team working on climate change did meet with CSOs with expertise on climate issues, but this meeting did not discuss issues concerned with work or labour. In the presentation delivered by IMF staff, 'just transition' was defined merely in terms of a need to 'compensate vulnerable households and regions', while collaboration was envisaged with the World Bank institutions and the World Health Organization, as well as other regional multilateral development banks, but not the ILO.[54] Instead, trade union organisations and NGOs representing those in precarious work may (as CSOs) have more success mobilising behind complaints made to the

---

[51] See the CSPF Program Schedule available at: https://thedocs.worldbank.org/en/doc/8a7600f2559437be138bf15ea6b5263b-0360012022/original/Public-schedule-CSPF-SM-2022-March-24.pdf. For analysis of what can and cannot be said at the CSPF, see Felix Anderl, *Broken Solidarities*: *How Open Global Governance Divides and Rules* (Bristol University Press 2022), 170–96.

[52] See www.worldbank.org/en/events/2021/10/08/civil-society-policy-forum#2.

[53] See https://thedocs.worldbank.org/en/doc/eb8b1a05fc5fd3c201efd0b06f6ba957-0440012023/related/WB-SpringMeetings-Day4-Publish.pdf.

[54] 'IMF's Engagement on Climate Issues, February 2023' resources available at: www.imf.org/en/About/Partners/civil-society.

World Bank Inspection Panel[55] and the Compliance Advisor/Ombudsman.[56] There may also be potential for domestic litigation, given the US Supreme Court judgment in *Jam* stating that the scope of immunity recognised for international organisations, such as the World Bank IFC, has declined to reflect reduced foreign sovereign immunity for 'commercial acts'.[57] However, the founding charter of the International Monetary Fund, which has its headquarters in Washington, does explicitly preserve absolute immunity.[58] Also, the IMF has historically been less readily accessible to independent external scrutiny through complaints, but after an Institutional Safeguards Review made a commitment in 2022 to taking a range of measures to strengthen investigatory procedures.[59]

2.3 The So-called Washington Consensus and Its Longevity

The IMF and World Bank Group are required by their constitutional Articles of Agreement to collaborate and this has remained a feature of their practice. That expectation of cooperation arguably enables these two institutions to

---

55 Jonathan Fox, 'Transnational Civil Society Campaigns and the World Bank Inspection Panel' in Alison Brysk (ed.), *Globalization and Human Rights* (University of California Press 2002); and Guy Fiti Sinclair, 'Beyond Accountability? Human Rights, Global Governance, and the World Bank Inspection Panel' (2019) SSRN available at: https://papers.ssrn.com/sol3/papers.cfm?abstract_id=3391646.

56 Lynn M.G. Ta and Benjamin A.T. Graham, 'Can Quasi-Judicial Bodies at the World Bank Provide Justice in Human Rights Cases' (2018) 50 *Georgetown Journal of International Law* 113, who at 128–9 identify a strong correlation between NGO involvement and complaint success.

57 *Jam v Int'l Fin. Corp.*, 139 S. Ct. 759, 759 (2019); for further analysis of the relevance of that judgment see Desiree LeClercq, 'A Rules-Based Approach to Jam's Restrictive Immunity: Implications for International Organizations' (2020) 58(1) *Houston Law Review* 55.

58 See Article IX of the IMF Articles of Agreement; also Chimène I. Keitner and Scott Dodson, 'Jam v. International Finance Corp.' (2019) 113(4) *American Journal of International Law* 805, 809.

59 Statement by the IMF Executive Board and Management on the Institutional Safeguards Review, 30 June 2022 available at: www.imf.org/en/News/Articles/2022/06/29/pr22238-statement-by-the-imf-executive-board-and-management-on-the-institutional-safeguards-review. See also the potentially pro-active role of the IMF Independent Evaluation Office (IEO), which does not however respond straightforwardly to complaints, evaluated in Catherine Weaver, 'The Politics of Performance Evaluation: Independent Evaluation at the International Monetary Fund' (2010) 5 *Review of International Organisations* 365. For the current operations of the IMF IEO, see: https://ieo.imf.org/en/our-work/Evaluations. Proposals for a scrutiny or complaints mechanism specifically in relation to Article V surveillance are discussed by Ebert n.17, 130–1.

wield considerable power jointly in the global economy. Article IV, Section 10 of the Articles of Agreement of the IBRD sets out what seems to have been a precaution against potential abuse of that power: 'The Bank and its officers shall not interfere in the political affairs of any member [...] Only economic considerations shall be relevant to their decisions.'[60] Article IV of the IMF Articles of Agreement, which establish processes of economic surveillance, requires the IMF to 'pay due regard' to domestic, social, and political affairs in its Article IV consultations, which again has led to adoption of the view that political intervention by the IMF is unacceptable.[61] These 'political prohibition' clauses have however arguably skewed the decision-making of the World Bank and the IMF, so that in their reluctance to intervene in the internal political sovereignty of member states, they have adopted a formalistic and thereby problematic assessment of their role. Their insistence on evaluation of the merits of policies in economic rather than social terms can obstruct access to development and amount to a breach of their human rights obligations as UN agencies.[62]

This concern was expressed in the 1990s when the manifestation of a 'Washington Consensus' was identified as guiding the policies of both these IEIs. John Williamson first coined this term in 1989 to refer to ten principles which he considered could and should be pursued by 'both the political Washington of Congress and senior members of the administration and the technocratic Washington of the international financial institutions, the economic agencies of the US government, the Federal Reserve Board, and the think tanks'.[63] It is interesting and perhaps not coincidental that he elided the policies of the US government and those of the IMF and World Bank.

---

60 See also IBRD Articles of Agreement, Article III, Section 5(b): 'The Bank shall make arrangements to ensure that the proceeds of any loan are used only for the purposes for which the loan was granted, with due attention to considerations of economy and efficiency and without regard to political or other non-economic influences or considerations.'

61 For discussion, see Daniel Bradlow, 'The World Bank, the IMF, and Human Rights' (1999) 6 *Transnational Law and Contemporary Problems* 47, 81.

62 John D. Ciorciari, 'The Lawful Scope of Human Rights Criteria in World Bank Credit Decisions: An Interpretive Analysis of the IBRD and IDA Articles of Agreement' (2000) 33 *Cornell International Law Journal* 331; Mac Darrow, *Between Light and Shadow: The World Bank, the International Monetary Fund and International Human Rights Law* (Bloomsbury/Hart, 2003) who argues that World Bank and the IMF have obligations to comply with human rights obligations stem from their role as UN agencies and their commitments under the UN Charter.

63 John Williamson, 'A Short History of the Washington Consensus' (2009) 15 *Law and Business Review of the Americas* 7, 8.

The ten 'policy instruments' that Williamson identified concerned: '1. Fiscal Discipline; 2. Reordering Public Expenditure Priorities; 3. Tax Reform; 4. Liberalizing Interest Rates; 5. A Competitive Exchange Rate; 6. Trade Liberalization; 7. Liberalization of Inward Foreign Direct Investment; 8. Privatization; 9. Deregulation; and 10. Property Rights.'[64] While concerned with important facets of trade and investment, there seemed to be nothing here directly concerning labour-related policies. However, as Williamson himself has observed, 'the liberalizing reforms that were embodied in the original Washington Consensus' would be extended 'to areas like the labor market where economic performance is being held back by excessive rigidity'.[65] He has used the example of Latin America, where there is a large informal labour market, members of which he suggested could be redirected to the formal labour market. The claim is that levels of informal employment could be reduced if formal labour markets are made cheaper and more flexible. The suggestion is that if states reduce 'the cost of employing labor in the formal sector' – for example, to make it easier to fire 'for good reason' and reduce social security contributions – that can 'lead to more hiring and greater efficiency'.[66] Whether such an ambition would be consistent with ILO standards or not was clearly not at the forefront of Williamson's mind, nor that of IMF and World Bank policy-makers. As Joseph Stiglitz has observed:

> The success of the Washington consensus as an intellectual doctrine rests on its simplicity: its policy recommendations could be administered by economists using little more than simple accounting frameworks. A few economic indicators – inflation, money supply growth, interest rates, budget and trade deficits – could serve as the basis for a set of policy recommendations.[67]

In this setting, trade union organisation and workers' participatory representation aimed at raising wages and labour standards, which increased costs and constrained managerial discretion, could be treated as labour market rigidities to be avoided.[68] IMF and World Bank lending conditions accompanied by numerous detailed policy prescriptions became emblematic of a shared

---

64 Ibid, 9–10.

65 Ibid, 18.

66 Ibid, 19.

67 Joseph Stiglitz, 'More Instruments and Broader Goals: Moving toward the Post-Washington Consensus', 7 January 1998, the 1998 WIDER Annual Lecture (Helsinki, Finland), 5. Available at: www.wider.unu.edu/publication/more-instruments-and-broader-goals-0.

68 Christine Kaufmann, *Globalisation and Labour Rights: The Conflict between Core Labour Rights and International Economic Law* (Hart 2007), 102.

concern with 'structural adjustment' programmes (SAPs).[69] In 1999, these institutions 'reformulated their much criticised SAPs as "Poverty Reduction Strategy Papers" (PRSPs), which were described as enabling "national ownership" and greater engagement with "broad based participation by civil society", although they are still reliant on social needs being met through economic growth, including privatisation and liberalisation'.[70]

IMF policies pursued in the wake of the global financial crisis from 2008 onwards were highly controversial. Financial assistance granted to EU member states experiencing severe sovereign debt was made conditional on policy prescriptions set out in the relevant Memoranda of Understanding.[71] These followed the familiar pattern set by the Washington Consensus, which had been understood by that time to be discredited and in decline, if not 'dead'.[72] Conditions requiring deregulation of labour markets were set by the so-called Troika: the European Central Bank, the European Commission and the IMF.[73] It may be that the enthusiastic embrace of the Washington Consensus can be attributed more to European institutions (the ECB and European Commission) than to IMF economists, who had started to indicate a desire to depart from

---

[69] M. Rodwan Abouharb and David L. Cingranelli, 'The Human Rights Effects of World Bank Structural Adjustment, 1981–2000' (2006) 50(2) International Studies Quarterly 233; and Jason Morgan-Foster, 'The Relationship of IMF Structural Adjustment Programs to Economic, Social and Cultural Rights: The Argentine Case Revisited' (2003) 24 *Michigan Journal of International Law* 577.

[70] Joe J. Wills, *Contesting World Order? Socioeconomic Rights and Global Justice Movements* (Cambridge University Press 2017), 39.

[71] Catherine Barnard, 'EU Employment Law and the European Social Model: The Past, the Present and the Future' (2015) 67 *Current Legal Problems* 199, 230.

[72] See Robin Broad and John Cavanagh, 'The Death of the Washington Consensus?' (1999) 16 *World Policy Journal* 79; James M. Cypher, 'The Slow Death of the Washington Consensus on Latin America' (1998) 25 *Latin American Perspectives* 47; Robert K. McCleery and Fernando De Paolis, 'The Washington Consensus: A Post-mortem' (2008) 19 *Journal of Asian Economics* 438. Cf. ongoing concern expressed by other commentators, such as Mark Anner and Teri Caraway, 'International Institutions and Workers' Rights: Between Labor Standards and Market Flexibility' (2010) 45 *Studies in Comparative International Development* 151, 161–4; and Bernhard Reinsburg, Thomas Stubbs, Alexander Kentikelenis and Lawrence King, 'The Political Economy of Labor Market Deregulation during IMF Interventions' (2019) 45(3) *International Interactions* 532 examining data from 1980 to 2014.

[73] Cinzia Alcidi, Alessandra Giovannini and Daniel Gros, 'History Repeating Itself: From the Argentine Default to the Greek Tragedy?' CEPS Commentary, 1 July 2011 available at: http://aei-dev.library.pitt.edu/32159/. For a less critical view of the overall desirability of IMF involvement, see Franz Seitz and Thomas Jost, 'The Role of the IMF in the European debt crisis' (2011) ECONSOR HAW im Dialog – Weidener Diskussionspapiere, No. 32 available at: https://web.archive.org/web/20170816170442/https://www.econstor.eu/bitstream/10419/56452/1/689266685.pdf.

such prescriptions.[74] Nevertheless, through what may be regarded as a form of normative isomorphism, these deregulatory policies did not only affect the eight member states engaged in borrowing arrangements, but were applied more generally through other EU mechanisms, such as the Europe 2020 Growth Strategy[75] and Country Specific Recommendations.[76] Overall, the aim was to address 'rigidities' in European labour markets, reducing access to employment rights and trade unions' role in setting wages or labour standards.[77]

Considerable alarm was expressed by ILO supervisory bodies regarding these interventions.[78] For example, the Greek government sought to defend non-compliance with the ILO Right to Organise and Collective Bargaining Convention, 1948 (No. 98) to the ILO Committee of Experts on the Application of Conventions and Recommendations (CEACR) with reference to 'the financial crisis and the measures found necessary to tackle it based on certain conditionalities set out in the Memoranda of Economic and Financial Policies and of Understanding on Specific Economic Policy Conditionality'. In response, the CEACR stated its 'deep concern' that the government's changes 'were likely to have a significant – and potentially devastating – impact on the industrial relations system in the country'. The CEACR 'trusted' that

> the social partners will be fully involved in the determination of any further alterations within the framework of the agreements with the EC, the IMF and the European Central Bank (ECB) that touch upon such aspects which go to the heart of

---

[74] See Susanne Lütz and Matthias Kranke, 'The European Rescue of the Washington Consensus? EU and IMF lending to Central and Eastern European Countries' (2014) 21(2) *Review of International Political Economy* 310; and Cornel Ban, 'Austerity versus Stimulus? Understanding Fiscal Policy Change at the International Monetary Fund Since the Great Recession' (2015) 28(2) *Governance: An International Journal of Policy, Administration, and Institutions* 167.

[75] See Communication from the Commission, EUROPE 2020: A strategy for smart, sustainable and inclusive growth COM(2010) 2020 final 3.3.2010.

[76] Commission, 'Recommendation for a Council Recommendation on the economic policy of the euro area' COM(2015) 992 final, 2.

[77] See Aristea Koukiadaki and Lefteris Kretsos, 'Opening Pandora's Box: The Sovereign Debt Crisis and Labour Market Regulation in Greece' (2012) 41 *Industrial Law Journal* 276; Imre Szabo, 'Between Polarization and Statism – Effects of the Crisis on Collective Bargaining Processes and Outcomes in Hungary' (2013) 19(2) *Transfer* 205; Hermes Augusto Costa, 'From Europe as a Model to Europe as Austerity: The Impact of the Crisis on Portuguese Trade Unions' (2012) 18 *Transfer* 397; Aurora Trif, 'Romania: Collective Bargaining under Attack' (2013) 19 *Transfer* 227, 231–2; and Stefan Clauwaert and Isabelle Schömann, *The Crisis and National Labour Law Reforms: A Mapping Exercise*. ETUI Working Paper 2012.04.

[78] Discussed in Claire Kilpatrick, 'Taking the Measure of Changing Labour Mobilization at the International Labour Organisation in the Wake of the EU Sovereign Debt Crisis' (2019) 68(3) *International & Comparative Law Quarterly* 665.

> labour relations, social dialogue and social peace, and that their views will be taken fully into account.[79]

Similarly, while the ILO Governing Body Committee on Freedom of Association (CFA) responded to the complaint of Greek trade unions by acknowledging that 'the measures giving rise to this complaint have been taken within a context qualified as grave and exceptional, provoked by a financial and economic crisis', the CFA recommendation was akin to that of the CEACR. The CFA insisted 'that the Government promote and strengthen the institutional framework for collective bargaining and social dialogue', urging that

> permanent and intensive social dialogue be held on all issues raised in the complaint and in its conclusions with the aim of developing a comprehensive common vision for labour relations in the country in full conformity with the principles of freedom of association and the effective recognition of collective bargaining and the relevant ratified ILO Conventions.[80]

Social dialogue might seem a very moderate and limited remedy for the harms done by austerity policies generated by financial conditionality,[81] but it is this remedial and constructive policy mechanism that the ILO in its distinctive way has sought to promote on the global stage.

What is perhaps curious regarding the IMF approach is that, despite the objections raised regarding the treatment of European states,[82] the IMF was in practice more lenient to them in terms of debt limits compared to those other IMF members, notably developing countries in the Global South.[83] Today 'debt limits' are not usually placed on 'countries that do not normally rely

---

[79] ILO Report of the Committee of Experts on the Application of Conventions and Recommendations (ILO 2012), ILC 101st Session ILC.101/III1A, 161.

[80] Case No. 2820 (Greece), ILO Governing Body Committee on Freedom of Association Report No. 365, November 2012) para. 784, at para. 1003. See also the fuller context covered in the *Report on the High Level Mission to Greece* (International Labour Office 2011), discussed *inter alia* by Koukiadaki and Kretsos n.77, 283–4, 289–90 and 293.

[81] Tonia Novitz, 'The Restricted Freedom to Strike: "Far-Reaching" ILO Jurisprudence on the Public Sector and Essential Services' (2017) 38(3) *Comparative Labor Law and Policy Journal* 353, 365–71.

[82] See Margot Salomon, 'Of Austerity, Human Rights and International Institutions' (2015) 21(4) *European Law Journal* 521.

[83] That differentiation is now 'baked in' to the IMF–World Bank Debt Sustainability Risk Framework for low-income countries, discussed in Danny Cassimon, Karel Verbeke, and Dennis Essers, 'The IMF–WB Debt Sustainability Framework: Procedures, Applications and Criticisms' (2017) 3(1) *Development Finance Agenda* (DEFA) 4.

on concessional financing' (normally in the Global North) as long as there is otherwise compliance with the terms of IMF lending, that is, the terms of fiscal conditionality imposed through agreement with the government concerned.[84] This has enabled extensive borrowing by countries, such as the UK and the US, during the COVID-19 pandemic.[85] By way of contrast, states which 'normally rely on concessional financing' from the IMF and World Bank will be assessed in terms of the risk of their default and debt limits are imposed accordingly.[86]

IMF and World Bank conditionality has been subjected to sustained criticism at the UN. Examples include reports published by the UN Independent Expert on Foreign Debt and Human Rights, Juan Pablo Bohoslavsky.[87] His primary report focused on labour-related issues, observing that the IMF and World Bank had promoted austerity measures which sought to make 'the labour market … more flexible through deregulation, downsizing the public sector and freezing or reducing wages and work-related social benefits in an effort to reduce government expenditure'.[88] He found that the economic case for dismantling labour standards was weak and indefensible in a financial crisis, given that such measures were also harmful, depriving people of their socio-economic rights.[89] As a consequence, his report recommended that these forms of lending conditionality be subjected in advance 'to robust human rights impact assessments' involving all stakeholders, 'in particular trade unions and employers' organizations, as well as relevant international organizations with relevant expertise, such as ILO'.[90] He advocated consultation of the social partners, respect for collective agreements reached and engagement with affected representatives of civil society such that there could be negotiation over the terms of sovereign debt restructuring.[91] In his view, IMF and World Bank conditionality must respect a trio of standards: 'freedom of

---

84 'Debt Limits Policy' (IMF 2021) available at: www.imf.org/en/Topics/sovereign-debt/debt-limits-policy.

85 IMF, *World Economic Outlook* (IMF 2023), ch 3. See also https://databank.worldbank.org/data/embed-int/Table-C1.-Total-Gross-Public-Sector-by-Sector/id/a90ed5c15b?ht=1500.

86 See the IMF Debt Limits Policy n.84 above.

87 Available at: https://ap.ohchr.org/documents/dpage_e.aspx?si=A/HRC/34/57; and https://ap.ohchr.org/documents/dpage_e.aspx?si=A/HRC/34/57/Add.1.

88 Report of the Independent Expert on the effects of foreign debt and other related international financial obligations of States on the full enjoyment of all human rights, particularly economic, social and cultural rights A/HRC/34/57, 27 December 2016, para. 2.

89 Ibid, paras 44–57.

90 Ibid, paras 58–9. For further elaboration of the role of the ILO, see para. 67.

91 Ibid, paras 61–3.

association and effective recognition of the right to collective bargaining and the right to strike.'[92]

In a supplementary report focusing on EU issues, the Independent Expert found that '[a]usterity policies have unfortunately all too often gone hand-in-hand with undermining economic, social and cultural rights'.[93] EU institutions and mechanisms were too concerned 'with whether economic and fiscal targets were met', providing limited 'analyses of adverse social impacts and how they could be better prevented in the future'.[94] His recommendation was to '[i]ncorporate the Sustainable Development Goals into the policy goals of the European Union and ensure that recommendations [...] are coherent with them'.[95] This UN human rights vision of labour standards seems to embrace the SDGs as a counterpoint to the 'Washington Consensus'.

Notably, following criticism of World Bank prescriptions and policy by Philip Alston in his role as UN Special Rapporteur on extreme poverty,[96] his successor, Olivier De Schutter, went on to observe in 2020 that '[t]he recipe of austerity failed after the 2008–2009 financial and economic crisis and would fail this time if tried again'.[97] De Schutter even cites IMF and World Bank sources from 2014 onwards in defence of his claim that the international community should be 'prioritizing the reduction of inequalities over the unsustainable quest for economic growth'.[98] De Schutter has advocated responding to sovereign debt following the COVID-19 pandemic with structural measures designed to promote sustainable development, including promotion of green jobs and decent jobs,[99] investment in training and reskilling,[100] and notably application of the 2015 ILO Just Transitions Guidelines.[101] Desirée LeClercq has observed that these objectives do not seem likely to be realised, at least as regards preservation of labour standards. She has observed that while 'some of

---

92 Ibid, para. 65.

93 Report of the Independent Expert on the effects of foreign debt and other related international financial obligations of States on the full enjoyment of all human rights, particularly economic, social and cultural rights on his mission to institutions of the European Union A/HRC/34/57/Add.1, 28 December 2016, para. 77.

94 Ibid, para. 79.

95 Ibid, para. 83(e).

96 Philip Alston, 'The World Bank as a Human Rights-Free Zone' (NYU School of Law, Public Law Research Paper No. 17-50 2017).

97 Interim report of the Special Rapporteur on extreme poverty and human rights, Olivier De Schutter, *The 'Just Transition' in the Economic Recovery: Eradicating poverty within planetary boundaries* A/75/181/Rev.1, 7 October 2020, para. 3.

98 Ibid, para. 56. See also paras 44–8.

99 Ibid, para. 34.

100 Ibid, paras 9–12.

101 Ibid, para. 10.

the IMF's COVID-19 loan arrangements authorized recipient governments to invest in public spending for labour-related policies, [t]hose arrangements also made clear that governments were to roll back that spending the moment conditions improved'.[102] These loan arrangements were, of course, merely temporary post-COVID, but we will have to see whether the normative shift towards sustainable development is more enduring, and can lead to longer-term commitments in subsequent arrangements. As De Schutter and his colleagues at the University of Louvain have observed: 'The inclusion of social policy into the Fund's programs relies to a great extent on their collaboration with the World Bank, which takes the lead.'[103]

2.4 ILO Influence at the World Bank? 'Doing Business', 'Performance Standards' and sustainable development

The ILO has not been without influence in the World Bank. For example, the ILO achieved initially some reform and now abolition of the World Bank's controversial 'Doing Business' prescriptions, which had placed pressure on countries to reduce labour standards so as to rank higher in the list of business-friendly states. Also, ILO 'core' labour standards, or fundamental principles and rights at work, have gradually and in a slightly modified form fed into the 'Performance Standards' that the IFC utilises in determining and managing project funding, now adapted and adopted more widely in the World Bank Group. The extent of these apparent successes and the prospects for future sustainability objectives, including labour standards protection in trade, are evaluated here.

2.4.1 ILO opposition to the 'Doing Business' Report and its outcomes

In 2003, the 'Doing Business' (DB) Report emerged as a way to provide indicators of 'the ease of doing business' in different countries and was targeted at potential investors. Not only did the DB Report establish so-called objective measures of business regulations and their enforcement, but the report ranked 133 countries in a composite index, covering initially five regulatory areas,

[102] Desirée LeClercq, 'Why Conflict Between International Economic and Rights-Based Governance Is Inevitable' (2022) 40(1) *Berkeley Journal of International Law* 7, 32.

[103] Olivier De Schutter, Nathalie Dubler, Paula Fernandez-Wulff and Anabella Sosa, *The IMF's Role in Social Protection: Promising Policy Shifts and Persisting Challenges* (University of Louvain 2021) CRIDHO Working Paper 2021/2 available at: https://sites.uclouvain.be/cridho/documents/Working.Papers/CRIDHO-WP-2021-2_DeSchutter.et.al_IMF.Social.protection.pdf.

including regulation of the labour market.[104] The following year, the 2004 DB Report listed 175 countries and contained 10 indicators.[105] The most controversial indicator was the 'Employing Workers Index' (EWI), which covered difficulty of hiring and firing, rigidity of hours, non-wage labour costs and firing costs.[106] In other words, the more flexible the labour market, the higher a country's ranking would be and the more likely it was to be seen as the place to do business (with implicit World Bank endorsement). This initiative reflected the prevalent economic orthodoxy that lowering labour regulation promoted employment, attracted foreign direct investment and reduced trade shocks for the economy.[107]

The DB Report prompted vehement objections from what was then the International Confederation of Free Trade Unions (ICFTU – a precursor to the current International Trade Union Confederation). An early report from Peter Bakvis at the ICFTU[108] raised concerns that, despite protestations of economic expert involvement in the design of the 'Doing Business' project, there were risks of misuse of data gathered for other purposes and misinterpretation of that data. Moreover, he strongly contested the assumption that deregulation would really cut costs for business. He also observed that the DB Report was being used as a catalyst for deregulation of labour laws and social security protections in Bolivia, Colombia, Ecuador, Lithuania, Nepal, Romania and South Africa, consistent with the ways in which the IMF and World Bank institutions were using conditionality for lending. The trade union movement was able to

---

[104] Timothy Besley, 'Law, Regulation, and the Business Climate: The Nature and Influence of the World Bank Doing Business Project' (2015) 29(3) *Journal of Economic Perspectives* 99, 99.

[105] Janine Berg and Sandrine Cazes, *The Doing Business Indicators: Measurement Issues and Political Implications* (ILO 2007), iii; available at: www.oit.org/public/english/employment/download/elm/elm07-6.pdf; also published as Janine Berg and Sandrine Cazes, 'Policymaking Gone Awry: The Labor Market Regulations of the Doing Business Indicators' (2008) 29(4) *Comparative Labor Law and Policy Journal* 349.

[106] Berg and Cazes (2007) n.105, 2–3; and see Appendix 1.

[107] See Juan C. Botero, Simeon Djankov, Rafael La Porta, Florencio Lopez-de-Silanes and Andrei Shleifer, 'The Regulation of Labor' (2004) 119(4) *Quarterly Journal of Economics* 1339; see also Simeon Djankov, 'The Doing Business Project: How It Started' (2016) 30(1) *Journal of Economic Perspectives* 247. A list of literature on which the EWI relied is available at: www.worldbank.org/en/research/employing-workers/research.

[108] See Peter Bakvis, 'How the World Bank & IMF use the Doing Business Report to Promote Labour Market Deregulation in Developing Countries' (ICFTU 2006). See also Peter Bakvis, 'The World Bank's Doing Business Report: A Last Fling for the Washington Consensus?' (2009) 15(3–4) *Transfer: European Review of Labour and Research* 419.

provide evidence that the World Bank had used the DB Report to pressure 23 countries to lower labour regulations on the basis of the EWI ratings.[109]

Those concerns were shared by International Labour Office staff.[110] They regarded the World Bank economic justifications as badly flawed, expressing concern regarding such methodological issues as selection bias, omitted variables (such as enforcement procedures), problematic aggregation and weighting systems, subjective indicators and limited coding methods.[111] Moreover, they saw the entire project as setting a 'race to deregulation of the labour market'.[112] A preferable approach suggested by Sangheon Lee and others was to resist a simple prescription of deregulation, but rather consider more carefully 'how individual countries can best promote labour laws and policies that respond to their current development challenges'. This need not 'retreat from substantive legal standards' so much as design 'procedural and implementation mechanisms to ensure that legal rights are realized in practice' and in so doing identify 'the most effective combinations of regulatory techniques to advance both social and economic objectives'.[113] This then was the development objection to the DB Report and the EWI.

The ICFTU and ILO eventually found an ally in the World Bank Independent Evaluation Group, whose 2008 Report recognises the lack of consensus among economists regarding labour market regulation and its impact on development, highlighting anomalies in the rankings.[114] A 'Doing Business Employing Workers Consultative Group' was established in 2009 and continued until 2011, engaging with the issues that had been raised, including alignment with the standards set out in relevant ILO Conventions, including on termination of employment.[115] In that respect, the scope of discussions went beyond

---

[109] Hannah Murphy, 'The World Bank and Core Labour Standards: Between Flexibility and Regulation' (2014) 22 *Review of International Political Economy* 399, 412.

[110] See Berg and Cazes n.105 above; also Sangheon Lee, Deirdre McCann, and Nina Torm, 'The World Bank's "Employing Workers" Index: Findings and Critiques: A Review of Recent Evidence' (2008) 147(4) *International Labour Review* 416.

[111] Berg and Cazes (2007) n.105, 9–13. Analysis supported subsequently by André Broome, Alexandra Homolar and Matthias Kranke, 'Bad Science: International Organizations and the indirect Power of Global Benchmarking' (2018) 24(3) *European Journal of International Relations* 514.

[112] Berg and Cazes (2007) n.105, 12.

[113] Lee et al, n.110, 428.

[114] World Bank Independent Evaluation Group, *Doing Business: An Independent Evaluation: Taking the Measure of the World Bank-IFC Doing Business Indicators* (World Bank 2008).

[115] Murphy n.109, 414; and Henner Gött, 'Interactions Between International Organizations: Approaching a Neglected Governance Dimension' (2020) 17(1) *International Organizations Law Review* 75, 88–91.

the so-called core labour standards identified in the 1998 ILO Declaration on Fundamental Principles and Rights at Work.[116] These debates reflected a broader concern relating to access to employment and social protection, which was evident in the ILO 'Decent Work Agenda' and the 2008 Declaration on Social Justice for a Fair Globalization.

As a result, initial modifications were made to the format of the DB Report, which in 2009 ceased to publish rankings of economies on the basis of the EWI but presented that data in a separate annex.[117] By 2015, the DB Report had conceded: 'Employment regulations are unquestionably necessary [...] They benefit both workers and firms [...] and can have a significant impact on economic growth and competitiveness. That impact can be negative where regulatory interventions are insufficient or excessive, so finding the right balance is essential.'[118] That notion of balance was consolidated in the 2017 DB Report, which observed that '[t]he challenge in developing labor policies is to avoid the extremes of over and under regulation by reaching a balance between worker protection and flexibility'.[119] Taking the case of the IMF country-specific report on South Africa under Article V surveillance from 2005 to 2018, a study conducted by Franz Christian Ebert has revealed long-term deference to DB Report findings, even after the termination of publication of the EWI rankings. Ebert concluded that this deference led to disregard for ILO standards and the recommendations of UN human rights bodies, such as the UN Committee on Economic, Social and Cultural Rights.[120] This assessment chimes with the view expressed by Lee and others in 2008 that the Doing Business project 'could be understood as providing an empirical basis for the "augmented Washington Consensus"'.[121]

In 2022, World Bank advocacy on 'Doing Business' was stopped after 'data irregularities' were identified in the DB Reports for 2018 and 2020.[122] This could be viewed as a vindication of labour-related objections, but any sense of victory should be tempered by the decision to replace this reporting process with a 'Business Enabling Environment' (BEE) project.[123] This has now been renamed 'Business Ready (B-READY)'.[124]

---

116 Discussed in Chapter 3 of this book at text accompanying n.79 et seq.

117 See Besley n.104, 101; and *Doing Business Report* (World Bank 2015), 231.

118 *Doing Business Report* (World Bank 2015), 231.

119 *Doing Business Report* (World Bank 2017), 95.

120 Ebert n.17, 118–19.

121 Lee et al n.110, 416.

122 See the statement available at: www.worldbank.org/en/news/statement/2021/09/16/world-bank-group-to-discontinue-doing-business-report.

123 Details are available at: https:// www .worldbank .org/ en/ programs/ business -enabling-environment.

124 See www.worldbank.org/en/businessready.

A BEE 'Pre-Concept Note' was published in February 2022. A later 'Concept Note' issued in June 2022 and revised in December the same year is available on the World Bank website alongside a new B-READY *Manual and Guide* and *Methodology Handbook*.[125] These documents demonstrate that there will once again be 'benchmarking' of labour-related factors by the World Bank Group, albeit approached differently. Three indicators will be used:

> (a) the quality of labor regulations (regulatory pillar); (b) the adequacy of public services for the labor market (public services pillar); and (c) the ease of employing labor which assesses how the two pillars (regulatory and public services) contribute in practice to the efficient functioning of labor markets from the perspective of both the firm and the employee.[126]

The World Bank has flagged the B-READY initiative as being different to the EWI. The crucial difference is said to be attention to the success of labour regulation from the perspective not only of the firm, but also the employee: 'BEE will consider more explicitly the perspective of employees.'[127] Additionally, the February 2022 Pre-Concept Note stated that 'unlike Doing Business the BEE indicators will include different types of firms and workers, including workers on different types of employment contracts', an approach that would have been more inclusive of those in a wider 'world of work'.[128] This commitment is not so evident in the more recent documentation, although there is reference to the failure for basic labour standards to be made available to those who work informally, albeit alongside the claim that reducing the costs of hire in the formal labour market will encourage employers to hire more workers on a formal basis that enables access to greater protections.[129] This is a view which obviously harks back to Williamson's description of the 'Washington Consensus'.[130] That said, reassurance was given in December 2022 in the 'concept note' that '[t]he Labor topic does not seek to promote deregulation

---

125 World Bank Group, 'Pre-Concept Note: Business Enabling Environment (BEE)', 4 February 2022; replaced by World Bank Group, 'Concept Note: Business Enabling Environment' (First version: June 2022 This version: December 2022) available at: https://thedocs.worldbank.org/en/doc/2250b12dfe798507f7b42064378cc616-0540012022/original/BEE-Concept-Note-December-2022.pdf.

126 Ibid, 47. See also *Business Ready Methodology Handbook* (World Bank Group 2023), ch 5 available at: https://thedocs.worldbank.org/en/doc/357a611e3406288528cb1e05b3c7dfda-0540012023/original/B-READY-Methodology-Handbook.pdf.

127 'Pre-Concept Note' n.125 above, 23.

128 Ibid, 48 and 50.

129 *Methodology Handbook* n.126, ch 5.

130 See Williamson n.63.

but rather to inform policies that encourage decent, sustainable, and productive job creation, considering the perspectives of the employer and the employee'.[131]

What is interesting in the BEE/B-READY documentation is the extent to which the language of sustainability has entered the frame. The 'Pre-Concept Note' stated that the indicator relating to 'worker protection' would 'build on applicable International Labor Standards drawn up by the ILO, in relation also to the 2030 Agenda for Sustainable Development and previous research on good practices conducted by the World Bank Group individually, and in cooperation with OECD, ILO, and other institutions'.[132] In the later 'Concept Note' connection between ILO standards and SDG 8 is relegated to a footnote.[133] In the B-READY *Methodology Handbook*, it is curious that gender equality and environmental sustainability are linked together to be addressed in tandem in relation to trade,[134] but no obvious connection is made with sustainable development and decent work in that context.

The BEE/B-READY mechanism provides 'three sets of indicators in the area of international trade'. These are: 'quality of regulations for international trade (regulatory framework pillar); quality of public services for the facilitation of international trade (public services pillar); and efficiency of importing goods, exporting goods, and engaging in digital trade (efficiency pillar).'[135] The regulatory framework pillar addresses 'the themes of digital adoption, environmental sustainability and gender' but not ostensibly labour.[136] However, a notable departure will be expansion of the indicators to encompass trade in services: 'whereas *Doing Business* focused on the ease of complying with trade regulations applicable only to goods, BEE indicators will expand the scope to include trade in services, as well as indicators on the regulatory framework and public services provided by governments.'[137] It will be argued later in this chapter that issues relating to migration and work arise in the context of trade in services that merit greater regulation, but at the time of writing it is difficult to know whether inclusion of this topic will be problematic or beneficial in relation to the protection of labour standards for workers who temporarily move across national borders. Much depends on how the BEE/B-READY plan operates in practice.

---

131 'Concept Note' n.125, 47.

132 'Pre-Concept Note' n.125, 23.

133 'Concept Note' n.125, 47.

134 *Methodology Handbook* n.126, e.g. at 505, 566–7 and 589.

135 'Concept Note' n.125, 60.

136 Ibid. See also *Methodology Handbook* n.126, ch. 6.

137 Ibid.

2.4.2 The ILO role in prompting inclusion of labour standards in project lending

The ILO has prompted inclusion of labour standards in the IFC Policy and Performance Standards on Environmental and Social Sustainability, which is now part of the IFC Sustainability Framework.[138] These Performance Standards were first adopted in 2006 and the use of the overarching term 'sustainability' is interesting as an instance of early institutional recognition of the potential interaction between economic, environmental and labour objectives.[139] The IFC Performance Standards also went beyond the standard terms in what was the 2003 World Bank 'Core Labor Standards Toolkit'.[140]

The first IFC Performance Standards were limited in terms of their initial content.[141] 'Labor and Working Conditions' were included as the second of eight 'Performance Standards' (PS2), as they still are today. They are purported to be based on all eight 'core' ILO Conventions and 'safe and healthy working conditions'.[142] Also 'reasonable working conditions' are to be applied and communicated transparently to workers.[143] Unfortunately, the central obligation with respect to freedom of association has been to comply with national law, with further limited duties arising where 'national law substantially restricts workers' organizations' or 'is silent'. This is a curiously limited obligation placed on IFC clients compared to the fuller obligations envisaged in ILO Conventions Nos 87 and 98.[144]

The ILO and IFC started to collaborate on the ILO 'Better Work Programme' from 2009 onwards, a manifestation of ILO determination to forge partnerships with other UN agencies, including IEIs,[145] and one might have expected

---

138 Information relating to their current content and application is available at: www .ifc .org/ wps/ wcm/ connect/ topics _ext _content/ ifc _external _corporate _site/ sustainability-at-ifc/policies-standards/performance-standards.

139 As discussed in Chapter 2 of this book.

140 Tonia Novitz, 'Core Labour Standards Conditionalities: A Means by which to Achieve Sustainable Development?' in Julio Faundez and Celine Tan (eds), *International Law, Economic Globalization and Developing Countries* (Edward Elgar Publishing 2010), 243–4; and Murphy n.109, 408 and 417.

141 *International Finance Corporation's Performance Standards on Social & Environmental Sustainability, 30 April 2006*, paras 9–10 available at: www .ifc .org/wps/wcm/connect/3f3419f4-6043-4984-a42a-36f3cfaf38fd/IFC%2BPerformance %2BStandards.pdf?MOD=AJPERES&CVID=jkC.Eka&id=1322803957411.

142 Ibid, PS2 paras 1–2. Accordingly, there is little apparent need to update PS2 following the 2022 ILO Resolution on the 1998 Declaration (discussed in Chapter 3 of this book at text accompanying n.90).

143 Ibid, PS2, paras 7–8.

144 Discussed in Novitz n.140, 244–5.

145 For example, ILO World Commission on the Social Dimension of Globalization, *A Fair Globalization, Creating Opportunities for All* (ILO, 2004), 124.

some enhancement of PS2 in response. Certainly, the Performance Standards were revised in 2012 following what the IFC officially described as 'comprehensive inputs and suggestions from a large number of stakeholders'.[146] The IFC was determined to demonstrate, for example, that it had been responsive to concerns regarding 'climate change', the emergence of 'business and human rights norms', the operation of supply chains in ways that were detrimental to workers and the environment, as well as concerns of indigenous peoples.[147] The obligations regarding freedom of association and collective bargaining did not substantially change,[148] but the inclusion of further protections for the most vulnerable including migrant workers and workers in the 'supply chain' could be significant.[149]

PS2 now makes provision for a client's responsibilities, not only to 'direct workers' but also 'contracted' and 'supply chain workers'.[150] This arguably amounts to an important recognition of a wider 'world of work' in ILO terms.[151] This concern with supply chains is not limited to labour-related matters but also applies in relation to PS6 concerned with 'Biodiversity Conservation and Sustainable Management of Living Natural Resources'. This means that under the procedure set out in PS1: 'Where the client can reasonably exercise control, the risks and impacts identification process will also consider those risks and impacts associated with primary supply chains, as defined in Performance Standard 2 (paragraphs 27–29) and Performance Standard 6 (paragraph 30).'[152] That initial risk assessment process carried out by IFC staff can lead to both positive and negative covenants to be undertaken by the client and included in any legal agreement. The client is then obliged to establish and manage mechanisms to assure compliance with these project conditions. A corrective action plan for emergencies should be anticipated and applied if need be to mitigate harms, and IFC staff can insist on its adaptation after reporting of such incidents which is required in a timely manner. The IFC will also be engaged in monitoring and in receiving annual progress reports and can request further information, with the Compliance Advisor/Ombudsman (CAO)

---

146 *Update of IFC's Policy and Performance Standards on Environmental and Social Sustainability, and Access to Information Policy* (IFC 2011), 3 at para. 12.

147 Ibid, iv–v.

148 *IFC Performance Standards on Environmental and Social Sustainability 1 January 2012*, PS2 paras 13–14, available at: www.ifc.org/wps/wcm/connect/24e6bfc3-5de3-444d-be9b-226188c95454/PS_English_2012_Full-Document.pdf?MOD=AJPERES&CVID=jkV-X6h.

149 Ibid, PS2, paras 2, 11 and 15 regarding migrant workers and paras 2, 4, 7 and 27–9 regarding supply chain workers.

150 Ibid, PS2, para. 10.

151 See Chapter 3 of this book, text accompanying n.129 and 249–50.

152 IFC Performance Standards n.148, PS1, para. 10.

providing additional oversight. The IFC will seek to re-establish compliance, but default can lead to cancellation of funding, recovery of monies paid and other legal action.[153] Stakeholder engagement is also anticipated at all stages of the process.[154]

What is interesting is that this principle, established gradually with respect to environmental and labour sustainability at the IFC, has since been extended to MIGA, which adopted almost identical Performance Standards in 2013.[155] In 2016 an overarching Environmental and Social Framework (ESF) was adopted by the Bank's Executive Board of Directors, apparently as a follow-up to UN SDG commitments.[156] This ESF has three inter-related aspects:

- A Vision for Sustainable Development, which sets out the Bank's aspirations regarding environmental and social sustainability.
- The World Bank Environmental and Social Policy for Investment Project Financing, which sets out the mandatory requirements that apply to the Bank.
- The Environmental and Social Standards, together with their Annexes, which set out the mandatory requirements that apply to the Borrower and projects.[157]

The ESF became effective from 1 October 2018, so that such standards apply now to public sector projects.[158] The second of the ten Environmental and Social Standards set out in the ESF requires that borrowers prevent use of child and forced labour and promote non-discrimination, but also 'support the principles of freedom of association and collective bargaining'. Also included (prior to the 2022 amendment of the 1998 ILO Declaration) is an obligation to

---

153 Ibid, see PS1: 'Assessment and Management of Environmental and Social Risks and Impacts'.

154 Ibid, PS1, para. 1: 'An effective Environmental and Social Management System (ESMS) is a dynamic and continuous process initiated and supported by management, and involves engagement between the client, its workers, local communities directly affected by the project (the Affected Communities) and, where appropriate, other stakeholders.'

155 MIGA Performance Standard on Environmental and Social Sustainability 1 October 2013 available at: www .miga .org/ sites/ default/ files/ archive/ Documents/ MIGA_Performance_Standards_October_2013.pdf.

156 LeClercq n.102, 30.

157 *The World Bank Environmental and Social Framework* (World Bank 2017), 2 available at: https://thedocs.worldbank.org/en/doc/837721522762050108-0290022018/original/ESFFramework.pdf.

158 See Franz Christian Ebert, 'Labour Standards and the World Bank: Analysing the potential of Safeguard Policies for protecting workers' in Henner Gött (ed.), *Labour Standards in International Economic Law* (Springer 2018), 282.

'promote safety and health at work'.[159] This can be seen as an incremental beneficial shift towards inclusion of international labour standards in World Bank activities, even 'a victory for ILO principles',[160] but some caution may be wise.

To date, there has been only qualified success in using the IFC PS2 to challenge the exploitation of labour in projects receiving IFC funding; it is not a model that is working well, or at least not yet. The CAO will determine eligibility of a complaint, which is often then referred to dispute resolution involving the IFC or MIGA. Mediation by the CAO may follow, or settlement through dispute resolution; there may be withdrawal of the complaint or there can be referral to an assessment and then, if appropriate, a compliance process, involving potentially appraisal and investigation. Past studies indicated that CAO engagement has been helpful, but that IFC (and MIGA) staff do not necessarily respond swiftly and appropriately to violations or even CAO recommendations.[161] Moreover, the supply chain provision has not been wholly successful, since the standards relating to compliance imposed on the borrower depend on the nature of their link with the workers (direct, contracted or in a supply chain, as discussed above).[162] This can lead to a situation, in which as Ebert says, borrowers are enabled 'to avoid the respective obligations by adjusting the structure of the project'.[163]

Current cases before the CAO which are a matter of public record indicate reliance on PS2 and the ESF in relation to labour standards by claimants, but also a process which may not have optimal outcomes.[164] For example, one case submitted in 2022 was brought by a complainant who was a former employee of the large Pakistan financial institution, Habib Bank Ltd (HBL), which received financial investment from the IFC for various purposes, including improvement of HBL's environmental and social performance and

---

[159] See the details of 'ESS2: Labor and Working Conditions' available at: https://thedocs.worldbank.org/en/doc/837721522762050108-0290022018/original/ESFFramework.pdf#page=45&zoom=80.

[160] Anne Trebilcock, 'The ILO as an Actor in International Economic Law: Looking Back, Gazing Ahead' in Marc Bungenberg, Markus Krajewski, Christian J. Tams, Jörg Philipp Terhechte and Andreas R. Ziegler (eds), *European Yearbook of International Economic Law 2019* (Springer 2020), 12.

[161] As outlined by Franz Christian Ebert, 'Labour Safeguards of International Financial Institutions: Can They Help to Avoid Violations of ILO Core Labour Standards?' in Bungenberg et al n.160, 125–8. See also *External Review of IFC/MIGA E&S Accountability, including CAO's Role and Effectiveness: Report and Recommendations* (World Bank 2020).

[162] Raised in the *External Review of IFC/MIGA E&S Accountability* n.158, 41–2.

[163] Ebert, n.158, 300.

[164] Case summaries and access to materials are available from the CAO at: www.cao-ombudsman.org/cases.

risk management.[165] The case raised issues of dismissal and protection from whistleblowing for a senior employee who had alleged 'greenwashing' while Deputy General Manager and Head of Planning and Implementation of HBL's Social and Environmental Management Systems (SEMS) unit. The case was referred to the IFC, but that process was unsuccessful from the complainant's perspective and the matter was returned to the CAO for a 'compliance appraisal', which found that the IFC had documented 'deficiencies in HBL's E&S performance' and there might have been non-compliance with PS1, but that this did not directly have any demonstrable 'harm'. The treatment of the employee under PS2 was a matter for the courts in Pakistan and no concern regarding IFC conduct was raised in this respect. Accordingly, the CAO closed the case. There was no mention in the CAO's reasoning of ILO standards (or indeed in any of the submissions appended to the CAO appraisal).[166]

A number of cases relating to breach of labour standards have been raised since 2019 relating to the Karot Power Company Limited (KPCL) and its development of a hydropower plant being developed on the Jhelum River, in Pakistan.[167] At the most recent count, this amounts to seven cases. For example, cases 2 and 3 raise the following PS2 concerns:

> working conditions and terms of employment (para.10); workers' accommodation (para. 12); workers' collective bargaining through a workers' union (para. 13 and 14); discrimination and fair treatment (para. 15); retrenchment (para. 18); grievance mechanism (para. 20), and safe work environment (para. 23). The complainants also allege that the presence of security personnel (PS4 para 12) is a concern since it creates an intimidating atmosphere that impacts the workers' ability to freely exercise their rights in the collective bargaining process.[168]

It is evident from the first report that the IFC were made aware of two deaths on site in 2017 and that health and safety had long been an issue, but also that repeated complaints had been made from various sources by the time this CAO case was filed and a time-bound remedial plan was put in place in 2019,

---

165 Pakistan: HBL-01, filed 3 April 2022.

166 CAO Compliance Appraisal of Complaint Regarding IFC Projects with Habib Bank Ltd, Pakistan, 13 June 2023 available at: www .cao -ombudsman .org/ sites/ default/ files/ downloads/ CAO %20Compliance %20Appraisal %20of %20Complaint %20Regarding %20IFC %20Projects %20with %20Habib %20Bank %20Ltd %2C %20Pakistan_1.pdf.

167 The first of these on record, Pakistan: Karot Hydro-02/Jhelum River, filed 24 August 2019, is now in the compliance investigation stage.

168 CAO Compliance Appraisal of Complaint Karot-02 & 03/Jhelum River, 21 January 2022, 18. Available at: www .cao -ombudsman .org/ sites/ default/ files/ downloads/ CAO _Compliance _Appraisal _Report %20Karot _Hydro _Pakistan -02_03_Jan2022_0.pdf.

but with only virtual inspections following due to COVID-19.[169] The CAO made the telling comment that 'considering that construction of the project has been ongoing for more than six years, CAO has questions as to whether IFC's supervision has been sufficient to identify and address E&S compliance issues as required by the Sustainability Policy'.[170] The most recent complaint was filed by the president of the trade union, Social Hydro Labor Union (SHU), in August 2023, alleging inability to access the plant site to carry out trade union activities and expressing concern regarding treatment of the workers.[171] The IFC has not commented extensively on this case (the contrast to the alleged 'greenwashing' whistleblower dismissal case is palpable). The CAO has duly recorded the facts but has not commented on PS2 or ESF compliance, let alone ILO standards. Instead, KPCL has recorded a commitment to take 'corrective action' and 'to positive relations with communities and stakeholders' and is agreeing to enter into 'dispute resolution' with the trade union president, and the case is to be transferred from the CAO accordingly.[172]

The World Bank seems to be actively trying to correct past limitations in staff training and expertise as well as administrative processes,[173] but there may be also deeper structural issues. By 2023, an independent report was recommending that additional action be taken to ensure that appropriate processes were followed and suitable remedies made available to claimants.[174] At the time of writing, consequent reforms have yet to be announced.

There is a danger that the standards included by the IFC, like those relating to freedom of association, do not altogether cohere with the content of ILO core conventions or ILO supervisory findings, to which as we have seen the CAO does not refer. As Ebert has observed, this use of ILO standards in PS2 and the ESF can be seen as a kind of 'appropriation' of labour standards from the 'social justice' setting of the ILO into a sphere where they are subjected to the World Bank Group's 'institutional logic' and 'market constraints'.[175]

---

169 Ibid, 17.

170 Ibid, 18.

171 Pakistan: Karot Hydro-07/Jhelum River, filed 13 August 2022.

172 CAO Assessment Report Regarding the Seventh Complaint Received in Relation to IFC's Investment in Karot Power Company Ltd. (IFC #36008) May 2023, 6.

173 The World Bank, *Environmental and Social Framework (ESF): Implementation Update* (World Bank 2020), 8–15 available at: https://thedocs.worldbank.org/en/doc/982711602165538091-0290022020/original/ESFImplementationUpdateOctober2020.pdf.

174 CAO Evaluation of Dispute Resolution and Assessment Processes: Concentric Alliance Report (World Bank 2023) available at: www.cao-ombudsman.org/sites/default/files/2023-07/230331_CAO_EvaluationReport_Clean%20%282%29.pdf.

175 Ebert, n.158, 300.

The ILO has undoubtedly had some influence, evident from the inclusion of core labour standards in PS2 and ESF, but not all that might be desired in terms of reference to ILO Conventions, Recommendations and past findings of supervisory bodies. The 'strategic partnerships' that the World Bank has identified in implementation of the ESF are with other international financial institutions and civil society organisations,[176] and although the latter consultations might seem promising, there is no clear or straightforward deference to ILO norms.

3. SUSTAINABILITY AT THE WTO AND EVASION OF ISSUES RELATING TO LABOUR STANDARDS

This section examines the sustainable development paradigm which currently operates at the WTO. The IMF and World Bank were created to enable the kinds of fiscal rules and financial equilibrium which could promote world trade. The WTO, having evolved from its origins in the trade rules established by the GATT, has set the parameters of world trade law alongside systems for its elaboration, evaluation, enforcement and expansion. What is notable is the ostensible avoidance of WTO engagement with issues relating to labour standards, while simultaneously crafting the trade norms that affect the livelihoods and modes of hire of those in the world of work – both traditional 'employees' and others whose services are hired in a myriad of other ways. We will see that, unlike the Bretton Woods institutions, the WTO is not formally a UN agency but operates under separate systems of governance, while retaining complex connections with both the IMF and the World Bank, without being bound by the UN Charter.

While it was initially intended that ILO standards could have significant influence within an 'International Trade Organization' (ITO), the first section examines how that notion was abandoned by 1948 and was never revived. The preamble to the 1994 Marrakesh Agreement made certain fundamental commitments to environmental protections and development, while avoiding the issue of labour – a stance confirmed in the 1996 Singapore Ministerial Declaration. This was a curious position to take, given that the overarching framework of trade rules will have profound effects on the ways in which labour is hired for manufacture of export goods and cross-border supply of services, but can probably be best understood in terms of the political battlefield

176 World Bank *Implementation Update* n.173, 16.

that the so-called trade–labour linkage had become.[177] Instead, the Marrakesh Agreement established a WTO enhancing regulation of international trade, for example setting rules for trade in services as well as trade in goods while strengthening dispute settlement. The second section outlines the basic trade rules established in the GATT, their application in a modified form in the GATS and potential implications for labour, especially in relation to mode 4 trade in services regarding temporary movement for work. The following section examines the scope for unilateral action to be taken by states to protect labour standards under the 'General Exceptions' clause in both the GATT and the GATS, as well as the scope to make tariff preferences introduced under the 'Enabling Clause'[178] conditional upon compliance with labour standards. This permissive approach to the protection of labour standards might seem a boon. It is, after all, consistent with the permission given in the GATT and GATS to establish preferential trade agreements (colloquially known as free trade agreements),[179] which may be conditional on protection of labour standards (to be examined further in chapter 5). It has been established that, at least in principle, some restrictions can be placed by the WTO on the application of such conditions, but in practice labour conditionality has yet to be subjected to such scrutiny. The consequences of this approach for North–South trade and labour relations will also be considered. This chapter concludes by considering avenues for worker voice in the WTO when compared with other IEIs.

3.1 The Constitutional Foundations of the WTO

This section begins by examining the constitutional foundations of the WTO, beginning with plans for an ITO, and the initial workings of the GATT. The relationship between the GATT and the eventual WTO with the UN is introduced, together with discussion of their governance. The reforms achieved through the Marrakesh Agreement are outlined here, alongside what the text of that instrument indicates regarding the potential role of the WTO in sustainable development, particularly as regards trade and labour. It will become apparent that initial plans to ensure collaboration of an ITO with the ILO were not replicated in 1994. Indeed, the political will to achieve this remains absent.

---

[177] See, for a historical perspective Clyde Summers, 'The Battle in Seattle: Free Trade, Labor Rights, and Societal Values' (2001) 22 *University of Pennsylvania Journal of International Economic Law* 61.

[178] The Enabling Clause: 'Differential and More Favourable Treatment Reciprocity and Fuller Participation of Developing Countries' – Decision of 28 November 1979 L/4903 – appended to GATT (which continues to apply as part of GATT 1994 under the WTO) available at: www.wto.org/english/docs_e/legal_e/enabling1979_e.htm.

[179] See the GATT, Article XXIV; and GATS, Articles V and Vbis.

3.1.1 From the inclusion of ILO standards in the Havana Charter to trade under the GATT

In 1945, an International Trade Organization (ITO) to manage trade relations was proposed by the US. This proposal was endorsed by the new UN Economic and Social Council (ECOSOC), which convened the 1946 conference that led to adoption of the Havana Charter. This was a smaller gathering than the Bretton Woods conference, representing, as Quinn Slobodian recalls, only 17 states out of what were then 71 independent sovereign nations.[180]

It should be noted that Article 7 of the Havana Charter, titled 'fair labour standards',[181] did not place obligations directly on the ITO but rather on its members, stating in Article 1(1):

> The Members recognize that measures relating to employment must take fully into account the rights of workers under inter-governmental declarations, conventions and agreements. They recognize that all countries have a common interest in the achievement and maintenance of fair labour standards related to productivity, and thus in the improvement of wages and working conditions as productivity may permit. The Members recognize that unfair labour conditions, particularly in production for export, create difficulties in international trade, and, accordingly, each Member shall take whatever action may be appropriate and feasible to eliminate such conditions within its territory.

So, the ITO would not gain competence over the application of fair labour standards but would acknowledge the entitlement (and obligation) of action by member states. Moreover, that action was not to be extra-territorial, but was to be addressed by a state 'within its territory'. This was not exactly a 'social clause' envisaged to be applied in the course of trade.[182] Instead, the Havana Charter did contain, in Article 45, the prototype for what is now the 'General Exceptions' clause applicable under both the GATT and GATS which permits unilateral action by member states of measures which were, for example, 'necessary to protect 'public morals', 'necessary to the enforcement of laws and regulations relating to public safety', 'necessary to protect human, animal or plant life or health' and 'relating to the products of prison labour'. There remains a debate today whether these unilateral measures are permissible where they have an intended extraterritorial effect,[183] and regarding their

180 Slobodian n.3, 125–6.

181 Havana Charter for an International Trade Organization available at: www.wto.org/english/docs_e/legal_e/havana_e.pdf.

182 Cf. Lance Compa, 'Labor Rights and Labor Standards in International Trade' (1993) 25(1) *Law and Policy in International Business* 165, 181 and 190.

183 Lorand Bartels, 'Article XX of GATT and the Problem of Extraterritorial Jurisdiction: The Case of Trade Measures for the Protection of Human Rights' (2002) 36(2) *Journal of World Trade* 353; Marieke Koekkoek, 'In Search of the Final Frontier

wording (such as the term 'necessary' and its implications),[184] which we will return to later in this part of the chapter.

ILO members did have particular responsibilities acknowledged in Article 7(2) of the Havana Charter: 'Members which are also members of the International Labour Organisation (sic) shall cooperate with that organization in giving effect to this undertaking.' Finally, under Article 7(3), where any ('all') 'matters relating to labour standards' were referred to the ITO, the ITO was obliged to 'consult and co-operate with the International Labour Organisation'.[185] Such cooperation would have been 'indispensable' in terms of crafting the coordinated treatment of labour and trade.[186]

The Havana Charter was interesting in respect of the elaboration of ITO aims in Article 8, which recognise the inter-related nature of economic and social (including labour) objectives:

> The Members recognize that the productive use of the world's human and material resources is of concern to and will benefit all countries, and that the industrial and general economic development of all countries, particularly of those in which resources are as yet relatively undeveloped, as well as the reconstruction of those countries whose economies have been devastated by war, will improve opportunities for employment, enhance the productivity of labour, increase the demand for goods and services, contribute to economic balance, expand international trade and raise levels of real income.

What was missing, however, was awareness of how those 'productive resources' might need to be applied sustainably in environmental as well as social and economic terms. There was also an unquestioning acceptance of the benefits of trade and, implicitly, economic growth.[187]

In the meantime, the original text of the GATT was prepared and adopted in 1947. The parties were eager for the instrument to become operative so it was agreed that it should be given provisional application from 1 January 1948.[188] It

– An Analysis of the Extraterritorial Effect of International Trade Measures from a Jurisdictional Perspective' (2018) 10(1) *Trade Law and Development* 65.

[184] See for example Filippo Fontanelli, 'Necessity Killed the GATT – Art XX GATT and the Misleading Rhetoric about Weighing and Balancing' (2012) 5(2) *European Journal of Legal Studies* 39.

[185] See the Havana Charter for an ITO, Article 7. Discussed by Clair Wilcox, 'The London Draft of a Charter for an International Trade Organization' (1947) 37(2) *The American Economic Review* 529, 8–9.

[186] See Adelle Blackett, 'Theorizing Emancipatory Transnational Futures of International Labor Law' (2019) 113 *American Journal of International Law* 390, 391.

[187] Cf. Chapter 2 of this book and text accompanying nn.53–4.

[188] Protocol of Provisional Application to the General Agreement on Tariffs and Trade, October 30, 1947, 61 Stat. pt.5 a2051, T.I.A.S. No. 1700, 55 U.N.T.S. 308.

was hoped that the ITO would also soon be operational, 'with the ITO forming the organizational structure, and the GATT being merely one among possibly several subsidiary specialized agreements'.[189] The Havana Charter was submitted to the US Congress for that purpose, but was blocked due to the fear that 'the Charter might establish too far-reaching restraints on the foreign policy of the United States'.[190] The International Chamber of Commerce and other key business interests were also opposed to its adoption, but possibly for different reasons.[191] As a result, the Interim Commission which had been established as the ITO secretariat was redeployed to assist with the administration of the GATT.[192]

The GATT was a small club whose members abided by its trading rules. It grew from an initial 23 ratifying signatories (the 'Contracting Parties'), operating without legal personality, struggling also to require states to abide by their obligations under the treaty.[193] These 'birth defects', as John H. Jackson described them, were to be (at least partially) corrected by the establishment of the WTO in the Marrakesh Agreement,[194] but there has been no return to engagement with labour-related issues as envisaged in the Havana Charter. Indeed, Slobodian provides an account of how any attempt to do so was resisted by a 'Geneva School' which sought global economic governance from a neo-liberal position, resisting redistributive social justice.[195]

---

[189] John H. Jackson, 'GATT and the Future of International Trade Institutions' (1992) 18 *Brooklyn Journal of International Law* 11, 17; and John H. Jackson, *Sovereignty, the WTO, and Changing Fundamentals of International Law* (Cambridge University Press 2006), 93.

[190] Matthias Herdegen, *Principles of International Economic Law*, 2nd ed. (Oxford University Press 2016), 196; discussed more fully in William Diebold, *The End of the ITO* (Princeton University Press 1952).

[191] Slobodian n.3, 128–33 attributes this to the reluctance to contemplate 'the decision-making parity' the ITO would have conceded to 'the poorer nations of the world'.

[192] See the exchange of letters between the then Executive Secretary of GATT and the then Secretary-General of the United Nations in August 1952 attached to UN document E/5476/Add.12 of 24 May 1974.

[193] John L. Jackson, *World Trading System: Law and Policy of International Economic Relations* (MIT Press 1989), 83–4; Pablo Zapatero Miguel, 'Level Up: A History of Regime-building at GATT Club' (2020) 12 *Cuadernos de Derecho Transnacional* 818, 818–21; and Gardner Patterson, 'The GATT: Categories, Problems and Procedures of Membership' (1992) *Columbia Business Law Review* 7.

[194] See n.10 above.

[195] Slobodian n.3, 123 and 133; see also a detailed summary of his findings and their implications in Adelle Blackett, 'On Social Regionalism in Transnational Labour Law' (2020) 159(4) *International Labour Review* 591, 594–6.

Starting from such modest beginnings, each Contracting Party at the GATT had an equal say and voice. This is a very different model to the IMF and institutions in the World Bank Group, and could be regarded as more 'democratic'.[196] There is no structural provision for CSOs, such as business and labour, to have a say in GATT or, now, WTO decision-making processes. These are reserved to state 'members'. Instead, a 'WTO Public Symposium' first held in 2001 has become an annual tradition, now renamed the 'WTO Public Forum'. This is a large event currently attracting more than 2,000 CSO participants over four days, including 'civil society, academia, business, government, international organisations and the media'.[197]

As increasing numbers of developing countries became contracting parties to the GATT, they were able to exercise some influence, establishing a 'special and differential treatment' (SDT) principle manifested in the insertion in 1964 of Part IV into the GATT.[198] This may have been due to numerical power, but also their collective determination to wield that power as demonstrated by the Declaration of the Group of 77 at the UN Conference on Trade and Development (UNCTAD) that same year.[199]

Nevertheless, ultimately, there was little change in the underlying rules of the club – which would pose problems in terms of their effects on the Global South, as we shall see.[200] A 'club' model of governance has continued in the WTO, where it has been observed that '[t]he reality of trade negotiations is that states with large market-shares enjoy significant input and influence over decisions; indeed one might describe them as decision-makers, while states with smaller market-share are effectively decision-takers'.[201]

The GATT was a treaty rather than an organisation and lacked the legal personality to be a UN agency.[202] The secretariat did however establish terms of

---

[196] Joint Declaration of the Seventy-Seven Developing Countries made at the Conclusion of the United Nations Conference on Trade and Development, Geneva, 15 June 1964, Article 6 available at: www.g77.org/doc/Joint%20Declaration.html.

[197] See www.wto.org/english/forums_e/public_forum_e/public_forum_e.htm.

[198] Uche Ewelukwa, 'Special and Differential Treatment in International Trade Law: A Concept in Search of Content' (2003) 79 *North Dakota Law Review* 831, 847.

[199] Robert E. Hudec, 'GATT and the Developing Countries' (1992) *Columbia Business Law Review* 67, 68–72 who also discusses the effect of the Enabling Clause examined further in this chapter below. See further Robert E. Hudec, *Developing Countries in the GATT Legal System* (Cambridge University Press 2010), 64–74 and 103–14.

[200] For a critical perspective of outcomes, see Elimma C. Ezeani, *The WTO and Its Development Obligation* (Anthem Press, 2012), 34–5.

[201] Ngaire Woods and Amrita Narlikar, 'Governance and the Limits of Accountability: The WTO, the IMF, and the World Bank' (2001) 53(170) *International Social Science Journal* 569, 573.

[202] Cf. Jackson (1992) n.189, 17–19.

cooperation with the UN, under which 'close de facto working arrangements' arose, such that formal 'agency' status was said to be 'unnecessary'.[203] 'On essentially political matters', the Contracting Parties to the GATT followed the policy set out in Article 86 of the Havana Charter, namely, 'to avoid passing judgement in any way on such matters and to follow decisions of the United Nations on such questions'.[204] There was also agreement on information sharing, reciprocal representation, coordination and cooperation; moreover, GATT staff are hired as UN staff and have benefited from the same UN pension fund.[205] Under exchanges of letters and through a practice of mutual consultations, the GATT and the IMF were able to 'pursue a co-ordinated policy with regard to questions of quantitative restrictions and other trade measures within the jurisdiction of GATT, and exchange questions within the jurisdiction of the Fund'.[206] The secretariat servicing the GATT also cooperated with UNCTAD to run the International Trade Centre (ITC).[207]

The WTO could have become a UN agency, but instead followed the precedent that there are no 'formal institutional links' but instead established 'cooperative ties', such as continuing collaboration with UNCTAD to operate the ITC.[208] In neither of the formal documents relating to GATT or WTO cooperation with the UN have the close ties with the ILO envisaged in the Havana Charter been replicated. Indeed, while it has been argued that the IMF and World Bank Group should be regarded, as UN agencies, as bound by the terms of the UN Charter,[209] and therefore the human rights instruments and supervisory findings relating to these, it is not straightforward to frame the same argument in respect of the WTO.

---

203 *Relations of the General Agreement on Tariffs and Trade with the United Nations*, Note by the Secretariat, UN General Assembly document of 9 March 1976 (A/AC.179/5); for discussion see: https://docs.wto.org/dol2fe/Pages/SS/directdoc.aspx?filename=q:/WT/GC/W10.pdf&Open=True. Cf Jackson (2006), n.189, 97 who described the GATT as being 'a de facto international organization'.

204 *Relations of the GATT with the UN* n.205, citing SR.22/3 of 8 March 1965.

205 Ibid.

206 Ibid, citing letters attached to document E/5476/Add.12.

207 Ibid. See also https://intracen.org/our-work.

208 *Arrangements for Effective Cooperation with other Intergovernmental Organizations: Relations Between the WTO and the United Nations* Communication from the Director-General, WT/GC/W/10, 3 November 1995, reporting the relevant exchange of letters, available at: https://docs.wto.org/dol2fe/Pages/SS/directdoc.aspx?filename=q:/WT/GC/W10.pdf&Open=True.

209 Darrow, n.62.

3.1.2 Sustainable development since the Marrakesh Agreement: the connection to Special and Differential Treatment (SDT)?

The Marrakesh Agreement establishing the WTO, adopted in 1994, starts by recognising the objective of 'sustainable development'. The preamble sets out objectives relevant to those in the world of work, namely that 'relations in the field of trade and economic endeavour should be conducted with a view to raising standards of living' as well as 'ensuring full employment'. Job creation is apparently prioritised over other facets of protection of those at work. There is also to be 'optimal use of the world's resources in accordance with the objective of sustainable development, seeking both to protect and preserve the environment and to enhance the means for doing so in a manner consistent with [...] respective needs and concerns at different levels of economic development'.[210] In this sense it is arguable that there is recognition here, not only of the importance of environmental sustainability, but also intra- and inter-generational justice based on the needs of present and future generations. However, there is not much more in the text of the Marrakesh Agreement itself to offer guidance as to how such objectives can be achieved.

Perhaps we should not be looking for great unity of purpose since, as Robert Wolfe has explained, 'the WTO is not one agreement but dozens'; so that it is not possible to 'find a singular place from which to see the WTO legal order as a whole, as if the WTO could mean the same thing for all actors, or be reflective of a single set of values'.[211] Appended to the Marrakesh Agreement were four annexes, themselves subdivided.[212] The GATT 1994 was appended together with the GATT 1947 in Annex 1A, alongside numerous other 'Understandings' and 'Agreements'. Many of those instruments have some significance in practice for labour, such as the Agreement on the Application of Sanitary and Phytosanitary Measures (SPS), which has potential relevance

[210] See the Marrakesh Agreement n.10. See also the Marrakesh Declaration of 15 April 1994. Available at: www.wto.org/english/docs_e/legal_e/marrakesh_decl_e.htm; and the more optimistic reading by Gabrielle Marceau, 'Trade and Labour' in Daniel Bethlehem, Isabelle Van Damme, Donald McRae and Rodney Neufeld (eds), *The Oxford Handbook of International Trade Law* (Oxford University Press 2009), 543.

[211] Robert Wolfe, 'An Anatomy of Accountability at the WTO' (2015) 6(1) *Global Policy* 13, 14.

[212] A full record made is made available on the WTO website at: www.wto.org/english/docs_e/legal_e/final_e.htm.

to workers' health and thereby SDG 3,[213] and the Agreement on Technical Barriers to Trade (or TBT).[214]

GATS was set out in Annex 1B, while the Agreement on Trade-Related Aspects of Intellectual Property Rights (TRIPs) was appended in Annex 1C (the latter being beyond the scope of this book, although its significance for labour has become obvious in relation to availability of vaccines and medicines, not least during the coronavirus pandemic, affecting the health and wellbeing of numerous workers disproportionately exposed to COVID-19).[215] Another notable instrument set out in Annex 2 was the Understanding on Rules and Procedures Governing the Settlement of Disputes (the Dispute Settlement Understanding or DSU), which established 'a rule-based adjudicatory process with compulsory jurisdiction over all WTO member countries, a broad jurisdictional scope over almost all of the WTO Agreements, a right of appeal to the seven-member Appellate Body, and procedures for assessing damages and authorizing retaliation'.[216] Annex 3 set out the Trade Policy Review Mechanism (TPRM).[217] Annex 4 consisted of the Plurilateral Trade

---

213 Hossain Mohammad Reza, 'Can the Concept of "Justice" Be Employed in North–South Trade to Serve the Interests of the South in Ways that Sustainable Development Cannot?' (2021) 48 *Journal of Malaysian and Comparative Law* 81, 91–3.

214 Cf. Joanna Langille, 'The Trade–Labour Relationship in the Light of the WTO Appellate Body's Embrace of Pluralism' (2020) 159(4) *International Labour Review* 569, 576–7.

215 See, for example, the roundtable discussion on a TRIPS waiver in Els Torreele and Joseph J. Amon, 'Equitable COVID-19 Vaccine Access' (2021) 23(1) *Health and Human Rights* 273; for the targeted five-year 'TRIPS waiver', see the Ministerial Decision on the TRIPS Agreement adopted on 17 June 2022, available at: https://docs.wto.org/dol2fe/Pages/SS/directdoc.aspx?filename=q:/WT/MIN22/30.pdf&Open=True. There is however no direct mention of work or workers in the document.

216 Rachel Brewster, 'WTO Dispute Settlement: Can We Go Back Again?' (2019) 113 *American Journal of International Law* 61, 61–2; and Joost Pauwelyn, 'WTO Dispute Settlement Post 2019: What to Expect?' (2019) 22(3) *Journal of International Economic Law* 297; both of whom discuss the current threat to the DSU by virtue of US obstruction of Appellate Body appointments from 2016 onwards. Regarding the latter, also see Joshua Paine, 'The WTO's Dispute Settlement Body as a Voice Mechanism' (2019) 20(6) *The Journal of World Investment and Trade* 820. For a full account, David Palmeter, Petros C. Mavroidis and Niall Meagher, *Dispute Settlement in the World Trade Organization*, 3rd ed. (Cambridge University Press 2022).

217 See regarding the forms of surveillance established by the TPRM, Petros C. Mavroidis, 'Surveillance Schemes: The GATT's New Trade Policy Review Mechanism' (1991) 13 *Michigan Journal of International Law* 374; and Mathias Kende, *The Trade Policy Review Mechanism: A Critical Analysis* (Oxford University Press 2018).

Agreements, which bind only those countries which consent to them individually, including the Government Procurement Agreement.[218]

The agreements, understandings and decisions in all these annexures are also supplemented by numerous other texts as agreed through the larger WTO apparatus and that established under, for example, the GATT, GATS and TRIPS. Continuous negotiations are envisaged as part of expansion of international trade, gradually not only lowering tariffs but removing 'non-tariff barriers' to access.[219] The process of bargaining has taken place through a variety of scheduled 'rounds', with the Uruguay Round being the last successfully completed with the adoption of the Marrakesh Agreement. The Doha Round, which was to focus on SDT and sustainable development, was never fully concluded, although some further significant instruments have since been adopted as a result.[220] Plurilateral negotiations now continue in the form of 'Joint Initiatives'[221] and commitment of more than 50 members to pursue 'Trade and Environmental Sustainability Structured Discussions' (TESSD) alongside the existing work of the Committee on Trade and Environment, reflecting the aspirations of the 2021 ministerial statement.[222] At present these discussions take place without apparent reference to ILO Just Transitions guidelines or active engagement with those in the world of work.

It will be apparent that there is an enormous volume of material informing the appropriate conduct of trade originating now under the WTO, which can

---

[218] For arguments now to extend the range of plurilateral agreements under Annex 4 as a WTO model (and an alternative to preferential or so-called 'free' trade agreements), see Bernard M. Hoekman and Petros C. Mavroidis. 'WTO "à la carte" or "menu du jour"? Assessing the Case for More Plurilateral Agreements' (2015) 26(2) *European Journal of International Law* 319; and Bernard Hoekman and Charles Sabel, 'Open Plurilateral Agreements, International Regulatory Cooperation and the WTO' (2019) 10(3) *Global Policy* 297.

[219] For example, Andrew Lang, *World Trade Law after Neoliberalism: Re-imagining the Global Economic Order* (Oxford University Press 2011) charts the extension in reach of the GATT and then the WTO.

[220] Documentation available at: www.wto.org/english/tratop_e/dda_e/dda_e.htm. For a critical view of the failure of the 'Doha Development Round' as symptomatic of 'the North's disregard of the Global South', see Aoife O'Donoghue and Ntina Tzouvala, 'TTIP: The Rise of the "Mega-market" Trade Agreements and Its Potential Implications for the Global South' (2016) 8(2) *Trade Law and Development* 30, 46. For a perhaps more optimistic view, see Destaw A. Yigzaw, 'On the Obituary of the Doha Round: A Path for Reinventing the WTO's Future' (2021) 22 *Estey Journal of International Law and Trade Policy* 31.

[221] For e.g. the proposed Investment Facilitation Agreement for Development; see https://www.wto.org/english/news_e/news23_e/infac_06jul23_e.htm. For a call to return to multilateral engagement, see Alan W. Wolff, *Getting Back to the Negotiating Table* (Peterson Institute for International Economics Working Paper 2022).

[222] See www.wto.org/english/tratop_e/tessd_e/tessd_e.htm.

pose problems for transparency and even access by those so-called developing countries in the Global South seeking to decipher the source and scale of their obligations as WTO Members and to utilise options open to them. In recognition of these difficulties, in 2014 the WTO Trade Facilitation Agreement Facility (TFAF) was created to offer assistance.[223] Other SDT allowances made for countries in the Global South include textual exceptions and timing of implementation, yet these are widely condemned as partial, limited and problematic.[224]

The principle of SDT has developed from its origins in the GATT. For example, since 1955 Article XVIII of the GATT has enabled developing countries to take measures to shield infant industries and respond to balance of payments (BoP) crises.[225] However, concerns have been raised regarding technicalities associated with the qualifications required for exemption under these provisions, as well as the required negotiation of compensation for other affected states (even those with a higher income). It is also apparent that IMF evidence as to whether there is a genuine BoP crisis or whether a change in policy could avert this can be regarded by the Appellate Body as persuasive.[226] Part IV of the GATT adopted in 1965 introduced a principle of non-reciprocity regarding concessions made to developing countries, apparently recognising the innate disadvantages experienced by states and the connections between trade and development.[227] Other dispensations have included the limited

---

[223] Further information regarding the origins and operations of the TFA is available at: https://www.tfafacility.org/facility.

[224] See Asoke Mukerji, 'Developing Countries and the WTO; Issues of Implementation' (2000) 34(6) *Journal of World Trade* 33; Lorand Bartels, 'WTO Reform Proposals: Implications for Developing Countries' in Teddy Subramanien, Brendan Vickers and Hilary Enos-Edu (eds), *WTO Reform: Reshaping Global Trade Governance for 21st Century Challenges* (The Commonwealth 2019).

[225] T. Ademola Oyejide, 'Development Dimensions in Multilateral Trade Negotiations' in M. Moore (ed.), *Doha and Beyond: The Future of the Multicultural Trading System* (Cambridge University Press 2004), ch 5, at 79; and Ezeani n.200, 26–33.

[226] *India—Quantitative Restrictions on Imports of Agricultural, Textile and Industrial Products* Appellate Body Report and Panel Report WT/DS90/14, 13 October 1999. For comment, see Chantal Thomas, 'Balance-of-Payments Crises in the Developing World: Balancing Trade, Finance and Development in the New Economic Order' (2000) 15(6) *American University International Law Review* 1249.

[227] See Ewelukwa n.198, 847: 'although Part IV asserted the principle of non-reciprocity, the exact meaning of the term was never too clear.' Cf. Ezeani n.200, 34–5 outlining the outcomes of certain disputes regarding compliance with Part IV, concluding that: 'Disputes brought under these provisions have not seen strenuous application thereof.'

application of 'safeguard' provisions to developing countries.[228] Nevertheless, commentators observe that there has since been a shift from making concrete exceptions for developing and least developed countries to merely providing them with more time to comply with WTO prescriptions.[229] Arguably more progress has been made regarding the evolving implementation of the least developed countries (LDC) services waiver, which enables preferential treatment to services and service suppliers from LDC WTO members; although, again, this initiative which was undertaken in 2013 is still the subject of continuing discussion and debate to enable its realisation.[230] In this sense, the aspirations of SDG 10 (regarding equality not only within but between states)[231] are present, but have yet to be fully realised within the WTO context.

There have been longstanding arguments made, particularly by Ernst-Ulrich Petersmann, that the WTO constitution could be further elaborated, for example by a WTO Declaration 'that all WTO members are committed to respect for universal human rights within the confines of WTO law and policy [...] and welcome the contribution of trade policy to the fulfilment of human rights'.[232] This recommendation might seem a way to include at least those labour standards recognised as human rights, whether under UN instruments or at the ILO, into the regulatory matrix of the WTO. However, this may not have been Petersmann's intention.

Petersmann has been identified in a recent historical study of 'the Globalists' as one of a trio of experts explicitly applying neoliberalism to the international economic order;[233] he has himself endorsed this vision of the WTO

---

[228] See Article XIX of the GATT and other examples of SDT provisions listed by the WTO at: www.wto.org/english/tratop_e/devel_e/teccop_e/s_and_d_eg_e.htm.

[229] Ewelukwa n.198, 833–4; and for an argument for SDT as delay (to ensure longer-term reciprocity of commitments) see Paola Conconi and Carlo Perroni, 'Special and Differential Treatment of Developing Countries in the WTO' (2015) 14 *World Trade Review* 67.

[230] For an outline of recent developments, see: www.wto.org/english/tratop_e/serv_e/ldc_mods_negs_e.htm. For the benefits that the LDC services waiver could bring see Sèna Kimm Gnangnon, *The Least Developed Countries' Services Waiver and the Stability of Least Developed Countries' Services Exports* (ECONSTOR Working Paper 2022) available at: www.econstor.eu/bitstream/10419/260587/1/Paper%20LDC%20Services%20Waiver-Export%20Volatility.pdf.

[231] See in this book Chapter 1, text accompanying n.118 et seq.

[232] Ernst-Ulrich Petersmann, 'The "Human Rights Approach" Advocated by the UN High Commissioner for Human Rights and by the International Labour Organization: Is It Relevant for WTO Law and Policy' (2004) 7 *Journal of International Economic Law* 605, 626.

[233] Slobodian n.3, 223 and 278; although for criticism of Slobodian's representation of Petersmann's influence, see Anne Orford, *International Law and the Politics of History* (Cambridge University Press 2021), 277–81.

as 'a crowning victory of the neo-liberal project'.[234] Petersmann's advocacy of 'constitutionalisation' of the WTO legal order seemed heavily biased towards recognising property rights and freedom of contract as constitutive of human rights, neither of which seem likely to operate as a foundation which might secure protection of workers' interests. Philip Alston responded to Petersmann's proposals by resisting what he described as the 'merger and acquisition' of human rights by economic objectives.[235] This objection was the forerunner of (and is comparable to) the concerns expressed by Ebert relating to of 'appropriation' of ILO labour standards to application within a World Bank 'institutional logic' and 'market constraints'.[236]

More compelling may be Petersmann's proposals for enhanced democratic participation in setting WTO objectives, on the basis that '[c]itizen participation in consultative WTO bodies and other multi-levelled international governance could strengthen the legitimacy and political support for the world trading system'.[237] However, at no time did he suggest that dedicated representatives of labour be given a meaningful role in decision-making, as they have been at the ILO. Nor have either of his bold proposals been adopted at the WTO.[238]

Henner Gött has argued that, even though the Marrakesh Agreement does not recognise labour standards and the Singapore 1996 Ministerial Declaration refused to contemplate a global 'social clause' for trade,

> even this explicit rejection had at least an indirect impact on labour governance, as it reinvigorated the ILO's work on core labour standards which resulted in the 1998 ILO Declaration on Fundamental Principles and Rights at Work. Moreover, it gave a boost to several important WTO members' efforts to include labour standards in bilateral and regional trade agreements.[239]

Those free trade agreements (FTAs) are the subject of Chapter 5 of this book.

The remainder of this chapter considers what the application of formal trade rules under GATT and GATS within the larger WTO framework has done for international labour standards, having set the parameters for what is regarded as fair competition and impacting on the ways in which work (or services) is costed and hired. It is argued that, despite the apparent collective decision to leave some scope for active defence of labour standards, this has been done

---

[234] See Orford n.233, citing Petersmann, 23 and 25.

[235] Philip Alston, 'Resisting the Merger and Acquisition of Human Rights by Trade Law: A Reply to Petersmann' (2002) 13 *European Journal of International Law* 815.

[236] See Ebert n.163 above.

[237] Ernst-Ulrich Petersmann, 'The WTO Constitution and Human Rights' (2000) 3(1) *Journal of International Economic Law* 19, 25; cited in Slobodian n.3, 280.

[238] Cf. Orford, n.233, at 281.

[239] Gött n.117, 79.

in a way which is highly discretionary. That discretion can, in reality, usually only be wielded by states with economic power, and therefore creates an ongoing imbalance between the Global North and Global South, with arguably increasing fracturing of interests and benefits for different so-called emerging economies.[240] Moreover, the lack of trade union and other civil society influence within WTO decision-making means that labour concerns have barely been heard and even environmental groups have struggled to be heard within the amicus curiae system in WTO dispute settlement. The result is, therefore, probably less promising than Gött has suggested.

3.2 The Rules Established by GATT and GATS and Their Impact on Labour

From the time of its provisional application in 1948 the GATT set the terms for trade in goods across national borders, establishing broad principles of non-discrimination, access and fair competition for those states who were members of the 'club' that then consisted of the 'Contracting Parties' of the GATT. Those same rules now apply across the entire membership of the WTO. Most fundamental are the 'most favoured nation' (MFN) principle (established under Article I of the GATT) which requires that the same tariff preferences and rights of access extended to one member be extended to all members, and national treatment (set out in Article III of the GATT), which ensures that there is no permissible discrimination after the goods enter national markets in terms of, for example, additional taxes on sale for foreign goods originating in another member state. Quantitative restrictions are also barred subject to certain limited exceptions (under Article XI of the GATT). Provision is made for 'special and differential treatment' in relation to developing countries (such as Article XVIII and Part IV of the GATT),[241] but also environmental and social purposes (including measures relating to 'prison labour') under Article XX of the GATT.[242] Scope for particular preferential tariff measures regarding

240 Cf. Clara Weinhardt and Till Schöfer, 'Differential Treatment for Developing Countries in the WTO: The Unmaking of the North–South Distinction in a Multipolar World' (2022) 43(1) *Third World Quarterly* 74; for comparable concerns raised some years previously, see Jagdish Bhagwati, *Termites in the Trading System: How Preferential Agreements Undermine Free Trade* (Oxford University Press 2008).

241 Ewelukwa n.198 above; also for useful background, Maria Jobim, 'Drawing on the Legal and Economic Arguments in Favour and Against "Reciprocity" and "Special and Differential Treatment" for Developing Countries within the WTO System' (2013) 6(3) *Journal of Politics and Law* 55.

242 Although these have yet to be applied outside the environmental sphere, as discussed in this chapter below. See also Robert Howse, 'Back to Court After Shrimp/Turtle? Almost But Not Quite Yet: India's Short Lived Challenge to Labor

developing and 'least developed' countries was further introduced under the 'Enabling Clause' appended to the GATT, the application of which has in practice been made conditional on compliance with certain labour standards.[243]

As noted above, the entire regulatory culture of the GATT and subsequently the WTO is based on rounds of negotiations in which members secure new or enhanced agreements normally to be applied to all members, or make concessions in schedules to, for example, gradually lower tariffs under the GATT or enhance market access to services under GATS. The aim is to lower the price of goods and widen accessibility of services on world markets, which could thereby mean that workers purchase more with their income.

The GATT does not require that a tariff be set by a member at any specific level, but rather establishes a mechanism whereby tariffs can be listed and then a country can 'bind' these so that all other members (in line with the MFN principle) can engage in trade with that country aware of the level of tariffs to be charged at the border.[244] The freedom to bind the level of one's own tariffs as a country enables flexibility according to the needs of the state in question. As such, the GATT regime may seem to be more concerned with consistency of application together with information transparency, rather than coercion. While the GATT (and the WTO) are ostensibly concerned only with the relationship between states, employers as producers can and will benefit from access to this information in terms of planning their budget, including employment costs.[245] The GATT rules are however also formalistic, subject to narrow exceptions, such as the SDT provisions outlined above, limiting opportunities for exceptions to ensure intra-generational distributional justice (under SDG 10, as discussed in Chapters 1 and 2 of this book). Issues relating to labour only arise expressly in relation to specific exceptions outlined below.

GATS follows a similar model. The MFN principle is outlined with respect to trade in services in Article II. Under paragraph (1), 'each Member shall accord immediately and unconditionally to services and service suppliers of any other Member treatment no less favourable than that it accords to like services and service suppliers of any other country'. Transparency is also

---

and Environmental Exceptions in the European Union's Generalized System of Preferences' (2003) 18 *American University International Law Review* 1333.

243 Olivier De Schutter, *Trade in the Service of Sustainable Development: Linking Trade to Labour Rights and Environmental Standards* (Bloomsbury/Hart 2015) ch 4; and Kofi Addo, *Core Labour Standards and International Trade: Lessons from the Regional Context* (Springer 2015) ch 5.

244 Wolfe n.211, 19.

245 Discussed in Clair Gammage and Tonia Novitz, 'Trade, Investment and Corporate Sustainability' in Beate Sjåfjell and Christopher M. Bruner (eds), *Cambridge Handbook of Corporate Law, Corporate Governance and Sustainability* (Cambridge University Press 2019).

required under Article III. However, the specificities of trade in services are also acknowledged.

Article I(2) of GATS defines 'trade in services' as the supply of a service:

> (a) from the territory of one Member into the territory of any other Member; (b) in the territory of one Member to the service consumer of any other Member; (c) by a service supplier of one Member, through commercial presence in the territory of any other Member; (d) by a service supplier of one Member, through presence of natural persons of a Member in the territory of any other Member.

These have come to be known as the 'four modes' of trade in services. Arguably, of most significance to labour are mode 3 relating to the 'commercial presence', or in other words local investment, that enables supply of services,[246] and mode 4, which entails temporary presence of 'a natural person' who may be an employee of or otherwise performing work for the 'service provider', or who can be the 'service provider' themselves if in business on their own account.[247]

The GATS Schedule of Specific Commitments enables member states to list their sector-based commitments, which are linked with 'market access' under Article XVI and 'national treatment' (or non-discrimination) under Article XVII. Commitments made on a sectoral basis are binding unless a state opts to be 'unbound', which enables that member to be free to 'introduce or maintain measures inconsistent with market access or national treatment'.[248] If bound, then the rights and privileges afforded to service providers from one member state must be extended to all the other members under the MFN rule. This leads states to be cautious in their commitments.[249] Exceptions again remain possible, for example in respect of certain 'safeguards' of vulnerable sectors.[250]

---

246 Dan Sarooshi, 'Investment Treaty Arbitration and the World Trade Organization: What Role for Systemic Values in the Resolution of International Economic Disputes?' (2014) 49 *Texas International Law Journal* 445.

247 Tonia Novitz, 'Evolutionary Trajectories for Transnational Labour Law: Trade in Goods to Trade in Services?' (2014) 67 *Current Legal Problems* 239, 245–6.

248 WTO, 'Guide to Reading the GATS Schedules of Specific Commitments and the List of Article II (MFN) Exemptions' available at: www.wto.org/english/tratop_e/serv_e/guide1_e.htm.

249 For example commitments under GATS mode 4 are commonly limited to 'professionals, managers and highly skilled workers', while so-called lower-skilled workers tend to be supplied through 'guest worker programmes'. Philip L. Martin, *GATS, Migration and Labour Standards* DP/165/2006 (ILO 2006), 14 available at: https://documents.pub/document/gats-migration-and-labor-migration-and-labor-standards-philip-l-martin-international.html?page=1.

250 All countries may rely on Art. X (Emergency Safeguard Measures) and Art. XXII (Restrictions to Safeguard the Balance of Payments) where domestic service

GATS mode 4 is governed in addition by an 'Annex on the Movement of Natural Persons Supplying Services under the Agreement'. This applies to both those people who are themselves 'service suppliers' (presumably in business on their own account) and also to 'natural persons of a member who are employed by a service supplier of a member' (paragraph 1). The Annex states that GATS does not cover measures relating to 'natural persons seeking access to the employment market of a Member', nor does it apply to 'measures regarding citizenship, residence or employment on a permanent basis' (paragraph 2). Instead, the terms of commitment relating to movement are governed by the GATS Schedule in relation to sectors and services affected. Mode 4 receives many fewer commitments than other modes of service contemplated in Article 1 of GATS[251] and has been estimated as constituting less than 5 per cent of global trade in services, although that volume has undoubtedly increased since then.[252]

It remains for each state still to determine its own immigration policies and manage its own borders. Under GATS mode 4, a state can apply immigration 'measures to regulate the entry of natural persons into, or their temporary stay in, its territory' – provided that 'such measures are not applied in such a manner as to nullify or impair the benefits accruing to any Member under the terms of a specific commitment'.[253] As I have argued elsewhere, in GATS mode 4 the WTO has introduced a regime akin to that operating in the European Union (EU) for posted workers,[254] but without the removal of immigration requirements or the imposition of minimum labour standards and other commitments which operate in the EU to protect this vulnerable group of temporary migrants. GATS seems to leave the length of any visa to the discretion of the host state and, unlike the EU posting of workers scheme as now amended, has no obvious time limit. Given the incidence of vulnerability and evidence of exploitation under the EU posting regime,[255] which the EU polit-

---

sectors are unexpectedly likely to come under threat from foreign service providers; cf. Articles XVIII and XIX of the GATT.

[251] Caf Dowlah, 'Mode 4 of WTO's General Agreement on Trade in Services: Can It Spur Cross-Border Labor Mobility from Developing Countries' (2012) 5 *Law & Development Review* 56, 58; and OECD Policy Brief, *Service Providers on the Move* (OECD 2003), 2.

[252] Pradip Bhatnagar, *GATS Mode 4: Movement of Natural Persons and Protection of Migrant Workers' Rights* (ILO 2014), 23.

[253] Annex on Movement of Natural Persons Supplying Services under the Agreement, Art 4.

[254] See Novitz n.247; see Directive 96/71 concerning the posting of workers in the framework of the provision of services [1997] OJ L18/1.

[255] EU Commission, 'Proposal to amend the Posted Workers Directive' COM(2016)128 final; and EU Commission, 'Staff Working Document, Impact

ical institutions have since taken measures to address,[256] it does seem curious that so little has been contemplated at the WTO.[257]

Under conflict of law rules, the temporarily sent workers may remain governed by the laws of their country of origin, relieving employers of the need to meet the usually higher costs these would entail in the host country, particularly in relation to social security. There is clear scope here to take jobs from host state workers, or undercut their wages as well as other terms and conditions, thereby reducing wages and the price of labour more generally in the country – or, in other words, to engage in 'social dumping'.[258] Arguably, GATS mode 4 workers should still be subject to host state jurisdiction in relation to *jus cogens*, such as slavery or child labour, but this has yet to be tested.[259]

Notably, the WTO and its members do not demand compliance with the terms of ILO Conventions Nos 97 and 143, which set out a general principle of 'equality' of treatment of home and migrant workers. The WTO stance is perhaps consistent with exceptions made in Article 11 of ILO Convention No 143 for

> employees of organisations or undertakings operating within the territory of a country who have been admitted temporarily to that country at the request of their employer to undertake specific duties or assignments, for a limited and defined period of time, and who are required to leave that country on the completion of their duties or assignments.[260]

Assessment, Strasbourg, 8.3.2016' SWD(2016)52final; discussed in Tonia Novitz and Rutvica Andrijasevic, 'Reform of the Posting of Workers Regime – An Assessment of the Practical Impact on Unfree Labour Relations' (2020) 58(5) *Journal of Common Market Studies* 1325.

256 Directive 2014/67 on the enforcement of the Posting of Workers Directive [2014] OJ L 159/ 11; and Directive 2018/957 amending the Posting of Workers Directive [2018] OJ L 173/16.

257 See Tonia Novitz, 'Trading in Services: Commodities and Beneficiaries' in Adelle Blackett and Anne Trebilcock (eds), *Research Handbook on Transnational Labour Law* (Edward Elgar Publishing 2015).

258 Magdalena Bernaciak, 'Social Dumping? Political Catchphrase or Threat to Labour Standards' (2016) ETUI Working Paper 2012/06, 26.

259 For discussion see Jessie Williams, 'Low Skill Temporary Migration in New Zealand: Labour market and human rights law as a framework for managing future migration' (VUW Working Paper 2009) available at: http:// hdl .handle .net/ 10063/ 2576; and Marion Panizzon, 'Temporary Movement of Workers and Human Rights Protection: Interfacing the Mode 4 of GATS with Non-Trade Bilateral Migration Agreements' (2010) 104 *Am. Soc'y Int'l L. Proc.* 131.

260 ILO Migration for Employment Convention (Revised), 1949 (No. 97); and Migrant Workers (Supplementary Provisions) Convention, 1975 (No. 143), analysed at length in Judy Fudge, 'Precarious Migrant Status and Precarious Employment: The

However, the potential injustice of the situation is manifest.

GATS facilitates expansion of markets for services for countries in the Global North, enabling investment accompanying extended service provision in mode 3, but also the importation of labour to deliver services. Notably, this can be via importation of skilled labour from the Global North, but also can involve redeployment of cheaper labour from MNE subsidiaries or temporary employment agencies in other emerging or developing countries in the Global South, often into the 'export processing zones' discussed in Chapter 2.[261] Given that GATS mode 4 movement could obstruct local training and access to skilled work, it has been argued that scheduled commitments should include provision for local training programmes, which they sometimes do.[262] An interest in securing training and remittances can also lead to skilled workers from the Global South taking advantage of recruitment opportunities in the Global North in the limited circumstances established through GATS mode 4 commitments. This can lead to the beneficial acquisition of valuable experience which can be brought home again to inform, for example, computer science or engineering, but there are also risks that this kind of movement can lead to labour shortages, such as the crises in health care already evident in African and Asian states,[263] made more problematic by the pandemic.[264] Low-skilled workers are not usually included in GATS schedule commitments, with their

---

Paradox of International Rights for Migrant Workers' (2012–13) 34 *Comparative Labor Law and Policy Journal* 95.

[261] See Chapter 2 of this book, text accompanying n.66 et seq. See also Jennifer Gordon, 'In the Zone: Work at the Intersection of Trade and Migration' (2022) 23(2) *Theoretical Inquiries in Law* 147; and Tonia Novitz, 'Supply Chains and Temporary Migrant Labour: The Relevance of Trade and Sustainability Frameworks' in Diamond Ashiagbor (ed.), *Re-imagining Labour Law for Development* (Hart 2019), 196.

[262] Marion Panizzon, Trade and Labor Migration: GATS Mode 4 And Migration Agreements (Friedrich-Ebert-Stiftung 2010), 26; available at: http://library.fes.de/pdf-files/iez/global/06955.pdf. Doing so would arguably be consistent with the UN Global Compact for Safe, Orderly and Regular Migration: Intergovernmentally Negotiated and Agreed Outcome, Morocco, 13 July 2018, objective 18, which encourages investment in 'skills development'.

[263] Martin n.249, 11–13; see also Churnrurtai Kanchanachitra et al., 'Human Resources for Health in Southeast Asia: Shortages, Distributional Challenges and International Trade in Health Services' (2011) 377 *The Lancet* 769; Johannes J. Fagan et al, 'COVID-19 Exposes Health Worker Shortages in the USA and UK, but Nationalism and Self-interest must not Exploit Medical Workforces from Low- and Middle-income Countries' (2020) 110(5) *South African Medical Journal* 335.

[264] See Panizzon n.262; Jane Kelsey, *Serving Whose Interests? The Political Economy of Trade in Services Agreements* (Routledge 2008), 200–6; and Laura Ritchie Dawson, 'Labour Mobility and the WTO: The Limits of GATS Mode 4' (2012) 51(1) *Labour Migration* 1, 13.

movement generally determined by ad hoc guest worker programmes.[265] This may be explained, at least in part, by the narrow scope of what are regarded as 'service sector occupations', such that agricultural work, for example, is not considered covered.[266] GATS mode 4 can also enable 'South–South' movement of natural persons, but even in these scenarios there may be a significant imbalance of power between countries, with some of the same issues arising.[267] The political and economic realities have, as yet, had no impact on the design of the formal trade rules set out in GATS.

There has been a more recent plea from Pierre Sauvé to liberate mode 4 trade 'from its current services shackle and allow the multilateral community to think harder about the pros and cons of a stand-alone and generic set of disciplines on trade-related labor movement divorced from the goods and services divide'.[268] This would be helpful, but that kind of political debate does not seem to be on the horizon. Instead, issues relating to labour are currently addressed only in relation to the discretion allowed to states under the 'General Exceptions' clause set out in Article XX of the GATT and Article XIV of GATS, and under the generalised systems (or schemes) of preferences established under the Enabling Clause, which merit careful and detailed consideration.

3.3 State Discretion regarding Labour Standards Conditionality and Promotion of Sustainable Development under 'General Exceptions' and the 'Enabling Clause'

While the WTO has fiercely resisted proposals from the EU and US to introduce forms of labour conditionality, there has been explicit recognition of the capacity of members to take unilateral measures to do so, albeit in certain

---

[265] See Martin n.249, 14; for examples of agricultural guest work programmes, see Manoj Dias-Abey, 'Justice on Our Fields: Can "Alt-Labor" Organizations Improve Migrant Farm Workers' Conditions?' (2018) 53 *Harvard Civil Rights-Civil Liberties Law Review* 167; and Joanna Howe, Stephen Clibborn, Alexander Reilly, Diane van den Broek and Chris F. Wright, *Towards a Durable Future: Tackling Labour Challenges in the Australian Horticulture Industry* (University of Adelaide 2019).

[266] Bhatnagar n.252 above; and OECD Policy Brief 'Service Providers on the Move' (OECD 2003).

[267] OECD n.266, 2. See J.B. Cronjé, *Innovating for Temporary Movement of Natural Persons in Africa: Leveraging the CFTA* (Tralec 2017), 10; available at: www.cuts-geneva.org/pdf/TAF087_CFTA-temporary_movement_natural_persons.pdf.

[268] Pierre Sauvé, 'To Fuse, Not to Fuse, or Simply Confuse? Assessing the Case for Normative Convergence Between Goods and Services Trade Law' (2019) 22(3) *Journal of International Economic Law* 355, 367.

limited circumstances.[269] The first and most notable example of this potential for exercise of discretion is Article XX of the GATT, which incorporates a political agreement reached in the Havana Charter (set out there in Article 45) to enable contracting parties to breach GATT obligations where these come within a particular list of acceptable aims (including environmental and labour objectives), subject to the criteria set out in the 'chapeau' regarding terms of fair competition. A comparable provision is to be found in Article XIV of GATS. We shall investigate the parameters of that permission here regarding protection of labour standards.

The second way in which labour conditionality is permitted is via the Enabling Clause appended to the GATT, which enables tariff preferences to be granted to developing and least developed countries on generalised and transparent terms. This is the basis, for example, of the 2012 Regulation governing the EU Generalised Scheme of Preferences, including the (GSP+) special incentive arrangements concerning sustainable development and good governance.[270] At the time of writing, the Commission has adopted a legislative proposal for the GSP system to continue to apply from the end of 2023.[271]

3.3.1 'General Exceptions' and unilateral state action

Article XX of the GATT set out 'General Exceptions' enabling 'adoption or enforcement' of measures for a listed set of purposes, subject to the 'chapeau' requirements that 'such measures are not applied in a manner which would constitute a means of arbitrary or unjustifiable discrimination between countries where the same conditions prevail, or a disguised restriction on international trade'. Article XIV of GATS contains a clause beginning with an identical

---

269 See Sandra Polaski, 'The Strategy and Politics of Linking Trade and Labor Standards: An Overview of Issues and Approaches' in Kimberly A. Elliott (ed.), *Handbook on Globalisation and Labour Standards* (Edward Elgar Publishing 2022), 204–8.

270 Regulation (EU) No 978/2012 of the European Parliament and of the Council of 25 October 2012 applying a scheme of generalised tariff preferences and repealing Council Regulation (EC) No 732/2008 OJ L 303/1 31.10.2012. See Preamble, recitals 4 and 11.

271 Proposal for a Regulation of the European Parliament and of the Council on applying a generalised scheme of tariff preferences and repealing Regulation (EU) No 978/2012 of the European Parliament and of the Council COM/2021/579 final 22.9.2021. The European Parliament has now adopted a position on the new Regulation, but at the time of writing discussions at the Council are still continuing. See the 'legislative train schedule' available at: www.europarl.europa.eu/legislative-train/theme-an-economy-that-works-for-people/file-new-gsp-regulation. If the negotiations are not completed in time, the Commission has proposed adoption of legislation extending the status quo until 31 December 2027. See COM(2023) 426 final.

introductory chapeau, but sets out a shorter list of permissible aims, arguably reflecting the more specific objectives and mechanics of trade in services.

The two clauses have in common the ability to take measures '(a) necessary to protect public morals' and '(b) necessary to protect human, animal or plant life or health'. While Article XX(d) of the GATT contemplates measures 'necessary to secure compliance with laws or regulations which are not inconsistent with the provisions of this Agreement', including for example 'the prevention of deceptive practices', Article XIV(c) of GATS contemplates measures

> necessary to secure compliance with laws or regulations which are not inconsistent with the provisions of this Agreement including those relating to: (i) the prevention of deceptive and fraudulent practices or to deal with the effects of a default on services contracts; (ii) the protection of the privacy of individuals in relation to the processing and dissemination of personal data and the protection of confidentiality of individual records and accounts; (iii) safety.

To this extent, it seems that measures consistent with the WTO SPS Agreement (in Annex B to the Marrakesh Agreement discussed above) would be permitted.[272] State action 'necessary' to protection of health and safety of those at work will be permitted under both the GATT and GATS. What is omitted from GATS is the provision in Article XX(e) of the GATT relating to 'the products of prison labour', presumably because GATS is only concerned with delivery of services and not products. However, it is perhaps worrying that the issue of hiring and subcontracting services of prison labour across borders is not addressed at all.[273] There does remain the possibility that any breach of internationally recognised fundamental labour standards could still be addressed

---

[272] See Article 2 of the SPS Agreement which also contemplates that: The WTO Agreement on Sanitary and Phytosanitary Measures provides that 'no Member should be prevented from adopting or enforcing measures necessary to protect human, animal or plant life or health' provided that the adoption of such measures 'is only to the extent necessary' to pursue the legitimate objective and is not applied in a manner that constitutes a 'disguised restriction on international trade'.

[273] As briefly acknowledged in Panagiotis Delimatsis and Léo Gargne, *General Exceptions under the GATS – A Legal Commentary on Article XIV GATS* (TILEC Discussion Paper 2020), para. 17. See, for broader concern regarding commercial use of prison labour, Adelle Blackett and Alice Duquesnoy, 'Slavery Is Not a Metaphor: US Prison Labor and Racial Subordination through the Lens of the ILO's Abolition of Forced Labor Convention' (2021) 67 *UCLA Law Review* 1504; Colin Fenwick, 'Private Use of Prisoners' Labour: Paradoxes of International Human Rights Law' (2005) 27(1) *Human Rights Quarterly* 249; and Faina Milman-Sivan and Yair Sagy, 'On the International Labour Organisation and Prison Labour: An Invitation for Recalculation' (2020) 159(4) *International Labour Review* 505.

through reliance on the 'public morals' exception,[274] although that assumes that any objection to 'extra-territoriality' can be overcome.[275]

Few cases have been raised or defended under Article XIV of GATS, but it was established from the outset that the same tests apply as for Article XX.[276] In the first Appellate Body determination under Article XIV(a) of GATS concerning the 'public morals' exception (akin to Article XX(a) of the GATT), the *US Gambling* case,[277] it was found that the US was entitled to restrict online supply of gambling services on the basis of 'prevailing social, cultural, ethical and religious values'. This would seem to be a very broad exception.[278] However, as those controls were not placed on US home-based internet gambling facilities, the measure failed to pass the test in the chapeau and amounted to a discriminatory disguised restriction on trade. This is indicative of the standard two-stage test which has been applied in dispute settlement: first, whether the defence comes with the list of permissible aims and second, whether the requirements of the chapeau are satisfied.

The *EC—Seal Products* case concerned the scope of the equivalent public morals exception under Article XX(a) of the GATT.[279] This was how the European Community (subsequently EU) sought to defend measures banning the importation and marketing in the EU of all seal products, with three narrowly defined exceptions: (1) those resulting from traditional hunting by Inuit and indigenous communities; (2) products derived from culls carried out for marine management purposes on a not-for-profit basis; and (3) those brought into the EU by travellers for their personal use.[280] This was then less a concern regarding the morality of the product in question, but rather the

---

[274] International Lawyers Assisting Workers (ILAW) Network, *WTO Law Aspects of Import Prohibitions on Products and Services Made using Forced Labour* (ILAW 2022), 14.

[275] See this chapter below, text accompanying n.293 et seq.

[276] Delimatsis and Gargne n.273 above, paras 7 and 8.

[277] *United States—Measures Affecting the Cross-Border Supply of Betting and Gambling Services* WT/DS285/AB/R (20 April 2005).

[278] See Robert Howse, 'The WTO and the Protection of Workers' Rights' (1999) 3 *Journal of Small and Emerging Business Law* 131; and Jenny Schultz and Rachel Ball, 'Trade as a Weapon? The WTO and Human Rights-Based Trade Measures' (2007) 12 *Deakin Law Review* 41, 61.

[279] *European Communities: Measures Prohibiting the Importation and Marketing of Seal Products* (*EC—Seal Products* case) – *Reports of the Appellate Body* WT/DS400/AB/R and WT/DS401/AB/R (22 May 2014).

[280] See for criticism Petros C. Mavroidis, 'Sealed with a Doubt: EU, Seals, and the WTO' (2015) 6 *European Journal of Risk Regulation* 388; also J. Ife Ogbonna, 'Protecting Human Rights as Public Morals under the General Agreement on Tariffs and Trade (GATT) 1994: A Review of EC—Seal Products' (2014) 3 *International Human Rights Law Review* 97.

process by which it was made and came to the EU. There was a preference here for protection of indigenous traditions, arguably consistent with respect for the working lives (broadly understood) in ILO Indigenous and Tribal Populations Convention, 1957 (No. 107); and ILO Indigenous and Tribal Peoples Convention, 1989 (No. 169). That approach would also seem to chime with the 2007 UN Declaration on the Rights of Indigenous Peoples (UNDRIP).[281] However, a distinction was made regarding indigenous communities' actions which had commercial benefits, so that Canadian Inuit seal products were not protected, while those deriving from subsistence hunts in Greenland were; to this was added a 'partial use' requirement, namely that to be exempt from the ban the seal products must be 'at least partly used, consumed or processed within the communities according to their traditions'.[282] These subsistence and partial use requirements pose an interesting question relating to whether a 'profit motive' can be seen as morally objectionable in relation to the treatment of animals, when other uses are acceptable.

The Appellate Body found that, while the EU ban was potentially justifiable under the 'public morals' exception relating to treatment of animals,[283] this distinction was indefensible under the chapeau, constituting 'arbitrary or unjustifiable discrimination between countries'.[284] First, the Appellate Body could not see logically how the absence of a commercial motive was relevant to the welfare of seals;[285] with respect, this is the weakest part of the judgment, which fails to acknowledge the importance of indigenous culture. Second, the Appellate Body found potential for exploitation of uncertainty as to what the term 'subsistence' and 'partial use' might mean, while also noting that insufficient administrative assistance was given to facilitate access to the scheme's exceptions for Inuit and other indigenous peoples across the world.[286]

To succeed in a defence under paragraphs (a) and (b) of Article XX of the GATT and Article XIV of GATS, it is evident that the test of 'necessity' must be met. As the *EC—Seal Products* case would seem to demonstrate, this is not perhaps as stringent a requirement as it might be. It has been acknowledged by the Appellate Body that there may be a range of degrees of 'necessity', such that the reasonable availability of alternatives can be considered along

281 See discussion of indigenous and peoples' rights in Chapter 2 of this book, text accompanying n.99 et seq.

282 *EC—Seal Products* case n.279, outlined at paras 5.324–5.326.

283 Ibid, paras 5.289–5.290.

284 Ibid, para. 5.291 et seq.

285 Ibid, para. 5.338.

286 Ibid.

a continuum.[287] Moreover, this would seem to be assessed on a case by case basis, such that 'the more vital or important the common interests or objectives pursued, the easier it will be to accept as "necessary" measures designed to achieve those ends'.[288] Notably, under the GATT no necessity test needs to be applied in relation to 'products of prison labour'. It would seem to be sufficient that their origins can be verified as such. While it has been argued that the absence of a necessity test for prison labour should be applied by analogy to child labour under the 'public morals' exception in (a) and 'human life or health' in (b),[289] there is no indication from the Appellate Body or any panel in the DSU that such a generous approach would be taken. It is however clear that both the GATT and GATS have to be interpreted 'in accordance with customary rules of interpretation of public international law' (under Article 3(2) of the Dispute Settlement Understanding (DSU), which means that principles of *jus cogens*, for example regarding slavery, which is universally condemned, could be relevant in determining what could be regarded as 'public morals'.[290]

It is also evident that NGOs with relevant competence in the subject matter at issue have the opportunity to make submissions by virtue of WTO Appellate Body rules, but as the vast majority of cases involve environmental issues we have seen few interventions from trade unions on labour matters and, when submitted, these are often in the form of 'joint briefs' with environmental and social NGOs.[291] There has been reluctance from countries in the Global South to concede this form of lobbying before the panels or Appellate Body, with the result that in the *EC—Asbestos* case, applications to submit briefs from the

---

[287] *Korea—Various Measures on Beef* WT/DS161/AB/R (10 January 2001), paras 161–6.

[288] *EC—Measures Affecting Asbestos and Asbestos-Containing Products* WT/DS135/AB/R (5 April 2001), para. 172; discussed in Donald H. Regan, 'The Meaning of "Necessary" in GATT Article XX and GATS Article XIV: The Myth of Cost–benefit Balancing' (2007) 6(3) *World Trade Review* 347.

[289] Matthew T. Mitro, 'Outlawing the Trade in Child Labor Products: Why the GATT Article XX Health Exception Authorizes Unilateral Sanctions' (2002) 51 *American University Law Review* 1223, 1259; cf. Tatjana Eres, 'The Limits of GATT Article XX: A Back Door for Human Rights' (2004) 35 *Georgetown Journal of International Law* 597.

[290] Sarah H. Cleveland, 'Human Rights Sanctions and International Trade: A Theory of Compatibility' (2002) 5(1) *Journal of International Economic Law* 133; Makane Moïse Mbengue and Apollin Koagne Zouapet, 'Ending the Splendid Isolation—Jus Cogens and International Economic Law' in Dire Tladi (ed.), *Peremptory Norms of General International Law (Jus Cogens)* (Brill Nijhoff 2021), 509–74.

[291] For the WTO's official outline of this practice, see: www.wto.org/english/tratop_e/dispu_e/disp_settlement_cbt_e/c9s3p1_e.htm. For comment, see Nicola Charwat, 'Who Participates as Amicus Curiae in World Trade Organisation Dispute Settlement and Why?' (2016) 27 *New Zealand Universities Law Review* 1, especially at 21.

International Confederation of Free Trade Unions (ICFTU) and the European Trade Union Confederation (ETUC) were refused, despite their obvious competence in the field of health and safety at work, which was at issue in that case.[292]

A further issue is that of extraterritoriality. Measures which relate to the impact of an unsafe product or delivery of service within the relevant state's own territory are permissible, but those which fall outside state jurisdiction, namely measures which seek to regulate 'process production methods' within another country, are generally regarded as impermissible.[293] Once again, it is evident that a bar on extraterritoriality cannot logically apply to the prison labour exception under the GATT, which expressly recognises the legitimacy of a response to the creation of a product by such means in another country. Whether such a bar extends to other *jus cogens* issues, such as forced labour or slavery, remains a moot question which has yet to be determined under the DSU.[294] Arguably, the problem of extraterritoriality would not arise in the scenario where a state takes measures to regulate the terms on which employees are hired when present in their territory under GATS mode 4, even though the fact that their contracts of service would still probably be governed under conflicts of laws rules by the home rather than the host state could potentially pose problems in this regard. The question also has yet to be tested under WTO dispute settlement.

Moreover, this resistance to extraterritorial regulation may also be misguided in a number of ways. Hannah Buxbaum has observed that there can be exercises of legal authority 'outside the lawmaker's territory' which serve worthy purposes 'as a matter of international law and policy', giving the example of the application of international human rights law.[295] Moreover, the ways in which powerful states and the commercial interests within them operate across borders mean that extraterritorial measures to promote decent work could be viewed more as a corrective of extraterritorial mischief than as problematic in and of themselves. For example, the expansion and outsourcing of digital services and platform work from the Global North into the Global South would seem to call for correctives from the countries and corporations

---

[292] Padideh Ala'i, 'Judicial Lobbying at the WTO: The Debate over the Use of Amicus Curiae Briefs and the U.S. Experience' (2000) 24 *Fordham International Law Journal* 62, 82; and Paine n.216, 840. Both discuss *EC—Measures Affecting Asbestos and Products Containing Asbestos* WT/DS135/AB/R (5 April 2001), para. 56.

[293] Bartels n.183.

[294] See this chapter, text accompanying n.290.

[295] Hannah L. Buxbaum, 'The Practice(s) of Extraterritoriality' in Hannah L. Buxbaum and Thibaut Fleury Graff (eds) *Extraterritoriality/L'extraterritorialite* (Brill Nijhoff 2022).

which benefit from such a form of commerce, given that 'a mismatch exists between digital technologies' global reach and geographically bounded states' legal authority'.[296] It is also evident that environmental pollution, including the effect of carbon emissions, does not respect national borders, meaning that extraterritorial measures may be appropriate to curb the effects of what one country does to its neighbours and other parts of the planet.[297] The problem may therefore be less the extraterritorial nature of the measures concerned and more the need for all those affected to take part in the decision-making processes through which they are crafted;[298] hence the case made in this book for collective voice from the wider 'world of work'.

A further restriction on utilising the 'General Exceptions' is that the measures must not only come within the scope of the list and the chapeau, but they also have to be proportionate and consistent,[299] which can be linked to the requirement that the measure must not constitute 'arbitrary or unjustifiable discrimination' or be a disguised restriction on trade under the chapeau.[300]

A case that deserves attention from a labour-related perspective is the *EC—Asbestos* case, referred to above.[301] This remains notable as the one case of successful reliance on Article XX of the GATT, although it should also be conceded that in many instances, reliance on Article XX as a justification for quantitative restrictions does in practice go unchallenged.[302] Joanna Langille has argued that through Appellate Body interpretation of WTO law, including

---

[296] Guillaume Beaumier, Kevin Kalomeni, Malcolm Campbell-Verduyn, Marc Lenglet, Serena Natile, Marielle Papin, Daivi Rodima-Taylor, Arthur Silve and Falin Zhang, 'Global Regulations for a Digital Economy: Between New and Old Challenges' (2020) 11(4) *Global Policy* 515, 516; see also ILO World Employment and Social Outlook (WESO) Report, *The Role of Digital Labour Platforms in Transforming the World of Work* (ILO 2021) available at: www.ilo.org/global/research/global-reports/weso/2021/WCMS_771749/lang--en/index.htm.

[297] See Ryan Turner, 'Transnational Supply Chain Regulation: Extraterritorial Regulation as Corporate Law's New Frontier' (2016) 17(1) *Melbourne Journal of International Law* 188.

[298] See discussion of the participatory decision-making advocated by SDG 16 in this respect, in Chapter 1 of this book, text accompanying nn.110 et seq.

[299] See *EC—Seal Products* n.279.

[300] Lorand Bartels, 'The Chapeau of the General Exceptions in the WTO GATT and GATS Agreements: A Reconstruction' (2015) 109(1) *American Journal of International Law* 95.

[301] *EC—Measures Affecting Asbestos and Asbestos-Containing Products* WT/DS135/AB/R (5 April 2001).

[302] WTO, 'Quantitative Restrictions: Factual Information on Notifications Received' Report by the Secretariat of 22 March 2022, G/MA/W/114/Rev.4, observes at para. 2.12: 'Under this Agreement, the "General Exceptions" of Article XX were the most frequently used: 1363 QRs, or 77% of the total. Particularly relevant is the reference to paragraph b of Article XX, which refers to measures "necessary to protect human,

Article XX, there has been an 'embrace of pluralism', whereby states can take measures to protect labour standards, even if this permission is largely hidden from view.[303]

In the *Asbestos* case, the determination of France to block imports of asbestos products was upheld on grounds of health and safety under Article XX(b) of the GATT, despite Canadian opposition. Notably, this decision was reached by the Appellate Body without entertaining the views of key international and trade union representatives as amicus curiae, as discussed above.[304] However, on grounds of 'necessity' and proportionality, the exception could be established and questions of extraterritoriality did not arise (as the harmful effects of asbestos would affect people inside French territory once imported). While this ban could be regarded as a 'technical barrier to trade' under the TBT Agreement (in Annex 1A to the Marrakesh Agreement), the terms of Article XX still applied. It would be enough for the member taking the measure to establish a *prima facie* case, providing quantitative or qualitative evidence of health risks and the need for the measures.[305] It may also have been helpful, as Robert Howse and Elisabeth Tuerk have observed, that Article 10(a) of the ILO Convention No. 162 recommends, wherever possible, 'replacement of asbestos or of certain types of asbestos or products containing asbestos by other materials or products or the use of alternative technology, scientifically evaluated by the competent authority as harmless or less harmful'.[306] However, there was no mention of the ILO in the Appellate Body decision issued.

While there has been extensive comment in the context of General Exceptions regarding environmental standards (and the relevance of the international multilateral agreements on which states can rely), there has been less said on the subject of 'sustainable development'. Where mentioned by the Appellate Body, as in the *Shrimp-Turtle* case on the basis of explicit reference to 'sustainable development' in the preamble to the Marrakesh Agreement,[307]

---

animal or plant life or health", which was cited for almost 54% of the QRs in the dataset.'

303 Langille n.214, especially at 580–6.

304 See this chapter, text accompanying nn.291–2.

305 *EC—Asbestos*, WT/DS135/AB/R n.301, para. 167.

306 Robert Howse and Elisabeth Tuerk, 'The WTO Impact on Internal Regulations—A Case Study of the Canada–EC Asbestos Dispute' in Gráinne de Búrca and Joanne Scott, *The EU and the WTO: Legal and Constitutional Issues* (Hart Publishing 2002), 283–328, 320.

307 Asbestos Convention, 1986 (No. 162); and see *United States—Import Prohibition of Certain Shrimp and Shrimp Products*, WT/DS58/AV/R (12 October 1998), at paras 127–31 adding 'colour, texture and shading' to the interpretative process; discussed by Virginie Barral, 'Sustainable Development in International Law: Nature and Operation

this has been solely in the sphere of environmental considerations arising under Article XX.

In *Brazil—Certain Measures Concerning Taxation and Charges (Brazil—Taxation)*,[308] Brazil sought to rely on the 'public morals' exception in Article XX(a), citing the 'digital divide' as a reason for its actions, making reference to target 8.F of the Millennium Development Goals (MDGs), which encouraged states to cooperate 'with the private sector' so as to 'make available the benefits of new technologies, especially information and communications' and thereby further social sustainable development (concerned with intra-generational justice).[309] Ultimately, Brazil's claim failed on the test of necessity.[310] There was however one single specific mention of 'sustainable development' in the panel report in a social sustainability context, notably not repeated in the Appellate Body reports.[311] That fleeting acknowledgment of social sustainability has given rise to claims that facets of sustainable development, such as social inclusion under SDG 10, can now be viewed as a 'fundamental moral imperative'; also, that the Sustainable Development Goals can (by way of analogy with the MDGs) be a significant source of reference regarding the ability of states to justify breach of GATT and GATS.[312] An even bolder claim has been made regarding social sustainability, namely that means advancing the welfare of women and girls could be protected under Article XX(a) with reference to Article 31 of the Vienna Convention on the Law of Treaties, SDG 5 and the WTO Buenos Aires Joint Ministerial Declaration on Trade and Women's Economic Empowerment 2017.[313] As the Appellate Body

---

of an Evolutive Legal Norm' (2012) 23(2) *European Journal of International Law* 377, at 386 and 395.

308 *Brazil—Certain Measures Concerning Taxation and Charges,* WT/DS472/R WT/DS497/R (30 August 2017).

309 Ibid, at para. 7.563 citing the MDG Report of 2015 which advocated more equal distribution of 'ICT access and use [...] within and between countries', such that 'the transformative power of ICTs and the data revolution be harnessed to deliver sustainable development for all'.

310 Caroline Foster, *Global Regulatory Standards in Environmental and Health Disputes: Regulatory Coherence, Due Regard, and Due Diligence* (Oxford University Press 2021), 155 and 317.

311 *Brazil—Certain Measures Concerning Taxation and Charges* WT/DS472/AB/R WT/DS497/AB/R (13 December 2018).

312 Gillian Moon, 'A "Fundamental Moral Imperative": Social Inclusion, the Sustainable Development Goals and International Trade Law after Brazil—Taxation' (2018) 52(6) *Journal of World Trade* 995.

313 Amrita Bahri and Daria Bokla, 'Not Just Sea Turtles, Let's Protect Women Too: Invoking Public Morality Exception or Negotiating a New Gender Exception in Trade Agreements?' (2022) 33(1) *The European Journal of International Law* 237, 246–50.

has stopped functioning at the WTO, at least for the time being,[314] there seems less prospect of there being momentum behind these claims. We will have to see how past findings and principles are applied under the Multiparty Interim Appeal-Arbitration Arrangement operating under Article 25 of the WTO DSU.[315]

3.4 The 'Enabling Clause' and GSP Conditionality

Immediately after the Second World War, previous colonial powers continued to grant special trade preferences to previous colonies, which also meant that previous colonial trade routes were preserved. This was an approach which trapped production in newly independent developing countries within previous expectations, preventing diversification away from primary produce and limiting the potential for development of industrialisation and skilled labour, which could secure more income both for the country concerned and its people.[316] In recognition of this problematic use of tariffs, it was agreed at the second UNCTAD conference in 1968 that instead developing countries should be able to gain preferential access under a 'generalised' scheme.[317] There was 'unanimous agreement' in favour of preferential arrangements, but legal authority was needed and this took time to agree. Within the OECD, 'developed' countries in the Global North sought to protect their discretion to determine tariff preferences, so as to determine rules of origin, decide the scope of any tariff reductions, determine product coverage, include safeguard mechanisms and exclude more developed countries (or emerging economies). A complex compromise emerged by virtue of the 1971 decision creating temporary waivers and later the 1979 'permanent' Enabling Clause was appended formally to the GATT.[318]

Paragraph 1 of the Enabling Clause establishes the principle of non-reciprocity, such that 'contracting parties may accord differential and more favourable treatment to developing countries, without according such

---

[314] Jean Galbraith, 'United States Continues to Block New Appellate Body Members for the World Trade Organization: Risking the Collapse of the Appellate Process' (2019) 113(4) *American Journal of International Law* 822.

[315] See, for comment on the factors that led to the status quo, Foster n.310, 138–9.

[316] Gene M. Grossman and Alan O. Sykes, 'A Preference for Development: The Law and Economics of GSP' (2005) 4(1) *World Trade Review* 41; also Maria Persson, 'Trade Preferences from a Policy Perspective' in Oliver Morrissey, Ricardo Lopez and Kishor Sharma (eds), *Handbook on Trade and Development* (Edward Elgar Publishing 2015), 111–28.

[317] Resolution 21(ii) taken at the UNCTAD II Conference, New Delhi 1968; see also De Schutter n.243, 102.

[318] Hudec (1992) n.199, 70–4.

treatment to other contracting parties'.[319] Paragraph 2(a) specifically contemplates the creation of '[p]referential tariff treatment accorded by developed contracting parties to products originating in developing countries in accordance with the Generalized System of Preferences' [sic]. The latter is described in footnote 3, as 'relating to the establishment of "generalized, non-reciprocal and non-discriminatory preferences beneficial to the developing countries"' as agreed in the Decision of 1971. Non-tariff preferential measures are covered by paragraph 2(b). Special measures for least developed countries are contemplated under paragraph 2(d) and paragraph 7.

The European Economic Community (EEC) – the forerunner to the EU – introduced a 'Generalised System of Preferences' (GSP) programme in July 1971.[320] Japan, Norway and the UK followed soon after, while the US scheme was first introduced in 1976.[321] All schemes are notified to UNCTAD and appear on the UNCTAD website.[322] It should be noted, and this is important for the analysis in Chapter 5, that paragraph 2(c) of the Enabling Clause also contemplates '[r]egional or global arrangements entered into amongst less-developed contracting parties for the mutual reduction or elimination of tariffs and [...] for the mutual reduction or elimination of non-tariff measures, on products imported from one another'. This provision opened up scope for South–South preferential trade agreements, with partial success.[323]

'Developed contracting parties shall therefore not seek, neither shall less-developed contracting parties be required to make, concessions that are inconsistent with the latter's development, financial and trade needs.'[324] So, any conditions imposed regarding labour or environmental standards, for example, must be compatible with 'development, financial and trade needs', which should constrain their application and operation. Whether meaningful

---

[319] Enabling Clause: 'Differential and More Favourable Treatment Reciprocity and Fuller Participation of Developing Countries' – Decision of 28 November 1979 L/4903 – appended to the GATT (which continues to apply as part of GATT 1994 under the Marrakesh Agreement). See further also Enabling Clause, para. 5: 'The developed countries do not expect reciprocity for commitments made by them.'

[320] James Harrison, 'Incentives for Development: The EC's Generalized System of Preferences, India's WTO Challenge and Reform' (2005) 42 *Common Market Law Review* 1663, 1666.

[321] Authorized by the Trade Act of 1974 and implemented on 1 January 1976, as discussed at: www.cbp.gov/trade/priority-issues/trade-agreements/special-trade-legislation/generalized-system-preferences. Cf. Addo n.243, 151.

[322] See the UNCTAD GSP Utilization Database available at: https://unctad.org/topic/trade-agreements/trade-preferences-utilization.

[323] Rolf J. Langhammer and Ulrich Hiemenz, *Regional Integration among Developing Countries: Opportunities, Obstacles, and Options* (J.C.B. Mohr/Westview Press 1990).

[324] Enabling Clause, paragraph 5.

constraint can be placed on the discretion of developed states utilising GSP options has only been tested once in WTO dispute settlement, culminating in a decision of the Appellate Body in a case brought by India with respect to the then European Communities' preferential 'drug arrangements'.[325] The European Communities (EC) tried to claim that the Enabling Clause did not merely create an exception to Article I of the GATT but removed GSP schemes entirely from the coverage of the GATT, giving wide-ranging discretion to developed nations in how they offered trade preferences, but the Appellate Body gave pause to that argument. That said, GSP schemes, despite suspected non-compliance were not challenged prior to this case and have not been challenged subsequently.

India benefited from the then EC GSP 'General Arrangements' but not 'drug arrangements' or 'special incentive arrangements' for protection of labour rights or the environment. India did initially challenge its exclusion from the latter (in 2002), but later limited its complaint to the drug arrangements under which preferences had been given only to 12 countries, within the Andean Community and the Central American Common Market, with the rationale being that the preferences would incentivise substitutions of legal for illegal crops and promote job creation outside drug production and trafficking. India's argument was that this degree of selectivity was in breach of the MFN principle but also the very notion of a 'generalised' system of preferences if the exception in the Enabling Clause was to be applied.

In response, the Appellate Body found that the GSP was an exception to the MFN principle provided that its operation 'is in accordance with the conditions set out in the Enabling Clause', with reference to the significance of non-reciprocal preferences for the promotion of developing country trade.[326] India accordingly had to point to the breach of specific terms in the Enabling Clause and then the onus fell on the EC to rebut those arguments.[327] The Appellate Body also determined that preferences need not be extended to all developing countries without differentiation. The test is that 'identical treatment is available to all similarly-situated GSP beneficiaries' or 'that identical tariff treatment must be available to all GSP beneficiaries with the "development, financial [or] trade need" to which the differential treatment is intended to respond'.[328]

The term 'generalised' might mean 'generally applicable' but there should be capacity for different treatment of specific states, in line with differential

---

[325] *EC—Conditions for the granting of Tariff Preferences to Developing Countries*, WT/DS246/AB/R (7 April 2004).

[326] Ibid, paras 89 – 90. See also paras 106 and 110.

[327] Ibid, para. 113.

[328] Ibid, paras 173 and 179.

needs.[329] Moreover, the term 'non-reciprocal' would not prevent attachment of conditions to preferences, if these reflected a legitimate objective established in the Enabling Clause which was reasonable and proportionate. However, explanations must be provided detailing why certain countries had not been selected for a GSP scheme. The EC therefore needed to demonstrate that the drug arrangements scheme was 'available to all GSP beneficiaries that are similarly affected by the drug problem'.[330] This was clearly not the case to the point that there was not even any mechanism to add further beneficiaries when they became eligible.[331] Although India abandoned its claims regarding to labour-related conditionality early in the proceedings, Langille has observed that 'the Appellate Body made an oblique reference to the European Communities' labour conditions, which suggested an openness to accepting labour conditionality that has a development-oriented purpose'.[332]

The GSP arrangements in the EU were revised accordingly to enable such transparency, regarding the terms of eligibility and scrutiny. They operate now on a three-track system. Alongside the standard GSP for developing countries defined as 'vulnerable', there are the special incentive arrangements for Sustainable Development and Good Governance (known as GSP+) which offer additional tariff reductions for countries that ratify and implement certain international conventions, including ILO Conventions. There is also the so-called Everything But Arms (EBA) arrangement, which provides entirely duty-free and quota-free access for all goods exported by least-developed countries apart from armaments.[333]

However, criticism of GSP schemes persists. For example, concerns have been raised regarding the capacity of states to demonstrate, after production through global supply chains, that rules of origin (ROO) obligations are met. The discretionary powers of developed states offering GSP preferences are

---

[329] Ibid, para. 160 citing paragraph 7 of the Enabling Clause.

[330] Ibid, para. 180.

[331] See, for more detailed analysis of the case, Harrison n.264; and Robert Howse, 'India's WTO Challenge to Drug Enforcement Conditions in the European Community Generalized System of Preferences: A Little Known Case with Major Repercussions for "Political" Conditionality in US Trade Policy' (2003) 4(2) *Chicago Journal of International Law* 385.

[332] Langille n.214, 587.

[333] See Council Regulation No. 980/2005 of 27 June 2005, OJ L169/1, especially Articles 9 and 16; and today EU Regulation 978/2012 operating from 1 January 2014 at n.226 above; also for helpful summaries, Addo n.243, ch 5; De Schutter n.243, ch 4; Manfred Weiss, 'The EU Generalised Scheme of Preferences and the Special Incentive Arrangement for Sustainable Development and Good Governance' in Adalberto Perulli and Tiziano Treu (eds), *Sustainable Development, Global Trade and Social Rights* (Wolters Kluwer 2018).

such that different rules can apply under different schemes, imposing unnecessary costs on developing countries and their producers and thereby arguably reducing profits available to pay wages. While, for example, the EU has recently relaxed its ROO requirements, the multiplicity of schemes and rules still causes problems.[334] Moreover, there are more than 1,200 EU tariff lines which impose no tariffs on MFN countries, which means that the relative benefits of the GSP and GSP+ schemes for developing countries are declining.[335]

Another problem remains the shock of 'graduation' for states when they are no longer deemed 'vulnerable' under GSP and GSP+, or LDCs under EBA, and have to move onto other trade rules, such as preferential trade agreements (which we will discuss further in Chapter 5) or default standard 'WTO rules' relying on the operation of the MFN rule in terms of tariff preferences and market access. The EU rule is that whenever an individual country's performance on the EU market over a three-year period exceeds or falls below a set threshold (whether 'vulnerable' status under GSP and GSP+ or LDC under the EBA scheme), preferential tariffs are either suspended or re-established, which provides a little insulation but has the potential to penalise newly successful country-based initiatives. This is an issue for Bangladesh as it graduates from LDC status, casting doubt on access for its garment industry, in which so many low-income workers are employed.[336] It is therefore interesting that the new GSP Regulation proposed by the Commission is said to be designed to ensure

> a smooth transition for all countries set to graduate from Least Developed Country (LDC) status in the next decade. They will be able to apply for the special incentive arrangement for sustainable development and good governance (GSP+) if they

[334] Tobias Sytsma, 'Rules of Origin and Trade Preference Utilization among Least Developed Countries' (2021) 39(4) *Contemporary Economic Policy* 701; Pramila Crivelli and Stefano Inama, *Improving Market for LDCs: The Impact of the EU Reform of Rules of Origin on Utilization Rates and Trade Flows under the Everything But Arms Initiative (EBA)* (UNCTAD Working Paper 2021).

[335] Addo n.243, 166.

[336] Mohammad A. Razzaque and Jillur Rahman. *Bangladesh's Apparel Exports to the EU: Adapting to Competitiveness Challenges following Graduation from Least Developed Country Status* (Commonwealth Secretariat Working Paper 2019); and Md Abu Saleh and Muhammad Omar Faruque, 'LDC graduation and WTO challenges' in Mohammad Shahabuddin (ed.), *Bangladesh and International Law* (Routledge 2021), 194–204; William A. Kerr, 'Generalized System of Preferences and Graduation: Is there a Parallel with Infant Industries?' (2021) 22(2) *The Estey Journal of International Law and Trade Policy* 68. For analysis of Bangladesh as a case study for GSP, see also Katrina Peake, *To What Extent do EU Trade and Sustainable Development Instruments Effectively Promote Labour Rights in the Ready-Made Garment Industry of South Asia*, PhD Thesis submitted to the University of Nottingham, December 2019.

commit to strong sustainability standards and can thus retain generous tariff preferences to access to the EU market.[337]

The difficulty may be for those graduating to afford to make such commitments without development-related assistance and aid in doing so. It will be interesting to see how these proposals and their implementation progress.

More importantly, it can be hard to find the nexus between the conditions imposed in the GSP scheme (such as labour conditions) and the terms for reciprocity established under paragraph 5 of the Enabling Clause. For example, Bruce Wardhaugh has argued that there are significant costs of compliance that have to be met before eligibility for trade preferences under GSP+, which may not be commensurate with the benefits, and he asks why, if expansion of human rights (or labour rights) protection actually benefits a country's development, countries should receive any special compensation for compliance.[338] He is certainly not alone in asking this question regarding linkage of conditionality to 'development, financial and trade needs'.[339] Further, Samantha Velluti has questioned the transparency of the basis on which third countries are selected as recipients of GSP+ preferences, raising 'issues of selective conditionality and double standards'.[340] She, like Wardhaugh, also observes that 'although suspensions are directed against a given government, they end up having negative effects on the country as a whole, including its population', including job losses for workers.[341]

Arguably, the EU system is at least more transparent than the US system by virtue of reference to ratification and implementation of specific ILO Conventions, which can be readily ascertained through consultation of the ILO database made available online.[342] There are options for temporary withdrawal where there is serious and systematic violation of principles set out in the Conventions and a need to judge eligibility for GSP+. Whether there is

---

[337] See https:// policy .trade .ec .europa .eu/ news/ commission -proposes -new -eu -generalised-scheme-preferences-promote-sustainable-development-low-income-2021 -09-22_en.

[338] Bruce Wardhaugh, 'GSP+ and Human Rights: Is the EU's Approach the Right One?' (2013) 16 *Journal of International Economic Law* 827, 838.

[339] For further concerns regarding the EU, see Lorand Bartels, 'The WTO Legality of the EU's GSP+ Arrangement' (2007) 10 *Journal of International Economic Law* 869; and regarding the US, see Omphemetse S. Sibanda Sr, 'Towards a Revised GATT/ WTO Special and Differential Treatment Regime for Least Developed and Developing Countries' (2015) 50 *Foreign Trade Review* 31, 37.

[340] Samantha Velluti, *The Role of the EU in the Promotion of Human Rights and International Labour Standards in Its External Trade Relations* (Springer 2020), 218.

[341] Ibid.

[342] See www.ilo.org/dyn/normlex/en/f?p=NORMLEXPUB:12000:0::NO:::.

adequate assessment is arguably less clear, given a tendency to revert to the findings of the political ILO institutions such as the Conference Committee on the Application of Standards, rather than the Committee of Experts on the Application of Conventions and Recommendations.[343] The overall utilisation of a 'scorecard' and 'dialogue' is not wholly transparent.[344]

The benefit of the US system would seem to be its engagement with collective worker voice. While the US requires compliance with certain labour standards without direct reference to core ILO Conventions,[345] its operation is arguably more participatory. The system allows the US administration to take unilateral action via the Office of the US Trade Representative (USTR), but there is also potential for petition by private organisations such as NGOs and trade unions. If the USTR accepts the petition, a public hearing will be held. Thereby, US GSP does at least offer the possibility of public scrutiny from interested parties, albeit in the US rather than the developing country concerned. Chapter 5 examines the EU innovation of the 'domestic advisory group' created to assist in scrutiny of implementation of sustainable development chapters in free trade agreements.

Reviewing these features of Article XX and the Enabling Clause, it becomes apparent that these are mechanisms which offer considerable discretion to countries in the Global North to make trade conditional on compliance with certain labour standards, albeit subject to some, but not many, tangible limitations. This is a compromise which would seem to take account of the statement in the ILO's first Constitution under the Treaty of Versailles that 'the failure of any nation to adopt humane conditions of labour is an obstacle in the way of other nations which desire to improve the conditions of their own countries'.[346] In that sense, the legitimacy of imposing internationally recognised labour standards on other states is conceded. The few limitations placed on such unilateral action under WTO trade rules are designed to prevent forms of obvious trade protectionism or political preferences, which developing

---

[343] See Chapter 2 above; also Jeffrey Vogt, 'A Little Less Conversation: The EU and the (Non) Application of Labour Conditionality in the Generalized System of Preferences (GSP)' (2015) 31(3) *International Journal of Comparative Labour Law and Industrial Relations* 285.

[344] Cf. Weiss n.333, 126.

[345] *GSP Renewal Act* 1984, Pub L No 98-577, 98 Stat 3019. See Bob Hepple, *Labour Laws and Global Trade* (Hart Publishing 2005), 93; Gene M. Grossman and Alan O. Sykes, 'A Preference for Development: The Law and Economics of GSP' in George A. Bermann and Petros Mavroidis, *WTO Law and Developing Countries* (Cambridge University Press 2007), 255–82.

[346] See Chapter 3 of this book, text accompanying n.19.

countries in the Global South have mobilised to prevent since the 1960s,[347] but they do not go very far. That said, rather than adoption of draconian unilateral measures regarding labour standards, there has in practice been some use of the ILO as an intermediatory, as the initiator of country programmes that provide the financial aid and foster the capacity to secure incremental change. The Better Factories Cambodia programme[348] is illustrative of the kinds of globally co-ordinated measures orchestrated at the ILO that ensure that there is not discriminatory treatment or sanctions for a failure to implement legal reform which the country lacks the ability to implement. However, while in practice such programmes, referred to in Chapter 3 of this book and discussed further in Chapter 5, meaningfully supplement the world trade rules, they do not change them.

4. FINAL OBSERVATIONS ON VOICE FROM THE WORLD OF WORK

Freedom of association and the effective right to collective bargaining can be promoted by the unilateral measures permissible (if not actively approved) at the WTO. However, these vital enabling fundamental principles and rights at work are only partially 'built in' to this system. It is evident that states can potentially rely on ILO core labour standards and supervisory findings when justifying the terms of trade they impose on other states; and governments can consult or be informed by complaints from workers' organisations, including both trade unions and NGOs. However, there is no obligation for states to do so, as long as they satisfy the minimal constraints placed on their terms and conditions of trade set out in GATT and GATS, the Enabling Clause and WTO Appellate Body prescriptions. Moreover, while both labour and environmental standards are permitted as bases for conditionality under these provisions, the combination of these in an overarching context of 'sustainable development' in a way that responds to the holistic approach to the 2030 Agenda has yet to receive any meaningful or detailed attention in the dispute settlement process.

The GATT and WTO governance structures have enabled developing countries to exercise some influence manifested in SDT principles, since 'the WTO remains one of the few international organizations which actually

---

347 See discussion of the role of the Group of 77 in this chapter, text accompanying n.199.

348 See for the ILO description of the Better Factories Cambodia Programme: www.ilo.org/asia/projects/WCMS_099340/lang--en/index.htm; and for a contemporary assessment, Kevin Kolben, 'Trade, Monitoring, and the ILO: Working to Improve Conditions in Cambodia's Garment Factories' (2004) 7 *Yale Human Rights & Development Law Journal* 79.

abides by the concept of state equality no matter the economic or other might of its members'.[349] Nevertheless, the reality is that both the formal rules which govern global operation and the exceptions to them do not operate in the interests of working people in the Global South. There remains significant scope for the exploitation of their labour, while the blockages on trade which can occur when instances are uncovered and publicised, would seem to do more to remove the likelihood of future jobs in an industry rather than improving terms and conditions in a given country. This means that, while the World Bank IFC Performance Standards (and now the ESF) system may seem flawed, it is at least adaptable and can allow for investment in capabilities, which may reap rewards for those in the wider world of work.

The difficulty with the World Bank system is that both the developing world and collective labour have such minimal voice that the likelihood of their achieving meaningful adaptation of the international economic system is stymied. Indeed, in all the IEIs discussed in this chapter, it would seem that voices from the wider world of work are most likely to enter through claims procedures and dispute resolution rather than within mainstream decision-making frameworks. The Civil Society Forum held twice a year by the IMF and the World Bank and the Public Forum hosted by the WTO each year do demonstrate some engagement with civil society, but not the kinds of direct structural access to decision-making for social partners which is available at the tripartite ILO. Instead, it is through complaints procedures (for example before the World Bank CAO) and in the WTO dispute settlement that trade union and NGO concerns can be heard, even if they do not necessarily sway the course of institutional operations by doing so. There would seem to be formal 'access to justice' as contemplated by SDG targets 16.3 and 16.6, and in that sense some sustainable development objectives are being met as regards the potential for promotion and protection of decent work. However, there is not the full compliance with SDG 16.7 that might be expected, namely 'responsive, inclusive, participatory and representative decision-making at all levels'. It is on this note of ongoing frustration that we turn to consider the scope for preferential or 'free' trade agreements to change the dynamics of trade and labour regulation so that no one is left behind.

[349] O'Donoghue and Tzouvala n.220, 47.

5. Regional trade regulation and labour standards: a European Union case study

1. INTRODUCTION

'Free trade agreements' (abbreviated as 'FTAs' here but also referred to as 'regional trade agreements' or 'preferential trade agreements') are permitted by the World Trade Organization (WTO). These agreements are permitted because they enable trade between bilateral and multilateral parties which exceeds the scope of scheduled commitments to the General Agreement on Tariffs and Trade (GATT) or the General Agreement on Trade in Services (GATS). Indeed, FTAs have been termed 'termites in the trading system',[1] threatening the 'most favoured nation principle' under the GATT and GATS, which is supposed to promote (at least formal) equality within the WTO between treatment of trading partners.

The European Union (EU), as a remarkably powerful customs union, has been identified as one of the leading culprits promoting FTAs, being 'the hub seeking spokes'.[2] The EU has sparked the proliferation of FTAs with (and later between) non-EU states. Simultaneously, the EU has encouraged other regional trading arrangements; one example is the process of drafting and ratification of the African Continental Free Trade Agreement (AfCFTA), a 'mega-regional' agreement which has received significant financial support

[1] Jagdish Bhagwati, *Termites in the Trading System: How Preferential Agreements Undermine Free Trade* (Oxford University Press 2008), 2.

[2] Ibid, 36; see also Clair Gammage, *North–South Regional Trade Agreements as Legal Regimes: A Critical Assessment of the EU–SADC Economic Partnership Agreement* (Edward Elgar Publishing 2017); Kholofelo Kugler and Mulualem Getachew Adgeh, 'Africa and Trade and Investment Liberalization' in Daniel Bethlehem, Donald McRae, Rodney Neufeld and Isabelle Van Damme (eds), *The Oxford Handbook of International Trade Law*, 2nd ed. (Oxford University Press 2022), 412–17; and Sanoussi Bilal and Isabelle Ramdoo, *Sustainability and Human Rights in EPAs: A Comparative Analysis between the Caribbean and African EPAs* (European Centre for Development Policy Management Discussion Paper 2016).

through EU funding, as well as technical assistance.[3] In this way, the EU also seeks to act as an exemplar in terms of regional social and economic governance.[4] In this respect, the EU has been viewed in idealistic terms as a 'normative power',[5] or in realist terms as creating a 'market power'[6] Europe. A third view is that the EU has a more subtle mimetic 'Brussels effect'.[7]

Trade conditionality in FTAs has been viewed as 'an opportunity to put muscle behind international norms and standards' that have been 'weakly respected, if not routinely flouted'.[8] While the WTO is bound to promote sustainable development – as stated in the preamble to the 1994 Marrakesh Agreement[9] – as seen in Chapter 4, trade relations between its members are not required to be compliant with environmental or labour standards. Instead, there is the opportunity for WTO contracting parties in bilateral or multilateral FTAs to mutually agree to adopt (and enforce) labour obligations. They may also do so with reference to a broader sustainable development framework.

---

3 See the records of the 7th EU–Africa Economic and Social Stakeholders Network European and Economic Social Committee, 2 March 2021 available at: www.eesc.europa.eu/sites/default/files/files/madame_synowiec_.pdf. This document records that the EU provided funding of more than EUR 74 million (EUR 26 million for 'the AfCFTA negotiation process and architecture' and EUR 40 million 'facilitating the future AfCFTA implementation') alongside 'significant technical support [...] sharing expertise in economic integration'. See also Axel Berger (DIE), Clara Brandi, Frederik Stender, Edward K Brown, Philomena Apiko and Sean Woolfrey, *Advancing EU–Africa Cooperation in Light of the African Continental Free Trade Area* (European Think Tanks Group (ETTG) 2020), 7. Cf. Katrin Kuhlmann and Akinyi Lisa Agutu, 'The African Continental Free Trade Area: Toward a New Legal Model for Trade and Development' (2020) 51 *Georgetown Journal of International Law* 753, which does not reflect on that influence.

4 Cf. Elaine Fahey and Isabella Mancini (eds), *Understanding the EU as a Good Global Actor: Ambitions, Values and Metrics* (Edward Elgar Publishing 2022).

5 Ian Manners, 'The European Union's Normative Power' in Richard Whitman (ed.), *Normative Power Europe: Empirical and Theoretical Perspectives* (Palgrave 2011), 235.

6 Chad Damro, 'Market Power Europe' (2012) 19(5) *Journal of European Public Policy* 682, 689–96.

7 Anu Bradford, 'The Brussels Effect' (2012) 107(1) *Northwestern University Law Review* 1, 9. Cf. Anu Bradford, *The Brussels Effect: How the European Union Rules the World* (Oxford University Press 2019), ch 3 which identifies the limited application of this theory to 'preferential trade agreements', that is, 'FTAs'.

8 Kerry Rittich, 'Trade Agreements in the Twenty-First Century: Rethinking the Trade–Labor Linkage' in Alvaro Santos, Chantal Thomas and David Trubek (eds), *World Trade and Investment Law Reimagined: A Progressive Agenda for an Inclusive Globalization* (Anthem Press 2019), 204.

9 The Marrakesh Agreement Establishing the World Trade Organization (the 'Marrakesh Agreement') concluded on 15 April 1994 available at: www.wto.org/english/docs_e/legal_e/04-wto.pdf.

Indeed, that practice is becoming increasingly common, promoted by states in the Global North, either via dedicated chapters on 'trade and sustainable development', a practice adopted by the EU, or through 'side agreements' on labour, the approach favoured by Canada and the US. Both are claimed to be designed to prevent competitive advantage in trade by undercutting established labour standards, and the provisions included in such FTAs tend to be linked to 'core labour standards' and a 'decent work' agenda promoted by the International Labour Organization (ILO).[10]

This chapter begins by explaining the basis on which two WTO instruments, the General Agreement on Tariffs and Trade (GATT) and the General Agreement on Trade in Services (GATS), allow contracting parties to conclude FTAs. These FTAs can enable the formation of 'customs areas' or 'free trade areas', involving substantial liberalisation of trade in goods and/or services. In practice, such FTAs may also include chapters relating to matters outside the remit of WTO activities, such as investment. The chapter then goes on to consider the ways in which FTAs can foster what has been described as 'social regionalism', which may be best understood as a form of regulatory 'experimental governance' that could enable the combination of trade and labour objectives to foster social justice and decent work.[11] The remainder of the chapter examines the opportunities for and barriers to the achievement of such aims through FTAs, with a focus on sustainable development as a normative vehicle for such initiatives.

The scope and span of contemporary FTAs is now so vast that it is not possible to exhaustively survey or summarise their implications for labour in a single chapter of this book, but it is possible to examine their potential treatment of labour standards in connection with sustainable development, with reference to the example of EU FTAs that contain 'trade and sustainable development' (TSD) chapters.[12] The significance of inclusion of ILO standards

---

[10] As documented in the ILO International Labour Office report, *Labour Provisions in G7 Trade Agreements: A Comparative Perspective* (ILO 2019), 3; see also Rittich n.8, 205; and the ILO online archive titled 'Labour Provisions in Trade Agreements Hub', available at: www.ilo.org/LPhub/.

[11] Adelle Blackett, 'Social Regionalism in Better Work Haiti' (2015) 31(2) *The International Journal of Comparative Labour Law and Industrial Relations* 163, 164. See also Adelle Blackett, 'On Social Regionalism in Transnational Labour Law' (2020) 159(4) *International Labour Review* 591.

[12] As discussed in Lore Van den Putte and Jan Orbie, 'EU Bilateral Trade Agreements and the Surprising Rise of Labour Provisions' (2015) 31(3) *International Journal of Comparative Labour Law and Industrial Relations* 263; James Harrison, Mirela Barbu, Liam Campling, Franz Christian Ebert, Deborah Martens, Axel Marx, Jan Orbie, Ben Richardson and Adrian Smith, 'Labour Standards Provisions in EU Free Trade Agreements: Reflections on the European Commission's Reform

and the principle of sustainable development in the FTA concluded between the EU and the Republic of South Korea (Korea) was analysed recently in the 2021 report of an expert panel, which is discussed below.[13] By highlighting the potential and the limitations of EU practice to date in TSD chapters, it may be possible to further probe the potential for 'sustainable development' to operate on the regional and global stage as a unifying rationale for regulation of trade and labour.

The chapter then goes on to consider the use in EU FTAs of provisions enabling temporary movement of natural persons for the delivery of services (as a feature of trade in services), which are not applicable to *all* other WTO members but only the contracting parties to the FTA.[14] This regime for temporary movement has parallels with GATS mode 4 outlined in Chapter 4.[15] Regulation of the terms on which workers are sent by their employers to another country to perform services is compared here with the posting of workers regime which operates internally in the EU.[16] It is argued that the (albeit minimal) protections offered under the posting of workers regime inside the EU should at least be applied more generally externally under its FTA chapters.

Furthermore, there is a difficulty with EU FTAs that incorporate investment chapters, which provide protections for investors from the EU and third countries. These, as we shall see, pursue ostensibly fair objectives, such as 'fair

---

Agenda' (2019) 18(4) *World Trade Review* 635. For analysis of current practice and proposals for its reform, see European Commission *Communication on the Power of Trade Partnerships: together for green and just economic growth* COM(2022) 409 final, 22.6.2022.

[13] Report of the Panel of Experts (2020) Proceeding constituted under Article 13.15 of the EU–Korea Free Trade Agreement, 25 January 2021, Panel: Dr Jill Murray (Chairperson), Professor Laurence Boisson de Chazournes and Professor Jaemin Lee; available at: https://trade.ec.europa.eu/doclib/docs/2021/january/tradoc_159358.pdf.

[14] See Tonia Novitz, 'Supply Chains and Temporary Migrant Labour: The Relevance of Trade and Sustainability Frameworks' in Diamond Ashiagbor (ed.), *Re-imagining Labour Law for Development* (Hart 2019); and Odin Ekman and Samuel Engblom, 'Expanding the Movement of Natural Persons through Free Trade Agreements? A Review of CETA, TPP and ChAFTA' (2019) 35(2) *International Journal of Comparative Labour Law and Industrial Relations* 163.

[15] See Chapter 4 of this book, text accompanying n.247 et seq.

[16] For critical analysis of the EU posting of workers regime, see for example Marco Rocca, *Posting of Workers and Collective Labour Law: There and Back Again* (Intersentia 2015); and Stein Evju (ed.), *Cross-Border Services, Posting of Workers, and Multilevel Governance* (University of Oslo 2013). Regarding recent reforms see Tonia Novitz and Rutvica Andrijasevic, 'Reform of the Posting of Workers Regime: An Assessment of the Practical Impact on Unfree Labour Relations' (2020) 58(5) *Journal of Common Market Studies* 1325.

and equitable treatment', and prevent 'expropriation' of investor property by the host state. The danger in this context is that the introduction of national sustainable development policies, whether aimed at environmental or labour protections, can be challenged on these bases. For example, introduction of a minimum wage could be treated as 'indirect' expropriation of an investor's assets, given the unexpected costs that a higher wage could impose. The enforcement of such provisions is commonly achieved through investor-state dispute settlement (ISDS), which is notorious for its *ad hoc* operation through arbitration mechanisms, although these are increasingly the subject of regulation at the World Bank through the International Centre for Settlement of Investment Disputes (ICSID) and at UNCITRAL.[17] The attempts made most recently by the EU to address these issues are also outlined and evaluated here.

Overall, taking the EU as an exemplar of promotion of sustainable development and, thereby, labour standards under FTAs, there are some issues regarding EU conduct of external relations that should be flagged. First, the EU, by playing a leading role in the proliferation of FTAs, could be seen to undermine the principle of parity of treatment (or equality) between states, which is arguably fundamental to sustainable development and is reflected in SDG 10 of the 2030 Agenda. Much depends on the extent to which the EU is prepared to respect the WTO 'special and differential treatment' (SDT) principle and the regional autonomy of third country states to promote their own brand of social regionalism. Second, it seems to be both desirable and appropriate to include freedom of association as a facet of the substance of 'sustainable development' in TSD chapters and collective voice processes to promote implementation of the substantive standards in those chapters. However, there remains a need to ensure that the power imbalance between the EU and many third countries (and between the manifold voices of labour across these states) does not lead to hypocritical enforcement of standards not required within the EU internal market. A precondition for the legitimacy of TSD chapters would seem to be that all those engaged in the wider world of work across national borders are represented within collective drafting and implementation processes. The new initiatives taken by the EU to promote decent work globally through internal market measures are also deserving of attention in this context.[18] Finally, the treatment of temporary movement in EU FTAs with other countries emerges as particularly problematic given the experience of the European Commission in documenting the need for greater protection of labour rights in the context

---

17 See Chapter 4 of this book, text accompanying nn.24–30.

18 European Commission, *Communication on Decent Work Worldwide for a Global Just Transition and a Sustainable Recovery* COM(2022) 66 final, 23.2.2022 and proposals discussed further below.

of posting of workers within the EU.[19] There is the potential for the EU to promote one standard for those workers originating from EU member states and another for those temporarily moving from elsewhere, which, in both labour and sustainability terms, is hard to defend.

2. THE TERMS OF WTO PERMISSION TO ENTER A FREE TRADE AGREEMENT (FTA)

FTAs allow differential treatment of WTO members, but are permitted because they are viewed as furthering the WTO objectives of 'free trade'. Article XXIV.4 of the GATT states: 'The contracting parties recognize the desirability of increasing freedom of trade by the development, through voluntary agreements, or closer integration between the economies of the countries parties to such agreements.' What is important is that FTAs do not inadvertently raise further trade barriers. So paragraph (4) goes on to say that 'the purpose of a customs union or free-trade area should be to facilitate trade between constituent territories and not to raise barriers to the trade of other contracting parties with such territories'. In this context, customs unions involve the creation of a common external commercial policy ('a single customs territory') and 'application of substantially the same duties and other regulations of commerce'.[20] Notably, the EU is itself a customs union par excellence but also has the competence to create customs unions with other states,[21] and, as observed above, has the resources to facilitate regional trade arrangements concluded between other states to which it will not be a party.[22] As Holger Hestermeyer has observed, the EU 'has created one of the largest networks of FTAs'.[23]

Free trade areas facilitate the free movement of goods without tariffs providing obstacles. For both customs unions and free trade areas there needs to be substantial liberalisation of trade. This means that, subject to certain limited exceptions, 'the duties and other restrictive regulations of commerce [...] are eliminated on substantially all the trade between the constituent territories in

[19] See European Commission, *Proposal to amend the Posted Workers Directive* COM(2016) 128 final 9.7.18; and Staff Working Document, Impact Assessment, Strasbourg, 8.3.2016 SWD(2016)52 final.

[20] See Article XXIV(8)(a) of the General Agreement on Tariffs and Trade (the GATT).

[21] See, for example the EU–Turkey Customs Union, discussed by Hüseyin Aytuğ, Merve Mavuş Kütük, Arif Oduncu and Sübidey Toganas, 'Twenty Years of the EU–Turkey Customs Union: A Synthetic Control Method Analysis' (2017) 55 *Journal of Common Market Studies* 419.

[22] See n.3 above.

[23] Holger P. Hestermeyer, 'Trade Law in Europe' in Bethlehem et al (eds) n.2, 310.

products originating in such territories'.[24] Subject to these 'internal requirements', both custom areas and free trade areas can be created by preferential (or 'free') trade agreements (FTAs). They are also subject to the 'external requirement' that their creation will not have negative effects on other WTO members; negotiations with affected third parties are expected to alleviate such harms.[25] The difficulty lies in the lack of certainty as to the precise meaning of these internal and external requirements and their appropriate application.[26]

FTAs concerned with trade in services can also be permitted where they can be demonstrated to comply with Article Vbis and Article V of the General Agreement on Trade in Services (GATS). Article Vbis of GATS enables integration of labour markets where the relevant agreement (a) exempts citizens of parties to the agreement from requirements concerning residency and work permits and (b) is notified to the WTO Council for Trade in Services.[27] The European Economic Area is one such labour integration agreement.[28] More common are FTAs permissible under Article V of the GATS, which contemplates 'substantial sectoral coverage' and non-discrimination measures. An Article V GATS agreement can include, for example, a chapter regarding temporary movement of natural persons, which is common in EU new generation trade agreements.[29]

FTAs, being 'reciprocal preferential trade agreements between two or more partners' (who are also WTO members), have to be examined by the WTO Committee on Regional Trade Arrangements (CRTA).[30] While often referred to as 'regional' trade agreements, that term is a misnomer, as there is no addi-

---

[24] Article XXIV(8)(a) and (b) of the GATT.

[25] Article XXIV(9) of the GATT.

[26] Owais Hasan Khan, *Strengthening Regional Trade Integration in South Asia: A SAARC Perspective* (Springer 2021), 12–23.

[27] See for the WTO description of the Council's functions: www.wto.org/english/tratop_e/serv_e/s_coun_e.htm#:~:text=The%20Council%20for%20Trade%20in%20Services%20is%20responsible,members%2C%20and%20can%20establish%20subsidiary%20bodies%20as%20appropriate.

[28] See also www.efta.int/eea. For exploration of different forms of labour mobility under regional trading systems, see Flavia Jurje and Sandra Lavenex, *ASEAN Economic Community: What Model for Labour Mobility?* (Swiss NCCR Trade Regulation Working Paper No 2015/02 2015) available at: www.wti.org/media/filer_public/24/f2/24f2c553-c4cc-4cc2-b670-6144e31d453c/nccr_working_paper_asean_jurje_lavenex__.pdf.

[29] Tonia Novitz and Clair Gammage, *Report on International Regulatory Complexity of EU Trade and Investment* (SMART/University of Oslo 2018), 72 available at: www.smart.uio.no/publications/reports/d2.2-smart-report-on-international-complexity.pdf.

[30] See www.wto.org/english/tratop_e/region_e/region_e.htm. This has been a requirement since 1996. On the work of the Committee and the attempts to make

tional requirement of geographical proximity between the parties, although in practice genuine regional FTAs (covering adjacent countries) are common for logistical reasons.[31] This freedom to conclude FTAs across different parts of the world could enable trade benefits to be more widely distributed, rather than creating distinct regional enclaves of different wealth and capabilities. Much, of course, depends on the relative wealth of the region concerned. Certainly, the option to collaborate regionally, and its convenience in terms of shared commercial and other values, and efficacy of the transport of goods (and services) means that regional trade and other agreements have been advocated as a path to self-determination and sustainable wealth creation.[32] Reduced need for transportation may also have effects regarding pollution caused by travel.[33]

WTO dispute resolution has been invoked to raise challenges to the legitimacy of FTAs under WTO agreements. For example, in 1999 India argued disadvantage by reason of Turkey's participation in what was then the EC–Turkey Customs Union, which had affected the terms of textile imports.[34] Notably, the panel was hesitant to provide an overall assessment of consistency of the FTA creating the customs union with WTO rules, as this was 'generally a matter for the CRTA'. However, the Appellate Body was more interventionist, finding that an Article XXIV defence under the GATT could only be applicable if: (1) the party claiming the defence could 'demonstrate that the measure at issue is introduced upon the formation of a customs union that fully meets the requirements of […] Article XXIV'; and (2) 'the formation of the customs union would be prevented if it were not allowed to introduce the measure at issue'.[35]

The onus seems to lie on a WTO member adopting (and invoking the provisions of) an FTA to show compliance with the GATT and GATS.[36] But, nev-

the provisional 2006 Transparency Mechanism more permanent, see www.wto.org/english/tratop_e/region_e/regcom_e.htm.

[31] Tesfaye B. Takele, 'The Relevance of Coordinated Regional Trade Logistics for the Implementation of Regional Free Trade Area of Africa' (2019) 13(1) *Journal of Transport and Supply Chain Management* 1; Sang-Wook Cho, Hansoo Choi and Julián P. Díaz, 'The Causal Effect of Free Trade Agreements on the Trade Margins: Product-level Evidence from Geographically Distant Partners' (2022) 88(4) *Southern Economic Journal* 1453.

[32] As discussed in Blackett (2020) n.11 above; cf. Sarah Ellis Barnekow and Kishore G. Kulkarni. 'Why Regionalism? A Look at the Costs and Benefits of Regional Trade Agreements in Africa' (2017) 18(1) *Global Business Review* 99.

[33] Cf. for example issues raised by Jonathan Köhler, 'Globalization and Sustainable Development: Case Study on International Transport and Sustainable Development' (2014) 23(1) *The Journal of Environment and Development* 66.

[34] *Turkey—Restrictions on Imports of Textiles and Clothing Products* WTO Doc. WT/DS34/R 31 May 1999.

[35] See WTO Doc WT/DS34/AB/R of 22 October 1999, paras 58–9.

[36] *US—Line Pipe* WTO Doc WT/DS202/R of 29 October 2001 – panel report.

ertheless, there are certain matters which the WTO does not regulate, such as investment, which is increasingly becoming a feature of large mega-regional FTAs. Such matters have significant implications for the protection of labour standards,[37] as shall be discussed further later in this chapter.

3. 'SOCIAL REGIONALISM' AS A BASIS FOR SUSTAINABLE TRADE AND LABOUR RULES

Since 2002, Adelle Blackett has offered a compelling vision of 'social regionalism' that enables experimental transnational regulation.[38] She is (rightly) critical of the 'contemporary trade architecture' crafted at the WTO, which, as demonstrated in Chapter 4, together with IMF and World Bank Group activities, does not deliver on 'promises of raised standards of living, full employment and sustainable development'.[39] In response, she advocates the utilisation of regional trade arrangements, which can offer an alternative to the WTO's neoliberal turn, enabling experimental transnationalism so that 'collective goals and values' can be pursued which operate in counter-hegemonic ways that enable 'development'.[40] Social regionalism, for Blackett, is a normative concept which offers opportunities to 'recast' established norms.[41] This approach enables resistance of the 'encasing' of economic priorities in international institutions, as observed for example by Quinn Slobodian.[42]

Blackett's desire to widen the scope of regulatory possibilities has been shared by Kerry Rittich, who describes how trade regimes could move beyond a narrow focus on fair competition and instead consider how they act as 'mechanisms for allocating risks and immunities, powers and disabilities, including among workers and those that employ them'.[43] Rittich also acknowledges the frustrations which have led to Dani Rodrik's insistence on the sole nation state as an actor, while recognising the limitations of such an approach.[44] Regional

---

37 See International Labour Office n.10 above, 3, 16, 25.

38 Adelle Blackett, 'Toward Social Regionalism in the Americas' (2002) 23(4) *Comparative Labour Law and Policy Journal* 901. See also n.11 above.

39 Blackett (2020) n.11, 591.

40 Blackett (2015) n.11, 165.

41 Blackett (2020) n.11, 607.

42 Blackett (2020) n.11, 594–5 and see also 607. For further discussion of Quinn Slobodian, *Globalists: The End of Empire and the Birth of Neoliberalism* (Harvard University Press 2018), see Chapter 4 of this book above.

43 Rittich n.8, 214.

44 Blackett (2020) n.11, 607–8. Cf. Dani Rodrik, *Straight Talk on Trade: Ideas for a Sane World Economy* (Princeton University Press 2018), 13–14; and discussion of his views in Chapter 2 of this book, text accompanying nn.195–201.

groupings have the capacity to be stronger; and she is not advocating reactive nationalism.

Blackett's advocacy of social regionalism draws on an understanding of international labour law as 'transnational', a vision shared by Anne Trebilcock.[45] They espouse exploration of alternative mechanisms for regulation at local, national, regional and international levels. In so doing, both are attentive to the power dynamics between labour and capital (as would be any two such experienced labour lawyers), but they also demonstrate awareness of the forces at work between states. In particular, Blackett has identified 'the regulatory consequences of the hardening asymmetry between trading partners, and the structural challenges that developing countries face when they attempt to experiment without redistributive capacity'.[46]

This is a potentially exciting vision for regional engagement with the trade–labour linkage. There remain however obstacles to its achievement, which are not always fully interrogated by other advocates of regulatory experimentalism.[47] One barrier could stem from WTO determination of what will be regarded as permissible FTAs, for example that they should substantially liberalise all trade, which may not be appropriate for certain countries that have exceptional vulnerabilities insofar as their trade focuses on particular products or services that cannot be readily diversified.[48]

Another problem is the EU's determination to simultaneously promote profitable trade and ethical terms in its relationships with third countries.[49] The

---

[45] Adelle Blackett and Anne Trebilcock, 'Conceptualising Transnational Labour Law' in Adelle Blackett and Anne Trebilcock (eds), *Research Handbook on Transnational Labour Law* (Edward Elgar Publishing 2015). See also Anne Trebilcock, 'Why the Shift from International to Transnational Law Is Important for Labour Standards' in Henner Gött (ed.), *Labour Standards in International Economic Law* (Springer 2018); Anne Trebilcock, 'The Rana Plaza Disaster Seven Years On: Transnational Experiments and Perhaps a New Treaty?' (2020) 159(4) *International Labour Review* 545; and Blackett (2020) n.11, 607 et seq.

[46] Blackett (2020) n.11, 608.

[47] See for example advocacy of 'regulatory cooperation' as a brand of experimentalism in Bernard Hoekman and Charles F. Sabel, *Trade Agreement, Regulatory Sovereignty and Democratic Legitimacy* (Columbia Law School 2017), which does not seem sensitive to the dynamics of North–South power dynamics or the complex constituencies which lie behind national 'self-determination'.

[48] See recognition of this issue in the 'Brundtland Report', discussed in Chapter 1 of this book at text accompanying nn.91 et seq; World Commission on Environment and Development (WCED), *Our Common Future* (Oxford University Press 1987).

[49] See Sophie Meunier and Kalypso Nicolaïdes, 'The European Union as a Conflicted Trade Power' (2006) 13(6) *Journal of European Public Policy* 906; and Billy Melo Araujo, 'Labour Provisions in EU and US Mega-regional Trade Agreements: Rhetoric and Reality' (2018) 67(1) *International and Comparative Law*

potential tension between these two EU external relations objectives and the difficulty entailed in disentangling them can lead to confusion and suspicion.

Moreover, there remains the potential for EU influence (whether mimetic or due to the exertion of market power and preferential conditionality) to limit genuine regional innovation.[50] Countries in the Global South may have a limited knowledge-base and little opportunity to set trade arrangements, when access to the EU market depends on compliance with certain market orthodoxies.[51] Moreover, while the EU has a number of funds accessible to EU member states, as well as social and commercial actors, which cushion the impact of trade agreements,[52] this is a luxury which other states in the Global South may not be able to afford; they will be imitating part of rather than the entire EU trade conditionality model.

Another difficulty is that, within any given region – for example, that of Southern Africa – there are notable differences between states in terms of wealth and influence, which can create significant imbalances of power between regional state actors.[53] This creates challenges for the socially redistributive dimension of regional trade, not only in North–South but also in South–South FTAs.

The question then is whether there are sufficient mechanisms in trade negotiations, the drafting of agreements, and processes of implementation which enable leverage to be exercised by less powerful actors, such as those in precarious work and their representatives, particularly from the Global South. Arguably, the greater the participatory capacity of mechanisms for civil society – such as trade unions, but also NGOs – to engage with the processes for the making and operation of trade rules, the more likely it is that brute

---

Quarterly 233, 250. For a contemporary example, compare the 'growth' agenda and the determination to promote 'European values in the world' in European Commission, *Communication on a Strong Social Europe for Just Transitions* COM(2020) 14 final 14.1.20 at 1–3 and 12.

[50] See text accompanying nn.3–7 above.

[51] See Maurizio Carbone, 'The EU and the Developing World: Partnership, Poverty, Politicization' in Christopher Hill and Michael Smith (eds), *International Relations and the European Union*, 2nd ed. (Oxford University Press 2011), cited by Aoife O'Donoghue and Ntina Tzouvala, 'TTIP: The Rise of the "Mega-market" Trade Agreements and Its Potential Implications for the Global South' (2016) 8(2) *Trade Law and Development* 30, 41 and 48 as they consider Global South capacity and influence in the content of FTAs.

[52] See https:// commission .europa .eu/ funding -tenders/ find -funding/ eu -funding -programmes_en; also the argument made for this kind of 'commitment to compensate the losers' and 'redistribute gains' made by Rittich n.8, 211–12.

[53] Jeffrey Herbst, *States and Power in Africa: Comparative Lessons in Authority and Control* (Princeton University Press 2014).

economic power will not prevail and that issues of importance to those at work are placed on the agenda.

That said, Lukes' identification of a third type of 'power' reminds us that the normalisation of inclusion of certain terms and dispute mechanisms in trade agreements by trading blocs by the EU and BRICS states (such as South Africa)[54] will have its own effects on what all parties are prepared to accept. Much may depend on whether the effects of trade rules spark objections and the processes via which they are heard. The latter can include dispute settlement, but also mechanisms like the 'domestic advisory groups' and civil society forums contemplated in EU trade agreements. Their relative successes are considered in this chapter.

That is not to say that there is no scope for agency for Global South states or private actors, including trade unions.[55] The point is rather that their capacity remains constrained by the structures currently created for engagement, which make it difficult to reach those most affected and vulnerable to the outcome of trade-related decisions. There is also a difficulty that those hired to do the most precarious work are often excluded from national, and even regional and international, representation by trade unions, due to limited recognition of their employment status, for example under domestic labour laws or even competition law.[56] We shall see that trade rules and their enforcement at the regional level could prompt correction in this respect, an example being the recent dispute concerning freedom of association principles set out in the EU–Korea FTA[57] and subsequent EU Commission action on enabling sole independent contractors in the EU to be represented by trade unions and engage in collective bargaining.[58]

The recent tripartite paralysis at the ILO on employment status and global supply chains has been unfortunate because it has impacted not just on claims to protection under national labour laws but also on representational mechanisms.[59] In the absence of ILO action, it has been tempting to look to innovations in the EU. The danger is that EU initiatives relating to the labour–trade

---

54 See Chapter 1 of this book, text accompanying n.60 et seq on 'BRICS' status and also text accompanying n.63 et seq on conceptions of 'power'.

55 Gammage n.2 highlights that potential for agency.

56 As discussed in Sanjukta Paul, Shae McCrystal and Ewan McGaughey (eds), *The Cambridge Handbook of Labor in Competition Law* (Cambridge University Press 2022).

57 See n.13 above.

58 European Commission, *Guidelines on the Application of Union Competition Law to Collective Agreements regarding the Working Conditions of Solo Self-employed Persons* C(2022) 6846 final, 29.9.22. Discussed further in this chapter below, at text accompanying n.135.

59 Discussed in Chapter 3 of this book, for example at n.188.

linkage may have influence and impact without social actors in third countries having much scope to participate in or affect those deliberations.[60]

4. TRADE AND SUSTAINABLE DEVELOPMENT CHAPTERS IN EUROPEAN UNION (EU) FTAS

Trade and sustainable development (TSD) chapters have become an established feature of EU FTAs.[61] This model was established in the 'new generation' FTA concluded between the EU and Korea,[62] continuing a tradition whereby the EU sought to connect the legitimacy of labour conditionality in trade with reference to norms established at the ILO, in particular those so-called core labour standards established by the 1998 Declaration on Fundamental Principles and Rights at Work, and associated 'fundamental' ILO Conventions.[63] This approach is already familiar from the EU Generalised System of Preferences (first GSP and later GSP+),[64] as discussed in Chapter 4.[65]

This endeavour is consistent with provisions set out in the Treaty on the EU (TEU) and the Treaty on the Functioning of the EU (TFEU), which provide the EU's constitutional foundations. Article 3(3) of the TEU states that the EU 'shall work for the sustainable development of Europe', while Article 3(5) requires the EU to contribute to 'the sustainable development of the Earth, solidarity and mutual respect among peoples, free and fair trade, eradication of poverty and the protection of human rights'. Under Article 21(2)(d) of the TEU, the EU is to 'foster the sustainable economic, social and environmental development of developing countries, with the primary aim of eradicating poverty'.

Under Article 207 TFEU, the EU enjoys the exclusive competence to adopt binding legislation and regulations in respect of trade in goods, services and

---

60 For historical review and critique, see Samantha Velluti, *The Role of the EU in the Promotion of Human Rights and International Labour Standards in Its External Trade Relations* (Springer 2020), ch 5.

61 Van den Putte and Orbie n.12, 281–2.

62 European Commission, *The EU–Korea Free Trade Agreement in Practice* (EU 2011), 3. See also Sunghoon Park, 'The New Politics of Trade Negotiations: The case of the EU-Korea FTA' (2017) 39(7) *Journal of European Integration* 827, 830–2.

63 Tonia Novitz, 'The European Union and International Labour Standards: The Dynamics of Dialogue Between the EU and the ILO' in Philip Alston (ed.), *Labour Rights as Human Rights* (OUP 2005).

64 Currently see Regulation (EU) No. 978/2012 of the European Parliament and of the Council of 25 October 2012 applying a scheme of generalised tariff preferences and repealing Council Regulation (EC) No. 732/2008 [2012] OJ L303/1, especially Articles 9–10.

65 See Chapter 4 above, text accompanying nn.316 et seq.

commercial aspects of intellectual property. Foreign direct investment falls within this competence,[66] and all other aspects of investment fall under the shared competence of the EU and its member states.[67] Article 208(2) of the TFEU requires that, in the context of development cooperation, the EU will comply with commitments and objectives 'approved in the context of the United Nations and other competent international organisations'. This would encompass standards endorsed by the ILO, presumably to the extent that they are consistent with those adopted by other UN bodies.

This part of the chapter outlines the 'model' for FTAs adopted by the EU in terms of its blend of economic, environmental and social (specifically labour) objectives. It then considers the treatment of 'sustainability' and freedom of association in the EU–Korea FTA dispute. Finally, it considers the broader implications of this model for sustainable development, considering how it could be further refined and developed.

4.1 A 'Template' for the TSD Chapter

No EU FTA is identical to another; in many ways this is reassuring in the sense that this would suggest that there is scope for contracting parties from third countries (outside the EU) to exercise influence over their content, scope and enforcement. However, the European Commission's approach to the content of TSD chapters has been remarkably consistent, from 2011 to the present date. To this extent, the EU–Korea FTA, provisionally applied from 2011 and ratified in 2015,[68] provides a helpful indication of what has been the model for TSD chapters that the European Commission has sought to promote.[69] The EU–Korea FTA seems to have established what have come to be described

---

[66] Opinion 2/15 on the Conclusion of the EU–Singapore FTA [2016] ECLI:EU:C:2016:992.

[67] Discussed by Clair Gammage, 'EU International Relations Law: The Power to Conclude International Trade Agreements' in Sangeeta Khorana and María García (eds), *Handbook on the EU and International Trade* (Edward Elgar Publishing 2018).

[68] See information provided on the EU Commission website at: https://ec.europa.eu/trade/policy/countries-and-regions/countries/south-korea/. See also https://webgate.ec.europa.eu/isdb_results/factsheets/country/details_south-korea_en.pdf.

[69] For more detailed analysis, see Tonia Novitz, 'Sustainable Labour Conditionality in EU Free Trade Agreements? Implications of the EU–Korea Expert Panel Report' (2022) 47(1) *European Law Review* 3, 9–12. See also Ludo Cuyvers, 'The Sustainable Development Clauses in Free Trade Agreements of the EU with Asian Countries: Perspectives for ASEAN' (2014) 22(4) *Journal of Contemporary European Studies* 427, 428 and 436; and Harrison et al n.12 above, 639.

as the essential features of (or a 'template' for) EU TSD chapters, in terms of substantive norms and procedures for disputes.[70]

4.1.1 A framework agreement

It is standard for an FTA to be accompanied by a 'framework agreement' including human rights and sustainable development provisions.[71] The EU–Korea Framework Agreement, for example, emphasises in Article 1 not only the parties' 'attachment to democratic principles, human rights and fundamental freedoms, and the rule of law [...] as laid down in the Universal Declaration of Human Rights and other relevant international human rights instruments' (in paragraph 1), but also their 'commitment to promoting sustainable development in all its dimensions' (in paragraph 2). As expected, the ILO has been a key reference point for the legitimacy of EU conditionality, and is mentioned expressly in Article 8 in relation to 'Cooperation in regional and international organisations', regarding obligations concerning 'decent work' arising under Article 22 and with the parties also affirming 'their commitments to respect, promote and realise internationally recognised labour and social standards, as laid down in particular in the ILO Declaration on Fundamental Rights and Principles at Work'.

4.1.2 Commitments to environmental but also labour standards

EU TSD chapters make clear commitments to environmental standards, but also recognise that sustainable development in trade extends to economic and social development, including the protection of labour standards. For example, chapter 13 on TSD in the EU–Korea FTA makes this explicit at the outset.[72] While there will be statements to the effect that there is no intention for such chapters to operate in a way that is 'protectionist'[73] and that the parties retain a 'right to regulate',[74] ILO norms can be expected to fall within the 'multilateral labour standards and agreements' governing the agreement.[75]

For example, in the EU–Korea FTA, Article 13.4.2 recognises 'a shared commitment to the International Labour Organization's core labour standards and decent work agenda', while Article 13.4.3 (at issue in the subsequent

---

70 Cuyvers n.69 above, 428 and 436; Harrison et al n.12 above, 639.

71 Full text available at: https://eeas.europa.eu/archives/docs/korea_south/docs/framework_agreement_final_en.pdf.

72 See Article 13.1 EU–Korea FTA; also the European Commission briefing note made available in 2009 at: https://trade.ec.europa.eu/doclib/docs/2009/october/tradoc_145203.pdf.

73 Article 13.2 EU–Korea FTA.

74 Article 13.3 EU–Korea FTA.

75 Article 13.4 EU–Korea FTA.

dispute) has two aspects: (1) 'respecting, promoting and realising, in their laws and practices, the principles concerning the fundamental rights', notably including '(a) freedom of association and the effective recognition of the right to collective bargaining'; and (2) 'continued and sustained efforts towards ratifying the fundamental ILO Conventions as well as the other conventions that are classified as "up-to-date" by the ILO'. This provision is distinct from the later 'non-regression clause' in Article 13.7 requiring effective enforcement of labour and environmental laws and stating that such protection should not be reduced 'in a manner affecting trade or investment between the Parties'.

It has become standard for these substantive terms to be inserted in EU FTAs (as they were in the EU–Korea FTA), without reference to other 'trade in services' or 'investment' chapters.[76] However, there are indications that this practice is likely to change, with the European Commission's most recent statement that 'sustainability considerations should also be proactively mainstreamed in different parts of trade agreements', at least as regards impact assessments.[77]

4.1.3 The role of Domestic Advisory Groups (DAGs)

'Monitoring' of EU FTAs tends to require transparency,[78] assessment of impact on sustainability[79] and 'cooperation' between the trading partners.[80] A further feature of these TSD chapters in EU FTAs is the creation of consultative bodies, designed to enable engagement with civil society organisations regarding their implementation. While the concrete substantive standards adopted by the ILO may lend legitimacy to the conditionality imposed in such FTAs, procedural legitimacy is also vital. That is what these participatory mechanisms are intended to promote. In doing so, they arguably hark back to the 'good governance' objectives of the Aarhus Convention.[81] EU FTAs typically require the creation of 'domestic advisory groups' (DAGs) both on the EU side and in the relevant partner country for each trade agreement. These

---

[76] Beate Sjåfjell, Jukka Mähönen, Tonia Novitz, Clair Gammage and Hanna Ahlström, Securing the Future of European Business: SMART Reform Proposals (University of Oslo Faculty of Law Research Paper No. 2020-11 2020), 48–51; available at: https://papers.ssrn.com/sol3/papers.cfm?abstract_id=3595048.

[77] *Communication on The Power of Trade Partnerships* n.12, 7 and 25.

[78] Article 13.9 EU–Korea FTA.

[79] Article 13.10 EU–Korea FTA.

[80] Article 13.11 EU–Korea FTA.

[81] United Nations Economic Commission for Europe (UNECE) Convention on Access to Information, Public Participation in Decision-Making and Access to Justice in Environmental Matters, 25 June 1998, which entered into force on 20 October 2001, available at: https://unece.org/DAM/env/pp/documents/cep43e.pdf. See Chapter 1 of this book, text accompanying n.100.

reflect civil society interests that include business and non-business representatives, the latter including trade unions and environmental NGOs. Civil society representatives also tend to meet in a 'Civil Society Forum' established by the FTA.

The intention is stated to be that these bodies raise economic, environmental and social issues that affect the groups that they represent. Their efficacy had been the subject of doubt.[82] These are only consultative bodies and, while they can raise issues and make recommendations, their influence depends on the majority view reached within each given constituency and the willingness of the trading partners to adhere to such views. DAG engagement with the concerns regarding treatment of freedom of association rights in Korea suggests that these bodies may be able to make sufficient noise to at least trigger complaints in certain circumstances, particularly when other key actors, such as the International Trade Union Confederation (ITUC), the European Trade Union Confederation (ETUC) and the national Korean Confederation of Trade Unions (KCTU), are allied,[83] and the European Parliament also supports action.[84]

Diana Potjomkina, Jan Orbie and Jamal Shahin have documented the various kinds of 'civil society resistance' emerging in the DAGs, observing both overt and more subtle practices. The authors suggest that civil society actors have not been naively co-opted but are well aware of their needs to pursue their

---

[82] Karin Ulmer, 'Trade Embedded Development Models' (2015) 31(3) *International Journal of Comparative Labour Law and Industrial Relations* 305, 320–1; and Harrison et al n.12, 644–5. See, regarding fears of co-optation and giving legitimacy to consultative processes without the ability to influence these, Jan Orbie, Deborah Martens, Myriam Oehri and Lore Van den Putte, 'Promoting Sustainable Development or Legitimising Free Trade? Civil Society Mechanisms in EU Trade Agreements' (2016) 1(4) *Third World Thematics: A TWQ Journal* 526, 531–2.

[83] See ITUC, *Annual Survey of Violations of Trade Union Rights* (ITUC 2010); and EU Domestic Advisory Group of the EU-Korea FTA, 'Update on Core Labour Standards in South Korea' (2016) available at: www.epsu.org/sites/default/files/article/files/ Update %20on %20Core %20Labour %20Standards %20in %20South %20Korea %20-%20Oct%202016.pdf. See also an interview with the International Director of the KCTU, 21 March 2021, available at: www.bilaterals.org/?fta-labour-rights-provisions; and María J. García, 'Sanctioning Capacity in Trade and Sustainability Chapters in EU Trade Agreements: The EU–Korea Case' (2022) 10(1) *Politics and Governance* 58, 62–3 and 65.

[84] European Parliament resolution of 18 May 2017 on the implementation of the Free Trade Agreement between the European Union and the Republic of Korea (2015/2059(INI)) P8_TA(2017)0225 available at: www .europarl .europa .eu/ doceo/ document/TA-8-2017-0225_EN.html?redirect.

own preferences both within the DAG mechanisms and outside these.[85] In this context, they observe the divergent agendas of different participants, differentiating between 'business' and 'non-business' actors, such that interviewees from the latter group 'prioritize sustainable development over trade' and see DG TRADE (the part of the European Commission responsible for trade relations) as treating sustainable development as 'secondary to commerce'.[86] Business representatives tend to seek to limit the role of sustainability to a 'voluntary' one, resisting criticism of partner countries, seeing 'themselves more as lobbyists of their own interests instead of watchdogs'.[87] A broader study conducted by Deborah Martens, Diana Potjomkina and Jan Orbie published in 2020 was revealing as regards the role that trade unions played in the DAGs. It emerges that business often dominates in decision-making and that key trade union actors can be excluded from third country partner DAGs, an example being the refusal to enable participation by the KCTU, one of the Korea's most important unions, in the EU–Korea FTA DAG.[88] Martens and colleagues also observed that 'environmental organisations are less active on trade issues in the EU and indeed are often underrepresented in the DAGs'.[89] This observation may also indicate that labour and environmental issues are perceived as operating alongside each other, rather than as interacting.

The European Commission has announced that in future there is to be greater involvement of the DAGs 'in monitoring the compliance stage'. The Commission also now advocates extension of 'the possibility to apply trade sanctions in cases of failure to comply with obligations that materially defeats the object and purpose of the Paris Agreement on Climate Change or in serious instances of non-compliance with the ILO fundamental principles and rights at work'.[90] European civil society will be able to prompt the European Commission to take forward complaints, for example through the new Single Entry Point facility introduced in 2020 for EU civil society and

---

85 Diana Potjomkina, Jan Orbie and Jamal Shahin, 'Forging Their Path in the Brussels Bubble? Civil Society Resistance within the Domestic Advisory Groups Created under the EU Trade Agreements' (2023) 36(3) *Cambridge Review of International Affairs*, 352, forthcoming available at: www.tandfonline.com/doi/full/10.1080/09557571.2020.1855110.

86 Ibid, 12.

87 Ibid, 13. This discrepancy between business and non-profit representatives in the DAGs had also been identified earlier in Orbie et al n.82, 540.

88 Deborah Martens, Diana Potjomkina and Jan Orbie, *Domestic Advisory Groups in EU Trade Agreements: Stuck at the Bottom or Moving Up the Ladder* (Friedrich Ebert Stiftung 2020), 20–2 and 46.

89 Ibid, 25.

90 *Communication on The Power of Trade Partnerships* n.12, 12.

its representatives.[91] Moreover, the Commission Communication of 2022 on 'The Power of Trade Partnerships' does recognise the differences between the power resources that different actors can access and seeks to promote measures that might address those differentials.[92] At the time of writing, the European Economic and Social Committee provides secretariat support for all 12 DAGs for the 2023–5 mandate.[93]

4.1.4 Dispute settlement

Where disputes arise, EU FTAs have to date adopted dispute settlement procedures particular to the TSD chapter and separate from those governing other parts of the agreement. For example, under the EU–Korea FTA, there could be 'government consultations' on issues arising from the TSD,[94] and an expert panel could be convened to provide a report for 'a matter that has not been satisfactorily addressed through government consultations'.[95] That report is to consist of advice and recommendations and will not be binding on the parties – a state of affairs which has caused frustration among academics who would like to see more efficacious enforcement of labour standards in TSD chapters.[96]

It may be unclear whether a dispute is a suitable subject for an expert panel under the TSD or the standard state–state dispute settlement (SSDS) provisions[97] available in respect of substantive entitlements arising under other FTA chapters. For example, the *Ukraine—Wood Products* case decided by an

---

[91] See 'Operating guidelines for the Single Entry Point and complaints mechanism for the enforcement of EU trade agreements and arrangements', available at https://trade.ec.europa.eu/access-to-markets/en/form-assets/operational_guidelines.pdf. Note that this procedure is not available to those at work in third countries.

[92] *Communication on The Power of Trade Partnerships* n.12, 10–11.

[93] See www.eesc.europa.eu/en/sections-other-bodies/other/all-domestic-and-joint-advisory-groups-dags.

[94] Article 13.14 EU–Korea FTA.

[95] Article 13.15 EU–Korea FTA.

[96] See Ciaran Cross, *Legitimising an Unsustainable Approach to Trade: A Discussion Paper on Sustainable Development Provisions in EU Free Trade Agreements* (PowerShift 2017); Marco Bronckers and Giovanni Gruni, 'Taking the Enforcement of Labour Standards in the EU's Free Trade Agreements Seriously' (2019) 56 *Common Market Law Review* 1591; and Peter-Tobias Stoll, Henner Gött and Patrick Abel, 'Model Labour Chapter for EU Trade Agreements – In cooperation with Bernd Lange MEP, Chairman of the Committee on International Trade and commissioned by Friedrich-Ebert Stiftung' (2020) available at: http://library.fes.de/pdf-files/bueros/singapur/16089.pdf.

[97] Regarding the use of SSDS provisions in FTAs, see Donald McRae, 'State-to-State Dispute Settlement in Megaregionals' in Benedict Kingsbury, David M. Malone, Paul Mertenskötter, Richard B. Stewart, Thomas Streinz and Atsushi Sunami (eds), *Megaregulation Contested: Global Economic Ordering after TPP, Law And Global Governance* (Oxford University Press 2019).

Arbitration Panel in 2020 illustrated how some trading partners might prefer resolution of a dispute through a non-binding decision from an expert panel under the TSD chapter, as opposed to the more stringent enforcement measures associated with state–state dispute settlement in FTAs.[98]

In 2022 the European Commission presented proposals to 'further align TSD enforcement with the general state-to-state dispute (SSDS) settlement' in FTAs and to 'extend the compliance stage to disputes under the TSD chapter'.[99] What this will mean in practice for the enhanced protection of labour standards has yet to be seen. A danger is that the specialist expertise of TSD expert panellists will be bypassed and that this may make a considerable difference to the outcome of the decision.[100] However, one would hope that it would be possible to engage suitably qualified members of an arbitration panel whose finding was binding. A remaining difficulty may be channelling the information that workers or their organisations have into the dispute resolution process.[101] At the time of writing, the Commission's proposed policy has now been implemented for the first time in the EU–New Zealand FTA signed on 9 July 2023, chapter 19 of which sets out a 'Trade and Sustainable Development' chapter that goes beyond the substantive commitments previously contained in the EU–Korea model. This chapter is also enforceable through mainstream SSDS by virtue of Article 26.2.2 in chapter 26 on 'Dispute Settlement'.[102] It is expected that the EU–Australia FTA will take a similar form, but that text is still subject to negotiation at the time of writing.[103]

---

[98] *Restrictions applied by Ukraine on exports of certain wood products to the European Union,* Final Report of the Arbitration Panel established pursuant to Article 307 of the Association Agreement between Ukraine and the EU and its Member States, 11.12.20. Ukraine argued that the dispute should have been brought to an expert panel, on the basis that its breach of a provision relating to trade in goods concerned 'forest products' covered by the TSD chapter. However, at para. 251 the Arbitration Panel found that provisions in the TSD chapter could not be regarded as 'self-standing or unqualified measures to justify measures that are in breach of other provisions'.

[99] *Communication on The Power of Trade Partnerships* n.12, 11.

[100] Rittich n.8, 208; Geraldo Vidigal, 'Regional Trade Adjudication and the Rise of Sustainability Disputes: *Korea—Labour Commitments* and *Ukraine—Wood Export Bans*' (2022) 116(3) *American Journal of International Law* 567, 575 and 578.

[101] Rittich n.8, 209.

[102] See Free Trade Agreement Between the European Union and New Zealand (EU–NZ FTA) signed on 9 July 2023 available at: www .mfat .govt .nz/ en/ trade/ free-trade-agreements/free-trade-agreements-concluded-but-not-in-force/new-zealand -european-union-free-trade-agreement/ nz-eu-free-trade-agreement-by-chapter/; and https://policy .trade.ec.europa.eu/ eu-trade-relationships-country-and-region/ countries -and-regions/new-zealand/eu-new-zealand-agreement/text-agreement_en.

[103] For the EU–Australia round reports as at August 2023, see https://policy.trade.ec .europa.eu/eu-trade-relationships-country-and-region/countries-and-regions/australia/ eu-australia-agreement/documents_en.

4.2 The EU–Korea FTA Expert Panel Report: On Sustainable Development and Freedom of Association

Concerns regarding freedom of association in Korea, even prior to conclusion of the FTA, had taken the form of complaints to the ILO, for example concerning decertification of trade unions for retaining members who had been dismissed for their trade union activities, as well as the punishment of trade union officials by imprisonment for organising protests and taking industrial action.[104] There was no precondition that Korea comply with these ILO standards relating to freedom of association prior to conclusion of the FTA, which would seem to have been a missed opportunity.[105] By 2017, the ILO Committee on Freedom of Association had found there to be numerous breaches of freedom of association, including with respect to the right to strike.[106] Indeed, the European Commission's reticence to call Korea to account under the TSD chapter was seen to be typical of a more 'general orientation to non-application of the labour clauses – whatever their specific textual content'.[107]

The EU's complaint regarding Korean conduct under the FTA related only to two matters. The first was Korea's non-ratification of several core ILO Conventions, including those concerning freedom of association (that is, Conventions Nos 87 and 98). The second concerned certain breaches of freedom of association which arose by virtue of the content of the Korean Trade Union and Labour Relations Act 1997 (the TULRAA),[108] none of which

---

[104] See EU Domestic Advisory Group of the EU–Korea FTA n.83. See also ILO CFA NORMLEX website, recording cases concerning Korea including: Case Nos 1865, 2602, 2620, 3047, 3138, 3237, 3238 and 3262.

[105] Cf. Franz Christian Ebert, 'Labour Provisions in EU Trade Agreements: What Potential for Channelling Labour Standards-related Capacity Building?' (2016) 155(3) *International Labour Review* 407; and Franz Christian Ebert, 'Increasing the Social Sustainability of Trade Agreements in Terms of Labour Standards: Insights from the TPP Experience' in Clair Gammage and Tonia Novitz (eds), *Sustainable Trade, Investment and Finance: Towards Responsible and Coherent Regulatory Frameworks* (Edward Elgar Publishing 2019).

[106] See ILO CFA Case No 3238 (Korea), Report No 383, October 2017.

[107] See for this general observation, Joo-Cheong Tham and K.D. Ewing, 'Labour Clauses in the TPP and TTIP: A Comparison without a Difference?' (2016) 17 *Melbourne Journal of International Law* 1, 24; on the EU–Korea FTA as emblematic of this reluctance to enforce, see Harrison et al n.12, 645; Park n.62, 836; and Demy van't Wout, 'The Enforceability of the Trade and Sustainable Development Chapters of the European Union's Free Trade Agreements' (2021) *Asia Europe Journal* 1, 2, 7 and 10 published online; available at: https://link.springer.com/article/10.1007/s10308-021-00627-1.

[108] For an English translation, see www.ilo.org/dyn/natlex/natlex4.detail?p_isn=46398.

touched on either the right to strike or the access of trade unions to peaceful protest, which had been the focus of CFA concern. Presumably, the controversy at the ILO regarding the right to strike had made this, even some years later, a difficult basis on which to present any complaint.[109] Aleydis Nissen regards the narrow scope of the EU complaint relating to the right to strike as a key failure of the European Commission, and an indication that the EU is still not willing to be *that* assertive, even in the face of the EU DAG's ongoing identification of 'persistent issues' regarding Korean legislative interference with the right to strike and access to collective bargaining.[110]

In referring the matter to an expert panel, the European Commission relied on Article 13.4 of the EU–Korea FTA, as opposed to the non-regression clause (Article 13.7), which would have required an effect on trade. The expert panel for the EU–Korea FTA dispute was established by December 2019, ultimately led by Jill Murray, a prominent labour law scholar based in Melbourne; her indisputable expertise would seem to be detectable in the report issued on 20 January 2021.[111]

On the one hand, there has been disappointment that the Expert Panel Report did not deliver criticism of Korea's tardy ratification of core ILO Conventions.[112] Article 13.4.3 required 'continued and sustained efforts' without setting any timeframe. In that context, the 'tangible, though slow' and 'less than optimal' action taken by Korea would suffice, at least for the time being.[113] Subsequent to publication of the Export Panel Report, Korea did ratify Conventions Nos 29, 87 and 98,[114] although Convention No. 105 remains outstanding and is the subject of ongoing pressure through the Civil Society Forum under the FTA. So, to that extent, the proceedings brought by the EU may have had some (if only partial) impact.

The Expert Panel Report's findings are more notable for their assertion of jurisdiction in the absence of an alleged effect on trade and their treatment of freedom of association, both of which arguably have significant and

---

109 See Chapter 3 in this book, text accompanying nn.171 et seq.

110 Aleydis Nissen, 'Not that Assertive: The EU's Take on Enforcement of Labour Obligations in Its Free Trade Agreement with South Korea' (2022) 33(2) *European Journal of International Law* 607, 623 and 629.

111 See for further details of the panel appointment and procedure, the EU–Korea FTA Expert Panel Report n.13 above, paras 4–41.

112 Jan Orbie, 'EU Trade Policy Meets Geopolitics: What about Trade Justice?' (2021) 26(2) *European Foreign Affairs Review* 197, 199.

113 EU–Korea FTA Expert Panel Report n.13 above, paras 291–2.

114 Celebrated in a virtual ceremony with the then ILO Director-General, Guy Ryder, as reported at: www.ilo.org/global/standards/WCMS_785448/lang--en/index.htm.

far-reaching effects.[115] In relation to the former, Korea had explicitly relied on the earlier arbitral findings in a case brought by the US against Guatemala under the Dominican Republic–Central American Free Trade Agreement (CAFTA-DR).[116] In the Guatemala case, US claims were founded on Article 16.2.1 of the CAFTA-DR FTA, which required that the alleged breaches of freedom of association occur in 'a manner affecting trade between the Parties'.[117] The Arbitration Panel found that there had been a 'sustained or recurring course of action or inaction' by the Guatemalan Ministry of Labour, but did not conclude that 'a failure to effectively enforce labor laws protecting the right to organize or the right to bargain collectively necessarily affects conditions of competition'.[118]

By way of contrast, the EU–Korea FTA Expert Panel Report took a different view. First, the three-member panel was confident that Article 13.4.3 did not require any trade effect; the non-regression clause which would have mirrored that in the *Guatemala* case was not at issue.[119] Yet, even if Article 13.7 had been at issue, it could not be assumed that Korean non-compliance with freedom of association would have no impact on trade. The Expert Panel Report stressed the connections between economic, social and environmental objectives connected to 'sustainable development' and their interaction in the EU–Korea FTA.[120] Trade and labour could in this way be seen as 'interdependent and mutually reinforcing'.[121] The CAFTA-DR agreement at issue

---

[115] For an earlier summary of these arguments, see Tonia Novitz, *Enforceable Social Clauses in Trade Agreements with 'Bite'? Implications of the EU–South Korea Panel of Experts Report of 20 January 2021* (ETUI Policy Brief 2021).

[116] Expert Panel Report n.13 above, para. 58, with reference to *Final Report of the Panel, Guatemala – Issues Relating to the Obligations Under Article 16.2.1(a) of the CAFTA-DR,* 14 June 2017.

[117] ILO, *Labour Provisions in Trade Agreements* (ILO 2016), 45–7.

[118] Final Report of the Panel, Guatemala n.116 above, at para. 485. For critical comment, see Blackett (2020) n.11 above, at 599–606; Tequila J. Brooks, 'Enforcement of Labor Standards in Trade Agreements: The Case of Guatemala' in Kimberly Ann Elliott (ed.), *Handbook on Globalisation and Labour Standards* (Edward Elgar Publishing 2022); and Lance Compa, Jeffrey Vogt and Eric Gottwald, *Wrong Turn for Workers' Rights: The US–Guatemala CAFTA Labor Arbitration Ruling – And What to Do about It* (Labour Rights 2018) available at: https://laborrights.org/sites/default/files/publications/Wrong%20Turn%20for%20Workers%20Rights%20-%20March%202018.pdf.

[119] Expert Panel Report n.13 above, at para. 92; a conclusion reached after application of Articles 31 and 32 of the Vienna Convention on the Law of Treaties, for which see also paras 42–53 and 61–73.

[120] Ibid, paras 74–9 and paras 90–4.

[121] Ibid, para. 77, citing Clair Gammage, 'Social Norms in EU Free Trade Agreements: Justiciable or Not?' in Gammage and Novitz n.105.

in the *Guatemala* case was said not to 'have the same contextual setting of sustainable development as the EU-Korea FTA'; nor did it 'refer to the range of multilateral and international agreements and declarations which the Parties have included in the EU-Korea FTA'.[122] A sustainable development agenda thereby was used to confer greater protection for labour standards than might have otherwise been the case. This is intriguing, given that the freedom of association issue apparently arose solely in a labour (and arguably an economic) context with no hint of environmental issues being at play. However, it may be useful in establishing a point of reference for viewing all three as interacting in future disputes.

Further, the treatment of freedom of association in the Expert Panel Report would seem to reflect the understanding and expertise of a chair who was an expert labour lawyer and could explain the relevance of the claims presented. First and perhaps foremost of these was that the Korean trade union legislation, the TULRAA, operated to exclude many of those in the wider world of work from trade union representation.[123] Article 2(1) of the TULRAA excluded from the Act's definition of 'worker' the self-employed, dismissed and unemployed, and Article 2(4)(d) of the TULRAA prevented union certification if non-workers were permitted to join and remain members. The Expert Panel Report found that the ILO 'principles of freedom of association' referred to in Article 13.4.3 contained certain tangible obligations, which became legally binding by virtue of their inclusion in the EU–Korea FTA.[124] While it could 'be difficult for States to obtain guidance on the precise legal implications of the fundamental principles' set out in the ILO 1998 Declaration, freedom of association was extensively examined by 'the ILO supervisory system', which had established sufficient content to be applied in this case.[125] In so doing, the Report referred to the general principles established by the ILO Committee on Freedom of Association (CFA) which have been recognised as authoritative, rather than its specific conclusions on Korean cases.[126] Also discussed were the findings of UN human rights supervisory bodies and decisions of other

[122] Expert Panel Report n.13 above, para. 93.

[123] Other concerns relating to freedom of association also arose, but are not addressed in full here. For more detailed treatment, see Novitz n.69 above, at 15–18; and Aleydis Nissen, 'And So It Begins: Trade and Sustainable Development Recommendations by a Panel of Experts under a European Union Free Trade Agreement' (2021) 7 *International Labor Rights Case Law* 257.

[124] Expert Panel Report n.13 above, paras 107 and 122.

[125] Expert Panel Report n.13, 138 citing Jordi Agusti-Panareda, Franz Christian Ebert and Desirée LeClercq, 'ILO Standards and Trade Agreements: A Case for Consistency' (2015) 36 *Comparative Labor Law and Policy Journal* 347, 365.

[126] For example, see Expert Report n.13, para. 146.

national and regional courts which supported the expert panel's reliance on the CFA as an authority on the meaning of freedom of association principles.[127]

On this basis, the expert panel concluded that self-employed workers should be entitled to form and join trade unions and that Korean legislation was in breach of freedom of association principles.[128] In particular, the definition of a 'worker' in TULRAA would have the effect of excluding those who worked for platforms or in the gig economy for a number of different clients.[129] The Expert Panel Report thereby made a powerful claim for far-reaching trade union representation of people engaged in many different types of work in a way which is consistent with established ILO supervisory jurisprudence.[130] Moreover, decertification of trade unions continuing to represent dismissed workers as members was regarded as illegitimate, as employers would be able to dismiss on grounds of trade union membership and activities with relative impunity.[131]

In terms of follow-up on these findings, the legal situation in Korea does not seem to have improved markedly for trade unions.[132] A Civil Society Forum meeting in September 2022 was still advocating legal implementation of the three newly ratified ILO Conventions in Korea and ratification of Convention No. 105.[133] In June 2023, the ILO CFA reported to the Governing Body that new guidelines for public sector collective bargaining in Korea 'had been developed without the full and meaningful participation of the trade unions and

---

[127] Ibid, paras 114 and 117, and illustrated by paras 131–2.

[128] Expert Report n.13, para. 148; see also Valerio De Stefano, 'Not as Simple as It Seems: The ILO and the Personal Scope of International Labour Standards' (2021) 160(3) *International Labour Review* 387.

[129] Expert Report n.13, para. 165.

[130] Tonia Novitz, 'Collective Labour Rights for Working People: The legal framework established by the International Labour Organization' in Paul et al n.56.

[131] Expert Report n.13, paras 203–7.

[132] See 'IndustriALL Global Union condemns arrest of KCTU president Yang Kyeung-soo and demands his immediate release', news release 4 September 2021, available at: www.industriall-union.org/industriall-global-union-condemns-arrest-of-kctu-president-yang-kyeung-soo-and-demands-his-immediate; also the Open Letter from International Lawyers Assisting Workers (ILAW), 12 September 2021, available at: www.ilawnetwork.com/wp-content/uploads/2021/09/ILAW-Letter-to-President-Moon-Sept-12-2021.pdf.

[133] The Civil Society Forum under the EU-Korea Free Trade Agreement 8th meeting in Seoul – 13 September 2022 Joint Conclusions of the Korea DAG and the EU DAG, paras 8–9 and 15, available at: www.eesc.europa.eu/sites/default/files/files/joint_conclusions_eu-korea_csf_2022_final_proofread_clean.pdf.

effectively interfered with collective bargaining'.[134] It does not seem that much progress is being made on freedom of association in Korea to date.

In this context, it is interesting that the European Commission is now taking the lead on permitting collective bargaining for certain self-employed workers as an exception to the usual operation of EU competition law.[135] At the time that proceedings were being brought against Korea before the expert panel, the EU had not contemplated, let alone introduced, these measures. Progress has been incremental and perhaps, apart from the obvious merits of intra-EU internal market and social policy reasons for such a step, it may have been helpful to demonstrate that reforms demanded from Korea are not hypocritical.

4.3 Prospects for EU FTAs and Their Treatment of Sustainable Development

The EU–Korea Expert Panel Report made certain determinations regarding the extent to which ILO standards can be legally binding when included in an FTA, and drew significant conclusions regarding the scope of rights to trade union representation under freedom of association principles. Both conclusions were drawn in the wider normative context of the incorporation of 'sustainable development' as an aspiration in that FTA, having combined and interconnected economic, environmental and social dimensions.

The Expert Panel Report was, however, only operative between the parties and clearly has been viewed as merely recommendatory by Korea. It did not have strict legal effect and could not (easily) be the subject of trade sanctions. The European Commission is doing its best to encourage Korea to change tack, particularly on treatment of trade union representation of platform workers, but is doing so more by example than coercion. While it has been observed optimistically that the Expert Panel Report 'demonstrated that the legal nature of many sustainability standards does not differ from other FTA norms that are subject to regular dispute settlement',[136] and this seems likely to prompt change to future mechanisms for enforcement in FTAs, progress seems slow.

---

[134] Minutes of the 348th Session of the Governing Body of the International Labour Office GB.348/PV, 17 June 2023, 10, para. 45.

[135] Commission Guidelines (2022) n.57. Cf. European Commission 'Draft Guidelines on the application of EU competition law to collective agreements regarding the working conditions of self-employed persons' (2021) available at: https:// competition -policy .ec .europa .eu/ public -consultations/ 2021 -collective -bargaining -2 _en. See Ricardo M. Buendia Esteban, 'Examining Recent Initiatives to Ensure Labour Rights for Platform Workers in the European Union to Tackle the Problem of Domination' (2022) 28(4) *Transfer: European Review of Labour and Research* 475.

[136] Marco Bronckers and Giovanni Gruni, 'Retooling the Sustainability Standards in EU Free Trade Agreements' (2021) 24 *Journal of International Economic Law* 25, 51.

Notably, the EU–UK Trade and Cooperation Agreement (TCA),[137] which was concluded prior to the decision of the expert panel in the EU–Korea FTA case, follows the standard EU FTA pattern by including what may be described as a TSD chapter.[138] Operative post-Brexit, the TCA states the importance of sustainable development[139] and makes reference expressly to the 2030 Agenda and Sustainable Development Goals.[140] Once again, 'multilateral labour standards and agreements', including ILO instruments, core labour standards and 'decent work', are treated as intrinsic to the achievement of sustainable development,[141] as are certain 'multilateral environmental agreements'.[142] Continuing compliance with labour or environmental standards previously established under EU law is notably not required.[143] However, there will still need to be a 'trade effect' of any breach of labour and environmental standards under the TCA for sanctions to be imposed by either side in the imposition of the intended 'level playing field'.[144] These matters will be overseen by a 'Trade Specialised Committee on Level Playing Field for Open and Fair Competition and Sustainable Development'.[145] The recent EU–NZ FTA, in chapter 19, also refers to the 2030 Agenda, compliance with ILO standards, human rights protections as well as environmental objectives such as those related to climate

---

[137] Trade and Cooperation Agreement (TCA) between the European Union and the European Atomic Energy Community, of the one part, and the United Kingdom of Great Britain and Northern Ireland, of the other part [2021] OJ L 149/10, version approved by European Parliament (following provisional application of the TCA from 1 January 2021).

[138] Part Two – Heading 1 – Title XI: Level playing field for open and fair competition and sustainable development'.

[139] Article 355.2 EU–UK TCA.

[140] Article 397 EU–UK TCA.

[141] Articles 397 and 399 EU–UK TCA. The 'multilateral' labour agreements also include Council of Europe instruments, as observed by K.D. Ewing, 'The EU–UK Trade and Cooperation Agreement: Implications for ILO Standards and the European Social Charter in the United Kingdom' (2021) 32(2) *King's Law Journal* 306.

[142] Article 400 EU–UK TCA.

[143] Discussed by Nicola Countouris, K.D. Ewing and John Hendy, *The EU–UK Trade and Cooperation Agreement and Workers' Rights* (ETUI Policy Brief 2021), 2.

[144] Article 411 EU–UK TCA. Otherwise, Article 399 is primarily to be enforced through consultations and potentially a 'panel of experts' under Article 409 in a manner similar to that contemplated in chapter 13 of the EU–Korea FTA. See Phil Syrpis, 'The Influence of the EU on UK Labour Law—Before and After Brexit' (2022) 51(4) *Industrial Law Journal* 802.

[145] For a full and helpful outline and analysis, see Federico Ortino, *Workers' Rights Commitments in the UK–EU Trade and Cooperation Agreement (TCA)* (Trades Union Congress 2021).

change. As observed above, that instrument even offers the promise of direct access to SSDS as a means of enforcement.[146]

There are however two overarching problems potentially with the continuing operational model of EU FTAs in terms of their treatment of labour standards in sustainable development chapters. One is conceptual and the other pragmatic.

The first conceptual difficulty is that while EU commitment to sustainable development in trade is manifested in a determination to promote protection of environmental standards and internationally agreed labour norms (especially those stemming from the ILO), the ways in which these two dimensions might engage, conflict or overlap are not addressed. There is nothing in the actual provisions set out in the FTA chapters that tells us anything about the ways in which these norms are expected to relate and be reconciled, let alone how they can be weighed against other economic objectives pursued through EU FTA chapters relating to goods, services or investment. Nor is there any dispute resolution decision or arbitral panel finding that gives us a clue. There is, for the time being, nothing to see here.

This is troubling because experience of just transitions debates indicates that instances will arise where they coalesce.[147] An example might be where restriction of entry of products may be based on both environmental concerns regarding their extraction and the use of forced labour. Presumably provisions relating to environmental and labour standards in a TSD chapter could be relied upon simultaneously and cited together in the dispute. More difficult may be the scenario where they conflict. It is possible to imagine the scenario where collective bargaining or a right to strike will not be permitted in respect of workers temporarily supplied by a service provider, due to host state requirements regarding environmental protections in that particular sector. These tensions will have to be given detailed consideration in due course, but the failure to begin to pre-empt or anticipate such disputes is arguably troubling. One wonders how long environmental and labour standards can play out on parallel tracks in EU FTAs and trade relations, given that sustainable development (at least in theory if not EU practice) demands attention to the ways in which they combine.

A second more pragmatic issue is the fact that the EU has maintained its own distinctive approach, without apparently learning from lessons learnt elsewhere. In particular, the Agreement between the United States of America,

---

[146] See this chapter n.102.

[147] See Béla Galgóczi, 'Just Transition on the Ground: Challenges and Opportunities for Social Dialogue' (2020) 26(4) *European Journal of Industrial Relations* 367; and Paolo Tomassetti, 'From Treadmill of Production to Just Transition and Beyond' (2020) 26(4) *European Journal of Industrial Relations* 439.

the United Mexican States and Canada (USMCA) which entered into force on 1 July 2020[148] could provide a useful reference point in several ways. As Federico Ortino has observed, the limitations of the current 'trade effect' requirement in the EU–UK TCA could be overcome were the provisions of the USMCA followed, which clarify the meaning of that term.[149] Under USMCA, a trade effect arises merely where a 'course of action or inaction' involves:

> (i) a person or industry that produces a good or supplies a service traded between the Parties or has an investment in the territory of the Party that has failed to comply with this obligation; or (ii) a person or industry that produces a good or supplies a service that competes in the territory of a Party with a good or a service of another Party.[150]

Also, he notes the presumption of an effect on trade established by USMCA: 'For purposes of dispute settlement, a panel shall presume that a failure is in a manner affecting trade or investment between the Parties, unless the responding Party demonstrates otherwise.'[151]

Moreover, the treatment of 'rules of origins' (ROO) under chapter 4 USMCA operates to ensure that certain goods (in the automobile sector) cannot be traded where they are produced without payment of the set minimum wage.[152] This is an innovative way to link trade to labour standards compliance.

Perhaps even more significantly, the Facility-Specific Rapid Response Labor Mechanism ('rapid response mechanism' or 'RRM') set out in Annex 31-A of the USMCA enables sanctions to be directed to a specific corporate facility which does not comply with workers' free association and collective bargaining rights.[153] Janice Bellace has observed that this mechanism 'avoids

---

[148] Text and supplementary materials are available at: https://ustr.gov/trade-agreements/free-trade-agreements/united-states-mexico-canada-agreement.

[149] Ortino n.145, 33.

[150] See USMCA n.148, Article 23.5.1 footnote 11.

[151] Ibid, Article 23.5.1 footnote 12.

[152] James Harrison, 'The Labour Rights Agenda in Free Trade Agreements' (2019) 20 *Journal of World Trade* 705, 723. See also Karen Curtis and Elizabeth Echeverría Manrique, 'Trade Arrangements and Labour Standards in a Supply Chain World: Current Issues and Future Considerations' in Guillaume Delautre, Elizabeth Echeverría Manrique and Colin Fenwick (eds), *Decent Work in a Globalized Economy: Lessons from Public and Private Initiatives* (ILO 2021), 116; and Franz Christian Ebert and Pedro A Villarreal, 'The Renegotiated "NAFTA": What Is in It for Labor Rights?' (EJIL: Talk!, 11 October 2018) available at: www.ejiltalk.org/the-renegotiated-nafta-what-is-in-it-for-labor-rights/.

[153] As Ortino n.145 observes, at 35, these mechanisms (between Canada and Mexico and the US and Mexico – not seemingly between Canada and the US) extend to 'priority sectors', manufacturing goods, supplying services or engaged in mining. Agriculture is not covered. Also the goods or services must either be traded between

penalizing good employers for the failures of some'.[154] A failing of EU country-based trade measures has been that they could be used to penalise workers across an entire sector or even state,[155] while the rapid response mechanism would seem to make a more targeted approach. It has been observed that the RRM could be a valuable addition to a new EU approach.[156] The Commission has to date proposed that RRM be incorporated into the new GSP Regulation but has not made a similar suggestion regarding utilisation in FTAs.[157] A problem with the RRM would seem to be that it is likely to be used by the US rather than its trading partners,[158] that it is difficult to challenge the evidential basis for its use[159] and that it can have a harsh impact on competitor industries.[160] The RRM operates swiftly without necessitating access to the representatives of those at work who will be affected in the third country concerned. This then may be a problematic mechanism to adopt without further critical engagement and modification.

In February 2022, the Commission's ambitions were extended in a Communication 'on Decent Work Worldwide for a Global Just Transition and a Sustainable Recovery'.[161] That Communication was however only linked with two internal market measures to be adopted not through trade instruments

---

the contracting parties or compete in the territory of a party with a good or a service of the other party, as set out in Articles 31-A.15 and 31-B.15.

[154] Janice R. Bellace, 'The 1998 ILO Declaration: Responding to Globalization and Impacting Corporate Labor Behavior' in Kimberly Ann Elliott (ed.), *Handbook on Globalisation and Labour Standards* (Edward Elgar Publishing 2022), 197. See also Curtis and Echeverría Manrique n.152, 116–17.

[155] Cf. Velluti n.60, 218.

[156] Eline Blot, Antoine Oger and James Harrison, *Enhancing Sustainability in EU Free Trade Agreements: The Case for a Holistic Approach* (Institute for European Environmental Policy (IEEP) 2022), 11–12 and 31–2; Ortino n.145, 37–9.

[157] Blot et al n.156, 12; Proposal for a Regulation of the European Parliament and of the Council on applying a generalised scheme of tariff preferences and repealing Regulation (EU) No 978/2012 of the European Parliament and of the Council COM/2021/579 final 22.9.2021, 3, 7 and 13.

[158] Six proceedings had been initiated by the US against Mexico private facilities by February 2023 and eleven by July 2023. See Marva Corley-Coulibaly, Gaia Grasselli and Ira Postolachi, *Promoting and Enforcing Compliance with Labour Provisions in Trade Agreements: Comparative analysis of Canada, European Union and United States approaches and practices* (ILO 2023), 52; and Desirée LeClercq, 'Integrating Non-binding Labour Standards in Binding Trade Agreements: The ILO's Feedback Loop' (2023) 26(3) *Journal of International Economic Law* 542–58.

[159] Corley-Coulibaly et al n.158, 90 on the timescale and reversal of the burden of proof.

[160] Desirée LeClercq, 'A Worker-Centered Trade Policy' (2023) 61(3) *Columbia Journal of Transnational Law* 733.

[161] *Communication on Decent Work Worldwide* n.18.

but by an EU Directive and a regulation, respectively. These are a proposal for a Directive 'on Corporate Sustainability Due Diligence' (released at the time of the 'Decent Work' Communication)[162] and a later proposal for a Regulation 'on prohibiting products made with forced labour on the Union market'.[163] We will return to these initiatives at the end of this chapter, considering their implications for collective voice including representation of the wider world of work in countries outside the EU.

To summarise for the time being, it emerges that EU practice regarding FTAs has involved, and will continue to entail, the inclusion of TSD chapters, which refer to ILO standards. Measures are being taken by the EU to promote collective worker voice, through DAGs and the Civil Society Forum created by each FTA. The relationship between environmental and labour standards in these chapters have yet to be fully explored, although we do have the statement of the Expert Panel Report in the EU–Korea FTA dispute that the economic, environmental and social dimensions of sustainable development should be regarded as inter-related. The further and highly significant practical difficulty is that participatory mechanisms for the implementation and enforcement of EU FTAs remain unwieldy and the EU does not, for the time being, seem willing to learn lessons from elsewhere, such as the novel and experimental provisions in the USMCA.

5. OTHER SIGNIFICANT FTA CHAPTERS AFFECTING LABOUR STANDARDS: TEMPORARY MOVEMENT AND INVESTMENT

While the primary concern of this chapter lies with the TSD provisions incorporated into EU FTAs, there remain other features of FTAs that also have obvious relevance to the protection of labour standards globally. The two identified here and discussed below relate to 'temporary presence of natural persons for business' and 'investment'. For example, provisions relating to the former, which permit forms of temporary migration to assist service providers, is set out in Article 7.17–7.20 of the EU–Korea FTA and chapter 10 of the Comprehensive Economic Trade Agreement (CETA) concluded between

---

162 European Commission, *Proposal for a Directive of the European Parliament and of the Council on Corporate Sustainability Due Diligence and amending Directive (EU) 2019/1937* COM(2022) 71 final, 23.2.2022.

163 European Commission, *Proposal for a Regulation of the European Parliament and of the Council on prohibiting products made with forced labour on the Union market* COM(2022) 453 final, 14.9.2022.

Canada and the EU.[164] No investment chapter was included in the EU–Korea FTA,[165] but this was a contentious feature of the CETA FTA (in chapter 8 of that instrument). There has been controversy over the extent to which labour standards can be applied by a host state to those workers temporarily in their jurisdiction under the FTA, whereas the question regarding investment has been the extent to which protections for investors can overwhelm 'the right to regulate' labour and environmental standards by the host state.

5.1 Temporary Presence of Natural Persons for Business Purposes

Chapter 4 of this book has outlined the regime applied under GATS relating to mode 4 trade in services, namely the ability of natural persons to enter another state to deliver services, whether as employees of a service provider or in business on their own account.[166] Under GATS, states will set out in the Schedule the obligations regarding market access for various sectors and occupations, according to which they wish to be bound. In so doing, their decisions are guided by the Annex to GATS on Temporary Movement of Natural Persons, which envisages that states retain their own discretion regarding immigration arrangements and proclaims that those who move in this way are not to be regarded as 'seeking access to the employment market' of a host state. FTAs offer an opportunity to embrace and further embellish or add 'disciplines' to the GATS mode 4 model.[167]

Chapter 7 of the EU–Korea FTA, for example, made provision for 'Trade in services, establishment and electronic commerce', which was to include 'Temporary presence of natural persons for business'.[168] This enabled 'the

---

[164] See the final text of the CETA, available at: www.international.gc.ca/trade-commerce/trade-agreements-accords-commerciaux/agr-acc/ceta-aecg/text-texte/toc-tdm.aspx?lang=eng. For the Joint Interpretative Instrument, see: www.international.gc.ca/trade-commerce/trade-agreements-accords-commerciaux/agr-acc/ceta-aecg/jii-iic.aspx?lang=eng. Note that there are three chapters in CETA which address TSD: chapter 22 on 'Trade and Sustainable Development', chapter 23 on 'Trade and Labour', and chapter 24 on 'Trade and Environment'.

[165] An agreement on investment was concluded separately between Korea and Iceland, Liechtenstein and Switzerland as European Free Trade Area (EFTA) states. See: www.efta.int/free-trade/free-trade-agreements/korea#anchor-12.

[166] See Chapter 4 of this book, text accompanying nn.247 et seq.

[167] Antonia Carzaniga and Swatu Sharma, *Regulatory Disciplines on the Mobility of Service Professionals – Lessons from Regional Trade Agreements*, Staff Working Paper ERSD-2022-12 (WTO, 2022). In the African context, see Xaver Keller, *AfCFTA and Trade in Services for Development* (German Cooperation/GIZ Discussion Paper 2019), 6 available at: www.giz.de/en/downloads/Policy%20Paper%20-%20Trade%20in%20Services.pdf.

[168] Article 17.17 EU–Korea FTA.

entry into, and temporary stay in' the parties' territories of 'key personnel, graduate trainees, business services sellers, contractual service suppliers and independent professionals', subject to certain requirements. These included a notable embellishment on the bare terms of the 'mode 4' annex to the GATS in the Annex to chapter 7 insofar as the EU made clear that 'commitments on key personnel and graduate trainees do not apply in cases where the intent or effect of their regulatory presence is to interfere with, or otherwise affect the outcome of, any labour/management dispute or negotiation'.[169] Moreover, '[a]ll requirements of the laws and regulations of the EU party regarding entry, stay, work and social security measures shall continue to apply', specifically including 'minimum wages as well as collective wage agreements'.[170] The Korean explanatory notes to the Schedule were more nuanced, containing a comparable provision on industrial disputes,[171] but requiring that the 'key personnel, graduate trainees and business sellers whose entries and temporary stays are permitted shall observe the immigration and labour laws of Korea'. This is not quite the same as requiring that their employers do so.

Another example is chapter 10 of CETA (titled 'Temporary Entry and Stay of Natural Persons for Business Purposes'), which makes provision for certain 'trained workers' to temporarily enter the EU or Canada for business purposes, setting out the types of 'professional' worker permitted and the maximum length of their stay.[172] In a manner similar to the Annex to GATS, Article 10.2.2 states: 'This Chapter shall not apply to measures affecting natural persons seeking access to the employment market of a Party, nor shall it apply to measures regarding citizenship, residence, or employment on a permanent basis.' However, Article 10.2.5 follows what is now a familiar precedent by stating that 'all requirements of the Parties' laws regarding employment and social security measures shall continue to apply, including regulations concerning minimum wages as well as collective wage agreements', although there does not seem yet to be a mechanism for coordinating social security provision.[173] Under standard transparency requirements, it would be expected that those national laws applicable would be supplied on request to service

169 EU–Korea FTA, Annex 7-A-3, EU Party List of Reservations, para. 3.

170 Ibid, para. 5.

171 EU–Korea FTA, Annex 7-A-3, Schedule of Specific Commitments Explanatory Notes, para. 5.

172 For a summary, see: https://policy.trade.ec.europa.eu/eu-trade-relationships-country-and-region/countries-and-regions/canada/eu-canada-agreement/ceta-chapter-chapter_en.

173 Cf. measures taken within the EU due to Regulation (EC) No 883/2004 on the coordination of social security systems [2004] OJ L 200/1. See also on transparency requirements, Carzaniga and Sharma n.167.

providers in a manner broadly compatible with the minimum requirements set by Article 3(1) of the Posting of Workers Directive 1996 applicable in the EU internal market to temporary movement of natural persons.[174]

Also embedded in the main text of CETA (in Article 10.2.6) is the statement that the chapter will not apply 'where the intent or effect of the temporary entry or stay is to interfere with or otherwise affect the outcome of a labour or management dispute or negotiation, or the employment of natural persons who are involved in such dispute or negotiation'. This term is also present in the EU's most recent FTA with New Zealand, which goes further to state that those moving temporarily are to receive no less favourable treatment than that accorded 'in like situations' to the host state's own natural persons. Normally, these provisions relating to favourable treatment (and non-discrimination) relate to the supply of services, not the persons engaged themselves. So, this could be regarded as a further breakthrough.[175]

EU temporary movement chapters tend to be restricted in their application to skilled professionals in particular sectors, arguably less likely to be subjected to exploitation or abuse and more useful to the host state concerned. They do however anticipate temporary movement for a much longer period than the maximum contemplated under the EU's most recent legislation governing such movement within its own internal market.[176] Under conflict of laws principles, these temporary migrants are likely to find that their contract (whether of employment or as an independent contractor) will remain governed by their home state in which their corporate employer is based. This may impede enforcement of their contractual terms in practice. Nor can they necessarily rely on their length of residence in the host state, as they have not entered the 'employment market' for immigration purposes.[177] This can impact in negative ways on private and family life, despite entitlements under international and

---

[174] Directive 96/71/EC of the European Parliament and of the Council of 16.12.96 concerning the posting of workers in the framework of the provision of services [1997] OJ L18/1 (PWD).

[175] See Article 10.20.2 of the EU–NZ FTA.

[176] Directive 2018/957 amending the Posting of Workers Directive [2018] OJ L 173/16. See Piet Van Nuffel and Sofia Afanasjeva, 'The Posting of Workers Directive Revised: Enhancing the Protection of Workers in the Cross-border Provision of Services' (2018) 3(3) *European Papers* 1401, 1421–2. See also discussion in Novitz and Andrijasevic n.16, 1332 and 1335.

[177] Philip L. Martin, *GATS, Migration and Labour Standards* DP/165/2006 (ILO 2006), 3 available at: https:// documents .pub/ document/ gats -migration -and -labor -migration -and -labor -standards -philip -l -martin -international .html ?page = 1; see also Jon Horgen Friberg, 'The Stages of Migration: From Going Abroad to Settling Down: Post-accession Polish Migrant Workers in Norway' (2012) 38(10) *Journal of Ethnic and Migration Studies* 1589.

regional human rights law.[178] Indeed, temporary visas issued to inter-corporate transferees under these kinds of FTA provisions may mean that, if personal ties have been forged in the host state, these workers may tolerate forms of ill-treatment to see the visa renewed.[179] These sources of vulnerability can be compounded where there is uncertainty regarding the appropriate country where a legal claim can be made, especially where transnational employment agencies are involved.[180]

In this scenario, one might have thought that the European Commission would be proposing that these types of chapters in FTAs be more closely integrated with TSD labour standard protections; and perhaps this will follow from the 2022 Commission Communication on 'The Power of Trade Partnerships' to the extent that the Commission endorses more explicit mainstreaming of TSD chapters.[181]

The terms of the TSD chapter 19 in the 2023 EU–NZ FTA are promising in terms of integration of the norms set out there into the operationalisation of the other chapters. An example is the statement in Article 19.3.1 of the parties' 'commitment to promote the development of international trade in a way that is conducive to decent work for all, as expressed in the ILO Declaration on Social Justice for a Fair Globalization', but also broader statements of intent in Article 19.11 on 'trade and investment supporting sustainable development' and Article 19.12 on 'trade and responsible business conduct and supply chain management'. What may also be crucial is whether, in the design and implementation of further policy and regulations under chapters 10 and 19, there is respect for SDGs 8 (in terms of decent work) and 16 (access to justice).

5.2 Investment Chapters

There is also a risk that sustainable development objectives can be undermined by the investment chapters incorporated into FTAs. International investment law largely falls outside the reach of the WTO, except perhaps as regards mode 3 trade in services, where delivery of services entails establishment in the host

---

[178] See for example the International Covenant on Civil and Political Rights 1966, Article 17 and rights and duties regarding the family in the African Charter of Human and Peoples' Rights, Article 18.

[179] Anna Boucher, 'Measuring Migrant Worker Rights Violations in Practice: The Example of Temporary Skilled Visas in Australia' (2019) 61(2) *Journal of Industrial Relations* 277, at 280 citing Judy Fudge, 'Precarious Migrant Status and Precarious Employment: The Paradox of International Rights for Migrant Workers' (2012) 34 *Comparative Labor Law and Policy Journal* 95.

[180] Jennifer Gordon, 'Regulating the Human Supply Chain' (2017) 102 *Iowa Law Review* 445.

[181] *Communication on The Power of Trade Partnerships* n.12, 7 and 25.

state, as discussed above in Chapter 4.[182] Instead, different investment-related obligations can be agreed by states under bilateral or multilateral investment agreements. Indeed, this is the approach which the EU is currently taking in negotiations with India, namely that the FTA will be discrete from the intended additional agreement on investment protection.[183] However, with increasing frequency, investment chapters are placed in FTAs alongside chapters relating to trade in goods and services.[184] There are also divergent mechanisms created for enforcement of these treaty commitments through ISDS. Chapter 4 introduced the International Centre for Settlement of Investment Disputes (ICSID), which is part of the World Bank Group,[185] while the United Nations Commission on International Trade Law (UNCITRAL) has adopted its own parallel Arbitration Rules.[186] Even then, state parties can choose to establish their own particular mechanism peculiar to any given agreement, as the EU did in chapter 10 of CETA with respect to a standing investment tribunal and appellate 'Court'.[187]

To reassure investors that their investments will be secure, there has been a tendency for investment agreements and chapters in FTAs to contain

---

[182] See Chapter 4 of this book, text accompanying n.246. In this way, GATS requirements regarding most favoured nation status, national treatment, market access and transparency become relevant.

[183] See https://policy.trade.ec.europa.eu/news/eu-and-india-kick-start-ambitious-trade-agenda-2022-06-17_en.

[184] Makson Usynin and Szilárd Gáspár-Szilágyi, 'The Growing Tendency of Including Investment Agreements in PTAs' [2017] *Netherlands Yearbook of International Law* 267.

[185] See Chapter 4 of this book, text accompanying nn.24–30.

[186] Ibid, text accompanying n.29. See also the collaboration of ICSID and UNCITRAL in publishing a Draft Code of Conduct for Adjudicators in International Investment Disputes on 19 April 2021, available at: https://icsid.worldbank.org/news-and-events/icsid-and-uncitral-release-version-two-draft-code-conduct-adjudicators and https://uncitral.un.org/en/news/icsid-and-uncitral-release-version-two-draft-code-conduct-adjudicators-international-investment. Cf. their different approaches to 'transparency', discussed in Gary J. Stewart, 'The 2022 ICSID Rules: A Leap toward Greater Transparency in ICSID Arbitration' (2022) *ICSID Review*, forthcoming available at: https://academic.oup.com/icsidreview/advance-article-abstract/doi/10.1093/icsidreview/siac016/6611548?redirectedFrom=PDF&casa_token=Guz57_8NQdgAAAAA: 7aq1d DZAELQI8xa 12aIP70hNP 7BWLDQgS0q SJTY1wLcSU 6naO0jJDHd-AoyYiHS876bFNiu1flHy.

[187] Subsequently also endorsed by the Court of Justice in *Opinion 1/17* (2019) EU:C:2019:341. See Christian Riffel, 'The CETA Opinion of the European Court of Justice and Its Implications—Not that Selfish After All' (2019) 22(3) *Journal of International Economic Law* 503.

a number of standard clauses.[188] For example, these instruments tend to recognise the 'legitimate expectations' of investors that states will not take action affecting the value of their investments and that there will be 'fair and equitable treatment' of external investors vis-à-vis each other and national private actors. Accordingly, the 'right to regulate' often acknowledged by states in relation to environmental and labour standards under TSD, environmental or labour chapters can come into tension with the terms of an investment chapter under the same agreement. In the *Bilcon* case,[189] a North American Free Trade Agreement (NAFTA) arbitral panel found that the Canadian government's rejection of an investor's environmental report relating to a mining and marine project could be challenged on the basis of the investor's 'legitimate expectations' stemming from official state endorsement at the outset of the project. Canada was obliged to compensate accordingly.[190] If a state engages in direct or even indirect expropriatory measures for sustainability reasons, it is common for ISDS to find that the investor must also be compensated.[191] This approach has also enabled corporations to bring claims where the introduction of environmental or labour standards creates costs for investors, which can be claimed to amount to 'indirect expropriation'. As a result, many have called for reform of the terms included in investment instruments and the ways in which such norms are applied.[192]

---

[188] For the gradual emergence of consensus in use of certain standard terms and their interpretation, see Stephan W. Schill, 'W(h)ither Fragmentation? On the Literature and Sociology of International Investment Law' (2011) 22(3) *European Journal of International Law* 875.

[189] *Clayton/Bilcon v Government of Canada*, (PCA) Case No. 2009-04 (17 March 2015) Award on Jurisdiction and Liability at paras 595–8, 602, 734–8, see: www.italaw.com/sites/default/files/case-documents/italaw4212.pdf.

[190] Ibid at 531–3. Discussed also in Clair Gammage and Tonia Novitz, 'Trade, Investment and Corporate Sustainability' in Beate Sjåfjell and Christopher M. Bruner (eds), *Cambridge Handbook of Corporate Law, Corporate Governance and Sustainability* (Cambridge University Press 2019), 25–7.

[191] *Compania del Desarrollode Santa Elena, S.A. v Republic of Costa Rica*, ICSID Case No. ARB/96/1, Final Award of 17 February 2002, paras 71-72 15 ICSID Rev. 167 (2000): 'where property is expropriated, even for environmental purposes, whether domestic or international, the State's obligation to pay compensation remains.' See also *Técnicas Medioambientales Tecmed, S.A. v United Mexican States*, ICSID Case No. ARB (AF)/00/2, Award of 29 May 2003, at 20, para. 63. See more recently *Eco Oro Minerals Corp v Republic of Colombia*, ICSID Case No ARB/16/41, Decision on Jurisdiction, Liability and Directions on Quantum, 9 September 2021 and analysis from Robert Garden, 'Eco Oro v Colombia: The Brave New World of Environmental Exceptions' (2023) 38(1) *ICSID Review* 17. Also the discussion regarding 'police powers' in Chapter 4 of this book, text accompanying n.25 et seq.

[192] On *Bilcon*, see for example Michael Carfagnini, 'Too Low a Threshold: Bilcon v Canada and the International Minimum Standard of Treatment' (2016) 53 *Canadian Yearbook of International Law/Annuaire canadien de droit international* 244.

Investors have notoriously relied on terms under bilateral or multilateral investment agreements, or investment chapters included in trade agreements, to bring claims in ISDS that seek to restrict a government's regulation of labour markets. For example, an investor may claim that the introduction of improved labour standards has a negative effect on their investment, such that they should be compensated. Even if ultimately unsuccessful, the investor can impose on the government the initial costs of defending the proceedings brought.[193]

In *Noble Ventures v Romania* the investor made a claim for indirect expropriation and a breach of fair and equitable treatment on the basis that the Romanian government had not adequately prevented or policed unlawful strikes, although that claim was ultimately unsuccessful.[194] In *Veolia v Egypt*, the investor required the Egyptian government to defend a rise in the monthly minimum wage, with the outcome of the claim now determined but remaining private.[195] From a rule of law perspective, ISDS is problematic in its lack of transparency,[196] working potentially to the advantage of the larger multinational corporations that engage in investment as opposed to more vulnerable countries in the Global South (and those who work there).[197]

Investment chapters can have a chilling effect on the improvements of labour standards where they are most needed. This would seem to contravene SDG target 10.a, which aims to '[e]ncourage official development assistance and financial flows, including foreign direct investment, to States where the need is greatest, in particular least developed countries' and which should be read as consistent with the 'decent work' objectives in SDG 8. The CETA investment chapter does seek to promote transparency through the standing tribunal and court system, while also stating in the Joint Interpretative Instrument that the parties aim to 'preserve the right of governments to regulate in the

---

193 See Tonia Novitz, 'SDG 8: Promote Sustained, Inclusive and Sustainable Economic Growth, Full and Productive Employment and Decent Work for All' in Jonas Ebbesson and Ellen Hey, *Cambridge Handbook of the Sustainable Development Goals* (Cambridge University Press 2020), 222–4.

194 *Noble Ventures, Inc. v Romania*, ICSID Case no. ARB/01/11 (12 October 2005), https://icsid.worldbank.org/en/Pages/cases/casedetail.aspx?CaseNo=ARB/01/11.

195 *Veolia Propreté v Arab Republic of Egypt*, ICSID Case no. ARB/12/15, (25 May 2018), https://icsid.worldbank.org/en/Pages/cases/casedetail.aspx?CaseNo=ARB/12/15.

196 Stephan W. Schill, 'Reforming Investor–State Dispute Settlement: A (Comparative and International) Constitutional Law Framework' (2017) 20(3) *Journal of International Economic Law* 649.

197 Thomas Schultz and Cédric Dupont, 'Investment Arbitration: Promoting the Rule of Law or Over-Empowering Investors? A Quantitative Empirical Study' (2014) 25(4) *European Journal of International Law* 1147.

public interest'.[198] Much will depend on how this chapter operates in practice, but it could be seen as a step towards greater recognition of sustainable development aspirations than other aspects of its external relations activities to date.

6. EU INTERNAL MARKET MEASURES AIMED EXTERNALLY

As part of the EU's common commercial policy, certain EU internal market regulatory measures may be adopted which have wider effects on the rest of the world. From 2019 onwards, the von der Leyen Commission stated its determination to embed sustainability into the corporate governance framework, so as to place constraints on EU corporate conduct related to production, services and trade.[199] Those ambitions were extended further in 2022 in the Commission Communication 'on decent work worldwide for a global just transition and a sustainable recovery',[200] which highlighted the urgency of promoting decent work 'in line with the UN 2030 Agenda for Sustainable Development', including in global supply chains.[201]

Accompanying the 2022 Communication was a proposed 'Corporate Sustainability Due Diligence' Directive.[202] This has since been followed by a further proposal for a Regulation 'on prohibiting products made with forced labour on the Union market'.[203] The latter would involve blocking such goods at the EU border and goes beyond the explicit permission to prevent entry of products made by prison labour (as set out in Article XX of the General Agreement on Trade and Services at the WTO), although the measure could be justified potentially on a 'public morals' basis.[204] These are trade but also

---

[198] See n.164, para. 6: 'Investment'.

[199] European Commission, *Communication on the European Green Deal* COM(2019) 640 11.12.2019, 17.

[200] *Communication on Decent Work Worldwide* n.18.

[201] Ibid, 1–2.

[202] *Proposal for a Directive on Corporate Sustainability* COM(2022) 71 final n.162. See for amendments made by the European Parliament in June 2023: www.europarl.europa.eu/doceo/document/TA-9-2023-0209_EN.html.

[203] *Proposal for a Regulation on prohibiting products made with forced labour* COM(2022) 453 final n.163.

[204] For debates over the 'product/process' distinction usually applied regarding 'public morals' and problems of extra-territoriality, see Olivier De Schutter, *Trade in the Service of Sustainable Development: Linking Trade to Labour Rights and Environmental Standards* (Hart Publishing 2015) ch 4; and Kofi Addo, *Core Labour Standards and International Trade: Lessons from the Regional Context* (Springer 2015) ch 5. See also Chapter 4 of this book, text accompanying nn.293 et seq. For an argument that it is possible to design measures to comply with the GATT and GATS general exception requirements, see International Lawyers Assisting Workers (ILAW)

corporate social responsibility (CSR) measures, traversing the divide between public and private regulation, which some welcome given frustration arising from the limitations of existing FTA conditionality.[205] However, these measures are also problematic, not so much in terms of content but by virtue of the limited participatory engagement they anticipate. They will not be adopted through agreement with other states or private actors, but rather as unilateral EU internal market regulation which have effects on trade and external relations.[206]

In both proposals, the EU's ambitions are limited to norms already endorsed on the global stage, being carefully tied not merely to SDGs but widely ratified international instruments, as set out in the annex to the proposal for a Due Diligence Directive. Part I of the annex lists in detail the pertinent 'violations of rights and prohibitions included in international human rights agreements', accompanied by the 'human rights and fundamental freedoms conventions' to which each potential violation relates. Part II has the same format, but focuses on 'violations of internationally recognized objectives and prohibitions included in environmental conventions'.[207] Notably, the right to strike is explicitly protected in Part I,[208] although the extent to which EU law protects such a right within the EU internal market remains questionable.[209] Further, the division between Parts I and II of the annex repeats the EU pattern of regarding environmental and labour issues as distinct, and does not address connections between them. However, at least some basic transparency requirements would seem to be met and the legitimacy of the labour standards to be imposed is determined with reference to ILO and other UN instruments.

Network, *WTO Law Aspects of Import Prohibitions on Products and Services Made Using Forced Labour* (ILAW 2022).

[205] Kevin Kolben, 'A Supply Chain Approach to Trade and Labor Provisions' (2017) 5(4) *Politics and Governance* 60.

[206] See, for further analysis of these 'hybrid measures' in the context of broader EU social policy objectives, Tonia Novitz, 'Challenges When Combining Labour and Environmental Objectives: Trade and Sustainable Development Chapters and Beyond' in Adalberto Perulli and Tiziano Treu (eds), *Labour Law and Climate Change: Towards a Just Transition* (Wolters Kluwer 2023), especially at 106–9.

[207] *ANNEX to the proposal for a Directive of the European Parliament and of the Council on Corporate Sustainability Due Diligence and amending Directive (EU) 2019/1937* COM (2022) 71 final, 23.2.2022.

[208] Ibid, 3.

[209] Jeffrey Vogt et al, *The Right to Strike in International Law* (Hart 2020), 106–18; see also Tonia Novitz, 'The EU and the Right to Strike: Regulation through the Back Door and Its Impact on Social Dialogue' (2016) 27(1) *King's Law Journal* 46.

The Commission proposal for a Regulation on forced labour products refers explicitly to SDG 8.7.[210] 'Forced labour' in Article 1(1) is defined in terms of Article 2 of the ILO Forced Labour Convention 1930 (No. 29). Once again, legitimacy for the EU regulatory action contemplated is derived from internationally agreed norms. Any difficulties lie less in the standards adopted and potentially more in their operationalisation.

In preparation of the proposed Due Diligence Directive, the Commission consulted with members of the public, business, social partners in the EU (comprising employer and trade union representatives), NGOs and company lawyers.[211] It is however difficult to detect evidence of engagement with worker representatives or other entities in third countries. Article 7(2) of the proposed Directive does seem to contemplate design of a 'prevention action plan' to be conducted with 'affected stakeholders', while Article 8(3)(b) states that a 'corrective action plan' is to be 'developed in consultation with stakeholders'. It seems that 'stakeholders' will include (under Article 3) 'the company's employees, the employees of its subsidiaries, and other individuals, groups, communities or entities whose rights or interests are or could be affected by the products, services and operations of that company, its subsidiaries and its business relationships'. So, stakeholders could include those at work even in third countries, but this is not made express and the mechanisms for implementation of Articles 7 and 8 are to be left to EU member states, potentially without consultative engagement with representatives of labour in those countries. Recital (49) however states that the Commission and Member States should act 'in partnership' with the governments and 'stakeholders' in the affected countries. How that is to be achieved remains unclear, at least for the time being.

The draft regulation on products made with forced labour was prefaced by extensive consultation with, for example, the ILO and the OECD.[212] It seems that '[t]here were disagreements between what evidence is needed by authorities to withhold a consignment at the point of entry'.[213] There is scope for cooperation between the Commission and relevant authorities in third countries (under Article 26) relating to forced labour violations which might affect the entry of particular goods, but the extent to which the concerns of those at work from third countries can feed into this process will be crucial. Instead, the aim stated in Article 4 is to comply with 'due diligence guidelines

---

210 *Proposal for a Directive on Corporate Sustainability* COM(2022) 71 final n.162, 1.

211 Ibid, 18–19.

212 *Proposal for a Regulation on prohibiting products made with forced labour* COM(2022) 453 final n.163, 5–8, with the summary reflecting differences of opinion.

213 Ibid, 6.

or recommendations of the UN, ILO, OECD or other relevant international organisations' and 'any other due diligence in relation to forced labour'; but we know that at present concerns have been raised regarding the extent to which local workers (and their representatives) feed into extant due diligence processes, as shall be discussed in Chapter 6 of this book.[214] What is notable is the European Commission's apparent ongoing determination to take both bilateral and unilateral action on trade conditionality relating to labour and environmental issues. Once again, the interaction between those issues seems to be glossed over, and the extent and scope of consultative engagement with those whose jobs and livelihoods at work will be affected by such policies has yet to be systematically considered, which is what arguably SDGs 8, 10 and 16 demand.[215] There is the possibility that the ILO could mediate to assist in accessing those voices, but this is not expressly contemplated in the proposal.

7. FINAL OBSERVATIONS ON THE EU AS AN EXEMPLAR

This chapter has examined the role of free trade agreements in promoting, implementing and even undermining labour standards. It has considered, in particular, how the EU as a powerful and prominent trade actor has navigated its role. It emerges that the EU has only been minimally constrained by the WTO architecture in pursuing its trade agreements and objectives. The EU has achieved its aims of growth and freer trade in ways that substantially benefit its member states.[216]

However, the EU has done more than this. The EU has also been an interesting ideological presence, insisting on the promotion of international labour standards as a facet of sustainable development, using ILO standards as its reference point to anchor the legitimacy of the terms imposed in FTAs on third countries. This has seemingly led to action internally in the EU to overcome potential (and actual) allegations of hypocrisy, arguably akin to compliance with the chapeau of Article XX of the GATT, for example seeking to enable

---

[214] See Chapter 6 of this book, text accompanying n.159 et seq.

[215] See Chapters 1 and 2 in this book above.

[216] See for example the European Commission's report on how the EU–Korea FTA has had beneficial effects for Korea but has brought more extensive benefits for the EU. See https://ec.europa.eu/trade/policy/countries-and-regions/countries/south-korea/ , which records that EU exports of goods to Korea increased by 77 per cent from 2010 to 2018, while EU exports of services to Korea increased by 82 per cent (compared to a 66 per cent increase in EU imports from Korea from 2010 to 2017).

collective bargaining by EU platform workers in the context of the EU–Korea FTA dispute.[217]

The EU has also used innovative methods to promote implementation of sustainable development, drawing on collective voice mechanisms engaging 'civil society' and 'stakeholders' in which workers and their representatives can play some part. These procedures tap the voices of established unions on the national, regional and global stage, but effective representation of those engaged in precarious and atypical work has probably yet to be achieved. As we have seen, in recent initiatives within the internal market the views of those at work in third countries were not sought, as they might have been.

Instead, labour from third countries can be utilised as temporary and expendable within a trade in services matrix played out in FTAs concluded by the EU and other states. The chapters on 'business persons' placed in EU FTAs enable short-term movement of employees and those providing services for a business into EU states, but are more limited than the EU internal market equivalent regulation of 'posted workers'. While it is not difficult to see why WTO members might fail to reach consensus to amend GATS provisions regarding Mode 4 trade in services, it is harder to explain why the EU does not include more extensive and explicit protections for those engaged in temporary movement who enter the EU. This could be more readily achieved if TSD chapters are 'mainstreamed' into the rest of the FTA and made more readily enforceable, as suggested by the European Commission in a 2022 Communication and apparently manifested in the EU–NZ FTA.[218] Already we are beginning to see more action on procedural and substantive reforms regarding investment protection, with chapter 10 of CETA illustrating the potential for change.

An interesting question in the context of the EU's 'normative power' is whether the EU approach taken to trade and sustainable development regarding labour standards can and should be more broadly applied. Certainly, the EU provides an interesting focus for attention and analysis. However, it is not wholly successful yet, for example, given its failure to consider how environmental and labour standards can combine or conflict. Moreover, norms and mechanisms which are in operation in EU FTAs do not yet reflect the input of the collective voice of those engaged in the wider 'world of work' in the Global South.[219] This is even more obviously true of recent EU regulatory proposals seeking to promote global delivery of the ILO's Decent Work

---

[217] See text accompanying n.58 above.

[218] See this chapter, text accompanying n.104.

[219] For comparable concern raised in a US context, see Desirée LeClercq, 'A Worker-Centred Trade Policy' (2023) 61(3) *Columbia Journal of Transnational Law* 733.

Agenda with reference to the SDGs, as explained above. We may need to look to the more organic evolution of labour standards and sustainable development clauses in South–South agreements to establish effective promotion of decent work, enhancing regional governance,[220] which could be sensitive to the needs of a wider variety of affected actors.

We might also wish to consider what kinds of participatory engagement should be contemplated in the context of FTAs. The assumption of the European Commission, enshrined in the constitution of DAGs and a Civil Society Forum, and even in the more recent proposals, is that labour's role is merely consultative. There remain greater possibilities for cross-border collective bargaining and even collective action,[221] which are entirely overlooked in the EU FTA context. It is this opportunity that is considered more fully in the next chapter of this book, which considers the scope for private alongside public regulation of corporate conduct in global supply chains.

---

[220] As proposed by Blackett (2015) n.11 163–5 and Blackett (2020) n.11, 607–9.

[221] Rittich n.8, 214 envisages 'rules and regimes that permit workers to organize more easily across borders and thereby capture more of the gains of their labor'.

6. Sustainable regulation of corporate conduct in global supply chains?

1. INTRODUCTION

Chapter 5 considered the potential for the content of free trade agreements (FTAs) to normalise the protection of environmental and social sustainability. That ambition may however be thwarted by 'the development of more far-flung supplier networks that trade enables', which is 'just as likely to normalize low labor standards and reliance on precarious forms of work'.[1] The difficulty, as Kerry Rittich has explained, is that global supply chains can detach and thereby insulate 'lead firms' – that is, multinational enterprises (MNEs) – from responsibilities (legal and ethical) to those who labour at some geographical and contractual distance.[2] These extensive and sophisticated contractual networks enable risks and costs to be shifted to other weaker parties down the chain, whether they be hirers or suppliers of labour.[3]

Olivier De Schutter has described this web of contractual relationships in trade as the 'international dispersal of production',[4] observing how 80 per cent of global trade could be attributed to such methods, in which different aspects of 'value' are added to goods in multiple countries so that they are made across the world.[5] Additionally, the complex contractual framework established with respect to so-called global value chains can also involve fragmentation of

[1] Kerry Rittich, 'Trade Agreements in the Twenty-First Century: Rethinking the Trade–Labor Linkage' in Alvaro Santos, Chantal Thomas and David Trubek (eds), *World Trade and Investment Law Reimagined: A Progressive Agenda for an Inclusive Globalization* (Anthem Press 2019), 205.

[2] Ibid.

[3] Ibid, 207.

[4] Olivier De Schutter, *Trade in the Service of Sustainable Development: Linking Trade to Labour Rights and Environmental Standards* (Bloomsbury/Hart 2015), 175.

[5] Ibid, citing Suzanne Berger, *How We Compete: What Companies Around the World Are Doing to Make it in Today's Global Economy* (Doubleday 2005).

supply of services through trade within and between states.[6] Standard 'rules of origin' in trade become difficult to apply.

The international trade regime was premised on understanding competition in trade as operating between states, but a more realistic view of the contemporary global economy is that trade may be more concerned with competition between corporate entities which operate in complex ways across national borders.[7] The question then becomes how such competition can be prevented from being destructive in environmental and social terms, in the sense of a 'race to the bottom' as described in Chapter 2,[8] when state actors are not the principal agents and may not be the most effective regulators.[9] For example, despite the introduction of a 'Human Trafficking Deterrence and Suppression Act' in Bangladesh in 2012, there was only one conviction under that legislation in 2017, while more than half a million people were then estimated to be held in forms of modern slavery.[10] The importance of making not just states but corporate actors responsible for implementing sustainability, including labour standards, in global supply chains has been the subject of emerging and accelerating regulatory attention on the world stage.[11]

Remedies for the current situation are now being designed, not only by states and international organisations, but also by private actors. Aristea Koukiadaki has described this regulatory matrix as a 'patchwork of rules', but one which has potential for improving efficacy through experimentation towards a more cohesive 'web'.[12] 'Corporate social responsibility' (CSR) has been fostered by

---

[6] Jane Kelsey, *Serving Whose Interests? The Political Economy of Trade in Services Agreements* (Routledge 2008); Jennifer Gordon, 'Regulating the Human Supply Chain' (2017) 102 *Iowa Law Review* 445; and Tonia Novitz, 'Evolutionary Trajectories for Transnational Labour Law: Trade in Goods to Trade in Services?' (2014) 67 *Current Legal Problems* 239.

[7] De Schutter n.4, 177.

[8] See Chapter 2 of this book, text accompanying n.42 et seq.

[9] Adelle Blackett, 'Global Governance, Legal Pluralism and the Decentered State: A Labor Law Critique of Codes of Corporate Conduct' (2001) *Indiana Journal of Global Legal Studies* 401; and Saskia Sassen, *Losing Control? Sovereignty in the Age of Globalization* (Columbia University Press 1996). More recently, see Kevin Kolben, 'A Supply Chain Approach to Trade and Labor Provisions' (2017) 5(4) *Politics and Governance* 60.

[10] Katrina Peake and Jeff Kenner, '"Slaves to Fashion" in Bangladesh and the EU: Promoting Decent Work?' (2020) 11(2) *European Labour Law Journal* 175, 177 and 186–7.

[11] For an impressive review from a range of contributors, see Guillaume Delautre, Elizabeth Echeverría Manrique and Colin Fenwick (eds), *Decent Work in a Globalized Economy: Lessons from Public and Private Initiatives* (ILO 2021).

[12] Aristea Koukiadaki, 'Global Supply Chains and Labour Standards: From a Patchwork of Rules to a Web of Rules?' in Barry Colfer, Brian Harney, Colm

MNEs seeking to self-regulate within their own corporate group or even the sector in which they operate. An alternative to such self-regulation, the outcomes of which have been variable, has been negotiation of broad overarching labour (and environmental) standards with global unions federations (GUFs).

We will see that the International Labour Organization (ILO) remains a source of normative legitimacy for corporate policy, so that core labour standards identified in Chapter 3[13] are commonly incorporated in codes of conduct promulgated by various international organisations, corporate social responsibility documents and even so-called international or global framework agreements (IFAs or GFAs) concluded between multinational enterprises and global union federations. It is also possible to detect increasing reference to 'sustainable development' as a source of norms, which is considered here with reference to the United Nations (UN) Sustainable Development Goals (SDGs) set out in the 2030 Agenda that were discussed in Chapters 1 and 2 of this book.[14]

An important question is what the normative framework of sustainable development could add to any future regulation of corporate conduct in global supply chains and the procedural mechanisms entailed. There is scope to explore here the potential for use of soft law mechanisms, navigating between different spheres or 'systems' of law (public and private, but also corporate, competition and labour law).[15] However, it will be argued in this chapter that, to leave no one behind, reflexive legal design needs to engage with those at work across the globe who have been affected by the ways in which trade has developed through these supply chains. Otherwise, corporate regulation will be created and enforced by those who have little material interest in making them effective, allowing sparse opportunity for transformational change in terms of economic, environmental or social justice (whether inter- or intra-generational). So much is evident from the analysis of power dynamics explored earlier in this book.[16]

McLaughlin, Chris F. Wright (eds), *Protecting the Future of Work: New Institutional Arrangements for Safeguarding Labour Standards* (Emerald Publishing Limited 2023).

13 See Chapter 3 of this book, text accompanying n.76 et seq.

14 United Nations (UN), Transforming our World: The 2030 Agenda for Sustainable Development, General Assembly, 70th Session, A/Res/70/1, New York, 2015 ('UN 2030 Agenda') available at: https://sustainabledevelopment.un.org/post2015/transformingourworld.

15 See Ralf Rogowski, *Reflexive Labour Law in the World Society* (Edward Elgar Publishing 2013), 246–50; and Gunther Teubner, 'Self-constitutionalizing TNCs? On the Linkage of "Private" and "Public" Corporate Codes of Conduct' (2011) 18(2) *Indiana Journal of Global Legal Studies* 617.

16 See Chapter 1 in this book, text accompanying n.63 et seq.

This chapter begins by discussing how our understanding of the dynamics of global supply chains has evolved and goes on to examine the emergence of voluntary corporate codes of conduct to protect brand reputation. The extent to which the corporate conduct could be influenced by international institutional initiatives is also considered. In this respect, the chapter outlines measures taken by the international community from the 1970s onwards, designed to address the growing power of MNEs in trade, and how these instruments have since been updated and embellished. In this context the chapter considers the current scale of 'due diligence' measures and their implications for lead firms, namely the extent to which they can be held to account for conduct of employers further down the supply chain. The difficulty of worker representation and participation within corporate due diligence systems is highlighted, before turning to an examination of the sphere within which trade unions (as well as other representatives of those at work) have been involved in the negotiation and implementation of GFAs. Finally, the potential role of the ILO in further contributing to the efficacy of all these corporate governance measures is considered. Throughout this chapter, my concern lies with tracking the increasing attention paid in this sphere to the notion of 'sustainable development', but also its limitations. Moreover, the significance of collective voice at work is highlighted as a means by which to tame corporate conduct in global supply chains, although there remain important questions regarding how emerging participatory mechanisms can foster inclusion of those engaged in all kinds of work across the globe.

2. THE DYNAMICS OF CORPORATE BEHAVIOUR WITHIN GLOBAL SUPPLY CHAINS

Supply chains have been defined at the ILO as 'the cross-border organization of the activities required to produce goods or services and bring them to consumers through inputs and various phases of development, production and delivery'.[17] The process of trade through supply chains can further be viewed through the prism of corporate conduct, which can include foreign direct investment in certain countries, to enable more profitable sites for production and service delivery. Supply chains can also operate through use of subsidiaries incorporated in various locations and subcontracting relating to 'goods, inputs and services'.[18] It has been reported by the ILO and OECD

[17] ILO, *Report IV: Decent Work in Global Supply Chains*, ILC, 105th Session (ILO 2016), 2; this definition being cited again in the ILO, *ILO Decent Work Interventions in Global Supply Chains: A Synthesis Review on Lessons Learned; What Works and Why, 2010–2019* (ILO 2019), 1.

[18] Ibid.

that, as of 2021, approximately 70 per cent of international trade involved 'global supply chains, as services, raw materials, parts, and components cross borders – often numerous times'.[19] The geographical and contractual distance between a so-called lead firm (usually the buyer with the brand reputation) and any environmental or social harms caused can be convenient. This distancing can circumvent legal liability (which would entail costs) while also keeping trade profitable for MNEs because they do not have to cover directly additional expenses that might be associated with ecological protections or, for example, living wages and other labour standards.

The results of current global supply chain arrangements have been exposed as highly detrimental to those at work in the Global South. One of the most potent emblematic events was the 2013 Rana Plaza disaster, the collapse of an eight-storey building containing five garment factories in Dhaka, Bangladesh, in which at least 1,132 people were killed and more than 2,500 were injured. The workers had been ordered by their employers to work in these premises, which had already been identified by an inspector as unsafe, under threat of dismissal.[20] Only five months prior to this catastrophe, 112 workers had died in a factory fire nearby.[21] These tragedies underscored the vulnerability of Global South workers in the ready-made garment (RMG) sector servicing brand consumers in the Global North.[22]

Nor should we assume that, because specific measures have been taken to address the situation in Bangladesh,[23] such incidents no longer arise. Just a year after the Rana Plaza disaster, a fire in a Pakistani RMG factory servicing a German brand led to a further 250 deaths.[24] More recently, concern

---

[19] ILO, *Gap Analysis of ILO Normative and Non-normative Measures to Ensure Decent Work in Supply Chains* WGDWS/2021 (ILO 2021), 7; and see www.oecd.org/trade/topics/global-value-chains-and-trade/.

[20] Anne Trebilcock, 'The Rana Plaza Disaster Seven Years On: Transnational Experiments and Perhaps a New Treaty?' (2020) 159(4) *International Labour Review* 545, 546.

[21] ILO, *The Rana Plaza Accident and Its Aftermath* (ILO 2018).

[22] Stephanie W. Barrientos, '"Labour Chains": Analysing the Role of Labour Contractors in Global Production Networks' (2013) 49(8) *The Journal of Development Studies* 1058; and Laura A. Carlson and Vera Bitsch, 'Social Sustainability in the Ready-made-garment Sector in Bangladesh: An Institutional Approach to Supply Chains' (2018) 21(2) *International Food and Agribusiness Management Review* 269.

[23] See discussion in Trebilcock n.20; Jennifer Bair, Mark Anner and Jeremy Blasi, 'The Political Economy of Private and Public Regulation in Post-Rana Plaza Bangladesh' (2020) 73(4) *ILR Review* 969; and Peake and Kenner n.10. See also section 5 of this chapter.

[24] Nicolas Bueno, 'Corporate Liability for Violations of the Human Right to Just Conditions of Work in Extraterritorial Operations' (2017) 21(5) *The International Journal of Human Rights* 565, 565.

has centred on the numerous unexplained deaths of migrant workers in Qatar, particularly in agriculture and construction.[25] The International Trade Union Confederation (ITUC) Global Labour Rights Index of 2022 has documented continuing decline of labour standards internationally, demonstrating that those performing work are becoming progressively less safe across the world.[26] These problems seem to have been compounded by the emergence of export processing zones (EPZs) or 'special economic zones',[27] where different labour standards may be applied. For example, the Dhaka EPZ in Bangladesh became notorious not only for a decline in labour standards but also for environmental pollution,[28] which has had further health and safety implications for workers and other members of the local community.[29]

The literature on 'supply chains' is extensive, awash with different definitions and analyses.[30] In the sphere of political economy, 'global commodity chains' (GCCs) are understood to refer to cross-border 'production processes

---

[25] ILO, *One Is Too Many: The Collection and Analysis of Data on Occupational Injuries in Qatar* (ILO 2021) reporting that in 2020 alone 50 workers died, with just over 500 severely injured, and 37,600 suffering mild to moderate injuries. Amnesty International, *'In the Prime of Their Lives': Qatar's Failure to Investigate, Remedy and Prevent Migrant Workers' Deaths* (Amnesty International 2021) links the high incidence of mortality to heat exposure and long working hours. See also the controversial article: 'Revealed: 6,500 migrant workers have died in Qatar since World Cup awarded' *The Guardian*, 23 February 2021.

[26] See ITUC Global Labour Rights index available at: www.globalrightsindex.org/en/2022.

[27] Blackett n.9, 403–6; see also Douglas Zeng, 'The Past, Present and Future of Special Economic Zones and Their Impact' (2021) 24 *Journal of International Economic Law* 259; and Jennifer Gordon, 'In the Zone: Work at the Intersection of Trade and Migration' (2022) 23(2) *Theoretical Inquiries in Law* 147, 151–7.

[28] M. Safiur Rahman, Narottam Saha and A. Hossain Molla, 'Potential Ecological Risk Assessment of Heavy Metal Contamination in Sediment and Water Body around Dhaka Export Processing Zone, Bangladesh' (2014) 71(5) *Environmental Earth Sciences* 2293; M.S. Islam, A. Sultana, M.S. Sultana, M. Shammi and M.K. Uddin, 'Surface Water Pollution around Dhaka Export Processing Zone and Its Impacts on Surrounding Aquatic Environment' (2016) 8(3) *Journal of Scientific Research* 413.

[29] M. Safiur Rahman, Yeasmin Nahar Jolly, Shirin Akter, Noshin Anjum Kamal, Rubina Rahman, Tasrina Rabia Choudhury, and Bilkis Ara Begum, 'Sources of Toxic Elements in Indoor Dust Sample at Export Processing Zone (EPZ) Area: Dhaka, Bangladesh; and Their Impact on Human Health' (2021) 28(29) *Environmental Science and Pollution Research* 39540.

[30] See for an earlier overview, particularly with reference to migrant work, Tonia Novitz, 'Supply Chains and Temporary Migrant Labour: The Relevance of Trade and Sustainability Frameworks' in Diamond Ashiagbor (ed.), *Re-imagining Labour Law for Development* (Hart 2019).

whose end is a finished commodity'.[31] The dynamics of these processes (and the chains that they constitute) is driven not only by states, but also by producer-driven and buyer-driven GCCs, which take distinctive forms. At various 'nodes' of each process, the utilisation of certain services may be vital. There could be demand to hire highly skilled workers to address supply-side problems, but more frequently there is demand for cheaper labour to enable profitable production of goods at a lower price.[32] The GCC literature has highlighted the significance of 'production chains', for example in relation to RMGs and electronic goods.[33] This focus on production of goods as opposed to trade in services may now be outdated. The OECD reported in 2021 that its members are trading significantly more in services, and that while manufacturing chains are shortening to take account of fewer suppliers, service chains are lengthening.[34] This is significant because the lengthening of supply chains, increasing distance between an MNE as the 'lead firm' and subcontractors, can lead to diminishing accountability.

The GCC analysis has since been supplemented by investigation of 'global production networks' (GPNs), an analytical perspective which does not so neatly distinguish states from markets. The claim is that identification of GPNs enables a more holistic view of markets as 'embedded' in states and political processes, so as to explore the ways in which firms connect ostensibly distinct countries and societies.[35] Jeffrey Henderson and colleagues sought to reconceptualise what have been regarded as linear 'chains' as 'highly complex network structures in which there are intricate links – horizontal, diagonal, as well as vertical – forming multi-dimensional, multi-layered lattices of economic activity'.[36] Moreover, the very idea of 'commodities' is critically interrogated, especially in the context of labour, while the distinction between the commercial interests of buyers and suppliers is found to be more fluid than

---

[31] Terence K. Hopkins and Immanuel Wallerstein, 'Commodity Chains in the World Economy prior to 1800' (1986) 10(1) *Review* 157, 159, cited in Gary Gereffi and Miguel Korzeniewicz (eds), *Commodity Chains and Global Capitalism* (Prager 1994), 2.

[32] Barrientos n.22.

[33] See Jim Glassman, 'The Geo-political Economy of Global Production Networks' (2011) *Geography Compass* 154, 156 citing Gereffi and Korzeniewicz n.31.

[34] OECD, *Trade Policy Implications of Global Value Chains: Preliminary observations from the 2021 TiVA database* (OECD 2021); and OECD, *Guide to OECD's Trade In Value Added Indicators 2021 Edition* Preliminary Version (OECD 2021) available at: www.oecd.org/industry/ind/oecd-trade-in-value-added-indicators-2021-guide.pdf.

[35] Glassman n.33, 156.

[36] Jeffrey Henderson, Peter Dicken, Martin Hess, Neil Coe and Henry Wai-Chung Yeung, 'Global Production Networks and the Analysis of Economic Development' (2002) 9(3) *Review of International Political Economy* 436, 442.

previously thought, with other institutions, such as government, trade unions and NGOs, possessing potential influence.[37]

The dominant discourse however remains concerned with 'global value chains' (GVCs), so named on the basis that value is added at each stage of production (and in each country).[38] The theory (endorsed by World Bank and other policy makers) is that this 'value-creation' in the Global South can boost development.[39] Similarly, the International Labour Office has observed that GVCs provide 'new opportunities for employment [...] including for workers who had difficulty accessing wage employment or formal jobs, such as women, young people and migrant workers'.[40] In this way, GVCs can be presented as inclusive and thereby compatible with the aspirations for decent work and equality set out in SDGs 5, 8 and 10.[41]

However, others disagree. For example, it has been convincingly argued that 'global care chains' demonstrate the gendered effects of the commodification of care across national borders.[42] Others have observed that supply chain practices create rather than alleviate poverty.[43] For this reason the term 'value' is omitted from usage in this book, so that reference is made to 'global supply chains' and not 'global value chains'. A further recurring theme in academic literature is the problem of power asymmetry, recognising the power vested in lead firms, as 'core actors in cross-border business networks' within corporate

---

37 Ibid, 444–7.

38 See Stefano Ponte, Gary Gereffi and Gale Raj-Reichert (eds), *Handbook on Global Value Chains* (Edward Elgar Publishing 2019).

39 Daria Taglioni and Deborah Winkler, *Making Global Value Chains Work for Development* (*The World Bank – Economic Premise* no. 143 2014), especially at 1–2 and 8.

40 ILO (2016) n.17, 17.

41 See Chapter 1 of this book, text accompanying n.110 et seq.

42 See Arlie Hochschild, 'Global Care Chains and Emotional Surplus Value in Will Hutton and Anthony Giddens (eds), *On the Edge: Living with Global Capitalism* (Jonathan Cape 2001); Nicola Yeates, 'Global Care Chains: A State-of-the-art Review and Future Directions in Care Transnationalization Research' (2012) 12(2) *Global Networks* 135; and Ann Stewart, *Gender, Law and Justice in Global Markets* (Cambridge University Press 2011).

43 Benjamin Selwyn, 'Poverty Chains and Global Capitalism' (2019) 23(1) *Competition & Change* 71; Charlotte Villiers, 'Collective Responsibility and the Limits of Disclosure in Regulating Global Supply Chains' (2018) 23 *Deakin Law Review* 143.

hierarchies,[44] and their capacity to normalise certain practices and standards which can override the objections of other stakeholders.[45]

The failure of global supply chains to protect those who work within them was exposed further during the COVID-19 pandemic.[46] The ILO has at least acknowledged (in 2016 and 2021) 'enforcement gaps' and 'fragmentation of norms' alongside particular difficulties for those 'in an irregular situation and in the informal economy'.[47] The question then is how this situation is best addressed.

3. VOLUNTARY CORPORATE CODES OF CONDUCT AND THEIR LIMITATIONS

One possibility is that MNEs devise their own corporate codes of conduct, which then would govern their conduct globally. There are some significant structural impediments to that course of action, as observed by Beate Sjåfjell. A shareholder primacy model prevalent in national company law seems to have deterred corporate policy engagement with wider environmental and labour standards, especially in countries where shareholders are unlikely to be located. This has led to advocacy of reform of company purposes and the duties of company directors,[48] but in the meantime there is little impetus to do more than what enables these commercial enterprises to be profitable for the benefit of shareholders, as opposed to 'stakeholders' or a wider group of

---

44 Stefano Ponte and Timothy Sturgeon, 'Explaining Governance in Global Value Chains: A Modular Theory-building Effort' (2014) 21(1) *Review of International Political Economy* 195, 200.

45 Ibid, 205–9; see also Frank Boons, Henrikke Baumann and Jeremy Hall, 'Conceptualizing Sustainable Development and Global Supply Chains' (2012) 83 *Ecological Economics* 134, 136–7 and 139–40.

46 See Shuvro Sen, Neel Antara, Shusmita Sen and Sunny Chowdhury. 'The Unprecedented Pandemic "COVID-19" Effect on the Bangladesh Apparel Workers by Shivering the Apparel Supply Chain' (2020) 11(3) *Journal of Textile and Apparel, Technology and Management* 1; and Alexander Trautrims, Martin C. Schleper, M. Selim Cakir and Stefan Gold, 'Survival at the Expense of the Weakest? Managing Modern Slavery Risks in Supply Chains during COVID-19' (2020) 23(7) *Journal of Risk Research* 1067; and Business and Human Rights Resource Centre, *Wage Theft and Pandemic Profits: The Right to a Living Wage for Garment Workers* (Business and Human Rights Resource Centre 2021) available at: https://media.business-humanrights.org/media/documents/Unpaid_wages_v9.pdf.

47 ILO (2016) n.17, 25 and 32; and see ILO n.19.

48 Beate Sjåfjell, 'How Company Law Has Failed Human Rights – and What to Do About It' (2020) 5 *Business and Human Rights Journal* 179; Beate Sjåfjell, 'Sustainable Value Creation within Planetary Boundaries – Reforming Corporate Purpose and Duties of the Corporate Board' (2020) 12 *Sustainability* 6245.

persons affected by an MNE's supply chains.[49] While attention to a restricted interest group is so prevalent, it may not be so surprising that the efficacy of voluntary codes adopted by MNEs has been limited.[50]

Historically, the content of corporate codes of conduct relating to CSR tended to be crafted to serve shareholders' commercial interests, often omitting standards such as entitlement to freedom of association and the effective right to collective bargaining.[51] For example, Nike, which adopted extensive CSR policies following negative publicity concerning its supply chain practices in the 1990s and early 2000s,[52] developed a practice of issuing statements focusing on forced labour and modern slavery in which collective labour rights are not mentioned.[53] While in most corporate codes there now tends to be reference to ILO standards as a source of legitimacy, 'the ambiguity of commitments to FOA [freedom of association] continues to draw critiques of symbolic adoption of codes as "window dressing" to protect brand reputations'.[54] A recent study by Sarosh Kuruvilla and his co-authors concluded that corporate institutional antagonism to freedom of association and collective bargaining continues and that the social auditing industry tends to overlook these standards, not recording levels of unionisation or collective bargaining coverage.[55]

More recently, MNEs have latched on to the catchphrase 'sustainability' and, since 2016, make reference to the Sustainable Development Goals (SDGs) set out in the 2030 Agenda. Today, 'sustainability' is prominent as

---

49 Maisam Abbasi, 'Towards Socially Sustainable Supply Chains – Themes and Challenges' (2017) 29(3) *European Business Review* 261, 263.

50 Beate Sjåfjell, 'When the Solution Becomes the Problem: The Triple Failure of Corporate Governance Codes' in Jean du Plessis and Chee Keong Low (eds), *Corporate Governance Codes for the 21st Century: International Perspectives and Critical Analyses* (Springer 2017).

51 Bob Hepple, 'A Race to the Top – International Investment Guidelines and Corporate Codes of Conduct' (1999) 20 *Comparative Labour Law and Policy Journal* 347, 358; Mark Anner, 'Corporate Social Responsibility and Freedom of Association Rights: The Precarious Quest for Legitimacy and Control in Global Supply Chains' (2012) 40(4) *Politics & Society* 609.

52 Randall L. Waller and Roger N. Conaway, 'Framing and Counterframing the Issue of Corporate Social Responsibility: The Communication Strategies of Nikebiz.com' (2011) 48(1) *Journal of Business Communication* 83.

53 See for example https://about.nike.com/en/newsroom/statements/statement-on-forced-labor.

54 See Sarosh Kuruvilla with Matt Fischer-Daly and Christopher Raymond, 'Freedom of Association and Collective Bargaining in Global Supply Chains' in Sarosh Kuruvilla, *Private Regulation of Labor Standards in Global Supply Chains* (Cornell University Press 2021), 151–2.

55 Ibid, 153–5.

an aspiration on the Nike website, while CSR is no longer visible as a term.[56] This emphasis on 'sustainability supply chain management' has become the focus for academic research, with initial findings indicating MNE lead firm commitment to realising the SDGs, but not necessarily full compliance across the supply chain.[57]

Currently, a lack of transformational change as regards environmental and social sustainability in practice has led to accusations of 'greenwashing', with a need for greater steps to be taken towards transparency that enables more rigorous scrutiny.[58] Moreover, while some corporate structures (such as B-corps) seem more amenable and responsive to environmental sustainability standards, current evidence suggests that 'their record of improving labor practices has been abysmal'.[59] The notion that environmental and labour norms are closely connected, potentially self-reinforcing or symbiotic, as discussed in Chapters 1 and 2 of this book, seems to be rejected by many corporate entities in practice. The interaction of these different pillars of sustainable development, which might be addressed by engagement with stakeholder views of 'just transitions',[60] has yet to be the subject of MNE action on any large scale.

Moreover, the operation of MNE voluntary codes is seldom subjected to external review mechanisms and, given a lack of corporate enthusiasm for freedom of association or trade union representation, is unlikely to engage meaningfully with the experience of the workers affected except perhaps on the occasion of an 'inspection' visit.[61] Such flaws are perhaps not inevitable. Mark Barenberg has, for example, highlighted ways in which transnational labour monitoring through the 'Workers' Rights Consortium' did not have to 'displace collective bargaining'; rather, private monitoring could 'open "social

---

56 See www.nike.com/gb/sustainability.

57 Dominik Zimon, Jonah Tyan and Robert Sroufe, 'Drivers of Sustainable Supply Chain Management: Practices to Alignment with UN Sustainable Development Goals' (2019) 14(1) *International Journal for Quality Research* 219; Cheree Topple, Jerome D. Donovan, Eryadi K. Masli and Thomas Borgert, 'Corporate Sustainability Assessments: MNE Engagement with Sustainable Development and the SDGs' (2017) 24(3) *Transnational Corporations* 61.

58 Addisu A. Lashitew, 'Corporate Uptake of the Sustainable Development Goals: Mere Greenwashing or an Advent of Institutional Change?' (2021) 4(1) *Journal of International Business Policy* 184; Constantin Blome, Kai Foerstl and Martin C. Schleper, 'Antecedents of Green Supplier Championing and Greenwashing: An Empirical Study on Leadership and Ethical Incentives' (2017) 152 *Journal of Cleaner Production* 339.

59 Kuruvilla n.54, 11.

60 See Chapter 2 of this book, text accompanying n.168 et seq.

61 Opi Outhwaite and Olga Martin-Ortega, 'Worker-driven Monitoring – Redefining Supply Chain Monitoring to Improve Labour Rights in Global Supply Chains' (2019) 23(4) *Competition & Change* 378.

and political space" that enables rather than displaces workers' exercise of rights of association'.[62] However, that aspect of collective worker voice needs to be operationalised more fully than seems to be contemplated under current practices, and, in the current global 'world of work', to be inclusive of those whose employment status is uncertain or whose immigration status is insecure.[63]

There is also a danger that the holistic nature of sustainable development can be exploited to gloss over tensions and problems. It has been reported that new 'integrated reporting strategies' addressing simultaneously financial, environmental and social sustainability have the potential to bypass scrutiny of problematic issues, becoming more of a confirmatory 'legitimation strategy'.[64] The problem here would seem to be less acknowledgement of the ways in which the three pillars of sustainability are inter-related and more a lack of specificity and transparent debate on how different objectives are to be reconciled.

Furthermore, voluntary codes tend to be operated by sidelined human resources (HR) and public relations (PR) and 'communications' departments, which have limited influence or control over the actual direction or substance of corporate policy globally.[65] Overall, there seems to be highly critical assessment of voluntary codes by those engaged in research in the field,[66] suggesting that corporate emphasis remains on brand management rather than promotion

---

[62] Mark Barenberg, 'Toward a Democratic Model of Transnational Labour Monitoring' in Brian Bercusson and Cynthia Estlund (eds), *Regulating Labour in the Wake of Globalisation: New Challenges, New Institutions* (Hart 2008), 60–1. A view shared by Manoj Dias-Abey, 'Using Law to Support Social Movement-Led Collective Bargaining Structures in Supply Chains' (2019) 32(2) *Australian Journal of Labour Law* 123, who also sees potential for collective agency in these forms of private regulation.

[63] As discussed in Chapters 1 and 2 of this book. See also Shelley Marshall, *Living Wage: Regulatory Solutions to Informal and Precarious Work in Global Supply Chains* (Oxford University Press 2019) for exploration of the dynamics that lead to precarity of those who work in supply chains and some national specific solutions.

[64] Alessandro Lai, Gaia Melloni and Riccardo Stacchezzini, 'Corporate Sustainable Development: Is "Integrated Reporting" a Legitimation Strategy?' (2016) 25(3) *Business Strategy and the Environment* 165.

[65] Zeeshan Mahmood and Shahzad Uddin, 'Institutional Logics and Practice Variations in Sustainability Reporting: Evidence from an Emerging Field' (2020) 34(5) *Accounting, Auditing & Accountability Journal* 1163; Günter K. Stahl, Chris J. Brewster, David G. Collings and Aida Hajro, 'Enhancing the Role of Human Resource Management in Corporate Sustainability and Social Responsibility: A Multi-stakeholder, Multidimensional Approach to HRM' (2020) 30(3) *Human Resource Management Review* 100708.

[66] Niklas Egels-Zandén and Henrik Lindholm, 'Do Codes of Conduct Improve Worker Rights in Supply Chains? A Study of Fair Wear Foundation' (2015) 107 *Journal of Cleaner Production* 31; Dima Jamali, Peter Lund-Thomsen and Navjote

globally of sustainable development policies, which would enhance environmental and labour standards – despite the assertions of the World Business Council for Sustainable Development (WBCSD).[67]

Anne Trebilcock regards 'the entrepreneurship of private law entities vying to influence market rules' with some scepticism. She observes that these involve not only the creation of corporate codes of conduct but also other collective initiatives. An example is the utilisation of the International Organisation for Standardization (ISO) to set employment standards for business, which she notes 'has increasingly encroached on traditional ILO territory'.[68] An example is the adoption of ISO 45001, which would seem to dilute norms established by the ILO applicable to health and safety,[69] and whose adoption did not reflect the kinds of rigorous representative participatory engagement which adoption of ILO standards demands.[70] The actions of ISO raise, as Janelle Diller observes, serious questions regarding the wisdom of 'private standard-setting authority on public policy issues', especially in the absence of transparency and accountability.[71]

MNEs may also shelter behind industry-wide codes to which they can refer as lending legitimacy to their own corporate practices, such as the Electronic Industry Citizenship Coalition, which has since been transformed into the 'Responsible Business Alliance', with again its own 'Code of Conduct' and 'Responsible Labor Initiative'.[72] Notably, the standards set out in the Code of Conduct are said to 'reference international norms and standards including the Universal Declaration of Human Rights, ILO International Labor Standards, OECD Guidelines for Multinational Enterprises, ISO and SA standards

---

Khara, 'CSR Institutionalized Myths in Developing Countries: An Imminent Threat of Selective Decoupling' (2017) 56 *Business and Society* 454.

67 See WBCSD, *Vision 2050 Time to Transform* (WBCSD 2021) available at: www.wbcsd.org/contentwbc/download/11765/177145/1; and Chapter 1 of this book, text accompanying nn.165–8.

68 Anne Trebilcock, 'The ILO as an Actor in International Economic Law: Looking Back, Gazing Ahead' in Marc Bungenberg, Markus Krajewski, Christian J. Tams, Jörg Philipp Terhechte and Andreas R. Ziegler (eds) *European Yearbook of International Economic Law 2019* (Springer 2020), 29.

69 Iñaki Heras-Saizarbitoria, Olivier Boiral and Ander Ibarloza, 'ISO 45001 and Controversial Transnational Private Regulation for Occupational Health and Safety' (2020) 159(3) *International Labour Review* 397.

70 Leading ultimately to withdrawal of ILO cooperation from ISO, regarding which see Janelle M. Diller, 'The Role of the State in the Exercise of Transnational Public and Private Authority over Labour Standards' (2020) 17(1) *International Organizations Law Review* 41, 56–9.

71 Ibid, 59.

72 See www.responsiblebusiness.org/ and for information regarding this transformation, see www.responsiblebusiness.org/news/rebrand/.

[Standards on Auditing], and many more'.[73] Here it is interesting that ISO standards feature, but are not regarded as sufficient to solely imbue legitimacy for corporate codes. It is this desire and willingness to engage with standards, guidelines and codes endorsed by international institutions to which this chapter now turns.

4. ATTEMPTS BY INTERNATIONAL INSTITUTIONS TO REGULATE CORPORATE GOVERNANCE

We have witnessed a rapid expansion in international instruments seeking to promote responsible corporate practices, which are now used as a reference point for voluntary corporate codes as well as global framework agreements (GFAs). These instruments include the Organisation for Economic Cooperation and Development (OECD) Guidelines for Multinational Enterprises (1976 and revised most recently in 2011),[74] the ILO Tripartite Declaration concerning Multinational Enterprises and Social Policy (1977 and revised most recently in 2022),[75] the UN Global Compact created in 2000 (revised in response to the 2015 UN SDGs)[76] and the UN Guiding Principles on Business and Human Rights (adopted 2011 and again in a process of revision and adaptation).[77]

There could be difficulties here with the sheer multiplicity of instruments to which a corporation may have reference, and the grievance and complaint procedures which may be utilised, such that it is possible to hide in not only the gaps but also the overlaps between their provisions.[78] However, at least to some extent these tensions have been arguably alleviated by common substantive reliance on international human rights and designated ILO core labour standards as stated in the original 1998 Declaration on Fundamental Principles

---

[73] Available at: www.responsiblebusiness.org/code-of-conduct/.

[74] OECD Guidelines for Multinational Enterprises available at: www.oecd.org/daf/inv/mne/48004323.pdf; regarding revision see Ashley L. Santner, 'A Soft Law Mechanism for Corporate Responsibility: How the Updated OECD Guidelines for Multinational Enterprises Promote Business for the Future' (2011) 43(2) *George Washington International Law Review* 375.

[75] The 2022 edition of the ILO Tripartite Declaration is available at: www.ilo.org/empent/Publications/WCMS_094386/lang--en/index.html.

[76] Based online at: www.unglobalcompact.org/.

[77] John Ruggie, *Guiding Principles on Business and Human Rights: Implementing the United Nations 'Protect, Respect and Remedy' Framework*, 17th sess, Agenda Item 3, UN Doc A/HRC/17/31, 21 March 2011 annex ('UNGPs').

[78] Rutvica Andrijasevic and Tonia Novitz, 'Supply Chains and Unfree Labor: Regulatory Failure in the Case of Samsung Electronics in Slovakia' (2020) 6(2) *Journal of Human Trafficking* 195, 204–5.

and Rights at Work.[79] There is also some procedural cross-referencing between these instruments as regards 'due diligence', although, as has been observed, 'they differ significantly in their scope, application and the obligations they impose on business'.[80] In the more recent revisions after the adoption of the 2030 Agenda in 2015,[81] the language of 'sustainability' and 'sustainable development' is entering the frame, although its actual influence is hard to detect in terms of a positive influence on the content of standards or the processes for their implementation. Concerns regarding the representation and participation of those in the wider world of work remain, both in the context of due diligence and enforcement procedures.

4.1 OECD Guidelines for Multinational Enterprises

The OECD Guidelines for Multinational Enterprises (as revised in 2011) set out ostensibly non-binding recommendations made by states to MNEs either originating or operating in OECD states or other countries which opt into the code.[82] The Guidelines are a curious mix of hard and soft law. On the one hand, with respect to MNEs, this code sets out 'voluntary principles and standards for responsible business conduct'; on the other, state parties 'make a binding commitment to implement them'.

The substance of the recommendations set out in the OECD Guidelines is largely based on other key international instruments. Part I, Chapter IV refers to 'the framework of internationally recognised human rights', which the accompanying Commentary makes clear will refer to the Universal Declaration and 1966 Covenants, as well as 'principles concerning fundamental rights set out in the 1998 International Labour Organisation Declaration on Fundamental Principles and Rights at Work'.[83] Those core labour standards are further elaborated in Chapter V on 'Employment and Industrial Relations', especially in relation to collective bargaining, but also mention is made of issues relating to training and collective dismissals. In this context, the particular competence of the ILO is acknowledged in the Commentary, as is the (then 2006) ILO Tripartite MNE Declaration.[84] Chapter VI addresses the 'Environment'. In this context, some overlap with labour concerns is acknowledged. For example,

---

79 See Chapter 3 of this book, text accompanying nn.79 et seq.

80 Shelley Marshall, Ingrid Landau, Hila Shamir, Tamar Barkay, Judy Fudge and Auret van Heerden, *Mandatory Human Rights Due Diligence: Risks and Opportunities for Workers and Unions* (RMIT/TraffLab/Monash 2023), 4.

81 See this chapter, n.14 above.

82 See OECD Guidelines for MNEs n.74, Preamble para. 1.

83 Ibid, Part I, Chapter IV, 'Commentary' para. 39.

84 Ibid, Part I, Chapter V, 'Commentary', para. 48 et seq.

workers should be informed (alongside the public) of 'potential environment, health and safety impacts of the activities of the enterprise' and workers are to have access to 'adequate education and training [...] in environmental health and safety matters'.[85] However, as observed in Chapter 2 of this book, there is scope to make reference to a wider range of labour-related environmental concerns and it is problematic that there does not necessarily seem to be any contemplation of collective bargaining on the subject of 'just transitions'.

The adoption of Chapter VI pre-dated the UN SDGs, but makes reference to the Rio Declaration on Environment and Development.[86] That reference should also be read in the light of other OECD sustainability initiatives, such as the Round Table on Sustainable Development operating from 1998 and the Guidance on Sustainability Impact Assessment issued in 2010.[87] Revision of the OECD MNE Guidelines in 2011 was accompanied by adoption of the OECD Due Diligence Guidance for Responsible Supply Chains of Minerals from Conflict-Affected and High-Risk Areas, which is now in its third 2016 edition.[88] The introduction of a 'due diligence' process via this instrument, and into the OECD MNE Guidelines, drew on the 2011 UN Guiding Principles on Business and Human Rights.[89] The most current instrument of note is the almost 100-page-long but more general OECD Due Diligence Guidance For

---

[85] Ibid, Part I, Chapter VI, paras 2 and 7, respectively.

[86] Ibid, Part I, Chapter VI, 'Commentary', para. 68 (referencing Principle 15); see Chapter 1 of this book, text accompanying nn.99 et seq.

[87] Valentina Cagnin, *Labour Law and Sustainable Development* (Wolters Kluwer 2020), 51–2 stresses the significance of 'sustainable development' in this instrument.

[88] Available at: www .oecd -ilibrary .org/ docserver/ 9789264252479 -en .pdf ?expires = 1672326581&id=id&accname=guest&checksum=6FD04E3F533F78F49E5DDA38B471151F. Since then the OECD has further adopted other Due Diligence Guidelines for various sectors, such as the OECD-FAO Guidance for Responsible Agricultural Supply Chains, 2016, OECD Due Diligence; OECD Responsible Business Conduct for Institutional Investors: Key Considerations for due diligence under the OECD Guidelines for MNEs, 2016; and OECD Due Diligence Guidance for Meaningful Stakeholder Engagement in the Extractive Sector, 2017. See Lise Smit, Claire Bright, Robert McCorquodale, Matthias Bauer, Hanna Deringer, Daniela Baeza-Breinbauer, Francisca Torres-Cortés, Frank Alleweldt, Senda Kara, Camille Salinier and Héctor Tejero Tobed, *Study on Due Diligence Requirements through the Supply Chain: Final Report* (European Commission 2020), 162.

[89] See UNGPs n.77; also the OECD Guidelines n.74, Foreword, 4, which also notes that in addition to the ILO and other international organisations, the UN Secretary-General's Special Representative on Business and Human Rights, Professor John Ruggie, 'provided extensive input on the Update'. See also Part I, Chapter II 'General Policies', paras A.10–A.13 and 'Commentary' paras 14–16; as well as Chapter IV, para. 5 and 'Commentary', paras 45–6. For further analysis, see Holly Cullen, 'The Irresistible Rise of Human Rights Due Diligence: Conflict Minerals and Beyond' (2016) 48(4) *George Washington International Law Review* 743.

Responsible Business Conduct.[90] The significance of the emergent human rights due diligence process will be discussed in greater detail below, but its inclusion in these OECD instruments does seem to have led to more stringent risk assessment, even though the extent to which due diligence has in practice engaged with collective voices at work remains the subject of controversy.[91]

Part II of the 2011 OECD Guidelines sets out the 'Implementation Procedures'. Central to implementation is the role of 'National Contact Points for Responsible Business Conduct' (NCPs): both to promote awareness of the Guidelines and to hear complaints brought by individuals, trade unions and NGOs relating to 'specific instances' of problematic corporate conduct.[92] NCPs report to the Investment Committee, which shall 'periodically invite the Business and Industry Advisory Committee to the OECD (BIAC), and the Trade Union Advisory Committee to the OECD (TUAC) (the "advisory bodies"), OECD Watch, as well as other international partners to express their views on matters covered by the Guidelines'.[93] In this way, some degree of trade union and NGO representation of those at work is embedded in the process, albeit in formal parity with that of employers as 'business and industry', so that disparities of power are not officially recognised in this context.[94]

While the OECD Guidelines have been lauded as the 'strongest code on MNEs in existence',[95] in practice states have had considerable discretion regarding how NCPs operate, including the transparency of their procedures and findings, so that NCP practices vary.[96] Moreover, while NCPs are to encourage 'constructive engagement' of MNEs with the complainant, and

---

[90] See OECD-Due-Diligence-Guidance-for-Responsible-Business-Conduct.pdf.

[91] See for example Sarosh Kuruvilla and Chunyun Li, 'Freedom of Association and Collective Bargaining in Global Supply Chains: A Research Agenda' (2021) 57(2) *Journal of Supply Chain Management* 43.

[92] 'Specific instances mechanism of the OECD Guidelines for Multinational Enterprises' available at: http://mneguidelines.oecd.org/specificinstances.htm. See also this chapter, n.74, Part II, especially 'Procedural Guidance'.

[93] See this chapter, n.74, Part II, 'Amendment of the Decision of the Council on the OECD Guidelines for Multinational Enterprises', II, para. 2.

[94] Cf. Chapter 1 of this book, text accompanying n.63 et seq.

[95] Angel Gurría, 'Preface', *OECD Guidelines for Multinational Enterprises: A Glass Half Full* (OECD 2018) 8; cited by Gabriele Buchholtz, 'Social and Labour Standards in the OECD Guidelines: Enforcement Mechanisms' (2020) 17(1) *International Organizations Law Review* 133, 134.

[96] Ingrid Landau and John Howe, 'State Extraterritorial Regulation and Decent Work in the Asia Pacific' in Janice Bellace and Beryl ter Haar (eds), *Research Handbook on Labour, Business and Human Rights Law* (Edward Elgar Publishing 2019), 483–5.

can arrange mediation, they cannot compel MNE involvement in the process.[97] Nevertheless, in this context, trade unions have mobilised to utilise OECD mechanisms to the extent that is possible, deploying their 'power resources' to effect meaningful change.[98] For example, a successful campaign for unionisation at Natixis involved requesting intervention by the French NCP under the OECD Guidelines,[99] while four trade unions and confederations were able to utilise the Netherlands NCP process in an attempt to prompt McDonald's to take action as a global employer to protect against gender-based violence and harassment at work.[100]

4.2 ILO Tripartite Declaration concerning Multinational Enterprises and Social Policy

The ILO has declared proudly that its Tripartite Declaration concerning Multinational Enterprises and Social Policy (the 'MNE Declaration') 'is the only global instrument in this area that was elaborated and adopted by governments, employers and workers from around the world'.[101] This Tripartite Declaration was adopted close to 40 years ago, repeatedly amended, and most recently revised in a sixth edition published in 2022.[102] It is declaratory and, as such, a soft law instrument, although its text provides much more detailed treatment of labour standards than the OECD Guidelines. All principles set out in the instrument build on international labour standards, with a focus on ILO conventions and recommendations, facilitating 'outreach and understanding

[97] For emphasis placed on these limitations, see Lucio Baccaro and Valentina Mele, 'For Lack of Anything Better? International Organizations and Global Corporate Codes' (2011) 89(2) *Public Administration* 451.

[98] Michele Ford and Michael Gillan, 'Power Resources and Supranational Mechanisms: The Global Unions and the OECD Guidelines' (2021) 27(3) *European Journal of Industrial Relations* 307.

[99] Jeremy Blasi and Samir Sonti, 'Private Equity, Human Rights Due Diligence and Global Labour Rights: The Case of "Hotel California"' (2021) 1(1) *The Global Labour Rights Reporter* 44.

[100] Mary Joyce Carlson, 'Unions Use the OECD Guidelines to Challenge Gender-based Violence and Harassment in the Global Operations of McDonald's Corp' (2021) 1(1) *The Global Labour Rights Reporter* 49. This specific instance complaint has been found by the Netherlands NCP to be admissible to be further pursued, for which see: www.oecdguidelines.nl/documents/publication/2021/05/20/initial-assessment-of-the-notification-of-4-trade-unions-vs-apg-asset-management.

[101] See www.ilo.org/empent/areas/mne-declaration/WCMS_570332/lang--en/index.htm.

[102] See ILO Tripartite Declaration, 6th edition n.75. See also Decision on taking stock five years after the adoption of the revised MNE Declaration GB.346/POL/5/Decision, 9 November 2022.

of the Decent Work Agenda in the private sector'.[103] The MNE Declaration consists of distinct principles directed to 'Governments' and to 'Enterprises'.[104]

The previous revision of the MNE Declaration in 2017 (the fifth edition) added principles addressing specific decent work issues: social security, forced labour, transition from the informal to the formal economy, wages, access to remedy and compensation of victims. That revised instrument was also notable for providing additional guidance on 'due diligence' processes, consistent with the UN Guiding Principles on Business and Human Rights,[105] while being focused not on the broader achievement of human rights but rather more specifically achieving decent work. The 2022 revision responded to 'the adoption of the ILC resolution on the inclusion of a safe and healthy working environment in the ILO's framework of fundamental principles and rights at work'.[106]

Moreover, the emphasis in the revised Tripartite Declaration is said to be on 'sustainable business' and achievement of SDG 8.[107] The 'Introduction' states that: 'The parties concerned have the opportunity to use the principles of the MNE Declaration as guidelines for enhancing the positive social and labour effects of the operations and governance of multinational enterprises to achieve decent work for all, a universal goal recognized in the 2030 Agenda for Sustainable Development.'[108] In this way the language of sustainable development is tied by the revised instrument to ILO standards for decent work. Under 'Aim and Scope' the Declaration says:

> Within the framework of sustainable development policies established by governments, [MNEs] can also make an important contribution to the promotion of economic and social welfare; to the improvement of living standards and the satisfaction of basic needs; to the creation of employment opportunities, both directly and indirectly; and to the enjoyment of human rights, including freedom of association, throughout the world.[109]

---

[103] Ibid.

[104] ILO, *What Is the ILO MNE Declaration?* (ILO 2022) available at: www.ilo.org/wcmsp5/groups/public/---asia/---ro-bangkok/---ilo-manila/documents/publication/wcms_842868.pdf.

[105] UNGPs n.77.

[106] See ILO Tripartite Declaration, 6th edition n.75, 7.

[107] Set out in ILO press release, 'ILO Revises Its Landmark Declaration on Multinational Enterprises' (17 March 2017), available at: www.ilo.org/global/about-the-ilo/newsroom/news/WCMS_547615/lang--en/index.htm. Cited in Smit et al n.88, 164–5.

[108] See ILO Tripartite Declaration n.75, 5.

[109] Ibid, 8.

However, in the main body of the Declaration, sustainable development and SDG 8 are only referred to briefly in relation to 'employment promotion'.[110]

A difficulty with the text of the MNE Declaration (even after recent revisions) is that, despite its focus on labour rights, the instrument uses 'general and conditional language even when referring to established international and national legal norms'.[111] This seems odd, given that 'most provisions that are included in the Tripartite Declaration have already been included in binding ILO Conventions or in domestic law and have thereby acquired binding effect at least against states'.[112] It may perhaps be explained by the diluting effect of tripartism within the current ILO governance framework, in which the employers' group is reluctant to cede influence over corporate conduct.[113]

Implementation and enforcement of the Declaration is set out in Annex II, which indicates that, in addition to 'promotional activities', there can be 'company–union dialogue' and a procedure for examination of disputes. The promotional activities operate *ex ante* to prevent violations. In this respect, the work of the ILO 'Helpdesk for Business on International Labour Standards' run by MULTI (the ILO's Multinational Enterprises and Enterprise Engagement Unit) would seem to have had notable successes in its outreach and advisory activities.[114]

However, concerns have been raised regarding the effectiveness of this mechanism, especially as regards access to 'remedies for workers' grievances'.[115] A difficulty is that while social dialogue has its uses, with the ILO Helpdesk operating as an important facilitator,[116] proceedings are kept confidential, which means that the exposure of embarrassing conduct does not necessarily act as a deterrent for MNEs.[117] In 2019, Jernej Letnar Černič argued that urgent reforms were needed to provide victims with a 'fair, impartial,

---

110 Ibid, 12, paras 13–14.

111 Peter Muchlinski, *Promoting Responsible Business through the Revised ILO Tripartite Declaration*, Columbia FDI Perspectives No. 231 (Columbia Center on Sustainable Investment 2021) available at: www.econstor.eu/bitstream/10419/254155/1/fdi-perspectives-no321.pdf.

112 Jernej Letnar Černič, 'The ILO Tripartite Declaration of Principles Concerning Multinational Enterprises and Social Policy Revisited: Is There a Need for Its Reform?' in Marc Bungenberg, Markus Krajewski, Christian J. Tams, Jörg Philipp Terhechte and Andreas R. Ziegler (eds), *European Yearbook of International Economic Law 2019* (Springer 2020), 197.

113 See Chapter 3 in this book, text accompanying nn.152 et seq.

114 Antonio Garcia-Muñoz Alhambra, Beryl Ter Haar and Attila Kun, 'Harnessing Public Institutions for Labour Law Enforcement' (2020) 17(1) *International Organizations Law Review* 233, 256.

115 Muchlinski n.111.

116 Garcia-Muñoz Alhambra et al n.114, 256–7.

117 Letnar Černič n.112, 203.

independent and transparent procedure, where they could enforce their rights'.[118] His conclusion was that 'the Declaration has so far not been a star in the global area of business and human rights'.[119]

Members of the ILO Governing Body which met in November 2022 took a more nuanced view. Collectively, they called on the new Director-General:

> (a) to scale up activities in support of constituents to make better use of the Tripartite Declaration in coordination with 'the comprehensive strategy on achieving decent work in supply chains', including: (b) to strengthen and promote operational tools, as outlined in Annex II to the MNE Declaration; (c) to further mainstream the MNE Declaration in relevant development cooperation programmes and ILO engagement with enterprises; (d) to strengthen ILO engagement with other international organizations to advance decent work through the promotion of the MNE Declaration in the context of trade, investment and supply chains; and (e) to facilitate resource mobilization to that effect.[120]

This is perhaps an admission that promotional and enforcement aspects of the MNE Declaration are not yet working as effectively as possible.

Moreover, some of the divisions between worker and employer representatives' views were stark. The workers' group had proposed the inclusion in the Governing Body Declaration of a commitment to a new 'ILO forum on business and decent work', which was opposed by the employers' group. The forum has the express support of the Multinational Enterprises and Enterprise Engagement Unit in the International Labour Office as a feature of the ILO's five-year strategy on achieving decent work in supply chains and the proposed Global Coalition for Social Justice. The employers' group's caution (and that of some other representative state groupings) meant that the initiative was not included in the joint Governing Body Declaration in November 2022, although the Office is committed to further consultations.[121]

Also, while both the employers' and the workers' groups were positive about building national and regional strategies for awareness and application of the MNE Declaration and the broader links with the ILO's five-year supply chain strategy, they took a different view of its role. While the worker spokesperson considered that the MNE Declaration 'should guide efforts to link trade, investment and supply chain matters more closely with decent

---

[118] Ibid, 206 and 210–11.

[119] Ibid, 194.

[120] ILO Governing Body, *Minutes of the Policy Development Section* GB.346/POL/PV 346th Session, Geneva, October–November 2022 (ILO 2022), 33.

[121] Ibid; see especially the Employer Spokesperson at para. 120, and the Office response on behalf of the Director-General at para. 136.

work priorities',[122] the employer response was that the Declaration 'was not a mandatory instrument and should not be used as such'.[123] On this basis, the employers' group expressed concern that 'the secretariat of the UN Global Compact had adopted the company–union dialogue in Annex II to the MNE Declaration as a dispute resolution mechanism', which 'might infringe on the voluntary, consensual and confidential nature of the mechanism' and 'must not be permitted or involve the diversion of ILO resources'.[124]

4.3 UN Global Compact

The Global Compact was an initiative adopted in 2000 by Kofi Annan, the then UN Secretary-General. This was a response to the emergence of global supply chains and the evident failure of global governance as highlighted by the 1999 anti-globalisation protests at Seattle.[125] This was to be a 'global compact' between UN public international law institutions and business, requiring the latter, whether individually in firms or collectively through 'business associations', to 'embrace, support and enact, within their sphere of influence, a set of core values in the areas of human rights, labour standards, and the environment'.[126] The Global Compact began with nine principles, extended to a tenth relating to corruption in 2004. The Global Compact's labour principles are derived from the original 1998 ILO Declaration on Fundamental Principles and Rights at Work, namely: Principle 3 (Businesses should uphold the freedom of association and the effective recognition of the right to collective bargaining); Principle 4 (the elimination of all forms of forced and compulsory labour); Principle 5 (the effective abolition of child labour); and Principle 6 (the elimination of discrimination in respect of employment and occupation). There is no reference to the relevant accompanying fundamental ILO Conventions or the issue of health and safety. Instead, the Global Compact

---

[122] Ibid, para. 116.

[123] Ibid, 112.

[124] Ibid.

[125] Janice Bellace, 'From Workers' Rights to Human Rights at Work' in Janice Bellace and Beryl ter Haar (eds), *Research Handbook on Labour, Business and Human Rights Law* (Edward Elgar Publishing 2019), 414; cf. Clyde Summers, 'The Battle in Seattle: Free Trade, Labor Rights, and Societal Values' (2001) 22 *University of Pennsylvania Journal of International Economic Law* 61.

[126] Kofi Annan's address to World Economic Forum in Davos, 1 February 1999 available at: www.un.org/sg/en/content/sg/speeches/1999-02-01/kofi-annans-address-world-economic-forum-davos. For restatement of that call in the contemporary Global Compact, see www.unglobalcompact.org.uk/the-ten-principles/.

has become enthusiastically engaged in promoting the SDGs, with sustainable development emerging as a key aspiration.[127]

The obligations placed on MNEs wishing to participate in the Global Compact are not insignificant. There is an annual and public 'Communication on Progress' (COP). This requires MNEs annually to provide: their renewed statement of support for the Global Compact; a concrete example of progress made for posting on the Global Compact website; and a statement of outcomes (actual and proposed).[128] This disclosure does not seem to require state scrutiny and is not subject to procedures enabling criticism or complaint. Instead, MNEs can choose their own level of compliance through a new differentiated system (applied since 2011) depending on whether they see themselves as 'Learner', 'Active' or 'Advanced'.[129] 'The Global Compact seeks to provide a contextual framework to encourage innovation, creative solutions, and good practices among participants.'[130] There is naming and shaming to the extent that (at the time of writing) more than 15,000 former participants have been 'delisted' for not following the 'COP' process by the required deadline and their names are recorded accordingly on the Global Compact website.[131] The curious feature of this list is that it reveals the sheer number of businesses who seem to only join the Global Compact as a temporary means to gain commercial credibility and do not subsequently endeavour to demonstrate their compliance with the ten principles in the longer term.

Overall, the main aim of the Global Compact at present seems to be assistance to MNEs, offered primarily on a discreet, confidential basis, especially as regards achieving SDG compliance by 2030.[132] The website for the Global Compact also sets out particular assistance for MNEs seeking to improve

---

[127] See www.unglobalcompact.org/sdgs.

[128] See www.unglobalcompact.org/what-is-gc/participants; and the detailed COP questionnaire available at: www.unglobalcompact.org/participation/report/cop#:~:text =Submitting%20an%20annual%20Communication%20on%20Progress%20%28CoP %29 %20is ,long %20as %20they %20meet %20the %20minimum %20requirements %20below.

[129] James Barresea, Cynthia Phillips and Victoria Shoa, 'Why do U.S. Public Companies Continue to Join the UN Global Compact: Ethics or Economics?' (2020) 50(3) *International Studies of Management and Organization* 209, 211.

[130] Stephanie Barrientos, *Global Production Systems and Decent Work* ILO working paper 77 (ILO 2007), 17.

[131] See www .unglobalcompact .org/ participation/ report/ cop/ create -and -submit/ expelled.

[132] See Edward T. Bristol-Alagbariya, 'The UN Global Compact as a Soft Law Business Regulatory Mechanism Advancing Corporate Responsibility towards Business Sustainability and Sustainable Development Worldwide' (2020) 94 *Journal of Law, Policy and Globalization* 27; cf. Štěpánka Zemanová and Radka Druláková, 'Mainstreaming Global Sustainable Development Goals through the UN Global

supply chain regulation.[133] This is said to be a sustainability 'cross-cutting' initiative applied 'across all four UN Global Compact issue areas (human rights, labour, environment and anti-corruption)'.[134] The website guidance includes a 'Decent Work Toolkit for Sustainable Procurement' devised by the Decent Work in Global Supply Chains Action Platform made up of Global Compact MNE members 'and UN partners, ILO and UNICEF'.[135] The ILO terminology of 'decent work' would therefore seem to have impact on the Global Compact and the broader SDG programmes and agendas,[136] although it remains difficult to assess the significance of this remodelling at the current stage in the context of the 'uneven' application and implementation of the Global Compact.[137]

4.4 UN Guiding Principles on Business and Human Rights

In 2008, Special Representative John Ruggie proposed to the UN Human Rights Council a framework on business and human rights based on three pillars: first, the duty of the state to *protect* against human rights abuses by third parties, including business; second, corporate responsibility to *respect* human rights; and finally, the principle of access by victims to effective *remedy*, both judicial and non-judicial. This has come to be known as the 'protect, respect and remedy' framework.[138] This would seem to have been his attempt to 're-embed' liberalism in markets by means of the UN human rights framework.[139] The adoption of the UN Guiding Principles in 2011 has also been seen as a 'positive development for the ILO', giving fresh impetus to core labour standards and setting in motion processes that provided 'opportunities for deepening understanding of effective measures for enhancing respect for labour rights in firms'.[140] However, the UN Guiding Principles do state that

---

Compact: The case of Visegrad Countries' (2020) 13(3) *Journal of Risk and Financial Management* 41.

[133] Available at: www.unglobalcompact.org/what-is-gc/our-work/supply-chain.

[134] Ibid.

[135] See www.unglobalcompact.org/take-action/sustainableprocurement for access to the training materials, case studies and e-courses.

[136] Cf. Cagnin, n.87, 47; and Peake and Kenner n.10.

[137] Dina Abdelzaher, Whitney Douglas Fernandez and William D. Schneper, 'Legal Rights, National Culture and Social Networks: Exploring the uneven adoption of United Nations Global Compact' (2019) 28(1) *International Business Review* 12.

[138] John Ruggie, *Protect, Respect and Remedy: A Framework for Business and Human Rights*, 8th sess, Agenda Item 3, UN Doc A/HRC/8/5, 7 April 2008.

[139] See Steen Vallentin and David Murillo, 'Ideologies of Corporate Responsibility: From Neoliberalism to "Varieties of Liberalism"' (2022) 32(4) *Business Ethics Quarterly* 635.

[140] Trebilcock n.68, 5.

'nothing in these Guiding Principles should be read as creating new international law obligations, or as limiting or undermining any legal obligations a State may have undertaken or be subject to under international law with regard to human rights'.[141] As such, the norms and processes generated are to be understood as 'voluntary'.

The 31 United Nations Guiding Principles (UNGPs) impose three-fold obligations consistent with the framework proposed in 2008. States are obliged to *protect* human rights, including with respect to the conduct of private parties such as business (under Principles 1–10). Business must *respect* human rights (by virtue of Principles 11–24). By virtue of Principle 12 and the accompanying 'Commentary', these human rights include the core labour standards set out in the 1998 ILO Declaration (as was) and as set out in the eight associated ILO 'fundamental' Conventions,[142] together with the International Bill of Human Rights (namely the Universal Declaration of Human Rights and the Covenants of 1966).[143] The latter enable extension beyond the core labour standards to at least include such rights as privacy and free speech at work, health and safety and holidays with pay,[144] although rights to protection from dismissal and of whistleblowing are not so self-evident.[145] The UNGPs make clear that 'respect' has three elements. First, there is to be a policy commitment. Second, and perhaps most importantly, there is to be a 'human rights due diligence process' which enables business to 'identify, prevent, mitigate and account for' risks of human rights breaches and take pre-emptive action (Principle 15). So, both respect for substantive norms and demonstration of that respect through a detailed process are required. Human rights risks and impacts have to be identified and assessed, those findings have to be acted upon and integrated into business plans, the effectiveness of the actions taken need to be evaluated and there needs to be communication of what has been done.[146] There has to be a 'remediation process' to address any such adverse

---

[141] Anne Trebilcock, 'Due Diligence on Labour Issues: Opportunities and Limits of the UN Guiding Principles on Business and Human Rights' in Adelle Blackett and Anne Trebilcock (eds), *Research Handbook on Transnational Labour Law* (Edward Elgar Publishing 2015), 96 and 105.

[142] See Chapter 3 in this book, text accompanying nn.76 et seq.

[143] As discussed in Chapter 2 of this book, see text accompanying nn.86–7.

[144] See James J. Brudney, 'Hiding in Plain Sight: An ILO Convention on Labor Standards in Global Supply Chains' (2023) 23(2) *Chicago Journal of International Law* 272, 314–15.

[145] Cf. Chapter 2 of this book, text accompanying nn.142 et seq.

[146] See the summary in Brudney n.144, 303; and Nicolas Bueno, 'Multinational Enterprises and Labour Rights: Concepts and implementation' in Janice Bellace and Beryl ter Haar (eds), *Research Handbook on Labour, Business and Human Rights Law* (Edward Elgar Publishing 2019), 422–7.

human rights impacts that business causes or to which it contributes.[147] Finally, both states and businesses have a joint obligation to enable access to a remedy for business-related human rights obligations.[148] That emphasis on availability of a remedy arguably chimes with the later Agenda 2030's emphasis on the rule of law and access to justice, set out in SDG 16.[149]

Human rights due diligence is a relatively recent invention, perhaps best understood as an 'evolution and transformation of the original concept of financial and legal due diligence as a business practice'.[150] This process involves assessment of risks not only to the business itself, but to third parties, including those at work. It has even been argued that due diligence is, in this context, less a process and more a 'standard of care' to those affected by business activities.[151] Moreover, due diligence tracing along corporate subsidiary and contractual links can enable genuine interrogation of transboundary harms, common in terms of environmental as well as labour cross-border effects.[152]

The UNGPs were adopted some years prior to the 2030 Agenda, but there has been recent recognition of the issue of sustainability in the UN Working Group on the issue of human rights and transnational corporations and other business enterprises. For example, the Working Group's 2018 report observed:

> For businesses, the most powerful contribution to sustainable development is to embed respect for human rights in their activities and across their value chains, addressing harm done to people and focusing on the potential and actual impacts [...] not having negative impacts is a minimum expectation and a positive contribution to the Goals.[153]

---

[147] Ingrid Landau, 'Human Rights Due Diligence and the Risk of Cosmetic Compliance' (2019) 20 *Melbourne Journal of International Law* 221, 224.

[148] Summarised in Trebilcock n.20, 557. For further exploration of access to remedies, especially regarding failure to perform due diligence, see Bueno n.24; and Nicolas Bueno and Claire Bright, 'Implementing Human Rights Due Diligence through Corporate Civil Liability' (2020) 69(4) *International and Comparative Law Quarterly Review* 789.

[149] Cagnin n.87, 23.

[150] Gabriela Quijano and Carlos Lopez, 'Rise of Mandatory Human Rights Due Diligence: A Beacon of Hope or a Double-Edged Sword?' (2021) 6 *Business and Human Rights Journal* 241, 246.

[151] Ibid, 247. See also Jonathan Bonnitcha and Robert McCorquodale, 'The Concept of Due Diligence in the UN Guiding Principles on Business and Human Rights' (2017) 28(3) *European Journal of International Law* 899, 900–1.

[152] Bonnitcha and McCorquodale n.151, 907 citing the judgment of *Case Concerning Pulp Mills on the River Uruguay*, ICJ Judgment (20 April 2010), discussed in Chapter 1 of this book at text accompanying n.106. See also Sassen n.9 above.

[153] UN Working Group on the issue of human rights and transnational corporations and other business enterprises, *Corporate human rights due diligence – emerging prac-*

The creation of a specific human rights-based due diligence process has had considerable influence, as seen above in the revision of OECD and ILO instruments, arguably 'as a meta-principle governing corporate actors in production chains'.[154] Ingrid Landau has observed that this process is 'emerging globally as a dominant, if not *the* dominant, conceptual frame through which business responsibility for human rights impacts is understood and operationalised'.[155] But, she adds: 'It should not be presumed, however, that the widespread institutionalisation of the concept will necessarily translate into significant improvements in corporate respect for human rights.'[156]

One difficulty is that the UNGPs remain merely voluntary; they are stated to be 'guidance'.[157] Even the due diligence approach is primarily 'defensive and reactional'.[158] It is a form of regulation less concerned with positive planning to fulfil human rights, and more related to taking minimal steps to deflect criticism. The due diligence process would seem to offer a defence against culpability of the lead firm for the actions of subcontracting parties, such as suppliers. The justification for that defence is that it encourages lead firm participation in the due diligence process, but arguably may also result in minimal engagement with that process sufficient to be seen to act, rather than being proactive.

A better option, in James Brudney's view, would be a vigorous monitoring system 'that assures direct and meaningful participation by workers and their representatives, along with other interested parties, at each stage of the process'.[159] Landau also warns against 'cosmetic compliance', in favour of an approach which would influence the *quality* of human rights due diligence as opposed to its mere quantity.[160] In this way, it is possible to see workers 'as agents of change – active actors in setting labour standards and enforcing them – rather than merely as passive victims requiring corporate care'.[161]

---

tices, challenges and ways forward, A/73/163 (16 July 2018), at para 10. Cited in Smit et al n.88, 190.

154 Etienne Pataut and Sophie Robin-Olivier, *The Future of Labour Law*, White Paper 23 (International Law Association 2022), 70. For a helpful overview of human rights due diligence, its effects for labour rights and the trajectory of implementation, see Olivier De Schutter, *Towards Mandatory Due Diligence in Global Supply Chains* (ITUC 2020) available at: www.ituc-csi.org/IMG/pdf/de_schutte_mandatory_due_diligence.pdf.

155 Landau n.147, 222.

156 Ibid.

157 Bellace n.125 above, 417.

158 Bueno n.146, 437.

159 Brudney n.144, 302.

160 Landau n.147, 223 and 235 et seq.

161 Marshall et al n. 80, 8, 27 and 29.

A key problem is that, unlike the ILO Tripartite Declaration, the UNGPs do not require any 'meaningful role for workers or their representatives';[162] this seems anomalous, given that 'the primary target of supply chain risks and possible abuses is the workers themselves'.[163] Research does indicate that 'interaction with third parties such as NGOs or local trade associations' will improve 'sustainability outcomes in GSCs [global supply chains]'.[164]

But, while there is academic consensus on the need to address participatory engagement, in line with SDG target 16.7, the difficulty remains implementation within the UNGP due diligence process. A first step towards this would be the transparent 'detailed disclosure' to civil society organisations (CSOs) which is advocated by Landau and others, enabling the collective organisation of those at work as they gain a systemic view of how and where supply chains operate.[165] More important are the rights to 'consultation and participation' that Landau further recommends.[166] The question remains whether due diligence could ever enable collective bargaining and action (or, in other words, negotiation), alongside bare representation or consultation that need not influence corporate processes and policies.[167] Trebilcock has suggested that remedies under the UNGP could be connected to grievance mechanisms under collective bargaining agreements or international framework agreements as suitable avenues for effective remedies.[168] This would be consistent with Guiding Principles 28, 30 and 31, which refer to non-state-based grievance mechanisms. However, for the time being, this is an option which lies at the discretion of MNEs but is by no means uniformly adopted; to do that, the UNGP and the 'respect, protect and remedy' framework would need to have binding force under international law.

---

162 Brudney n.144, 291.

163 Ibid, 310.

164 Esteban Koberg and Annachiara Longoni, 'A Systematic Review of Sustainable Supply Chain Management in Global Supply Chains' (2019) 207 *Journal of Cleaner Production* 1084, 1094.

165 Landau n.147, 241; Marshall et al n.80, 17–18.

166 Landau n.147, 243.

167 See the notion of a 'representation pyramid' presented in K.D. Ewing, 'Trade Union Recognition – A Framework for Discussion' (1990) 19 *Industrial Law Journal* 209, 212; cf. the regulatory pyramid proposed by Ian Ayres and John Braithwaite, *Responsive Regulation: Transcending the Deregulation Debate* (Oxford University Press 1992), 38–41; discussed in a labour law context in Colin Fenwick and Tonia Novitz, 'Conclusion: Regulating to Protect Workers' Human Rights' in Colin Fenwick and Tonia Novitz (eds), *Human Rights at Work: Perspectives on Law and Regulation* (Hart Publishing 2010).

168 Trebilcock n.68, 557.

A UN 'Open-ended Intergovernmental Working Group' has now been tasked with drafting what would be an 'internationally legally binding instrument on transnational corporations and other business enterprises with respect to human rights'. The first preliminary draft emerged in 2018 and has since been debated and revised.[169] At the time of writing, the most recent draft was published in July 2023.[170] In the meantime, as noted in Chapter 5, the European Commission is seeking to make human rights due diligence mandatory for companies incorporated in EU member states.[171] At national level, there have been new legislative initiatives in certain states. Notable among these are the Dutch Child Labor Due Diligence Act, France's Duty of Vigilance Law and a German Law on Supply Chain Due Diligence.[172] In this sense it could be said that there is a trajectory towards harder regulation,[173] although this trend seems inconsistent and has yet to ensure engagement with social dialogue and representation of those at work.

5. COLLECTIVE BARGAINING TO REGULATE GLOBAL SUPPLY CHAINS

Collective bargaining at the global level, addressing the conduct of MNEs in supply chains, is a relatively recent phenomenon. Initial attempts in the 1980s to coordinate cross-border collective bargaining[174] led to the conclu-

[169] Ibid, 558.

[170] This version makes reference in the preamble to the 'nine core international human rights treaties adopted by the United Nations, and the eight fundamental conventions adopted by the International Labour Organization, as well as other relevant international human rights treaties and conventions adopted by the United Nations and by the International Labour Organization' and also the 2030 Agenda, but does not expressly refer to freedom of association, collective bargaining or the right to strike. See www.business-humanrights.org/en/big-issues/binding-treaty/.

[171] European Commission, Proposal for a Directive of the European Parliament and of the Council on Corporate Sustainability Due Diligence and amending Directive (EU) 2019/1937 COM(2022) 71 final, 23.2.2022. Discussed in Chapter 5 of this book, text accompanying nn.200 et seq.

[172] Bueno n.146, 430–6. Discussed also by Brudney n.144, 295–339; and Landau n.147, 231–2.

[173] Landau n.147, 222; and Charlotte Villiers, 'Global Supply Chains and Sustainability: The Role of Disclosure and Due Diligence Regulation' in Beate Sjåfjell and Christopher M. Bruner (eds), *Cambridge Handbook of Corporate Law, Corporate Governance and Sustainability* (Cambridge University Press 2019).

[174] Konstantinos Papadakis, 'Globalizing Industrial Relations: What role for International Framework Agreements?' in Susan Hayter (ed.), *The Role of Collective Bargaining in the Global Economy: Negotiating for Social Justice* (Edward Elgar Publishing 2011), 280.

sion of the first international framework agreement (IFA) in 1994. By 1995 the International Confederation of Free Trade Unions (ICFTU) had set up a joint committee to explore the possibility of global collective bargaining, issuing a first code of practice in 1998.[175] The aim was to promote the conclusion of agreements, based on negotiations between MNEs and what were called 'International Trade Secretariats' (since 2002 termed 'Global Union Federations' or GUFs). IFAs are now more commonly titled 'global framework agreements' (GFAs).[176]

It has been suggested that 'global collective agreements can balance the existing power relation in favour of unions',[177] and may even be 'a key trade union tool for addressing the growth of corporate power'.[178] The difficulty has been to enable access to influence from all those in the world of work, beyond workers affiliated to established trade unions, to represent those whose work is precarious and informal, and based in the Global South rather than the North. However, there are some indications that IFAs and GFAs do aid organisation of those who are involved in these forms of work and can enable them to enforce the terms of the agreement.[179] Moreover, experiments with new forms of collective agreement, involving NGO as well as international and national trade union representation, have been promising.[180]

This section of the chapter outlines the standard content of IFAs and GFAs, with reference to their capacity to promote ILO core labour standards and 'decent work', and examines the extent to which they include standards relating to sustainable development. It then goes on to consider the relationship

---

[175] See http://training.itcilo.it/actrav_cdrom1/english/global/guide/icftuco.htm.

[176] For background, see Tonia Novitz, 'Exploring Multi-level Collective Bargaining: Transnational Legal Frameworks that Promote Worker Agency' in Julia López López (ed), *Collective Bargaining and Collective Action: Labour Agency and Governance in the 21st Century?* (Oñati/Hart 2019).

[177] Fabiana Avelar Pereira, *Global Framework Agreements: A Response to Urgent Global Labour Concerns*, PhD Thesis, Lund University, 2021.

[178] This was a UK Trades Union Congress (TUC) statement, cited by K.D. Ewing, 'International Regulation of the Global Economy – The Role of Trade Unions' in Brian Bercusson and Cynthia Estlund (eds), *Regulating Labour in the Wake of Globalisation: New Challenges, New Institutions* (Hart 2008), 205.

[179] See Lone Riisgaard, 'International Framework Agreements: A New Model for Securing Workers Rights?' (2005) 44(4) *Industrial Relations* 707; and Rüdiger Krause, 'The Promotion of Labour Standards through International Framework Agreements' in Henner Gött (ed.), *Labour Standards in International Economic Law* (Springer 2018), 329, who views IFAs as part of 'an emerging global labour governance regime'.

[180] Reingard Zimmer, 'International Framework Agreements: New Developments through Better Implementation on the Basis of an Analysis of the Bangladesh Accord and the Indonesian Freedom of Association Protocol' (2020) 17(1) *International Organizations Law Review* 178.

between these collectively negotiated agreements and MNE voluntary codes of conduct. The processes for enforcement of these agreements are considered, alongside new innovative multi-partner 'sustainability' agreements, such as those recently adopted in Bangladesh, which contain arbitration clauses. The section concludes by considering the relative success of these collectively bargained initiatives in terms of redressing power imbalances in global supply chains.

5.1 The Content of IFAs and GFAs

A list of IFAs and GFAs has been kept in a 'database on transnational company agreements' compiled by the ILO and the European Commission.[181] Defining features of these agreements are contested,[182] but are commonly understood to require inclusion of one or more GUFs as a party, and inclusion of ILO standards as a key source of reference. Unlike many voluntary corporate codes of conduct, they refer to freedom of association and the right to collective bargaining. They are also usually expected to incorporate obligations for MNEs to inform supply chains and subsidiaries of the content of the agreement, involving worker representatives in that process, alongside obligations regarding monitoring and even potentially complaints procedures. These agreements may take a general form, with more specific agreements concluded subsequently on specific issues, such as health and safety or education and training.[183]

IFAs and GFAs tend to refer explicitly to ILO Conventions, and almost invariably 'fundamental' Conventions, especially those relating to freedom of association and collective bargaining.[184] However, some IFAs contain only a 'clause of neutrality of union organizing'.[185]Also, certain IFAs do not refer

---

[181] See http://ec.europa.eu/social/main.jsp?catId=978&langId=en.

[182] For some consensus, see Nikolaus Hammer, 'International Framework Agreements: Global Industrial Relations between Rights and Bargaining' (2005) 11(4) *Transfer* 511; and Owen E. Herrnstadt, 'Are International Framework Agreements a Path to Corporate Social Responsibility?' (2007/8) 10 *University of Pennsylvania Journal of Business and Employment Law* 187.

[183] Michael Whittall, Miguel Martinez Lucio, Stephen Mustchin, Fernando Rocha, Volcker Telljohann, 'Workplace Trade Union Engagement with European Works Councils and Transnational Agreements: The Volkswagen Europe' (2017) 23(4) *European Journal of Industrial Relations* 397, 400.

[184] See the IFA signed between ICEM, BWI, PSI and GDF SUEZ (2010); IFA between ThyssenKrupp AG, the Group Works Council of Thyssenkrupp AG, IG Metall and IndustriALL Global Union (2015); and GFA between Aeon Co Ltd, UNI Global Union, UA Zenzen and the Federation of Aeon Group Workers' Unions (2014).

[185] Papadakis n.174, 281; the GFA on social, societal and environmental responsibility between the Renault Group, the Renault Group Works' Council and IndustriALL Global Union (2013) states that: 'Every employee is free to join a trade union or not.

in detail to ILO Conventions, but do mention obligations under the corporate governance instruments referred to in this chapter, such as the OECD Guidelines and the ILO Tripartite Declaration concerning MNEs,[186] and may even when referring to ILO Conventions include mention of mechanisms like the UN Global Compact.[187] Further protections can be included in these framework agreements for 'migrants and posted workers' to enjoy the conditions applicable to national workers.[188] Terms in IFAs and GFAs can refer to 'sustainable development',[189] and there seems to be a higher incidence of such provisions since the UN adopted the 2030 Agenda. In 2018, the GFA on the EDF Group's Corporate Social Responsibility made express reference to both the SDGs and the ways in which 'just transition' could be operationalised.[190]

5.2 The Scope and Impact of Negotiations

Bargaining to secure IFAs or GFAs depends on the engagement of GUFs, but also the capacity of local and regional trade unions and confederations to bring MNEs to the bargaining table.[191] The success of these multilevel campaigns is therefore likely to turn on the national and regional labour laws which enable collective representation, bargaining and action.[192] Keith Ewing has observed that 'although legal support is not a precondition for the concluding of an IFA, it is hard to escape the conclusion that it is helpful'.[193] Arguably, IFAs and

---

The Renault Group also undertakes to respect the terms of the ILO No. 98 Right to Organise and Collective Bargaining Convention, 1949. As such, the Renault Group respects the right of its employees to organise themselves collectively, and remains strictly neutral. The signatories undertake to respect the choice of each employee on this matter.'

[186] IFA between Ford Motor Company and Global IMF/Ford Global Information Sharing Network (2012).

[187] See IFA between Siemens AG, the Central Works Council of Siemens AG, the IG Metall and the IndustriAll Global Union (2012).

[188] IFA between Salini-Impreglio and BWI, Feneal-UIL, Filca-CISL and Fillea-CGIL (2014).

[189] See the Ford IFA n.186 and the Renault IFA n.185.

[190] GFA on the EDF Group's Corporate Social Responsibility between EDF and IndustriALL Global Union and PSI (2018).

[191] Tonia Novitz, 'Big Unions and Big Business: Can International Framework Agreements Promote Sustainable Development at a Local Level?' in Tonia Novitz and David Mangan (eds), *The Role of Labour Standards in Development: From Theory to Sustainable Practice?* (OUP/British Academy 2011).

[192] See Whittall et al n.183; and Silvana Sciarra, 'Collective Exit Strategies: New Ideas in Transnational Labour Law' in Guy Davidov and Brian Langille (eds), *The Idea of Labour Law*. (Oxford University Press 2011), 417.

[193] Ewing n.178, 224.

now GFAs are negotiated in 'the shadow of the law',[194] so legal norms remain relevant. This means that the state re-enters the picture as an important actor at this point, as does the ILO to the extent that this Organization can influence state practice.

The ways in which collective negotiations in an IFA can influence the terms of a corporate code of conduct have been examined by Maayan Menashe, who reaches some revealing conclusions regarding the potential scale of trade union power in a global collective bargaining setting.[195] His analysis involved a comparison of H&M's CSR code of conduct, which now takes the form of a 'Sustainability Commitment' adopted in 2016, with H&M's international framework agreements. The suppliers and business partners of H&M have had to sign up to the Sustainability Commitment, which sets out basic legal requirements alongside more 'aspirational' objectives, which contractors are required to follow.[196] An initial IFA was concluded in 2004 with the GUF UNI (at a ceremony conducted at the ILO) and the second was signed in 2015 with another GUF, IndustriALL.[197]

What Menashe points to is the limited impact that the 2015 IFA had on the 2016 Sustainability Commitment, which were in fact drafted contemporaneously. Notably, the 2015 IFA was itself limited, containing no recognised right to strike but placing emphasis on dispute resolution procedures.[198] The 2015 IFA did contain a provision against acts of interference with workers' freedom of association, which was then omitted in the Sustainability Commitment. Menashe concluded that shareholders had a considerable influence on the terms of the 2015 IFA and 'when H&M had the opportunity to decide unilaterally on a set of commitments without any influence from global union federations, the result did not deviate much from the agreement with the global union federations'.[199] The result was limited promotion of international labour rights.

This suggests that the language of 'sustainable development' does not necessarily enhance the content of voluntary corporate codes or IFAs. Moreover, being seen to conclude an IFA may be more a way of keeping trade unions

---

[194] Gunther Teubner, 'Substantive and Reflexive Elements in Modern Law' (1983) 17 *Law and Society Review* 242; cf. Diamond Ashiagbor, 'Evaluating the Reflexive Turn in Labour Law' in Alan Bogg, Cathryn Costello, A.C.L. Davies and Jeremias Prassl (eds), *The Autonomy of Labour Law* (Oxford University Press 2015), 128.

[195] Maayan Menashe, 'Private Actors as Transnational Regulators: The Case of Freedom of Association' (2020) 49(1) *Industrial Law Journal* 1.

[196] Ibid, 16–18 and 23–4. This Commitment is linked to scrutiny from the Sustainable Apparel Coalition 'Sustainability Index', which will give positive points to coverage by a collective agreement.

[197] Ibid, 17.

[198] Ibid, 26.

[199] Ibid, 29.

(GUFs and others) pacified than of making meaningful change to corporate governance.

That said, recent empirical research regarding the implementation of the H&M 2015 IFA in Cambodia is more promising in terms of indicating engagement with promotion of collective agreements at factories and a genuine effort to make 'national monitoring committees' operative.[200] It is also notable that in 2019 H&M signed a 'partnership agreement' with the ILO,[201] although the operation of that partnership and its mechanics are not fully transparent at the date at the time of writing. The impetus for H&M to act would seem to be based on its role as a brand implicated in the Bangladesh RMG and as a signatory to the Bangladesh Accord.[202]

5.3 How the Bangladesh 'Sustainability Compact' and 'Accord' Refashioned Understandings of Global Collective Agreement

Initially, it was largely European-based MNEs that negotiated IFAs,[203] and global collective bargaining was often seen as a 'culturally specific' European phenomenon.[204] This seems to be changing. César Rosado Marzán has argued that IFAs could be helpful as a means by which to bypass formal National Labour Relations Act (NLRA) requirements, enabling recognition of 'minority unions' in the US.[205] However, minority unions sometimes struggled to rely on clauses in IFAs, for example regarding rights to trade union organisation.[206] This was because the practical effect of earlier IFAs tended to depend on extra-legal procedures and mechanisms. They were regarded as 'gentlemen's agreements'.[207] There was 'no international legal framework [...] to provide

---

200 Avelar Pereira n.177, although she does not consider the processes to be unproblematic.

201 Reported at: www.ilo.org/wcmsp5/groups/public/---dgreports/---exrel/documents/publication/wcms_765661.pdf. See Chapter 3 of this book, text accompanying nn.267–8.

202 See https://bangladeshaccord.org/signatories. Note that H&M has also announced its signature of the 2021 Accord: https://hmgroup.com/news/hm-group-signs-new-agreement-on-bangladesh-fire-and-building-safety/.

203 See Hammer n.182, 525.

204 Papadakis n.174, 281; Hans-Wolfgang Platzer and Stefan Rüb, *International Framework Agreements: An Instrument for Enforcing Social Human Rights?* (Friedrich Ebert Stiftung Working Paper 2014), 6.

205 See César F. Rosado Marzán, 'Organizing with International Framework Agreements: An Exploratory Study' (2014) 4 *UC Irvine Law Review* 727.

206 Christina Niforou, 'International Framework Agreements and the Democratic Deficit of Global Labour Governance' (2014) 35(2) *Economic and Industrial Democracy* 367.

207 Reynauld Bourque, 'International Framework Agreements and the Future of Collective Bargaining' (2008) 12 *Multinational Companies Just Labour: A Canadian*

a guaranteed legal status to any labour/management agreement reached at international level'.[208]

Recent developments in Bangladesh would seem to have challenged previous assumptions regarding the remit of global collective bargaining, both in geographical terms and in relation to efficacy of agreements reached. On the one hand, the Bangladesh Accord as an innovative form of regulation appears more reflexive and situationally sensitive than clumsier international trade-based mechanisms. Such an agreement also seems to be indicative of the capacity for alliances to be forged between trade unions and NGOs and between these CSOs across the Global North and Global South.[209] As such, these types of agreement have also been described as the 'embryo of a new transnational labour law' offering renewed capacity to 'regulate global value chains'.[210]

The Bangladesh Accord arose as one pillar of a three-pronged 'Sustainability Compact' aimed at improving labour standards in Bangladesh after the Rana Plaza disaster.[211] Previously, the language of sustainability had been widely used in the RMG sector, but less attention has been paid to its implementation, while treatment of social and environmental sustainability seem to have been artificially divided.[212] In recent years, the Bangladesh Accord has been treated as illustrative of the potential for sustainable development in action, blending concern with the working environment and labour standards, and as a qualified success in this respect.

Journal of Work and Society 30, 37.

[208] Dan Gallin, *Transnational Companies: International Framework Agreements: A Reassessment* (Global Labour Institute 2008), 10–11 available at: www.globallabour.info/.

[209] Pataut and Robin-Olivier n.154, 26–8.

[210] Ibid, 69.

[211] See 'Joint Statement – Staying Engaged: A Sustainability Compact for Continuous Improvements in Labour Rights and Factory Safety in the Ready-made Garment and Knitwear Industry in Bangladesh' 8 July 2013; available at: https://trade.ec.europa.eu/doclib/docs/2013/july/tradoc_151601.pdf; also Jeff Kenner and Katrina Peake, 'The Bangladesh Sustainability Compact: An Effective Exercise of Global Experimentalist EU Governance?' (2017) 19 *Cambridge Yearbook of European Legal Studies* 86. For the Alliance as a further 'prong' of that Compact, see Trebilcock n.20, 552–3.

[212] See Dorothée Baumann-Pauly, Sarah Labowitz and Nate Stein, 'Transforming the Garment Industry in Bangladesh: Sharing Responsibility' in Sarah Margaretha Jastram and Anna-Maria Schneider (eds), *Sustainable Fashion: Governance and New Management Approaches* (Springer International Publishing 2018); cf. plans for a UN Charter for Sustainable Fashion discussed at: https://unfccc.int/news/fashion-industry-un-pursue-climate-action-for-sustainable-development and www.theguardian.com/fashion/2018/nov/29/stella-mccartney-to-launch-un-charter-sustainable-fashion.

Reingard Zimmer has argued that the Accord changed the paradigm for IFAs (and GFAs), which were previously considered merely to operate as legally unenforceable agreements on the world stage. She has argued that the Accord should be regarded as meeting the criteria for an IFA because: more than one GUF was involved in the conclusion and negotiation of the agreement; the IFA was based upon rights derived from ILO standards (concerned with health and safety); and the agreement contains a mechanism to monitor the implementation, namely factory inspections.[213]

There are some distinctions that could be made. The Accord did not give the standard attention to freedom of association and collective bargaining usually expected of an IFA, but arguably did so implicitly by involving trade unions as parties. Also, IFAs normally apply internationally or globally, and the Bangladesh Accord has been concerned only with one country. Moreover, the Accord was not an unenforceable gentlemen's agreement but could be implemented through arbitration.[214] However, these do not prevent Zimmer from classification of the initiative as an IFA; instead, she suggests that the 'specificities' of the instrument offer ways to understanding how IFAs and global collective bargaining can be strengthened.[215] Similarly, Manoj Dias-Abey has argued that 'while the Bangladesh Accord materialised very quickly after the Rana Plaza disaster', being prompted by those specific circumstances, 'it would be a mistake not to connect this to the preceding decades of transnational activism aimed at eliminating sweatshop conditions in the global garment industry'.[216] This initiative has been indicative of what global collective bargaining can achieve whether in terms of sectoral or social responsibility agreements, whether they are termed IFAs, GFAs or other.[217]

The original Accord was concluded between RMG brands, primarily but not only exclusively based in Europe, two GUFs and local trade unions, while four prominent NGOs (including the Workers' Rights Consortium) were witnesses.[218] Implementation included capacity building and remediation following

---

[213] Zimmer n.180, 199.

[214] In accordance with the UNCITRAL rules and the New York Convention, regarding which and the threat of two potential arbitration claims which were settled, see Zimmer n.180, 200.

[215] Zimmer n.180, 199.

[216] Dias-Abey n.62, 130. Cf. Zimmer n.180, 201 who sees the crisis as a major factor in the adoption of the Accord: 'the Accord was concluded in a specific situation, when the attention of world public was directed towards the purchasing policies of transnational brands in Bangladesh, a constellation that is not so easily repeatable.'

[217] For a broader view of this promise, see Marshall et al n.80, 29–32.

[218] Zimmer n.180, 190 and at 198 regarding the survival of the Accord (albeit in a modified form) after court proceedings. See, regarding the role of the 'Workers' Rights Consortium' globally, Barenberg n.62.

failed inspections and was widely regarded as successful, at least initially. The Accord was generated by a crisis, but operated in many ways effectively in its aftermath. The Accord facilitated health and safety inspections in factories, especially with respect to the immediate suppliers of brands, and, although more could have been done to foster collective bargaining in the text of the Accord, it may indirectly have been of assistance in this respect.[219] The Accord was intended to operate for five years, but is now continued in a different guise under the RMG Sustainability Council operated through the Bangladesh government via a revised 'International Accord'.[220] The Bangladeshi RMG industry suffered extensively in the context of the COVID-19 pandemic, as did the workers, who – being employed often on a casual basis – struggled to remain in work and thereby maintain the terms and conditions of employment established previously.[221] But there do now seem to be some signs of recovery and, as noted above with respect to H&M, a determination of key brands to continue their contribution to the next manifestation of the Accord.[222] 'Better Work Bangladesh' also remains a significant part of the ILO's Programme on 'Improving Conditions in the Ready-Made Garment Sector', set for completion in 2023.[223]

The Accord's successes have been attributed to engagement of a blend of global and local actors (with the involvement of GUFs having potential to empower local unions). Arguably, the forms of participatory engagement encouraged regarding scrutiny of corporate conduct reflect SDG target 16.7 and the global partnership envisaged by SDG 17. It may also have helped that the Accord was formally a legally binding instrument, operative through inspection but ultimately through arbitration. Another important factor may have been involvement of the ILO as a source of informal advice and guidance.[224] The ILO was also engaged in delivering the Arrangement for payment of victims.[225] This involvement of the ILO poses the question as to what the ILO could contribute further as a regulator in the field of corporate governance in the context of global supply chains.

---

219 Trebilcock n.20, 548. Cf. Kuruvilla et al n.54, 168.

220 See www.rsc-bd.org/en.

221 See Sen et al n.46.

222 See this chapter above, text accompanying n.202.

223 Trebilcock n.20, 549.

224 Zimmer n.180, 190–1.

225 The 'Understanding for a Practical Arrangement on Payments to the Victims of the Rana Plaza Accident and their Families and Dependents for Their Losses' was a multi-party mechanism for payment of some compensation for surviving workers and the dependants of those who died. The ILO also set up a subsequent Trust Fund to manage the process. See Diller n.70, 60–5 and Trebilcock n.20, 553–5.

6. WHAT FURTHER ROLE FOR THE ILO?

An interesting remaining question is the extent to which the corporate governance initiatives discussed above can be supported and boosted by more meaningful ILO engagement. Can the ILO promote further 'due diligence' strategies which foster genuine participatory engagement from all spheres of the world of work across the globe? A starting point was the Due Diligence Toolkit on Fair Recruitment created by the ILO in conjunction with the Global Business Network on Forced Labour,[226] but other interventions may now be feasible, such as further ILO regulation relating to global supply chains.[227] Another possibility is that the ILO can offer a labour inspection service or even a mediation and arbitration service, which would facilitate the transparent operation of CSR and sustainability codes.[228] The suggestion is that connection with the ILO would enhance the credibility of regulation and reform of corporate governance.[229]

This chapter has illustrated how ILO standards already provide an important source of reference in voluntary corporate codes of conduct, collectively negotiated 'framework' agreements and various international instruments adopted as a means by which to promote responsible corporate conduct in supply chains. The ILO has also been fostering programmes and public–private partnerships whereby it lends assistance in perhaps tangible but less visible ways.[230] The interesting question is how this interaction between ILO public and private (or state and non-state) initiatives could be more systematically addressed.[231]

An enhanced role for the ILO could reflect various aspects of its reputation and expertise. For example, following adoption of the SDGs, the ILO has emerged as a site of information gathering, knowledge and expertise on various indicators.[232] In the context of the crisis in Bangladesh, the ILO emerged as neutral and authoritative, reflecting what Janelle Diller has termed

---

226 See https://flbusiness.network/library/due-diligence-toolkit-for-fair-recruitment/, based on the 2016 ILO General Principles and Operational Guidelines for Fair Recruitment available at: www.ilo.org/global/topics/fair-recruitment/WCMS_536755.

227 See the emergence of the five-year ILO strategy on global supply chains, outlined in Chapter 3 of this book, text accompanying n.288.

228 Garcia-Muñoz Alhambra et al, n.114.

229 Ibid, 234.

230 See section 4 of Chapter 3.

231 Cf. Pataut and Robin-Olivier n.154, 77.

232 Huw Thomas and Peter Turnbull, 'From Horizontal to Vertical Labour Governance: The International Labour Organization (ILO) and Decent Work in Global Supply Chains' (2018) 71(4) *Human Relations* 536, 546 et seq. See also Chapter 1 of this book, text accompanying nn.131; and section 5 of Chapter 3 of this book.

'a global public authority'.[233] Her assessment is that the ILO possesses 'recognized authority and expertise in standard-setting in the labour sphere', which can then 'contribute to the effectiveness of the outcome and enforceability' of a transnational labour governance process.[234] For example, in Bangladesh, 'the ILO contributions of expertise, independence, and authority [...] helped to bridge conflicting interests and deeply-rooted distrust among various private-public actors concerned'.[235]

Trebilcock has been less optimistic. She has acknowledged the swift and creative way[236] in which the ILO responded to the challenges posed by the situation in Bangladesh. Like Diller, she also considers that the ILO's 'roles of convener, neutral broker, trustee and expert adviser in response to the Rana Plaza disaster' made the value of ILO intervention readily apparent. 'However, with 187 member States, most of which are developing countries, ILO resource levels would not permit replication of a response on this scale every time such a need arose.'[237]

The problem would seem to be that, to date, the ILO has tended to act in an 'ad hoc' or at least a highly selective manner in relation to specific country-based violations, rather than in a holistic way, offering structural regulation of global supply chains.[238] Time-limited programmes such as the Bangladesh Accord may have impressive short-term effects but do not address the power relations which lead to asymmetries in the global supply chains and longer-term regulatory failures.[239] The challenge then for the ILO is to initiate structural change. The 'governance gaps' arising from 'private, voluntary and deregulatory standards, with a focus on compliance by business (rather than governments)' need to be addressed systematically.[240] There is a need for 'sustainable' in the sense of durable solutions,[241] as well as measures which reflect a combination of economic, environmental and social objectives.

---

[233] See Diller n.70, 47. Cf. Maayan Menashe's view of international labour law as a 'global public good' in Maayan Menashe, *International Labour Law as a Global Public Good: Enhancing Labour Regulation in an Era of Globalisation.* PhD Diss. University of Cambridge, 2021.

[234] Diller n.70, 52.

[235] Ibid, 64.

[236] Trebilcock n.20, 563.

[237] Ibid, 555–6.

[238] Thomas and Turnbull n.232, 548.

[239] See Fahreen Alamgir and Subhabrata Bobby Banerjee, 'Contested Compliance Regimes in Global Production Networks: Insights from the Bangladesh Garment Industry' (2019) 72(2) *Human Relations* 272, 293.

[240] Thomas and Turnbull n.232, 537.

[241] See Chapter 1 of this book, text accompanying n.138.

Brudney has highlighted some measures taken by the ILO to date which suggest that the Organization is ready to engage with this regulatory feat. For example, he observes that the ILO Convention No. 190 on violence and harassment revealed the ILO's 'capacity and willingness to include a multi-stage obligatory due diligence process aimed at preventing a particular kind of workplace abuse and also its appreciation for the value of consultation with workers as an integral part of that process'.[242] Another mark of ILO capabilities, highlighted by several commentators, is the Maritime Labour Convention 2006, in which the 'economic employer' can be held accountable through cross-border regulatory cooperation.[243] Brudney also claims that ILO experience in monitoring labour standard compliance as part of its 'Better Work' and other programmes could be helpful, because this demonstrates that the ILO is familiar with not simply following a blanket punitive approach where there is non-compliance, but is used to the kinds of remediation and encouragement of changes to practices realised during the currency of the Bangladesh Accord.[244]

Brudney has argued that 'the ILO should take the lead in formulating a global supply chain convention'. This would include a requirement that 'workers and their representatives must be directly and substantially engaged with other interested parties in the formulation and implementation of the multi-stage due diligence process' accompanied by an obligation to protect 'all workers engaged in supply chain activities, regardless of their formal employment or contractual status under relevant national law'.[245] While not explicitly engaging with the language of sustainable development, which is now becoming dominant in the CSR discourse, Brudney's proposal tackles two of the concerns raised in this chapter. The first is the erratic treatment of collective worker voice in corporate governance procedures to date, whether in due diligence or enforcement procedures. It has been argued in this book that systematic engagement with those affected in the world of work is vital for any sustainable development. The second is the concern with the need to take a more inclusive view of the world of work, which, as has been demonstrated in this book, would be consistent with the 2030 Agenda's insistence that no one is left behind.[246] In this respect, Brudney envisages alliances between trade unions, which may still take a leading role, and NGOs and other CSOs

---

242 Brudney n.144, 312.

243 Ibid, 327; Thomas and Turnbull n.232, 552 Cf. analysis of this aspect of the Maritime Labour Convention in Diller n.70, 49–53 who also sees this instrument as promoting 'power-sharing' between states and non-state actors, given credibility by the ILO.

244 Brudney n.144, 71–2.

245 Ibid, 278.

246 See chapter 1 of this book, text accompanying n.144.

that 'may speak more effectively than traditional trade unions to address working conditions for supply chain workers who are migrants, homeworkers, or otherwise part of the informal economy'.[247] He suggests that this form of 'co-governance' could achieve more far-reaching outcomes,[248] citing alliances in the sphere of domestic work as illustrations of what can be achieved.[249] His proposals also of course raise other important issues, such as the scope of vicarious liability and meaningful remedies. In particular, he advocates arbitration as a means by which to resolve disputes which traverse borders,[250] which echoes the identification of arbitration as a means of placing pressure on parties to the Bangladesh Accord to ensure implementation.[251]

The difficult question is whether tripartite consent to such a course of action can be achieved at the ILO. Brudney argues that 'the ILO's unique tripartite governance structure is well suited to generating and justifying expectations applicable to employers and their organizations as well as governments'.[252] However, employers have been remarkably resistant to efforts to regulate global supply chains, acting as a 'break' on the adoption of a convention.[253] This attitude was evident in the 2016 International Labour Conference,[254] and even now it seems that the creation of 'a new policy paradigm' would be 'prolonged and contested process'.[255] Brudney does acknowledge the resistance of the International Organisation of Employers at present.[256]

It may be that smaller incremental steps can be taken in the meantime, for example focusing on the effects that supply chains have on one particular issue, such as wages. The centrality of pay as an issue for workers has become readily apparent since the peak of the pandemic as inflation soars across the globe.[257] The level of real wages is of course relevant to SDG 1 concerning poverty, SDG 8 insofar as pay is a feature of decent work and SDG 10 regard-

---

[247] Brudney n.144, 338.
[248] Ibid.
[249] Ibid, 80. Cf Adelle Blackett, *Everyday Transgressions: Domestic Workers' Transnational Challenge to International Labor Law* (ILR Press 2019).
[250] Brudney n.144, 317.
[251] See this chapter, text accompanying n.214.
[252] Brudney, n.144, 279.
[253] See Francis Maupain, *The Future of the International Labour Organisation in the Global Economy* (Hart 2013), 123–4.
[254] Thomas and Turnbull n.232, 552–3.
[255] Ibid, 538.
[256] Brudney n.144, 337.
[257] Reported at the World Economic Forum in 2022 at: www.weforum.org/agenda/2022/06/inflation-stats-usa-and-world/.

ing equality within and between states.[258] Shelley Marshall sees a role for the ILO in 'orchestrating' regulation of a global living wage to operate within supply chains. In other words, the ILO can act as an 'orchestrator of decentralized regulation', engaging with relevant social, political and economic actors.[259]

In her book, Marshall draws on the emerging orchestration literature that has been used to explain governance and implementation of the SDGs.[260] She sees international organisations, and presumably the ILO among these, as acting as 'honest brokers' acceptable to multiple stakeholders. She considers that such organisations bring 'strong legitimacy and expert support' which enables them to wield 'significant authority to convene multi-stakeholder groups and reap the benefits of the increased participation—including a range of civil society organizations in transnational governance that soft law initiatives have fostered'.[261] Arguably the World Bank Group is already, through lending conditionality, in the context of the International Finance Corporation 'Performance Standards' and later the more generally applicable 'Environmental and Social Framework', beginning to shape the contours of MNE lead firm corporate governance. However, Chapter 4 explained how, at the World Bank, scrutiny of compliance with these labour and sustainability standards needs to be further enhanced.[262]

---

[258] See Ruth Mhlanga, Uwe Gneiting and Namit Agarwal, *Walking the Talk: Assessing Companies' Progress from SDG Rhetoric to Action* (Oxfam Discussion Papers 2018), especially at 23 (regarding wages and SDG 8) and 37 (relating to wages and SDG 10); and Murray R. Hall, 'The Living Wage Gap—A Quantitative Measure of Poverty in Global Supply Chains' (2021) 26(9) *The International Journal of Life Cycle Assessment* 1867 (with reference to SDG 1).

[259] Marshall n.63, 153.

[260] See Chapter 1 of this book, text accompanying n.108. See also Kenneth W. Abbott and Duncan Snidal, 'International Regulation without International Government: Improving IO Performance through Orchestration' (2010) 5(3) *The Review of International Organizations* 315; and Kenneth W. Abbott, Philipp Genschel, Duncan Snidal and Bernhard Zangl, 'Orchestration: Global Governance through Intermediaries' in Kenneth W. Abbott and Duncan Snidal (eds), *The Spectrum of International Institutions: An Interdisciplinary Collaboration on Global Governance* (Routledge 2021). See discussion of concerns regarding this 'orchestration' process in the UN High Level Political Forum in Tonia Novitz and Margherita Pieraccini, 'Agenda 2030 and the Sustainable Development Goals: "Responsive, Inclusive and Participatory Decision-making"?' in Margherita Pieraccini and Tonia Novitz (eds), *Legal Perspectives on Sustainability* (Bristol University Press 2020), 53–60.

[261] Marshall n.63, 153.

[262] See Franz Christian Ebert, 'Labour Standards and the World Bank: Analysing the Potential of Safeguard Policies for Protecting Workers' in Henner Gött (ed.), *Labour Standards in International Economic Law* (Springer 2018). Discussed in Chapter 4 of this book, text accompanying nn.164–76.

Marshall's modest proposal for fusion of public ILO regulation with private corporate governance may yet have some sway to the extent that international organisations, such as the ILO, 'can act as bridges between local, national, and international regulatory scales'.[263] Marshall's view is that this embellishment of ILO functions would build on prior experimentation in its project-related work and ensure the Organization's 'international relevance'.[264] Nevertheless, while this measure may gain some political traction among certain states, trade unions and NGOs, employer group consent at the ILO cannot be taken for granted. There is no immediate sign that the 'hardening' of due diligence sought by Landau is genuinely afoot.[265] It may be that business is content with more minimal World Bank intervention at this stage, which does not in the context of the Environmental and Social Framework (ESF) currently contemplate extensive engagement with the ILO.[266]

7. CONCLUDING COMMENTS

In voluntary corporate codes relating to global supply chain management, there is growing awareness of the language of sustainable development. To this extent there seems to be acceptance that '[t]o better align sustainability within business, society, and global SDGs, organizations can enable sustainability activities as a catalyst for change in their supply chains'.[267] However, detailed attention to specific SDGs in corporate codes or even global framework agreements is rare, so that the term 'sustainable development' seems more of a gloss on existing practices or a signal of goodwill as opposed to a signal of meaningful change in terms of substantive content and effect. Health and safety protections have emerged as significant concerns and an illustration of how labour standards can intersect with environmental agendas, but other labour-related issues pertinent to overlap between the three pillars of sustainability seem to be absent from mainstream corporate governance discussion. There is little or no discussion of protection for whistleblowers; nor is there the exploration one might expect of 'just transitions' with trade unions, NGOs and other stakeholders. The latter omission could be understood as the latter-day manifestation of past corporate resistance to freedom of association

---

263 Marshall n.63, 153.

264 Ibid, 181.

265 Landau n.147, 222.

266 The World Bank, *Environmental and Social Framework (ESF): Implementation Update* (World Bank 2020), 16; discussed in Chapter 4 of this book, text accompanying nn.156 et seq.

267 Zimon et al n.57, 228.

and collective bargaining, arguably evident in different forms throughout this chapter.

Due diligence has the potential to promote labour standards as a facet of social sustainability, but that process of risk assessment would then have to be more rigorous in terms of scrutinising the ways in which different SDGs intersect and clash; tensions between the economic, social and environmental would have to be teased out. This could be done through transparent, participatory processes, for example through inclusion of trade unions and NGOs within due diligence consultations or even where there is meaningful collective negotiation leading to the conclusion of GFAs. However, there seems to be resistance on the employer side to transparent disclosure, complaints procedures involving multiple stakeholders and these kinds of deliberation.

Further ILO intervention could be helpful, whether focused on a particular issue such as wages in supply chains (moving on from recruitment) or in even more ambitious ways. The ILO could add value as a neutral body with expertise, as an orchestrator of systems and even as a labour inspector called on to give credence to MNE corporate codes. However, here a tripartite system of governance and employer resistance is posing problems. This means that, until greater political will is evident and mobilised, the current flouting of basic core labour standards is likely to continue down the supply chain and lead firms seem unlikely to be held accountable. The transparent interrogation of sustainable development priorities and application of norms through engagement with representatives of a wider world of work is still to be fully realised in a corporate governance setting in relation to global supply chains.

7. Conclusion: preconditions for realising the promise of sustainable development

1. INTRODUCTION

> Global trade relies on a hidden labour force that represents up to 94 per cent of the world's total labour force – condemning people to accept low-paying, unsafe and sometimes hazardous work.[1]

> Where we already have law in place, we need to work toward effective implementation and build effective models […] Where we don't have laws, we need to identify their specific needs, understand the local institutions, and design laws and systems that will guarantee their rights and facilitate their respect and protection.[2]

As these voices of trade unionists indicate, there is a crisis globally which stems from how those who work are treated and the ways in which that treatment is perpetuated through forms of trade. There is a clear need to do more to acknowledge the legal structures which reinforce rather than correct intra- and inter-generational injustices and to represent those most affected in the creation of any legal architecture which might change the status quo. This is a mission pursued, as observed in Chapter 6 of this book, by international trade union organisations, such as the International Trade Union Confederation (ITUC) and the global union federations (the GUFs), as well as by organisations such as International Lawyers Assisting Workers (ILAW), which supports strategic

[1] Marta Pujadas (General Counsel Unión Obrera de la Construcción de la República Argentina and Asesora de la CGT-RA – Argentinian General Workers' Confederation) and Mónica Tepfer (Attorney Member of the Secretariat of International Relations of the CGT-RA), 'The Impact of a New Framework of Fundamental Principles and Rights at Work on Global Supply Chains' in International Lawyers Assisting Workers (ILAW) (2021) *The Global Labour Rights Reporter: Special Issue on Accountability and Remedy in Global Supply Chains: Considerations for Workers and Unions* 42, 45.

[2] Elizabeth Tang (General Secretary, International Domestic Workers Federation – IDWF) in 'A Conversation with Elizabeth Tang' reported in ILAW (2022) *The Global Labour Rights Reporter: Special Issue on Protection of the Rights of Workers in the Informal Economy* 8, 12.

litigation and policy initiatives pursued by workers and their organisations in all parts of the world. While the International Labour Organization (ILO) Global Commission on the Future of Work has called on trade unions to do more,[3] and they seek to do so at all levels (international, regional, national and local), it may be more sensible first to look critically at what is wrong with the current legal order. After all, everybody has a responsibility to fix this – governments and employers too.

This book has examined the mutually reinforcing relationship between trade and labour, reflected in the regulatory decisions taken in various public and private international fora. The problems with the current legal texts and the interplay of international institutional and corporate activities have been highlighted, from the shocking impact on workers at Rana Plaza in Bangladesh to the failure to provide protections for those at work in, for example, the platform economy. My aim has been to interrogate the implications of current trade and labour regimes for bilateral and multilateral relations between states and for standards of corporate conduct for employers. In particular, this book has explored the capacity of sustainable development to offer an alternative unifying narrative, offering a vision for the regulation of trade and labour that could be shared, for example, by the ILO and the World Trade Organization (WTO), but also other international institutions, state actors and regional organisations, as well as representatives of management and labour across the globe, regardless of the countries in which they are situated.

Given the increasing normative sway of sustainable development on the world policy stage, as reflected in the Sustainable Development Goals (SDGs) adopted by the General Assembly in 2015,[4] I have sought to explore where that approach to policy and law-making *could* lead. Accordingly, this book has examined the claims made for sustainable development as a guide for policy development and legal reform in relation to its economic, environmental and social pillars in the specific context of trade and labour. I have reviewed the use of 'sustainable development' as a source of reference in the ILO, in international economic institutions, in free trade agreements focusing on the particular case study of the European Union (EU), and in contemporary regulation of corporate governance, to see what sustainable development may add as a normative foundation. In each context, I found a growing trend towards reference to sustainable development, but usually only superficially. My suspicion is that, at present, its potential has not been realised.

---

[3] ILO Global Commission on the Future of Work, *Work for a Brighter Future* (ILO 2019), Report issued 22 January 2019 available at: www.ilo.org/global/publications/books/WCMS_662410/lang--en/index.htm.

[4] United Nations (UN), Transforming our World: The 2030 Agenda for Sustainable Development, General Assembly, 70th Session, A/Res/70/1, New York, 2015.

This concluding chapter reviews the evidence and arguments presented in this book, with reference to a sustainable development agenda for a trade–labour linkage. A common theme that arises throughout is the lack of attention in various institutional settings paid to the ways in which environmental and labour objectives intersect. The two subjects of trade conditionality (labour and the environment) are often pursued alongside each other, without recognising their connections and tensions. Their status vis-à-vis economic objectives is also not fully articulated. More may need to be done to address this, if a sustainable development approach is in fact to be realised. A second, even more palpable observation is that inadequate attention has been paid to aspirations for 'good governance' and 'global partnership'. These aims are present in the SDGs 16 and 17, but have been applied only in limited and partial ways in the institutional settings explored in this book. The powerful injunction in the 2030 Agenda to 'leave no one behind' cannot be realised, and transparent resolution of tensions between the three pillars cannot be achieved, unless policy-making, the creation of legal standards and their application includes the voices of those at work in different jobs and in all parts of the globe.

2. NORMATIVE FOUNDATIONS AND THE PROMISE OF SUSTAINABLE DEVELOPMENT

Chapters 1 and 2 of this book considered whether it could be helpful to utilise the concept of 'sustainability', identifying various possible ways in which this could be done. The first way is to challenge the lack of durability of current trade operations which reflect a form of short-term capitalism, as well as the precarity experienced in labour markets that such operations encourage. There is scope within the sphere of sustainable development to engage with both 'intra-generational' justice (promoting equity in distribution of social goods today) and 'inter-generational' justice (preserving the world and its environment, alongside the welfare of future generations for the longer term).[5] Sustainability could thereby offer a helpful vantage point through which to view previous economic, social and human rights-based justifications for the terms of trade.

Chapter 1 explored the historical connections between trade and labour, supporting the view potently stated by Adelle Blackett that '[l]abour is not a trade "add-on" but an essential part of how we understand the social in the

[5] World Commission on Environment and Development (WCED), *Our Common Future* (Oxford University Press 1987) also known as 'the Brundtland Report'; see Chapter 1 of this book, text accompanying nn.91 et seq.

economic'.[6] This chapter sought to challenge the view that this relationship between trade and labour is merely static or pre-determined, exploring the complex relationships between countries across the so-called developing and developed worlds, also termed the Global South and the Global North respectively. Chapter 1 also highlighted the power dynamics at play, not only between different states and groups of states, but also between capital and labour (and between capital and states). Finally, the chapter probed the potential relevance of sustainable development for understanding the connections between trade and labour.

There is no doubt that the normative framework in the 2030 Agenda could have potential value for those at work: addressing poverty (in SDG 1); tackling gender inequality (in SDG 5); promoting and expanding the concept of decent work (in SDG 8, for example responding to the concerns of migrant workers); and demanding equality within and between states (in SDG 10, which responds to the current divisions between the Global North and South). The collection of goals, targets and indicators in the 2030 Agenda further assemble a host of environmental protections which benefit everyone. They include protections for the rule of law, access to justice and fundamental rights, which one would expect to include freedom of association (SDG 16.10) and participatory democratic engagement (SDG 16.7 and SDG 17). This part of the chapter also acknowledged possible connections between the 2030 Agenda and promotion of human capabilities. That instrument was also significant in recognising (repeatedly) the role that trade can play in realising not only economic goals, but also environmental and social justice (for example in SDG targets 10.8 and 17.10), so that no one will be left behind.

Chapter 2 proceeded to probe more carefully and systematically the economic, social and environmental objectives underlying a sustainable development approach to trade. These three 'pillars' of sustainable development can be demonstrated to be deeply connected, interacting in complex ways which the chapter aimed to expose. Moreover, Chapter 2 sought to demonstrate how the application of sustainable development can be understood as a dynamic process, which under SDG 16.7 should include those at work in different ways in diverse parts of the globe. Tensions between the three pillars are susceptible to prompt reactive counter-movement in response to perceptions of injustice, such that their resolution will require engagement with the perspectives of those constituencies at work affected by recent events and new policy designs.

---

6 Adelle Blackett, 'On Social Regionalism in Transnational Labour Law' (2020) 159(4) *International Labour Review* 591, 610. To which we might add 'how we understand the social in the environmental'.

3. THE ILO AND TRADE REGULATION

This book has examined the role that the ILO has sought to play in regulation of trade over the past century and the difficulties that the Organization has faced in asserting competence to do so. This is perhaps ironic, given the origins of the ILO in 1919 and its ongoing concern with fair competition in trade between states. Chapter 3 accordingly examined tensions arising between an economic justification for ILO regulation in a global capitalist economy and the overarching constitutional ambition of 'social justice'.

There are two facets of ILO activity that have particular significance for the purposes of this book. The first regards the treatment of freedom of association, which is integral to a tripartite institution. In this way, the ILO has sought to nurture durable, even sustainable, collective worker representation. Inclusion of trade union voice has ensured that standards set are rigorously reviewed, that important contributions are made to construction of a viable regulatory frame and that supervision of the implementation of standards is scrutinised by those most profoundly affected by any omission or absence. In this sense the ILO offers an important reference point for considering how we might feed the collective voices of those at work into international level discussions around trade. We can compare and contrast the treatment of 'civil society' at the International Monetary Fund (IMF) and the World Bank with the more extensive access to decision-making provided at the ILO.

The ILO has also begun in recent years to embrace the message of 'sustainable development', initially treating this as a matter of primarily environmental or green policy, but has taken a more extensive view of the implications of social sustainability in the 2019 Centenary Declaration. Moreover, in *Time to Act for SDG 8*, the International Labour Office posits that freedom of association and collective bargaining are a vital means to achievement of social and environmental objectives.[7] However, the ILO also presents a cautionary tale, since the ILO has struggled to include representatives of those engaged in informal work and to overcome employers' determination to block certain initiatives within a tripartite governance structure. Alliances between trade unions and NGOs representing different forms of labour may be possible, but also further action by the ILO on tangible issues such as employment status and global supply chains might secure more engagement of those in precarious and informal work at the ILO and in other transnational settings. It appears that these regulatory possibilities are now being explored at the ILO in the wake of agreement to place the issue of treatment of 'platform workers' on the inter-

---

[7] ILO International Labour Office, *Time to Act for SDG 8: Integrating Decent Work, Sustained Growth and Environmental Integrity* (ILO 2019).

national labour conference agenda in 2025 and the launch of a new five-year strategy on decent work in supply chains in 2023.[8] The question remains how to secure effective representation of the most vulnerable in the world of work across the globe at the ILO.

The ILO has sought to act in partnership with the Bretton Woods institutions and the WTO. This has not been oriented so much towards joint achievement of sustainable development objectives, but has been more pragmatic and *ad hoc*, addressing specific concerns affecting labour as they arise. One suspects that the ILO and international economic institutions (IEIs) have played a mutually validating role for their development of specific policies, without perhaps achieving much shared substantive ground. This may be due to the constitutional underpinnings of IEIs, which are not tied to respect for ILO standards despite the foiled attempt to secure connections in the Havana Charter with an International Trade Organisation.[9]

The ILO seems to have been interested in facilitating policy dialogues and debates at global, regional and national levels. This is arguably consistent with the overall decline in the rate of standard-setting through adoption of ILO Conventions following employer caution in the period after the Cold War. It is also an approach which fits with the Organization's technical assistance function, as well as the emergence of private transnational governance. The soft promotional and programmatic aspects of ILO activities seem likely to expand in the future and the challenge in these public–private partnerships may be to continue to engage employers, while maintaining the degree of transparency and worker group engagement apparent in other ILO standard-setting and supervisory functions (as noted above).

What has been interesting in relation to a broader sustainable development agenda has been the ways in which the normative framework of ILO core labour standards, ILO Conventions and a broader notion of 'decent work' still operate as a reference point for 'sustainable' trade conditionality, as illustrated in Chapter 5. These ILO norms also provide the substance of many corporate 'sustainability' codes governing MNE conduct in global supply chains, as demonstrated in Chapter 6. This suggests that what the ILO still does in terms of standard setting such as, for example, its recent inclusion of a right to a 'safe and healthy working environment' as a 'fundamental principle' in 2022 may have palpable flow-on effects which are not linked to the formal supervision of implementation of Conventions Nos 155 and 187 or even the 1998 Declaration

[8] ILO Governing Body, Minutes of the Policy Development Section GB.347/POL/PV, 347th Session, Geneva, 13–23 March 2023 (ILO 2023), 3–16; and ILO Strategy on Decent Work in Supply Chains GB.347/INS/8, 27 February 2023.

[9] Havana Charter for an International Trade Organization available at: www.wto.org/english/docs_e/legal_e/havana_e.pdf.

on Fundamental Principles and Rights at Work, in which core labour standards were initially elaborated as principles.[10] How the ILO engages with and applies the notion of sustainable development may also be significant, and in particular its role in the formation of any 'Global Coalition for Social Justice'.[11]

4. RESPONSES OF INTERNATIONAL ECONOMIC INSTITUTIONS TO LABOUR STANDARDS AND DEVELOPMENT

The IMF and World Bank have been devoted to securing financial stability and the financing of trade ventures, while the WTO is more directly engaged in the regulation of many (if not all) terms of trade. Both the IMF and the World Bank, the focus of discussion in the first section of Chapter 4, became notorious for their negative impact on labour standards. The first reason was the tacit adoption of a 'Washington Consensus', which viewed labour laws and collective bargaining as rigidities in markets which should be reformed. The second was the part played by both institutions in endorsing structural adjustment following the global financial crisis from 2007 onwards. These issues were compounded by systems of governance at the IMF and World Bank that give priority to the interests of wealthier states in the Global North, which have contributed more to their funds, while no arrangement is made for direct policy influence from trade unions or other representatives of those in the world of work.

The IMF is known for the ways in which it has used its surveillance powers and lending conditionality to promote structural adjustment, including reduction of the scope of effective collective bargaining and application of labour laws. This was initially a policy agenda pursued in respect of developing states in the Global South, but the IMF also participated in drafting Memoranda of Understanding for conditional lending in European countries regarding excessive sovereign debt following the global financial crisis. Both are outlined in Chapter 4.

The World Bank Group has played a more inconsistent role in the context of work. In part, this can be attributed to the diversity of its component institutions,

---

[10] See Resolution on the inclusion of a safe and healthy working environment in the ILO's framework of fundamental principles and rights at work, ILC.110/Resolution1, 10 June 2022 available at: www.ilo.org/wcmsp5/groups/public/---ed_norm/---relconf/documents/meetingdocument/wcms_848632.pdf.

[11] See ILO, *Report of the Director-General First Supplementary Report: A Global Coalition for Social Justice* (ILO 2022); *Update on the Global Coalition for Social Justice* GB.347/INS/4, 20 February 2023, 6–7; and *Report of the Director-General: Advancing Social Justice* (ILO 2023).

which range from the International Development Agency (IDA), concerned primarily with development aid and issues of sustainability, to more commercial World Bank components such as the International Finance Corporation (IFC) and the International Centre for Settlement of Investment Disputes (ICSID), the latter also having relevance to terms of bilateral and multilateral investment agreements (and investment chapters in FTAs). It is notable that the IFC introduced Environmental and Social 'Performance Standards' (which include core and other labour standards) for projects to which it lends: a practice which has been expanded under a wider 'Environmental and Social Framework'.[12] However, concerns have been raised regarding access to the complaints mechanisms established for the enforcement of this social and environmental sustainability mechanism, which is of considerable importance given the limited access of civil society organisations (at both the World Bank and IMF) otherwise to influence in policy-making. Moreover, the IFC initially crafted the Performance Standards while simultaneously recommending forms of deregulation of labour standards, including trade union engagement, in its original 'Doing Business' report, and an important issue will be the implementation of a new plan to promote a 'Business Enabling Environment', the 'B-READY' project.[13] While a commitment to 'sustainable development' is detectable in World Bank policy documentation, the level of engagement with labour-related issues could be improved and it will be interesting to see how future cooperation now planned with the ILO may secure that.

The second section of Chapter 4 examined the evolution of the WTO from the period after the Second World War and into the twenty-first century. This part began by examining the initial preoccupation with trade in goods under the General Agreement on Tariffs and Trade (GATT)[14] and implications for protection of labour standards. In this context, the effect of abandonment of the Havana Charter was highlighted, alongside the preservation of some public policy measures which could be taken unilaterally by state contracting parties, with reference to labour and environmental protections as 'general exceptions'.

The survey conducted in Chapter 4 engaged with the challenges of de-colonisation and the ways in which the desirability of enabling voice for

---

[12] *The World Bank Environmental and Social Framework* available at: https://thedocs.worldbank.org/en/doc/837721522762050108-0290022018/original/ESFFramework.pdf.

[13] See www.worldbank.org/en/programs/business-enabling-environment.

[14] GATT, Enabling Clause: 'Differential and More Favourable Treatment Reciprocity and Fuller Participation of Developing Countries' – Decision of 28 November 1979 L/4903 – appended to GATT (which continues to apply as part of GATT 1994 under the WTO).

so-called developing countries started to be acknowledged.[15] A related issue was the failure of formal parity of legal treatment to take sufficient account of the vulnerability of working people in the Global South. Their call for 'special and differential treatment' (SDT) was only gradually reflected in legal texts, such as Article XVIII of the GATT as amended in 1955 and the insertion of Part IV into the GATT in 1965.[16] The emergence of the UN Conference on Trade and Development (UNCTAD) in 1964 and its role in establishing a Generalised System of Preferences (under an Enabling Clause) freer from previous colonial dependent trading ties (permanently appended to the GATT some years later in 1979) were significant here. By the 1970s, developing countries were being given an opportunity to 'trade their way out of poverty' with assistance from the IFIs. It is evident that this became a debt trap for those governments and the workers within those States, which has not yet been overcome.[17] Later on, a decision was taken to opt out of a social clause and defer instead to the ILO as a regulator of labour standards, even though the ILO would struggle to do so effectively and directly in the sphere of trade. The potential offered by the Doha Declaration of 2001 to promote development objectives,[18] which could have had significant implications for workers, did not meet the expectations expressed at the start of the millennium.

Another pertinent issue is the way in which the WTO has sought to regulate trade in services, including temporary migrant labour. The terms of the General Agreement on Trade in Services (GATS) appended to the WTO Agreement[19] and provision made for the temporary movement of natural persons under mode 4 service delivery, as explained in an Annex on Movement of Natural Persons,[20] has enabled employers (and the states in which they are based) to import a pliable and cheaper workforce which can be prevented from

---

[15] Adelle Blackett, *Trade Liberalization, Labour Law, and Development: A Contextualization* (ILO Discussion Paper Series 2007); and David M. Trubek and Alvaro Santos (eds), *The New Law and Economic Development – A Critical Appraisal* (Cambridge University Press 2006).

[16] See, for the texts of GATT 1947 and 1994, WTO website at: www.wto.org/english/docs_e/legal_e/final_e.htm.

[17] See UNCTAD, *Debt Vulnerabilities in Developing Countries: A New Debt Trap?* (UNCTAD 2018) available at: https://unctad.org/webflyer/debt-vulnerabilities-developing-countries-new-debt-trap-volume-i-regional-and-thematic.

[18] See documentation available at: www.wto.org/english/tratop_e/dda_e/dda_e.htm.

[19] General Agreement on Trade in Services (GATS), Annex IB to the World Trade Organisation Agreement, available at: www.wto.org/english/docs_e/legal_e/26-gats.pdf.

[20] See GATS, Art 1(b) and Annex on Movement of Natural Persons Supplying Services under the Agreement.

making claims to longer-term immigration status or naturalisation. It becomes extremely difficult to secure effective trade union representation and collective bargaining for those engaged in such temporary movement across borders. While GATS in some ways seems to simply echo familiar terms in the GATT, such as non-discrimination and the most favoured nation principle, the shift in context is not adequately addressed. Formal parity of norms does not secure justice in this setting, serving some interests more than others. What emerges starkly is the appropriation and commodification of labour as 'services' and the extinguishing of worker voice implicit in this form. The commercialisation of work, as it becomes merely a 'service' to be traded, neglects the lived experience of the people who move temporarily, their needs and their voices.

That is made manifest by the limited opportunities for collective worker representation in WTO dispute settlement under the amicus curiae system, despite emergent reference to sustainable development as a source of norms.[21] Arguably, such interventions are now made even less likely following the blocking of Appellate Body (AB) appointments, seemingly in response to the frustration of the US and other WTO members with alleged AB activism, including the willingness to hear unsolicited amicus curiae briefs (under particular conditions).[22] Much will depend on the outcome of contemplated reforms to be agreed.[23]

5. LABOUR STANDARDS AND SUSTAINABLE DEVELOPMENT IN FREE TRADE AGREEMENTS

Free trade areas and customs unions can be exempt from usual WTO rules under the GATT (Article XXIV) and GATS (Article V and Vbis) subject to certain provisos. FTAs have become more common, resulting in a 'spaghetti bowl' web of reciprocal bilateral and multilateral obligations.[24] FTAs tend to build upon WTO obligations regarding goods and services, but also have now begun to set out other matters beyond the remit of the WTO, such as invest-

---

21 Trade union engagement seems to have been largely limited to the WTO case, *European Communities – Measures Affecting Asbestos and Asbestos-Containing Products* (known as *EC—Asbestos*), Report of the Appellate Body (12 March 2001) WT/DS135/AB/R, and even then the application of the ITUC/ETUC was treated as being too late to be considered (at para. 55).

22 Joshua Paine, 'The WTO's Dispute Settlement Body as a Voice Mechanism' (2019) 20 *Journal of World Investment and Trade* 820. See Chapter 4 of this book, text accompanying nn.291–2.

23 See for the present aim of concluding reforms by 2024, www.wto.org/english/thewto_e/minist_e/mc12_e/briefing_notes_e/bfwtoreform_e.htm.

24 Jagdish Bhagwati, *Termites in the Trading System: How Preferential Agreements Undermine Free Trade* (Oxford University Press 2008).

ment. What has emerged over time is that FTAs can and often do make specific provision for protection of labour standards. The content of such provisions and the procedures attached to them (and their adequacy in terms of implementation) remains a live subject of research and policy experimentation, which was discussed in Chapter 5.

Using the EU as a case study, Chapter 5 examined how a ‘new generation’ of FTAs have included ‘trade and sustainable development’ (TSD) chapters, with reference to ILO standards. While these were once considered to be barely enforceable, given the difficulty of demonstrating how labour standards ‘affect trade’ – especially freedom of association and the effective right to collective bargaining[25] – the enforcement landscape may be changing. So much is evident from a recent expert panel decision in the EU–Korea FTA dispute, which gives as one of the reasons for its findings the overall context of the sustainable development provisions in the FTA.[26] This suggests promise for sustainable development as a basis for enforcement of labour standards, but needs to be tempered by acknowledgement of the importance of *how* implementation of FTA labour standards takes place. The representation of collective voice of those at work, both in and beyond the EU, is likely to be significant.

Other FTA chapters may also be relevant to those at work. An example is the tendency to make provision for temporary movement of natural persons as a feature of trade in services. Investment chapters in FTAs may also have implications for labour to the extent that investors can challenge a state’s improvement of labour standards or the adoption of new policies relating more broadly to sustainable development. There is considerable potential for engagement with the interests of corporate actors as employment agencies, investors and employers, but not usually those in the world of work who are affected.

Finally, Chapter 5 considered how far the sustainability initiatives to be pursued by ‘normative power Europe’ can or should extend. The chapter closed by considering proposals from the European Commission to adopt measures which would block import of products of forced labour and promote corporate responsibility of EU companies abroad, all with reference to the principle of sustainable development. The extent of engagement with those at work in what are termed ‘third countries’ was considered here, and issues were raised regarding whether the scope of social dialogue anticipated outside

---

[25] *Final Report of the Panel, Guatemala – Issues Relating to the Obligations Under Article 16.2.1(a) of the CAFTA-DR,* 14 June 2017.

[26] Report of the Panel of Experts (2020) Proceeding constituted under Article 13.15 of the EU–Korea Free Trade Agreement, 25 January 2021, Panel: Dr Jill Murray (Chairperson), Professor Laurence Boisson de Chazournes and Professor Jaemin Lee; available at: https://trade.ec.europa.eu/doclib/docs/2021/january/tradoc_159358.pdf.

the EU could be sufficient for achievement of the objectives in SDGs 8, 10, 16 and 17.

6. REGULATION OF CORPORATE GOVERNANCE IN GLOBAL SUPPLY CHAINS

Chapter 6 addressed international public and private codes for corporate conduct and the emergence of global collective bargaining that may regulate labour standards in global supply chains, constraining the actions of multinational enterprises (MNEs). The chapter set out problems for labour standards and broader environmental and social sustainability objectives posed currently by corporate conduct in supply chains, especially but not exclusively in the readymade garment (RMG) sector. The chapter then investigated the ways in which various corporate governance instruments and initiatives refer to and, more importantly, give effect to sustainable development norms. The processes through which such norms were set and implemented were also examined, with reference once again to collective representation of those at work in the Global North and South.

Corporate codes have for some considerable period of time been voluntarily adopted by MNEs operating transnationally to improve their brand reputation. Chapter 6 highlighted how the content of these codes tended to refer to ILO standards for legitimacy and more recently to sustainable development, but often sought to evade obligations relating to freedom of association and collective bargaining. Some pressure has been placed on 'lead firms' in supply chain regulation through a variety of so-called soft international legal instruments, designed to guide corporate conduct with reference to labour standards, with varying degrees of success.[27]

The most significant development has been the 'respect, protect and remedy' framework supplemented by a 'due diligence' framework in the UN Guiding Principles on business and human rights.[28] In other contexts, namely the OECD Guidelines on Multinational Enterprises, the ILO Declaration relating to multinational enterprises and social policy and the UN Global Compact,[29] the language of sustainable development has been included as

---

[27] OECD Guidelines for Multinational Enterprises available at: www.oecd.org/daf/inv/mne/48004323.pdf; and the 6th edition of the ILO Tripartite declaration of principles concerning multinational enterprises and social policy available at: www.ilo.org/empent/Publications/WCMS_094386/lang--en/index.html.

[28] John Ruggie, *Guiding Principles on Business and Human Rights: Implementing the United Nations 'Protect, Respect and Remedy' Framework*, 17th sess, Agenda Item 3, UN Doc A/HRC/17/31, 21 March 2011 annex.

[29] Based online at: www.unglobalcompact.org/.

texts and procedures have been revised after the 2030 Agenda. However, the revisions do not seem to have improved the transparency of the procedures under these instruments or secured access to justice for those most vulnerable in the global world of work, especially in the RMG industry. It is perhaps not surprising that the OECD, with a tradition of standing business and trade union representatives engaged in policy-making, comes closest to doing so – with some excellent examples of trade union representation before National Contact Points – but even there, practice is variable.

More significant may be the evolution of global collective bargaining regarding corporate supply chain management regarding labour and even environmental standards. This has developed from the first international framework agreement in 1994 into more wide-ranging 'global framework agreements' and initiatives like the Bangladesh Accord. These initiatives can incorporate sustainable development as a source of reference, although they tend to do so in a general and vague way, with more concrete inclusion of ILO standards. Collectively bargained agreements can enable more effective regulation of supply chains, but depend on national, regional and international structural and legal support to address the power imbalances between those at work and lead firms as employers. Here the role of the ILO as an 'orchestrator' and facilitator re-enters the frame, given its neutrality and expertise. So far, ILO interventions have been limited and *ad hoc*. Several commentators envisage and demand enhanced ILO standard setting on global supply chains, relating to wages or more generally, requiring due diligence with reference to the voices of all those at work in the Global North and South.[30] However, despite the potential for greater regulatory engagement, employer opposition in a tripartite ILO may still poses a significant obstacle to more systematic and structural intervention.

7. CONCLUSION

Various themes arise from this historical and normative excursus into the regulation of trade systems which impact upon labour from the perspective

[30] Ingrid Landau, 'Human Rights Due Diligence and the Risk of Cosmetic Compliance' (2019) 20 *Melbourne Journal of International Law* 221; Shelley Marshall, *Living Wage: Regulatory Solutions to Informal and Precarious Work in Global Supply Chains* (Oxford University Press 2019); Shelley Marshall, Ingrid Landau, Hila Shamir, Tamar Barkay, Judy Fudge and Auret van Heerden, *Mandatory Human Rights Due Diligence: Risks and Opportunities for Workers and Unions* (RMIT/TraffLab/Monash 2023); and James J. Brudney, 'Hiding in Plain Sight: An ILO Convention on Labor Standards in Global Supply Chains' (2023) 23(2) *Chicago Journal of International Law* 272.

of sustainable development. The then UN Secretary-General, Kofi Annan, observed in 2001: 'Our biggest challenge in this new century is to take an idea that seems abstract – sustainable development – and turn it, too, into a daily reality for all the world's people.'[31] That reality has yet to become manifest. Instead, what becomes apparent are the failures of modes of existing national, regional and international trade regulation to protect the interests of working people. The results are palpable social and environmental harms and diminishing economic prosperity. Those failures have been harshly exposed by first the global financial crisis and then the COVID-19 pandemic. We are witnessing ever greater challenges posed by transnational trade law to maintenance of international, regional and national labour laws and human rights laws, while emergent trade and investment practices (facilitated by the current global legal matrix) prompt new patterns of work excluding increasing numbers of people from the protection of basic labour standards and agency over their labour. The global regulatory design of IEIs provides restricted access to voice for governments in the Global South and very little engagement with those in the world of work within these countries.

This book has analysed the status quo, considering coordinated global solutions to problems that traverse national boundaries. Change might be achieved by recognising the role of international, regional and transnational institutions (public, private and 'blended') in mediating tensions between trade, labour and other human rights. The obvious problem is that each institution and legal framing, whether within the UN framework or outside, is representative of its own institutional objectives and systemic values. Common ground could be found in the idea of 'sustainable development' as endorsed by the international community in the 2030 Agenda, offering a prism for rethinking and departure. Sustainable development encourages consideration of longer-term plans based on inter- and intra-generational justice, as opposed to short-term capitalist ventures based only on immediate financial gain. The content of the SDGs, targets and indicators, including the inclusion of the ILO term 'decent work' in SDG 8, could prompt more rigorous interrogation of interactions between economic, environmental or social objectives in practice. However, this could only be a viable strategy, generating legal and institutional change, if a wider range of voices in the world of work receive attention within that larger matrix. Otherwise progress will be elusive and indeed illusory.

The current UN Secretary-General, António Guterres, speaking at COP 27 in 2022, observed that 'justice and ambition require the essential voice of

---

[31] See 'Secretary-General Calls for Break in Political Stalemate over Environmental Issues' 14 March 2001, Press Release, SG/SM/7739, ENV/DEV/561; available at: https://press.un.org/en/2001/sgsm7739.doc.htm.

civil society. The most vital energy source in the world is people power.'[32] It is precisely that power which has been identified as lacking in this book. The reasons would seem to be manifold, but also inter-related. Capital is creative and has eked out opportunities for profit, at the expense of labour and the environment, that have evaded democratic regulation and even the protection of the most fundamental human rights which have been apparently 'universally' recognised by the international community. Labour and the environment have tended to be viewed as instrumental means to economic ends, rather than deserving of specific attention. Likewise, the relationships between the social and ecological have been largely neglected by policy-makers at the international level.

The SDGs as a statement of intent are only as effective as the multi-level institutions put in place to secure their effectiveness. At a first preliminary level, in terms of the relationship between trade and labour, this requires recognition of all those in the world of work in all parts of the globe affected by current modes of production, service delivery and investment for trade. The need for solidarity has never been stronger, and there is an urgent need to secure transformation of internationally recognised labour standards to enable those in precarious employment to organise and act in concert regardless of formal employment status. To support those who are most vulnerable at work, there have to be protections for those at work who collectively bargain and strike in sympathy with others – whether they be colleagues and fellow-workers, or members of their communities seeking environmental protections, or even people in different countries impacted by the way that they work.[33] This is the essential basis of meaningful participation in decision-making contemplated by the 2030 Agenda, given current imbalances of power in the global economy between capital and labour, between capital and states and between the Global North and Global South.

Further, in the crafting of these norms aimed at collective engagement, the different experiences of those in the Global South, compared to the dominant Global North, need to be explored in greater depth. The informal economy in so-called developing countries, ostensibly lying outside the regulated labour market, has not been and seems unlikely to be extinguished.[34] If anything, the

---

32 Statement by the Secretary-General at the conclusion of COP27 in Sharm el-Sheikh, 19 November 2022 available at: www.un.org/sg/en/content/sg/statement/2022-11-19/statement-the-secretary-general-the-conclusion-of-cop27%C2%A0-sharm-el-sheikh%C2%A0%C2%A0.

33 Julia López López (ed.), *Inscribing Solidarity: Debates in Labor Law and Beyond* (Cambridge University Press 2022).

34 See Donatella Alessandrini, Johanna del Pilar Cortes-Nieto, Luis Eslava and Anil Yilmaz Vastardis, 'The Dream of Formality: Racialization Otherwise and International Economic Law' (2022) 25 *Journal of International Economic Law* 207.

incidence of informality has merely expanded in the Global North. Rather, strategies need to be devised that can affect current exigencies, and this may mean revisiting connections between labour, jobs, dismissal and social security, as posited by Juan Somavia as part of his original ILO Decent Work Agenda.[35] The terms of global lending, the ways in which temporary migration is regulated (whether at the WTO or under FTAs), the power of the WTO to place conditions on terms of FTAs and the scope of norms prevalent in international investment law could all helpfully be revisited.

There are glimmers of hope. The emergence of 'sustainable development chapters' in EU FTAs may not yet attend to the interactions between environmental and labour concerns, but they have been accompanied by new participatory mechanisms for engaging with those affected by the terms of trade, including trade unions, which is a norm that could usefully be adopted elsewhere. Yet, even in the EU setting, there remains a need to enable more active participation at the negotiation as well as the implementation stage and to ensure that those most vulnerable gain access to these systems and are suitably represented. Further, unilateral action by trading blocs such as the EU to promote various facets of decent work, arguably permitted by WTO instruments, should be crafted with more attention to the views of those at work in third countries, and their input should be incorporated in any application and enforcement. Utilising a richer global understanding of sustainable development, which encompasses protection of human rights and capabilities in the sense of voice and agency, there may be better choices to be made collectively than those currently contemplated by politicians and trade lawyers in our current crises. Indeed, there are palpable dangers in the trade-based vulnerability, impoverishment and silencing of those engaged in work.

Seeking to take a sustainable development approach in which 'no one is to be left behind' inevitably begs questions as to the institutional scope for the enabling the voices of those who work in many ways and different places, alongside their effective representation in international public governance, crafting and execution of regional measures and in a corporate governance setting. How can collective voice be encouraged alongside sensitivity to divergent origins and experiences within a labour market in high and low-income occupations across low and high-income countries? How can the dynamics which sway power be managed? It is hoped that by exposing the need for these questions from a sustainable development perspective in the current complex global legal matrix which shapes the interaction between trade and labour, we can begin to craft answers. Otherwise, sus-

---

35 ILO, *Report of the Director-General: Decent Work* (ILO 1999).

tainable development will remain only a superficial gloss on current global practices, where trade and labour remain linked in effect but their connections are poorly regulated, to the continued detriment of those in the wider world of work.

Bibliography

Maisam Abbasi, 'Towards Socially Sustainable Supply Chains – Themes and challenges' (2017) 29(3) *European Business Review* 261.

Kenneth W. Abbott and Steven Bernstein, 'The High-level Political Forum on Sustainable Development: Orchestration by default and design' (2015) 6(3) *Global Policy* 222.

Kenneth W. Abbott, Philipp Genschel, Duncan Snidal, Bernhard Zangl, 'Orchestration: Global governance through intermediaries' in Kenneth W. Abbott and Duncan Snidal (eds), *The Spectrum of International Institutions: An Interdisciplinary Collaboration on Global Governance* (Routledge 2021).

Kenneth W. Abbott and Duncan Snidal (eds), *The Spectrum of International Institutions: An Interdisciplinary Collaboration on Global Governance* (Routledge 2021).

Kenneth W. Abbott and Duncan Snidal, 'International Regulation without International Government: Improving IO performance through orchestration' (2010) 5(3) *The Review of International Organizations* 315.

Dina Abdelzaher, Whitney Douglas Fernandez and William D. Schneper, 'Legal Rights, National Culture and Social Networks: Exploring the uneven adoption of United Nations Global Compact' (2019) 28(1) *International Business Review* 12.

M. Rodwan Abouharb and David L. Cingranelli, 'The Human Rights Effects of World Bank Structural Adjustment, 1981-2000' (2006) 50(2) *International Studies Quarterly* 233.

Judson Abraham, 'Just Transitions for the Miners: Labor environmentalism in the Ruhr and Appalachian coalfields' (2017) 39(2) *New Political Science* 218.

Fikret Adaman, Pat Devine, and Begum Ozkaynak, 'Reinstituting the Economic Process: (Re)embedding the economy in society and nature' (2003) 13(2) *International Review of Sociology/Revue Internationale de Sociologie* 357.

Abi Adams-Prassl, Teodora Boneva, Marta Golin and Christopher Rauh, 'Inequality in the Impact of the Coronavirus Shock: Evidence from Real Time Surveys' IZA DP No. 13183 (2020) available at: https://covid-19.iza.org/wp-content/uploads/2020/04/dp13183.pdf.

Kofi Addo, *Core Labour Standards and International Trade: Lessons from the regional context* (Springer 2015).

Kofi Addo, 'The Correlation Between Labour Standards and International Trade' (2002) 36(2) *Journal of World Trade* 285.

Jordi Agusti-Panareda, Franz Christian Ebert and Desiree LeClercq, 'ILO Standards and Trade Agreements: A Case for Consistency' (2015) 36 *Comparative Labor Law and Policy Journal* 347.

Jordi Agusti-Panareda, Franz Christian Ebert and Desiree LeClercq, *Labour Provisions in Free Trade Agreements: Fostering their Consistency with the ILO Standard System* (ILO 2014).

Padideh Ala'i, 'Judicial Lobbying at the WTO: The Debate over the Use of Amicus Curiae Briefs and the U.S. Experience' (2000) 24 *Fordham International Law Journal* 62.

Fahreen Alamgir and Subhabrata Bobby Banerjee, 'Contested Compliance Regimes in Global Production Networks: Insights from the Bangladesh garment industry' (2019) 72(2) *Human Relations* 272.

Cinzia Alcidi, Alessandra Giovannini and Daniel Gros, 'History Repeating Itself: From the Argentine default to the Greek tragedy? CEPS Commentary, 1 July 2011 available at: http://aei-dev.library.pitt.edu/32159/.

Antony E. Alcock, *History of the International Labour Organisation* (Macmillan 1971).

Donatella Alessandrini, 'Global Value Chains, Development and the *Long Duree* of Trade and Investment Law' (2022) 35 *Leiden Journal of International Law* 619.

Donatella Alessandrini, Johanna del Pilar Cortes-Nieto, Luis Eslava and Anil Yilmaz Vastardis, 'The Dream of Formality: Racialization Otherwise and International Economic Law' (2022) 25 *Journal of International Economic Law* 207.

Robert Alexy, *A Theory of Legal Argumentation: The Theory of Rational Discourse as Theory of Legal Justification* Translated by Ruth Adler and Neil MacCormick (Clarendon Press 1989).

Philip Alston, 'The World Bank as a Human Rights-Free Zone' (2017) NYU School of Law, Public Law Research Paper No. 17-50, Available at SSRN: https://ssrn.com/abstract=3079899.

Philip Alston, 'Facing Up to the Complexities of the ILO's Core Labour Standards Agenda' (2005) 16 *European Journal of International Law* 457.

Philip Alston (ed.), *Labour Rights as Human Rights* (Oxford University Press (OUP) 2005).

Philip Alston, '"Core Labour Standards" and the Transformation of the International Labour Rights Regime' (2004) 15 *European Journal of International Law* 457.

Philip Alston, 'Resisting the Merger and Acquisition of Human Rights by Trade Law: A reply to Petersmann' (2002) 13 *European Journal of International Law* 815.

Philip Alston and James Heenan, 'Shrinking the International Labour Code' (2004) 36(2/3) *International Law and Politics* 221.

Christoph Aluttis, Tewabech Bishaw, and Martina W. Frank, 'The Workforce for Health in a Globalized Context – Global shortages and international migration' (2014) 7(1) *Global Health Action* 23611.

Felix Anderl, *Broken Solidarities: How Open Global Governance Divides and Rules* (Bristol University Press 2022).

Peter Andersson, Niklas Bruun, Petra Herzfeld Olsson, Tonia Novitz and Erik Sjödin, 'Assessing the Swedish Labour Law Model through a Social Sustainability Lens' (2022) 2 *Retfærd* 75.

Rutvica Andrijasevic and Tonia Novitz, 'Supply Chains and Unfree Labor: Regulatory Failure in the Case of Samsung Electronics in Slovakia' (2020) 6(2) *Journal of Human Trafficking* 195.

Konstantinos Angelopoulos, Spyridon Lazarakis, Rebecca Mancy and Max Schroeder, *Pandemic-Induced Wealth and Health Inequality and Risk Exposure* CESifo Working Paper No. 9474 available at SSRN: http://dx.doi.org/10.2139/ssrn.3985772.

Richard Anker, Igor Chernyshev, Philippe Egger and Farhad Mehran, 'Measuring Decent Work with Statistical Indicators' (2003) 142 *International Labour Review* 147.

Mark Anner, 'Corporate Social Responsibility and Freedom of Association Rights: The precarious quest for legitimacy and control in global supply chains' (2012) 40(4) *Politics & Society* 609.

Mark Anner and Teri Caraway, 'International Institutions and Workers' Rights: Between labor standards and market flexibility' (2010) 45 *Studies in Comparative International Development* 151.

Billy Melo Araujo, 'Labour Provisions in EU and US Mega-regional Trade Agreements: Rhetoric and reality' (2018) 67(1) *International and Comparative Law Quarterly* 233.

Diamond Ashiagbor, 'Race and Colonialism in the Construction of Labour Markets and Precarity' (2021) 50(4) *Industrial Law Journal* 506.

Diamond Ashiagbor (ed.), *Re-imagining Labour Law for Development* (Hart 2019).

Diamond Ashiagbor, 'Evaluating the Reflexive Turn in Labour Law' in Alan Bogg, Cathryn Costello, A.C.L. Davies and Jeremias Prassl (eds), *The Autonomy of Labour Law* (OUP 2015).

Diamond Ashiagbor, 'Unravelling the Embedded Liberal Bargain: Labour and Social Welfare Law in the Context of EU Market Integration' (2013) 19(3) *European Law Journal* 303.

Diamond Ashiagbor, Prabha Kotiswaran, Amanda Perry-Kessaris, 'Introduction: Moving towards an Economic Sociology of Law' (2013) 40 *Journal of Law and Society* 1.

Ed Atkins, *A Just Energy Transition: Getting Decarbonisation Right in a Time of Crisis* (Bristol University Press 2023).

Fabiana Avelar Pereira, *Global Framework Agreements: A Response to Urgent Global Labour Concerns*, PhD Thesis, Lund University, 2021.

Ian Ayres and John Braithwaite, *Responsive Regulation: Transcending the Deregulation Debate* (OUP 1992).

Hüseyin Aytuğ, Merve Mavuş Kütük, Arif Oduncu, Sübidey Toganas, 'Twenty Years of the EU-Turkey Customs Union: A Synthetic Control Method Analysis' (2017) 55 *Journal of Common Market Studies* 419.

Lucio Baccaro and Valentina Mele, 'For Lack of Anything Better? International organizations and global corporate codes' (2011) 89(2) *Public Administration* 451.

Peter Bachrach and Morton S Baratz, 'Two Faces of Power' (1962) 56 *The American Political Science Review* 947.

Amrita Bahri and Daria Bokla, 'Not Just Sea Turtles, Let's Protect Women Too: Invoking Public Morality Exception or Negotiating a New Gender Exception in Trade Agreements?' (2022) 33(1) *The European Journal of International Law* 237.

Jennifer Bair, Mark Anner, and Jeremy Blasi, The Political Economy of Private and Public Regulation in post-Rana Plaza Bangladesh' (2020) 73(4) *ILR Review* 969.

Peter Bakvis, 'The World Bank's Doing Business Report: A Last Fling for the Washington Consensus?' (2009) 15(3–4) *Transfer: European Review of Labour and Research* 419.

Peter Bakvis, 'How the World Bank & IMF use the Doing Business Report to promote Labour Market Deregulation In Developing Countries' (ICFTU 2006).

Cornel Ban, 'Austerity versus Stimulus? Understanding Fiscal Policy Change at the International Monetary Fund Since the Great Recession' (2015) 28(2) *Governance: An International Journal of Policy, Administration, and Institutions* 167.

Bernard Barber, 'All Economies are "Embedded": The Career of a Concept and Beyond' (1995) 62(2) *Social Research* 387.

Mark Barenberg, 'Toward a Democratic Model of Transnational Labour Monitoring' in Brian Bercusson and Cynthia Estlund (eds), *Regulating Labour in the Wake of Globalisation: New Challenges, New Institutions* (Hart 2008).

Catherine Barnard, 'EU Employment Law and the European Social Model: The Past, the Present and the Future' (2015) 67 *Current Legal Problems* 199.

Sarah Ellis Barnekow and Kishore G. Kulkarni. 'Why Regionalism? A look at the costs and benefits of regional trade agreements in Africa' (2017) 18(1) *Global Business Review* 99.

George N. Barnes, *History of the International Labour Office* (London: Williams and Norgate, 1926).

Virginie Barral, 'Sustainable Development in International Law: Nature and Operation of an Evolutive Legal Norm' (2012) 23(2) *European Journal of International Law* 377.

James Barresea, Cynthia Phillips, and Victoria Shoa, 'Why do U.S. Public Companies Continue to Join the UN Global Compact: Ethics or economics?' (2020) 50(3) *International Studies of Management and Organization* 209.

Stephanie W. Barrientos, '"Labour Chains": Analysing the role of labour contractors in global production networks' (2013) 49(8) *The Journal of Development Studies* 1058.

Stephanie Barrientos, *Global Production Systems and Decent Work* ILO working paper 77 (ILO 2007).

Christian Barry and Sanjay G. Reddy, 'International Trade and Labor Standards: A proposal for linkage' (2006) 39 *Cornell International Law Journal* 545.

Lorand Bartels, 'WTO Reform Proposals: Implications for developing countries' in Teddy Subramanien, Brendan Vickers and Hilary Enos-Edu (eds), *WTO Reform: Reshaping Global Trade Governance for 21st Century Challenges* (The Commonwealth 2019).

Lorand Bartels, 'The Chapeau of the General Exceptions in the WTO GATT and GATS Agreements: A Reconstruction' (2015) 109(1) *American Journal of International Law* 95.

Lorand Bartels, 'Human Rights and Sustainable Development Obligations in EU Free Trade Agreements' (2012) *Legal Studies Research paper Series, University of Cambridge Faculty of Law,* Paper No. 24/2012.

Lorand Bartels, 'The WTO Legality of the EU's GSP+ Arrangement' (2007) 10 *Journal of International Economic Law* 869.

Lorand Bartels, *Human Rights Conditionality in the EU's International Agreements* (OUP 2005).

Lorand Bartels, 'Article XX of GATT and the Problem of Extraterritorial Jurisdiction: The Case of Trade Measures for the Protection of Human Rights' (2002) 36(2) *Journal of World Trade* 353.

Dorothée Baumann-Pauly, Sarah Labowitz and Nate Stein, 'Transforming the Garment Industry in Bangladesh: Sharing Responsibility' in Sarah Margaretha Jastram and Anna-Maria Schneider (eds), *Sustainable Fashion: Governance and New Management Approaches* (Springer International Publishing 2018).

Guillaume Beaumier, Kevin Kalomeni, Malcolm Campbell-Verduyn, Marc Lenglet, Serena Natile, Marielle Papin, Daivi Rodima-Taylor, Arthur Silve, and Falin Zhang, 'Global Regulations for a Digital Economy: Between new and old challenges' (2020) 11(4) *Global Policy* 515.

Janice R. Bellace, 'The 1998 ILO Declaration: Responding to globalization and impacting corporate labor behavior' in Kimberly Ann Elliott (ed.), *Handbook on Globalisation and Labour Standards* (Edward Elgar 2022).

Janice Bellace, 'From Workers' Rights to Human Rights at Work' in Janice Bellace and Beryl ter Haar (eds), *Research Handbook on Labour, Business and Human Rights Law* (Edward Elgar Publishing 2019).

Janice Bellace, 'The ILO and Tripartism: The Challenge of Balancing the Three-Legged Stool' in George P. Politakis, Tomi Kohiyama and Thomas Lieby (eds), *ILO 100: Law for social justice* (ILO 2019).

Janice R. Bellace, 'Pushback on the Right to Strike: Resisting the thickening of soft law' in Adelle Blackett and Anne Trebilcock (eds), *Research Handbook on Transnational Labour Law* (Edward Elgar 2015).

Janice Bellace, 'The ILO and the Right to Strike' (2014) 153(1) *International Labour Review* 29.

Janice Bellace, 'The ILO Declaration of Fundamental Principles and Rights at Work' (2001) 17 *International Journal of Comparative Labour Law and Industrial Relations* 269.

Janice Bellace and Beryl ter Haar (eds), *Research Handbook on Labour, Business and Human Rights Law* (Edward Elgar Publishing 2019).

Erik Bengtsson, 'Social Dumping Cases in the Swedish Labour Court in the Wake of *Laval*, 2004–2010' (2016) 37(1) *Economic and Industrial Democracy* 23.

Yakoub Benziane, Siong Hook Law, Anitha Rosland, Muhammad Daaniyall Abd Rahman, 'Aid for Trade Initiative 16 Years On: Lessons learnt from the empirical literature and recommendations for future directions' (2022) 21(1) *Journal of International Trade Law and Policy* 79.

Brian Bercusson and Cynthia Estlund, 'Regulating Labour in the Wake of Globalisation: New Challenges, New Institutions' in Brian Bercusson and Cynthia Estlund (eds), *Regulating Labour in the Wake of Globalisation: New Challenges, New Institutions* (Hart 2008).

Brian Bercusson and Cynthia Estlund (eds), *Regulating Labour in the Wake of Globalisation: New challenges, new institutions* (Hart 2008).

Janine Berg and Sandrine Cazes, 'Policymaking Gone Awry: The Labor Market Regulations of the Doing Business Indicators' (2008) 29(4) *Comparative Labor Law and Policy Journal* 349.

Janine Berg and Sandrine Cazes, *The Doing Business Indicators: Measurement issues and political implications* (ILO 2007).

Axel Berger (DIE), Clara Brandi, Frederik Stender, Edward K Brown, Philomena Apiko, and Sean Woolfrey, *Advancing EU-Africa cooperation in light of the African Continental Free Trade Area* (European Think Tanks Group (ETTG) 2020).

Suzanne Berger, *How We Compete: What Companies Around the World Are Doing to Make it in Today's Global Economy* (Doubleday 2005).

Isaiah Berlin, 'Two Concepts of Liberty' in *Four Essays on Liberty* (OUP 1969).

George A. Bermann and Petros Mavroidis, *WTO Law and Developing Countries* (Cambridge University Press (CUP) 2007).

Magdalena Bernaciek, *Social Dumping: Political Catchphrase or Threat to Labour Standards?* (ETUI 2012).

Timothy Besley, 'Law, Regulation, and the Business Climate: The Nature and Influence of the World Bank Doing Business Project' (2015) 29(3) *Journal of Economic Perspectives* 99.

Daniel Bethlehem, Isabelle Van Damme, Donald McRae, Rodney Neufeld (eds), *The Oxford Handbook of International Trade Law* 1st ed. (OUP 2009).

Daniel Bethlehem, Donald McRae, Rodney Neufeld, Isabelle Van Damme, (eds), *The Oxford Handbook of International Trade Law*, 2nd ed. (OUP 2022).

Jagdish Bhagwati, *Termites in the Trading System: How preferential agreements undermine free trade* (OUP 2008).

Pradip Bhatnagar, *GATS Mode 4: Movement of Natural Persons and Protection of Migrant Workers' Rights* (ILO 2014).

Andreas Bieler and Jörg Nowak (eds), *Labour Conflicts in the Global South* (Routledge 2022).

Sanoussi Bilal and Isabelle Ramdoo, '*Sustainability and Human Rights in EPAs: A comparative analysis between the Caribbean and African EPAs* (European Centre for Development Policy Management Discussion Paper 2016).

Anna Biondi, 'New Life for the ILO Tripartite Declaration on Multinational Enterprises and Social Policy' (2015) 7(1-2) *International Journal of Labour Research* 105.

Adelle Blackett, 'Racial Capitalism and the Contemporary International Law on Slavery: (Re)membering *Hacienda Brasil Verde* (2022) 25 *Journal of International Economic Law* 334.

Adelle Blackett, 'On Social Regionalism in Transnational Labour Law' (2020) 159(4) *International Labour Review* 591.

Adelle Blackett, *Everyday Transgressions: Domestic Workers' Transnational Challenge to International Labor Law* (Cornell University Press/ ILR Press 2019).

Adelle Blackett, 'Theorizing Emancipatory Transnational Futures of International Labor Law' (2019) 113 *American Journal of International Law* 390.

Adelle Blackett (ed.), 'Symposium on Transnational Futures of International Labor Law special issue' (2019) 113 *AJIL Unbound* available at: <https://www.cambridge.org/core/journals/american-journal-of-international-law/ajil-unbound-by-symposium/transnational-futures-of-international-labor-law.

Adelle Blackett, 'Social Regionalism in Better Work Haiti' (2015) 31(2) *The International Journal of Comparative Labour Law and Industrial Relations* 163.

Adelle Blackett, *Trade Liberalization, Labour Law, and Development: A contextualization* (ILO Discussion Paper Series 2007).

Adelle Blackett, 'Toward Social Regionalism in the Americas' (2002) 23(4) *Comparative Labour Law and Policy Journal* 901.

Adelle Blackett, 'Global Governance, Legal Pluralism and the Decentered State: A labor law critique of codes of corporate conduct' (2001) *Indiana Journal of Global Legal Studies* 401.

Adelle Blackett and Alice Duquesnoy, 'Slavery is not a Metaphor: US Prison Labor and Racial Subordination through the lens of the ILO's Abolition of Forced Labor Convention' (2021) 67 *UCLA Law Review* 1504.

Adelle Blackett and Colleen Sheppard, 'Collective Bargaining and Equality: Making Connections' (2003) 142 *International Labour Review* 419.

Adelle Blackett and Anne Trebilcock, 'Conceptualising Transnational Labour Law' in Adelle Blackett and Anne Trebilcock (eds), *Research Handbook on Transnational Labour Law* (Edward Elgar 2015).

Adelle Blackett and Anne Trebilcock (eds), *Research Handbook on Transnational Labour Law* (Edward Elgar 2015).

Alysia Blackham, Miriam Kullmann, and Ania Zbyszewska (eds), *Theorising Labour Law in a Changing World: Towards Inclusive Labour Law* (Hart 2019).

Jeremy Blasi and Samir Sonti, 'Private Equity, Human Rights Due Diligence and Global Labour Rights: The case of "Hotel California" (2021) 1(1) *The Global Labour Rights Reporter* 44.

Mark Blaug, *The Methodology of Economics: Or how economists explain* (CUP 2009).

Fred Block, 'Karl Polanyi and the Writing of *The Great Transformation*' (2003) 32 *Theory and Society* 275.

Constantin Blome, Kai Foerstl, and Martin C. Schleper, 'Antecedents of Green Supplier Championing and Greenwashing: An empirical study on leadership and ethical incentives' (2017) 152 *Journal of Cleaner Production* 339.

Eline Blot, Antoine Oger and James Harrison, *Enhancing sustainability in EU Free Trade Agreements: The case for a holistic approach* (Institute for European Environmental Policy (IEEP) 2022).

Alan Bogg, 'Economic Coordination as Freedom of Association' in Sanjukta Paul, Shae McCrystal and Ewan McGaughey (eds), *The Cambridge Handbook of Labor in Competition Law* (CUP 2022).

Alan Bogg, 'Republican Non-Domination and Labour Law: New Normativity or Trojan Horse?' (2017) 33(3) *International Journal of Comparative Labour Law and Industrial Relations* 391.

Alan Bogg, *The Democratic Aspects of Trade Union Recognition* (Hart 2011).

Alan Bogg, Cathryn Costello, A.C.L. Davies and Jeremias Prassl (eds), *The Autonomy of Labour Law* (OUP 2015).

Alan Bogg and Mark Freedland, 'Labour Law in the Age of Populism: Towards Sustainable Democratic Engagement' in Julia López López (ed.), *Collective Bargaining and Collective Action: Labour Agency and Governance in the 21st Century?* (Hart 2018).

Alan Bogg and Tonia Novitz (eds) *Voices at Work: Continuity and Change in the Common Law World* (OUP 2014).

Alan Bogg, Jake Rowbottom, and Alison Young (eds), *The Constitution of Social Democracy: Essays in Honour of Keith Ewing* (Hart 2020).

James Bohman, 'International Regimes and Democratic Governance: Political Equality and Influence in Global Institutions' (1999) 75 *International Affairs* 499.

James Bohman and Matias Lutz-Bachmann (eds), *Perpetual Peace: Essays on Kant's Cosmopolitan Ideal* (MIT 1997).

Nicole Bolleyer and Patricia Correa, 'Member Influence and Involvement in Civil Society Organizations: A resource dependency perspective on groups and parties' (2022) 70(2) *Political Studies* 519.

Jonathan Bonnitcha and Robert McCorquodale, 'The Concept of Due Diligence in the UN Guiding Principles on Business and Human Rights' (2017) 28(3) *European Journal of International Law* 899.

Jean-Michel Bonvin and Francesco Laruffa, 'Deliberative Democracy in the Real World: The contribution of the capability approach' (2018) 28(2) *International Review of Sociology* 216.

Frank Boons, Henrikke Baumann and Jeremy Hall, 'Conceptualizing Sustainable Development and Global Supply Chains' (2012) 83 *Ecological Economics* 134.

Eileen Boris, 'From Sexual Harassment to Gender Violence at Work: The ILO's Road to Convention #190' (2022) 19(1) *Labor* 109.

Klaus Bosselmann, *The Principle of Sustainability: Transforming law and governance*, 2nd ed. (Routledge, 2016).

John Boswell and Jack Corbett, 'Deliberative Bureaucracy: Reconciling Democracy's Trade-off Between Inclusion and Economy' (2018) 66(3) *Political Studies* 618.

Juan C. Botero, Simeon Djankov, Rafael La Porta, Florencio Lopez-de-Silanes and Andrei Shleifer, 'The Regulation of Labor' (2004) 119(4) *Quarterly Journal of Economics* 1339.

Anna Boucher, 'What is Exploitation and Workplace Abuse? A classification schema to understand exploitative workplace behaviour towards migrant workers' (2022) 27(4) *New Political Economy* 629.

Anna Boucher, 'Measuring Migrant Worker Rights Violations in Practice: The example of temporary skilled visas in Australia' (2019) 61(2) *Journal of Industrial Relations* 277.

Reynauld Bourque, 'International Framework Agreements and the Future of Collective Bargaining' (2008) 12 *Multinational Companies Just Labour: A Canadian journal of work and society* 30.

Anu Bradford, 'The Brussels Effect' (2012) 107(1) *Northwestern University Law Review* 1.

Anu Bradford, *The Brussels Effect: How the European Union rules the world* (OUP 2019).

Daniel Bradlow, 'Global Economic Governance and IMF Governance Reform: A Proposal' African Sovereign Debt Justice Paper Series, Paper III, Afronomicslaw (2021) available at: https://www.afronomicslaw.org/sites/default/files/pdf/Danny%20Bradlow%20IMF%20Governance%20Reform-Bradlow%20(times%20new%20roman).pdf.

Daniel Bradlow, 'The World Bank, the IMF, and Human Rights' (1999) 6 *Transnational Law and Contemporary Problems* 47.

Willy Brandt, 'North-South: A programme for survival: report of the Independent Commission on International Development Issues' (MIT Press 1980).

Willy Brandt, 'Common Crisis North-South: cooperation for world recovery' (1983) available at http://agris.fao.org/agris-search/search.do?recordID=XF2015040077.

Rachel Brewster, 'WTO Dispute Settlement: Can we go back again? (2019) 113 *American Journal of International Law* 61.

Edward T. Bristol-Alagbariya, 'The UN Global Compact as a Soft Law Business Regulatory Mechanism Advancing Corporate Responsibility towards Business Sustainability and Sustainable Development Worldwide' (2020) 94 *Journal of Law, Policy and Globalization* 27.

Robin Broad and John Cavanagh, 'The Death of the Washington Consensus?' (1999) 16 *World Policy Journal* 79.

André Broome, Alexandra Homolar and Matthias Kranke, 'Bad Science: International organizations and the indirect power of global benchmarking' (2018) 24(3) *European Journal of International Relations* 514.

Marco Bronckers and Giovanni Gruni, 'Retooling the Sustainability Standards in EU Free Trade Agreements' (2021) 24 *Journal of International Economic Law* 25.

Marco Bronckers and Giovanni Gruni, 'Taking the Enforcement of Labour Standards in the EU's Free Trade Agreements Seriously' (2019) 56 *Common Market Law Review* 1591.

Tequila J. Brooks, 'Enforcement of Labor Standards in Trade Agreements: The case of Guatemala' in Kimberly Ann Elliott (ed.), *Handbook on Globalisation and Labour Standards* (Edward Elgar 2022).

James J. Brudney, 'Hiding in Plain Sight: An ILO Convention on Labor Standards in Global Supply Chains' (2023) 23(2) *Chicago Journal of International Law* 272.

Alison Brysk (ed.), *Globalization and Human Rights* (University of California Press 2002).

Ruth Buchanan and Peer Zumbansen, *Law in Transition: Human Rights, Development and Transitional Justice* (Bloomsbury 2014).

Gabriele Buchholtz, 'Social and Labour Standards in the OECD Guidelines: Enforcement mechanisms' (2020) 17(1) *International Organizations Law Review* 133.

Ricardo M. Buendia Esteban, 'Examining Recent Initiatives to Ensure Labour Rights for Platform Workers in the European Union to Tackle the Problem of Domination' (2022) 28(4) *Transfer: European Review of Labour and Research* 475.

Nicolas Bueno, 'Multinational Enterprises and Labour Rights: Concepts and implementation' in Janice Bellace and Beryl ter Haar (eds), *Research Handbook on Labour, Business and Human Rights Law* (Edward Elgar Publishing 2019).

Nicolas Bueno, Corporate Liability for Violations of the Human Right to Just Conditions of Work in Extraterritorial Operations' (2017) 21(5) *The International Journal of Human Rights* 565.

Nicolas Bueno and Claire Bright, 'Implementing Human Rights Due Diligence through Corporate Civil Liability' (2020) 69(4) *International and Comparative Law Quarterly Review* 789.

Marc Bungenberg, Markus Krajewski, Christian J. Tams, Jörg Philipp Terhechte and Andreas R. Ziegler (eds) *European Yearbook of International Economic Law 2019* ((Springer 2019).

Philip Burton, 'Ordering Institutions: The Judicial Function of the Permanent Court of International Justice in Relation to Interwar Organizations' (2021) *International Organizations Law Review* 540.

Business and Human Rights Resource Centre, *Wage Theft and Pandemic Profits: The right to a living wage for garment workers* (Business and Human Rights Resource Centre 2021) available at: https://media.business-humanrights.org/media/documents/Unpaid_wages_v9.pdf.

Business and Human Rights Resource Centre, *Qatar: Fears that poor living conditions for migrant workers linked to sharp rise in coronavirus cases* (2020) available at: https://www.business-humanrights.org/en/qatar-fears-that-poor-living-conditions-for-migrant-workers-linked-to-sharp-rise-in-coronavirus-cases.

Harold Butler, *The International Labour Organization* (OUP 1939).

Hannah L. Buxbaum, 'The Practice(s) of Extraterritoriality' in Hannah L. Buxbaum and Thibaut Fleury Graff (eds) *Extraterritoriality/L'extraterritorialite* (Brill Nijhoff 2022).

David Cabrelli and Rebecca Zahn, 'Civic Republican Political Theory and Labour Law' in Hugh Collins, Gillian Lester and Virginia Mantouvalou, *Philosophical Foundations of Labour Law* (OUP 2018).

David Cabrelli and Rebecca Zahn, 'Theories of Domination and Labour Law: An Alternative Conception for Intervention?' (2017) 33(3) *International Journal of Comparative Labour Law and Industrial Relations* 339.

Valentina Cagnin, *Labour Law and Sustainable Development* (Wolters Kluwer 2020).

Damien Cahill, 'Polanyi, Hayek and Embedded Neoliberalism' (2018) 15(7) *Globalizations* 977.

Maurizio Carbone, 'The EU and the Developing World: Partnership, poverty, politicization' in Christopher Hill and Michael Smith (eds), *International Relations and the European Union* 2nd ed. (OUP 2011).

Laura A. Carlson and Vera Bitsch, 'Social Sustainability in the Ready-made-garment Sector in Bangladesh: An institutional approach to supply chains' (2018) 21(2) *International Food and Agribusiness Management Review* 269.

Mary Joyce Carlson, 'Unions use the OECD Guidelines to Challenge Gender-based Violence and Harassment in the Global Operations of McDonald's Corp' (2021) 1(1) *The Global Labour Rights Reporter* 49.

Chios Carmody, 'Theory and Theoretical Approaches to WTO Law' (2016) 13(2) *Manchester Journal of International Economic Law* 152.

Antonia Carzaniga and Swatu Sharma, *Regulatory Disciplines on the Mobility of Service Professionals – Lessons from Regional Trade Agreements*, Staff Working Paper ERSD-2022-12 (WTO 2022).

Danny Cassimon, Karel Verbeke, and Dennis Essers, 'The IMF-WB debt sustainability framework: Procedures, applications and criticisms' (2017) 3(1) *Development Finance Agenda* (DEFA) 4.

Conseulo Chacartegui, 'Workers' Participation and Green Governance' (2018) 40(1) *Comparative Labor Law and Policy Journal* 89.

Iheb Chalouat, Carlos Carrión-Crespo and Margherita Licata, *Law and Practice on Protecting Whistle-Blowers in the Public and Financial Services Sectors* (ILO 2019).

Simone Chambers, 'Deliberative Democratic Theory' (2003) 6 *Annual Review of Political Science* 307.

Steve Charnovitz, 'Trade, Employment and Labour Standards: The OECD Study and Recent Developments: The OECD Study and Developments in the Trade and Labour Standards Debate' (1997) 11 *Temple International and Comparative Law Journal* 131.

Steve Charnovitz, 'The Influence of International Labour Standards on the World Trading Regime - A Historical Overview' (1987) 126 *International Labour Review* 565.

Nicola Charwat, 'Who Participates as Amicus Curiae in World Trade Organisation Dispute Settlement And Why?' (2016) 27 *New Zealand Universities Law Review* 1.

Vincent Chetail, 'The Global Compact for Safe, Orderly and Regular Migration: A kaleidoscope of international law' (2020) 16(3) *International Journal of Law in Context* 253.

Archibald Chisholm, *Labour's Magna Charta: A Critical Study of the Labour Clauses of the Peace Treaty and of the Draft Conventions and Recommendations of the Washington International Labour Conference* (Longmans 1925).

Sang-Wook Cho, Hansoo Choi, and Julián P. Díaz, 'The Causal Effect of Free Trade Agreements on the Trade Margins: Product-level evidence from geographically distant partners' (2022) 88(4) *Southern Economic Journal* 1453.

John D. Ciorciari, 'The Lawful Scope of Human Rights Criteria in World Bank Credit Decisions: An Interpretive Analysis of the IBRD and IDA Articles of Agreement' (2000) 33 *Cornell International Law Journal* 331.

Richard Clark, and Lindsay R. Dolan. 'Pleasing the Principal: US influence in World Bank policymaking' (2021) 65(1) *American Journal of Political Science* 36.

Stefan Clauwaert and Isabelle Schömann, *The Crisis and National Labour Law Reforms: A mapping exercise* ETUI Working Paper 2012.04.

Christophe Clerc, The French 'Duty of Vigilance' Law: Lessons for an EU Directive on Due Diligence in Multinational Supply Chains (January 13, 2021). ETUI Research Paper - Policy Brief 1/2021, Available at SSRN: https://ssrn.com/abstract=3765288 or http://dx.doi.org/10.2139/ssrn.3765288.

Sarah H. Cleveland, 'Human Rights Sanctions and International Trade: A theory of compatibility' (2002) 5(1) *Journal of International Economic Law* 133.

Joshua Cohen and Charles Sabel, 'Directly-Deliberative Polyarchy' (1997) 3 *European Law Journal* 313.

Italo Colantone and Piero Stanig, *Global Competition and Brexit* (2016) BAFFI CAREFIN Centre for Applied Research on International Markets, Banking, Finance and Regulation available at: https://papers.ssrn.com/sol3/papers.cfm?abstract_id=2870313.

Barry Colfer, Brian Harney, Colm McLaughlin, Chris F. Wright (eds), *Protecting the Future of Work: New Institutional Arrangements for Safeguarding Labour Standards* (Emerald Publishing Limited 2023).

Hugh Collins, Gillian Lester and Virginia Mantouvalou, *Philosophical Foundations of Labour Law* (OUP 2018).

Lance Compa, 'Labor Rights and Labor Standards in International Trade' (1993) 25(1) *Law and Policy in International Business* 165.

Lance Compa and Stephen Diamond, (eds.), *Human Rights, Labour Rights and International Trade* (University of Pennsylvania Press 1996).

Lance Compa, Jeffrey Vogt and Eric Gottwald, *Wrong Turn for Workers' Rights: The US-Guatemala CAFTA Labor Arbitration Ruling – And what to do about it* (Labour Rights 2018) available at: https:// laborrights .org/ sites/ default/ files/ publications/ Wrong%20Turn%20for%20Workers%20Rights%20-%20March%202018.pdf.

Paola Conconi and Carlo Perroni, 'Special and Differential Treatment of Developing Countries in the WTO' (2015) 14 *World Trade Review* 67.

Steve Connelly, 'Mapping Sustainable Development as a Contested Concept' (2007) 12(3) *Local Environment* 259.

Heather Connolly, Stefania Marino and Miguel Martinez Lucio, *The Politics of Social Inclusion and Labor Representation: Immigrants and trade unions in the European context* (Cornell University Press 2019).

Efren Cordova, 'Some Reflections on the Overproduction of International Labour Standards' (1993) 14 *Comparative Labor Law Journal* 138.

Marva Corley-Coulibaly, Gaia Grasselli and Ira Postolachi, *Promoting and Enforcing Compliance with Labour Provisions in Trade Agreements: Comparative analysis of Canada, European Union and United States approaches and practices* (ILO 2023).

Hermes Augusto Costa, 'From Europe as a Model to Europe as Austerity: The impact of the crisis on Portuguese trade unions' (2012) 18 T*ransfer* 397.

Thomas Cottier, Joost Pauwelyn, and Elisabeth Bürgi Bonanomi (eds), *Human Rights and International Trade* (OUP 2005).

Nicola Countouris, K.D. Ewing and John Hendy, *The EU-UK Trade and Cooperation Agreement and Workers' Rights* (Brussels: ETUI, 2021) available at: https:// www .etui .org/ sites/ default/ files/ 2021 -03/ The %20EU -UK %20Trade %20and %20Cooperation%20Agreement%20and%20workers%27%20rights_2021.pdf.

Christopher R. Coxson, 'The 1998 ILO Declaration on Fundamental Principles and Rights at Work: Promoting Labor Law Reforms Through the ILO as an Alternative to Imposing Coercive Trade Sanctions' (1998) 17 *Dickinson Journal of International Law* 469.

James Crawford, *The Rights of Peoples* (OUP 1988).

Breen Creighton and Shae McCrystal, 'Who is a Worker in International Law' (2016) 37(3) *Comparative Labor Law and Policy Journal* 691.

Michael Cremens and Michael Kremer, 'The New Role for the World Bank' (2016) 30(1) *Journal of International Economic Perspectives* 53.

Pramila Crivelli and Stefano Inama, *Improving Market for LDCs: The impact of the EU Reform of Rules of Origin on Utilization Rates and Trade Flows under the Everything But Arms Initiative (EBA)* (UNCTAD Working Paper 2021).

J.B. Cronjé, *Innovating for Temporary Movement of Natural Persons in Africa: Leveraging the CFTA* (Tralec 2017) available at: http://www.cuts-geneva.org/pdf/ TAF087_CFTA-temporary_movement_natural_persons.pdf.

Ciaran Cross, *Legitimising an Unsustainable Approach to Trade: A discussion paper on sustainable development provisions in EU Free Trade Agreements* (PowerShift 2017).

Holly Cullen, 'The Irresistible Rise of Human Rights Due Diligence: Conflict Minerals and Beyond' (2016) 48(4) *George Washington International Law Review* 743.

Roy Culpeper, 'Regional Development Banks: Exploiting their specificity (1994) 15(3) *Third World Quarterly* 459.

Nicole Curato, Marit Hammond and John B. Min, *Power in Deliberative Democracy: Norms, Forums, Systems* (Palgrave Macmillan 2019).

Karen Curtis and Elizabeth Echeverría Manrique, 'Trade Arrangements and Labour Standards in a Supply Chain World: Current issues and future considerations' in Guillaume Delautre, Elizabeth Echeverría Manrique and Colin Fenwick (eds), *Decent Work in a Globalized Economy: Lessons from public and private initiatives* (ILO 2021).

Ludo Cuyvers, 'The Sustainable Development Clauses in Free Trade Agreements of the EU with Asian Countries: Perspectives for ASEAN' (2014) 22(4) *Journal of Contemporary European Studies* 427.

James M. Cypher, 'The Slow Death of the Washington Consensus on Latin America' (1998) 25 *Latin American Perspectives* 47.

Yossi Dahan, Hanna Lerner and Faina Milman-Sivan (eds), *Global Justice and International Labour Rights* (CUP 2016).

Robert A. Dahl, 'The Concept of Power' (1957) 2(3) *Behavioral Science* 201.

Gareth Dale, 'In Search of Karl Polanyi's International Relations Theory' (2016) 42 *Review of International Studies* 401.

Mark P. Dallas, Stefano Ponte, and Timothy J. Sturgeon, 'Power in Global Value Chains' (2019) 26(4) *Review of International Political Economy* 666.

Chad Damro, 'Market Power Europe' (2012) 19(5) *Journal of European Public Policy* 682.

Mac Darrow, *Between Light and Shadow: The World Bank, the International Monetary Fund and International Human Rights Law* (Hart 2003).

Guy Davidov, 'Who is a Worker?' (2005) 34 *Industrial Law Journal* 57.

Guy Davidov and Brian Langille (eds), *The Idea of Labour Law* (OUP 2011).

Rosie Day, 'A Capabilities Approach to Environmental Justice' in Ryan Holifield, Jayajit Chakraborty and Gordon Walker (eds), *The Routledge Handbook of Environmental Justice* (Routledge 2017).

Gopal Dayaneni, 'Carbon Fundamentalism vs. Climate Justice' (2009) 16(2) *Race, Poverty & the Environment* 7.

Grainne de Búrca, *Reframing Human Rights in a Turbulent Era* (OUP 2021).

Gráinne de Búrca and Joanne Scott, *The EU and the WTO: Legal and Constitutional Issues* (Hart 2002).

Olivier De Schutter, Nathalie Dubler, Paula Fernandez-Wulff and Anabella Sosa, *The IMF's Role in Social Protection: Promising policy shifts and persisting challenges* (University of Louvain 2021) CRIDHO Working Paper 2021/2 available at: https://sites.uclouvain.be/cridho/documents/Working.Papers/CRIDHO-WP-2021-2_DeSchutter.et.al_IMF.Social.protection.pdf.

Olivier De Schutter, *Towards Mandatory Due Diligence in Global Supply Chains* (ITUC 2020) available at: https://www.ituc-csi.org/IMG/pdf/de_schutte_mandatory_due_diligence.pdf.

Olivier De Schutter, *The 'Just Transition' in the Economic Recovery: Eradicating poverty within planetary boundaries* A/75/181/Rev.1, 7 October 2020.

Olivier De Schutter, *Trade in the Service of Sustainable Development: Linking Trade to Labour Rights and Environmental Standards* (Bloomsbury/Hart 2015).

Valerio De Stefano, 'Not as Simple as it Seems: The ILO and the personal scope of international labour standards' (2021) 160(3) *International Labour Review* 387.

Valerio De Stefano, 'Non-Standard Work and Limits on Freedom of Association: A Human Rights-Based Approach' (2017) 46(2) *Industrial Law Journal* 185.

Simon Deakin, 'Legal Evolution: Integrating Economic and Systemic Approaches' (2011) 7(3) *Review of Law and Economics* 659.

Simon Deakin and Frank Wilkinson, 'Rights versus Efficiency? The Economic Case for Transnational Labour Standards' (1994) 23 *Industrial Law Journal* 289.

Simon Deakin and Frank Wilkinson, 'The Law and Economics of the Minimum Wage' (1992) *The Journal of Law and Society* 379.

Christopher Deeming (ed.), *The Struggle for Social Sustainability: Moral Conflicts in Global Social Policy* (Policy Press 2021).

Julia Dehm, 'Reflections on Paris: Thoughts Towards a Critical Approach to Climate Law' (2018) *Quebec Journal of International Law* 61.

Natalia Delgado, 'Towards Work Liberalization: The WTO Discourse on Labour Standards and Policy' (2019) 35(4) *International Journal of Comparative Labour Law and Industrial Relations* 455.

Guillaume Delautre, Elizabeth Echeverría Manrique and Colin Fenwick (eds), *Decent Work in a Globalized Economy: Lessons from public and private initiatives* (ILO 2021).

Panagiotis Delimatsis and Léo Gargne, *General Exceptions under the GATS - A Legal Commentary on Article XIV GATS* (TILEC Discussion Paper 2020).

Manoj Dias-Abey, 'Mobilizing for Recognition: Indie Unions, Migrant Workers, and Strategic Equality Act Litigation' (2022) 38(2) *International Journal of Comparative Labour Law and Industrial Relations* 137.

Manoj Dias-Abey, 'Using Law to Support Social Movement-Led Collective Bargaining Structures in Supply Chains' (2019) 32(2) *Australian Journal of Labour Law* 123.

Manoj Dias-Abey, 'Justice on Our Fields: Can "Alt-Labor" Organizations Improve Migrant Farm Workers' Conditions?' (2018) 53 *Harvard Civil Rights-Civil Liberties Law Review* 167.

William Diebold, *The End of the ITO* (Princeton University Press 1952).

Peter Digeser, 'The Fourth Face of Power' (1992) 54(4) *The Journal of Politics* 977.

Janelle M. Diller, 'The Role of the State in the Exercise of Transnational Public and Private Authority over Labour Standards' (2020) 17(1) *International Organizations Law Review* 41.

Simeon Djankov, 'The Doing Business Project: How it started: correspondence' (2016) 30(1) *Journal of Economic Perspectives* 247.

Virginia Doellgast, Nathan Lillie, and Valeria Pulignano (eds), *Reconstructing Solidarity: Labour unions, precarious work, and the politics of institutional change in Europe* (OUP 2018).

David Doorey, 'Just Transitions Law: Putting labour law to work on climate change' (2017) 30(2) *Journal of Environmental Law and Practice* 201.

Filip Dorssemont, Klaus Lörcher, and Isabelle Schömann (eds), *The European Convention on Human Rights and the Employment Relation* (Hart 2013).

Caf Dowlah, 'Mode 4 of WTO's General Agreement on Trade in Services: Can It Spur Cross-Border Labor Mobility from Developing Countries' (2012) 5 *Law and Development Review* 56.

Anna Drake, *Activism, Inclusion and the Challenges of Deliberative Democracy* (UBC Press 2021).
John S. Dryzek, *Deliberative Democracy and Beyond: Liberals, critics, contestations* (OUP 2002).
John S. Dryzek, 'Transnational Democracy' (1999) 7 *Journal of Political Philosophy* 30.
Jean du Plessis and Chee Keong Low (eds), *Corporate Governance Codes for the 21st Century: International Perspectives and Critical Analyses* (Springer 2017).
Ruth Dukes and Wolfgang Streeck, *Democracy at Work: Contract, status and post-industrial justice* (Polity 2022).
R-J Dupuy (ed.), *Mélanges en l'honneur de Nicolas Valticos* (Éditions A. Pedone 1999).
Adeolu Durotoye, 'The MINT countries as emerging economic power bloc: Prospects and challenges' (2014) 4(5) *Developing Country Studies* 1.
Ronald Dworkin, *Taking Rights Seriously* (Duckworth 1977).
Franz Christian Ebert, 'A Public Law Perspective on Labour Governance by International Financial Institutions: The Case of the IMF's Article IV Consultations' (2020) 17(1) *International Organizations Law Review* 105.
Franz Christian Ebert, 'Labour Safeguards of International Financial Institutions: Can They Help to Avoid Violations of ILO Core Labour Standards?' in Marc Bungenberg, Markus Krajewski, Christian J. Tams, Jörg Philipp Terhechte and Andreas R. Ziegler (eds) *European Yearbook of International Economic Law 2019* (Springer 2019).
Franz Christian Ebert, 'Labour Standards and the World Bank: Analysing the potential of Safeguard Policies for protecting workers' in Henner Gött (ed.), *Labour Standards in International Economic Law* (Springer 2018).
Franz Christian Ebert and Pedro A Villarreal, 'The Renegotiated "NAFTA": What Is in It for Labor Rights?' (EJIL: Talk!, 11 October 2018) available at: www.ejiltalk.org/the-renegotiated-nafta-what-is-in-it-for-labor-rights/.
Jonas Ebbesson and Ellen Hey (eds), *Cambridge Handbook on the United Nations Sustainable Development Goals and International Law* (CUP 2022).
Niklas Egels-Zandén and Henrik Lindholm, 'Do Codes of Conduct Improve Worker Rights in Supply Chains? A study of Fair Wear Foundation' (2015) 107 *Journal of Cleaner Production* 31.
Odin Ekman and Samuel Engblom, 'Expanding the Movement of Natural Persons Through Free Trade Agreements? A Review of CETA, TPP and ChAFTA' (2019) 35(2) *International Journal of Comparative Labour Law and Industrial Relations* 163.
Kimberley Elliott (ed.), *Handbook on Globalisation and Labour Standards* (Edward Elgar 2022).
Stephen Elstub, 'The Third Generation of Deliberative Democracy' (2010) 8 *Political Studies Review* 291.
Anthony M. Endres and Grant Fleming, 'International Economic Policy in the Interwar Years: The special contribution of ILO economists' (1996) 135 *International Labour Review* 207.
Tatjana Eres, 'The Limits of GATT Article XX: A Back Door for Human Rights' (2004) 35 *Georgetown Journal of International Law* 597.
Erik O. Eriksen, 'Getting to Agreement: Mechanisms of deliberative decision-making' (2018) 10(3) *International Theory* 374.

Johannes Euler, 'The Commons: A social form that allows for degrowth and sustainability' (2019) 30(2) *Capitalism Nature Socialism* 158.
Stein Evju (ed.), *Cross-border Services, Posting of Workers, and Multilevel Governance* (University of Oslo 2013).
Uche Ewelukwa, 'Special and Differential Treatment in International Trade Law: A Concept in Search of Content' (2003) 79 *North Dakota Law Review* 831.
K.D. Ewing, 'The EU-UK Trade and Cooperation Agreement: Implications for ILO Standards and the European Social Charter in the United Kingdom' (2021) 32(2) *King's Law Journal* 306.
K.D. Ewing, 'International Regulation of the Global Economy – The role of trade unions' in Brian Bercusson and Cynthia Estlund (eds), *Regulating Labour in the Wake of Globalisation: New challenges, new institutions* (Hart 2008).
K.D. Ewing, 'The Function of Trade Unions' (2005) 34(1) *Industrial Law Journal* 1.
K.D. Ewing, 'Trade Union Recognition – A Framework for Discussion' (1990) 19 *Industrial Law Journal* 209.
K.D. Ewing and John Hendy, 'The Dramatic Implications of Demir and Baykara' (2010) 39 *Industrial Law Journal* 2.
Elimma C. Ezeani, *The WTO and its Development Obligation* (Anthem Press 2012).
Johannes J. Fagan, Lydia Cairncross, Bruce Biccard, Graham Fieggen and Salome Maswime, 'COVID-19 Exposes Health Worker Shortages in the USA and UK, but Nationalism and Self-Interest must not Exploit Medical Workforces from Low-And Middle-Income Countries' (2020) 110(5) *South African Medical Journal* 335.
Elaine Fahey and Isabella Mancini (eds), *Understanding the EU as a Good Global Actor: Ambitions, values and metrics* (Edward Elgar 2022).
Richard Falk, *Predatory Globalization: A Critique* (Wiley 1999).
Anne-Laure Fayard, 'Notes on the Meaning of Work: Labor, Work, and Action in the 21st Century' (2021) 30(2) *Journal of Management Inquiry* 207.
Gabriel Felbermayr, Feodora Teti, and Erdal Yalcin, 'Rules of Origin and the Profitability of Trade Deflection' (2019) 121 *Journal of International Economics* 103248.
Colin Fenwick, 'Private Use of Prisoners' Labour: Paradoxes of international human rights law' (2005) 27(1) *Human Rights Quarterly* 249.
Colin Fenwick and Tonia Novitz, 'Conclusion: Regulating to Protect Workers' Human Rights' in Colin Fenwick and Tonia Novitz (eds), *Human Rights at Work: Perspectives on Law and Regulation* (Onati/Hart 2010).
Colin Fenwick and Tonia Novitz (eds) *Human Rights at Work: Perspectives on Law and Regulation* (Onati/Hart 2010).
Janice Fine and Jennifer Gordon, 'Strengthening Labor Standards Enforcement through Partnerships with Workers' Organizations' (2010) 38(4) *Politics & Society* 552.
Tony Fitzpatrick, 'Paradigm Lost? Blocking the path to ecosocial welfare and post-productivism' in Christopher Deeming (ed.), *The Struggle for Social Sustainability: Moral Conflicts in Global Social Policy* (Policy Press 2021).
Thomas M. Flaherty, and Ronald Rogowski, 'Rising Inequality as a Threat to the Liberal International Order' (2021) 75(2) *International Organization* 495.
Frances Flanagan and Caleb Goods, 'Climate Change and Industrial Relations: Reflections on an emerging field' (2022) 64(4) *Journal of Industrial Relations* 479.
Meraiah Foley and Rae Cooper, 'Workplace Gender Equality in the Post-pandemic Era: Where to next?' (2021) 63(4) *Journal of Industrial Relations* 463.

Filippo Fontanelli, 'Necessity Killed the GATT - Art XX GATT and the Misleading Rhetoric about Weighing and Balancing' (2012) 5(2) *European Journal of Legal Studies* 39.

Michael Ford and Tonia Novitz, 'There is Power in a Union? Revisiting trade union functions in 2019' in Alan Bogg, Jake Rowbottom, and Alison Young (eds), *The Constitution of Social Democracy: Essays in Honour of Keith Ewing* (Hart 2020).

Michele Ford and Michael Gillan, 'Power Resources and Supranational Mechanisms: The global unions and the OECD Guidelines' (2021) 27(3) *European Journal of Industrial Relations* 307.

Anthony Forsyth, *The Future of Unions and Worker Representation: The Digital Picket Line* (Bloomsbury Publishing 2022).

Caroline Foster, *Global Regulatory Standards in Environmental and Health Disputes: Regulatory Coherence, Due Regard, and Due Diligence* (OUP 2021).

Jonathan Fox, 'Transnational Civil Society Campaigns and the World Bank Inspection Panel' in Alison Brysk (ed.), *Globalization and Human Rights* (University of California Press 2002).

Isaiah Frank, 'The Graduation Issue for LDCs' (1979) 13 *Journal of World Trade Law* 289.

Nancy Fraser, 'Can Society be Commodities All the Way Down? Post-Polanyian reflections on capitalist crisis' (2014) 43(4) *Economy and Society* 541.

Sandra Fredman, *Working Together: Human Rights, the Sustainable Development Goals and Gender Equality* (The British Academy 2018).

Sandra Fredman, *Human Rights Transformed: Positive Rights and Positive Duties* (OUP 2008).

Sandra Fredman, 'The New Rights: Labour Law and Ideology in the Thatcher Years' (1992) 12(1) *Oxford Journal of Legal Studies* 24.

Mark Freedland, 'The Contract of Employment and the Paradoxes of Precarity' (2016) University of Oxford Legal Research Paper Series Paper No 37/2016.

Mark Freedland. 'Application of Labour and Employment Law Beyond the Contract of Employment' (2007) 146(1) *International Labour Review* 3.

Mark Freedland and Jeremias Prassl (eds), *Viking, Laval and Beyond* (Hart 2014).

Duncan French and Louis J. Kotzé, *Sustainable Development Goals: Law, Theory and Implementation* (Edward Elgar 2018).

Caroline Freund, Maryla Maliszewska, Aaditya Mattoo, and Michele Ruta. 'When Elephants Make Peace: The impact of the China-US trade agreement on developing countries' (World Bank 2020) available at: https://elibrary.worldbank.org/doi/abs/10.1596/1813-9450-9173.

Diane F. Frey, 'Economic Growth, Full Employment and Decent Work: The means and ends in SDG 8' (2017) 21(8) *The International Journal of Human Rights* 1164.

Diane F. Frey and Gillian MacNaughton, 'A Human Rights Lens on Full Employment and Decent Work in the 2030 Sustainable Development Agenda' (2016) 6(2) *Journal of Workplace Rights* 1.

Jon Horgen Friberg, 'The Stages of Migration: From going abroad to settling down: Post-accession Polish migrant workers in Norway' (2012) 38(10) *Journal of Ethnic and Migration Studies* 1589.

Judy Fudge, 'Precarious Migrant Status and Precarious Employment: The paradox of international rights for migrant workers' (2012-13) 34 *Comparative Labor Law and Policy Journal* 95.

Judy Fudge, 'The New Discourse of Labour Rights: From Social to Fundamental Rights?' (2007) 29 *Comparative Labor Law and Policy Journal* 29.

Deirdre McCann and Judy Fudge, 'Unacceptable Forms of Work: A multidimensional model' (2017) 156(2) *International Labour Review* 147.

Francis Fukyama, *The End of History and the Law Man* (Free Press 1992).

Jean Galbraith, 'United States Continues to Block New Appellate Body Members for the World Trade Organization: Risking the Collapse of the Appellate Process' (2019) 113(4) *American Journal of International Law* 822.

Fred P. Gale, *The Political Economy of Sustainability* (Edward Elgar 2018).

Béla Galgóczi, 'Just Transition on the Ground: Challenges and opportunities for social dialogue' (2020) 26(4) *European Journal of Industrial Relations* 367.

Béla Galgóczi, 'The Changing Role of Trade Unions in the Sustainable Development Agenda' (2014) 24 *International Review of Sociology* 59.

Gregor Gall (ed.), *Handbook of the Politics of Labour, Work and Employment* (Edward Elgar 2019).

Dan Gallin, 'Transnational Companies: International Framework Agreements: A Reassessment' (2008) policy paper released on www.globallabour.info/.

Clair Gammage, 'Social Norms in EU Free Trade Agreements: Justiciable or not?' in Clair Gammage and Tonia Novitz (eds), *Sustainable Trade, Investment and Finance: Towards responsible and coherent regulatory frameworks* (Edward Elgar 2019).

Clair Gammage, 'EU International Relations Law: The Power to Conclude International Trade Agreements' in Sangeeta Khorana and María García (eds), *Handbook on the EU and International Trade* (Edward Elgar 2018).

Clair Gammage, *North-South Regional Trade Agreements as Legal Regimes: A Critical Assessment of the EU-SADC Economic Partnership Agreement* (Edward Elgar 2017).

Clair Gammage and Tonia Novitz, 'The Concept of Sustainability and its Application' in Clair Gammage and Tonia Novitz (eds), *Sustainable Trade, Investment and Finance: Toward responsible and coherent regulatory frameworks* (Edward Elgar 2019).

Clair Gammage and Tonia Novitz (eds), *Sustainable Trade, Investment and Finance: Toward responsible and coherent regulatory frameworks* (Edward Elgar 2019).

Clair Gammage and Tonia Novitz, 'Trade, Investment and Corporate Sustainability' in Beate Sjåfjell and Christopher M. Bruner (eds), *Cambridge Handbook of Corporate Law, Corporate Governance and Sustainability* (CUP 2019).

Gabriel Garcia, 'The Rise of the Global South, the IMF and the Future of Law and Development' (2016) 37(2) *Third World Quarterly* 191.

María J. García, 'Sanctioning Capacity in Trade and Sustainability Chapters in EU Trade Agreements: The EU–Korea Case' (2022) 10(1) *Politics and Governance* 58.

Antonio Garcia-Muñoz Alhambra, Beryl ter Haar and Attila Kun, 'Harnessing Public Institutions for Labour Law Enforcement' (2020) 17(1) *International Organizations Law Review* 233.

Robert Garden, 'Eco Oro v Colombia: The brave new world of environmental exceptions' (2023) 38(1) *ICSID Review* 17.

Gary Gereffi and Miguel Korzeniewicz (eds), *Commodity Chains and Global Capitalism* (Prager 1994).

Navraj Singh Ghaleigh, *Just Transitions for Workers: When climate change met labour justice*. Edinburgh School of Law Research Paper No. 2019/30 (University of Edinburgh 2019).

Victor-Yves Ghebali, *The International Labour Organization: A Case-Study on the Evolution of UN Specialised Agencies* (Martinus Nijhoff 1989).

Christophe Gironde and Gilles Carbonnier (eds), *The ILO@100: Addressing the Past and Future of Work and Social Protection* (Brill Nijhoff 2019).

Jim Glassman, 'The Geo-political Economy of Global Production Networks' (2011) *Geography Compass* 154.

Sèna Kimm Gnangnon, *The Least Developed Countries' Services Waiver and the Stability of Least Developed Countries' Services Exports* (ECONSTOR Working Paper 2022) available at: https://www.econstor.eu/bitstream/10419/260587/1/Paper%20LDC%20Services%20Waiver-Export%20Volatility.pdf.

Sèna Kimm Gnangnon, 'Effect of Aid for Trade Policy and Regulations on Tariff Policy Volatility: Does institutional and governance quality matter?' (2019) 7(1) *Economies* 6.

Uwe Gneiting, Nicholas Lusiani and Irit Tamir, 'Power, Profits and the Pandemic: From Corporate Extraction for the Few to An Economy that Works for All' (2021) available at: http://dx.doi.org/10.2139/ssrn.3956244.

Carter Goodrich, 'Labor Legislation and the International Frontier' (1941) 15(4) *Social Service Review* 661.

Jennifer Gordon, 'In the Zone: Work at the Intersection of Trade and Migration' (2022) 23(2) *Theoretical Inquiries in Law* 147.

Jennifer Gordon, 'Regulating the Human Supply Chain' (2017) 102 *Iowa Law Review* 445.

Henner Gött, 'Interactions Between International Organizations: Approaching a Neglected Governance Dimension' (2020) 17(1) *International Organizations Law Review* 75.

Henner Gött, *The Law of Interactions Between International Organizations* (Springer 2020).

Henner Gött (ed.), *Labour Standards in International Economic Law* (Springer 2018).

Alvin W. Gouldner, 'Marx's Last Battle: Bakunin and the First International' 11(6) *Theory and Society* 853.

Mark Graham and Mohammed Anwar, 'The Global Gig Economy: Towards a planetary labour market?' (2019) 24(4) *First Monday* 21.

Anna Grear, 'Towards "Climate Justice"? A critical reflection on legal subjectivity and climate injustice: warning signals, patterned hierarchies, directions for future law and policy' (2014) 5 *Journal of Human Rights and the Environment* 103.

Erich Grießler and Beate Littig, 'Social Sustainability: A catchword between political pragmatism and social theory' (2005) 8(1-2) *International Journal of Sustainable Development* 65.

Gene M. Grossman and Alan O. Sykes, 'A Preference for Development: The Law and Economics of GSP' in George A. Bermann and Petros Mavroidis, *WTO Law and Developing Countries* (CUP 2007).

Gene M. Grossman and Alan O. Sykes, 'A Preference for Development: The law and economics of GSP' (2005) 4(1) *World Trade Review* 41.

Elspeth Guild, Tugba Basaran and Kathryn Allinson, 'From Zero to Hero? An analysis of the human rights protections within the Global Compact for Safe, Orderly and Regular Migration (GCM)' (2019) 57(6) *International Migration* 43.

Rebecca Gumbrell-McCormick, 'The International Trade Union Confederation: From Two (or More?) Identities to One' (2013) 51(2) *British Journal of Industrial Relations* 240.

Angel Gurría, 'Preface' *OECD Guidelines for Multinational Enterprises: A glass half full* (OECD 2018).

Juan Escribano Gutierrez, 'Labour and Environmental Sustainability: Summary of Literature Reviews' (2020), available at: http:// agreenment .adapt .it/ wp -content/ uploads/2020/11/comparative_report_agreenment_final.pdf.

Amy Gutmann and Dennis F. Thompson, *Why Deliberative Democracy?* (Princeton University Press 2004).

Amy Gutmann and Dennis F. Thompson, *Democracy and Disagreement* (The Belknap Press 1996).

Jürgen Habermas, 'Why Europe Needs a Constitution' (2001) *New Left Review* 11.

Jürgen Habermas, 'The European Nation-State and the Pressures of Globalization' (1999) *New Left Review* 46.

Jürgen Habermas, 'A Short Reply' (1999) 12 *Ratio Juris* 445.

Jürgen Habermas, 'Kant's Idea of Perpetual Peace, with the Benefit of Two Hundred Years' Hindsight' in James Bohman and Matias Lutz-Bachmann (eds), *Perpetual Peace: Essays on Kant's Cosmopolitan Ideal* (MIT 1997).

Jürgen Habermas, *Between Facts and Norms: Contributions to a Discourse Theory of Law and Society* transl. William Rehg (MIT 1996).

Jürgen Habermas, *Communication and the Evolution of Society* (Beacon Press 1979).

Peter A. Hall and David Soskice (eds), *Varieties of Capitalism: The Institutional Foundations of Comparative Advantage* (OUP 2001).

Nikolaus Hammer, 'International Framework Agreements: Global industrial relations between rights and bargaining' (2005) 11(4) *Transfer* 511.

Marit Hammond, 'Sustainability as a Cultural Transformation: The role of deliberative democracy' (2020) 29(1) *Environmental Politics* 173.

Gordon H. Hanson, 'The Rise of Middle Kingdoms: Emerging economies in global trade' (2012) 26(2) *Journal of Economic Perspectives* 41.

Ivan Hare, 'Social Rights as Fundamental Human Rights' in Bob Hepple (ed.), *Social and Labour Rights in a Global Context: International and comparative perspectives* (CUP 2002).

Ann Harrison, John McLaren, and Margaret McMillan, 'Recent Perspectives on Trade and Inequality' (2011) 3(1) *Annual Review of Economics* 261.

James Harrison, 'The Labour Rights Agenda in Free Trade Agreements' (2019) 20 *Journal of World Trade* 705.

James Harrison, 'Incentives for Development: The EC's Generalized System of Preferences, India's WTO Challenge and Reform' (2005) 42 *Common Market Law Review* 1663.

James Harrison, Mirela Barbu, Liam Campling, Franz Christian Ebert, Deborah Martens, Axel Marx, Jan Orbie, Ben Richardson, and Adrian Smith, 'Labour Standards Provisions in EU Free Trade Agreements: Reflections on the European Commission's Reform Agenda' (2019) 18(4) *World Trade Review* 635.

Ann-Christine Hartzén, Andrea Iossa and Elena Karageorgiou (eds), *Law, Solidarity and the Limits of Social Europe: Constitutional Tensions for EU Integration* (Edward Elgar 2022).

Friedrich A. Hayek, *1980s Unemployment and the Unions: Essays on the Impotent Price Structure of Britain and Monopoly in the Labour Market*, 2nd ed., (Institute of Economic Affairs, 1984).

Friedrich A. Hayek, *The Road to Serfdom* (Dymock's 1944).

Friedrich A. Hayek, 'Economics and Knowledge' (1937) 4(13) *Economica* 33.

Lydia Hayes and Tonia Novitz, 'Trade Unions and Economic Inequality' (2021) 4(1) *Institute of Employment Rights Journal* 118.

Susan Hayter (ed.), *The Role of Collective Bargaining in the Global Economy: Negotiating for Social Justice* (Edward Elgar 2011).

Gunnar Heckscher, Eli Filip Heckscher, and Bertil Ohlin. *Heckscher-Ohlin Trade Theory* (MIT Press 1991).

Edmund Heery, 'Unions and the Organising Turn: Reflections after 20 years of organising works' (2014) 26(4) *The Economic and Labour Relations Review* 545.

Pasi Heikkurinen, Toni Ruuska, Anna Kuokkanen, and Sally Russell, 'Leaving Productivism Behind: Towards a holistic and processual philosophy of ecological management' (2021) 20(1) *Philosophy of Management* 21.

Laurence Helfer, 'The ILO at 100: Institutional innovation in an era of populism' (2019) 113 *American Journal of International Law* 396.

Laurence R. Helfer, 'Monitoring Compliance with Unratified Treaties: The ILO Experience' (2008) 71 *Law and Contemporary Problems* 193.

Jeffrey Henderson , Peter Dicken , Martin Hess , Neil Coe and Henry Wai-Chung Yeung, 'Global Production Networks and the Analysis of Economic Development' (2002) 9(3) *Review of International Political Economy* 436.

Bob Hepple, 'Does Law Matter? The Future of Binding Norms' in George P. Politakis, (ed.), *Protecting Labour Rights as Human Rights: Present and Future of International Supervision* (ILO 2007).

Bob Hepple, *Labour Laws and Global Trade* (Hart 2005).

Bob Hepple (ed.), *Social and Labour Rights in a Global Context: International and comparative perspectives* (CUP 2002).

Bob Hepple, 'A Race to the Top - International Investment Guidelines and Corporate Codes of Conduct' (1999) 20 *Comparative Labour Law and Policy Journal* 347.

Bob Hepple, 'New Approaches to International Labour Regulation' (1997) 26 *Industrial Law Journal* 353.

Iñaki Heras-Saizarbitoria, Olivier Boiral and Ander Ibarloza, 'ISO 45001 and Controversial Transnational Private Regulation for Occupational Health and Safety' (2020) 159(3) *International Labour Review* 397.

Jeffrey Herbst, *States and Power in Africa: Comparative lessons in authority and control* (Princeton University Press 2014).

Matthias Herdegen, *Principles of International Economic Law*, 2nd ed. (OUP 2016).

Owen E Herrnstadt, 'Are International Framework Agreements a path to corporate social responsibility?' (2007/8) 10 *University of Pennsylvania Journal of Business and Employment Law* 187.

Petra Herzfeld Olsson, 'The Role of Effective Enforcement in International Law on Labour Migration' (2020) 17(1) *International Organizations Law Review* 206.

Holger P. Hestermeyer, 'Trade Law in Europe' in Daniel Bethlehem, Donald McRae, Rodney Neufeld, Isabelle Van Damme, (eds), *The Oxford Handbook of International Trade Law*, 2nd ed. (OUP 2022).

Ellen Hey, 'The MDGs Archeology, Institutional Fragmentation and International Law: Human Rights', International Environmental and Sustainable (Development) Law (March 21, 2009). Available at SSRN: https://ssrn.com/abstract=1366345 or http://dx.doi.org/10.2139/ssrn.1366345.

Jason Hickel, 'What Does Degrowth Mean? A few points of clarification' (2021) 18(7) *Globalizations* 1105.

Will Hickey, *The Sovereignty Game: Neo-Colonialism and the Westphalian System* (Palgrave Macmillan 2020).

Richard Higgott and Eva Erman, 'Deliberative Global Governance and the question of Legitimacy: What can we learn from the WTO?' (2010) 36(2) *Review of International Studies* 449.

Christopher Hill and Michael Smith (eds), *International Relations and the European Union* 2nd ed. (OUP 2011).

Arlie Hochschild, 'Global Care Chains and Emotional Surplus Value in Will Hutton and Anthony Giddens, (eds), *On the Edge: Living with Global Capitalism* (Jonathan Cape 2000).

Bernard M. Hoekman and Petros C. Mavroidis. 'WTO 'à la carte'or 'menu du jour'? Assessing the case for more plurilateral agreements' (2015) 26(2) *European Journal of International Law* 319.

Bernard Hoekman and Charles Sabel, 'Open Plurilateral Agreements, International Regulatory Cooperation and the WTO' (2019) 10(3) *Global Policy* 297.

Bernard Hoekman and Charles F. Sabel, *Trade Agreement, Regulatory Sovereignty and Democratic Legitimacy* (Columbia Law School 2017).

Onno Hoffmeister, *Development Status as a Measure of Development* UNCTAD Research Paper no. 46 (UN 2020).

Erling Holden, Kristin Linnerud, and David Banister, 'Sustainable Development: Our common future revisited' (2014) 26 *Global Environmental Change* 130.

Patrick Holden, 'Finding Common Ground? European Union and European civil society framing of the role of trade in the sustainable development goals' (2019) 57(5) *Journal of Common Market Studies* 956.

Ryan Holifield, Jayajit Chakraborty and Gordon Walker (eds), *The Routledge Handbook of Environmental Justice* (Routledge 2017).

Breena Holland, 'Justice and the Environment in Nussbaum's "Capabilities Approach": Why sustainable ecological capacity is a meta-capability' (2008) 61(2) *Political Research Quarterly* 319.

Terence K. Hopkins and Immanuel Wallerstein, 'Commodity Chains in the World Economy prior to 1800' (1986) 10(1) *Review* 157.

Ruth Houghton, 'Looking at the World Bank's Safeguard Reform through the Lens of Deliberative Democracy' (2019) 32(3) *Leiden Journal of International Law* 465.

Joanna Howe, Stephen Clibborn, Alexander Reilly, Diane van den Broek and Chris F Wright, *Towards a Durable Future: Tackling Labour Challenges in the Australian Horticulture Industry* (University of Adelaide 2019).

Joanna Howe and Rosemary Owens (eds), *Temporary Labour Migration in the Global Era: The Regulatory Challenges* (Hart 2016).

Robert Howse, 'Back to Court After Shrimp/Turtle? Almost But Not Quite Yet: India's Short Lived Challenge to Labor and Environmental Exceptions in the European Unions' Generalized System of Preferences' (2003) 18 *American University International Law Review* 1333.

Robert Howse, 'India's WTO Challenge to Drug Enforcement Conditions in the European Community Generalized System of Preferences: A Little Known Case with Major Repercussions for "Political" Conditionality in US Trade Policy' (2003) 4(2) *Chicago Journal of International Law* 385.

Robert Howse, 'The WTO and the Protection of Workers' Rights' (1999) 3 *Journal of Small and Emerging Business Law* 131.

Robert Howse and Elisabeth Tuerk, 'The WTO Impact on Internal Regulations—A Case Study of the Canada–EC Asbestos Dispute' in Gráinne de Búrca and Joanne Scott, *The EU and the WTO: Legal and Constitutional Issues* (Hart 2002).

Robert E. Hudec, *Developing Countries in the GATT Legal System* (CUP 2010).

Robert E. Hudec, 'GATT and the Developing Countries' (1992) *Columbia Business Law Review* 67.

Steve Hughes, 'The International Labour Organisation' (2005) 10(3) *New Political Economy* 413

Stephen Hughes and Nigel Haworth, *The ILO Involvement in Economic and Social Policies in the 1930s* (ILO 2019).

Will Hutton and Anthony Giddens, (eds), *On the Edge: Living with Global Capitalism* (Jonathan Cape 2000).

Richard Hyman and Rebecca Gumbrell-McCormick, '(How) can International Trade Union Organisations be Democratic?' (2020) 26(3) *Transfer* 253.

International Law Commission (Study Group), *Fragmentation of International Law: difficulties arising from the diversification and expansion of international law: Report of the Study Group of the International Law Commission / finalized by Martti Koskenniemi* (UN 2006) Doc. A/CN.4/L.682.

International Lawyers Assisting Workers (ILAW), 'A Conversation with Elizabeth Tang' reported in ILAW (2022) *The Global Labour Rights Reporter: Special Issue on Protection of the Rights of Workers in the Informal Economy* 8.

International Trade Union Confederation (ITUC), *Qatar: Profit and Loss* (ITUC 2016) available at: https://www.ituc-csi.org/new-ituc-report-qatar-profit-and?lang=en.

Mark F. Imber, *The USA, ILO, UNESCO and IAEA: Politicization and Withdrawal in the Specialised Agencies* (Macmillan 1989).

International Lawyers Assisting Workers (ILAW) Network, *WTO Law Aspects of Import Prohibitions on Products and Services Made Using Forced Labour* (ILAW 2022).

M.S. Islam, A. Sultana, M.S. Sultana, M. Shammi and M.K. Uddin, Surface Water Pollution Around Dhaka Export Processing Zone and its Impacts on Surrounding Aquatic Environment (2016) 8(3) *Journal of Scientific Research* 413.

Markus Jachtenfuchs, 'The Governance Approach to European Integration' (2001) 39 *Journal of Common Market Studies* 245.

John Jackson, *Sovereignty, the WTO and Changing Fundamentals of International Law* (CUP 2006).

Merle Jacobs, 'Sustainable Development and Deep Ecology: An analysis of competing traditions' (1994) 18(4) *Environmental Management* 477.

John H. Jackson, *Sovereignty, the WTO, and Changing Fundamentals of International Law* (CUP 2006).

John H. Jackson, 'GATT and the Future of International Trade Institutions' (1992) 18 *Brooklyn Journal of International Law* 11.

John L. Jackson, *World Trading System: Law and policy of international economic relations* (MIT Press 1989).

Velibor Jakovleski, Scott Jerbi and Thomas Biersteke, 'The ILO's Role in Global Governance: Limits and Potential' in Christophe Gironde and Gilles Carbonnier (eds), *The ILO@100: Addressing the Past and Future of Work and Social Protection* (Brill Nijhoff 2019).

Dima Jamali, Peter Lund-Thomsen, and Navjote Khara, 'CSR Institutionalized Myths in Developing Countries: An Imminent Threat of Selective Decoupling' (2017) 56 *Business and Society* 454.

Sarah Margaretha Jastram and Anna-Maria Schneider (eds), *Sustainable Fashion: Governance and New Management Approaches* (Springer International Publishing 2018).

Florence Jaumotte, Ksenia Koloskova and Sweta C. Saxena, 'This is the Impact of Migration on Productivity' (2017) *World Economic Forum* available at: https://www.weforum.org/agenda/2017/01/this-is-the-impact-of-migration-on-productivity/.

Florence Jaumotte and Carolina Buitron, *Inequality and Labor Market Institutions* (IMF Staff Discussion Note 15/14, 1 July 2015).

C. Wilfred Jenks, 'The Challenge of Universality' (1959) 53 *American Society of International Law Proceedings* 85.

C. Wilfred Jenks, 'Co-ordination in International Organization: An Introductory Survey' (1951) 28 *British Yearbook of International Law* 29.

Maria Jobim, 'Drawing on the Legal and Economic Arguments in Favour and Against "Reciprocity" and "Special and Differential Treatment" for Developing Countries within the WTO System' (2013) 6(3) *Journal of Politics and Law* 55.

Christian Joerges, 'Deliberative Supranationalism'—Two defences' (2002) 8(1) *European Law Journal* 133.

Peter Jones, 'Human Rights, Group Rights, and Peoples' Rights' (1999) 21 *Human Rights Quarterly* 80.

Flavia Jurje and Sandra Lavenex, *ASEAN Economic Community: What model for labour mobility?* (Swiss NCCR Trade Regulation Working Paper No 2015/02 2015) available at: https://www.wti.org/media/filer_public/24/f2/24f2c553-c4cc-4cc2-b670-6144e31d453c/nccr_working_paper_asean_jurje_lavenex__.pdf.

Humayun Kabir, Myfanwy Maple, and Kim Usher, 'The Impact of COVID-19 on Bangladeshi Readymade Garment (RMG) Workers' (2021) 43(1) *Journal of Public Health* 47.

Otto Kahn-Freund, *Labour and the Law* (Stevens 1972).

Giorgos Kallis, 'In Defence of Degrowth' (2011) 70(5) *Ecological Economics* 873.

Evance Kalula, Ada Okoye Ordor, and Colin Fenwick, *Labour Law Reforms that Support Decent Work: The case of Southern Africa* (ILO 2008).

Churnrurtai Kanchanachitra, Magnus Lindelow, Timothy Johnston, Piya Hanvoravongchai, Fely Marilyn Lorenzo, Nguyen Lan Huong, Siswanto Agus Wilopo, Jennifer Frances dela Rosa, 'Human Resources for Health in Southeast Asia: Shortages, Distributional Challenges and International Trade in Health Services' (2011) 377 *The Lancet* 769.

Ilan Kapoor, 'Deliberative Democracy and the WTO' (2004) 11(3) *Review of International Political Economy* 522.

Christine Kaufmann, *Globalisation and Labour Rights: The conflict between core labour rights and international economic law* (Hart 2007).

Chimène I. Keitner and Scott Dodson, 'Jam v. International Finance Corp.' (2019) 113(4) *American Journal of International Law* 805.

Xaver Keller, *AfCFTA and Trade in Services for Development* (German Cooperation/GIZ Discussion Paper 2019).

Hilary Kellerson, 'The ILO Declaration of 1998 on Fundamental Principles and Rights: A challenge for the future' (1998) 137 *International Labour Review* 223.

Jane Kelsey, *Serving Whose Interests? The Political Economy of Trade in Services Agreements* (Routledge 2008).

Mathias Kende, *The Trade Policy Review Mechanism: A critical analysis* (OUP 2018)

Jeff Kenner and Katrina Peake, 'The Bangladesh Sustainability Compact: An Effective Exercise of Global Experimentalist EU Governance?' (2017) 19 *Cambridge Yearbook of European Legal Studies* 86.

Jeff Kenner, Isabella Florczak and Marta Otto (eds). *Precarious Work. The Challenge for Labour Law in Europe* (Edward Elgar 2019).

Alexander Kentikelenis, Daniela Gabor, Isabel Ortiz, Thomas Stubbs, Martin McKee, and David Stuckler. 'Softening the Blow of the Pandemic: Will the International Monetary Fund and World Bank make things worse?' (2020) *The Lancet Global Health* available at: https://doi.org/10.1016/S2214-109X(20)30135-2.

William A. Kerr, 'Generalized System of Preferences and Graduation: Is there a Parallel with Infant Industries?' (2021) 22(2) *The Estey Journal of International Law and Trade Policy* 68.

Owais Hasan Khan, *Strengthening Regional Trade Integration in South Asia: A SAARC Perspective* (Springer 2021).

Sangeeta Khorana and María García (eds), *Handbook on the EU and International Trade* (Edward Elgar 2018).

Claire Kilpatrick, 'Taking the Measure of Changing Labour Mobilization at the International Labour Organisation in the wake of the EU Sovereign Debt Crisis' (2019) 68(3) *International & Comparative Law Quarterly* 665.

Mwangi S. Kimenyi, 'Time to Rethink the Future World Bank President Appointment Process' (2012) *Brookings* available at: https://www.brookings.edu/opinions/time-to-rethink-the-future-world-bank-president-appointment-process/.

Benedict Kingsbury, David M. Malone, Paul Mertenskötter, Richard B. Stewart, Thomas Streinz, and Atsushi Sunami (eds), *Megaregulation Contested: Global Economic Ordering After TPP, Law And Global Governance* (OUP 2019).

Esteban Koberg and Annachiara Longoni, 'A Systematic Review of Sustainable Supply Chain Management in Global Supply Chains' (2019) 207 *Journal of Cleaner Production* 1084.

Marieke Koekkoek, 'In Search of the Final Frontier - An analysis of the extraterritorial effect of international trade measures from a jurisdictional perspective' (2018) 10(1) *Trade Law and Development* 65.

Beate Kohler-Koch and Christine Quittkat, 'What is Civil Society and who Represents Civil Society in the EU?—Results of an online survey among civil society experts' (2009) 28(1) *Policy and Society* 11.

Jonathan Köhler, 'Globalization and Sustainable Development: Case study on international transport and sustainable development' (2014) 23(1) *The Journal of Environment and Development* 66.

Kevin Kolben, 'A Supply Chain Approach to Trade and Labor Provisions' (2017) 5(4) *Politics and Governance* 60.

Kevin Kolben, 'Transnational Labor Regulation and the Limits of Governance' (2011) 12(2) *Theoretical Inquiries in Law* 403.

Kevin Kolben, 'Labour Rights as Human Rights?' (2010) 50 *Virginia Journal of International Law* 449.

Kevin Kolben, 'Trade, Monitoring, and the ILO: Working to Improve Conditions in Cambodia's Garment Factories' (2004) 7 *Yale Human Rights & Development Law Journal* 79.

Faradj Koliev and James H. Lebovic, 'Shaming into Compliance? Country reporting of convention adherence to the International Labour Organization' (2022) 48(2) *International Interactions* 258.

Walter Korpi, 'Power Resources Approach vs. Action and Conflict: On Causal and Intentional Explanations in the Study of Power' (1985) 3(2) *Sociological Theory* 31.

Martti Koskenniemi and Päivi Leino, 'Fragmentation of International Law? Postmodern anxieties' (2002) 15(3) *Leiden Journal of International Law* 553.

Sandrine Kott, 'ILO: Social Justice in a Global World? A History in Tension' in Christophe Gironde and Gilles Carbonnier (eds), *The ILO@100: Addressing the Past and Future of Work and Social Protection* (Brill Nijhoff 2019).

Aristea Koukiadaki, 'Global Supply Chains and Labour Standards: From a patchwork of rules to a web of rules?' in Barry Colfer, Brian Harney, Colm McLaughlin, Chris F. Wright (eds), *Protecting the Future of Work: New Institutional Arrangements for Safeguarding Labour Standards* (Emerald Publishing Limited 2023).

Aristea Koukiadaki and Lefteris Kretsos, 'Opening Pandora's Box: The sovereign debt crisis and labour market regulation in Greece' (2012) 41 *Industrial Law Journal* 276.

Rüdiger Krause, 'The Promotion of Labour Standards Through International Framework Agreements' in Henner Gött (ed.), *Labour Standards in International Economic Law* (Springer 2018).

Halliki Kreinin and Ernest Aigner, 'From "Decent Work and Economic Growth" to "Sustainable Work and Economic Degrowth": A new framework for SDG 8' (2022) 49(2) *Empirica* 281.

Kholofelo Kugler, Mulualem Getachew Adgeh, 'Africa and Trade and Investment Liberalization' in Daniel Bethlehem, Donald McRae, Rodney Neufeld, Isabelle Van Damme (eds), *The Oxford Handbook of International Trade Law*, 2nd ed. (OUP 2022).

Katrin Kuhlmann and Akinyi Lisa Agutu, 'The African Continental Free Trade Area: Toward A New Legal Model For Trade And Development' (2020) 51 *Georgetown Journal of International Law* 753.

Vidya Kumar, 'Rethinking the Convergence of Human Rights and Labour Rights in International Law: Depoliticisation and Excess' in Ruth Buchanan and Peer Zumbansen, *Law in Transition: Human Rights, Development and Transitional Justice* (Bloomsbury 2014).

Sarosh Kuruvilla, *Private Regulation of Labor Standards in Global Supply Chains* (Cornell University Press 2021).

Sarosh Kuruvilla and Chunyun Li, 'Freedom of Association and Collective Bargaining in Global Supply Chains: A research agenda' (2021) 57(2) *Journal of Supply Chain Management* 43.

Claire La Hovary, 'The ILO's Employers' Group and the Right to Strike' (2016) 22(3) *Transfer: European Review of Labour and Research* 401.

Claire La Hovary, 'A Challenging Ménage à Trois? Tripartism in the International Labour Organization' (2015) 12(1) *International Organizations Law Review* 204.

Claire La Hovary, 'Employers' Group 2012 Challenge to the Right to Strike' (2013) 42(4) *Industrial Law Journal* 338.

Claire La Hovary and Jordi Agustí Panareda, 'What is Work? A malleable notion in the ILO's legal pursuit of social justice' in George P. Politakis, Tomi Kohiyama and Thomas Lieby (eds), *ILO 100: Law for social justice* (ILO 2019).

William M. Lafferty and Oluf Langhelle, 'Sustainable Development as Concept and Norm' in William M. Lafferty and Oluf Langhelle (eds) *Towards Sustainable Development* (Palgrave Macmillan 1999).

William M. Lafferty and Oluf Langhelle (eds) *Towards Sustainable Development* (Palgrave Macmillan 1999).

Alessandro Lai, Gaia Melloni, and Riccardo Stacchezzini, 'Corporate Sustainable Development: Is "integrated reporting" a legitimation strategy?' (2016) 25(3) *Business Strategy and the Environment* 165.

Ingrid Landau, 'Human Rights Due Diligence and the Risk of Cosmetic Compliance' (2019) 20 *Melbourne Journal of International Law* 221.

Ingrid Landau and Tess Hardy, 'Transnational Labour Governance in Global Supply Chains: Asking Questions and Seeking Answers on Accountability' in Guillaume Delautre, Elizabeth Echeverría Manrique and Colin Fenwick (eds), *Decent Work in a Globalized Economy: Lessons from public and private initiatives* (ILO 2021).

Ingrid Landau and John Howe, 'State Extraterritorial Regulation and Decent Work in the Asia Pacific' in Janice Bellace and Beryl ter Haar (eds), *Research Handbook on Labour, Business and Human Rights Law* (Edward Elgar Publishing 2019).

Andrew Lang, *World Trade Law after Neoliberalism: Re-Imagining the Global Economic Order* (OUP 2011).

Rolf J. Langhammer and Ulrich Hiemenz, *Regional Integration among Developing Countries: Opportunities, obstacles, and options* (J.C.B. Mohr/Westview Press 1990).

Brian Langille (ed.), *The Capability Approach to Labour Law* (OUP 2019).

Brian Langille, '"Hard Law Makes Bad Cases": The International Labour Organization (Nervously) Confronts New Governance Institutions' (2016) 32(4) *International Journal of Comparative Labour Law and Industrial Relations* 407.

Brian Langille, 'Imagining Post Geneva Consensus Labor Law for Post Washington Consensus Development' (2009) 31 *Comparative Labor Law and Policy Journal* 523.

Brian Langille, 'Core Labour Standards – The True Story (Reply to Alston)' (2005) 16 *European Journal of International Law* 409.

Brian A. Langille, 'Eight Ways to Think about International Labour Standards' (1997) 31 *Journal of World Trade* 27.

Joanna Langille, 'The Trade–Labour Relationship in the Light of the WTO Appellate Body's Embrace of Pluralism' (2020) 159(4) *International Labour Review* 569.

Ernst Langthaler and Elke Schüßler, 'Commodity Studies with Polanyi: Disembedding and Re-Embedding Labour and Land in Contemporary Capitalism' (2009) 44(2) *Österreichische Zeitschrift für Soziologie* 209.

Addisu A. Lashitew, 'Corporate Uptake of the Sustainable Development Goals: Mere greenwashing or an advent of institutional change?' (2021) 4(1) *Journal of International Business Policy* 184.

John Lawler and Chokechai Suttawet, 'Labour Unions, Globalization and Deregulation in Thailand' (2000) 6(3) *Asia Pacific Business Review* 214.

Virginia Leary, 'The Paradox of Workers' Rights as Human Rights' in Lance Compa and Stephen Diamond, (eds.), *Human Rights, Labour Rights and International Trade* (University of Pennsylvania Press 1996).

Virgina A. Leary, 'Lessons from the Experience of the ILO' in Philip Alston (ed.), *The United Nations and Human Rights: A Critical Reappraisal* (OUP 1992).

Desirée LeClercq , 'A Worker-Centered Trade Policy (2023) 61(3) *Columbia Journal of Transnational Law* 733.

Desirée LeClercq, 'Integrating Non-Binding Labour Standards in Binding Trade Agreements: The ILO's Feedback loop' (2023) *Journal of International Economic Law*, forthcoming.

Desirée LeClercq, 'Invisible Workers' (2022) 116 *AJIL Unbound* 107.

Desiree LeClercq, 'Occupational Safety and Health as a New Fundamental Labour Right: Opportunities and Challenges' (July 12, 2022), Korea Labor Institute, International Labor Brief, Vol. 20(9) (2022), available at: https://ssrn.com/abstract=4161060 or http://dx.doi.org/10.2139/ssrn.4161060.

Desirée LeClercq, 'Why Conflict Between International Economic and Rights-Based Governance is Inevitable' (2022) 40(1) *Berkeley Journal of International Law* 1.

Desiree LeClercq, 'A Rules-Based Approach to Jam's Restrictive Immunity: Implications for International Organizations' (2020) 58(1) *Houston Law Review* 55.
Eddy Lee, 'Globalization and Labour Standards: A Review of Issues' (1997) 136(2) *International Labour Review* 173.
Sangheon Lee, Deirdre McCann, and Nina Torm, 'The World Bank's "Employing Workers" Index: Findings and critiques–A review of recent evidence' (2008) 147(4) *International Labour Review* 416.
Jernej Letnar Černič, 'The ILO Tripartite Declaration of Principles Concerning Multinational Enterprises and Social Policy Revisited: Is There a Need for Its Reform?' Marc Bungenberg, Markus Krajewski, Christian J. Tams, Jörg Philipp Terhechte and Andreas R. Ziegler (eds) *European Yearbook of International Economic Law 2019* (Springer 2020).
Jernej Letnar Černič, 'Corporate Responsibility for Human Rights: Analyzing the ILO Tripartite Declaration of principles concerning multinational enterprises and social policy' (2009) 6(1) *Miskolc Journal of International Law* 24.
Christian Lévesque and Gregor Murray, 'Understanding Union Power: Resources and capabilities for renewing union capacity' (2010) 16(3) *Transfer: European review of labour and research* 333.
Judith Levine, 'Navigating the Parallel Universe of Investor-State disputes under the UNCITRAL Rules' (2017) 14(1) *Transnational Dispute Management* (TDM) available at: www.transnational-dispute-management.com/article.asp?key=2434.
Marieke Louis, 'Who Decides? Representation and Decision-making at the International Labour Organization' in Christophe Gironde and Gilles Carbonnier (eds), *The ILO@100: Addressing the Past and Future of Work and Social Protection* (Brill Nijhoff 2019).
Li Li, 'BRICS: A Limited Role in Transforming the World' (2019) 43(6) Strategic Analysis 499.
Alain Lipietz, 'Fears and Hopes: The crisis of the liberal-productivist model and its green alternative' (2013) 37(1) *Capital & Class* 127.
Julia López López (ed.), *Inscribing Solidarity: Debates in Labor Law and Beyond* (CUP 2022).
Julia López López (ed.), *Collective Bargaining and Collective Action: Labour Agency and Governance in the 21st Century?* (Hart 2018).
Klaus Lörcher, 'The New Social Dimension in the Jurisprudence of the European Court of Human Rights (ECtHR): The Demir and Baykara Judgment, its Methodology and Follow-up' in Filip Dorssemont, Klaus Lörcher, and Isabelle Schömann (eds), *The European Convention on Human Rights and the Employment Relation* (Hart 2013).
Marieke Louis, 'The ILO, Social Partners and the G20: New prospects for social dialogue at the global level?' (2016) 16(3) *Global Social Policy* 235.
Elli Louka, *The Global Economic Order: The International Law and Politics of the Financial and Monetary System* (Edward Elgar 2020).
Frank Lovett, *A General Theory of Domination and Justice* (OUP 2010).
Frank Lovett and Philip Pettit, 'Neorepublicanism: A Normative and Institutional Research Program' (2009) 12 *Annual Review of Political Science* 11.
Andreas F. Lowenfeld, *International Economic Law* (OUP 2008).
Jonathan Z. Ludwig, 'Chernobyl, Coronavirus, and the Art of the Authoritarian Cover-Up: Who is to Blame, and What is to be Done?' *SAGE* 1 (2020).
Niklas Luhmann, 'Operational Closure and Structural Coupling: The differentiation of the legal system' (1992) 13 *Cardozo Law Review* 1419.

Niklas Luhmann, *Social Systems* (first printed 1984 (in German), Stanford University Press, 1995).

Steven Lukes, *Power: A Radical View* 1st ed. (Macmillan 1974).

Susanne Lütz and Matthias Kranke, 'The European Rescue of the Washington Consensus? EU and IMF lending to Central and Eastern European countries' (2014) 21(2) *Review of International Political Economy* 310.

Dáire MacCormack-George, 'Philip Pettit's Republicanism and Labour Law; A Defence' (2021) 37(4) *International Journal of Comparative Labour Law and Industrial Relations* 417.

Rowena Maguire, 'The Role of Common But Differentiated Responsibility in the 2020 Climate Regime (2013) 4 *Carbon and Climate Law Review* 260.

Zeeshan Mahmood and Shahzad Uddin, 'Institutional Logics and Practice Variations in Sustainability Reporting: Evidence from an emerging field' (2020) 34(5) *Accounting, Auditing & Accountability Journal* 1163.

Ian Manners, 'The European Union's Normative Power' in Richard Whitman (ed.), *Normative power Europe: Empirical and theoretical perspectives*, (Palgrave 2011)

Virginia Mantouvalou, 'Are Labour Rights Human Rights?' (2012) 3 *European Labour Law Journal* 151.

Gabrielle Marceau, 'Trade and Labour' in Daniel Bethlehem, Isabelle Van Damme, Donald McRae, Rodney Neufeld (eds), *The Oxford Handbook of International Trade Law* (OUP 2009).

Shelley Marshall, *Living Wage: Regulatory Solutions to Informal and Precarious Work in Global Supply Chains* (OUP 2019).

Shelley Marshall, Ingrid Landau, Hila Shamir, Tamar Barkay, Judy Fudge, Auret van Heerden, *Mandatory Human Rights Due Diligence: Risks and Opportunities for Workers and Unions* (RMIT/TraffLab/Monash 2023).

T.H. Marshall, *Citizenship and Social Class* (CUP 1950).

Deborah Martens, Diana Potjomkina and Jan Orbie, *Domestic Advisory Groups in EU Trade Agreements: Stuck at the bottom or moving up the ladder* (Friedrich Ebert Stiftung 2020).

Philip L. Martin, *GATS, Migration and Labour Standards* DP/165/2006 (ILO 2006) available at: http://www.ilo.org/inst/publication/discussion-papers/WCMS_193612/lang--en/index.htm.

Miguel Martinez Lucio and Stephen Mustchin, 'The Politics and Diversity of Worker Representation: The increasing fluidity and challenge of representation' in Gregor Gall (ed.), *Handbook of the Politics of Labour, Work and Employment* (Edward Elgar 2019).

Karl Marx, *Capital* (Wordsworth 2013).

Francis Maupain, 'A Second Century for What? The ILO at a regulatory crossroad' (2020) 17(1) *International Organizations Law Review* 291.

Francis Maupain, *The Future of the International Labour Organization in the Global Economy* (Hart 2013).

Petros C. Mavroidis, 'Sealed with a Doubt: EU, Seals, and the WTO' (2015) 6 *European Journal of Risk Regulation* 38.

Petros C. Mavroidis, 'Surveillance Schemes: The GATT's New Trade Policy Review Mechanism' (1991) 13 *Michigan Journal of International Law* 374.

Makane Moïse Mbengue and Apollin Koagne Zouapet, 'Ending the Splendid Isolation—Jus Cogens and International Economic Law' in Dire Tladi (ed.), *Peremptory Norms of General International Law (Jus Cogens)* (Brill Nijhoff 2021).

Stephen McBride and Scott Smith, 'In the Shadow of Crisis: Economic Orthodoxy and the Response of Global Labour' (2013) 4(3) *Global Labour Journal* 206.

Deirdre McCann, Sangheon Lee, Patrick Belser, Colin Fenwick, John Howe and Malte Luebker (eds), *Creative Labour Regulation: Indeterminacy and Protection in an Uncertain World* (ILO/Palgrave Macmillan 2014).

Christopher McCrudden and A.C.L. Davies, 'A Perspective on Trade and Labour Rights' (2000) *Journal of International Economic Law* 43.

Robert K. McCleery and Fernando De Paolis, 'The Washington Consensus: A post-mortem' (2008) 19 *Journal of Asian Economics* 438.

Brendan McGivern, 'The WTO Seal Products Panel: The Public Morals Defense' (2014) 9(2) *Global Trade and Customs Journal* 73.

Donald McRae, 'State-to-State Dispute Settlement in Megaregionals' in Benedict Kingsbury, David M. Malone, Paul Mertenskötter, Richard B. Stewart, Thomas Streinz, and Atsushi Sunami (eds), *Megaregulation Contested: Global Economic Ordering After TPP, Law And Global Governance* (OUP 2019).

Maayan Menashe, *International Labour Law as a Global Public Good: Enhancing Labour Regulation in an Era of Globalisation*. PhD Diss. University of Cambridge, 2021.

Maayan Menashe, 'Private Actors as Transnational Regulators: The Case of Freedom of Association' (2020) 49(1) *Industrial Law Journal* 1.

Maayan Menashe, 'The Race to the Bottom Revisited: International labour law, global trade and evolutionary game theory' (2020) 40(1) *Oxford Journal of Legal Studies* 53.

Justice Mensah, 'Sustainable Development: Meaning, history, principles, pillars, and implications for human action' (2019) 5(1) *Cogent Social Science* 1653531.

Sophie Meunier and Kalypso Nicolaïdes, 'The European Union as a Conflicted Trade Power' (2006) 13(6) *Journal of European Public Policy* 906.

Pablo Zapatero Miguel, 'Level up: A History of Regime-Building at GATT Club' (2020) 12 *Cuadernos de Depeche Transnacional* 818.

Branko Milanovic, *Global Inequality: A New Approach for the Age of Globalization* (Harvard University Press 2016).

Faina Milman-Sivan, 'Representativity, Civil Society, and the EU Social Dialogue: Lessons from the International Labor Organization' (2009) 16 *Indiana Journal of Global Legal Studies* 311.

Faina Milman-Sivan and Yair Sagy, 'On the International Labour Organisation and Prison Labour: An invitation for recalculation' (2020) 159(4) *International Labour Review* 505.

Matthew T. Mitro, 'Outlawing the Trade in Child Labor Products: Why the GATT Article XX Health Exception Authorizes Unilateral Sanctions' (2002) 51 *American University Law Review* 1223.

Gillian Moon, 'A "Fundamental Moral Imperative": Social Inclusion, the Sustainable Development Goals and International Trade Law After Brazil-Taxation' (2018) 52(6) *Journal of World Trade* 995.

Mike Moore (ed.), *Doha and Beyond: The Future of the Multicultural Trading System* (CUP 2004).

Lilian Moncrieff, 'Karl Polanyi and the Problem of Corporate Social Responsibility' (2015) 42(3) *Journal of Law and Society* 434.

Edouard Morena, Dunja Krause and Dimitris Stevis (eds), *Just Transitions: Social justice in the shift towards a low-carbon world* (Pluto Press 2020).

Jason Morgan-Foster, 'The Relationship of IMF Structural Adjustment Programs to Economic, Social and Cultural Rights: The Argentine Case Revisited' (2003) 24 *Michigan Journal of International Law* 577.

Jonathan Morris, Jean Jenkins and Jimmy Donaghey, 'Uneven Development, Uneven Response: The relentless search for meaningful regulation of GVCs' (2021) 59(1) *British Journal of Industrial Relations* 3.

Oliver Morrissey, Ricardo Lopez and Kishor Sharma (eds), *Handbook on Trade and Development* (Edward Elgar 2015).

Peter Muchlinski, *Promoting Responsible Business through the Revised ILO Tripartite Declaration*, Columbia FDI Perspectives No. 231 (Columbia Center on Sustainable Investment 2021) available at: https://www.econstor.eu/bitstream/10419/254155/1/fdi-perspectives-no321.pdf.

Asoke Mukerji, 'Developing Countries and the WTO; Issues of implementation' (2000) 34(6*)* *Journal of World Trade* 33.

Ronaldo Munck, *Globalization and Contestation: The New Great Counter-Movement* (Routledge 2006).

Guy Mundlak, *Organizing Matters: Two Logics of Trade Union Representation* (Edward Elgar/ILO 2020).

Guy Mundlak, 'Tri-Plus: Reflections on Opening the ILO's Tripartite Structure' in George P. Politakis, Tomi Kohiyama and Thomas Lieby (eds), *ILO 100: Law for social justice* (ILO 2019).

Hannah Murphy, 'The World Bank and Core Labour Standards: Between flexibility and regulation' (2014) 22 *Review of International Political Economy* 399.

Jill Murray, Taking Social Rights Seriously: Is there a Case for Institutional Reform of the ILO?' in Colin Fenwick and Tonia Novitz (eds.), *Human Rights at Work: Perspectives on Law and Regulation* (Hart 2010).

Mpoki Mwakagali, *International Financial Institutions and Labour Standards: A legal study of the role of these institutions in the promotion of freedom of association and collective bargaining* (Stockholm University 2018).

V.P. Nanda, 'The Journey from the Millennium Development Goals to the Sustainable Development Goals' (2016) 44 *Denver Journal of International Law and Policy* 389.

Christina Niforou, 'International Framework Agreements and the democratic deficit of global labour governance' (2014) 35(2) *Economic and Industrial Democracy* 367.

Aleydis Nissen, 'Not That Assertive: The EU's take on enforcement of labour obligations in its free trade agreement with South Korea' (2022) 33(2) *European Journal of International Law* 607.

Aleydis Nissen, 'And So It Begins: Trade and Sustainable Development Recommendations by a Panel of Experts under a European Union Free Trade Agreement' (2021) 7 *International Labor Rights Case Law* 257.

Tonia Novitz, 'Challenges When Combining Labour and Environmental Objectives: Trade and Sustainable Development Chapters and Beyond' in Adalberto Perulli and Tiziano Treu (eds), *Labour Law and Climate Change: Towards a Just Transition* (Wolters Kluwer 2023).

Tonia Novitz, 'Human Rights as a Regulatory Tool for "Just Transition" in Europe and Beyond' (2023) 39(3/4) *International Journal of Comparative Labour Law and Industrial Relations* 439.

Tonia Novitz, 'Addressing "Social Dumping" and "Unfair Competition": An analysis of EU pillar initiatives from a sustainability perspective' in Ann-Christine. Hartzén, Andrea Iossa and Elena Karageorgiou (eds), *Law, Solidarity and the Limits of Social Europe: Constitutional Tensions for EU Integration* (Edward Elgar 2022).

Tonia Novitz, 'Collective Labour Rights for Working People: The Legal Framework Established by the International Labour Organization' in Sanjukta Paul, Shae McCrystal and Ewan McGaughey (eds), *The Cambridge Handbook of Labor in Competition Law* (CUP 2022).

Tonia Novitz, 'Sustainability as Solidarity Unbound: Labour Rights and Collective Voice in the United Nations Sustainable Development Goals and the European Union' in Julia López López (ed.), *Inscribing Solidarity: Debates in Labor Law and Beyond* (CUP 2022).

Tonia Novitz, 'Sustainable Development Goal 8: Promote Sustained, Inclusive, and Sustainable Economic Growth, Full and Productive Employment, and Decent Work for All' in Jonas Ebbesson and Ellen Hey (eds), *Cambridge Handbook on the United Nations Sustainable Development Goals and International Law* (CUP 2022).

Tonia Novitz, 'Sustainable Labour Conditionality in EU Free Trade Agreements? Implications of the EU-Korea Expert Panel Report' (2022) 1 *European Law Review* 3.

Tonia Novitz, *Enforceable Social Clauses in Trade Agreements with 'Bite'? Implications of the EU–South Korea Panel of Experts Report of 20 January 2021* (Brussels: ETUI Brief, 2021).

Tonia Novitz, 'Engagement with Sustainability at the International Labour Organization and Wider Implications for Collective Worker Voice' (2020) 159(4) *International Labour Review* 463.

Tonia Novitz, 'Multi-level Disputes relating to Freedom of Association and the Right to Strike: Transnational Systems, Actors and Resources' (2020) 36(4) *International Journal of Comparative Labour Law and Industrial Relations* 471.

Tonia Novitz, 'Past and Future Work at the International Labour Organization: Labour as a Fictitious Commodity, Countermovement and Sustainability' (2020) 17(1) *International Organizations Law Review* 10.

Tonia Novitz, 'The Potential for International Regulation of Gig Economy Issues' (2020) 31(2) *King's Law Journal* 275.

Tonia Novitz, 'Social Sustainability, Labour and Trade: Forging Connections' in Margherita Pieraccini and Tonia Novitz (eds), *Legal Perspectives on Sustainability* (Bristol University Press 2020).

Tonia Novitz, 'Changing Collective Representation and Action to Meet the Challenges: Historical lessons and contemporary learning' in Alysia Blackham, Miriam Kullmann, and Ania Zbyszewska (eds), *Theorising Labour Law in a Changing World: Towards Inclusive Labour Law* (Hart 2019).

Tonia Novitz, 'Freedom of Association: Its Emergence and the Case for Prevention of its Decline' in Janice Bellace and Beryl ter Haar (eds), *Research Handbook on Labour, Business and Human Rights Law* (Edward Elgar Publishing 2019).

Tonia Novitz, 'Supply Chains and Temporary Migrant Labour: The Relevance of Trade and Sustainability Frameworks' in Diamond Ashiagbor (ed.), *Re-imagining Labour Law for Development* (Hart 2019).

Tonia Novitz, 'Tripartism as Sustainable Governance' in George P. Politakis, Tomi Kohiyama and Thomas Lieby (eds), *ILO 100: Law for social justice* (ILO 2019).

Tonia Novitz, 'Collective Bargaining and Social Dumping in Posting and Procurement – What Might Come from Recent Court of Justice Case Law and the Proposed Reform of the Posting of Workers Directive?' in Albert Sanchez-Graells (ed.), *Smart Public Procurement and Labour Standards: Pushing the Discussion after RegioPost* (Hart 2018).

Tonia Novitz, 'Labour Standards and Trade: Need we choose between "human rights" and "sustainable development"?' in Henner Gött (ed.), *Labour Standards in International Economic Law* (Springer 2018).

Tonia Novitz, 'The Restricted Right to Strike: "Far-Reaching" ILO Jurisprudence on the Public Sector and Essential Services' (2017) 38(3) *Comparative Labor Law and Policy Journal* 353.

Tonia Novitz, 'Changes in Employment Status under Austerity and Beyond – Implications for freedom of association' (2016) 39(1) *Dublin University Law Journal* 27.

Tonia Novitz, 'The EU and the Right to Strike: Regulation through the back door and its impact on social dialogue' (2016) 27(1) *King's Law Journal* 46.

Tonia Novitz, 'Trading in Services: Commodities and Beneficiaries' in Adelle Blackett and Anne Trebilcock (eds), *Research Handbook on Transnational Labour Law* (Edward Elgar 2015).

Tonia Novitz, 'Evolutionary Trajectories for Transnational Labour Law: Trade in Goods to Trade in Services?' (2014) 67 *Current Legal Problems* 239.

Tonia Novitz, 'Big Unions and Big Business: Can international framework agreements promote sustainable development at a local level?' in Tonia Novitz and David Mangan (eds.), *The Role of Labour Standards in Development: From theory to sustainable practice?* (OUP/British Academy 2011).

Tonia Novitz, 'Connecting Freedom of Association and the Right to Strike: European Dialogue with the ILO and its Potential Impact' (2010) 15(3) *Canadian Labour and Employment Law Journal* 465.

Tonia Novitz, *International and European Protection of the Right to Strike* (OUP 2003).

Tonia Novitz, 'Are Social Rights Necessarily Collective Rights? A critical analysis of the Collective Complaints Protocol to the European Social Charter' (2002) *European Human Rights Law Review* 50.

Tonia Novitz, 'The European Union and International Labour Standards: The Dynamics of Dialogue Between the EU and the ILO' in Philip Alston (ed.), *Labour Rights as Human Rights* (OUP 2005).

Tonia Novitz and Rutvica Andrijasevic, 'Reform of the Posting of Workers Regime – An Assessment of the Practical Impact on Unfree Labour Relations' (2020) 58(5) *Journal of Common Market Studies* 1325.

Tonia Novitz and Colin Fenwick, 'The Application of a Human Rights Discourse to Labour Relations: Translation of Theory into Practice' in Colin Fenwick and Tonia Novitz (eds) *Human Rights at Work* (Onati/Hart 2010).

Tonia Novitz and Clair Gammage, *Report on International Regulatory Complexity of EU Trade and Investment* (SMART/University of Oslo 2018).

Tonia Novitz and David Mangan (eds), *The Role of Labour Standards in Development: From theory to sustainable practice?* (OUP/British Academy 2011).

Tonia Novitz and Margherita Pieraccini, 'Agenda 2030 and the Sustainable Development Goals: 'Responsive, Inclusive, Participatory and Representative Decision-Making?' in Margherita Pieraccini and Tonia Novitz (eds), *Legal Perspectives on Sustainability* (Bristol University Press 2020).

Tonia Novitz and Phil Syrpis, 'Assessing Legitimate Structures for the Making of Transnational Labour Law: The Durability of Corporatism' (2006) 35(4) *Industrial Law Journal* 367.

Martha Nussbaum, 'Labour Law and the Capabilities Approach' in Brian Langille (ed.), *The Capability Approach to Labour Law* (OUP 2019).

Martha Nussbaum, *Creating Capabilities: The human development approach* (Harvard University Press 2011).

Martha Nussbaum, 'Capabilities as Fundamental Entitlements: Sen and Social Justice' (2003) 9 *Feminist Economics* 33.

Martha Nussbaum, *Women and Human Development: The capabilities approach* (CUP 2000).

Martha Nussbaum, 'Capabilities and Human Rights' (1997) 66 *Fordham Law Review* 273.

Aoife O'Donoghue and Ntina Tzouvala, 'TTIP: The rise of the "mega-market" trade agreements and its potential implications for the Global South' (2016) 8(2) *Trade Law and Development* 30.

Claus Offe and Helmut Wiesenthal, 'Two Logics of Collective Action: Theoretical notes on social class and organizational form' (1980) 1(1) *Political Power and Social Theory* 67.

J. Ife Ogbonna, 'Protecting Human Rights as Public Morals under the General Agreement on Tariffs and Trade (GATT) 1994: A Review of EC – Seal Products' (2014) 3 *International Human Rights Law Review* 97.

G. Chike Okogwu, 'Labour Standards Across Different Levels of Development' in Werner Sengenberger and Duncan Campbell (eds.), *International Labour Standards and Economic Interdependence* (ILO International Institute for Labour Studies 1994).

Jan Orbie, 'EU Trade Policy Meets Geopolitics: What about trade justice?' (2021) 26(2) *European Foreign Affairs Review* 197.

Jan Orbie, Deborah Martens, Myriam Oehri and Lore Van den Putte, 'Promoting Sustainable Development or Legitimising Free Trade? Civil society mechanisms in EU trade agreements' (2016) 1(4) *Third World Thematics: A TWQ Journal* 526.

Anne Orford, *International Law and the Politics of History* (CUP 2021).

Ebru Orhan, 'The Effects of the Russia-Ukraine War on Global Trade' (2022) 8(1) *Journal of International Trade, Logistics and Law* 141.

Federico Ortino, *Workers' Rights Commitments in the UK-EU Trade and Cooperation Agreement (TCA)* (Trades Union Congress 2021).

Ebere Osieke, 'The Exercise of the Judicial Function with respect to the International Labour Organization' (1974 - 1975) LXVII *British Yearbook of International Law* 315.

Opi Outhwaite and Olga Martin-Ortega, 'Worker-driven Monitoring – Redefining supply chain monitoring to improve labour rights in global supply chains' (2019) 23(4) *Competition & Change* 378.

T. Ademola Oyejide, 'Development Dimensions in Multilateral Trade Negotiations' in Mike Moore (ed.), *Doha and Beyond: The Future of the Multicultural Trading System* (CUP 2004).

Joshua Paine, 'Autonomy to Set the Level of Regulatory Protection in International Investment Law' (2021) 70 *International and Comparative Law Quarterly* 697.

Joshua Paine, 'The WTO's Dispute Settlement Body as a Voice Mechanism' (2019) 20(6) *The Journal of World Investment and Trade* 820.

David Palmeter, Petros C. Mavroidis and Niall Meagher, *Dispute Settlement in the World Trade Organization*, 3rd ed. (CUP 2022).

Cristiana Panella and Thierry De Putter, 'The Invisible Lives of Cobalt Miners and Green Traceability Discourses' (2022) 38(5) *Anthropology Today* 13.

Marion Panizzon, 'Temporary Movement of Workers and Human Rights Protection: Interfacing the Mode 4 of GATS with Non-Trade Bilateral Migration Agreements' (2010) 104 *Am. Soc'y Int'l L. Proc.* 131.

Marion Panizzon, Trade and Labor Migration: GATS Mode 4 And Migration Agreements (Friedrich-Ebert-Stiftung 2010) available at: http://library.fes.de/pdf-files/iez/global/06955.pdf.

Konstandinos Papadakis, 'Globalizing Industrial Relations: What role for International Framework Agreements?' in Susan Hayter (ed.), *The Role of Collective Bargaining in the Global Economy: Negotiating for Social Justice* (Edward Elgar 2011).

Sunghoon Park, 'The New Politics of Trade Negotiations: The case of the EU-Korea FTA' (2017) 39(7) *Journal of European Integration* 827.

Etienne Pataut and Sophie Robin-Olivier, *The Future of Labour Law*, White Paper 23 (International Law Association 2022).

Gardner Patterson, 'The GATT: Categories, Problems and Procedures of Membership' (1992) *Columbia Business Law Review* 7.

Sanjukta Paul, Shae McCrystal and Ewan McGaughey (eds), *The Cambridge Handbook of Labor in Competition Law* (CUP 2022).

Joost Pauwelyn, 'WTO Dispute Settlement Post 2019: What to expect?' (2019) 22(3) *Journal of International Economic Law* 297.

Katrina Peake, *To What Extent do EU Trade and Sustainable Development Instruments Effectively Promote Labour Rights in the Ready-Made Garment Industry of South Asia*, PhD Thesis submitted to the University of Nottingham, December 2019.

Katrina Peake and Jeff Kenner, '"Slaves to Fashion" in Bangladesh and the EU: Promoting decent work?' (2020) 11(2) *European Labour Law Journal* 175.

Antoine Pécoud, 'Philosophies of Migration Governance in a Globalizing World' (2021) 18(1) *Globalizations* 103.

Maria Persson, 'Trade Preferences from a Policy Perspective' in Oliver Morrissey, Ricardo Lopez and Kishor Sharma (eds), *Handbook on Trade and Development* (Edward Elgar 2015).

Adalberto Perulli and Tiziano Treu (eds), *Labour Law and Climate Change: Towards a Just Transition* (Wolters Kluwer 2023).

Adalberto Perulli and Tiziano Treu (eds), *Sustainable Development, Global Trade and Social Rights* (Wolters Kluwer 2018).

Ernst-Ulrich Petersmann, 'The "Human Rights Approach" Advocated by the UN High Commissioner for Human Rights and by the International Labour Organization: Is It Relevant for WTO Law and Policy' (2004) 7 *Journal of International Economic Law* 605.

Ernst-Ulrich Petersmann, 'The WTO Constitution and Human Rights' (2000) 3(1) *Journal of International Economic Law* 19.

Philip Pettit, 'Depoliticizing Democracy' (2004) 17(1) *Ratio Juris* 52.

Philip Pettit, *Republicanism: A Theory of Freedom and Government* (OUP 1999).

Margherita Pieraccini and Tonia Novitz, 'Sustainability and Law: A Historical and Theoretical Overview' in Margherita Pieraccini and Tonia Novitz (eds), *Legal Perspectives on Sustainability* (Bristol University Press 2020).

Margherita Pieraccini and Tonia Novitz (eds), *Legal Perspectives on Sustainability* (Bristol University Press 2020).

Thomas Piketty *Capital in the Twenty-First Century* (Harvard University Press 2014).

Lou Pingeot, *Corporate Influence in the Post-2015 Process* Working Paper (Misereor, Brot für die Welt and Global Policy Forum, 2014).

Hans-Wolfgang Platzer and Stefan Rüb, *International Framework Agreements: An Instrument for Enforcing Social Human Rights?* (Friedrich Ebert Stiftung Working Paper 2014).

Thomas Pogge, 'Recognized and Violated by International Law: The human rights of the global poor' (2005) 18(4) *Leiden Journal of International Law* 717.

Thomas Pogge and Mitu Sengupta, 'The Sustainable Development Goals (SDGs) as Drafted: Nice idea, poor execution' (2015) 24(3) *Washington International Law Journal* 571.

Karl Polanyi, *The Great Transformation: The Political and Economic Origins of our Time* (Beacon Press 2001) 2nd paperback ed.

Sandra Polaski, 'The Strategy and Politics of Linking Trade and Labor Standards: An overview of issues and approaches' in Kimberly A. Elliott (ed.), *Handbook on Globalisation and Labour Standards* (Edward Elgar 2022).

George P. Politakis, Tomi Kohiyama and Thomas Lieby (eds), *ILO 100: Law for social justice* (ILO 2019).

Stefano Ponte, *Business, Power and Sustainability in a World of Global Value Chains* (Zed Books 2019).

Stefano Ponte, Gary Gereffi and Gale Raj-Reichert (eds), *Handbook on Global Value Chains* (Edward Elgar 2019).

Stefano Ponte and Timothy Sturgeon, 'Explaining Governance in Global Value Chains: A modular theory-building effort' (2014) 21(1) *Review of International Political Economy* 195.

Richard A. Posner, 'Some Economics of Labor Law Author' (1984) 51(4) *The University of Chicago Law Review* 988.

Diana Potjomkina, Jan Orbie and Jamal Shahin, 'Forging Their Path in the Brussels Bubble? Civil society resistance within the domestic advisory groups created under the EU trade agreements' (2020) *Cambridge Review of International Affairs*, forthcoming available at: https://www.tandfonline.com/doi/full/10.1080/09557571.2020.1855110.

Jeremias Prassl, *The Concept of the Employer* (OUP 2015).

Tyler Pratt, 'Angling for Influence: Institutional proliferation in development banking (2021) 65(1) *International Studies Quarterly* 95.

Marta Pujadas and Mónica Tepfer, 'The Impact of a New Framework of Fundamental Principles and Rights at Work on Global Supply Chains' in International Lawyers Assisting Workers (ILAW) (2021) *The Global Labour Rights Reporter: Special Issue on Accountability and Remedy in Global Supply Chains: Considerations for Workers and Unions* 42.

Ben Purvis, Yong Mao and Darren Robinson, 'Three Pillars of Sustainability: In Search of Conceptual Origins' (2019) 44(3) *Sustainability Science* 681.

Qerim Qerimi, 'The Ambitious Modesty of the High-Level Political Forum on Sustainable Development' (2022) 13(2) *Global Policy* 281.

Gabriela Quijano and Carlos Lopez, 'Rise of Mandatory Human Rights Due Diligence: A Beacon of Hope or a Double-Edged Sword? (2021) 6 *Business and Human Rights Journal* 241.

Sarah A. Radcliffe, 'Geography and Indigeneity III: Co-articulation of colonialism and capitalism in indigeneity's economies' (2020) 44(2) *Progress in Human Geography* 374.

Mustafizur Rahman and Debapriya Bhattacharya, *Graduating LDCs in an Evolving WTO: Options and Strategies* (Friedrich-Ebert-Stiftung & Centre For Policy Dialogue 2019).

M. Safiur Rahman, Yeasmin Nahar Jolly, Shirin Akter, Noshin Anjum Kamal, Rubina Rahman, Tasrina Rabia Choudhury, and Bilkis Ara Begum, 'Sources of Toxic Elements in Indoor Dust Sample at Export Processing Zone (EPZ) Area: Dhaka, Bangladesh; and their impact on human health' (2021) 28(29) *Environmental Science and Pollution Research* 39540.

M. Safiur Rahman, Narottam Saha, and A. Hossain Molla. 'Potential Ecological Risk Assessment of Heavy Metal Contamination in Sediment and Water Body Around Dhaka Export Processing Zone, Bangladesh' (2014) 71(5) *Environmental Earth Sciences* 2293.

William Rasch, 'A Just War? Or Just a War?: Schmitt, Habermas and the Cosmopolitan Orthodoxy' (2000) 21 *Cardozo Law Review* 1665.

Nora Räthzel, Dimitris Stevis and David Uzzell (eds), *The Palgrave Handbook of Environmental Labour Studies* (Springer 2021).

Kate Raworth, *Doughnut Economics: Seven Ways to Think Like a 21st Century Economist* (Cornerstone Books 2017).

Mohammad A. Razzaque and Jillur Rahman. *Bangladesh's Apparel Exports to the EU: Adapting to competitiveness challenges following graduation from least developed country status* (Commonwealth Secretariat Working Paper 2019).

Donald H. Regan, 'The Meaning of 'Necessary' in GATT Article XX and GATS Article XIV: The myth of cost–benefit balancing' (2007) 6(3) *World Trade Review* 347.

Bernhard Reinsburg, Thomas Stubbs, Alexander Kentikelenis and Lawrence King, 'The Political Economy of Labor Market Deregulation During IMF Interventions' (2019) 45(3) *International Interactions* 532.

Hossain Mohammad Reza, 'Can the Concept of 'Justice' Be Employed in North-South Trade to Serve the Interests of the South in Ways That Sustainable Development Cannot?' (2021) 48 Journal of Malaysian and Comparative Law 81.

David Ricardo, *On the Principles of Political Economy and Taxation* (Penguin 1971).

Benjamin J. Richardson (ed.), *From Student Strikes to the Extinction Rebellion: New protest movements shaping our future* (Edward Elgar Publishing 2020).

Christian Riffel, 'Indirect Expropriation and the Protection of Public Interests' (2022) 71 *International and Comparative Law Quarterly* 945.

Christian Riffel, 'The CETA Opinion of the European Court of Justice and its Implications—not that selfish after all' (2019) 22(3) *Journal of International Economic Law* 503.

Lone Riisgaard, 'International Framework Agreements: A New Model for Securing Workers Rights?' (2005) 44(4) *Industrial Relations* 707.

Laura Ritchie Dawson, 'Labour Mobility and the WTO: The Limits of GATS Mode 4' (2012) 51(1) *Labour Migration* 1.

Kerry Rittich, 'Trade Agreements in the Twenty-First Century: Rethinking the Trade-Labor Linkage' in Alvaro Santos, Chantal Thomas and David Trubek (eds), *World Trade and Investment Law Reimagined: A Progressive Agenda for an Inclusive Globalization* (Anthem Press 2019).

Marco Rocca, *Posting of Workers and Collective Labour Law: There And Back Again* (Intersentia 2015).

Gerry Rodgers, Eddy Lee, Lee Swepston, and Jasmien Van Daele, *The ILO and the Quest for Social Justice 1919-2009* (International Labour Office 2009).

Dani Rodrick, 'A Response to the Comments by Thomas, Gallagher, Shaffer and Santos' in Alvaro Santos, Chantal Thomas and David Trubek (eds), *World Trade and*

Investment Law Reimagined: A Progressive Agenda for an Inclusive Globalization (Anthem Press 2019).
Dani Rodrik, *Straight Talk on Trade: Ideas for a Sane World Economy* (Princeton University Press 2018).
Ralf Rogowski, *Reflexive Labour Law in the World Society* (Edward Elgar 2013).
Miriam Ronzoni, 'Global Labour Injustice: A Critical Overview' in Yossi Dahan, Hanna Lerner and Faina Milman-Sivan (eds), *Global Justice and International Labour Rights* (CUP 2016).
César F. Rosado Marzán, 'Organizing with International Framework Agreements: An Exploratory Study' (2014) 4 *UC Irvine Law Review* 727.
James N. Rosenau, 'Governance, Order and Change in World Politics' in James N. Rosenau and Ernst-Otto Czempiel (eds.), *Governance Without Government: Order and Change in World Politics* (CUP 1992).
James N. Rosenau and Ernst-Otto Czempiel (eds.), *Governance Without Government: Order and Change in World Politics* (CUP 1992).
Supriya Routh, 'Examining the Legal Legitimacy of Informal Economic Activities' (2022) 31(2) *Social and Legal Studies* 282.
Supriya Routh and Vando Borghi (eds), *Workers and the Global Informal Economy: Interdisciplinary perspectives* (Routledge 2016).
Neville N. Rubin, *Code of International Labour Law: Law, Practice and Jurisprudence* (CUP 2005).
John Ruggie, *Guiding Principles on Business and Human Rights: Implementing the United Nations 'Protect, Respect and Remedy' Framework*, 17th sess, Agenda Item 3, UN Doc A/HRC/17/31, 21 March 2011.
John Ruggie, *Protect, Respect and Remedy: A Framework for Business and Human Rights*, 8th sess, Agenda Item 3, UN Doc A/HRC/8/5, 7 April 2008.
John Ruggie, 'International Regimes, Transactions and Change: Embedded liberalism in the post-war economic order' (1982) 36(2) *International Organization* 385.
Anna Saave and Barbara Muraca, 'Rethinking Labour/Work in a Degrowth Society' in Nora Räthzel, Dimitris Stevis and David Uzzell (eds), *The Palgrave Handbook of Environmental Labour Studies* (Palgrave Macmillan 2021).
Sebastian Sabato and Boris Fronteddu, *A Socially Just Transition through the European Green Deal?* (European Trade Union Institute 2020).
Md Abu Saleh and Muhammad Omar Faruque, 'LDC graduation and WTO challenges' in Mohammad Shahabuddin (ed.), *Bangladesh and International Law* (Routledge 2021).
Margot Salomon, 'Of Austerity, Human Rights and International Institutions' (2015) 21(4) *European Law Journal* 521.
Albert Sanchez-Graells (ed.), *Smart Public Procurement and Labour Standards: Pushing the Discussion after RegioPost* (Hart 2018).
Jan Sändig, Jochen von Bernstorff and Andreas Hasenclever, 'Affectedness in International Institutions: Promises and pitfalls of involving the most affected' (2018) 3(5)-(6) *Third World Thematics: A TWQ Journal* 587.
Ashley L. Santner, 'A Soft Law Mechanism for Corporate Responsibility: How the Updated OECD Guidelines for Multinational Enterprises Promote Business for the Future' (2011) 43(2) *George Washington International Law Review* 375.
Alvaro Santos, 'Reflecting on *Straight Talk on Trade*' in Alvaro Santos, Chantal Thomas and David Trubek (eds), *World Trade and Investment Law Reimagined: A Progressive Agenda for an Inclusive Globalization* (Anthem Press 2019).

Alvaro Santos, Chantal Thomas and David Trubek (eds), *World Trade and Investment Law Reimagined: A Progressive Agenda for an Inclusive Globalization* (Anthem Press 2019).

Dan Sarooshi, 'Investment Treaty Arbitration and the World Trade Organization: What Role for Systemic Values in the Resolution of International Economic Disputes?' (2014) 49 *Texas International Law Journal* 445.

Saskia Sassen, *The Mobility of Labour and Capital: A Study in International Investment and Labor Flow* (University of Cambridge Press 1998).

Saskia Sassen, *Losing Control?: Sovereignty in the age of globalization* (Columbia University Press 1996).

Lowell J. Satre, 'After the Match Girls' Strike: Bryant and May in the 1890s' (1982) 26(1) *Victorian Studies* 7.

Pierre Sauvé, 'To Fuse, Not to Fuse, or Simply Confuse? Assessing the Case for Normative Convergence Between Goods and Services Trade Law' (2019) 22(3) *Journal of International Economic Law* 355.

Laura Scherera, Paul Behrensa, Arjan de Koninga, Reinout Heijungsa, Benjamin Sprechera, Arnold Tukkera, 'Trade-offs between Social and Environmental Sustainable Development Goals' (2018) 90 *Environmental Science and Policy* 65.

Regina Scheyvens, Glenn Banks, Emma Hughes, 'The Private Sector and the SDGs: The need to move beyond "business as usual" ' (2016) 24(6) *Sustainable Development* 371.

Stephan W. Schill, 'Reforming Investor–State Dispute Settlement: A (Comparative and International) Constitutional Law Framework' (2017) 20(3) *Journal of International Economic Law* 649.

Stephan W. Schill, 'W(h)ither Fragmentation? On the Literature and Sociology of International Investment Law' (2011) 22(3) *European Journal of International Law* 875.

Stephen I. Schlossberg, 'United States Participation in the ILO' (1989) 11 *Comparative Labor Law Journal* 48.

Stefan Schmalz, Carmen Ludwig, Edward Webster, 'The Power Resources Approach: Developments and challenges' (2018) 9 *Global Labour Journal* 113.

Thomas J. Schoenbaum and Daniel CK Chow, 'The Peril of Economic Nationalism and a Proposed Pathway to Trade Harmony' (2019) 30 *Stanford Law and Policy Journal* 115.

Jenny Schultz and Rachel Ball, 'Trade as a Weapon? The WTO and Human Rights-Based Trade Measures' (2007) 12 *Deakin Law Review* 41.

Thomas Schultz and Cédric Dupont, 'Investment Arbitration: Promoting the Rule of Law or Over-Empowering Investors? A Quantitative Empirical Study' (2014) 25(4) *European Journal of International Law* 1147.

Silvana Sciarra, 'Collective Exit Strategies: New Ideas in Transnational Labour Law' in Guy Davidov and Brian Langille (eds), *The Idea of Labour Law*. (OUP 2011).

Sara Seck, 'Relational Law and the Reimagining of Tools for Environmental and Climate Justice' (2019) 31(1) *Canadian Journal of Women and Law* 151.

Sara Seck, 'Transnational Labour Law and the Environment: Beyond the bounded autonomous worker' (2018) 33(2) *Canadian Journal of Law and Society* 137.

Franz Seitz and Thomas Jost, 'The Role of the IMF in the European debt crisis' (2011) ECONSOR HAW im Dialog - Weidener Diskussionspapiere, No. 32 available at: https://web.archive.org/web/20170816170442/https://www.econstor.eu/bitstream/10419/56452/1/689266685.pdf.

Niklas Selberg, 'The Laws of Illegal Work and Dilemmas in Interest Representation on Segmented Labor Markets: A propos irregular migrants in Sweden' (2014) 35 *Comparative Labor Law and Policy Journal* 247.
Benjamin Selwyn, 'Poverty Chains and Global Capitalism' (2019) 23(1) *Competition & Change* 71.
Amartya Sen, *Development as Freedom* (OUP 1999).
Amartya Sen, *Commodities and Capabilities* (North-Holland 1985).
Shuvro Sen, Neel Antara, Shusmita Sen, and Sunny Chowdhury. 'The Unprecedented Pandemic "COVID-19" Effect on the Bangladesh Apparel Workers by Shivering the Apparel Supply Chain' (2020) 11(3) *Journal of Textile and Apparel, Technology and Management* 1.
Werner Sengenberger and Duncan Campbell (eds.), *International Labour Standards and Economic Interdependence* (ILO International Institute for Labour Studies 1994).
Jean-Michel Servais, *International Labour Law*, 6th ed (Kluwer 2020).
Mohammad Shahabuddin (ed.), *Bangladesh and International Law* (Routledge 2021).
James Thompson Shotwell, *The Origins of the International Labour Organization* (Columbia University Press 1934).
Omphemetse S. Sibanda Sr, 'Towards a Revised GATT/WTO Special and Differential Treatment Regime for Least Developed and Developing Countries' (2015) 50 *Foreign Trade Review* 31.
Vicente Silva, 'The ILO and the Future of Work: The politics of global labour policy' (2022) 22(2) *Global Social Policy* 341.
Guy Fiti Sinclair, 'C. Wilfred Jenks and the Futures of International Organizations Law' (2020) 31(2) *European Journal of International Law* 525.
Guy Fiti Sinclair, 'Beyond Accountability? Human Rights, Global Governance, and the World Bank Inspection Panel' (2019) SSRN available at: https://papers.ssrn.com/sol3/papers.cfm?abstract_id=3391646.
Guy Fiti Sinclair, *To Reform the World: International organizations and the making of modern states* (OUP 2018).
Beate Sjåfjell, 'How Company Law has Failed Human Rights – and What to Do About It' (2020) 5 *Business and Human Rights Journal* 179.
Beate Sjåfjell, 'Sustainable Value Creation Within Planetary Boundaries—Reforming Corporate Purpose and Duties of the Corporate Board (2020) 12 *Sustainability* 6245.
Beate Sjåfjell, 'When the Solution Becomes the Problem: The Triple Failure of Corporate Governance Codes' in Jean du Plessis and Chee Keong Low (eds), *Corporate Governance Codes for the 21st Century: International Perspectives and Critical Analyses* (Springer 2017).
Beate Sjåfjell and Christopher M. Bruner (eds), *Cambridge Handbook of Corporate Law, Corporate Governance and Sustainability* (CUP 2019).
Beate Sjåfjell, Jukka Mähönen, Tonia Novitz, Clair Gammage and Hanna Ahlström, *Securing the Future of European Business: SMART Reform Proposals* (University of Oslo Faculty of Law Research Paper No. 2020-11 2020), available at: https://papers.ssrn.com/sol3/papers.cfm?abstract_id=3595048.
Quinn Slobodian, *Globalists: The End of Empire and the Birth of Neoliberalism* (Harvard University Press 2018).
Lise Smit, Claire Bright, Robert McCorquodale, Matthias Bauer, Hanna Deringer, Daniela Baeza-Breinbauer, Francisca Torres-Cortés, Frank Alleweldt, Senda Kara and Camille Salinier and Héctor Tejero Tobed, *Study on Due Diligence Requirements through the Supply Chain: Final Report* (European Commission 2020) available at:

https://op.europa.eu/en/publication-detail/-/publication/8ba0a8fd-4c83-11ea-b8b7-01aa75ed71a1/language-en.

Adam Smith, *An Inquiry into the Nature and Causes of the Wealth of Nations* Rev. ed. (Penguin, 1979).

Darryn Snell, 'Trade Unions and Environmental Justice' in Nora Räthzel, Dimitris Stevis and David Uzzell (eds), *The Palgrave Handbook of Environmental Labour Studies* (Springer 2021).

L.B. Sohn, 'The Contribution of the International Labour Organization to the Development of the Concept of Economic, Social and Cultural Rights' in R-J Dupuy (ed.), *Mélanges en l'honneur de Nicolas Valticos* (Éditions A. Pedone 1999).

Elena Sondermann and Cornelia Ulbert, 'Transformation through "Meaningful" Partnership? SDG 17 as metagovernance norm and its global health implementation' (2021) 9(1) *Politics and Governance* 152.

Atul Sood, Paaritosh Nath and Sangeeta Ghosh, 'Deregulating Capital, Regulating Labour: The dynamics in the manufacturing sector in India' (2014) 49 (26/27) *Economic and Political Weekly* 58.

Benjamin K. Sovacool, 'When Subterranean Slavery Supports Sustainability Transitions? Power, patriarchy, and child labor in artisanal Congolese cobalt mining' (2021) 8(1) *The Extractive Industries and Society* 271.

Matthew Sparke, 'Comparing and Connecting Territories of Illiberal Politics and Neoliberal Governance' (2020) 8(1) *Territory, Politics, Governance* 95.

Clive L. Spash, 'The Economy as if People Mattered: Revisiting critiques of economic growth in a time of crisis' (2021) 18(7) *Globalizations* 1087.

Günter K. Stahl, Chris J. Brewster, David G. Collings, and Aida Hajro, 'Enhancing the Role of Human Resource Management in Corporate Sustainability and Social Responsibility: A multi-stakeholder, multidimensional approach to HRM' (2020) 30(3) *Human Resource Management Review* 100708.

Constantin Stamatis, 'The Idea of Deliberative Democracy: A Critical Appraisal' (2001) 14 *Ratio Juris* 390.

Guy Standing, *The Precariat: The New Dangerous Class* (Bloomsbury 2014).

Guy Standing, 'The International Labour Organization' (2010) 15(2) *New Political Economy* 307.

Guy Standing, 'The ILO: An Agency for Globalization' (2008) 39(3) *Development and Change* 355.

G. M. Stekloff, *History of the First International* (Martin Lawrence Limited 1928).

Dimitris Stevis, Edouard Morena and Dunja Krause, 'Introduction: The genealogy and contemporary politics of just transitions' in Edouard Morena, Dunja Krause and Dimitris Stevis (eds), *Just Transitions: Social justice in the shift towards a low-carbon world* (Pluto Press 2020).

Dimitris Stevis and Romain Felli, 'Global Labour Unions and Just Transition to a Green Economy' (2015) 15(1) *International Environmental Agreements* 29.

Ann Stewart, *Gender, Law and Justice in Global Markets* (CUP 2011).

Gary J. Stewart, 'The 2022 ICSID Rules: A Leap Toward Greater Transparency in ICSID Arbitration' (2022) *ICSID Review*, forthcoming available at: https://academic.oup.com/icsidreview/advance-article-abstract/doi/10.1093/icsidreview/siac016/6611548?redirectedFrom=PDF&casa_token=Guz57_8NQdgAAAAA:7aq1d DZAELQI8xa 12aIP70hNP 7BWLDQgS0q SJTY1wLcSU 6naO0jJDHd-AoyYiHS876bFNiu1fIHy.

Joseph Stiglitz, 'More Instruments and Broader Goals: Moving Toward the Post–Washington Consensus', 7 January 1998, the 1998 WIDER Annual Lecture (Helsinki, Finland).
Joseph E. Stiglitz and Andrew Charlton. 'Aid for Trade' (2006) 5(2) *International Journal of Development Issues* 1.
Peter-Tobias Stoll, Henner Gött, Patrick Abel, 'Model Labour Chapter for EU Trade Agreements - In cooperation with Bernd Lange MEP, Chairman of the Committee on International Trade and commissioned by Friedrich-Ebert Stiftung' (2020) available at: http://library.fes.de/pdf-files/bueros/singapur/16089.pdf.
Jonathan R. Strand and Kenneth J. Retzl, 'Did Recent Voice Reforms Improve Good Governance within the World Bank?' (2016) 47(3) *Development and Change* 410.
Wolfgang Streeck, *How will Capitalism End?* (Verso 2016).
Diana Stuart, Ryan Gunderson, and Brian Petersen, 'Climate Change and the Polanyian Counter-movement: Carbon markets or degrowth?' (2019) 24(1) *New Political Economy* 89.
Teddy Subramanien, Brendan Vickers and Hilary Enos-Edu (eds), *WTO Reform: Reshaping Global Trade Governance for 21st Century Challenges* (The Commonwealth 2019).
Clyde Summers, 'The Battle in Seattle: Free Trade, Labor Rights, and Societal Values' (2001) 22 *University of Pennsylvania Journal of International Economic Law* 61.
Alain Supiot, *The Spirit of Philadelphia: Social Justice vs the Total Market* (Verso 2012).
Alain Supiot, 'A Legal Perspective on the Economic Crisis of 2008' (2010) 149(2) *International Labour Review* 151.
Lee Swepston, 'Crisis in the ILO Supervisory System: Dispute over the Right to Strike' (2013) 29(2) *International Journal of Comparative Labour Law and Industrial Relations* 199.
Lee Swepston, 'Human Rights and Freedom of Association: Development through ILO Supervision' (1998) 137 *International Labour Review* 169.
Lee Swepston, 'Supervision of ILO Standards' (1997) 13 *International Journal of Comparative Labour Law and Industrial Relations* 327.
Phil Syrpis, 'The Influence of the EU on UK Labour Law—Before and after Brexit' (2022) 51(4) *Industrial Law Journal* 802.
Phil Syrpis, *EU Intervention in Domestic Labour Law* (OUP 2007).
Tobias Sytsma, 'Rules of Origin and Trade Preference Utilization among Least Developed Countries' (2021) 39(4) *Contemporary Economic Policy* 701.
Imre Szabo, 'Between Polarization and Statism – Effects of the crisis on collective bargaining processes and outcomes in Hungary' (2013) 19(2) *Transfer* 205.
Lynn M.G. Ta and Benjamin A.T. Graham. 'Can Quasi-Judicial Bodies at the World Bank Provide Justice in Human Rights Cases' (2018) 50 *Georgetown Journal of International Law* 113.
Daria Taglioni and Deborah Winkler, 'Making Global Value Chains Work for Development' (2014) *The World Bank – Economic Premise*, Number 143.
Tesfaye B. Takele, 'The Relevance of Coordinated Regional Trade Logistics for the Implementation of Regional Free Trade Area of Africa' (2019) 13(1) *Journal of Transport and Supply Chain Management* 1.
Gunther Teubner, 'Self-Constitutionalizing TNCs? On the Linkage of "Private" and "Public" Corporate Codes of Conduct' (2011) 18(2) *Indiana Journal of Global Legal Studies* 617.
Gunther Teubner, *Law as an Autopoietic System* (Blackwell 1993).

Gunther Teubner, 'Substantive and Reflexive Elements in Modern Law' (1983) 17 *Law and Society Review* 242.

Joo-Cheong Tham, 'Equality and Community for Migrant Workers' in Alan Bogg, Jacob Rowbottom and Alison Young (eds), *The Constitution of Social Democracy: Essays in Honour of Keith Ewing* (Bloomsbury Publishing 2020).

Joo-Cheong Tham and K.D. Ewing, 'Labour Clauses in the TPP and TTIP: A comparison without a difference?' (2016) 17 *Melbourne Journal of International Law* 1.

Nik Theodore, 'Regulating Informality: Worker centers and collective action in day-labor markets' (2020) 15(1) *Growth and Change* 144.

Albert Thomas, 'Preface' in *The International Labour Organization: The First Decade* (Allen & Unwin 1931).

Albert Thomas, 'The International Labour Organisation-Its Origins, Development and Future' (1921) 1 *International Labour Review* 5.

Chantal Thomas, 'Migration and International Economic Asymmetry' in Alvaro Santos, Chantal Thomas and David Trubek (eds), *World Trade and Investment Law Reimagined: A Progressive Agenda for an Inclusive Globalization* (Anthem Press 2019).

Chantal Thomas, 'Convergences and Divergences in International Legal Norms on Migrant Labor' (2010) 32 *Comparative Labor Law and Policy Journal* 405.

Chantal Thomas, 'Balance-of-Payments Crises in the Developing World: Balancing Trade, Finance and Development in the New Economic Order' (2000) 15(6) *American University International Law Review* 1249.

Huw Thomas and Mark Anner, 'Dissensus and Deadlock in the Evolution of Labour Governance: Global Supply Chains and the International Labour Organization (ILO)' (2023) 184 *Journal of Business Ethics* 33.

Huw Thomas and Peter Turnbull, 'From Horizontal to Vertical Labour Governance: The International Labour Organization (ILO) and decent work in global supply chains' (2018) 71(4) *Human Relations* 536.

Kyla Tienhaara, Rachel Thrasher, B. Alexander Simmons and Kevin P. Gallagher, 'Investor-State Dispute Settlement: Obstructing a just energy transition' (2022) *Climate Policy* DOI: 10.1080/14693062.2022.2153102.

Dire Tladi (ed.), *Peremptory Norms of General International Law (Jus Cogens)* (Brill Nijhoff 2021).

Paolo Tomassetti, 'Energy Transition: A Labour Law Retrospective' (2022) 52(1) *Industrial Law Journal* 34.

Paolo Tomassetti, 'From Treadmill of Production to Just Transition and Beyond' (2020) 26(4) *European Journal of Industrial Relations* 439.

Paolo Tomassetti, 'Labor Law and Environmental Sustainability' (2018) 40 *Comparative Labour Law and Policy Journal* 61.

Cheree Topple, Jerome D. Donovan, Eryadi K. Masli, and Thomas Borgert, 'Corporate Sustainability Assessments: MNE engagement with sustainable development and the SDGs' (2017) 24(3) *Transnational Corporations* 61.

Els Torreele and Joseph J. Amon, 'Equitable COVID-19 Vaccine Access' (2021) 23(1) *Health and Human Rights* 273.

Alexander Trautrims, Martin C. Schleper, M. Selim Cakir & Stefan Gold, 'Survival at the Expense of the Weakest? Managing modern slavery risks in supply chains during COVID-19 (2020) 23(7) *Journal of Risk Research* 1067.

Anne Trebilcock, 'The Rana Plaza Disaster Seven Years On: Transnational experiments and perhaps a new treaty?' (2020) 159(4) *International Labour Review* 545.

Anne Trebilcock, 'What the New Convention on Violence and Harassment tells us about Human Rights and the ILO' in George P. Politakis, Tomi Kohiyama and Thomas Lieby (eds), *ILO 100: Law for social justice* (ILO 2019).

Anne Trebilcock, 'The ILO as an Actor in International Economic Law: Looking Back, Gazing Ahead' in Marc Bungenberg, Markus Krajewski, Christian J. Tams, Jörg Philipp Terhechte and Andreas R. Ziegler (eds) *European Yearbook of International Economic Law 2019* ((Springer 2019).

Anne Trebilcock, 'Why the Shift from International to Transnational Law is Important for Labour Standards' in Henner Gött (ed.), *Labour Standards in International Economic Law* (Springer 2018).

Anne Trebilcock, 'Due Diligence on Labour Issues: Opportunities and Limits of the UN Guiding Principles on Business and Human Rights' in Adelle Blackett and Anne Trebilcock (eds), *Research Handbook on Transnational Labour Law* (Edward Elgar 2015).

Aurora Trif, 'Romania: Collective bargaining under attack' (2013) 19 *Transfer* 227.

David M. Trubek and Alvaro Santos (eds), *The New Law and Economic Development - A critical appraisal* (CUP 2006).

Eric Tucker, "Can Worker Voice Strike Back? Law and the Decline and Uncertain Future of Strikes" in Alan Bogg and Tonia Novitz (eds) *Voices at Work: Continuity and Change in the Common Law World* (OUP 2014).

Eric Tucker, 'Labor's Many Constitutions (and Capital's Too)' (2011-12) 33 *Comparative Labor Law and Policy Journal* 355.

Ryan Turner, 'Transnational Supply Chain Regulation: Extraterritorial regulation as corporate law's new frontier' (2016) 17(1) *Melbourne Journal of International Law* 188.

Aneta Tyc, *Global Trade, Labour Rights and International Law* (Routledge 2021).

Karin Ulmer, 'Trade Embedded Development Models' (2015) 31(3) *International Journal of Comparative Labour Law and Industrial Relations* 305.

Roberto M. Unger, 'The Critical Legal Studies Movement' (1983) 96 *Harvard Law Review* 563.

Makson Usynin and Szilárd Gáspár-Szilágyi, 'The Growing Tendency of Including Investment Agreements in PTAs' (2017) *Netherlands Yearbook of International Law* 267.

Areli Valencia, *Human Rights Trade-Offs in Times of Economic Growth: The long-term capability impacts of extractive-led development* (Palgrave Macmillan 2016).

Areli Valencia, 'Human Rights Trade-offs in a Context of "Systemic Lack of Freedom": The case of the smelter town of La Oroya, Peru' (2014) 13(4) *Journal of Human Rights* 456.

Steen Vallentin and David Murillo, 'Ideologies of Corporate Responsibility: From Neoliberalism to "Varieties of Liberalism"' (2021) *Business Ethics Quarterly* 1.

Nicolas Valticos, 'International Labour Standards and Human Rights: Approaching the Year 2000' (1998) 138 *International Labour Review* 135.

Lore Van den Putte and Jan Orbie, 'EU Bilateral Trade Agreements and the Surprising Rise of Labour Provisions' (2015) 31(3) *International Journal of Comparative Labour Law and Industrial Relations* 263.

Paul van der Heijden, 'The ILO Stumbling towards Its Centenary Anniversary' (2018) 15(1) *International Organizations Law Review* 203.

Kees van der Ree, 'Promoting Green Jobs: Decent Work in the Transition to Low-carbon, Green Economies' in Christophe Gironde and Gilles Carbonnier (eds),

The ILO@100: Addressing the Past and Future of Work and Social Protection (Brill Nijhoff 2019).

Piet Van Nuffel and Sofia Afanasjeva, 'The Posting of Workers Directive Revised: Enhancing the protection of workers in the cross-border provision of services' (2018) 3(3) *European Papers* 1401.

Jan Vandemoortele, 'The MDG Conundrum: Meeting the targets without missing the point' (2009) 27(4) *Development Policy Review* 355.

Demy van't Wout, 'The Enforceability of the Trade and Sustainable Development Chapters of the European Union's Free Trade Agreements' (2021) *Asia Europe Journal* 1.

Daniel Vaughan-Whitehead (ed.), *The European Social Model in Crisis: Is Europe losing its soul?* (Edward Elgar/ILO 2015).

Daniel Vaughan-Whitehead, *EU Enlargement versus Social Europe? The Uncertain Future of the European Social Model* (Edward Elgar Publishing 2003).

Samantha Velluti, *The Role of the EU in the Promotion of Human Rights and International Labour Standards in Its External Trade Relations* (Springer 2020).

Geraldo Vidigal, 'Regional Trade Adjudication and the Rise of Sustainability Disputes: *Korea – Labour Commitments* and *Ukraine – Wood Export Bans*' (2022) 116(3) *American Journal of International Law* 567.

Charlotte Villiers, 'Global Supply Chains and Sustainability: The Role of Disclosure and Due Diligence Regulation' in Beate Sjåfjell and Christopher M. Bruner (eds), *Cambridge Handbook of Corporate Law, Corporate Governance and Sustainability* (CUP 2019).

Charlotte Villiers, 'Collective Responsibility and the Limits of Disclosure in Regulating Global Supply Chains' (2018) 23 *Deakin Law Review* 143.

Jeffrey Vogt, Janice Bellace, Lance Compa, K.D. Ewing, Lord Hendy QC, Klaus Lörcher and Tonia Novitz, *The Right to Strike in International Law* (Hart 2020).

Jeffrey Vogt, 'A Little Less Conversation: The EU and the (non) application of labour conditionality in the generalized system of preferences (GSP)' (2015) 31(3) *International Journal of Comparative Labour Law and Industrial Relations* 285.

Christina Voigt (ed.), *Sustainable Development as a Principle of International Law: Resolving conflicts between climate measures and WTO law* (Brill 2009).

Leah Vosko, *Managing the Margins: Gender, citizenship and the international regulation of precarious employment* (OUP 2010).

Leah Vosko, *Temporary Work: The gendered rise of a precarious employment relationship* (University of Toronto Press 2000).

Tom Waas, Jean Hugé, Aviel Verbruggen, and Tarah Wright, 'Sustainable Development: A bird's eye view' (2011) 3(10) *Sustainability* 1637.

Randall L. Waller and Roger N. Conaway, 'Framing and Counterframing the Issue of Corporate Social Responsibility: The Communication Strategies of Nikebiz.com' (2011) 48(1) *Journal of Business Communication* 83.

Angela Ward, 'International Order, Political Community, and the Search for a European Public Philosophy' (1999) 22 *Fordham International Law Journal* 930.

Bruce Wardhaugh, 'GSP+ and Human Rights: Is the EU's Approach the Right One?' (2013) 16 *Journal of International Economic Law* 827.

Catherine Weaver, 'The Politics of Performance Evaluation: Independent Evaluation at the International Monetary Fund' (2010) 5 *Review of International Organisations* 365.

David Weil, *The Fissured Workplace: Why work has become so bad for so many and what can be done to improve it* (Harvard University Press 2014).

Pauline Weil, and Georg Zachmann, 'The Impact of the War in Ukraine on Food Security' Bruegel-Blogs (2022) available at: https://go.gale.com/ps/i.do?id=GALE%7CA697951850&sid=googleScholar&v=2.1&it=r&linkaccess=abs&issn=&p=AONE&sw=w&userGroupName=anon%7Ec387d5ac.

Clara Weinhardt and Till Schöfer, 'Differential Treatment for Developing Countries in the WTO: The unmaking of the North–South distinction in a multipolar world' (2022) 43(1) *Third World Quarterly* 74.

Manfred Weiss, 'The EU Generalised Scheme of Preferences and the Special Incentive Arrangement for Sustainable Development and Good Governance' in Adalberto Perulli and Tiziano Treu (eds), *Sustainable Development, Global Trade and Social Rights* (Wolters Kluwer 2018).

Lord Wedderburn, 'Labour Law and the Individual in Post-Industrial Societies' in Lord Wedderburn, Max Rood, Gerard Lyon-Caen, Wolfgang Däubler and Paul van der Heijden, *Labour Law in the Post-Industrial Era* (Dartmouth 1994).

Lord Wedderburn, Max Rood, Gerard Lyon-Caen, Wolfgang Däubler and Paul van der Heijden, *Labour Law in the Post-Industrial Era* (Dartmouth 1994).

Vera Weghmann, 'Theorising Practice: Independent trade unions in the UK' (2022) 2(1) *Work in the Global Economy* 132.

Peter Wells, Wessam Abouarghoub, Stephen Pettit and Anthony Beresford, 'A Socio-technical Transitions Perspective for Assessing Future Sustainability following the COVID-19 pandemic' (2020) 16(1) *Sustainability: Science, Practice and Policy* 29.

Philipp Wetzel and Erik Hofmann, 'Supply Chain Finance, Financial Constraints and Corporate Performance: An explorative network analysis and future research agenda' (2019) 216 *International Journal of Production Economics* 364.

Michael Whittall, Miguel Martinez Lucio, Stephen Mustchin, Fernando Rocha, Volcker Telljohann, 'Workplace Trade Union Engagement with European Works Councils and Transnational Agreements: The Volkswagen Europe' (2017) 23(4) *European Journal of Industrial Relations* 397

Richard Whitman (ed.), *Normative Power Europe: Empirical and theoretical perspectives*, (Palgrave 2011).

Clair Wilcox, 'The London Draft of a Charter for an International Trade Organization' (1947) 37(2) *The American Economic Review* 529.

Kim M. Willey, *Stock Market Short-Termism: Law, Regulation, and Reform* (Palgrave Macmillan 2019).

Jessie Williams, 'Low Skill Temporary Migration in New Zealand: Labour market and human rights law as a framework for managing future migration' (2009) VUW Working Paper available at: http://hdl.handle.net/10063/2576

John Williamson, 'A Short History of the Washington Consensus' (2009) 15 *Law and Business Review of the Americas* 7.

Joe J. Wills, *Contesting World Order? Socioeconomic Rights and Global Justice Movements* (CUP 2017).

Alfred Wisskirchen, 'The Standard-setting and Monitoring Activity of the ILO: Legal questions and practical experience' (2005) 144 *International Labour Review* 253.

Robert Wolfe, 'An Anatomy of Accountability at the WTO' (2015) 6(1) *Global Policy* 13.

Alan Wm. Wolff, *Getting Back to the Negotiating Table* (Peterson Institute for International Economics Working Paper 2022).

Hans-Michael Wolffgang and Wolfram Feuerhake, 'Core Labour Standards in World Trade Law: The Necessity for Incorporation of Core Labour Standards in the World Trade Organization' (2002) 36(5) *Journal of World Trade* 883.

Ngaire Woods, *The Globalizers: The IMF, the World Bank and their Borrowers* (CUP 2006).

Ngaire Woods and Amrita Narlikar, 'Governance and the Limits of Accountability: the WTO, the IMF, and the World Bank' (2001) 53(170) *International Social Science Journal* 569.

Stephen Woolcock, *Reforming the WTO, part 1: why world trade rules are looking shaky. LSE Brexit* (2020) available at: http://eprints.lse.ac.uk/104285/.

World Business Council for Sustainable Development (WBCSD), *Vision 2050* (WBCSD 2010) available at: https://www.wbcsd.org/Overview/About-us/Vision_2050/Resources/Vision-2050-The-new-agenda-for-business.

WCBSD, *Vision 2050 Time to Transform* (WBCSD 2021) available at: https://www.wbcsd.org/contentwbc/download/11765/177145/1.

World Commission on Environment and Development (WCED), *Our Common Future* (OUP 1987).

Chris F. Wright, Nick Wailes, Greg J. Bamber and Russell D. Lansbury, 'Beyond National Systems, Towards a "Gig Economy?" A Research Agenda for International and Comparative Employee Relations' (2017) *Employee Responsibilities and Rights Journal* 247.

David A. Wuttke, Constantin Blome, and Michael Henke, 'Focusing the Financial Flow of Supply Chains: An empirical investigation of financial supply chain management' (2013) 145(2) *International Journal of Production Economics* 773.

Fangjin Ye, 'The Impact of Bilateral Investment Treaties (BITs) on Collective Labor Rights in Developing Countries' (2020) 15(4) *The Review of International Organizations* 899.

Nicola Yeates, 'Global Care Chains: A state-of-the-art review and future directions in care transnationalization research' (2012) 12(2) *Global Networks* 135.

Destaw A. Yigzaw, 'On the Obituary of the Doha Round: A Path for Reinventing the WTO's Future' (2021) 22 *Estey Journal of International Law and Trade Policy* 31.

Iris Marion Young, 'Activist Challenges to Deliberative Democracy' (2001) 29(5) *Political Theory* 670.

Zahra Yusifli and Colin Fenwick, 'Workers' Rights and Human Rights: Toward a new fundamental principle?' in Kimberley Elliott (ed.), *Handbook on Globalisation and Labour Standards* (Edward Elgar 2022).

Ania Zbyszewska, 'Regulating Work with People and 'Nature' in Mind: Feminist reflections' (2018) 40(1) *Comparative Labor Law and Policy Journal* 9.

Štěpánka Zemanová and Radka Druláková, 'Mainstreaming Global Sustainable Development Goals through the UN Global Compact: The case of Visegrad countries' (2020) 13(3) *Journal of Risk and Financial Management* 41.

Douglas Zeng, 'The Past, Present and Future of Special Economic Zones and their Impact' (2021) 24 *Journal of International Economic Law* 259.

Reingard Zimmer, 'International Framework Agreements: New Developments through Better Implementation on the Basis of an Analysis of the Bangladesh Accord and the Indonesian Freedom of Association Protocol' (2020) 17(1) *International Organizations Law Review* 178.

Dominik Zimon, Jonah Tyan and Robert Sroufe, 'Drivers of Sustainable Supply Chain Management: Practices to Alignment with UN Sustainable Development Goals' (2019) 14(1) *International Journal for Quality Research* 219.

Danilo Zolo, 'A Cosmopolitan Philosophy of International Law? A Realist Approach' (1999) 12 *Ratio Juris* 428.
Ariel Zylberman, 'The Indivisibility of Human Rights' (2017) 36(4) *Law and Philosophy* 389.

Index